Harmonic Trading Volume Three:

Reaction vs. Reversal

By Scott M. Carney

Copyright 2016

Harmonic Trader Press
Printed in the United States of America

COPYRIGHT HARMONICTRADER, L.L.C. 2016

Harmonic Trading Volume 3: Reaction vs. Reversal

By Scott M. Carney

Library of Congress
Cataloging-in-Publication Data

This publication is designed to provide accurate and authoritative information in regard to the subject matter covered.

It is sold with the understanding that the publisher is not engaged in rendering legal, accounting, or other professional service.

If legal advice or other expert assistance is required, the services of a competent professional person should be sought.

From a Declaration of Principles Jointly Adopted by a Committee of the American Bar Association and a Committee of Publishers and Associations.

This material is protected under all copyright laws.
This material may not be reprinted or reused in any manner without written consent of Scott M. Carney. All rights reserved!

Harmonic Trader Press 2016

Printed in the United States of America

Table of Contents

Dedication

Acknowledgments

Foreword

Introduction p.17

Chapter 1:
- **Core Principles of Harmonic Trading** p.39

Chapter 2:
- **Standardized Harmonic Pattern Identification** p.57

Chapter 3:
- **Advanced Harmonic Trading Execution Strategies** p.147

Chapter 4:
- **Harmonic Trading Reversal Types** p.183

Chapter 5:
- **Advanced Indicator Analysis in Harmonic Trading** p.211

Chapter 6:
- **Harmonic Strength Index (HSI)** p.235

Chapter 7:
- **Advanced Harmonic Trading Management Strategies** p.281

Chapter 8:
- **Harmonic Trading Timeframes** p.313

Conclusion p.331

Bibliography

Dedication

For Priscila,

If Not for You,

This Would Not Be.

Acknowledgments

Throughout my journey of work, I have encountered many outstanding Harmonic Traders - fantastic individuals whom are dedicated to the financial markets and understanding how they tick. I have immense respect for those whom have dedicated themselves to the study of harmonic phenomenon in the financial markets. I encourage future generations to pick up the mantle of harmonic patterns and move forward with this advanced material to continue to unlock even deeper relationships. The most important acknowledgement to all Harmonic Traders is my appreciation to the standard of character that most uphold. Harmonic Traders possess motivated and pragmatic perspectives regarding the financial markets. They seem willing to share ideas in good faith, promote a larger positive engagement and do the work required to be successful. This represents the essence of the work that I have presented and the core values of Harmonic Trading

I would like to thank all of the people that I have thanked in prior material again. Many of these individuals – family and friends - continue to be tremendous influences on my life and have helped directly and indirectly supported the development of Harmonic Trading material since its inception.

I would like to thank all of the fantastic friends and family that I have in Brazil. My experiences and connection to this amazing culture and these incredible people has made a profound difference my life. Obrigado!

I want to recognize Stephanie Kramer for being one of the essential individuals who has been integral to the cause of realizing a larger effort over the past several years.

Robert Troy Hulmes – You lead by an example that has taught me much.

Michael Hausmann – It's always happening. Never forget!

Alan Kuenhold – It started because you opened your door. Much appreciated!

Mark Douglas, in memory. Your honest insights helped me bypass many avoidable mistakes.

Foreword

Next trade. Win, lose or draw – it is always about the NEXT TRADE! This perspective keeps us open to new opportunities and helps to maintain a balanced mindset with respect to current positions. As traders seeking to define market conditions from a natural framework of price movements, we must always be open the flow of opportunity available to us. There is unlimited opportunity in the financial markets but it requires a comprehensive measurement approach to effectively define clear possibilities. This has been my underlying purpose throughout my work with Harmonic Trading.

It has been quite a bit of time since I have written a book. I never intended to produce books and other resource material to this degree. But, my discoveries in harmonic patterns have continued to evolve. Over the past 20 years, I have expanded upon the initial concepts that define unique technical situations. As more natural cyclical relationships have been distilled, the basic tenets of harmonic pattern recognition have solidified the foundation of measurements that comprises this methodology while integrating advanced strategies to refine those characteristics that consistently provide reliable signals and technical information.

Initially, trading was a personal endeavor that I experienced alone and was a passion that few in my life shared. From time to time, I would meet individuals whom had experience trading markets or were employed in the industry to some degree. This was a time before the Internet and all of the devices that now seamlessly connect us. For someone whom most would not consider old, I find myself continually repeating things that my grandparents said to me growing up about how the world has changed. But, the world has changed, and it continues to evolve on a larger *digital* paradigm.

When I initially released *The Harmonic Trader*, the Internet was exploding but only as fast as your dial-up connection would permit. In the early 2000's, I released both *Harmonic Trading Volume 1* and a few years later, *Harmonic Trading Volume 2* that established the principles of the harmonic pattern framework. In my opinion, the amount of technological progress in the financial industry since the release of *Volume 2* – which was nearly a decade ago – has surpassed the total of the preceding 25 years combined. It is important to emphasize this phenomenon, as it is changing not only the way information is disseminated in the markets but it has transformed how money is even transacted. The barriers are gone. Anyone on the entire planet within reach of an internet connection can participate in the financial markets and attempt to be a successful trader.

Harmonic Trading Volume 3: Reaction vs. Reversal

New Ideas and Applications of Harmonic Trading

Over the past two decades, I have experimented with combinations of measurements to define unique situations that offer a great deal of reliable information regarding the future probable price action of any market relative to the natural limits of the prior trading history. Initially, these ideas were founded in harmonic pattern rules which now have been readily accepted by traders as an effective analytical framework. Once people are introduced to harmonic patterns and apply the measurement strategies, they quickly realize the predictive value of these techniques. Remarkably, the patterns and confirmation strategies enable an understanding of natural limits of price action within any market. Although the trend is always your friend, opportunities are omnipresent depending upon the timeframe considered. The key understanding to getting the most out of harmonic patterns is derived from their categorization and expected outcomes to differentiate nominal reactions versus larger reversals.

One of the greatest advantages measuring harmonic market movements is the derived understanding and set of expectations that provide a framework to explain price action. As we know, the market can only move so far within a period of time. Therefore, a basic awareness of the market's trading history is a critical foundation for any methodology that is looking to buy and sell for profit with some degree of reasonable understanding of what is possible. Within the Harmonic Trading approach, the measured strategies define unique and precise market conditions that validate opportunities unlike any other approach. When combined with traditional Technical Analysis, the entire structure of market movements can be identified, classified and quantified accurately to define price levels that effectively price the opportunity.

The remarkable accuracy of harmonic patterns is well-known. Although I do feel that some statistical claims have been manipulated by other online outfits for marketing gain, I believe that the high degree of accuracy associated with harmonic patterns is valid due to the sheer impact it has had on numerous traders' lives. One of the reasons why these methodologies have grown so immensely over the years is because they DO provide an accurate and effective framework to outline potential opportunities. However, price pattern recognition requires an enhanced set of conditions to truly capitalize on this phenomenon consistently.

Many have stated that harmonic patterns are 80 to 90% accurate. But what does this mean? Does this mean that 90% of all harmonic patterns will make you rich? No - 90% of all harmonic patterns will not make you rich! 90% of all harmonic patterns will give you a framework to analyze specific price zones that represent the completion of a specific set of trading history that comprises a prescribed structural alignment to denote a change in future direction. With all that being said, the only question to consider is <u>how far does the price action move in the desired direction before testing the prescribed stop loss limit</u>. This is an important consideration for any overall measure of accuracy.

Harmonic Trading Volume 3: Reaction vs. Reversal

There must be a measured parameter that explains how much of a price move could be expected following the completion of harmonic pattern. Upon further inspection, it is easy to see that a standardized assessment of multiple markets, timeframes and pattern structures must be analyzed more specifically to offer consistently accurate results.

As the creator of the harmonic patterns, it is difficult to quietly watch others misrepresent the true value of these measurements. Yes, the patterns can be extremely accurate but there must be a realistic and reasonable rationale to attempt to trade these opportunities successfully. The notion that a trader can click a button and employ a methodology that works 90% of the time is extremely suspect. Confirmation variables are required to separate minor reactions from substantial trading opportunities but the "home-run" outcome for every situation - unfortunately being circulated by less informed actors in the industry - is simply not the norm.

What is the Harmonic Norm?

As a proponent of understanding market strategies that define precise expectations, I am always looking for phenomenon in price action that can consistently guide my decisions. My understanding of harmonic patterns and the realistic expectations that I possess regarding possible outcomes facilitate my decisions and dictate how I handle each situation. From the very beginning, I have stressed the importance of a realistic perspective and the need to use the pattern structures as a starting point. I am a firm believer that multiple confirmation of market analysis frequently yields accurate and reliable signals. Therefore, I understand that not all patterns are valid opportunities and the possible candidates that I consider must possess multiple elements to be a valid consideration.

This perspective is derived from the fundamental understanding that harmonic patterns offer a reaction on the initial test of a distinct pattern followed by experience a secondary retest before exhibiting a larger price move. I will discuss this in detail later in this material. However, this is an example of just one expectation, and a standardized model of how harmonic patterns exhibit definable and repeatable behavior. There are other expectations involved with execution and trade management, as well as advanced identification considerations we will uncover in this material. Most important, all situations can be categorized and classified according to their proportional structure to an even more refined degree. In my opinion, these exact types of trading cycles can be considered thought of as "micro–price mechanisms" within the overall functioning process of the market. We know that the market ebbs and flows, moves up and down, and money flows in and out. This is the market in action. This is the market's primary function – to exist! It does not matter if the market trend is up or down. The basic function of the market is to exist and prices must fluctuate to create such an environment. Therefore, the fundamental function of markets is driven by cyclical trading phenomenon that frequently exhibit harmonic pattern properties. When we identify these situations, there

Harmonic Trading Volume 3: Reaction vs. Reversal

are specific expectations that are associated with the completion of the structure. This demands that we accurately measure and understand which ratios are significant, especially within structures that may appear the same.

Harmonic Standardization

My main interest in this book is to establish a standardized measurement basis that crystallizes the material initially presented in the first three books. These rules have become the industry standard for harmonic patterns. Although others have attempted to present alternative interpretations, these variations only distort the effectiveness of the natural structural measures. Simply stated, these MISinterpretations are mostly for marketing purposes offered by less reputable trading educators seeking to benefit from the popularity of the popularity of harmonic strategies. It is impossible to improve upon the explicit harmonic metrics that actually define true natural levels of support and resistance. For example, some of these outfits have argued that the 1.667 ratio is better than the 1.618. Anyone who understands the essence of Phi in nature and the universe knows that this ratio represents the essence of *Divine Proportion* of this phenomenon. I do not nor will I remark on these *Harmonic Traitors* other than to say "Google it" but I have found that sooner or later most eventually learn the proper way to measure the structures.

Personally, I have rededicated myself to the work to create a standardized start-to-finish framework and provide the thorough explanation for traders to learn this measured approach correctly. In particular, my focus with the material in this book has been to clarify the proper expectations while explaining why certain harmonic patterns work. The strategies presented throughout this material seek to foster this basic understanding and share the insights regarding those situations where the patterns have maximum significance.

Most traders sooner or later realize the significance of the harmonic pattern ratios that are exhibited in nature manifest themselves in the financial markets. Hence, traders realize the advantage of these natural cyclical turning points. Although the patterns represent an ideal structural model, valid trade opportunities unfold precisely within this framework. The measures provide a price range with "natural limits" to assess execution opportunities and profit objectives while reducing risk. These measurements serve as the foundation for any potential opportunity to differentiate when price action will slightly react from the targeted level as opposed to providing a significant reversal shortly after completing the measured area. The key is to know what factors are critical at the completion of distinct patterns to guide decisions and provide the proper expectations of what will happen to optimize the opportunity.

Harmonic Trading Volume 3: Reaction vs. Reversal

Once You Know What to Look for...

As I have said from the very beginning – even in *The Harmonic Trader* back in 1998 – harmonic patterns are a starting point but an effective means to analyze price movements that exhibit these properties. Of course, harmonic patterns are not going to appear in every market all the time but these structures inevitability materialize time and time again to mark important changes in the future price action. However, I must stress that the proper measurements are required to realize such success. It seems that other interpretations that been promoted as improvements are merely distortions from immutable basic harmonic ratios that categorize price action as such. The key point within the whole pattern debate is to always apply those measures that are directly related to the elements of natural cyclical harmonic phenomenon. Simply stated, the harmonic measurements serve as primary framework which can not be skewed without distorting results and destabilizing the essence of analyzing the markets from this perspective.

When I released the initial pattern rules in my first book, *The Harmonic Trader*, the entire subject of Technical Analysis lacked respect. However, two vicious bear markets in the first decade of this century and the advent of trading technology has changed the market's focus from opinion-based advisors to chart studies and quant-style computational analysis. These factors have altered "The Street's" focus from reputation-based advisors to more of a meritocracy where market perspectives are assessed upon quality and not zip code of origin. I believe that the strategies have proven themselves through challenging environments and continue to gain credibility in the trading world. Incredibly, nearly 20 years has already passed and the once obscure harmonic pattern discoveries are now common knowledge within the trading community.

As the industry continues to migrate most of its operations online, market participants will find themselves looking for advantages by analyzing price action and chart history. As the trading community continues to embrace Harmonic Patterns, the online discussion and interpretations have expanded the total engagement to the point where my initial work is now a separate entity from me. In my opinion, <u>I encourage interpretations and advancements that seek to improve the overall understanding</u> of what I have put forth over the past two decades. I can only stress that the primary pattern measurements that are founded in the essence of what is harmonic remain as the standard for future application. Otherwise, traders will find themselves attempting to identify random movements as repeatable behavior that simply is not a true phenomenon.

Realistically Harmonic

Many traders often search for one tool or strategy that can tell them when to buy and sell. It seems that these individuals are overwhelmed by the market in general and are looking for a lottery ticket more than a logical approach to understanding price action. Like anyone who has spent countless hours in front of the screen looking at endless of charts, it becomes apparent that certain market conditions possess clearer signals than others. I think one of the biggest misnomers of the market is that to be successful one must understand everything that is unfolding all at the same time. Certainly, the news outlets attempt to tie all of the various market moves together to package one big story. Real traders understand that not all markets can be traded all of the time. In fact, successful traders are typically spending as much of their time preparing for the trade than actual trading itself. If you're not spending as much time preparing for trade than trading, you're probably going to make mistakes. This type of discipline can be difficult for most as they are unable to be patient and wait for prescribed conditions to develop. A degree of selectivity is mandatory to focus on only those opportunities that present overwhelming evidence of a successful trade. All of these considerations are critical throughout the trading process, and such assessments must be made to minimize risk and maximize profit. Most important, I believe that a realistic perspective of what is possible is an essential to stay grounded and navigate a professional course in your trading endeavors. In my opinion, most people who are dedicated to measuring the market do realize that it takes more than one strategy or simple tool to develop the skills necessary to succeed.

Remarkably, there are broad elements within the industry that still operate on this type of unrealistic hype. I do believe that the larger public is becoming more aware of these unsavory elements, especially as more traders are dedicated to learning the proven strategies to succeed in the financial markets. I have spoken about my general disdain for the bad actors in the industry in each of my books. I have been forced to address a variety of issues, especially due to the unusual degree of disregard for fiduciary responsibility up and down Wall Street. Ultimately, I want the harmonic pattern work to speak for itself and always remain the focus of what is important. Although sometimes these distractions must be dealt with, the fiduciary responsibility that I maintain to consistently put forth the best work that I can create is a driving principle of Harmonic Trading.

Harmonic Trading History - My Story

In my own life, I have experienced a variety of positive and negative relationships that have had a profound impact on my personal trading journey as well as my perspective of the industry that I love. I feel that I have created a special foundation where individuals can actually learn predictive strategies that help them understand future probable price direction. However, it is important to share the personal journey that has shaped me to advance my work with harmonic patterns within the knowledge base of Technical Analysis in general. I believe it is an essential exercise to finally explain how the strategies were developed, where I initially released the rules of this work and provide the proper citation of those who came before what is now known as Harmonic Trading.

Harmonic Trading Volume 3: Reaction vs. Reversal

From the inception of my initial discoveries, it has been important for me personally to clearly delineate the Harmonic Trading advancements that have been put forth over the past two decades. So, let's start at the beginning – my beginning. The history of Harmonic Trading has its roots in my initial market endeavors nearly 30 years ago. Although I studied primarily fundamental analysis, my foray into Technical Analysis was fueled by observations about repeating price fluctuations in the fundamental values of companies. Basic seasonal trends in certain markets became apparent and led me to focus on more on price action and ranges of support and resistance. In this pursuit, I expanded formal study of all books related to Technical Analysis and price action as well as reading numerous pop-culture market books during this time. Probably the most infamous of these was Peter Lynch's *One up on Wall Street*. In its simplicity, the book highlighted a clear framework for regular people – non-professionals – to recognize obvious consumer trends as valid long-term investment opportunities. Mr. Lynch was always looking for that good story where he could make his "multi-bagger" on trades – that means making many times his money. Also, the book espoused a self-reliant and diligent perspective to do your homework, understand your investment and rely on one's own judgement than solely on others' opinions. This proactive perspective shaped my thinking to begin to look for relationships that were outside of traditional concepts. The book ignited an excitement where I started to pay close attention to what was happening in the economy and the financial markets. I became an avid reader of any recommended financial book. I found myself increasingly wanting to know more about the indicators and other technical measures that were frequently discussed by traders more so than the latest brokers' recommendations. I understood early on that the answers were not going to be handed to me and there was much to consider when it came to the world of trading.

This became ever apparent for me during a college summer internship on the floor of the Philadelphia Stock Exchange in 1987. As a CRT (computer) operator, I was in the Options pits manually adjusting the quote prices displayed at the market maker's terminal as he barked them out. (Of course, today it is all automatic.) I spent the first few weeks trying to keep up with the regular employees whom had been there for a while. I was intrigued by the overall operation, the excitement of busy sessions and the basic notion that people were making large sums of money working at a dynamic place of employment. For me, it was clear that those who understood probable future price direction were able to successfully navigate the chaos that was the trading floor of this time. Albeit a physically small exchange, the floor in Philadelphia was as busy as any frenetic day in New York. I learned a lot during this time, and a few individuals took the time to teach me some complex option strategies even though I barely knew what a put or a call was. It was all special and certainly different from any other corporate environment that I had previously experienced. I came away from that internship with a passion to further explore what this industry was all about.

I rededicated myself to studying books on charting and Technical Analysis. The more I investigated the measurement of the market using technical tools, the more I realized that this was the true means to know when to buy and sell for profit. In those early days, I was considering fundamental information but quickly into the journey, I learned that these metrics described what already unfolded, and actually had little value when it comes to determining day to day price fluctuations. Soon after, Technical Analysis became my exclusive means of determining trade opportunities in the market. Although this was the right direction, there were a few years of study required of all methodologies before I could fully grasp which technical tools worked the best. In this research, I spent tens of thousands of dollars on books and seminars to discover which systems were effective. Unfortunately, most methodologies failed to be reliable over time.

I was fortunate to encounter a retired former floor trader as I was finishing my college degree who mentored me on many old-school methods of Technical Analysis. I have mentioned him before but I would like to recognize him again. Although he never wrote a book and he was an extremely private person in nature, Bill Sourbey was my primary mentor in Technical Analysis. He was a former floor trader in the Minneapolis grains pit in the late 1950s. He shared many stories of the old days – and this was back when they were still writing quote changes on a chalkboard! Regardless, he showed me unique charting methods. In particular, he created elaborate charts by hand, plotting each day's price values. He stressed the importance of trendlines, channels and various price action phenomenon that he painstakingly measured. His discipline and focus on measuring every data point of individual price action showed me that charts were merely a collection of information that told a story. He believed that specific points and price levels were critical to finding the limits of possibility for any market. These all helped to shape my predictive abilities and understand that price action moves within definable constraints that can be and must be measured! In fact, I did not truly understand the full nature of what he taught me until I had a few years of experience studying his charts.

Despite our 30-year age difference, Bill and I formed a special friendship, sharing our interest of Technical Analysis. Bill was an "old-school" market guy who kept meticulous notes, developed his own indicators and was able to predict market moves with phenomenal accuracy. He developed proprietary indicators such as Viscosity – combining Volume with price ranges. This is a very interesting concept that tries to measure the "thickness or thinness" of support or resistance within the market in a similar way to Market Profile analysis. Bill has since passed in my life, and he never imparted to me the entire formula of how to determine this. I do have numerous charts and I have been analyzing for years trying to figure out the formulae but the concept unto itself has led to a few proprietary discoveries. Although he was always somewhat cryptic and vague in general, he was an influence. He encouraged me to tinker with proprietary strategies derived from my technical studies which I did in earnest.

Bill shared many personal (hand-drawn) charts with me. He illustrated various pattern formations such as simple wedge and triangle formulations that denoted breakouts or breakdowns with impressive accuracy. His trend analysis proved quite effective, and became the starting point for my studies, as well. The simple fact that I

Harmonic Trading Volume 3: Reaction vs. Reversal

could analyze a price action by drawing a basic trendline along the general direction was a breakthrough unto itself for me as simple as it may seem. It opened up the perspective that actually monitoring price action is the most effective means of gauging what potentially could occur. From this, I then began to focus on the phenomenon that markets frequently trade within ranges and cycles. In my discussions with him, Bill constantly reminded me of the importance of certain trendline violations as important structural signals. In fact, he referred me to the work of Richard Wyckoff, and I studied his material closely – much of these books were written in the early 1900s. Also, another trader from decades ago - Ted Warren – wrote a remarkable but relatively unknown book, *How to Make Money in the Stock Market*. This material is an in-depth discussion that explains why the market is always in a process of moving through stages. Armed with all of this information, I began to formulate the essence of my strategic approach and generate a more precise plan regarding each opportunity. I knew certain measurement combinations were consistently yielding the proper technical information and correct predictive price limits within a reasonable range. Although I made a great deal of mistakes in those early years and lost quite a bit of money – probably more money than I even had to lose, I knew that this was all in the endeavor to eventually make breakthroughs to become a consistently profitable trader. To do so, I needed a framework of strategies so I could understand market action in any environment on any timeframe.

The Gartley Group

During this time, I started to encounter other traders in my area, especially as the internet provided a direct means of reaching other people unlike ever before. In the mid-1990s, I was living in Tucson, Arizona where I encountered a group of traders that met once a month to talk about the markets. Although initially intended as a local group support group for Tradestation users, the discussion soon focused mostly on trading strategies relevant to the unfolding bull market mania of this decade. Founded by Alan Kuenhold who was a broker with UBS Advisors, the initial group of 10-15 people met at the Williams Center regularly to talk about the markets. It was a great discussion group and it is also the first place where I publicly began to divulge many of the strategies that became Harmonic Trading. After a few months, we officially named ourselves *The Gartley Group*.

Many a night, we debated the remarkable bull market of the time. I introduced a variety of ideas that were working for me at the time. Exact pattern alignments, trade management strategies such as the 38.2% trailer, and general price action analysis eventually became the foundation of Harmonic Trading. I am grateful to Alan and the group for giving me the format to present the ideas. I must admit this was during a time where the market was moving straight up. So, anything that you bought had a good chance of actually working out. It seemed as if nearly every retracement pattern led to a significant reversal. This made (bullish) harmonic patterns look great. Therefore, I was

Harmonic Trading Volume 3: Reaction vs. Reversal

able to differentiate which patterns were the most significant and where to execute the trades with a unique level of precision. The overall effectiveness and clarity of each opportunity increased over time as did the number of people attending the Gartley Group. After about two years, the Gartley Group tripled in size as we started meeting nearly every week. On average, we would see nearly 30 or 40 people show up. Although various opinions were bantered about, the core discussion evolved into mostly strategies that focused on THE PATTERNS. (Remember, harmonic pattern rules such as Potential Reversal Zone, Terminal Bar, Type I&II as well as the names – Bat, Crab, Shark - did not exist.) Many talked about ratios with respect to Elliott Wave. But I was only interested in the M&W-Type formations, stressing adamantly the importance of DIFFERENTIATION. Although Elliott Wave and earnings reports can have value, I was interested in the critical decision variables of a trade opportunity based upon the structural measures of price movements exclusively.

The ability of the early pattern strategies to consistently define DIRECTION was undeniable. At the group meetings, I would go through any chart people wanted to review based upon the general framework of measures I employed to differentiate patterns. For me, I simply applied the measured parameters to define not only patterns that were unfolding but applied these results to serve as price targets. Admittedly, the discussion focused mostly on what to buy. However, the bearish patterns were continually accurate signals when to take profits. As the Volatility and trading action increased through those few years, the public increasingly took notice, and soon the market was a pop culture phenomenon. The Gartley Group continued to grow in size and frequency, as we now met almost weekly AND some Saturday's! Unfortunately, the group's focus shifted in an extremely unusual manner as other individuals in the group began to talk about certain penny stocks and speculate wildly that it was different this time. The future of technology was endless and it was only the beginning. This was in the year 1999 – 10 months before the index topped out and lost over 80% of its value. The NASDAQ Composite tripled during these few years, and it was quickly on its way to test the 5000 level. The mania gripped the masses, and soon several people in the group all-in on speculative penny Tech stocks.

E-Digital (EDIG): The Epitome of Dotcom Mania

There was one stock that actually worked – for a few months. The company was named - eDigital (EDIG) – and had all of the labels of the time. First, we have the "e" for electronic (as in email) that was mixed with DIGITAL – in a combination that couldn't lose - right!?! There was one guy in the group who said that this was going to be the next Microsoft and recommended everyone buy the stock at about $0.05, then more at $0.10 and more at $0.20. Shying away from such penny stocks, I preferred to follow the leaders of the market and the more heavily traded issues of the time. For me, I felt that this mania was problematic. Furthermore, the fact that the group went from a

Harmonic Trading Volume 3: Reaction vs. Reversal

constructive discussion of technical methods to focusing on penny Tech stocks was another signal of the end.

E-Digital (EDIG): Jumping the Shark

This was a classic case where the group "Jumped the Shark" and I knew the end was near EDIG. Incredibly, it all culminated over the course of six weeks where this penny stock started to move from $.50 to a $1 to $3 to $7 to $11 and higher.

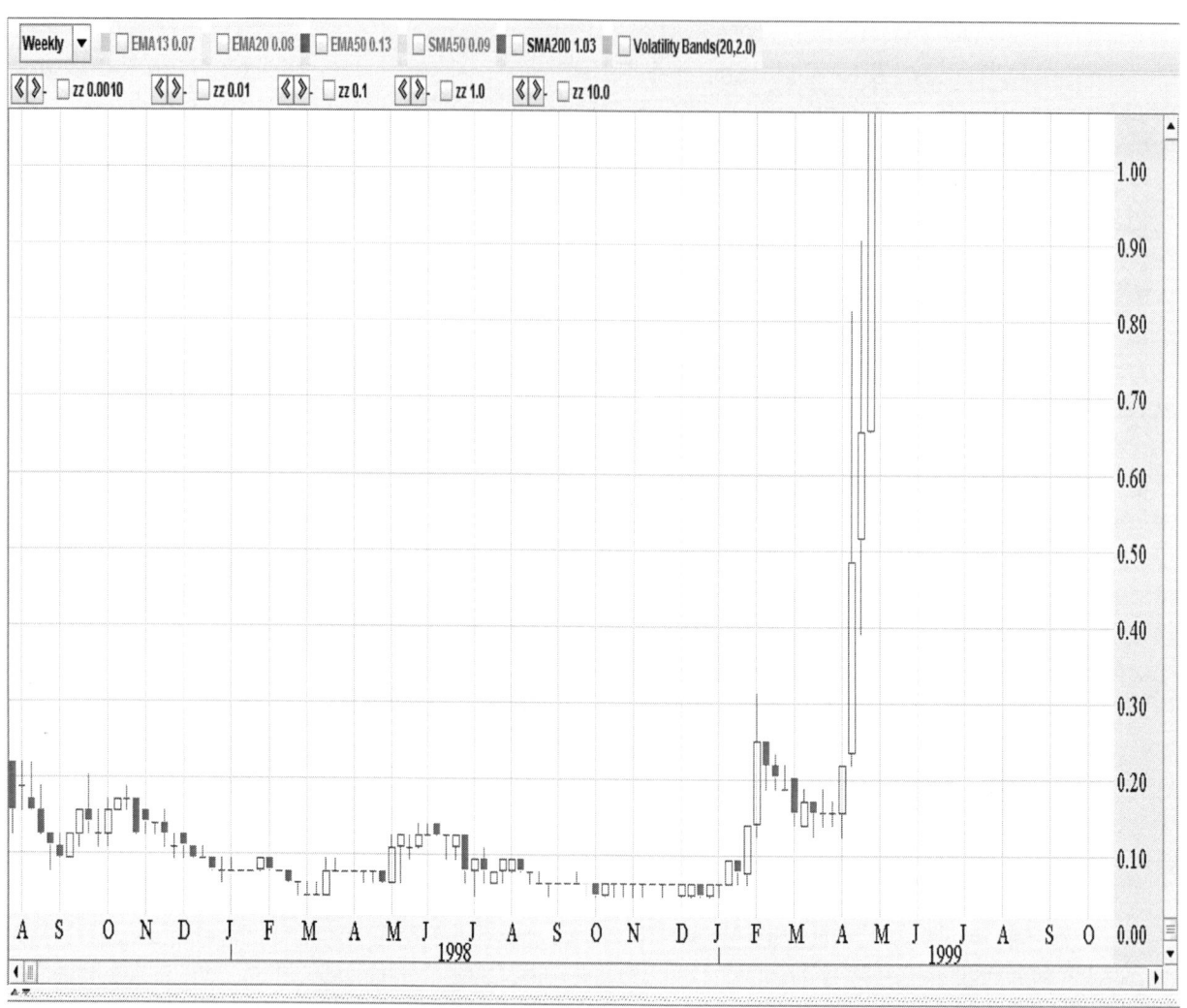

Soon, the stock went parabolic as it rallied from pennies to dollars a share. The individual who initially recommended the stock announced at one meeting that he had put his whole life savings into it because he predicted that this stock would go to $200. Many people jumped in, rode the stock up and all of the way down.

Harmonic Trading Volume 3: Reaction vs. Reversal

E-Digital (EDIG): The Meltdown

After some time, it was still being recommended as a buy. And people bought! Eventually, the stock went to $21 a share. I remember the exact meeting on the day it hit the $21 mark. There were approximately 50 people in the room that night. I was late getting there and there were so many that I couldn't even get into the room. I watched from outside the door. At that point, I knew that the Gartley Group was over. I also knew that this eDigital stock would not end well. People were asking me if I had bought the stock and I said that I didn't touch those types of positions.

Despite my concerns, many people continued to buy. The stock peaked out at the $21 level and then quickly lost half its value back to $10 a share. It was only a matter of time before the whole stock would collapse and that's exactly what happened. It was

Harmonic Trading Volume 3: Reaction vs. Reversal

a train-wreck in slow motion! Even though the stock was up 1000% in a short period of time, many assumed it would continue on the linear 90-degree uptrend. Well, nothing goes straight up! Wrecking day was near and I stayed clear.

EDIG @ 3.14 Bearish Extension: Weekly

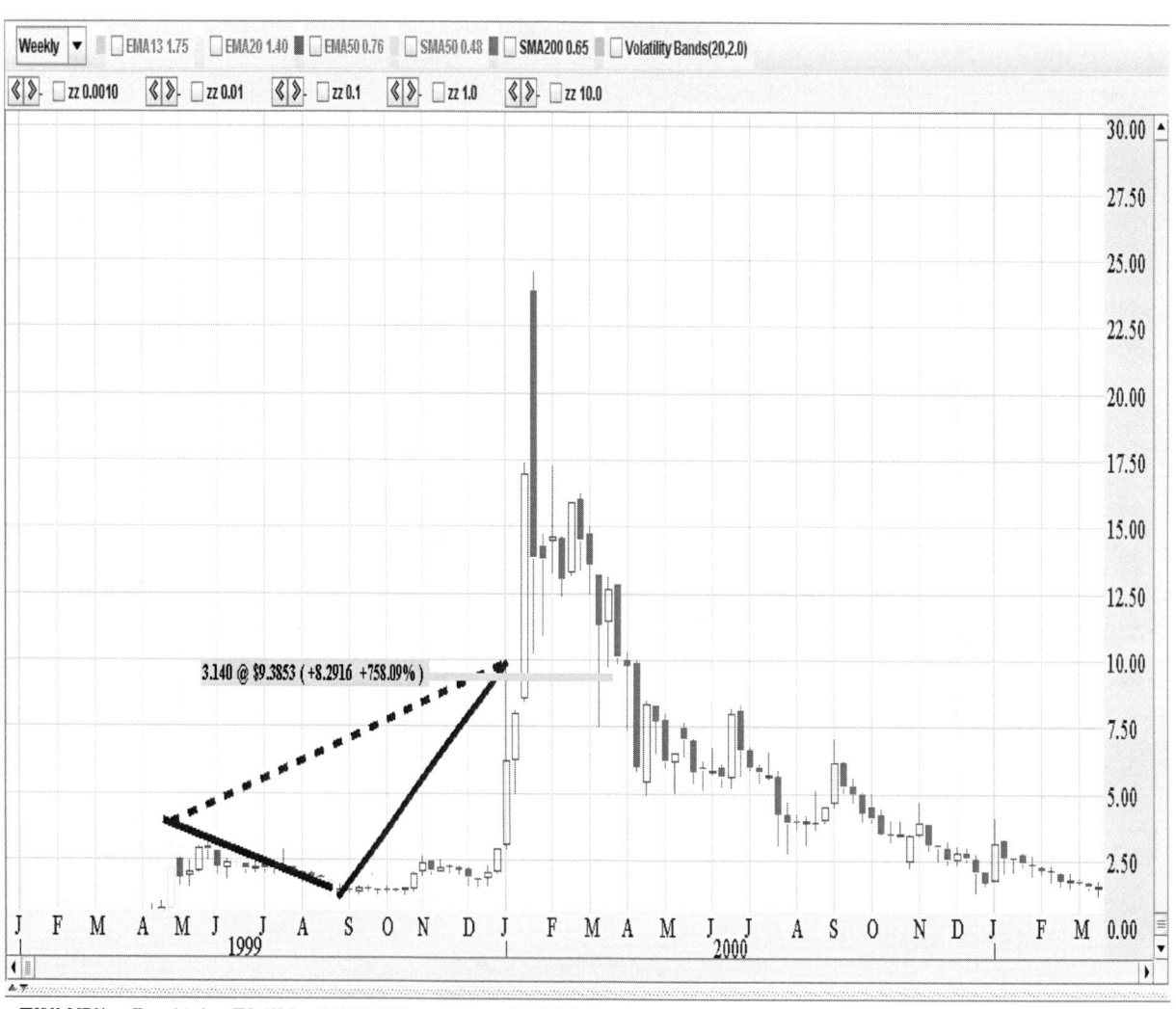

Being known as the harmonic guy in the group, the only analysis within the scope of measures I employed was a simple 3.14 extension that projected immediate resistance at the $10 level. After the stock rallied vigorously through this price, I distinctly remember hearing comments such is the fact that harmonic measurements don't work in situations like this. Nothing could be further from the truth because the 3.14 extension typically signals a parabolic move that is unsustainable beyond the measured level. Even in the early days, I understood that each ratio measurement

Harmonic Trading Volume 3: Reaction vs. Reversal

13

maintained certain expectations. In the case of this stock, the move was clearly parabolic, resulting in only one conclusion. After peaking above $22 a share, the imminent collapse was marked by an immediate haircut where the price lost half its value within a few weeks. By the end of the year, the entire bull run was over as the stock was trading back under $1.

Many were burned. Despite the post-crash squabbles, the entire experience was the perfect case study in Dot Com mania! I won't even go into the other details of what ensued, including potential legal action from one person to the next. The clear lesson to be learned from a mania like that taught me how to read the public and understand when certain market periods are exhausted.

Many in the group lost a ton of money – some even their life savings! Although I felt bad, I had nothing to do with it and I knew that things had to change. So, the remaining core Gartley Group actually decided to disband and begin to meet "secretly." It was during this time that I started to get serious with the pattern rules and refine the differentiations of all of the retracement and extension patterns to an exact degree. I was even working on new harmonic structures such as the 5-0 and the Shark pattern. I also was beginning to investigate which indicators served as the greatest confirmation techniques for the patterns. Most importantly, I started work on the Harmonic Analyzer – the first-of-its-kind harmonic pattern program. Despite the group's demise, I was able to work out many ideas during those years. It is important to remember that even simple pattern rules that are obvious today were not clearly established and required immense manual scrutiny to apply these strategies and identify opportunities.

The overall understanding of harmonic pattern phenomenon has evolved into an entire framework of measures that provides reliable decision metrics at each stage of the process. Integrating a variety of established technical measures with proprietary advancements, the strategic harmonic plan effectively delineates price parameters – entry, exit, stop loss – in advance. The harmonic relationships have become even more refined with the advent of the new harmonic pattern software and additional confirmation variables that separate random structures from valid opportunities. All of these strategies have coalesced into a comprehensive methodology that seeks to isolated and identify specific natural limits of price action.

Harmonic Pattern Framework – A Complete Methodology

The proprietary discoveries of harmonic pattern rules and related measures would not be possible without the decades of technical work put forth by so many traders from the past. I go out of my way to cite those technical forefathers whom have laid the foundation for what modern Technical Analysis is today. Most of my inspiration for these ideas has been derived from the "old-school" books. Based from this technical foundation, I created the system of trade identification, execution and management strategies that effectively that outlines the entire trading process. These strategies create a framework so that traders understand what to do in each step of every trade. From this perspective, an entire skill set has been established based on harmonic measures. Although these are some of the most accurate means of measuring, the business of trading is not easy. If you do the work and you want to understand which strategies are vital, a professional skill set that identifies harmonic opportunities facilitates the ability to execute with an optimal efficiency. This comprehension takes time. Furthermore, I urge everyone to do their own research, look at the materials and assess what I have done as a unique system in way to look at the market, especially now that it is now widely embraced.

After I released *The Harmonic Trader*, people began to take notice. I was having great success, and I was sharing chart ideas freely with many people. Maybe this was a bit naïve of my behalf, but I believed in sharing ideas with people that I knew and others whom requested it for feedback and constructive criticism. I felt that most of my trading friends at the time were on the same boat trying to succeed during chaotic times. Everyone was attempting to navigate the wild price action, especially during a time when the Internet stocks were going through a historic bull market. Against the backdrop of this frenzied market environment, my goal was to share the information to make it available so that people could understand the power of harmonic patterns. More importantly, the patterns provided a measured means to consider any opportunity. People realized that they could pinpoint opportunities with accuracy as long as they were disciplined and precise in following the plan. From this, I was motivated to expand upon the subject, refine the strategies and develop the most accurate harmonic tools possible. I was confident from the start I was using the right measures to analyze price action and it was only a matter of time before we would have the most advanced trading technology to automate the entire methodology.

Harmonic Mystique

Although it is easy to get caught up in the mystique of this phenomenon, I have always focused on relating the theory of these natural cycles with harmonic ratio proportions into actionable price levels in the financial markets. My goal has always been to take this knowledge into new areas of experimentation and further capitalize on the natural reactive aspects that harmonic measures offer. Even from the beginning, I wanted to differentiate patterns structures, interpret price action at those completion points and make larger assessments of probable future trend direction. From these concepts, Harmonic Trading has thrived and led to the subsequent discoveries presented *Harmonic Trading Volume 1* and *Volume* 2. In 2010, I received an offer from Financial Times Press to publish and internationally distribute a second edition of these books. As the material found an audience globally, more traders embraced these concepts. The ability of traders to integrate harmonic pattern strategies with success added to the overall validity of this approach and reinforced its reputation regarding the effectiveness of harmonic patterns, as its popularity has grown.

Harmonic Trading Volume 3: Reaction vs. Reversal

On a final note, I want to stress that for me it is always about the work – not the mystique. I always felt that if the work was excellent people would respond people. Traders have responded! For that Harmonic Traders, I thank you. This is become something far greater than I could ever imagine. I feel that with the limited time that I have left on this planet that I want to share this knowledge and I want to leave behind a legacy where people can not only trade the markets effectively but actually realize the amazing natural wonders and natural cycles that are occurring in the universe and in the world, every day.

Harmonic Character

For me, personal integrity and character are tantamount to everything else. There are too many charlatans hawking worthless products and services in the trading industry – especially the harmonic domain – as if they were selling vacuum cleaners door-to-door. This work is extremely personal to me and I will do everything within my ability to prevent the distortion and ridiculous manipulation to call any trading strategy harmonic in the attempt to catch the popular wave. There are no harmonic gimmicks and the true essence of this approach lies within the understanding of the very measures applied to define opportunities. Therefore, the degree of detail and strategic consideration is deep and has been tested for years before even being released. In this material, my goal is to preserve the value of the Harmonic Trading approach that highlights a standardized means to measure the markets not just recite the well-chosen examples. Unfortunately, I have seen quite a bit harmonic misinformation in recent years. Some individuals are teaching harmonic patterns based straight out of my book but they are still doing it incorrectly. And in most cases, few are able to do it in real time because they fail to understand and follow the entire natural process.

My goal is to expose the gimmicks and counter the faulty misappropriation by setting forth the entire process in a manner that traders can understand. Harmonic patterns are effective but individuals must be able to clarify the ambiguity in the execution and trade management stages of the process to optimize trading decisions. Most people aware of harmonic understand the general definitions of the ratio alignments and measurements required. But as I've always said, the harmonic patterns are a starting point, as their application requires a precision and a dedication above and beyond simple identification. Although I have presented in-depth material in my prior books, *Volume Three* brings it all together in an unprecedented manner. Furthermore, we now have the most sophisticated and precise harmonic pattern software program that can automatically provide all price parameters in advance. Together, this material and the new trading technology have refined these effective strategies even further. All of these endeavors have been a positive and proactive manner that attests to character of what being Harmonic is all about – absolute excellence. In that manner, this material solidifies all stages of the Harmonic Trading process unlike ever before.

Harmonic Trading Volume 3: Reaction vs. Reversal

Introduction

A Reintroduction to Harmonic Trading

My main goal in this book is to set the whole record straight, to reinforce the established structural measures and to emphasize the need to precisely confirm harmonic pattern opportunities with what I like to refer as "environmental technical indicators" that optimize all situations. I have been reluctant to write another book, as I knew that it would take quite a bit of time to put together a comprehensive advancement of the existing material. Although I have been aware of many advanced techniques for years, I have not shared these with too many people. Initially, I needed a great deal of time to test each strategy and completely refine the rules to effectively complement the basic Harmonic Trading approach. This book is comprised of nearly 80% new material that builds upon the existing strategies and optimizes specific pattern situations to improve overall results.

The advancements presented in this material represent a new stage in the evolution of the harmonic pattern methodology. The material in this book picks up right where *Harmonic Trading Volume 2* left off, and defines unprecedented situations that are as distinct as harmonic patterns themselves. These advanced conditions improve the effectiveness of the entire approach. Although many of these strategies can be learned as individual concepts, I reference the material from *Volume 1* and *Volume 2* as the foundation of strategies that are combined to isolate exact situations. Simple pattern rules, trade execution strategies and other guidelines still serve as the essential model for the Harmonic Trading process. In fact, this book represents an advancement of that process, especially in the area of Trade Execution and Trade Management. Although my first few Harmonic Trading books detailed effective strategies to comprise the identification aspect of the approach, this material coalesces a variety of individual techniques to define an even more comprehensive perspective of the harmonic pattern framework.

Harmonic Trading Volume 3: Reaction vs. Reversal

Over the years, my studies evolved to measure the market's price movements as the source for all trading decisions. Opportunities must be derived from the price action alone rather than any outside influences. Although most traders will consider a variety of sources of information to formulate a strategic approach to define opportunities, ultimately every participant is trying to profit from price fluctuations. Therefore, the business of harmonic pattern trading measures and predicts future movements based solely from the price analysis of buying and selling of these defined opportunities. Harmonic Traders realize that financial reports and news stories are less relevant as signals for trading opportunities are based upon the readings of the market's own movements. These measurements define the trade parameters and outline plan before the opportunity is even executed. In effect, the harmonic pattern framework – Potential Reversal Zone (PRZ), Terminal Bar, Management targets - define the limits of any possibility. Since harmonic patterns provide a strategic approach to measure these opportunities relative to prior price action, these structures can define the exact price levels where other technical measures provide secondary confirmation. In particular, a market's extreme indicator readings can denote the proper expectations that are reflected in something other than price.

These techniques are designed to gauge the natural limits of any movement relative to the immediate timeframe. In doing so, we can measure some sense of order within the chaos and randomness of price movements. For example, a market that moves decisively to test a clear 1.618 extension is a price movement that should ALWAYS be respected as an extreme move by harmonic definition but still requires additional criteria to determine the potential for something more than a brief reaction. For example, the analysis of Relative Strength readings is one confirmation strategy that helps to monitor type of "environment" in which patterns complete. We will look at this integration in detail later in this material, as we will examine price behavior within measured technical environments to show those conditions that possess the optimal characteristics for positive confirmation.

The Harmonic Learning Curve

Despite my attempts to simplify all of this, I know that there are many points of contention that may arise when assessing harmonic pattern concepts initially. There is a great deal of information to consider but I stress the importance of learning the process not just the pattern. For anyone that is new to this perspective, I like to use the phrase "live with it for a little while" where you observe the analytical steps to realize that sequence of steps these structures exhibit repeatedly. The common experience for most is a "lightbulb" that goes on, as the harmonic pattern relationships become almost obvious. Therefore, I recommend that traders whom are new to this approach take the time to develop a thorough comprehension of identification strategies. Although these methods require a period of study to truly grasp the entire harmonic pattern framework, the ratio relationships and structural proportions are quickly recognized more clearly with experience. I will thoroughly explain details and finer relationships that will answer most questions that typically arise in the discovery phase of these strategies. However, there is a Harmonic Learning Curve that all traders must go through. The common experience for most Harmonic Traders to gain a clear comprehension of the identification of pattern opportunities but lack execution and management skills to capitalize on the situation. Much of the material in *Volume Three* bridges the gaps in these stages of the Harmonic Trading process. Regardless, these strategies instill discipline to make decisions in an effective and proactive manner.

Consistency in the Application of Identification

Harmonic patterns provide a quantifiable technical model to define opportunities in the financial markets. This means that the prescribed measurements merely serve as a minimum framework upon which the actual expression of real trading must be compared. I emphasize this point in an attempt to reduce unrealistic expectations of patterns as signals on their own and implore traders to intelligently assess other market conditions that clearly contribute to the overall understanding of any harmonic opportunity. Furthermore, the true advantage of these identification strategies is founded upon the consistency in the definition of what is a potential HARMONIC opportunity. Specifically, each pattern has its own set ratios. Regardless of the timeframe or the price of the structure, each situation is defined by the relative harmonic measurements that validate random price movements as specific opportunities.

Harmonic pattern strategies can be applied to all markets on any timeframe. That is, all techniques possess the same interpretive qualities and must be applied in a uniform manner in every market and timeframe. From stocks to futures to currencies, Harmonic Trading principles possess the same implications in all markets. Although some argue that certain markets may behave differently than others, our primary concern with analyzing price action is to discover consistent relationships that can be derived with distinction. This is critical because the strategies are hence standardized, and define market opportunities in the same manner. Furthermore, the same relationships that occur on a daily or weekly chart can be found on intraday or even tick price movements.

Some structural market approaches have tendencies to adjust their analysis and fit derived results to conform to the overall picture. This type of interpretive analytical approach is dangerous when it comes to assessing price action because such variation of measurements leads to inconsistent results. Harmonic patterns employ proportional measurements that can be deciphered regardless of the price range. This is one of the true advantages that separates Harmonic Trading from all other methodologies. Finally, such universal application possesses enormous strengths in deciphering market movements that can frequently diverge from the norm. When this happens, traders tend to adjust their analytical findings and begin to create a biased assessment of what is

Harmonic Trading Volume 3: Reaction vs. Reversal

happening. Essentially, when a trader is confused they start guessing and nothing is more expensive than trying to guess which way the market will go. Nine times out of ten that guess will be wrong. Therefore, any market approach must have the ability to be uniformly applied and assess price action from an unwavering basis.

This was one of my guiding principles throughout my research. I am always looking for the market relationships that consistently and clearly present readings that can reliably define probable future price action. Many of the market methodologies that I have studied make room for slight variation of the application of their principles. However, I found that these circumstances led to incorrect assumptions and created even more confusion within the trading process. As I mentioned previously, Elliott Wave is a prime example where traders will conform their structural counts to best fit the current market environment, adjusting their structural calculations in the event that the market does not adhere to the ideal situation.

Founders of M&W-Type Structural Wave Analysis

There are many people that have discussed price patterns in the market, however few assigned ratios to the structures. Robert Prechter and A.J. Frost advanced Wave Theory analysis and were among the first to discuss 61.8% and 1.618% ratios with price structures. As most people know, Elliott wave counts can be quite subjective. For me, wave counts were insufficient as an accurate and consistent predictive system to pinpoint the PRICE of the opportunity. Admittedly, it is a great structural model but it is can be less than reliable as actionable trade information. Regardless, the principles of Elliott Wave theory provide general structural differentiation advantages that has been an essential focus throughout the history of Harmonic Trading. Therefore, R.N. Elliott and others must be recognized as the vital predecessors that laid the foundation for harmonic pattern analysis.

It is incredible to think that a bit more than 100 years ago people first started writing about technical strategies to decipher market movements. Although simple in the early years, basic technical methods such as Dow Theory was among the first to describe market movements and ratio measures. Later technicians focused more on simple percentage moves and identified trendline phenomenon. It is important to understand that Technical Analysis has not evolved much beyond the trendline and channel analysis that was introduced over 100 years ago. Some of the more prominent advancements such as Relative Strength, Stochastics, harmonic patterns, Elliott Wave, ratio analysis and other measured strategies technical in nature have advanced the initial tenets that quantify market movements. Personally, I feel there is plenty of room for the advancement of Technical Analysis to focus on the realization that market movements possess all of the answers that traders need to facilitate trading decisions. It is within this principle that I believe Harmonic Trading derives its greatest strength.

XABCD->Harmonic Patterns

There are a number of technicians over the past century whom have presented individual concepts that have inspired harmonic pattern discoveries and provided the primary foundation of market research to advance technical price strategies. Harmonic Trading encompasses parts of many theories and expands upon a variety of basic technical measurement strategies. I have studied most of the prominent technicians of the past hundred years and I have learned a great deal from their initial insights. I believe that it is imperative to recognize these individuals for their contribution. They have created a basic science around the recognition of market movements and these works have created the body of knowledge that is Technical Analysis today.

Harmonic patterns are an advancement of a vague identification strategy that labeled structures as five-point XABCD formations. Although the initial principles of wave structures were first outlined by R.N. Elliott, the notion that complex price formations can provide relevant predictive value of future direction has been refined by many other technicians since then. Furthermore, the application of ratio measurements has evolved ever since Charles Dow first introduced his rules for Dow Theory that analyzed the market in relation to standard percentages (1/3, 2/3). Other practitioners of Technical Analysis have added to this foundation and expanded the envelope of understanding over the past hundred years.

The Technical Pioneers (1890-1970s)

Once I was committed to the study of Technical Analysis, I researched the oldest materials I could find. Historic market insights that were presented decades ago have relevance to modern-day markets. In fact, many of the pioneers of Technical Analysis were keen to emphasize the importance of price analysis over advisor opinion. Illegal speculation and manipulation were rampant 100 years ago, necessitating that the actual trading history be analyzed. In my opinion, the following technicians must be sought out and researched.

- *Charles Dow & Dow Theory*
- *R.N. Elliott*
- *Elliott Wave Principle (Prechter and Frost)*
- *W.D. Gann*
- *Richard Wyckoff*
- *H.M. Gartley "Profits in the Stock Market"*
- *Arthur Merrill (& Edward Levy) = Merrill Waves*
- *Welles Wilder*

Harmonic Trading Volume 3: Reaction vs. Reversal

Most are known for a seminal book or method that distinguished their work from many others. In fact, most people do not know that there are dozens of technical pioneers whom have presented amazing work but never received the recognition they deserve. I mention a few of these individuals throughout this material and recommend their works, as well.

Modern Day Technicians (1980-Present)

- *Robert Miner "Dynamic Trading"*
- *Bryce Gilmore "Geometry of Markets"*

There are numerous individuals whom have put forth a dearth of resources but most have simply regurgitated the works of the past masters. It is important though that I recognize two individuals in particular, whom have distinguished themselves and were immensely inspirational in my work to create harmonic pattern rules. Robert Miner's book, *Dynamic Trading* is an Elliott Wave masterpiece that introduces new applications of the standard rules, including unique time and price projections. I had the pleasure of meeting Mr. Miner at a presentation he generously gave to the Gartley Group. Bryce Gilmore's *Geometry of Markets* is another must-have technical book that correlated ratios with wave analysis in an unprecedented manner. Mr. Gilmore's application of Gann-style ratios and trendlines were applied to his comprehensive explanation of the XABCD framework. In fact, he presented unique structural measurements related to various types of complex five-wave formations. Additionally, his *Wave Trader* was the first program to scan for M & W-type formations. In fact, Mr. Gilmore deserves the primary credit for establishing the general measurement principles for XABCD structures in the modern era. I am immensely grateful for his contributions and I recognize his work as a direct forerunner to harmonic patterns.

Harmonic Patterns - Two Schools of Technical Thought

It is important to outline the basis of measurement for harmonic structures. The strategies are founded upon two general categories of Technical Analysis. General ratio measures and structural wave classifications define the foundation of all technical approaches and comprise the foundation for Harmonic Trading. Harmonic patterns employ both ratios with structural wave analysis in a unique manner that incorporate many of the principles established by the past masters. I recommend these resources for any serious student of the market.

Harmonic Trading Volume 3: Reaction vs. Reversal

1. Wave Theory/Market Structure: Elliott/Dow/Others

Charles Dow was among the earliest of technicians who categorized market movements and proposed general percentage retracements (1/3, 1/2, 2/3, etc.) in his articles for *The Wall Street Journal*. A few decades later, the writings of R.N. Elliott were some of the most comprehensive structural analysis ever presented at this time. His classifications of three and five wave price phenomena were the first prescribed structural analysis that identified the importance of multiple segments. Although the wave structures lacked ratio measures, the general structural rules did provide an effective framework to assess the state of the larger trend.

In the same manner, harmonic patterns distinguish structural opportunities in the markets. The refinement of M&W-type patterns was a significant step forward in the structural analysis of five-wave price formations. The proprietary concepts of harmonic patterns advanced the primary body of knowledge as it relates to structural analysis of price segments based upon a simple differentiation principle, as the following exemplifies:

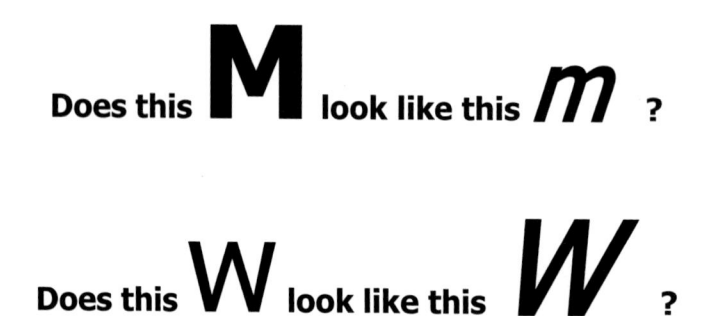

Does this **M** look like this *m* ?

Does this **W** look like this *W* ?

I have outlined this concept in prior material but this key recognition of structural differences is the essence of harmonic pattern analysis. When validated by specific ratio alignments and other harmonic measures, these structures quantify all relevant parameters in the determination of any trade.

Harmonic Trading Volume 3: Reaction vs. Reversal

2. "Sacred Geometry" Ratios (W.D. Gann)

William Delbert (W.D.) Gann presented numerous measures that have become a primary discipline within Technical Analysis. Tools such as Gann angles, Square of 9, Hexagon, and Circle of 360 became his primary market forecasting methods. Although I agree with many of his Geometric principles, Harmonic Trading has nothing to do with his other areas of study, most notably Astrology.

Although cyclical in nature, Astrology has little relevance to exact price structures, regardless of what its proponents might argue! In my opinion, the Gann mystique is overblown while I feel his essential technical contributions do not receive the credit due. W.D. Gann can be considered as the forefather of ratio differentiation, as he effectively refined concepts from Ancient Mathematics into trend analysis. In this regard, harmonic patterns and their measurements respect the natural phenomenon of cyclical movements of growth and decline in the same manner as Gann's principles. When related to the market, Harmonic Trading considers trendline analysis similarly, as well. In these regards, immense respect is due to Mr. Gann.

H.M. Gartley

Most popular of all harmonic patterns, the origins of the Gartley have been mired in a haze of misinformation and misrepresentation. I have discussed this previously in a variety of materials, including an article entitled "The Great Gartley Controversy." (Google it). First let me say, I have the utmost respect for his book, *Profits in the Stock Market* (1935). This masterpiece was ahead of its time and it is one of the most detailed technical resources I've ever read. The problem that I had with the initial interpretations of the Gartley pattern was the lack of precision to define exactly what was valid trading opportunity. This was not Mr. Gartley's fault, especially since he mentioned little in regards to patterns and did not integrate ratios with their measurements, despite contrary opinion. The Gartley pattern that many improperly attribute to his book does not resemble anything to what the industry standard is today. The following illustration is a recreation of the structural outline he presented in his book, *Profits in the Stock Market* (1935).

I encourage all serious students of the market to purchase this book. The painstaking detail and explanation provide accurate technical insights that are still relevant to this day. However, most will be surprised to learn that the material possesses little in the way of ratios or any of the work that is commonly attributed to him. The illustration represents what he presented in his book - no harmonic ratios, no AB=CD structures, and it is the extent of his identification of pattern structures. I have studied this book intensely and learned much from his work. However, the core focus of his material has been more on cycles and general wave structures than patterns. This is immensely important as a clarification of the source of harmonic patterns.

Although others have presented various interpretations, the personal breakthrough in my first book, *The Harmonic Trader* integrated the M&W-type structures on an unprecedented level. Whether I fully understood the uniqueness of this integration or not, the complex rules that defined harmonic opportunities advanced the general XABCD knowledge to convert this structural analysis into predictive trading capabilities. For my purposes, I experimented with combinations of measures to distinguish each as a unique situation. This pursuit led to distinct classifications of M&W formations as actionable trade opportunities.

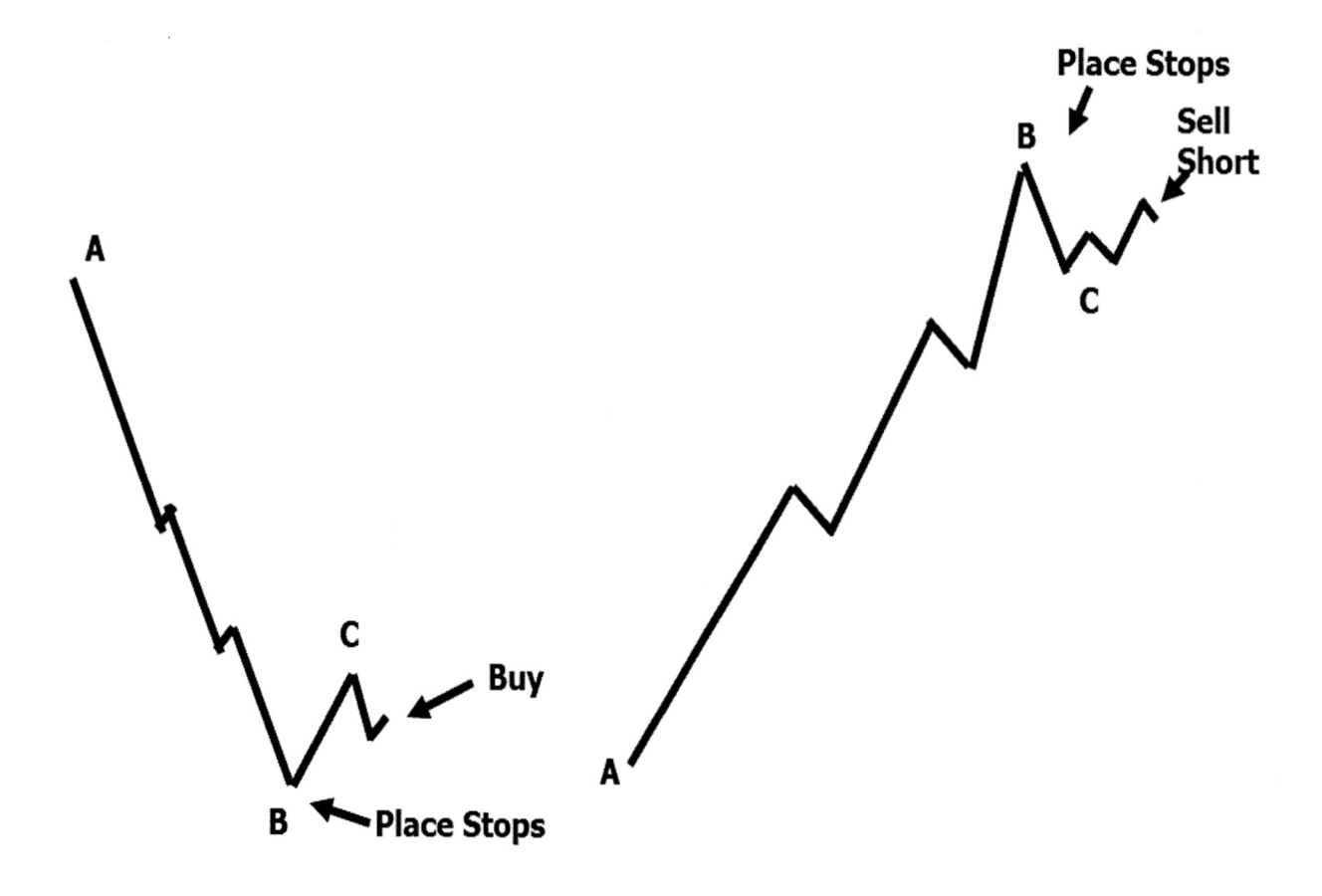

Profits in the Stock Market (1935) Gartley, H.M. Lambert-Gann Publishing, p.222.

Harmonic Trading Volume 3: Reaction vs. Reversal

Merrill Waves

Arthur Merrill authored his book, *Filtered Waves* and presented illustrations of a few dozen different M&W-type structures. Although his price formations were more Zig-Zag type market movements and lacked any ratio measurements, his basic premise of categorizing 5-point structures in this regard was unique interpretation of Wave Theory. The number of classifications that Mr. Merrill presented possessed a clear intention to structurally differentiate similar price movements. His approach attempted to distinguish 5-point wedge and consolidation formations, while incorporating basic rules of Elliott Wave. Also, Edward Levy contributed to this work and distinguished various segments as discernable formations. These contributions along with a host of other technicians bridged the writings of R.N. Elliott to the modern-day advancements of what has generally become known as a 5-point XABCD structure.

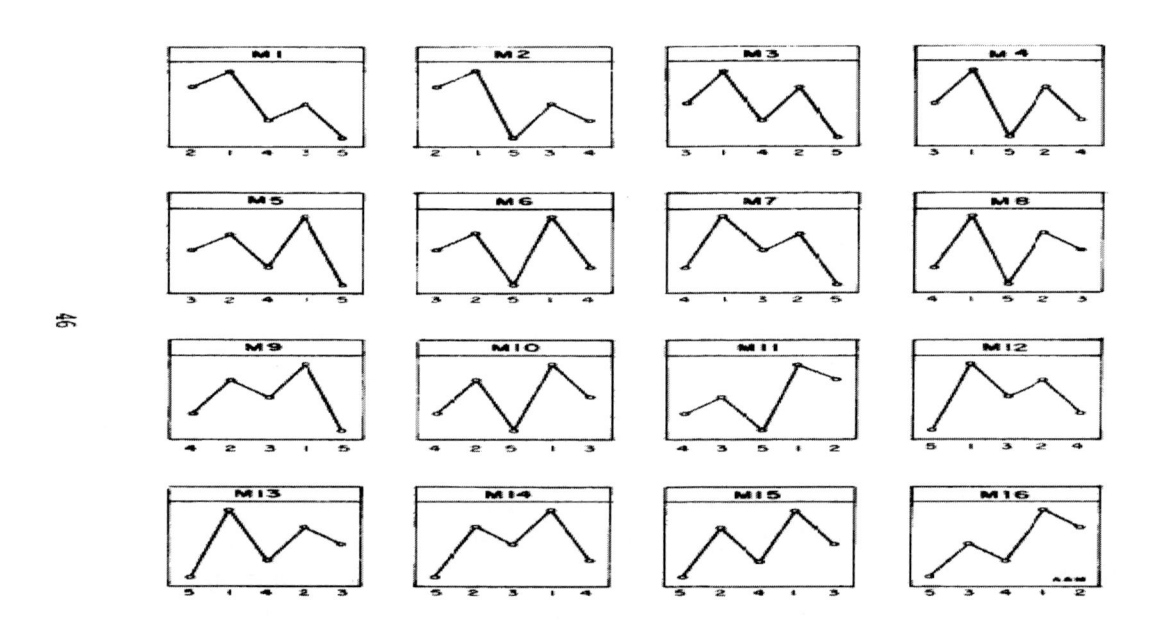

"*Filtered Waves, Basic Theory: A Tool for Stock Market Analysis*"
pg. 46 Analysis Press, 19

This illustration from *Filtered Waves* exemplifies one of dozens of 5-point formations which he believed to be unique patterns. His illustrations and categorization of M&W-types was a critical step in the advancement of price formations as predictive

Harmonic Trading Volume 3: Reaction vs. Reversal

pattern recognition signals. Although not all of the M&W pattern illustrations he proposed were precise, his attempt to validate and distinguish these market movements as relevant technical signals was an important step in the evolution of pattern recognition.

Welles Wilder

In the discussion technical indicators, the name Welles Wilder is atop the list of pioneers whom defined some of the most effective charting measures ever conceived. I like to refer to these readings as "technical ENVIRONMENTAL measures" more than just indicators, as these measures provide insight beyond simple price action. I have long cited Welles Wilder for his ground-breaking work with the Relative Strength formula. He presented the indicator in his book, *New Concepts in Technical Trading Systems* (1978). He is a legend in the technical indicators and developed some of the most popular tools available today. In *New Concepts*, he presented Average True Range, the Relative Strength Index, Directional Movement, Parabolic Stop & Reverse, Pivot Points, and Volatility among others measures that are now available on every major software platform, including my own.

His work has been an immense inspiration to me and it was a driving force behind the creation of my proprietary indicator, the *Harmonic Strength Index.* The Relative Strength concepts were revolutionary when he released it nearly 50 years ago. Mr. Wilder's contributions will always be lauded for such remarkable insights. Although it may have been difficult to foresee the magnitude back at this time, he shared a wealth of knowledge that has been a game-changing technical strategy for many traders. You could call Mr. Wilder a disruptor long before disrupters existed for his simple yet effective indicator formulae. Furthermore, I personally learned from his work that an integrative perspective will always find new relationships and clarify analysis.

Harmonic Patterns > *Harmonics*

The evolution of my research led me to realize that a more precise classification of market movements was required to advance my comprehension and improve the consistency of my analysis. Throughout my technical studies, I was disappointed in the vagueness of many well-popularized methods of the day. Certain indicators and methodologies were accurate in some situations but lacked the uniform success required to be consistently reliable.

Over the past 30 years, I have continually sought to create rules that clarified random movements and related indicator readings to define situational strategies. In fact, other concepts were adapted and combined with harmonic measurement techniques to create a greater standardization of price structure. As they say, "*Necessity is the mother of invention.*" For me, I realized that price action history could be measured and categorized. Initially, the categorization of price structures as harmonic patterns created specific guidelines for the identification of a trade opportunity. Beyond this, my analysis evolved as I was able to further define unique states of price action, especially relative to measured price environments.

The combination of harmonic pattern rules and related measures has carved a niche within Technical Analysis. From a general perspective, these measures have defined unique relationships of structural wave behavior in price action in the financial markets. The definable situations possess unique technical conditions as measured by harmonic ratio formulae. These pattern rules and larger technical measures have become collectively known as the study of *Harmonics* in the financial markets.

Theory of Market Mechanisms

My journey into Technical Analysis was the result of following daily stock prices in the newspaper when I was barely a teenager. This was long before the Internet and for most beginners. If you wanted analyze charts, you had to track the prices by hand and plot the results manually. As charting technology was introduced in the late 80s and early 90s, the ability to quantify market movements expanded rapidly. Well-known concepts such as Elliott Wave, wedge patterns and standard indicators could finally be automated. I know that sounds like talking about ancient history. However, in relation to what was happening today, those were antiquated markets. Now, the awareness has shifted. Traders are more statistically driven to look at those strategies that can be mathematically proven.

Anything that can have a definable edge is of value. Gone are the days of whispering trade tips. Technology has removed many blatant inefficiencies and the next generation of online trading will likely the replace the need for even the physical trading exchange floor. Maybe someday the New York Stock Exchange will be a museum? The pace of technology is helping to facilitate this revolution and the focus of market analysis has shifted to unlock those price action characteristics that define consistent situations and possess predictive value. In the markets, it is essential to follow a standardized rules-based approach that applies uniform measurements required to define consistent price action behavior. In essence, trading behavior can manifest repeatable movements that unfold in the same manner for most markets. Regardless of the metric employed, the future of trading systems will incorporate more complex but identifiable market conditions that possess predictive value.

Any repeatable phenomenon must possess basic rules that describe the behavior. These movements must be distinguished as unique but various definable cycles in price action represent a type of market mechanism within the buying and selling of trading. When we can categorize these movements, unique relationships can be measured and statistically validated. Market mechanisms such as harmonic pattern structures are one example of strategies that identify the type price movements to predict future possible outcomes and establish unique expectations unto the situation. When combined with distinct indicator strategies, these structural types can be refined further to provide even more precise technical insights.

All of these definable phenomena are micro price action mechanisms that facilitate the functional buying and selling that makes the market go. The collection of various technical events manifested by the population of price data provides the relevant signals to define the possibilities of future trend direction. Remember, it is not essential to have every possible harmonic phenomenon to validate an opportunity but the recognition of the primary elements regardless of type will always confirm a trade opportunity.

The Natural Harmonic Reaction Principle

The Natural Harmonic Reaction is the mechanical response of trading behavior at prescribed measurements of ratios that are related to the Fibonacci sequence and structural assessments that possess basic wave properties in the same manner as is manifested throughout nature. I believe this to be the common advantage all Harmonic Traders initially realize but it is a concept that needed to be labeled to better understand this phenomenon. Simply stated, correctly measured harmonic patterns provide important inflection points – whether temporary or permanent in their strength – defining material cyclical points that affect natural growth processes and trend changes in the market. Depending upon the structures themselves, the simple phenomenon the Natural Harmonic Reaction is a pausing behavior at the completion of patterns that can be quantified to determine its effectiveness in advance. That is, there are important structural areas that measure the extent of how far any market can go in one direction without some type of countertrend. This is simplifying the theory however this is the basic structural harmonic measurement technique to provide a uniform means of quantifying random price structures. The key to determining patterns with the greatest potential begins with the understanding that all price moves can be categorized within precise technical classifications. A potential opportunity as defined by harmonic patterns will always provide either an early signal of impending failure or demonstrative confirmation in most harmonic states of price action.

The Reaction Mechanism

In the financial markets, this harmonic reaction is the natural mechanism of buying and selling that makes it possible for the entire system to exist. This natural mechanism that makes the financial markets go is the exact process that creates opportunity. A market can only move so far in one direction within a certain period of time. Price action must go up to go down and vice versa. Price action must fluctuate to create opportunities for participants to buy and sell. This behavior is cyclical and finite. This price action exhibits a frequency over time that can be charted, analyzed and categorized to define opportunities that possess probable reactive properties. What does that mean? Essentially, it is possible to look at a market's trading history, analyze critical turning points that have previously dictated predominant trends and seek to capitalize on this repetitive nature.

Within the framework of harmonic patterns, these ratio measurements effectively quantify the finite nature of price action. It is possible to measure the market within such a model and optimize those situations that possess the ideal technical elements to define those price levels that precede significant profitable moves. Harmonic patterns present "signposts of future price action" that provide a framework to separate the noise from the meaningful signals in the market. In fact, most price action is merely a reaction within the larger reversal or continuation of a predominant trend. The reaction of price movements can be affected by a number of technical levels that define mini-cycles that play tug of war between buyers and sellers as the market attempts to discover equilibrium. The culmination of all my years of work have led me to realize the market provides such measurable natural reaction opportunities, where the market can move only so far within a certain period of time. These patterns and larger measurements encompass that limitation and exploit the "natural finiteness" of any market situation within a certain period of time.

Reactive Rates

This has led to the ability of programmers and researchers to quantify statistically what we can expect from each pattern. This has been a goal of mine for a long time. Technology has progressed to the point where we have the functionality and access to data that makes it easy to crunch these numbers. I spent a great deal of time analyzing and isolating situations that proves that certain situations are more favorable than others. There are many combinations of technical factors that can be considered in an attempt to find the best reactive situations. Nothing is absolute and the understanding of statistics like these must be mindful of the importance in considering any real-life event. That is, anything can happen at any time during the trading process. Therefore, if an aberrational event occurs that affects decisions positively or negatively, it is essential to focus on the readings at hand relative to the measured opportunity. Although nothing is 100% guaranteed, certain other factors can influence the reactive rate of rice action that may have not previously been considered. With that in mind, the research that I sought out was geared with the notion that it is important to provide some type of reliable baseline reactive success rate of each pattern, regardless of outside variables that might randomly affect performance. In addition, other more complex reactive situations can offer higher degrees of accuracy but require greater patience since these situations take time to develop. Simply stated, there are many types of natural harmonic reactive price action unfolding in the markets every day. The key is to focus on those strategies that define the most reliable price action relative to the pattern framework.

Harmonic Trading Volume 3: Reaction vs. Reversal

The major breakthrough that Harmonic Trading presented was the notion that the market can be structurally measured to a more complex degree based upon proportional relationships. Furthermore, the differentiation of price formations that appear similar but possess different ratios resulted in a specialization that defined pattern-specific strategies. In essence, the defined structures needed to be treated differently. Once categorized, it was important to discover exactly which measurements were most important for each pattern. The classification of harmonic patterns provided this. After many structures were distinguished, other complementary measures were integrated and refined to improve the accuracy of the patterns. Throughout all of the refinements of this methodology, the ability to decipher even more precise information and increasing effectiveness of the harmonic pattern framework has been the primary goal.

Fundamental vs. Technical Analysis

Historically, market analysis has been classified into two disciplines – fundamental and technical. From a fundamental perspective, there are numerous sources to consider. Actionable trading information disseminated from market news including analyst reports, media commentators and company events, are rarely reliable. Furthermore, there is no clear-cut means to even prioritize all of these information sources. In most cases, they can be interpreted and twisted to fit the story being told/sold. In particular, fundamental information such as earnings and business forecasts may possess the valid information about what has happened or currently unfolding. In some cases, the fundamental story can accurately describe the larger progress of the markets but price swings are difficult to measure based upon news headlines and industry reports.

The most intriguing part of the entire trading process is the fact that most individuals focus on fundamental news reports as their primary decision variable while mostly ignoring price analysis. The prevailing wisdom seems to dismiss that technically-derived strategies can provide reliable signals. Unfortunately, failure to accept the recognition that certain sources of fundamental information – although still popular – rarely reflects the true progress in the future trend of the price action. Eventually, most traders realize that this is the point where the comparison of actual analysis of trading history deviates from media mantra. In terms of technical expectations, the importance of measuring the history of price action has little subjectivity and greater reliability. In my opinion, the purity of the mathematical expression that the harmonic measures encompass provide an unbiased means of assessing the character of the market than relying on subjective data sources.

Harmonic Trading Volume 3: Reaction vs. Reversal

The Quest for Equilibrium

The market is always seeking to find value. Buyers and sellers are competing against each other because of perceived value. One participant may believe that a certain asset is worth more for the future while another may believe that same asset will be worth less. This is what makes a market. Therefore, the willingness of buyers and sellers to put a value on to the market comprises the process of price action where an equilibrium value satisfies all participants. Discovering value within price is pursued by traders because equilibrium is never actually fully achieved. If it was, there would be no price movement and no desire to participate due to lack of any perceived opportunity.

This is the eternal market struggle. The market moves up and down seemingly in a random manner while other times does nothing at all. This can be confounding to those market participants who do not understand that the notion of market equilibrium that actually unfolds in repeated proportional structures. Although the overall fluctuations may seem random, most markets exhibit definable characteristics within each opportunity that can be quantified and distinguish each as unique. Whether a pattern or extreme indicator reading, harmonic metrics define the natural limits that can be expected as the market moves too far to one side of the equilibrium spectrum.

One example, the 1.618 measurement exemplifies this concept clearly. Countless natural phenomena manifest this proportion as the limit of each growth cycle (i.e. Fibonacci Phyllotaxis: Plants, Nautilus Shell, etc). The 1.618 is a proportional limit that is a universal natural law of that repeats in the market, since it represents an overextended, unsustainable move that requires a countertrend pause as the overall all price adjusts to a new equilibrium. No market can move straight up or straight down (unless bankruptcy) within a trend without experiencing brief consolidations within the larger move.

I refer to these as "harmonic pauses" that are common reactions, even in the strongest of trends. Even in trending market moves, prices still must adjust within this force to continue to change the equilibrium of the market. Simply stated, market movements – up, down, sideways – can be understood to recognize not only possible price objectives but understand how these parameters fit within the market's equilibrium mechanism. The measures of the harmonic pattern framework categorize different stages of the market's fluctuations and ascertain clear direction by actually limiting the overall possibilities. Certain pattern situations represent ideal natural extremes where the price must return/retrace to the equilibrium point. Again, the 1.618 measure exemplifies this principle. Most important, the combination of the market's constant battle to determine an equilibrium price combined with the understanding of the market's natural limits comprises the harmonic foundation of comprehension. As traders, our job is to act upon these conditions when they materialize and follow the measured strategies precisely as your primary trading plan.

Harmonic Trading Volume 3: Reaction vs. Reversal

Fail to Plan...Plan to Fail!

Regardless of methodology, all traders need a plan. Albeit a bit abstract, concepts such as "Market Equilibrium" and other descriptive labels help to create situational-specific strategies. Those methodologies with a plan outlined according to a set of conditions that define an opportunity in advance typically lead to more consistent results and establishes a framework of strategies with true predictive value. Again, a planned approach helps to even avoid invalid opportunities if basic conditions are not met. Many traders have difficulty following a plan, especially when their trading executions are nowhere near the defined opportunity. Those who are unaware of the necessity of a rules-based system eventually realize that random decisions lead to a trading approach ripe with mistakes and inconsistencies. Regardless of the methodology, identification variables that define opportunities must recognize each stage of the trading process.

Within the Harmonic Trading approach, potential opportunities are mostly validated by the natural metrics that define the parameters of the trading plan in advance. These strategic plans can anticipate defined possibilities and effectively ascertain the likely outcome to optimize decisions. Furthermore, a plan that isolates unique technical situations can instill the proper expectation regarding the anticipated move. Although I discuss the proper perspective of realistic expectations throughout this book, it represents the underlying mindset required to capitalize on any trading opportunity.

This is a basic concept that most traders fail to realize. Whether they know it or not, every person has a prescribed set of expectations when they are making decisions in the market. A trader's propensity to buy, sell or do nothing can involve a variety of factors that shape their outlook. Although such individuals tend to distort their decisions based upon a prevailing preconceived notion. For most, the general expectations of market performance are shaped by what they hear from other people. It may be a financial news channel or an investment advisor. Regardless, there is a problem that arises from regurgitated analysis that does not properly assess the true possibilities within any situation. Therefore, professional traders develop precise skill sets and rely on their own decision framework to define opportunity in the financial markets.

Defining Direction

The collection of Harmonic Trading measurement strategies is all designed to provide insight to the probable future price direction of the market being analyzed. As I mentioned previously, one of the advantages of basing decisions upon measurements of the market's movements is the defined categorization of expectations that are derived from each ratio. For example, a price segment that reaches a 1.618 extension can be deemed as having moved too far in one direction. Although the price action can continue beyond a 1.618 level, the expectation to favor some type of countertrend move within this general vicinity will guide the proper trading decisions due to the expected natural limits of the market.

It is important to remember that these ratios are employed within the Harmonic Trading approach because they best reflect the natural growth cycles within many of life's processes. There are numerous examples of such natural cycles that manifest these ratio relationships. Applied to the markets, the analysis of price action considers the "living organism" that is the market. Comprised of buying and selling, the total sum of these actions possesses natural cyclical elements that can be measured and anticipated. It is in this purest application of Harmonic Trading measurements that we can consistently define the state of the market and relevant targets that ascertain future price action possibilities. These situations limit possibilities and clarify potential trend direction. As defined by the rules within the approach, each measurement possesses its own meaning to the overall technical picture. Whether it is a distinct harmonic pattern structure or a significant retracement/extension level or a combination of both, certain price formations and their relevant technical readings distinguish the conditions of what is within the realm of possibility.

Technical Entities

A harmonic pattern must be regarded as a specific *Technical Entity* that possesses precise numeric ranges, where all elements, such as execution points, stop loss limits and profit objectives, are defined relative to the price structure. Reversals must be allotted a certain time period relative to the size of the pattern. In addition to the price parameters, all patterns possess ideal harmonic time constraints - as measured from the structure – that create a defined range of duration to gauge the action following the reversal. I have discussed this concept in previous material and stressed the importance of defining expectations within a specific limit to guide trading decisions. I believe this transition of converting analysis into concrete scenarios is an important aspect of Technical Analysis in general. Essentially, we must search for those overwhelmingly clear situations as defined by prescribed strategies that define future market movements in a consistent and effective manner with a high degree of certainty.

One of the biggest mistakes most traders make is that they only look for the one tool or one strategy that represents the "Holy Grail" to blindly follow. My perspective has always been different – realistic. In that vein, I have avoided those types of pursuits and have always sought to develop an arsenal of skills that are comprised of precise measurements that signal common characteristics that precede the most substantial price movements. Many of the harmonic confirmation strategies are often smaller complementary measurements that can enhance the probabilities of a potential pattern. At a minimum, patterns with price levels that have multiple readings that are confirming each other provide a substantial advantage than a random structure. In fact, the harmonic pattern opportunities with the greatest potential are distinct technical entities that include a conglomeration of market measurements that distinguish a unique environmental scenario. Later in this material, we will outline the exact conditions that distinguish these exact opportunities with favorable risk-to-reward parameters.

Harmonic patterns can be considered as the primary technical entity of the entire methodology. In this regard, the structural measurements represent the starting point for any opportunity and define the general price range that encompasses the totality of the pattern signal. However, other price action mechanisms such as trend considerations, indicator calculations and timeframe applications are essential in further categorizing these unique technical entities. In concert, the conclusion derived from the structural information provided by harmonic patterns can be clarified to an advance degree.

One of my early challenges was simply categorizing all of the combinations that the harmonic measurements offer. In fact, I frequently found myself in situations where my analysis of certain patterns tended to indicate price objectives and ultimate possibilities that were seemingly unattainable. For me, I had to change what I assumed might happen and focus on the possibilities that the measured harmonic scenario presented to me. I know that many others have shared a similar learning experience. However, the harmonic pattern framework encompasses the technical entity and tells a story of where the market has been and where it must go in its quest for price equilibrium.

For many individuals learning these techniques for the first time, the basic ability to calculate harmonic patterns and predict their resulting possibility ignites an awareness of possibility. This typically leads to an experience where their ability in measuring these scenarios motivates them to further understand the harmonic phenomenon. I have seen this in numerous students and I have received many emails from people who begin to realize the importance of understanding these market mechanisms. Once they begin to put together the foundation of measurements, a broader understanding quickly emerges.

Confirming Structural Readings

Although distinct signals help define when to capitalize on structural opportunities, the general focus should always be on the immediate progress of the price action relative to the support/resistance levels established by the pattern. In actuality, the entire concept of technical confirmation in Harmonic Trading is relatively new. Much of my work in this technical area did not begin until several years after the basic rules for harmonic patterns were defined. Once I was able to integrate effective measures, the importance of confirming pattern structures in this regard became more apparent. In the beginning, I was somewhat of a staunch purist – stating the importance of price action alone. However, the "student-of-the-market" in me always sought to research other perspectives and refine those consistent variables that provided reliable predictive capabilities.

It is important to note that although many market measures can be applied to harmonic patterns, I have found most lack a consistent ability to filter the best opportunities. In *Harmonic Trading: Volume 2*, I detailed the advantages of Relative Strength and presented new ideas that integrated harmonic measurements with basic structural interpretations. Furthermore, the concepts of Divergence and Confirmation have been expanded to quantify the exact technical environments that best foster a valid reversal of a harmonic pattern. This is achieved through the complex integration of indicator readings, individual price action and trendline assessments. These strategies serve the basic structural identification principles well, as they define unique conditions where pattern signals are most likely to yield profitable moves.

Triggers and Signals

As I have defined the strategies within the Harmonic Trading approach over the years, I realized that certain points and specific subsets of data history frequently marked important turning points that signal potential future price action well in advance. One of the earliest strategies that I developed was the identification of individual price bars. Specifically, the Terminal Price Bar relies on one specific interval for the determination of behavior at that measured price level. I defined the Terminal Price Bar in *Harmonic Trading Volume 1*, primarily as a means to define the exact point where harmonic patterns complete. The execution process can be tricky at the completion of harmonic pattern since the real trading action frequently exceeds the measured range. I realized the need to navigate these realities, especially when it can be difficult to know which exact number is the most important within the specific range of Potential Reversal Zone (PRZ).

Although I believe specific numbers in certain situations are more significant than secondary measures, the importance of analyzing the entire zone is in the ability in knowing exactly when the pattern has completed. In doing so, this definitive price point establishes expectations that go a long way to guiding the overall decision-making process. In the same way that defined patterns provide specific price levels to execute a trade, other aspects of this process must be defined to clarify the parameters and the probability of the opportunity.

Confirmation strategies within the completion zones of harmonic patterns serve as the additional conditions that validate a potential execution. Essentially, specific signals MUST OCCUR at a pattern's completion point to trigger the trade. If price action does not act properly at the initial completion of a pattern, the nature of this behavior in the area of these important technical measures usually provides a warning sign of something other than what is expected that is actually unfolding. It can be difficult to trust that individual price bars can have such an impact and signal potential future price action but the evidence is quite clear. We will look at precise Terminal Bar situations that define these levels and the signals that initiate the anticipated price reversal.

Harmonic Trading Volume 3: Reaction vs. Reversal

It is important to note that the significance of the price action depends upon the nature of the structural measurements in that area. The optimal harmonic confirmation signals are typically encountered when extreme indicator readings are realized at the completion of multiple important structural measurements. Other structures that are not essentially at extreme readings still can still define opportunities but tend to provide less reactive responses to harmonic levels. The true character of any opportunity is assessed and anticipated upon monitored readings and specific price objectives. These are the strategies that signal an execution. In this regard, the arsenal of measurements explains the character of a particular market's action and highlight the conditions a trader responds to more than a subjective conclusion of what might happen. Therefore, the categorization of these situations provides the framework of substantial technical information to trigger decisions and defines the possibilities of any situation.

Conclusion

As we examine the advanced material - especially trade execution and management strategies, the importance of uniformly defining pattern structures will become more apparent. I go to great lengths in this book to outline exact specifications for each pattern in an unprecedented manner. Although I have been aware of these distinctions since the inception of harmonic patterns, I have not disclosed these concepts in any previous material. I believe it is important to share these strategies to further refine harmonic structures as precisely as possible. Not to mention, the categorization of harmonic patterns has effectively defined the proper expectations of price behavior. For those new to harmonic patterns, it is imperative to learn the structural–specific strategies that require a specialized treatment of situations depending upon the measures at hand. From an identification perspective, this book outlines those advanced measurements and goes to great lengths to describe why these specifications work in each situation.

As you begin to study the following material, it is important to be aware from the start that we are quantifying immutable mechanisms of price action in the financial markets. The perspective of harmonic measurements provides a natural framework to assess market movements. Although markets can be influenced by a variety of factors and even manipulated for finite periods of time, the natural function of buying and selling experiences a variety of price behavior phases that are immutable.

Simply stated, the market manifests harmonic patterns related measures without regard to external influences including news events, analyst reports and even artificial trading behavior. Any trader who understands the basic measurement parameters of harmonic patterns does realize this fact regardless of timeframe or market traded. The most important insight to it all is the fact that our ability to succeed depends upon a framework of measures that reflect very natural element we are trying to define. Therefore, the harmonic strategies employed cannot be altered or modified because they represent the essence of identifying these natural opportunities in price action.

Harmonic Trading Volume 3: Reaction vs. Reversal

Chapter 1
Core Principles of Harmonic Trading

The Foundation of Harmonic Trading

This book establishes the foundation of the entire methodology to define each step in the Harmonic Trading process. The new strategies in this material is integrated with the basic harmonic pattern identification principles to clarify exact trading opportunities to an even more precise degree. I think it is important and I want to take a minute to review the established Harmonic Trading material.

My initial work with harmonic patterns required a great deal of research to discover the optimal ratio combinations that defined structural signals. Although many of these techniques are common knowledge today, the basic understanding of pattern measurement specifications was vague and the analytical tools were quite limited back then. Most of the work was developed by hand, manually measuring each point. It was an even greater challenge to back-test the ideas to validate the correct parameters.

My first two books, *The Harmonic Trader* and *Harmonic Trading Volume 1* were similar in nature, as they focused on the identification rules for harmonic patterns. The identification rules alone required years before these could be perfected. Although this material outlined strategies for execution and management, most of the initial material focused mostly upon the identification of patterns.

After nearly 10 years of Harmonic Trading, I released *Harmonic Trading Volume 2* in 2007. This was an important advancement of the identification rules. In fact, I was concerned during this time that many were overlooking the importance of confirmation strategies to validate harmonic patterns as trading opportunities. I wanted to share these insights as I discovered more about the relationships of harmonic measurements with respect to price action in the financial markets. In fact, I have been refining many of the new ideas presented in this book for the past decade. As I tested new combinations of technical possibilities, I was able to unlock deeper relationships that function like automatic price mechanisms. Of course, many of these situations require a variety of conditions to be met but the derived analysis has become as reliable as harmonic patterns.

From a general standpoint, I have been able to clarify important concepts within my own journey of market research over the years that have guided my trading decisions in a more efficient manner. Starting from the primary assumption that the market can be measured, more complex harmonic situations that I have identified still manifest characteristics that continually repeat. Many of the new strategies consider conditions

Harmonic Trading Volume 3: Reaction vs. Reversal

outside of the basic pattern strategies but they have proven to be extremely effective when distinct pattern structures are present.

The Market's Signal

The important consideration in this pursuit is to understand that the market is providing its own answers every day. As traders, we must measure and define such price action phenomenon that consistently repeat. Understandably, it can be easy to get overwhelmed within this process but we must never forget that these signals can be unlocked. Although this is not an easy task, as many are overwhelmed by the pace of the financial markets, it is this type of chart analysis that separates noise in the markets from the valid signals that price action can generate.

Although fundamental and quantitative analysts frequently cite disdain for technical methods, it seems short-sighted for these individuals to overlook the trading history of a particular market as irrelevant. Within the record of price history, charts clearly exhibit the material trading events that help to define important levels support and resistance. In my opinion, any technical information that helps clarify the total picture to facilitate the trading decision-making process must be considered. Beyond this, the collection of harmonic measurements provides an accurate framework of reliable indications of future probable price direction based upon the market's own action. While other conditions must exist to confirm what any price measurement indicates, Harmonic Trading's predictive ability to define levels of harmonic support and resistance is the primary advantage that makes the difference between success and failure.

The Process of Reaction versus Reversal

I think this one dilemma, one challenge, one conceptual framework – analyzing the difference between a price reaction and a price reversal – describes how to gauge the strength of any harmonic pattern opportunity. That is, what is the likelihood the pattern structure will yield a profitable reaction while assessing the potential for a larger result? I believe there are essential analytical strategies that facilitate these assessments and effectively guide decisions in a disciplined manner that optimizes the process. It is this extent of precision that can avail traders whom are relying on harmonic patterns as a sole decision module for trade opportunities to properly distinguish nominal reactions from true reversals. Although we will discuss these differences later in this material, the *Reaction vs. Reversal* concepts enable traders to capitalize on opportunities with a balanced perspective.

It seems that many – especially traders with less experience – who discover harmonic patterns community seem entrenched in the singular possibility of a "magic box" – a one trick pony approach - to easily uncover the homerun trades unlike any other approach. Whether this is some hot story from *The Wall Street Journal* or a "Wolf of Wall

Street" type scam outfit, it is easy for the uninitiated to fall into the trap of false claims. When it comes to others whom seek to hype harmonic patterns for marketing gain, it is common for new traders to lose sight of reality. Although many are actually promoting the harmonic pattern cause, they are doing more harm than good by broadcasting unrealistic expectations with an incomplete understanding of the entire strategic process. It is true harmonic patterns provide some type reaction – a countertrend pause at a minimum - at the completion of distinct structures. In my opinion, this phenomenon tends to create an image of higher success than what is truly happening. Furthermore, the failure to adequately recognize reactions from reversals can lead to faulty management of these situations and disappointing results. Much of the material in this book is geared towards the clarification and specification of precise scenarios to help traders understand the importance of a comprehensive execution and management plan as well as identification that clarifies the reaction vs. reversal conundrum.

The reaction vs. reversal assessment process is essential to optimize all stages of the Harmonic Trading process. I must emphasize that blind execution of any harmonic pattern without regard to other technical considerations sows the seeds of failure. To truly distinguish those opportunities with the best chance for success, it is essential to analyze the larger picture relative to the pattern being considered. Furthermore, those who promote the notion of "set and forget" automatically executed trades ignore the majority of factors that must be considered to navigate the entire process profitably.

A trading plan that is designed to automatically sell or buy a position based solely upon harmonic pattern identification rules ignores the essential execution and management strategies that are required to understand when price is merely reacting as opposed to establishing a more substantial reversal. I go to great lengths to clarify these issues in this book but it is a fundamental issue that many new Harmonic Traders face. Obviously, traders will make mistakes as they integrate new strategies into their trading plan. However, I feel that many of the errors committed today are a result of distorted information rather than one's ability to execute the prescribed strategies. Therefore, I will emphasize these important points and stress a clear understanding of the concepts that distinguish smaller reactive moves versus substantial reversals.

Throughout the process of writing this book, I have realized "how" traders are learning this material as much as "what" they are focused on. I have spent the past several years talking to dozens of traders to improve my own communication of the strategies that I have initially presented. Clearly, there were many things that I had yet to discuss in any book previously that I considered every day in my analysis. Some of the ideas were proprietary that I wanted to keep to myself but I realized there were a number of other factors that I needed to communicate to traders so they could see the same picture I was envisioning in my mind. Without this clarification of properly instructing and educating the full realities of how to turn this analysis into profitable trading, I believe that the identification strategies would eventually become distorted due to others' inaccurate interpretations.

Harmonic Trading Volume 3: Reaction vs. Reversal

The Harmonic Trading Process

The steps that outline the Harmonic Trading approach present a simplistic but effective means in navigating any opportunity. I discussed this three-step trading process in my *Harmonic Trading Volume 2*, and I always emphasize the procedural importance that these steps engender. Within each step, a set procedure defines the decision-making process throughout the entire trade. From the identification of an opportunity to the closing of the position of particular profit target, these are the defined rules that foster consistency and success over the long-term.

Three Steps to Harmonic Trading

1. Trade Identification
2. Trade Execution
3. Trade Management

HarmonicTrader, L.L.C.

Harmonic Trading Volume 3: Reaction vs. Reversal

Phases of Trading

Clearly, identification strategies are the most important aspect of the process to FIRST identify the correct price level to enter positions that benefit from the natural reaction that the market exhibits every day. As price action "breathes" to buy and sell as its basic functional mechanism, I employ harmonic measures to define the finite limits of possibility. Since the market can only move so far so fast, the signals that are generated at the completion of a harmonic opportunity will typically provide a pausing phenomenon which represents the initial change in character of the current trend. No matter what time interval is traded, this is the starting point for every opportunity where I seek to capitalize on this limit as I assess other confirmation factors to manage the larger reversal that may be possible. These situations must be quantified and classified further but these conditions can be measured with precision.

Most Harmonic Traders are able to quickly incorporate identification strategies and predictive capabilities. However, most fall short in confirming reactions to ascertain the larger reversal potential at hand. However, I feel that over the years and now in this material, I have closed this gap to pinpoint the early signs that provide insight to know when to be aggressive in profit anticipation versus allowing more time for positions to materialize. Again, this is an area that all traders must deal with but I believe charting technology such my harmonic software has optimized these variables to make high-probability decisions with the proper input variables even more efficiently.

Each stage in the trading process possesses its own framework of decision-making guidelines to facilitate and optimize actions. It is important to break down the trading process and define various segments within the process to focus on important sequential events that must occur to ensure success. First, the trading opportunity must be identified second the execution must be determined and finally the management of that trade must be defined in advance to optimize results. Anything outside these three considerations is meaningless. From a Harmonic Trading perspective, I have been always focused on those strategies that decipher and highlight the overall picture of each stage in the process and the relevant confirmation strategies along the way.

Harmonic Trading Volume 3: Reaction vs. Reversal

1. **Trade Identification:** The prescribed harmonic pattern measurements define unique conditions that possess overwhelming predictive capabilities. In fact, any trading system must possess uniform requirements that identify particular market conditions as a potential opportunity. These techniques utilize historically proven and repetitive price patterns that capitalize on overbought and oversold signals generated by the market's technical price action. The consistent ratio framework facilitates identifying and differentiating harmonic price patterns as quantified by their structural alignment aspects. Understanding these identification parameters is critical in defining the proper expectations among the various harmonic patterns as an essential trading skillset to capitalize on specific opportunities.

2. **Trade Execution:** At the completion of the harmonic structure, a hyper-focused perspective must assess immediate factors that provide the confirmation of the actual trade. Several factors must be analyzed within a specific time period that is defined by the potential opportunity. The validity of the pattern must be determined and the final action of executing of the trade or not must be considered.

3. **Trade Management:** A prescribed set of guidelines and price objectives dictate actions once a position has been executed. Although a variety of general considerations may be involved within the process, the position must be managed according to specific rules that maximize the profit while minimizing the risk. Most harmonic pattern situations require a degree of responsive management to maximize the result from the featured opportunity.

Breaking Down the Process

Throughout the evolution of my research, it has always been my goal to clarify the existing principles of the Harmonic Trading approach and to integrate the new concepts that enhance the effectiveness of the entire methodology. I have stressed in each of my books the importance of understanding the three steps of the trading process. Trade identification, execution and management are the three primary steps for this decision-making process. In this book, I go to extensive lengths to discuss trading within the three-step process of identification, execution and management because it represents the fundamental process that all market participants experience - win, lose or draw. More importantly, this is the framework we must revisit when performance is lacking and mistakes are experienced. It is only through such examination can we break down the process of trading to analyze each element of the experience to isolate issues and devise specific strategies that corrects faulty behavior.

Harmonic Trading Volume 3: Reaction vs. Reversal

In the past, students have mentioned to me that they felt like these classifications were not necessary and confusing for beginners. I typically respond that such terminology helps to distinguish elements of the decision-making process where traders can examine each stage as a building block within a larger sequence of events required to realize a profitable move. Quite frankly, I feel that there is a lack of understanding regarding these technical stages, although they are clearly evident every day, in all markets and on all timeframes. Also, this analytical breakdown has been helpful in my own understanding, as each concept has coalesced into a larger comprehension that has transformed complex analytical situations into clear and concise situations. In fact, when mistakes are made and trading results are negative, it is possible to examine the behaviors at each stage and correct the actions that were the cause of the losses. Moreover, these can be identified over the course of a population of trades to isolate issues and integrate improvements in future opportunities.

Measure the Market

More than being a proponent of Harmonic Trading, I am an avid fan of recommending that all traders learn to measure the market, regardless of methodology. It is the singular phase that I repeat for anyone interested truly learning effective trading skills. Any technical approach employs a measured-style of trading. It is critical to emphasize that traders who focus on measuring the market's movements to determine opportunities are typically less dependent on the validation of news stories or outside opinions. The clearest of trends can easily be identified within the overall outlook on any particular timeframe and other relationships comprehended by simply analyzing a chart and measuring its history.

Measured Expectations

The "*Measure the Market*" philosophy instills a degree expected outcome and expectation that facilitates decisions within the trading process. Most technical methods employ some type of measured framework that analyzes price action history in the financial markets and categorizes movements to explain what is unfolding and possible. From a harmonic perspective, this framework assesses possibilities to natural cyclical limits (i.e. 1.618) and manifests comparatively the net result. Simple assessments such as the price behavior at specific harmonic pattern zones or confirmation strategies that outline relative indicator extremes are types of analysis that can indicate what to expect and respond accordingly.

Within the *Reaction vs. Reversal* considerations of trading, such expectations are essential when assessing harmonic price phenomena of the financial markets. Pre-defined price parameters according to the Harmonic Trading approach distinguish a character of the movements to anticipate a realistic outcome. In fact, one of the primary expectations on the initial completion of any harmonic pattern is a counter-trend reaction that is typically short-lived and requires other conditions before a larger reversal can unfold. Expectations like these underscores why it is essential to analyze market movements within a measured relevant range at all times no matter what.

The measurement of Harmonic Trading strategies such as the Potential Reversal Zone (PRZ), RSI BAMM and reversal types, establish common characteristics that repeat within each scenario and help to define where the anticipated price action can possibly unfold. At a minimum, pattern rules and harmonic confirmation strategies guide expectations during times particularly when price action behaves unexpectedly or varies from what is anticipated. Situation-specific strategies shape the proper expectations associated with each harmonic pattern, and facilitates the execution and trade management process by establishing price objectives in advance that are outlined quite clearly. When all actions are defined in advance, the collection of measured moves defines the situation and facilitates analysis to interpret specific technical events that can be anticipated. This approach effectively defines the critical "action spots" within any trend that can indicate the future potential direction with consistent accuracy.

Expectations in the Harmonic Trading Process

In general, properly identified Harmonic Trading opportunities that possess ideal structural measurements and other confirmation elements provide a tradeable execution within a definitive price limit will yield some type of anticipated and measurable REACTION in nearly 80% of all cases. This reaction can be a brief pause or larger reversal. However, other important considerations distinguish valid harmonic patterns from random price structures. Clearly, this is a generalization but represents an accurate rate of price behavior at the completion of ideally proportional harmonic structures. Although the initial *reaction* expectation can seem small-sighted, this temporary phenomenon of minor consolidation at the completion of a harmonic price level instills a critical anticipatory perspective that facilitates trade decisions effectively. The degree of this reaction will vary but the pausing phenomenon is one of the basic expectations once a properly measured pattern has completed.

It is important to emphasize that quantifiable (trade management) limits that ascertain what is a successful result (profit/loss) of a measured harmonic pattern must be delineated clearly. The initial reaction phenomenon related to these measures is merely one example that is consistently reliable but requires precise execution and management that employ predetermined measures, as well. Complementary confirmation strategies and standard price objectives help to formulate proper expectations in these stages of the process. We will focus on a variety of pattern-specific strategies later in the book. For now, the important take away before we even measure a pattern is to understand that we are following a step-by-step procedure where all actions are defined in advance and employ anticipatory strategies at each point within the harmonic framework.

After comprehending this framework of expectations, most traders are able to assess complex harmonic environments within the measured natural limits of possibility. At a minimum, these metrics must yield an accurate and consistent understanding of what to expect. However, traders whom are having a problem even being in the "ballpark" of being right in a majority of their positions are likely doing something fundamentally wrong and/or need to take a look at how they are identifying trading opportunities. This is extremely important because any system that is unable to even quantify the uniform variables that comprise their method of determining what represents a potential opportunity is inherently flawed. Again, the ability to analyze each step within the Harmonic Trading process and assess decisions to improve future results is a unique conceptual advantage that helps to improve performance.

Harmonic measurements distinguish that phenomenon in their ability to not only read the natural cyclical movements that most markets manifest but establish limits of possibility where the opportunity is finite relative to the completed pattern. More on that later, however it is possible to define exact price levels that establish reliable markers of direction even in the most confusing situations. Although this is a simplistic outline of the general trading process, it is important to note a few specific conditions regarding each phase. When harmonic patterns form the foundation as the means in determining trading opportunities, those parameters serve as the finite possibility of price within the situation upon which other measures can be assessed. For example, the importance of a pattern's completion point is profound in the determination of proper expectations, especially since the anticipated change in price action is one of the fundamental phenomena we are attempting to predict. Again, the harmonic strategies speak to the ability to categorize price movements as specific entities, understand their nature and even more so to this measurability of the market to generate its own relevant signals of future potential price direction.

Within the framework of a harmonic pattern, expectations within each stage – identification, execution, management - vary in time and character. For example, the execution phase of most harmonic patterns is typically much shorter than the identification and management of the position. The recognition of this fact alone underscores the importance of preparing in advance to properly measure the market, identify all variables relevant to the trade and manage the position optimally. Furthermore, the identification phase of the trading process can vary immensely depending upon the price action at the completion point. Therefore, there are instances in the process where one must be more diligent while at other times passive, as opportunities develop. At other times, obvious early signals will clearly invalidate the pattern considered. Although rigid in form, the harmonic pattern framework provides a type of "flow chart" analysis that effectively serves as the foundation for even the most advanced strategies.

Bullish Phases of Trading

The following illustration of a Bullish Gartley outlines the procedural stages of the Harmonic Trading process. As a pattern begins to form, the final leg of the structure will not trigger an opportunity until the B point has been violated. Many people attempt to project patterns immediately from the C point but fail to realize the larger complex structure does not officially become a valid opportunity until four of the five price points have been established. In nearly every instance, the trade execution phase will be the shortest aspect of the process but there are considerations that facilitate this decision, as identification rules and management parameters clarify the harmonic situation.

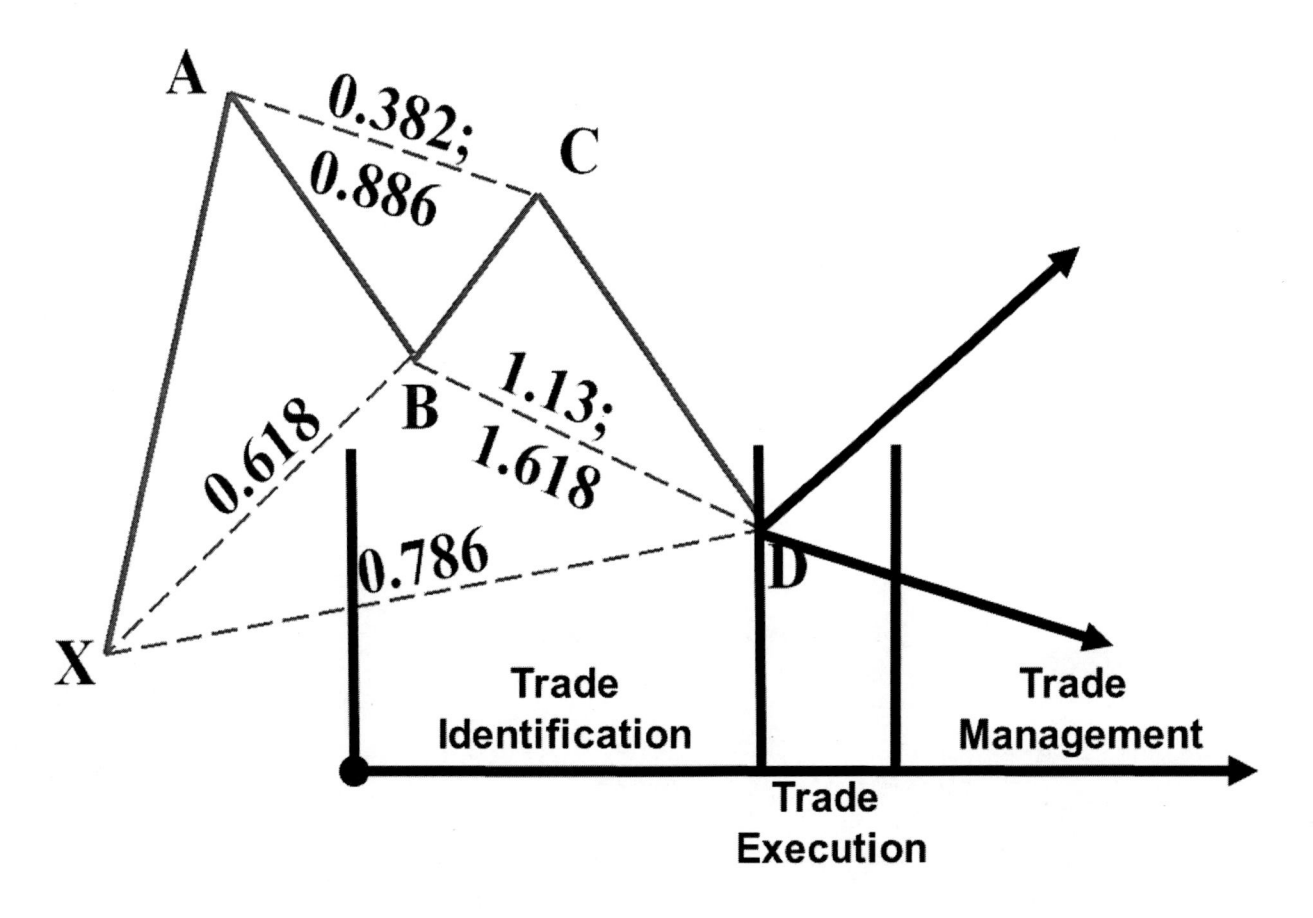

Harmonic Trading Volume 3: Reaction vs. Reversal

This chart of the US Dollar/Japanese Yen exemplifies the phases of the Harmonic Trading process. Regardless of timeframe, the identification of the opportunity is uniform. In this case, it was quite clear and unfolded over the course of a few hours during an intraday session on the following 5-minute chart. The price action tested this area and reversed relatively quickly in comparison to the total amount of time required for the pattern to complete. In fact, the pattern required nearly 4 hours to develop while the reversal unfolded over the course of less than 30 minutes.

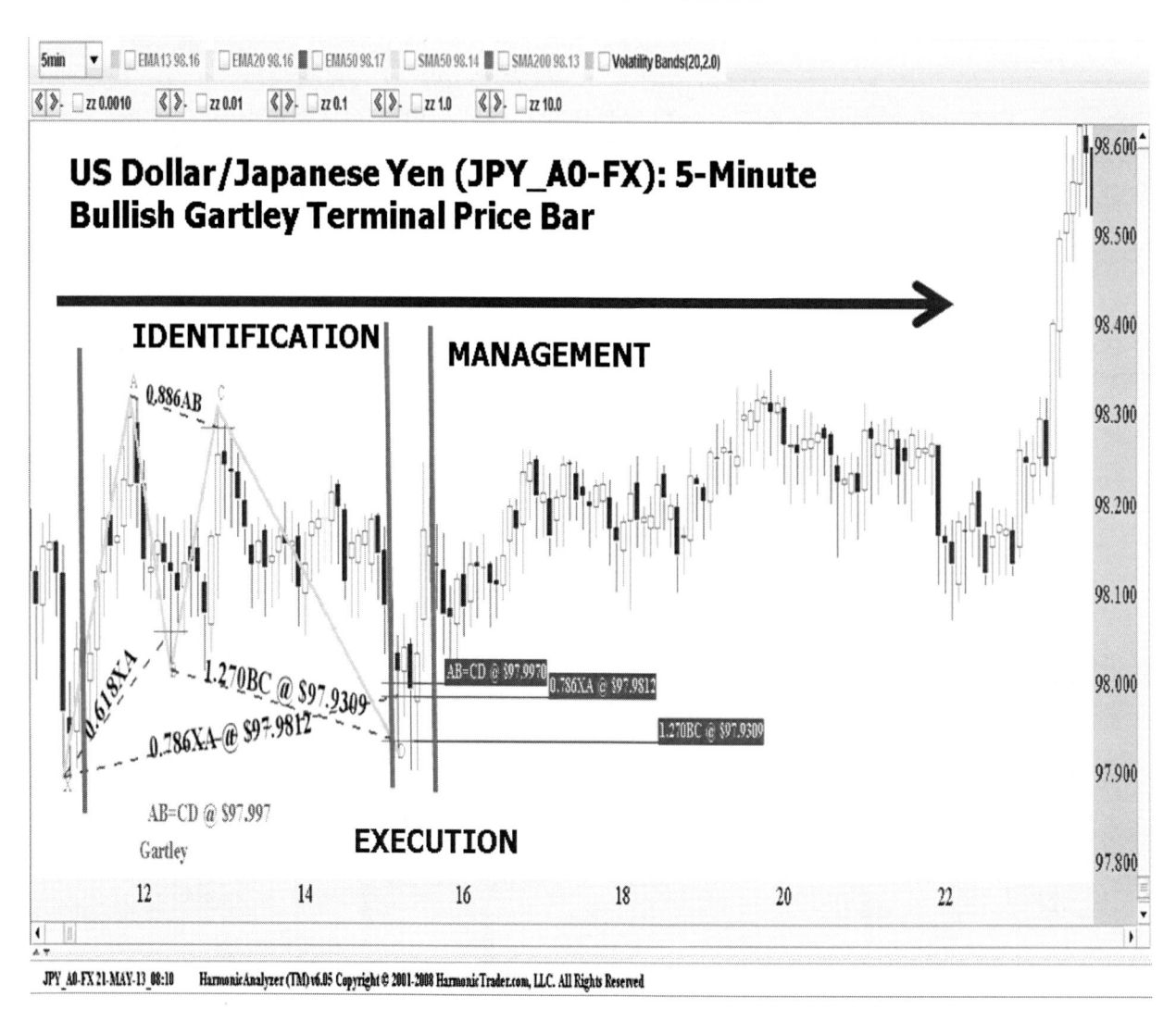

Although my harmonic pattern software can automatically signal when these situations are developing, the understanding of these time constraints facilitates executions and creates a perspective where the analysis of price action at the completion of the pattern must occur within a specific period of time. Meanwhile, the management

Harmonic Trading Volume 3: Reaction vs. Reversal

of the position was fairly simple, accelerating shortly after completing the pattern and continuing higher after a brief period of consolidation.

Bearish Phases of Trading

As we examine the advanced strategies in this book, we always analyze each step of the trading process utilizing specific harmonic measurements depending upon the situation. For this material, it is assumed that traders have a basic knowledge of harmonic patterns. Beyond this simple pattern recognition, traders must consider critical execution and management parameters to maximize each opportunity.

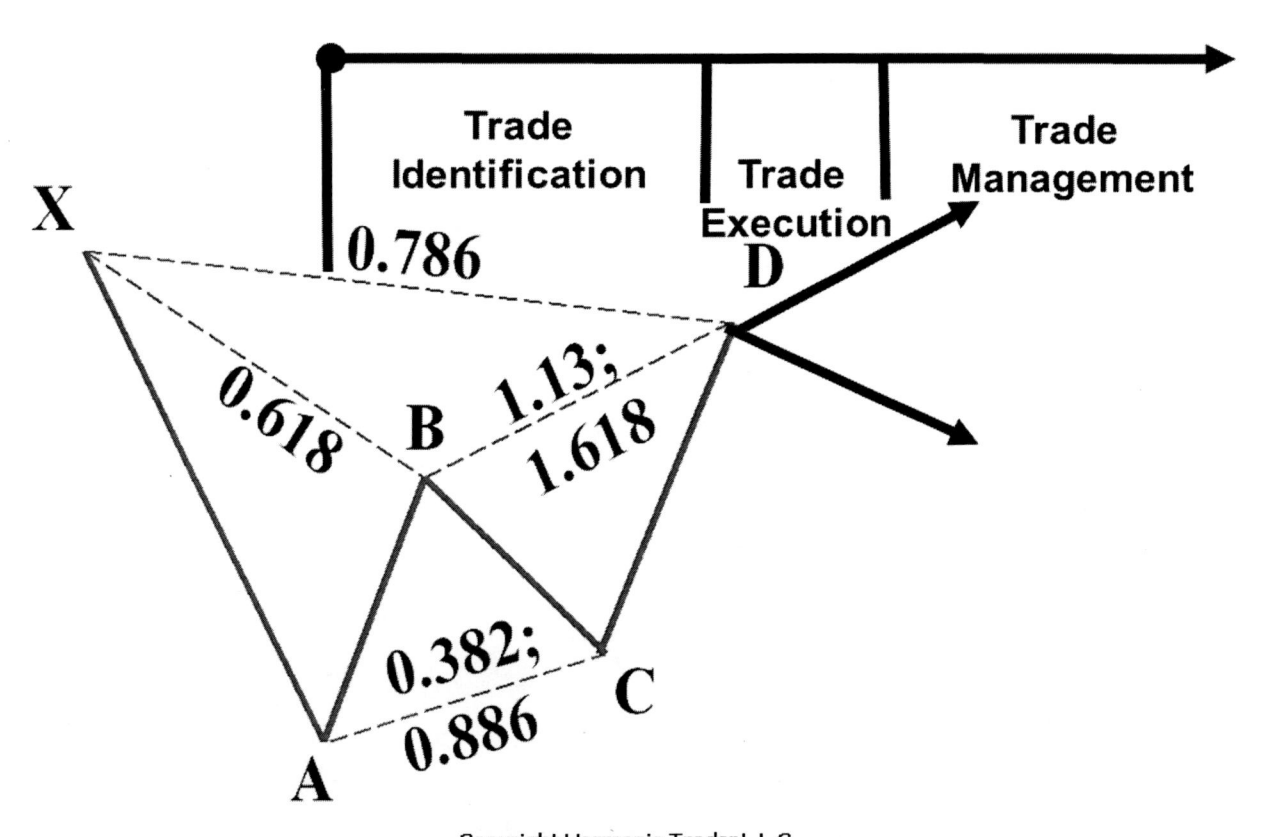

Copyright Harmonic Trader L.L.C

Of all the other technical approaches that I have studied throughout my life, I have noticed that there are unique measurement strategies each of these methods employ to be consistently successful. The goal of this book is to impart the most effective harmonic measurement strategies as well as a more precise framework for traders to assess price action. At a minimum, harmonic patterns provide this framework for all decisions –

Harmonic Trading Volume 3: Reaction vs. Reversal

identification, execution and management. This example of the Australian Dollar/Canadian Dollar shows a distinct Bearish Gartley on a 15-minute chart. Clearly, the execution phase was quite narrow. Although these can be tricky at times, the simple awareness of a finite window of opportunity facilitates decisions when the price action reaches the measured harmonic level. This is one example of how expectations can dictate decisions. Although a rapid execution may be required, traders whom are prepared for such realities will be able to pull the trigger when the pattern completes without hesitation.

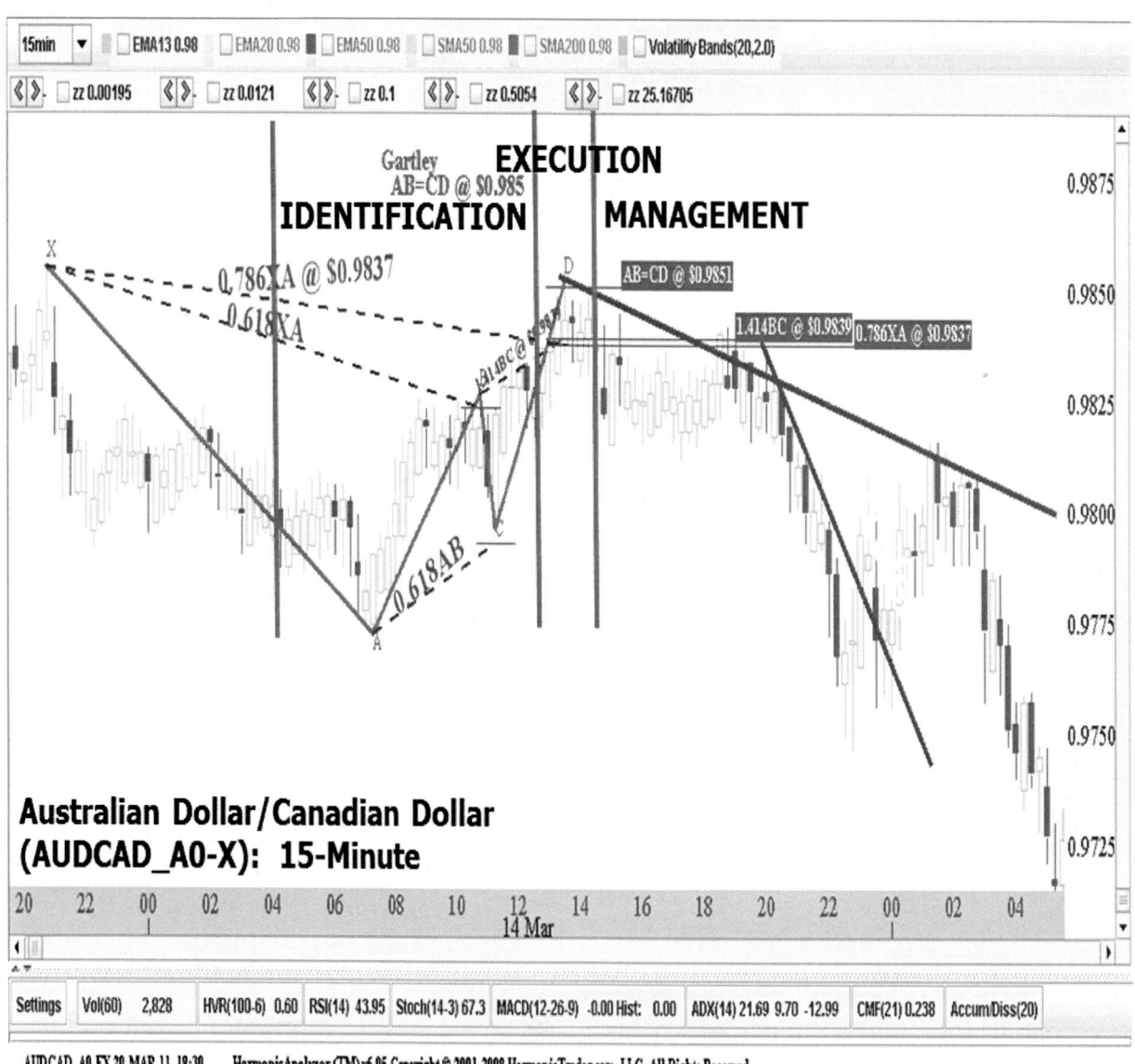

Harmonic Trading Volume 3: Reaction vs. Reversal

In the case of AUD/CAD, the larger reversal ensued after an initial reaction and consolidation phase. This is common in many reversals as the change in the primary trend frequently requires more time to realize a larger price move. Regardless of your level of Harmonic Trading comprehension, I encourage all traders to assess the specific strategies of each stage to optimize opportunities. It is important to note that not every measure is applicable in every situation. However, an arsenal of reliable metrics provides the framework required to understand what is possible in most situations. I will present several detailed scenarios that exemplify these conditions but the most important consideration is the clear delineation of what validates an opportunity. Furthermore, these measurements are defined in advance and provide a prescribed framework that is not subjective.

Compared to other market approaches, Harmonic Trading is quantifiable and measurable to a detailed degree that is unparalleled. This is a common distinction that new traders realize quickly, especially as they are able to discover their own strengths and weaknesses within each step in the process. Again, it is not necessary to integrate every aspect of each strategy presented herein. Rather, the broader comprehension of price action and the critical measurements that define important targets will outline a larger framework that is most effective when the clearest technical readings confirm the primary structural measurements.

Price Reaction

One of the initial breakthroughs in my early work was to provide explanations for specific measurements of harmonic price movements. Although the most substantial discovery was the differentiation of M&W-type formations, the larger breakthrough of execution and management strategies complemented the reliable framework of anticipated price behavior based upon harmonic pattern measurements. Furthermore, the direct link of prescribed expectations with exact measured situations started to create a detailed understanding of what is possible in these categorized trading scenarios. Of course, anything can happen in the markets but the majority of the time, the markets will exhibit normal price behavior that will be contained within the harmonic limits of what is possible within any period of time.

For me, I realized the combination of price measurements was the key to accurate assessments and expectations. The patterns are one example of these combinations of measurements. These initial breakthroughs were quite effective but their focus was predominantly measuring the price reaction. Any simple harmonic measurement – a projection or a retracement – possesses the potential to be an important level of support or resistance enough to provide a minimum reaction that can be profitably defined. Important ratios such as the 61.8% or 161.8% frequently will realize some degree of consolidation. As previously mentioned, this is the natural harmonic price reaction phenomenon experienced by these measures. Even new Harmonic Traders are able to

Harmonic Trading Volume 3: Reaction vs. Reversal

understand readily what these measurements mean, incorporate them in their existing strategies and begin to realize the larger dynamic that this approach provides.

Technical Environmental Measures

Much of my work has focused on the factors that consistently materialize that provide the highest degree of confirmation to capitalize on harmonic reactions in the markets at a minimum. These strategies analyze price and other relative measures to define the degree of a particular price movement. As I mentioned previously, all markets must "breathe" as the buying and selling fluctuates throughout each session, and price action can only move so far in one direction within a limited period of time. Although structural signals of harmonic patterns are powerful, my research has shown that indicator measures are required to differentiate where these patterns form on the chart. This correlation is as important as which pattern forms. So, the combination of both types of these measures properly integrates the price and environmental reaction that can be anticipated.

Although the price action of most reversals provides a minimum reaction – the harmonic pausing effect that offers immense predictive capabilities in its own right, the larger integration of environmental assessments such as Relative Strength and now the Harmonic Strength Index limits structural possibilities to highlight only the optimal situations. Furthermore, the material in this book reveals the precision that such integration provides, as these advanced strategies optimize trade decisions at each point in the process.

Harmonic Expectations vs. Harmonic Decisions

One of the most important concepts that I will emphasize throughout this book stresses the use of expectations to facilitate trading decisions in definable situations. Some of my earliest discoveries were relationships that identified and consistently provided the proper set of expectations of probable future price action when precise measurement conditions were present. If it was a unique pattern, important ratio measurement or a clear confirmation trigger, all of this analysis had to yield uniform results for me to be of value. I tested various relationships in my attempt to validate consistently reliable measurement parameters and develop strategies to assess any situation. Personally, the assignment of expectations and guidelines associated with specific measurements provided me with a plan to handle nearly every situation. Although anything can happen in the markets, the realm of possibility in most situations is actually quite small. In fact, the catastrophic "Black Swan" situation (big loss) and the "Home-Run" situation (big win) are often feared but rarely realized. Most important, the measured pattern guidelines instill the PROPER EXPECTATIONS to facilitate PROFITABLE DECISIONS, especially when market conditions may seem uncertain. Regardless, the conclusions derived from the expectations of the harmonic pattern framework are the most important factors in the ultimate decisions of the trading process. The comprehension of proper expectations is the key to breaking through, executing decisions with clarity and always understanding your relative position in any trade.

Misunderstood Expectations

If some of these concepts seem new, I encourage a thorough review of harmonic pattern basics. The introductory principles instill a realistic perspective required to maintain proper expectations. Although other people may employ different confirmation methods with harmonic patterns, there is a primary understanding and required attitude to remain focused and disciplined at all times. Many traders seem to misunderstand the essentials that maximize harmonic pattern opportunities. Although past successful patterns may engender confidence, the minute a trader loses reality within the defined parameters of a trade, they become vulnerable to emotional response and ultimately bad trade management. The inability of traders to "keep it real" can be the death-nail regardless of strategy. Within the harmonic pattern framework, we know what to expect at all times of the trading process.

Although I encourage "the whatever works" theory in relation to harmonic patterns, I have my own case studies and strategies – proprietary and otherwise – that I have shared over the years. Others have misrepresented results in unauthorized representations of what harmonic patterns are truly about. These distortions have tainted their reputation that has led to questioning of the effectiveness of these measurement techniques. Furthermore, there has been an unrealistic expectation that has been promoted by other individuals that does not promote the proper mindset for converting patterns into trading opportunities. I always stress a conservative approach to Harmonic Trading and integrate these strategies only after they are clearly understood to avoid mistakes. Finally, a realistic approach to the markets always fosters a balanced attitude to handle any trading situation.

Harmonic Confidence

Although it may take some practical experience to build confidence in these measurements, it won't take long before the essential relationships that define distinct opportunities becomes apparent. Although not every pattern will unfold as expected, the critical reality that price action does tend to adhere to these natural proportional ratio levels provides an immense degree of certainty to measure where a market may be headed. Harmonic ratio measurements can be used to identify trading opportunities, confirm executions and optimize management decisions as long as the proper metrics are employed. Within the remarkable software advancements in recent years, we can now feature consistently reliable situation with complex confirmation readings in an easily understood program. Furthermore, distinct pattern formations with specific price objectives as measured by the complex structure are now automated to generate only those conditions that satisfy the exact algorithmic constraints. Again, the most effective confirmation situations do not unfold all the time but we can now pinpoint the clearest of circumstances to define these trading opportunities in an unprecedented manner.

Core Principles of Harmonic Trading Conclusion

The necessity of developing proper expectations as a core competency of any trading methodology in unquestionable. The core principles of the Harmonic Trading approach are founded in such realistic expectation perspectives. This realism comes from a thorough recognition of what is possible in the market relative to the prescribed gamut of natural measures. I have outlined examples through the material in this book and go to great lengths to detail other complex strategies that are designed to identify those consistently reliable factors that outline unique opportunities.

Many of the strategies that I have created to describe the phenomenon of Harmonic Trading measurements arose from great deal of trial and error. My goal was to advance that framework to describe the unique market mechanisms that were manifested in specific instances of price action. However, the simple acknowledgment of this phenomenon has been thoroughly presented in my previous efforts, especially as it relates to harmonic ratio measures. Therefore, I will not review any basic Harmonic Trading concepts such as the Fibonacci sequence or other examples in nature. I encourage all Harmonic Traders to investigate the numerous examples of harmonic phenomenon throughout the universe. I share numerous resources on my website including a basic foundation of pattern measures. These resources provide overwhelming substantiation of this phenomenon and reaffirm the importance of basing all measures from a harmonic framework.

Chapter 2
Standardized Harmonic Trading Identification Measurements

What Makes Patterns Harmonic?

In my first book, *The Harmonic Trader*, I outlined a checklist of requirements and guidelines for a trading plan that validated harmonic patterns as definitive opportunities. I believe that book is an excellent resource, especially for new traders as they learn the importance of specific rules for every step of the trading process. I actually make that available for free as a PDF download on my website www.HarmonicTrader.com so that traders can learn the basic foundation of this approach the correct way. It is an important resource to learn the measurement foundation of harmonic patterns. In fact, I would like to review the essence of *Harmonics* in this material before addressing more advanced strategies. Basic pattern rules serve as the starting point for a more complex integration of other harmonic measures that validates structural signals as significant. When we combine distinct harmonic patterns with overwhelming technical readings, a clearer opportunity can be defined and the anticipated reaction from the pattern completion can be gauged for a larger reversal.

I think it is important to understand the measurements and technical considerations that validate certain trades as highly probable opportunities in advance. Also, I think it is important to emphasize the exact measurements that constitute appropriate price levels associated within the tenets of Harmonic Trading. These measurements are part of a larger skillset that must be studied and carefully reviewed before being put into real action.

As I have mentioned previously, it is important that structural signals contain multiple elements to define the situations as reliable opportunities more than focusing on a single measure or pattern. This comprehension comes with experience and practice. Although the strategies can be integrated quickly, the larger understanding and real trading experience take time to coordinate the various aspects of the entire process. So, I recommend going slow until a thorough recognition of all expectations throughout the trading process is fully understood. Once obtained, the insights and framework of these measures outline those natural areas of support and resistance that are typically overlooked by most.

Harmonic Trading Volume 3: Reaction vs. Reversal

Random Ratios = Random Results

As the Harmonic Trading techniques have become more popular, I have noticed that others' interpretations have failed to include certain required harmonic elements that validate these situations as unique. In fact, it seems that many people are attempting to simply combine multiple ratio measurements without much regard to other structural considerations. The general notion that any combination of ratio measurements can define a potential opportunity is a dangerous proposition. When random ratios are continually attributed to price action, the only possible result is a skewed performance that possesses undefined risk parameters. There are reasons why the harmonic patterns I presented work. At a minimum, their general acceptance throughout the trading world has substantiated the basic framework to quantify these structures when they possess the proper characteristics. Later in the look, I will focus on the exact reason why these measures work and why the metrics employed may not be altered.

If price structures do not possess the proper elements that validate these situations, Harmonic Traders are effectively comparing apples to oranges. I believe this is a subject that deserves further discussion but I will simply stress that traders must follow the prescribed measurements that make patterns harmonic. Although others may argue differently, as creator of the standard rules for harmonic patterns, I understand and I will explain why particular elements of trading behavior quantify the structures as harmonic in detail later in this material.

Generally, the relation of price proportions within the scale of harmonic ratios cannot be altered. We utilize the 1.618 and 0.618 measures due to their relation to natural cyclical growth cycles as exemplified by the Fibonacci sequence. I have outlined these reasons in previous works and I offer numerous resources on my website for more information. I will not present a Fibonacci review here. However, I will stress the importance of using only those ratios that are derived from this foundation. Otherwise, defined trading opportunities will be based on random measurements which is a recipe for disaster.

Harmonic Trading Identification Strategies

The first step in the Harmonic Trading process is to properly identify structural possibilities and validate them as harmonic patterns. The validation process involves several critical measurements that must exist to define the opportunity. It is important to review the basics of trade identification. My first two books covered the majority of the measurement techniques that define structures as harmonic patterns. In this material, I introduced new measures and effective combinations that quantify structures to differentiate random price movements from valid Harmonic Pattern Trading opportunities. As well as addressing execution and management situations sufficiently. Although

Harmonic Trading: Volume 2 expanded on the pattern foundation and added new insights into advanced harmonic strategies that complemented the system of pattern identification, this material presents new strategies that complement the primary advantages of the system.

Harmonic Pattern Size

Throughout the years, I have been frequently asked about the proper size for a pattern. It is quite common for smaller structures to form and yield reactive moves but these situations often do not possess the sheer size in terms of number of price bars or the entire range to be a profitable opportunity. As I previously stated, harmonic patterns are specific sets of data points that comprise a collective signal. However, the minimum size of the structure must be established to measure patterns of significance and ignore irrelevant formations.

Each individual price bar represents the recorded history of trading within a certain time interval. Although the completion of most patterns includes several price bars, there are definitive data points that define the opportunity. Further in this material, we will examine some precise strategies that capitalize on these individual price bars. For now, the general question of how many price bars any harmonic pattern should possess must be answered with respect to a basic scientific assessment of what constitutes a sufficient sample size. For statistical studies, most require a minimum sample size of 30 data points. Related to harmonic patterns, this means that each pattern should possess 30 price bars regardless of the timeframe. Founded in the principle of the *Central Limit Theorem,* the 30-sample size is designed to ensure a normal distribution of probable outcomes. That is, we can expect a normal reaction at the completion of harmonic pattern opportunity more so in the structures than those that possess less than the ideal sample size amount.

In *The Harmonic Trader*, I established basic guidelines about pattern sizes. For example, I put forth the notion that the larger the pattern, the more significant possible reversal. In another instance, a market opportunity that has multiple calculations converging in a specific area will likely favor the largest measured price leg is the most significant over smaller sized formations. Those are valid assumptions. However, I feel it is important to establish a standardize means of determining the proper sample size for harmonic patterns. If we postulate that 30 price bars will satisfy the requirements of normal expectations, it serves us to focus on those opportunities with at least this amount if not more. The problem arises when multiple time intervals have the same pattern. For example, a pattern that forms on a 60-minute chart will also be visible on a 15-minute chart. Of course, the 15-minute chart will have four times the number of hourly bars. If the hourly chart has 20 bars, the 15-minute chart would be favored having 60 bars and being closer to the 30-statistical minimum. However, when an hourly chart has 30 bars or something close to the minimum, sometimes the 15-minute chart more accurately

Harmonic Trading Volume 3: Reaction vs. Reversal

reflects the possibilities of the situation. Simply stated, it is important to utilize that timeframe which is closest to 30 bars as the primary time interval to analyze parameters of the harmonic pattern.

Central Limit Theorem

I personally feel that the future of all market approaches will be optimized statistical analysis that emerges as the primary source of decision variables. As technological improvements put more power into the hands of the individual trader, a more scientific approach to assess market strategies focuses on quantifiable situations that can be measured and repeat with a consistent outcome. I have presented some research regarding harmonic phenomenon financial markets previously but I have withheld a great deal of statistical discoveries because these findings represent the ultimate realization of decades of work. Although one does not need to be a PhD statistician to incorporate these concepts into your decision framework, it is essential to understand principles of statistical probability as it relates to trading behavior. Ultimately, we are all executing definable market conditions that will someday be quantified and categorized into mathematically proven processes.

Since we have established harmonic patterns as a collection 30 or more individual price bars that possesses prescribed ratio proportions, we can analyze these results in a scientific manner that focuses on distinct price parameters where normal expectations of possible outcomes can be realized. Simply stated, this means that patterns with the required minimum sample size are much less likely to get "blown out of the water" from unexpected events, reducing vulnerable conditions that may arise from more random structures. Therefore, the principles of the Central Limit Theorem provide the basis of establishing normal expectations of price behavior outcomes.

According to Wikipedia, "*...the Central Limit Theorem (CLT) states that, given certain conditions, the arithmetic mean of a sufficiently large number of iterates of independent random variables, each with a well-defined (finite) expected value and finite variance, will be approximately normally distributed, regardless of the underlying distribution. To illustrate what this means, suppose that a sample is obtained containing a large number of observations, each observation being randomly generated in a way that does not depend on the values of the other observations, and that the arithmetic average of the observed values is computed. If this procedure is performed many times, the Central Limit Theorem says that the computed values of the average will be distributed according to the normal distribution (commonly known as a 'bell curve').*"

https://en.wikipedia.org/wiki/Central_limit_theorem

Theory of Normal Distribution Returns

All patterns should possess at least 30 bars on the timeframe that they are identified. In fact, I find myself utilizing the 30 number to approximate a sufficient number of bars can encompass any trading situation. As I stated before, the pattern that is closest to 30 bars on any timeframes should be considered the most suitable for the primary pattern. Since all patterns serve as the basic measuring basis for entry points and stop loss considerations, we can assess the completion of patterns within this 30-bar limit as a minimum time constraint to allow the reversal to take hold. There are other examples where this approximation does work but the principle is founded in expectation of normal price behavior no matter what.

Albeit quite simple, this 30-bar limit has helped to confirm smaller patterns on shorter timeframe for that effectively optimize entries of larger structures. It is only in the past several years that I have been able to effectively explain the need for a minimum pattern size. However, as I have experimented with its application over the years, I know that this basic rule of 30 price bars has been quite effective as a means in differentiating those structures that are smaller and insignificant. If you are a long-term trader, I believe it is important to be aware of the last 30 days at 30 months no matter what the market. If you are a short-term trader, I would suggest always be aware of the prior day's action – that is, the last 30 hours. Finally, the simple technique is yet another important principle to effectively analyze and monitor pattern progress.

Potential Reversal Zone (PRZ) Review

The Potential Reversal Zone was the most important breakthrough concept that put harmonic measurements on the map in general. The Potential Reversal Zone (PRZ) represents a definitive statement of structural analysis where the measured movements pinpoint an exact price level with clear anticipated behavioral change is expected to unfold. Although I have stressed that this is merely a starting point, the precision of the measured levels of the Potential Reversal Zone (PRZ) provides a framework in a unique manner.

This concept was one of the first harmonically measured means to define some type of expectations with respect to future price action. In this matter, the collection and convergence of measurements define levels of support and resistance in a unique framework that provided tremendous insight and consistently accurate possibilities relative to the structural assessments being considered. Furthermore, each pattern possesses a combination of measurements that defines the character for each opportunity. A Crab pattern for example would have different trading expectations as opposed to a Shark pattern.

These measures have served to become the foundation of harmonic patterns. Although there are a variety of statistical reports regarding the accuracy of the patterns,

I have presented the alignments based upon an exact sequence of ratios as well as an assumed tolerance level for each pattern point that reflects the optimal combinations from my research. Although discovering precise tolerance levels can unlock more powerful pattern opportunities, these are typically found less.

The Three Elements of Harmonic Trading Opportunities

The original breakthrough that I realized 20 years ago was the importance of applying proper ratio measurements and structural analysis to define natural cyclical behavior of any market movement over time. I must emphasize that certain minimum timeframes are preferable to exploit these opportunities as well as understanding basic liquidity requirements of any market. Certain minimum requirements are important to avoid those markets which can be prone to irrational volatility swings. In essence, not every market interval or instrument should be traded. For example, tick charts can form distinct harmonic patterns but they typically do not provide a sufficient price range to capitalize on the opportunity relative to the required stop loss limit. These situations are obvious but if in doubt stay out. For most major markets, the elements of harmonic patterns should exhibit ideal relationships and adhere closely to the prescribed definition of the opportunity allowing plenty of time to capitalize on the situation. Regardless of the time interval, the ability to validate these opportunities depends on the following three conditions – Ratios, Sine Wave structures and "environmental" indicators.

1. Harmonic Ratio Relationships

Related to the numerous examples throughout nature, the importance of which ratios are employed is critical to define the natural harmonic cycles in the market. Many people are aware of the importance of the "Golden Ratio" phenomenon throughout nature. The 61.8% and the 161.8% proportions are merely a starting point. My initial research tested variations of these ratio relationships. Most notable, discoveries of the 88.6% and 113% measures - and other related reciprocal proportions – have yielded interesting and effective harmonic relationships.

Later in this chapter, I outline the exact list of the harmonic ratios employed that define retracements and projections within pattern structures as well as their derivations related to natural Geometric proportions. We will review each of the pattern elements in this material but the singular measurements do not need to be reviewed. If you would like to review more material on individual ratio measurements of retracements and projections, please visit my website at www.HarmonicTrader.com where you will find a great deal of information on basic subject matter such as this. Furthermore, the derivation of these numbers and its significance to the Fibonacci numeric sequence can be reviewed there. I want to focus more on the complex scenarios that these ratio measures manifest to define the harmonic pattern opportunities with the greatest.

Harmonic Trading Volume 3: Reaction vs. Reversal

The important point is not to get caught up in the mystique of these ratio metrics. It is true that the relationships and properties they identify are quite interesting. However, measures such as 1.618 properly define natural cyclical phenomenon in a variety of other examples outside the market. As I stated in previous discussions, I am more focused with what works, testing those ideas and refining them for effective optimization of these strategic proportions. Furthermore, most metrics are applied in pattern-specific situations that employ predetermined expectations within the analytical framework to assess price action.

One of the most remarkable historic examples of a singular ratio affecting a major market that I've ever witnessed unfolded in 2015. Ever since the bear market low that was established in 2009, the recovery of the past decade has been questioned continually. I believe this is typical uncertainty most long-term bull market's face throughout history but the severity of the prior bear market left an indelible mark which remains to this day. Situations like these demonstrate the need to measure price history to understand how far any market has moved relative to past history.

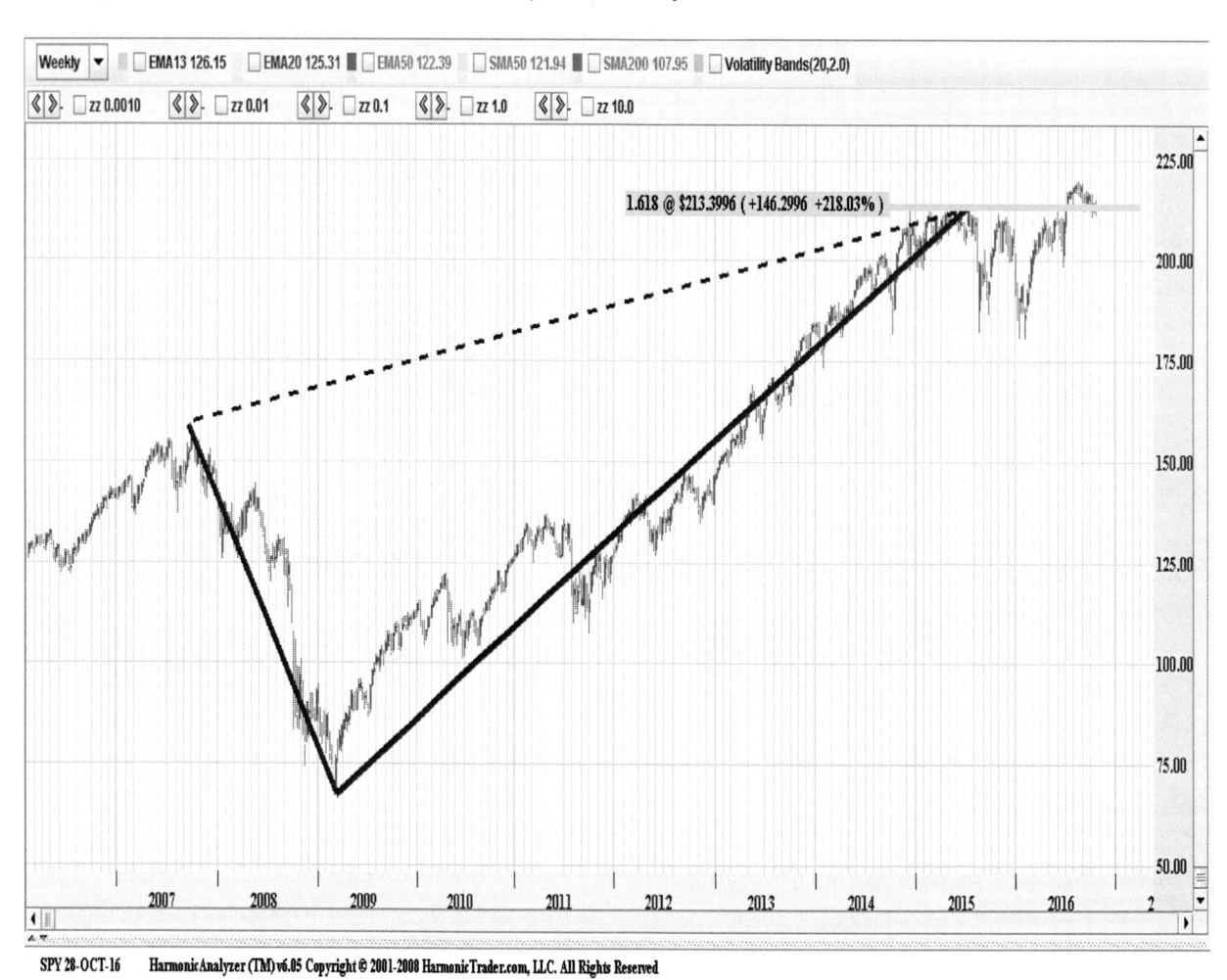

Harmonic Trading Volume 3: Reaction vs. Reversal

Simply stated, sentiment has remained skeptical after what happened during the financial crisis of 2009. Regardless, harmonic measurements defined that bear market in advance, the eventual low of that move, and they have effectively gauged the progress over the past 10 years. Remarkably, the 1.618 weekly limit was an initial challenge to this mutli-year recovery and marked an important pause in the long-term trend.

Although the decline from the 2007 peak was quite severe, it has served as a significant and relevant measurement basis to define long-term targets even to today. This remarkable example of ideal price behavior unfolding exactly where the 1.618 extension completed is evidence of harmonic resistance in action. This measure served as a clear target throughout the recovery and an important technical initial objectine.

Harmonic Trading Volume 3: Reaction vs. Reversal

Personally, I had been monitoring this measurement for nearly 18 months prior to its realization, as I covered it over the course of many of my monthly reports. The ETF possessed a 1.618 extension that completed at 213.40. After nearly 8 years of trading history, the price action tested this level and reversed on the exact day that it reached the 1.618 level. Over the next 15 months, the market slowly declined and lost 15% from the initial completion of that projection. Although the price action has since rebounded, the initial reaction provided a significant opportunity.

I must emphasize that this is more than an excellent well-chosen example. I know that the industry is ripe with people showing well-chosen examples that fit their promoted strategy. However, harmonic phenomenon like this occurs every day on all timeframes. Even after my years of experience observing such phenomenon, I still find these situations to be fascinating structures, and when these measurements materialize on long-term weekly and monthly patterns, I pay particular attention. Furthermore, it is important to note that all measurement strategies are applied in the same no matter what the timeframe or market. Price action unfolds in a uniform manner where the framework of measurements provides a consistent basis to analyze trading opportunities. The only difference is the amount of time permitted to make decisions.

One of the most misunderstood concepts about harmonic patterns is they are based upon ratio measurements alone. Since my introduction of harmonic pattern rules, there have been a number of interpretations that focus on different ratio combinations without respect to the primary structure. In fact, some have altered the harmonic ratios - claiming they have improved their effectiveness. Unfortunately, these immutable measures are the required elements that make patterns harmonic. This has created confusion and led traders away from the universal metrics that comprise the true harmonic advantage. With the proper ratios, traders can identify the correct harmonic price levels to facilitate decisions.

2. AB=CD Phenomenon: Sine Waves in the Financial Markets

Structural analysis of any market movement must recognize that phenomenon which repeats. Although some price formations may seem simplistic, distinct structures can define extended trends, areas of consolidation and pinpoint key changes that may otherwise be overlooked. In fact, technical traders can effectively recognize price movements as distinct waves. The Elliott Wave approach is a classic analytical approach that categorizes wave structures as unique. In general, Wave Theory views any price movement as a chartable frequency that exhibits various characteristics.

The "physics" behind such natural price movements can be expressed in terms of Sine Wave properties. Before we look at the advanced concepts, it is important to introduce basic Sine Wave concepts.

Harmonic Trading Volume 3: Reaction vs. Reversal

"A sine wave or sinusoid is a mathematical curve that describes a smooth periodic oscillation. A sine wave is a continuous wave...It is named after the function sine, of which it is the graph... It occurs often in pure and applied mathematics, as well as physics, engineering, signal processing and many other fields...
The sine wave is important in physics because it retains its wave shape when added to another sine wave of the same frequency and arbitrary phase and magnitude. It is the only periodic waveform that has this property."
https://en.wikipedia.org/wiki/Sine_wave

The Sine Wave concept can easily be more complicated that it really is. Although measurable frequencies – radio waves, cardiograms, etc. - exhibit these properties, it is important to consider that sine waves in the financial markets represent price movements that possess finite possibilities. When we categorize definable sine waves (patterns), we can differentiate larger price mechanisms of buying and selling that manifest these properties. Each price movement – up, down, sideways – possesses particular characteristics that dictate the parameters of the respective move. For our purposes, it is not necessary to dive into a deep mathematical discussion regarding the physics and the derived formula that quantify such movements.

The Sine Wave concept in the price action of the financial markets examines the structural expression of multi-segmented moves to distinguish uniquely repeatable situations. As we consider relative proportional measures and the force of individual segments within sine wave price movements, more complex conditions can be clearly defined, clarifying the possible price direction. Therefore, these structural harmonic sine wave types represent unique technical patterns that require all conditions to be satisfied to validate each opportunity. In addition, many structural pattern rules have been optimized in this material to exclude those types that do not express minimum wave proportions as a means of eliminating minor fluctuations from significant moves. The material in this book expands upon the initial rules of harmonic patterns presented in *The Harmonic Trader* and *Harmonic Trading Volume One*.

The Sine Wave concept comprises one of the most important assessments for any harmonic pattern opportunity - the AB=CD pattern. Although technician pioneers such as H.M. Gartley and J.M. Hurst presented basic sine wave relationships in their work decades ago, this analysis respective to harmonic price formations has defined more precise pattern alignments as well as eliminated many invalid situations that might have been previously considered. For our purposes, all HARMONIC sine wave types - a basic AB=CD or an Alternate AB=CD pattern – outline the critical structural measurement within any measured zone. Although I recommend the work of Gartley and Hurst, I believe that much of their detailed metrics – amplitude, cycle length, variation – are encompassed within the harmonic pattern framework.

Although each opportunity has measured implications, the structural sine wave of an AB=CD pattern defines minimum price objectives. This completion point serves as an essential minimum requirement for all M&W-type patterns while Alternate AB=CD variations are typically employed with distinct formations such as Bat and Crab patterns. Regardless, the structural measure is only effective when distinct harmonic proportions distinguish these situations.

"Market Sine-ature"

The AB=CD element is a simplified term for what I refer to as the phenomenon in price action termed *Market Sine-ature*. The Market Sineature concept encompasses the study of all AB=CD wave structures as independent price signals first and foremost. The ability of these structures to define important levels of support and resistance serve as the minimum price objective in most harmonic scenarios. Furthermore, additional harmonic pattern structural measures serve to complement what these minimum wave movements establish.

The Market Sineature concept espouses a certain set of expectations in regards to the price parameters each pattern possesses. In particular, early identification of these pattern types enables measurement of predictive completion points well in advance. When minimum AB=CD patterns take shape, their price action can unfold quite clearly and define direction effectively. These are the preferred situations, especially when price action possesses ideal harmonic ratio proportions.

The basic AB=CD sine wave phenomenon frequently unfolds like a magnet as the final leg of the pattern approaches a pattern's completion point. In fact, I have talked about this "Magnet Effect" of price behavior as it relates to the final leg of a harmonic pattern. In combination with complex patterns, there are defined acceleration situations where the CD leg of the structure highlights a highly probable completion point.

One of the magnet phenomena that I have described previously in my *Volume 2* was the BAMM strategy that outlined clear harmonic breakouts /breakdowns. BAMM is an acronym that means *Bat Action Magnet Move*. Simply stated, when a Bat pattern begins to enter the final (CD) leg, it accelerates into the Potential Reversal Zone once it exceeds the midpoint at B. This primary phenomenon serves as an effective basis for a variety of automatic reactions that can occur within harmonic limits. In fact, all sine wave structures possess this BAMM phenomenon, except they fall within the AB=CD framework. As the price action enters the final leg, the CD leg begins to form and exceeds the B point. The projected minimum completion point for the AB=CD structure defines the targeted objective. In essence, the equivalent AB=CD structure represents one completed harmonic cycle. When the formation is properly identified, it is possible to position trades accordingly. These situations depend upon the pattern at hand but the "magnet phenomenon" becomes clearer with a comprehensive understanding of each pivot points within the structure.

One of the most remarkable examples in recent memory of a singular the AB=CD structure defining critical price levels in impressive fashion was the long-term peak in the weekly chart of the iShares Energy ETF, the XLE. This remarkable sine wave structure defined the area just under $98 as the weekly harmonic resistance, and the price action reversed aggressively two weeks after completing the structure.

Harmonic Trading Volume 3: Reaction vs. Reversal

As this example demonstrates, AB=CD patterns must be analyzed with respect to the clarity of the price segments that are forming. Although AB=CDs can materialize as consolidation structures or they can mark important inflection points, they serve as the minimum limits to define potential inflection points. As the basic AB=CD formation is nearing completion, it is possible to measure these structures with harmonic ratios to anticipate the reversal with an understanding of the natural limits that pattern implies. That is, the AB=CD is a minimum cyclical completion point where a countertrend move can be anticipated.

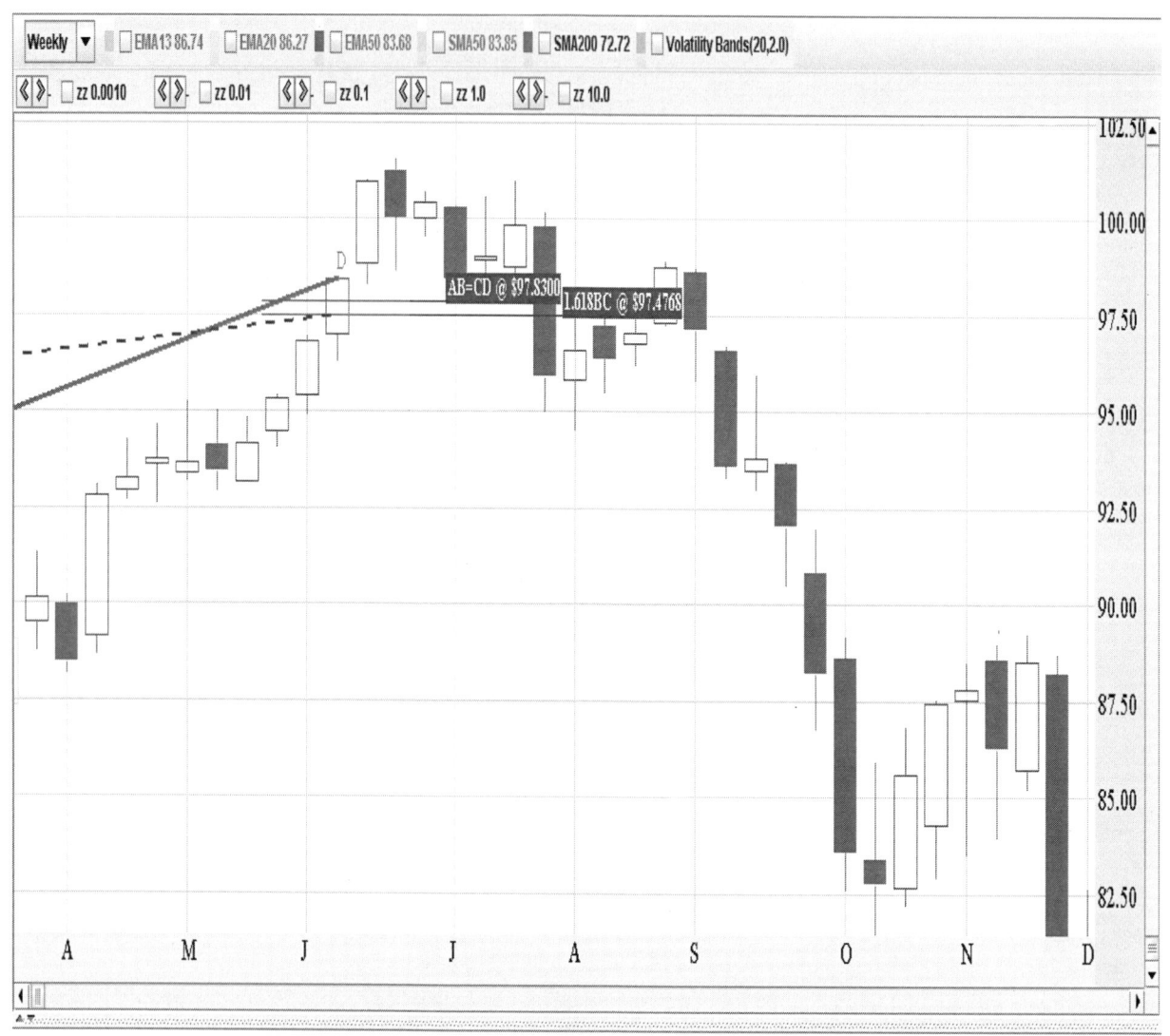

Harmonic Trading Volume 3: Reaction vs. Reversal

The basic AB=CD structural assumption - where the market will at least take a breather no matter how strong the trend – is a general yet effective principle of the Sine Wave concept. Although it is common for the minimum pattern to be exceeded, this recognition helps to clarify those situations when the objectives for a particular move are unclear. Furthermore, these assessments create a means to define basic expectations and validate minimum price objectives in any market on any timeframe.

3. Harmonic Indicator Measures: RSI, HSI

Although I am known for harmonic patterns, my work in this material - much of what I have not released previously - involves an advanced understanding of measuring market movements to determine oversold and overbought conditions. Initially, price measurements such as the 1.618 served as one of the metrics to define such extremes. However, my research into technical indicators was inspired by the fundamentals of harmonic pattern measures. I focused on those tools that complemented the basic expectations within the harmonic pattern framework. In fact, I introduced many of these in my *Harmonic Trading Volume Two* book in 2007. It was an immense advancement within my own understanding of harmonic price behavior as this research has led to remarkable proprietary advancements in recent years. Discoveries such as the Harmonic Strength Index (HSI) and new harmonic indicators have defined harmonic pattern opportunities to an unprecedented degree. However, I want to review some of the essential harmonic applications of indicators that I presented in *Volume Two* before introducing the new concepts.

As many already know, Relative Strength (RSI) is one of the most effective confirmation methods at the completion of harmonic patterns. I spent a great deal of time refining and categorizing Welles Wilder's Relative Strength Index, which I feel is still one of the most accurate indicators available today. I credit his technical measure for opening my eyes to many relationships, and without Mr. Wilder's contribution, I would not have been able to integrate price movements with indicator readings to the degree that I have. Upon this foundation, I have introduced several new strategies to optimize its effectiveness. Furthermore, I have expanded upon this analysis and optimized the essence of what a harmonic pattern indicator should define. These new applications led to measures that better reflect extreme harmonic price behavior and could be expressed as an individual reading. The most notable of all, the Harmonic Strength Index (HSI) is the culmination of years of research to develop a proprietary indicator that quantified this behavior.

Most traders are aware of the standard indicators. Aside from RSI, most software programs include Stochastics, MACD, Market Profile and many other technical methods. Not to mention, it is incredible to see the number of proprietary programs that have been developed by individual traders. In today's world where all transactions are online, the focus has shifted to chart analysis and statistical back testing. There is an accelerating trend emerging, as it seems that the industry is on the edge of a renaissance in terms of how it will determine asset allocation in the future. Individual advisors are certainly an endangered species in the years to come, as methodology will replace personality. Those who can consistently and effectively assess opportunities based upon the market's trading history - derived mostly from chart analysis - will be the dominating managers of future capital. Therefore, technology will become an increasing necessity, especially as artificial intelligence and statistically-proven strategies enable unprecedented insights into market behavior.

I believe that such technology has been an empowering benefit for individual traders. Most market participants now have access to nearly the same level of resources and tools as the biggest firms in the industry. There have already been many computer programmers whom have exploited market inefficiencies via extensive mathematical studies with mountains of statistical evidence to define high probability situations. In the same regard, the advancements in this book outline those conditions (based upon years of statistical analysis) to highlight which strategies have the best probability for success.

As more traders rely on chart analysis, visual methods such as pattern recognition have become accepted illustrative tools to facilitate decisions. Advanced charting technology is changing the game for not only harmonic patterns but Technical Analysis in the industry as a whole. In fact, throughout most of Wall Street's history, asset allocation was based more upon a company's zip code as much as a firm's capabilities. However, the demise of once reputable firms such as Lehman Brothers and Bear Sterns in the 2008 financial crisis was one of the seminal events that marked this change. Not to mention, the unthinkable fraud committed by Bernie Madoff & Associates will forever scar the once venerable world of New York's trusted advisors. In my opinion, the general interest in harmonic patterns and the related ratio measurements employed within Harmonic Trading grew immensely after these meltdowns, as the methodology actually benefited from these events.

Regardless the events of years ago, it is now an online trading world exclusively. Over the past decade, I have refined the measurement strategies with tools such as harmonic indicators and dynamic pattern targets that speak to these technological advancements. Automated trading software has provided unprecedented analytical capabilities to the individual trader unlike ever before. Furthermore, this progress has enabled individuals to devise and program general strategies into precise algorithms. As statistical and computational power expands, traders can isolate those situations with the highest probabilities and avoid unfavorable opportunities that may have been previously unrecognized.

Much of the new material in this book focuses on these advancements. Harmonic strategies that confirm structural signals can identify valid price behavior early in the reversal process. Specifically, indicator readings at the completion of harmonic patterns are essential such confirmation rather than focusing solely on price action. As I will outline later in this material, tools such as RSI and Harmonic Strength Index can be applied to specific situations to optimize decisions within the trading process. Furthermore, the combination of these strategies facilitates the overall understanding of what conditions define the best opportunities.

Most of my research has focused on harmonic environments that possess both indicator measures and structural price levels for all stages of the trading process. However, I feel that the gamut of potential patterns that can be measured has been exhausted and sufficiently covered by the existing structures that I have presented in most of my identification material. Other harmonic measurements that applied to management parameters and execution triggers have immensely clarified the harmonic process to a precise degree. In this book, we will breakdown complex strategic scenarios to integrate the best of both patterns and indicator analysis. Ultimately, the ability to decipher reactions from reversal depends upon those additional metrics that confirm the primary structural assessment provided by the harmonic pattern.

One of the problems that I have with people who are attempting to analyze opportunities based strictly on ratio measurements is that they fail to incorporate other critical elements that comprise valid structural signals. It is very easy to measure random various points and outline those levels where multiple ratios converge. Often referred to as "Confluence", these measurements tend to outline valid yet temporary support/resistance levels. Although I like the idea of multiple metrics completing in the same area, these projections lack other aspects required to highlight the most important harmonic zones. Substantial opportunities come from a combination of proportional ratio measurements and clear structural elements completing at the same price level. The advanced Harmonic Trading material in this book explains why ratio AND structure are the integrated advantage to the entire approach. These essential elements work together to properly assess the harmonic levels within valid situations.

Sine Wave

In the same way that we apply the harmonic ratios manifested throughout cycles in nature, we analyze price action within a framework of measurements. These metrics possess predictive behavioral expectations within the structure Sine Waves provide. Again, it's not my point to get into a long mathematical discussion about the mechanics of wave frequencies. Rather, price movements manifest these relationships continually and their proportional possibilities of expected targets and defined stop loss limits establishes the natural limit of any opportunity. Applied in the financial markets, we can isolate specific pattern situations as unique wave types.

Price behavior is just an expression of the trading energy waves – up/down – that can be analyzed over specific periods of time. Assuming the basic phenomenon of Sine Wave (M&W-Type) structural properties, these formations possess a relatively constant proportional expression in any normal environment (think Central Limit Theorem). For example, the AB=CD pattern is a type of minimum energy wave in the financial markets where each leg represents a component of one complete vibration, the associated price objectives and completion targets can be accurately measured. These are the basic assumptions that help us define price behavior, especially when conditions seem erratic. Regardless, the Sine Wave properties of any harmonic patterns will dictate which ratios should be employed to define true harmonic price zones.

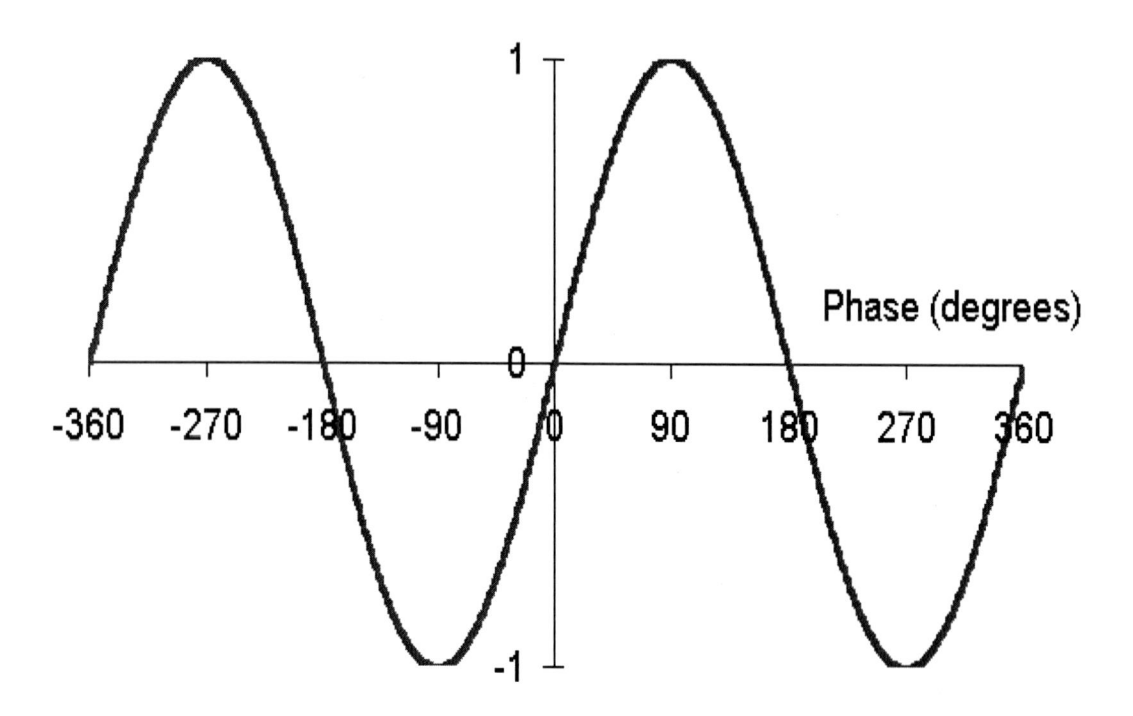

Cosine Wave

A cosine wave is a signal waveform that represents the complementary function the Sine Wave. An ideal frequency movement possesses S-shaped properties that can be measured and projected over any time interval. Much like a Sine Wave, the form expresses a "phase-shift" in that a cosine wave is variation of the primary metric upon which the related movement can be expected. Essentially, these sine concepts encompass the concept of Vibration where any movement over a particular interval will possess degrees of frequency. Again, it is not my desire to breakdown the Trigonometry that explains this phenomenon. Rather, the basics of Wave Theory such as this possesses measurable and definable segments. Within the analysis of harmonic price action, these structural considerations enable predictive strategies to capitalize on these situations once validated.

Cosine Waves in the Financial Markets

The combination of buying AND selling waves in the markets combine to produce a multi-component chartable frequency that possesses clear minimum price objectives when multiple harmonic proportions are manifested. Although the equation mathematically explains the wave structure and the constraints of the move, the key concept is to be aware of the minimum structural parameters for any price segment.

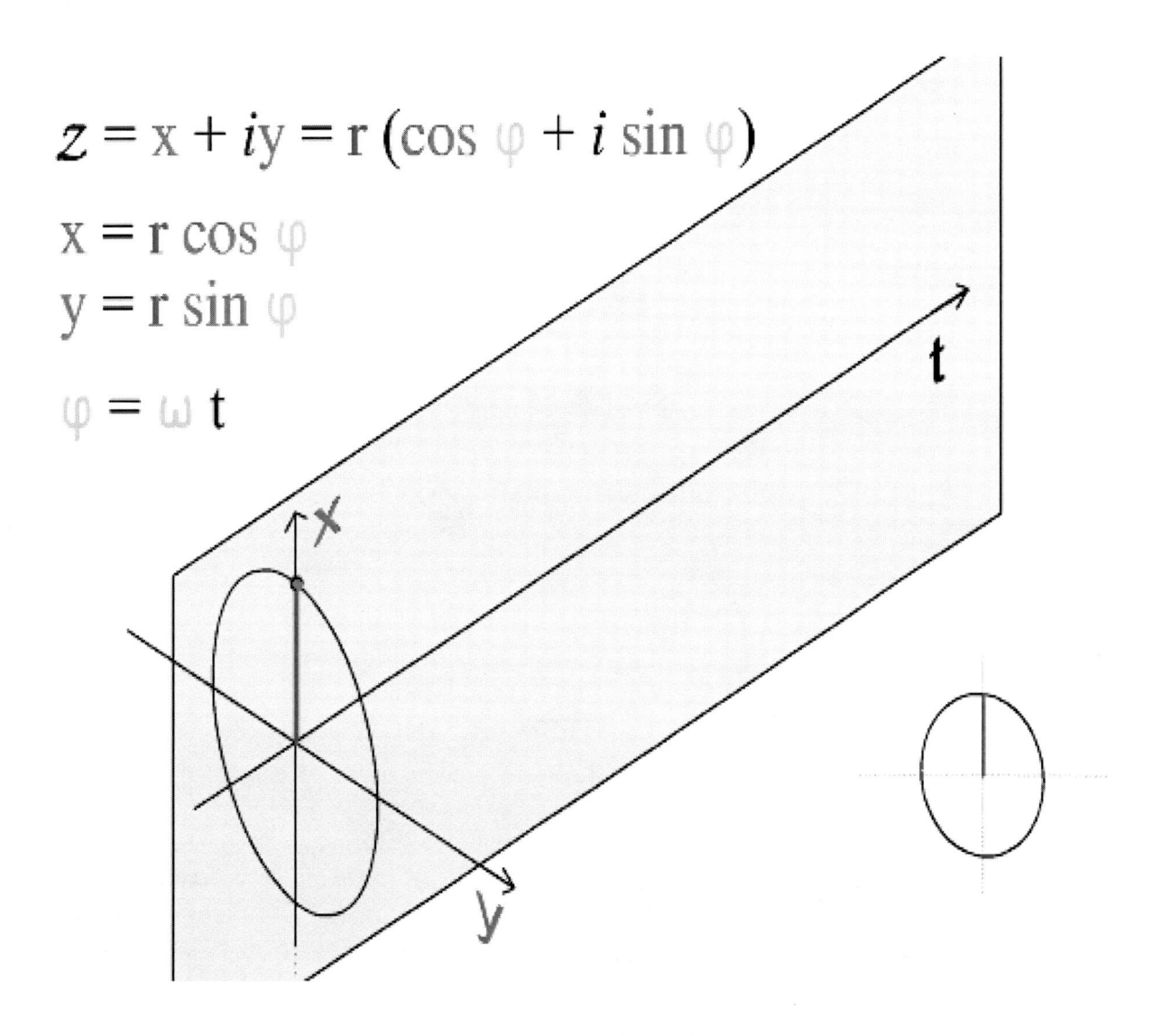

$$z = x + iy = r(\cos \varphi + i \sin \varphi)$$
$$x = r \cos \varphi$$
$$y = r \sin \varphi$$
$$\varphi = \omega t$$

Of course, not every movement in the financial markets is going to form this structure. However, it is an effective approximation tool when distinct movements possess the properties to validate its structure.

Harmonic Trading Volume 3: Reaction vs. Reversal

Cosine Waves as AB=CD Patterns

The AB=CD pattern represents a buying and selling sine wave formation where each leg is equal in magnitude and time. The AB=CD represents a structural MINIMUM in most harmonic patterns. This requirement is extremely important because it serves as a cyclical structural signal expressed within any defined trading period. Therefore, the AB=CD pattern minimum must be an essential of any trade opportunity.

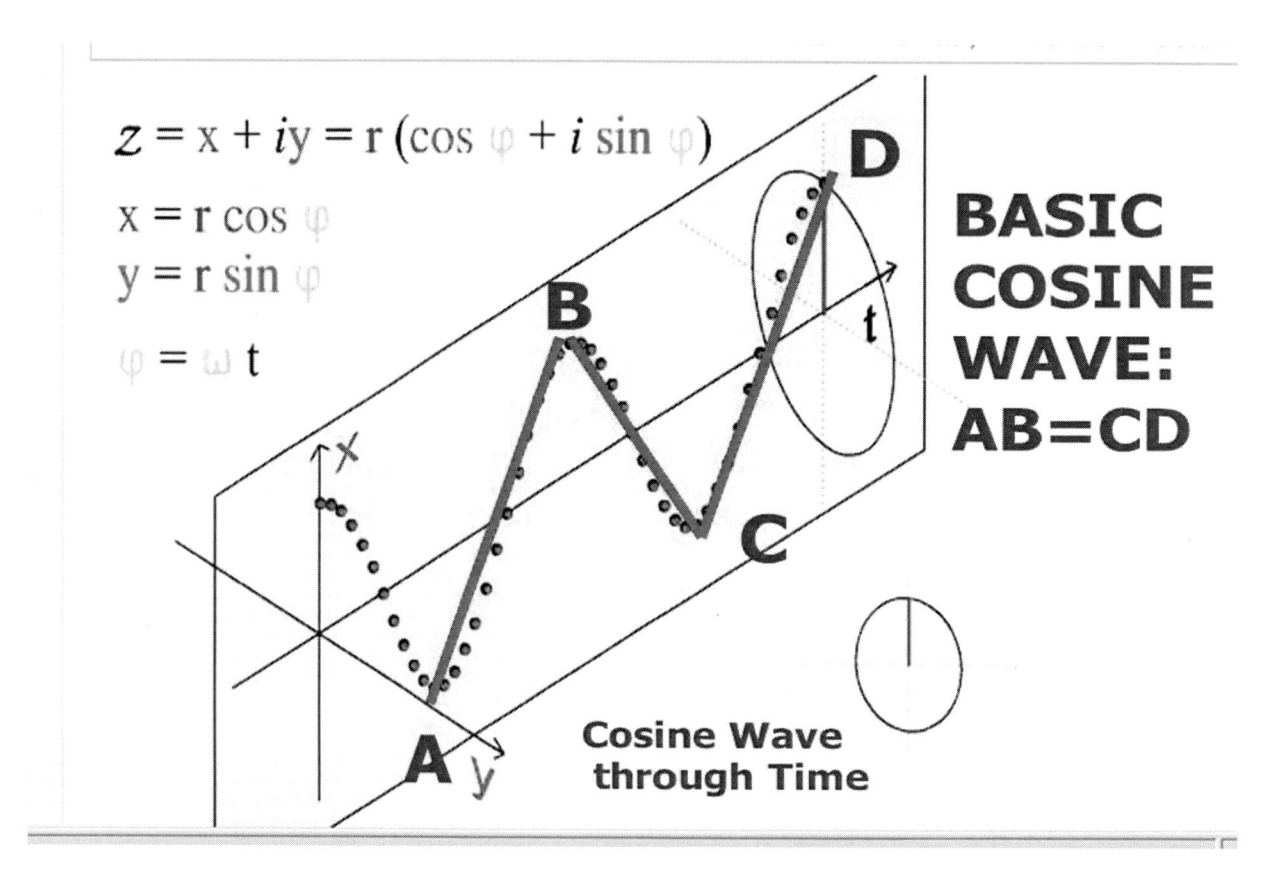

$$z = x + iy = r(\cos \varphi + i \sin \varphi)$$
$$x = r \cos \varphi$$
$$y = r \sin \varphi$$
$$\varphi = \omega t$$

BASIC COSINE WAVE: AB=CD

Cosine Wave through Time

In my opinion, harmonic patterns represent various types of natural cycles in the financial markets. Price action that forms clear structural patterns is signaling a special type of consolidation, where the data set of trades forms a unique mechanical phenomenon. Like leaves that turned their color during the Fall to signal the onset of Winter, the most distinct patterns consistently signal the correct probable future price action in this regard well before their fruition. The AB=CD is the minimum natural cycle that defines the minimum level of the structural phenomenon that has formed. Although ratio measurements are extremely important in any harmonic pattern, without the element of the AB=CD structure, they possess little significance.

Harmonic Trading Volume 3: Reaction vs. Reversal

AB=CD Pattern Elements

- The AB=CD pattern is a 4-point price structure that is a minimum requirement for most harmonic pattern setups.
- The AB=CD pattern is a structure comprised of two equidistant price segments that possess harmonic ratios.
- The exact completion point of the AB=CD is the most significant price level, while the BC projection complements the area.
- The C point will be a defining level for the completion of the pattern, establishing the Reciprocal Ratio.

Bullish AB=CD Pattern

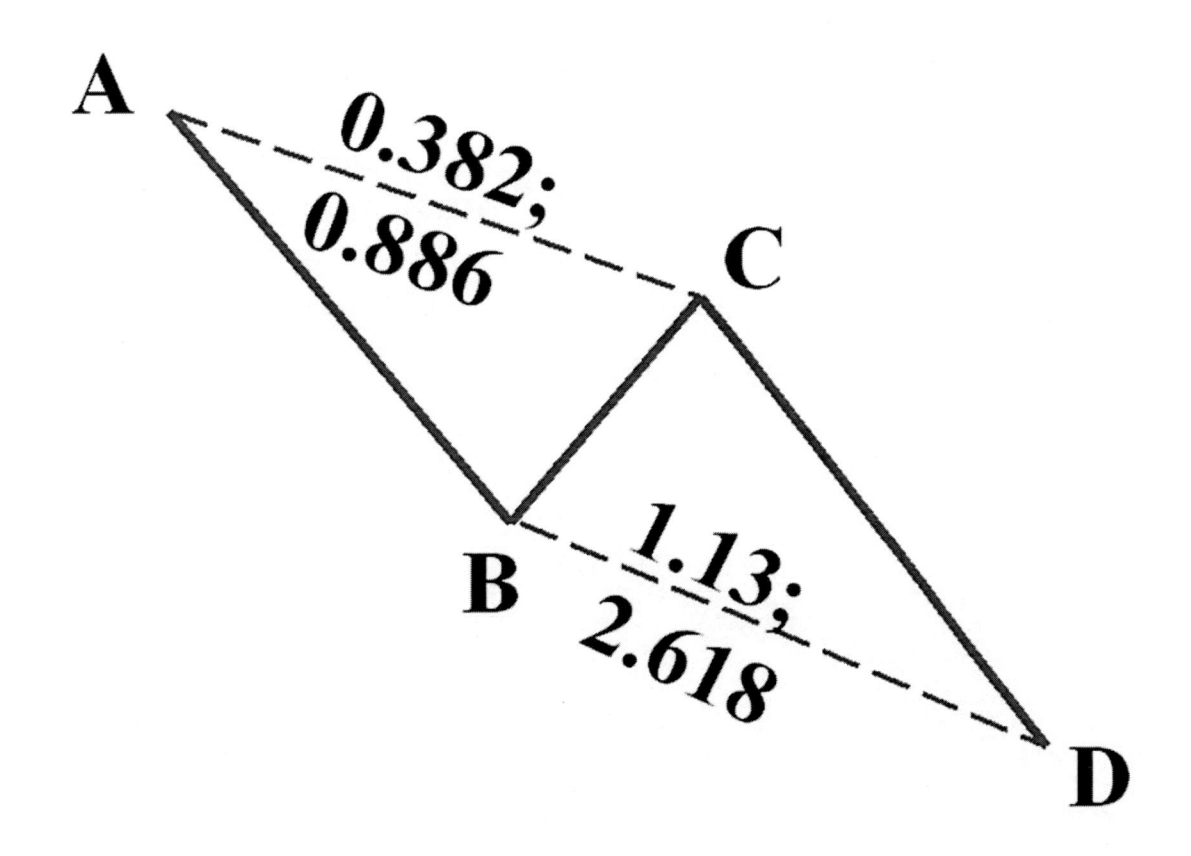

Harmonic Trading Volume 3: Reaction vs. Reversal

The Bullish AB=CD structure is a minimum component in any pattern opportunity. The key element in all valid patterns is found in the distinct symmetry of the formation. The harmonic ratios that comprise the structure are critical in complementing the completion point for the pattern. The BC projection measurement is critical in confirming the completion point for the structure as well. Although the AB=CD completion point is the most important minimum for any pattern consideration, it will typically be exceeded as the price action tests the entire support zone.

Euro/U.S. Dollar (EUR_A0-FX): 60-Minute
Bullish AB=CD Pattern

This 60-minute chart in the Euro/Dollar exemplifies what an intraday AB=CD pattern looks like. The structure possesses two distinct legs that were each approximately 125 pips in length. On the exact hour that the price action tested this zone, the market reversed. The most important point of this chart is to notice the distinct structure. These are the type of ideal formations that should be considered.

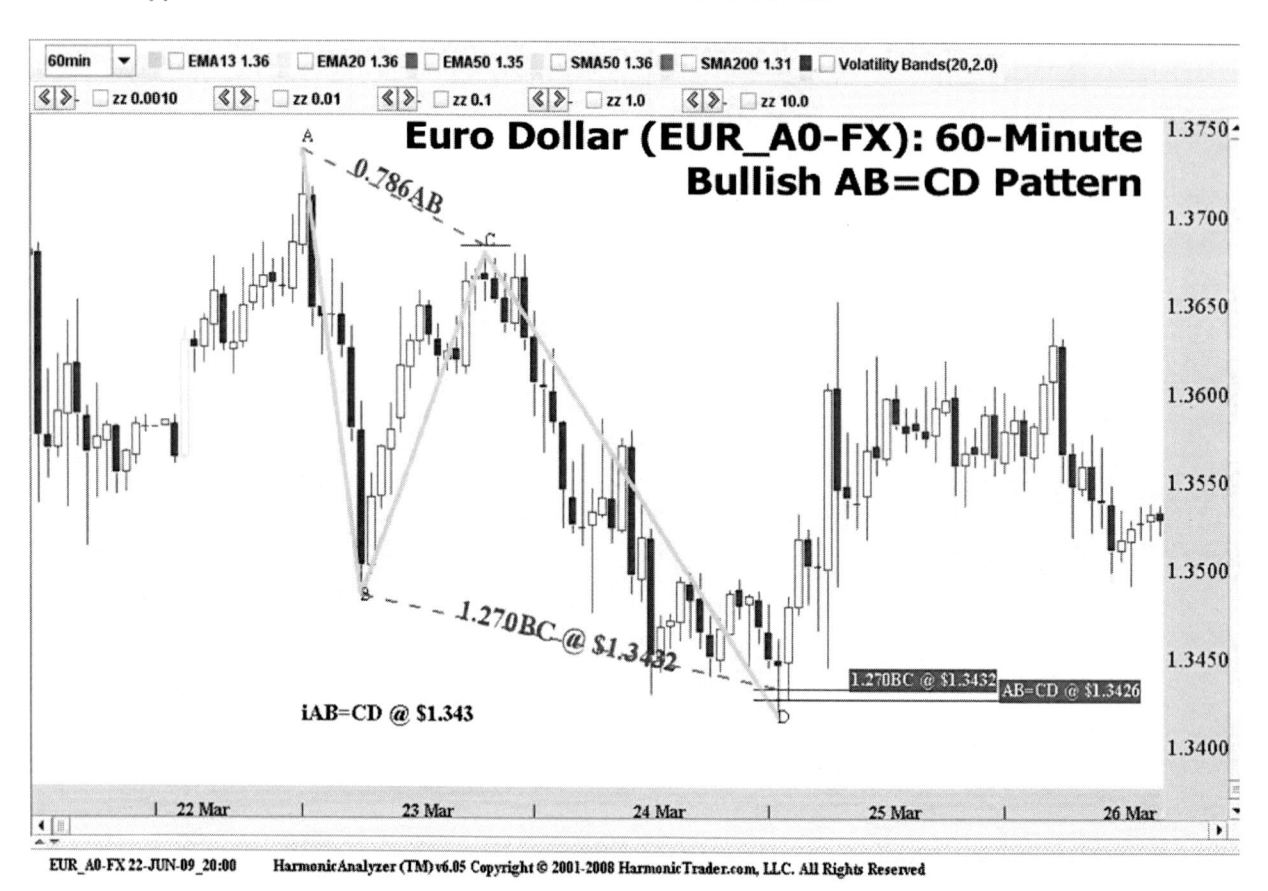

Harmonic Trading Volume 3: Reaction vs. Reversal

Bearish AB=CD Pattern

The following bearish illustration serves as an important minimum target in all M and W formations. The structure should be distinct and possesses a limited range of BC ratio projections to complement the exact completion.

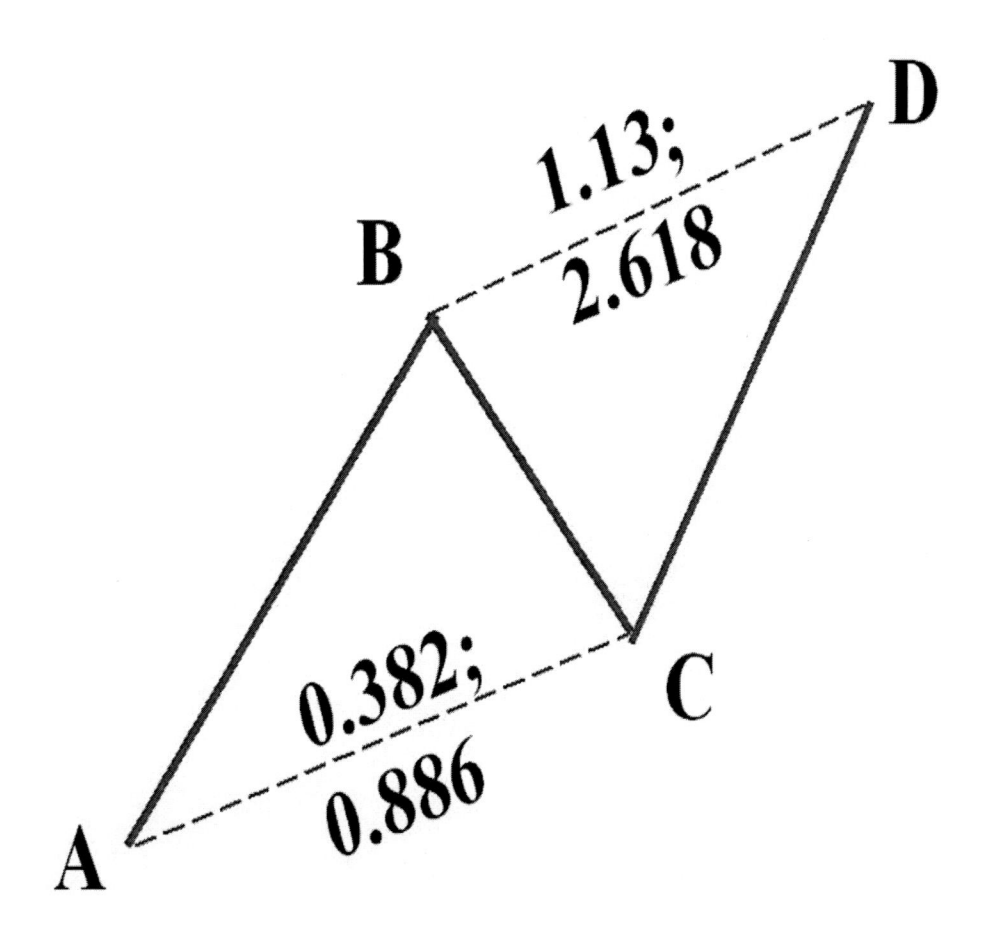

Harmonic Trading Volume 3: Reaction vs. Reversal

Euro/U.S. Dollar (EUR_A0-FX): 15-Minute Bearish AB=CD Pattern

The following 15-minute Euro/Dollar chart exemplifies what an ideal structure should look like. The symmetry of the pattern was quite distinct and the exact AB=CD completion point capped the strong intraday rally. The structure was projected to complete at 1.4933 and the reversal topped out at 1.4940. Also, the price action stalled immediately after testing all the numbers in the Potential Reversal Zone. After a few sideways individual price bars, the reversal accelerated.

Harmonic Trading Volume 3: Reaction vs. Reversal

Harmonic Ratios -> Reciprocal Ratios

Reciprocal Ratios are based upon the inverse relationships of retracements versus extensions. These are generally employed to measure and complement pattern completion points. In terms of the AB= CD structure, the retracement ratio can identify the expected extension measurement. We will look at these relationships in detail when we review the 5-0 pattern but for these purposes, we will review their significance.

Retracement		Extension
0.382	>	2.24, 2.618, 3.14, 3.618
0.50	>	2.0
0.618	>	1.618
0.707	>	1.414
0.786	>	1.272
0.886	>	1.13
1.0	>	2.0

Perfect AB= CD

The most symmetrical and harmonic of all structures is the Perfect AB=CD pattern. Although other ratio combinations signal valid starting points, this particular structure was initially identified in my book *Harmonic Trading Volume 1*. Previously, I have presented a number of perfect pattern alignments but the most important of all of these is the basic AB=CD structure with the 61.8% and 161.8% harmonic ratios. In fact, the perfect pattern alignments do present the most ideal structures as they relate to the harmonic ratios. Clearly, the AB=CD element is critical to all structures but without the harmonic proportions of the 0.618 and 1.618 measures for example, we would simply be assessing random structures. We know that these elements are essential to define structures as harmonic.

The premise of capitalizing on the natural cyclical phenomenon within the financial markets requires that we respect the measurements and execute trades at the prescribed levels. The perfect structures give us the ideal symmetrical model that is closest to what the natural model exhibits. From general standpoint, these measurement structures can be overlaid with real-time scenarios with a tolerance for some deviation from the ideal. This guides decisions and provides accurate information regarding the predominant trend to optimize executions, reduce risk and maximize profit. Therefore, these perfect

Harmonic Trading Volume 3: Reaction vs. Reversal

structures give us unique situations that have greater potential than other patterns. However, there will be typically less opportunities.

BC Layering Technique

One of the secondary measurement considerations that is useful is to assess the larger possibilities utilizing a secondary BC measurement in each pattern. This might be slightly different with each ratio combination but there are other complementary measures that help create more defined execution zones when two BC measures are employed. When we are talking about primary BC measurements, in most cases it will be focused upon the completion of a basic AB=CD structure. These are helpful in the clearest of cases and best integrated with the clearest ratio combinations. For example, an AB=CD structure that possesses a 1.13 extension will be rather tight. However, the 1.27 level effectively complements these pattern types. Although the AB=CD point is frequently exceeded in most pattern cases, the layering measurement defines the permissible level of tolerance for price action to exceed this area.

Bullish AB=CD Pattern with BC Layering Technique

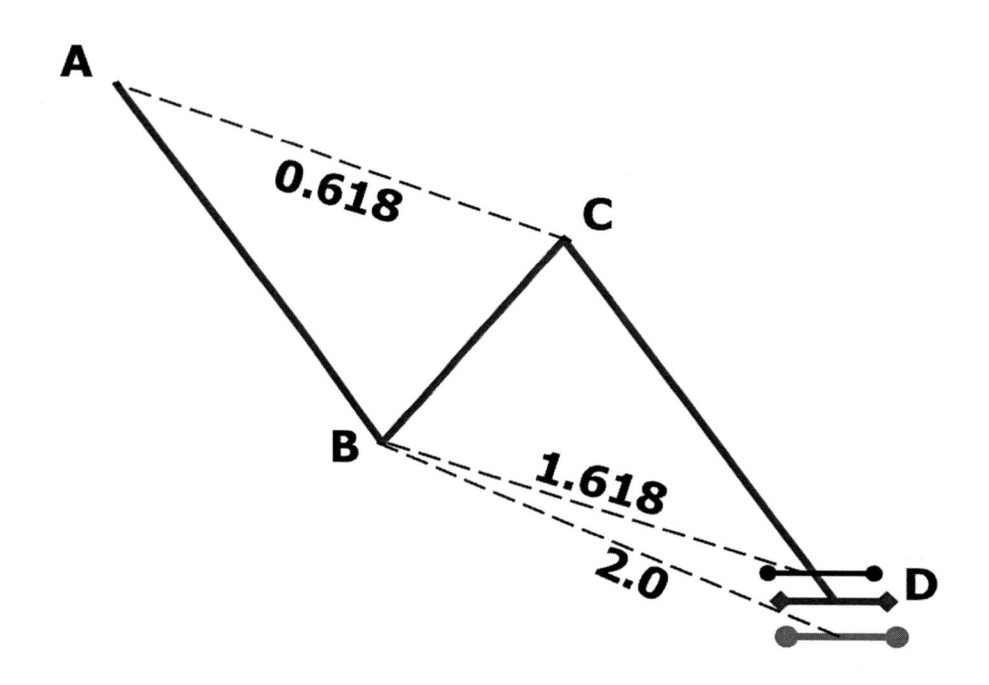

Although the technique can be applied to all harmonic ratios that define patterns, specific combinations of measures are more effective than others. I will show some basic relationships and try to keep it simple. I could go through dozens of possibilities but I feel

Harmonic Trading Volume 3: Reaction vs. Reversal

that the basic concept can be best represented in the perfect harmonic ratio situations. Employing the most common BC layer situation that utilizes a 1.618 and a 2.0 BC extension with the AB=CD pattern, we can create an effective tolerance to facilitate decisions at support/resistance. In the bullish harmonic support zone, the 1.618BC extension will precede the exact completion point pattern. In these situations, the AB=CD is the most important point within the range but the real-world trading action can exceed this area. This is when 2.0 BC measurement serves to gauge how far the opportunity can tolerate this trading action beyond the ideal measured level. In other situations, the BC layering technique can help to optimize stop loss measures as well.

Bullish AB=CD Pattern Potential Reversal Zone (PRZ) with BC Layering Technique

Since the AB=CD is a mandatory minimum, it is common for price action to exceed this area on the initial test and indicate that the Potential Reversal Zone will not be valid support. We will look at confirmation strategies later in this material however, the additional BC layer at the pattern's completion point adds a degree of precision to these situations.

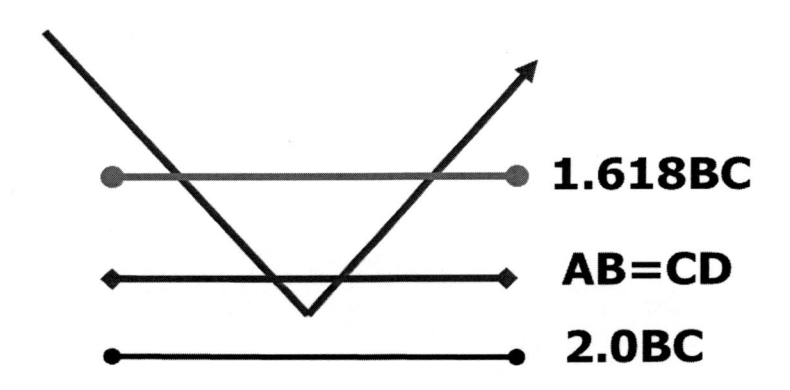

Harmonic Trading Volume 3: Reaction vs. Reversal

British Pound/US Dollar (GBP/USD): 15-Minute
Bullish AB=CD Pattern with BC Layering Technique

The following chart of the British Pound/US Dollar exemplifies how real world trading action can exceed ideal patterns. This situation exemplifies how price action can be somewhat skewed and reverse in irregular fashion. Clearly, the AB=CD structure defined support at the 1.4430 level yet the price action stabilized below this area before reversing significantly. The AB=CD structure possessed a 2.0BC extension and the next harmonic level of the 2.24 serve to gauge the excessive action beyond the ideal support.

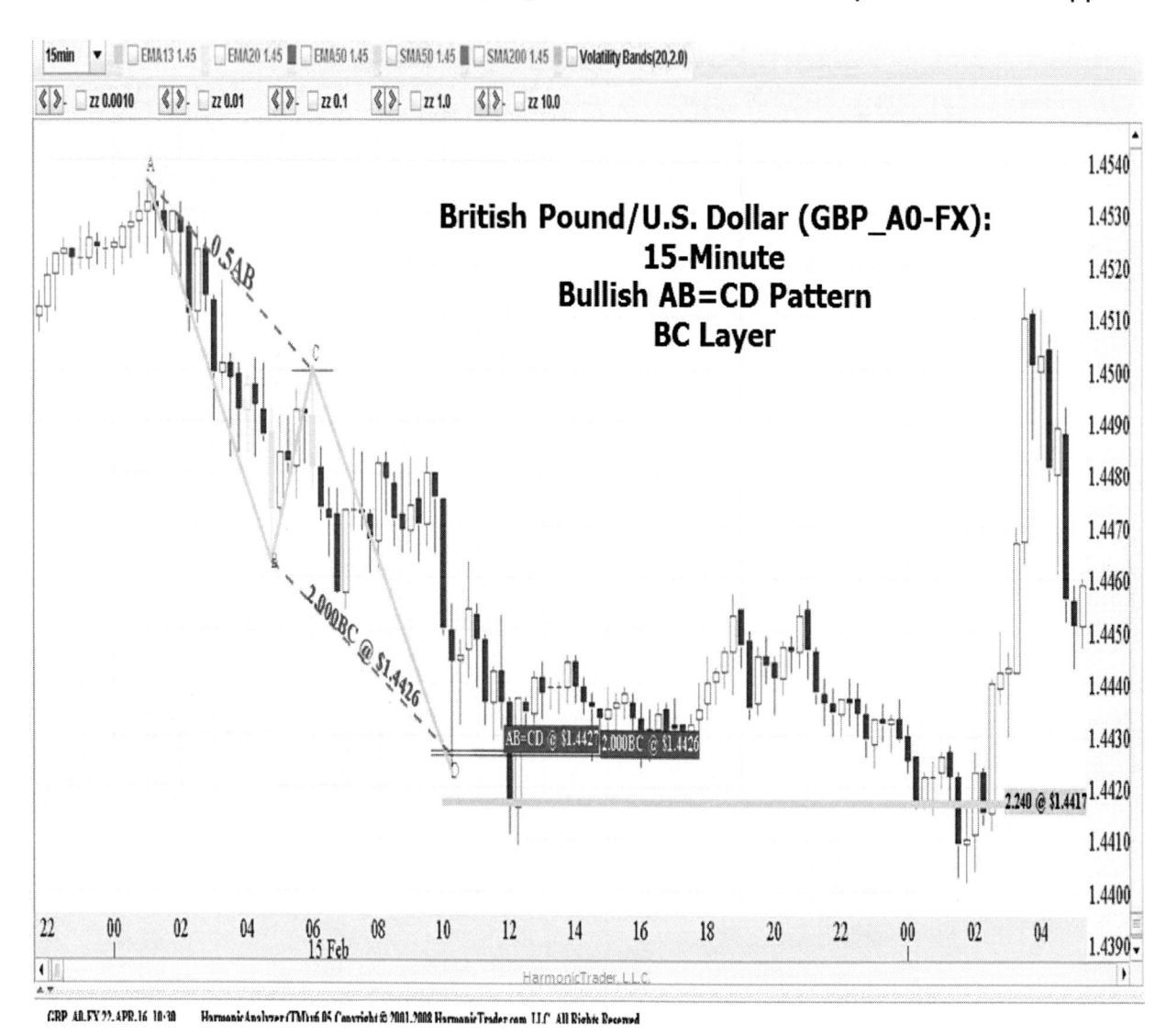

Harmonic Trading Volume 3: Reaction vs. Reversal

Bearish AB=CD Pattern with BC Layering Technique

In the bearish harmonic zone, the 1.618BC extension will precede the exact pattern completion point. In these situations, the AB=CD is always the most important MINIMUM OBJECTIVE within the range. This is when 2.0 BC measurement serves to gauge how far the opportunity can tolerate this trading action beyond the ideal measured level.

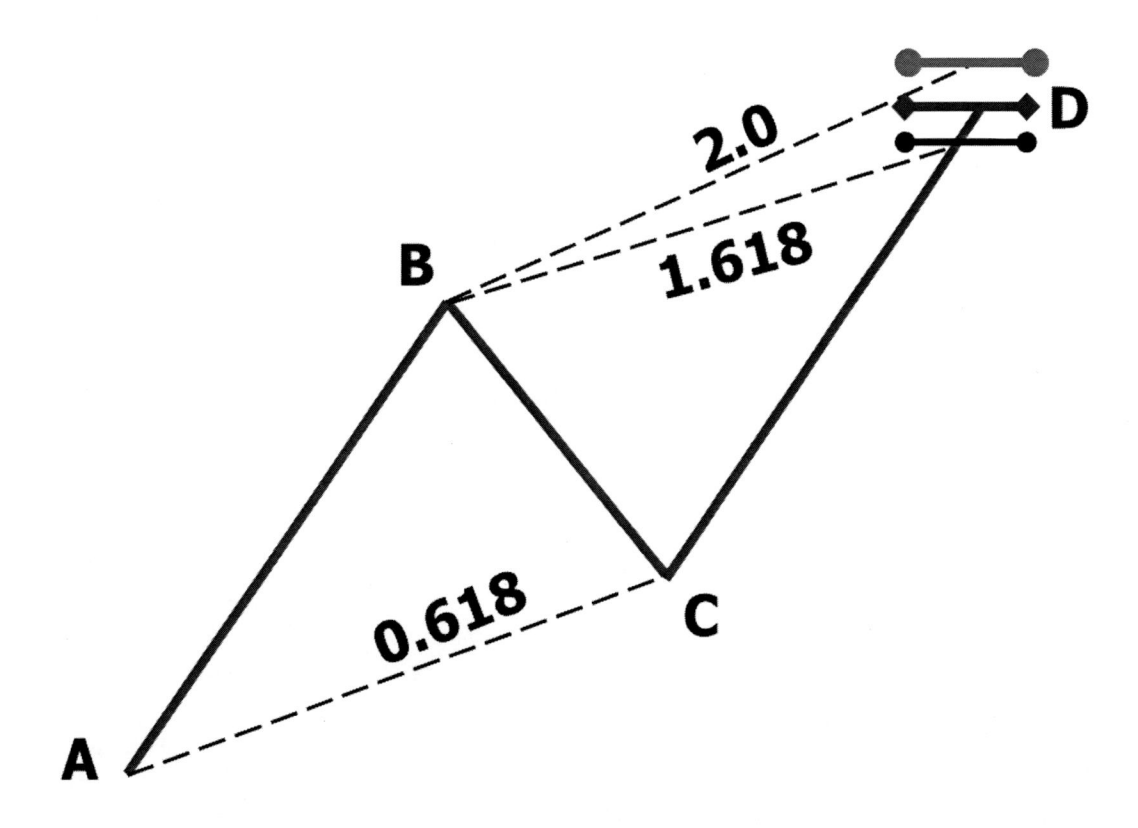

Harmonic Trading Volume 3: Reaction vs. Reversal

Bearish AB=CD Pattern with BC Layering Technique
Potential Reversal Zone (PRZ)

The AB=CD is a mandatory minimum but it is typically exceeded. The initial test will validate the Potential Reversal Zone as important resistance. The additional BC layer creates an additional tolerance to gauge the price action at the completion of the pattern.

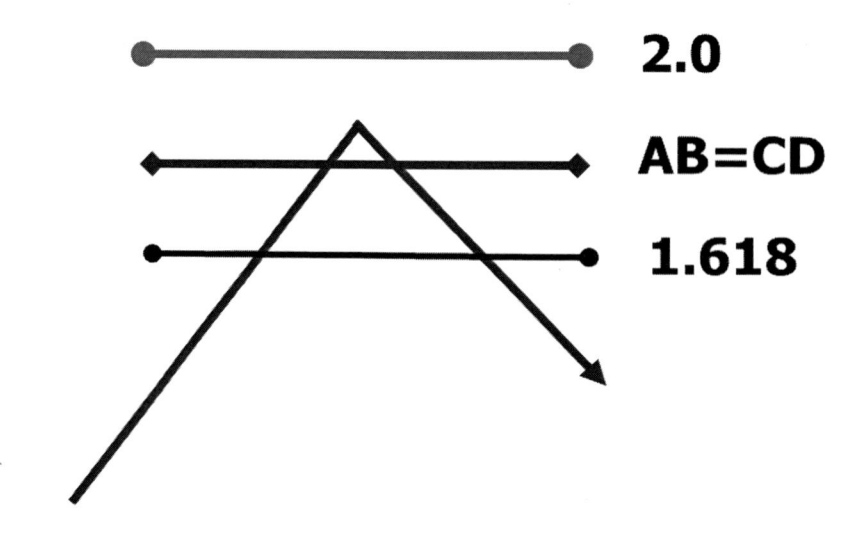

2.0

AB=CD

1.618

Harmonic Trading Volume 3: Reaction vs. Reversal

NASDAQ 100 (NQ): Daily
Bearish AB=CD Pattern with BC Layering Technique

The following example of a Bearish AB=CD in the NASDAQ 100 index possesses a 1.618 and 2.0 BC extension with the AB=CD completion point in the middle. Although this is a perfect AB=CD structure, the 2.0 BC layer provides a critical gauge of tolerance beyond the ideal measure. The completion point of the pattern and the 1.618 BC extension defined the area just above 4700 as critical harmonic resistance while the 2.0 measurement serve to define the limit of the structural possibility.

Harmonic Trading Volume 3: Reaction vs. Reversal

Alternate AB=CD Pattern

Originally outlined in my first book *The Harmonic Trader*, I believe it is important to review Alternate AB=CD variations that work well in specific situations, especially when the formation varies among patterns. Alternate AB=CD types represent different structural forms of a sine wave in price action expression. Depending upon each type, there are specific expectations that must be employed to define situation. Although sometimes more complementary than other structures, they are as effective specific pattern situations.

Bullish Alternate AB=CD Pattern

The Bullish Alternate AB=CD pattern was derived from my research of structural differentiation. In patterns such as the Alternate Bat and Crab, this extended formation has been a reliable measure when the equivalent AB=CD possibility is not relevant.

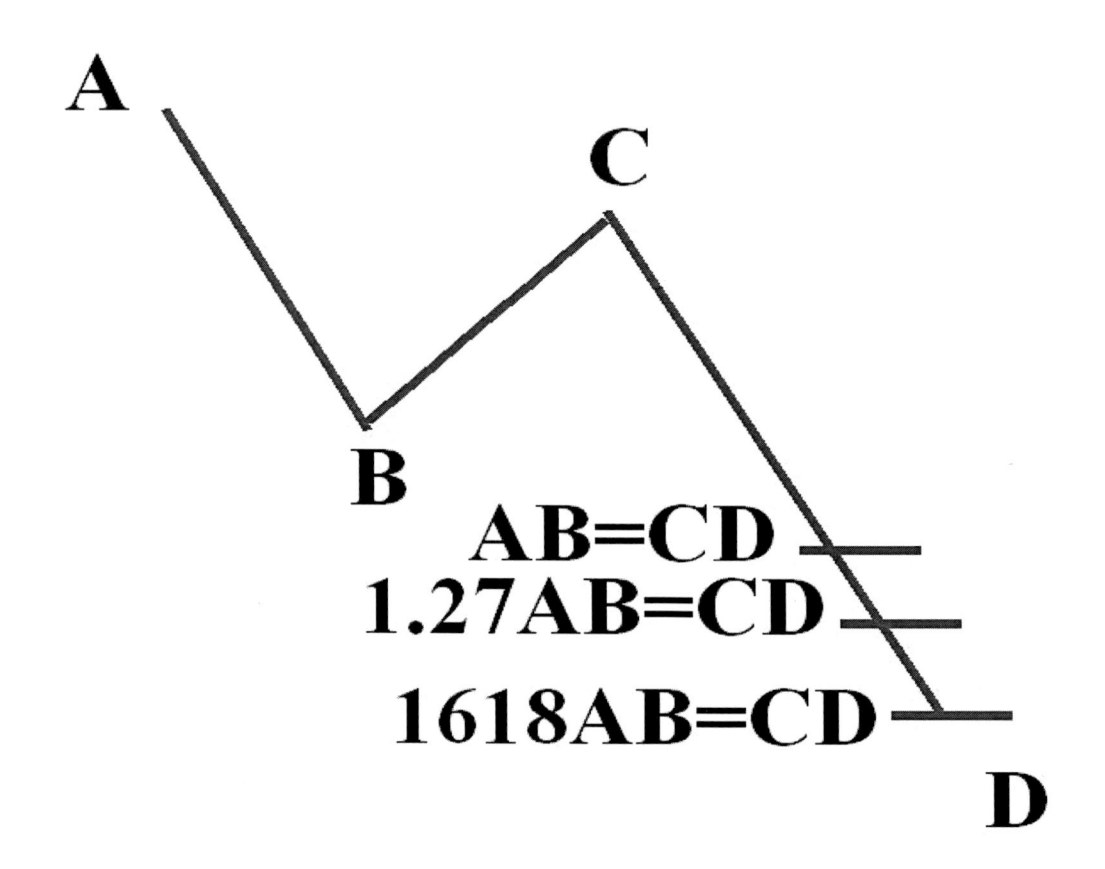

Harmonic Trading Volume 3: Reaction vs. Reversal

Austrailian Dollar/Japanese Yen (AUD/JPY): 15-Minute
Bullish Alternate 1.618AB=CD Pattern

In all of my software, I have programmed various combinations of alternate structures. These can include 1.13, 1.27, 1.41, 2.0, etc. These are more complementary measures in specific situations however I must stress that the 1.618 AB=CD is a unique creature unto itself. The following 15-minute chart of the Australian Dollar versus the Japanese Yen shows an ideal Alternate 1.618 AB=CD formation.

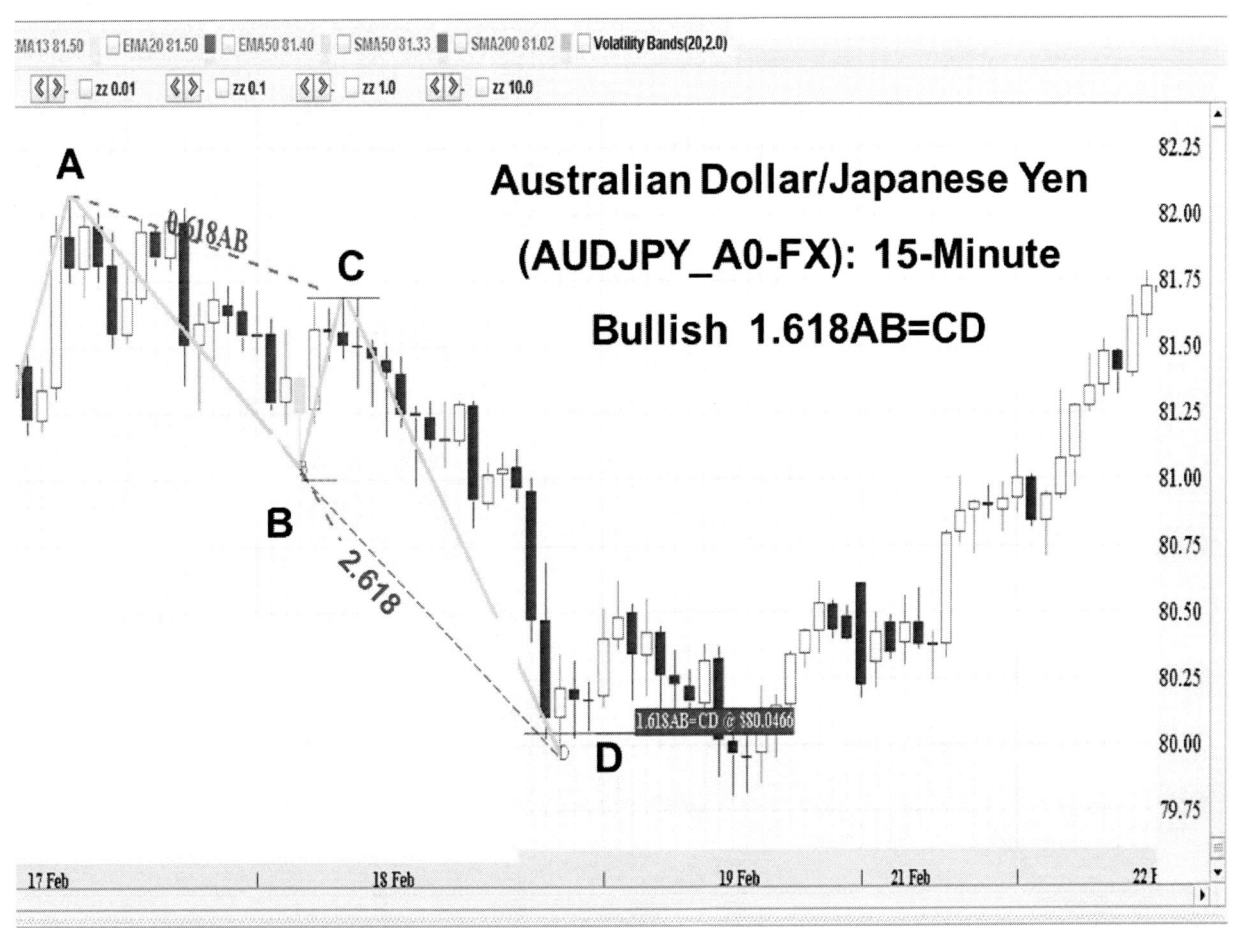

This pattern completed at 80.05. The interesting aspect of this decline was the price action as it tested the equivalent completion point for the AB=CD which was projected approximately at 80.75. When the price action tested the equivalent level, it continued sharply lower and accelerated to the alternate 1.618 calculated level. This is an oversimplification of utilizing the alternate measure but exemplifies how the market

Harmonic Trading Volume 3: Reaction vs. Reversal

will manifest failed signals of demonstrative price action when the particular possibility is not valid. In this instance, the acceleration beyond the exact equivalent AB=CD was the immediate warning sign.

Bearish Alternate AB=CD Pattern

As we outlined the different rules for pattern structures, these alternate types will become readily apparent as to their most effective situational application. The simple awareness as an alternate possibility above and beyond the equivalent formation also provides price objectives when price action exceeds the minimum completion point.

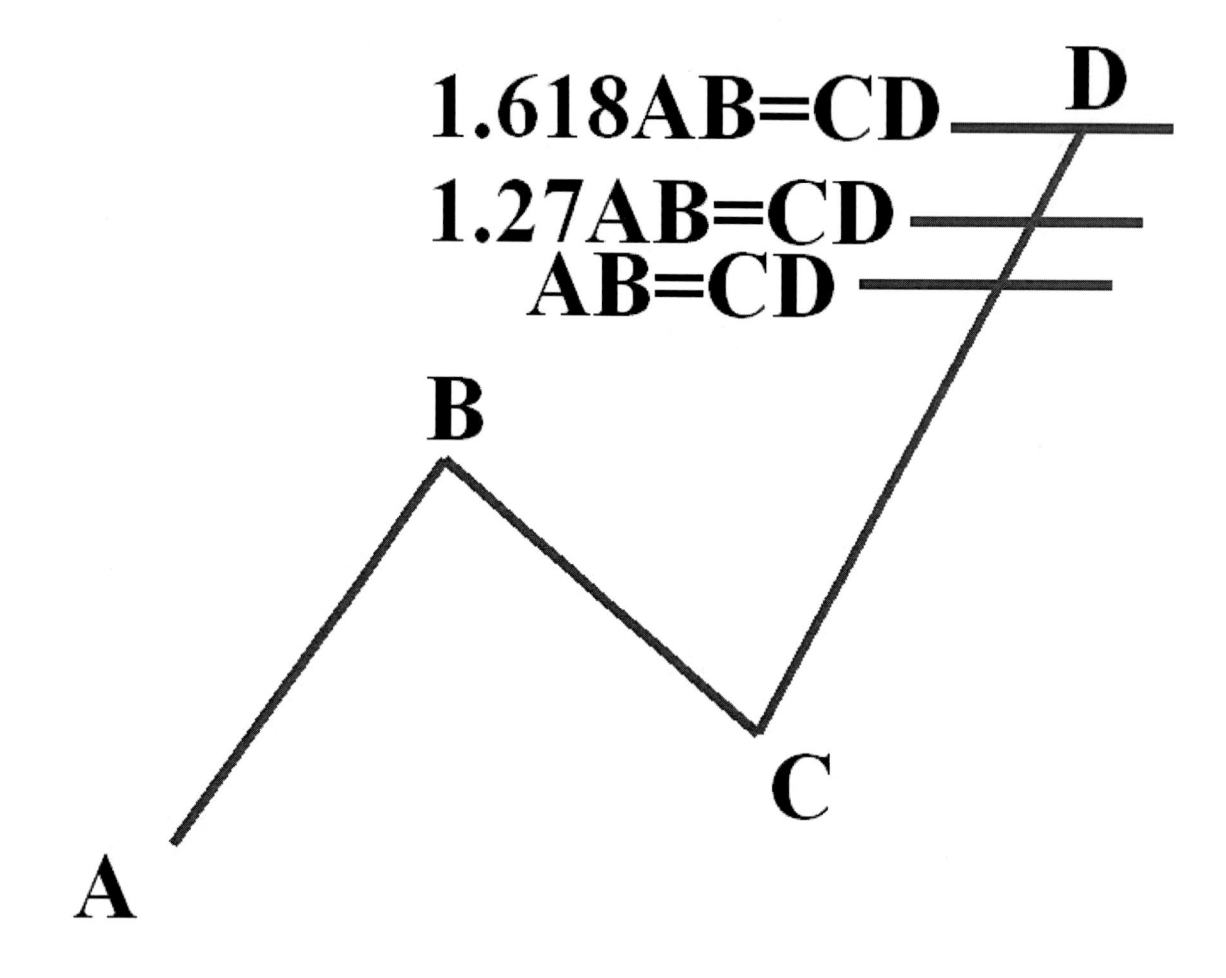

Harmonic Trading Volume 3: Reaction vs. Reversal

British Pound/Japanese Yen (GBPJPY_A0-FX): 5-Minute Bearish Alternate 1.618AB=CD Pattern

The following chart of the British Pound/Japanese Yen exemplifies the extended structure that alternates AB=CD types exemplify. Despite the lack of symmetry, the initial AB leg possessed relevant measures that can be projected. In this case, the 1.618 AB=CD structure at the 157.35 level served as short-term resistance on the intraday chart.

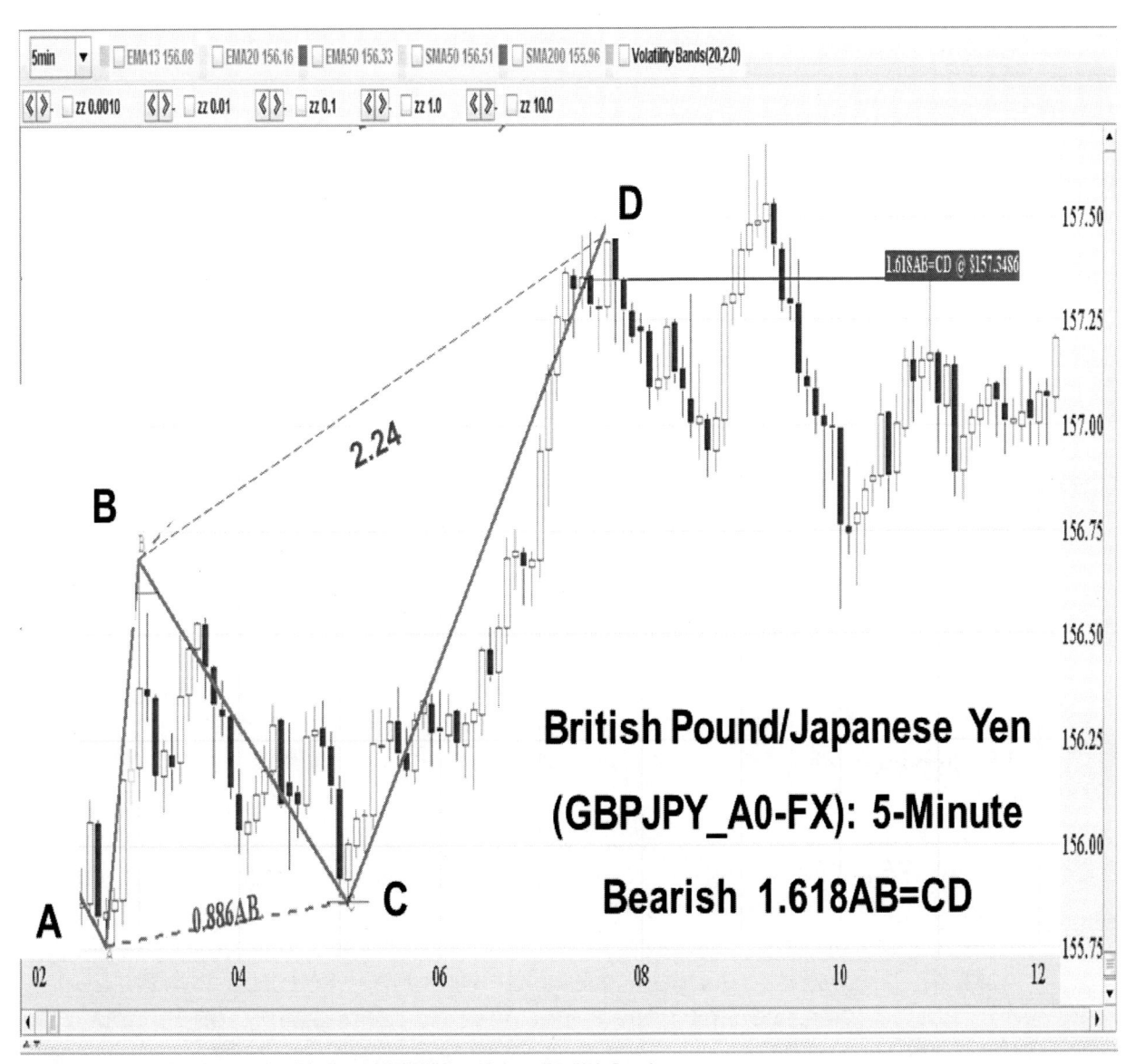

Harmonic Trading Volume 3: Reaction vs. Reversal

B Point Tolerance Classification

One of the earliest breakthroughs in my classification of M and W formation types was the specification of their alignment with particular attention to the B point. The AB=CD structural variation was an important price differentiation to distinguish similar possibilities. However, it was not until the release of my first harmonic scanner software, the Harmonic Analyzer that I was able to finally research and distinguish each structural pattern point.

Released in 2001, this is the first harmonic pattern program ever created. The rules for pattern algorithms were programmed from my first book *The Harmonic Trader* and design to find valid opportunities automatically. The program enabled me to test pattern alignments with unprecedented precision and refine the structures immensely. One of the most profound breakthroughs was the specification of the prescribed ratio alignments at the B point. Although this was one of my primary tenets to differentiate similar price structures, I was not able to exactly define acceptable tolerance limits until we had the power of the Harmonic Analyzer software to reveal the optimal results.

- **+/- ≤3%:** One of the first M&W structural types that I differentiated was the Gartley versus the Bat pattern. Essentially, my initial research showed that the Gartley only worked when the B point was within a close proximity to the 61.8% limit. We will look at the specifications later in this chapter but the results were profound. My research proved that those Gartley structures that had a B point that was +/-3% of the ideal 61.8% level yielded opportunities with the greatest potential. This means that any M or W structure with a B point between 58.8 – 64.8% possesses a valid tolerance for variation beyond the ideal measure to validate it as a harmonic pattern. In all other cases, it would typically default to a Bat pattern if it was less than the 3% tolerance or become invalid above the upper limit. I must emphasize that this strict definition also applies to Butterfly patterns. These small distinctions have been instrumental in eliminating those structures that appear similar but do not possess the proper proportions to validate as harmonic.

- **+/- ≤5%:** The 5% tolerance is applied to B points of most other structures. Although the Gartley and the Butterfly are two strict examples, the 5% tolerance at the B point is effective when analyzing Bat and Crab patterns in particular. Again, the purpose is to generally categorize what type of structure we are dealing with but the tolerance limit goes a long way to creating finite of defining valid opportunities.

Harmonic Trading Volume 3: Reaction vs. Reversal

Gartley Pattern

Elements:
B Point Ratio: 0.618 (+/-3% Tolerance)
AB=CD Type: AB=CD-1.27AB=CD
BC: 1.13-1.618
XA = 0.786
Stop Loss >1.0 (Depends upon AB=CD)

Bullish Gartley

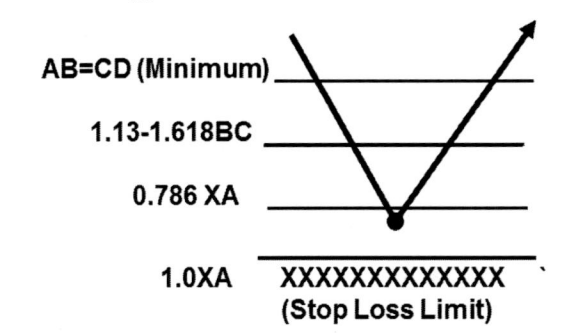

Bearish Gartley

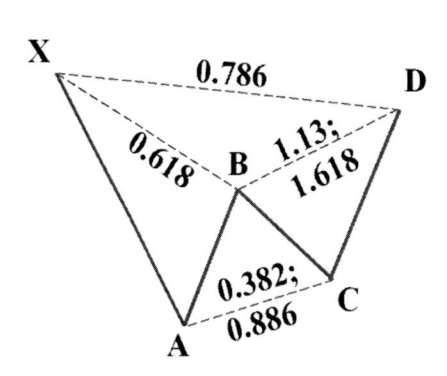

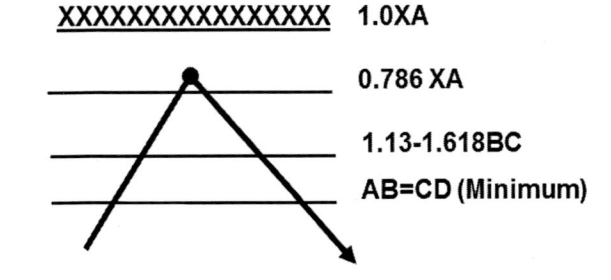

Notes:

- Wait for entire PRZ test – especially the 0.786 XA Retracement and the AB=CD – to be tested before executing the trade.
- Initial test of pattern completion SHOULD NOT extend BEYOND PRZ = Valid Gartley patterns exhibit decisive reversal behavior.
- Utilize area beyond 1.0 XA as make-or-break stop loss limit measure and include the 88.6% level, especially when AB=CD completes beyond the 78.6% area.
- Price action MUST REVERSE immediately after testing the entire PRZ.
- B Point Alignment @ 61.8%XA +/- 3 max.

Harmonic Trading Volume 3: Reaction vs. Reversal

Bullish Gartley Pattern

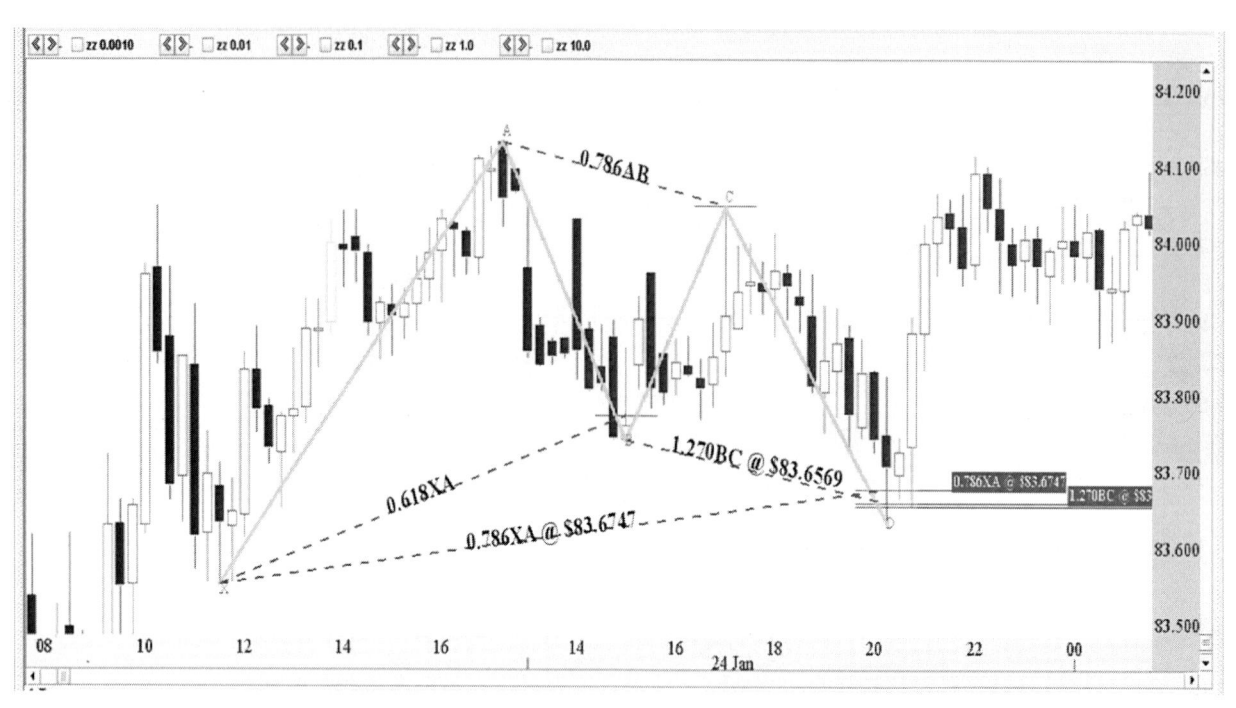

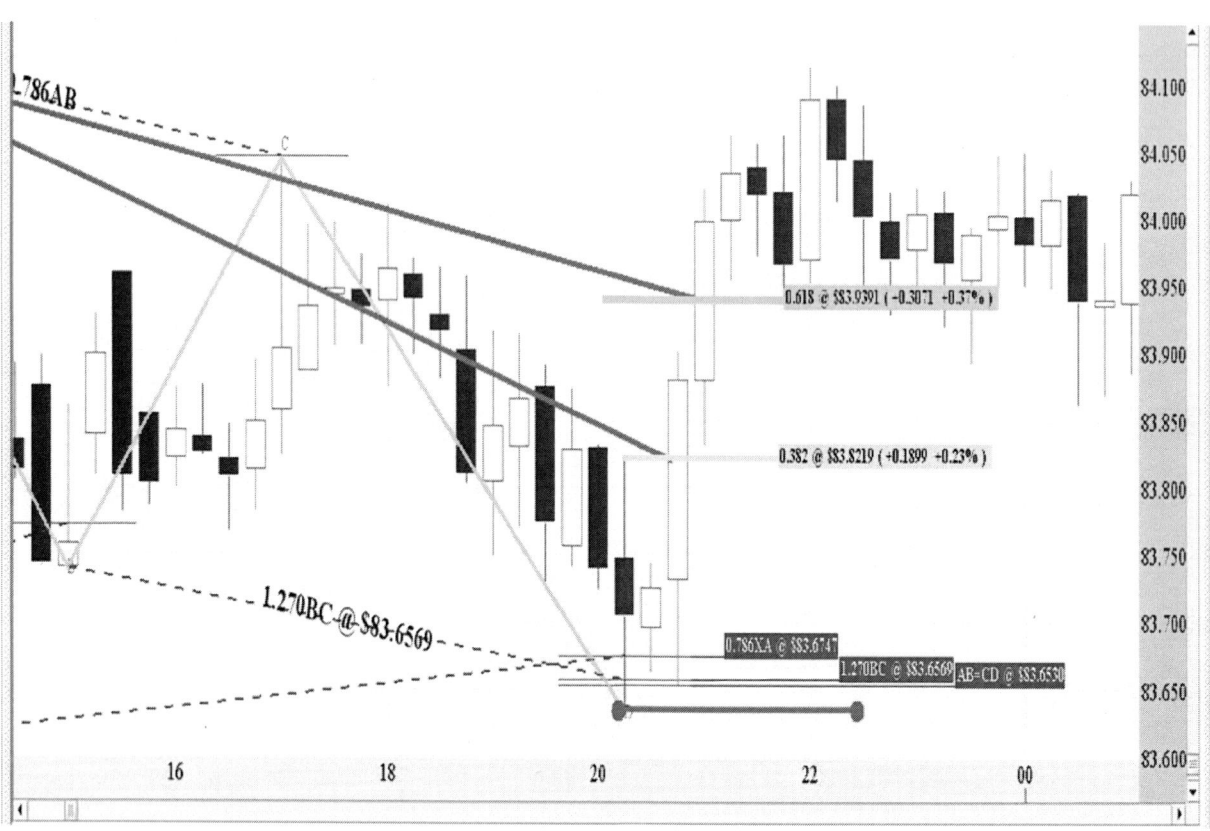

Harmonic Trading Volume 3: Reaction vs. Reversal

Bearish Gartley Pattern

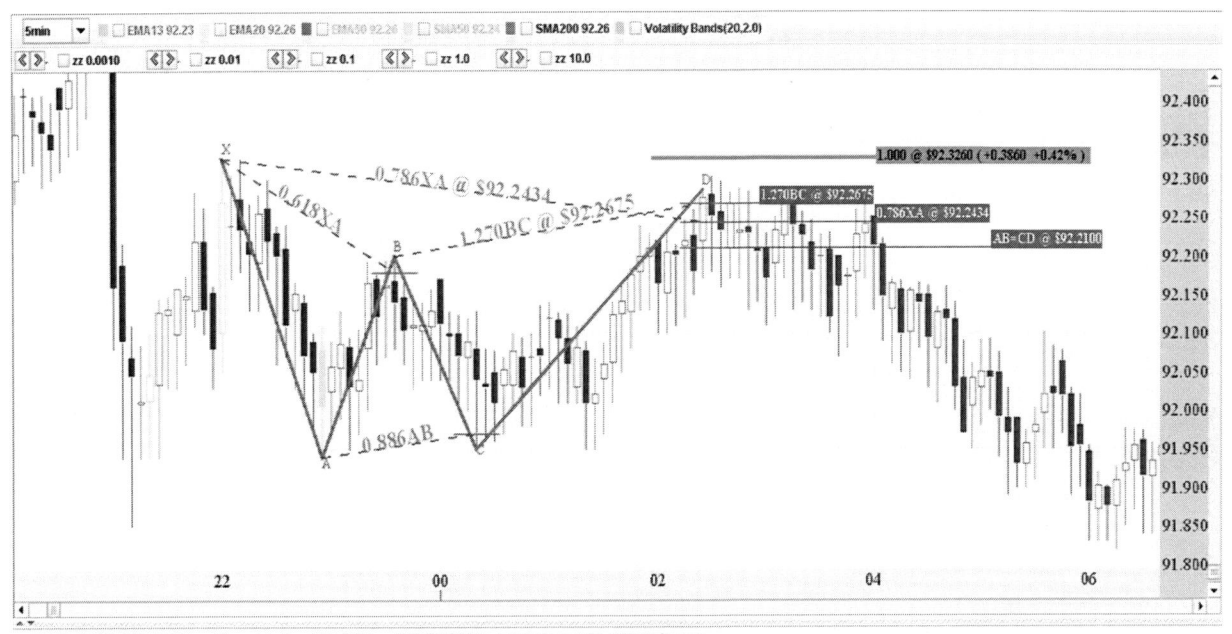

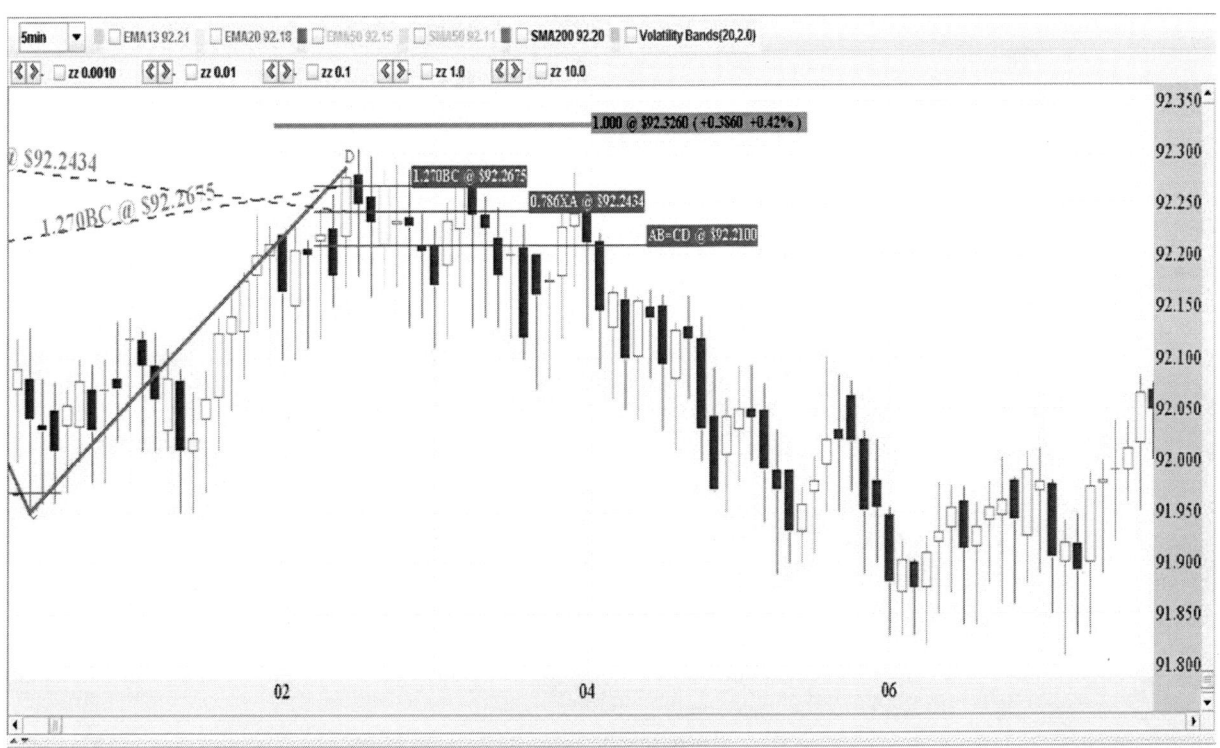

Harmonic Trading Volume 3: Reaction vs. Reversal

SPECIAL SITUATION:
Deep Gartley Pattern @ 88.6% XA Retracement

When AB=CD pattern completion extends past 78.6% retracement, other measures and a larger tolerance must be employed to gauge the real-time action relative to the parameters of the Gartley. In these cases, the 88.6% XA retracement defines a Deep Gartley for the ideal price level for the execution of the trade.

Elements:
B Point Ratio= 0.618 (+/-3% Tolerance)
AB=CD Type: AB=CD
BC: 1.618-2.618
XA: 0.786-0.886
Stop Loss > 1.0-1.13X (Depends upon AB=CD)

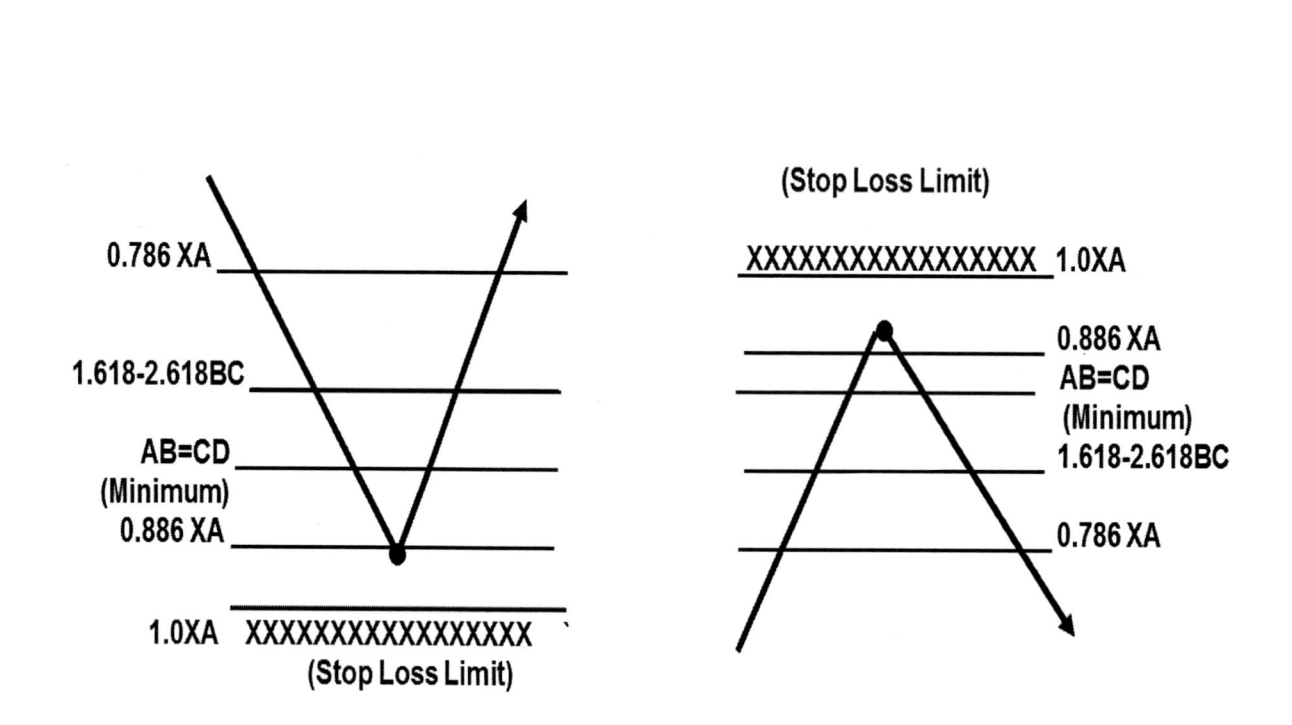

Bullish

0.786 XA

1.618-2.618 BC

AB=CD (Minimum)
0.886 XA

1.0XA XXXXXXXXXXXXXXXX
(Stop Loss Limit)

Bearish

(Stop Loss Limit)
XXXXXXXXXXXXXXXX 1.0XA

0.886 XA
AB=CD
(Minimum)
1.618-2.618 BC

0.786 XA

Harmonic Trading Volume 3: Reaction vs. Reversal

Bullish Gartley Pattern with 88.6% Retracement

Harmonic Trading Volume 3: Reaction vs. Reversal

Bearish Gartley Pattern with 88.6% Retracement

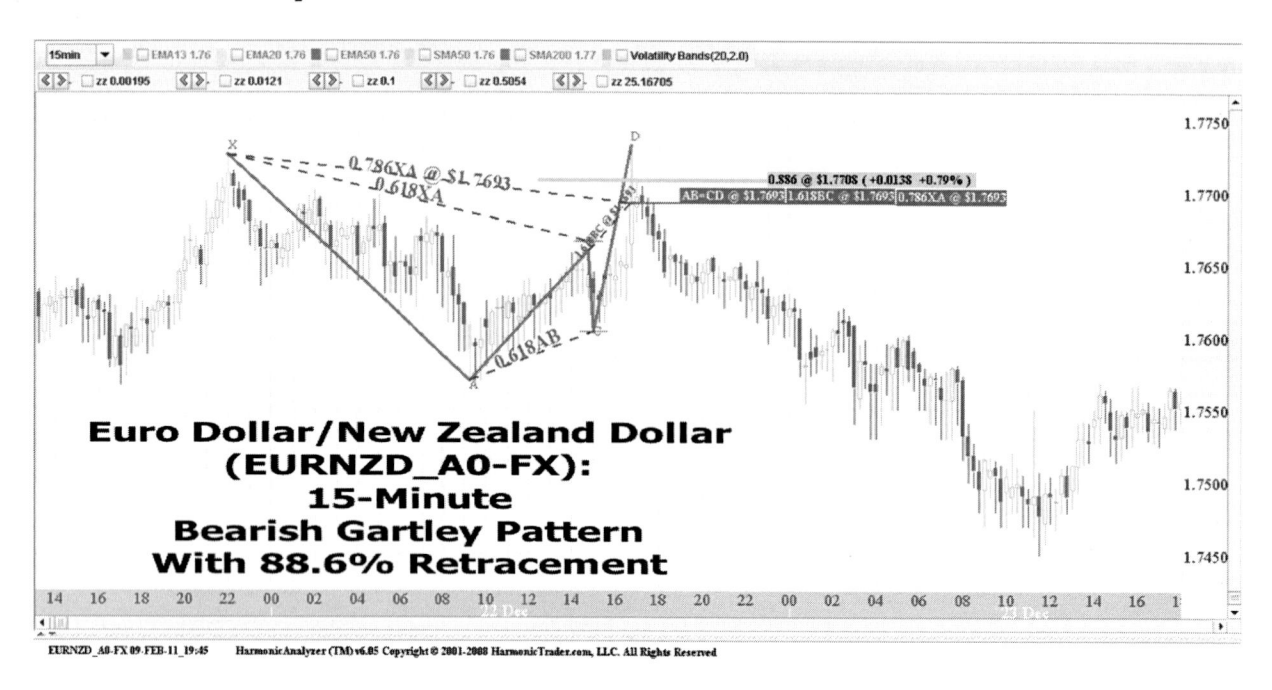

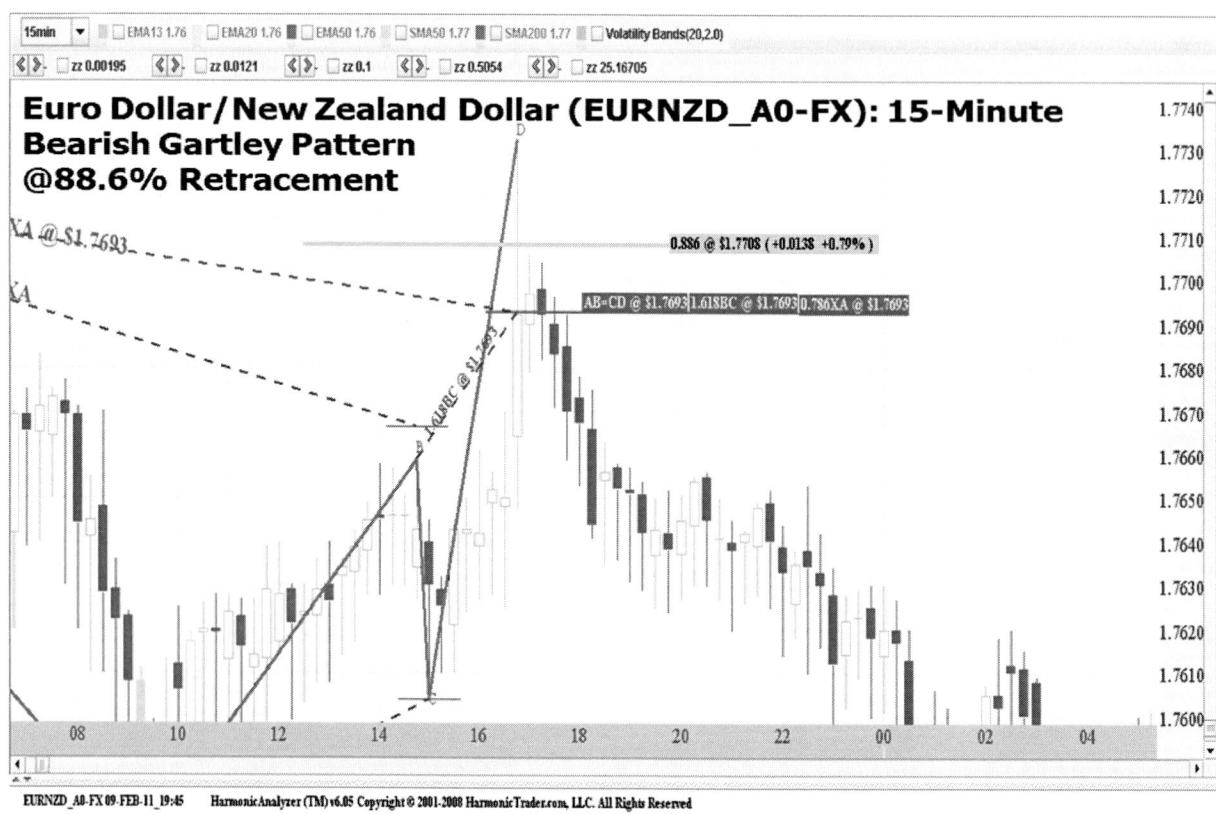

Harmonic Trading Volume 3: Reaction vs. Reversal

Bat Pattern

Elements:
B Point Ratio: 0.382-0.50
AB=CD Type: AB=CD-1.618AB=CD
BC: 1.618-2.618
XA: 0.886
Stop Loss > 1.13X (Depends upon AB=CD)

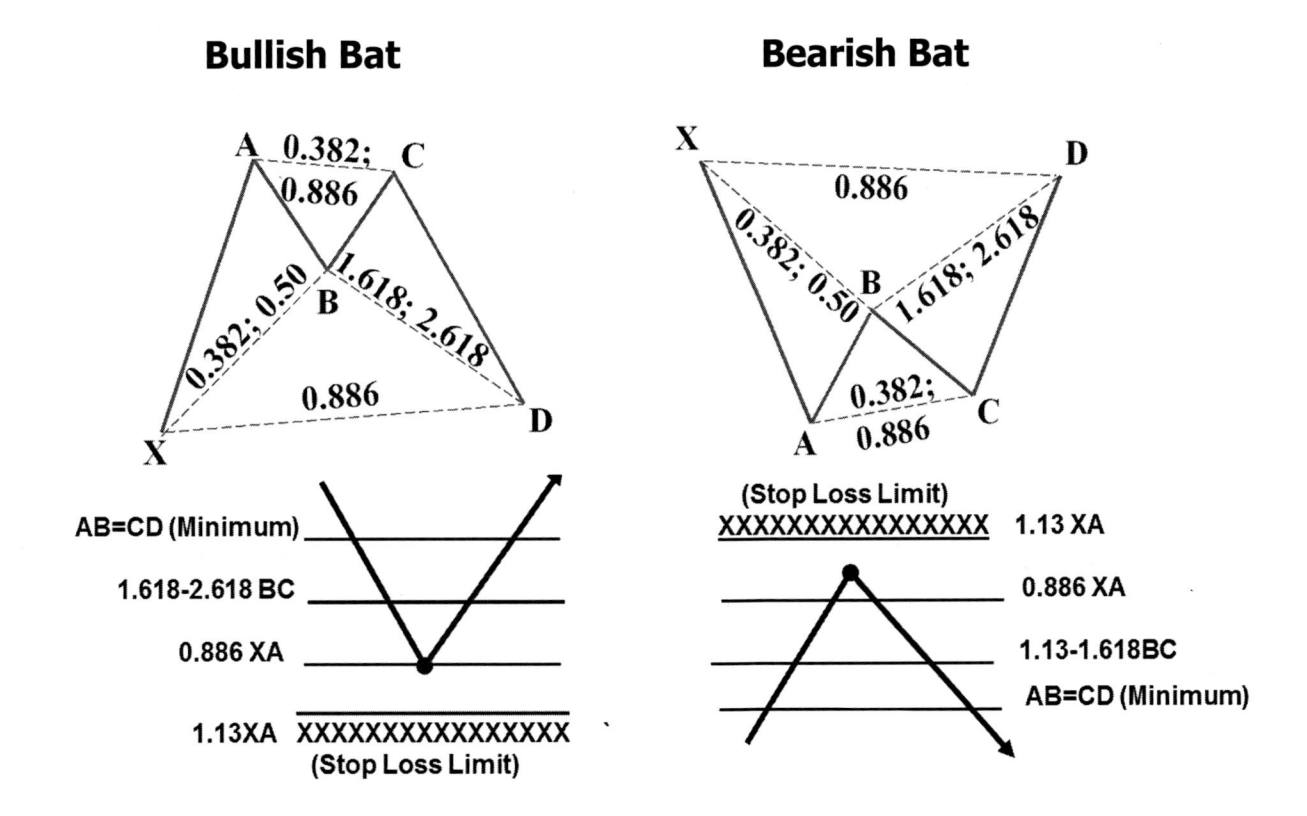

Bullish Bat

Bearish Bat

Notes:

- Expect PRZ test of 0.886 XA Retracement with minimum AB=CD (Typically 1.27AB=CD).
- Initial test of pattern completion can test close to 1.0XA.
- Utilize 1.13 XA as make-or-break stop loss limit measure.
- Price action MUST REVERSE immediately after testing the 0.886 XA Retracement.
- B Point Alignment @ 50%XA +/-5% Maximum Tolerance

Harmonic Trading Volume 3: Reaction vs. Reversal

Bullish Bat Pattern

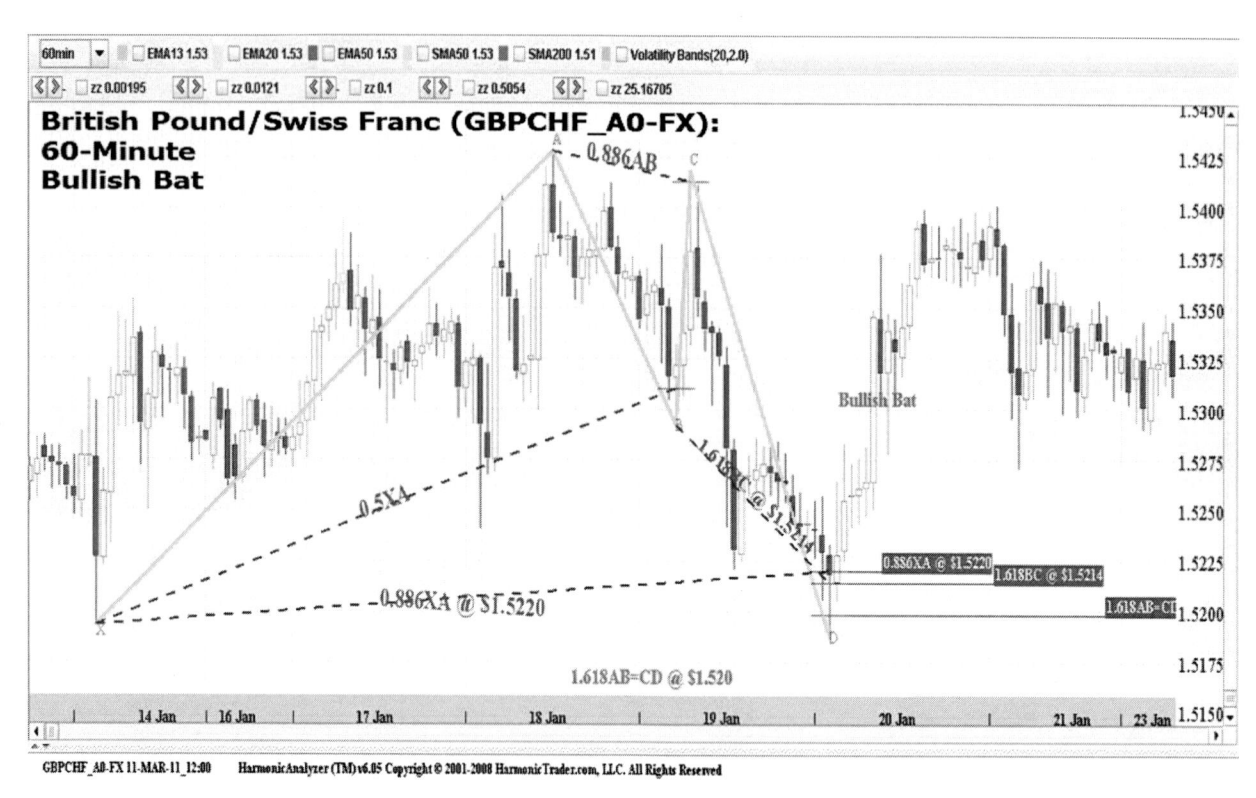

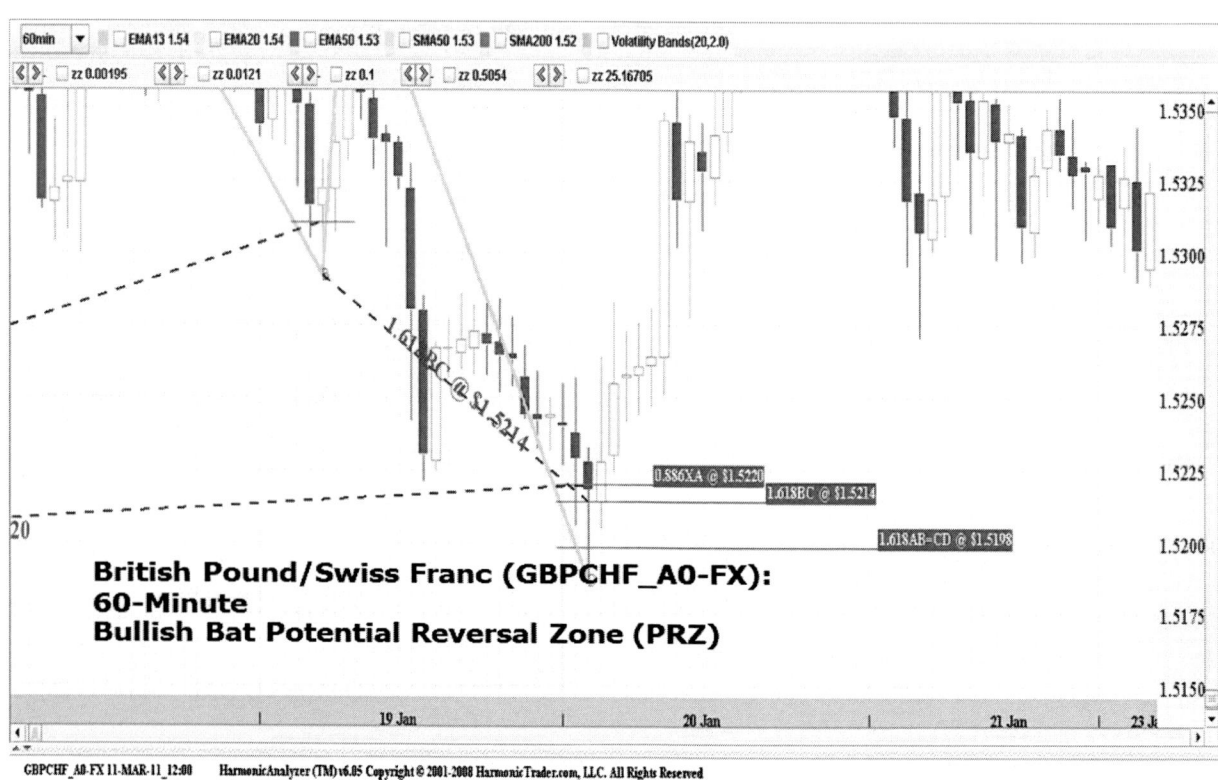

Harmonic Trading Volume 3: Reaction vs. Reversal

Bearish Bat Pattern

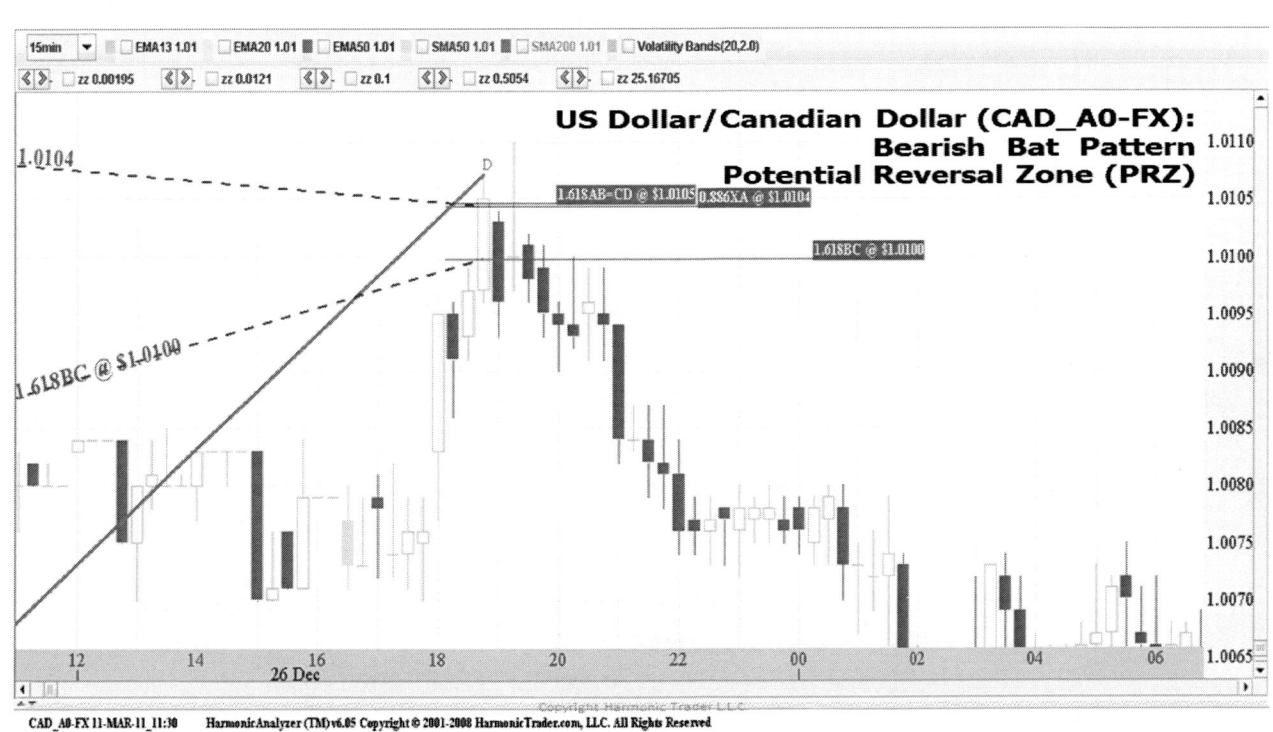

Harmonic Trading Volume 3: Reaction vs. Reversal

Alternate Bat Pattern

Elements:
B Point Ratio: 0.382 Max (-3% Tolerance)
AB=CD Type: 1.618AB=CD
BC: 2.0-3.618
XA: 0.886-1.13
Stop Loss > 1.27X (Depends upon XA Measurement)

Bullish Alternate Bat

Bearish Alternate Bat

Notes:
- Expect PRZ test of 0.886 XA Retracement as minimum but these situations must incude the 1.0XA.
- Utilize 1.27 XA as make-or-break stop loss limit measure espeecially when the 1.13XA level is relevant.
- Price action MUST REVERSE immediately after exceeding 1.0 XA general retracement area.
- B Point Alignment @ 38.2%XA or LESS with 3% tolerance max.

Harmonic Trading Volume 3: Reaction vs. Reversal

Bullish Alternate Bat Pattern

Harmonic Trading Volume 3: Reaction vs. Reversal

Bearish Alternate Bat Pattern

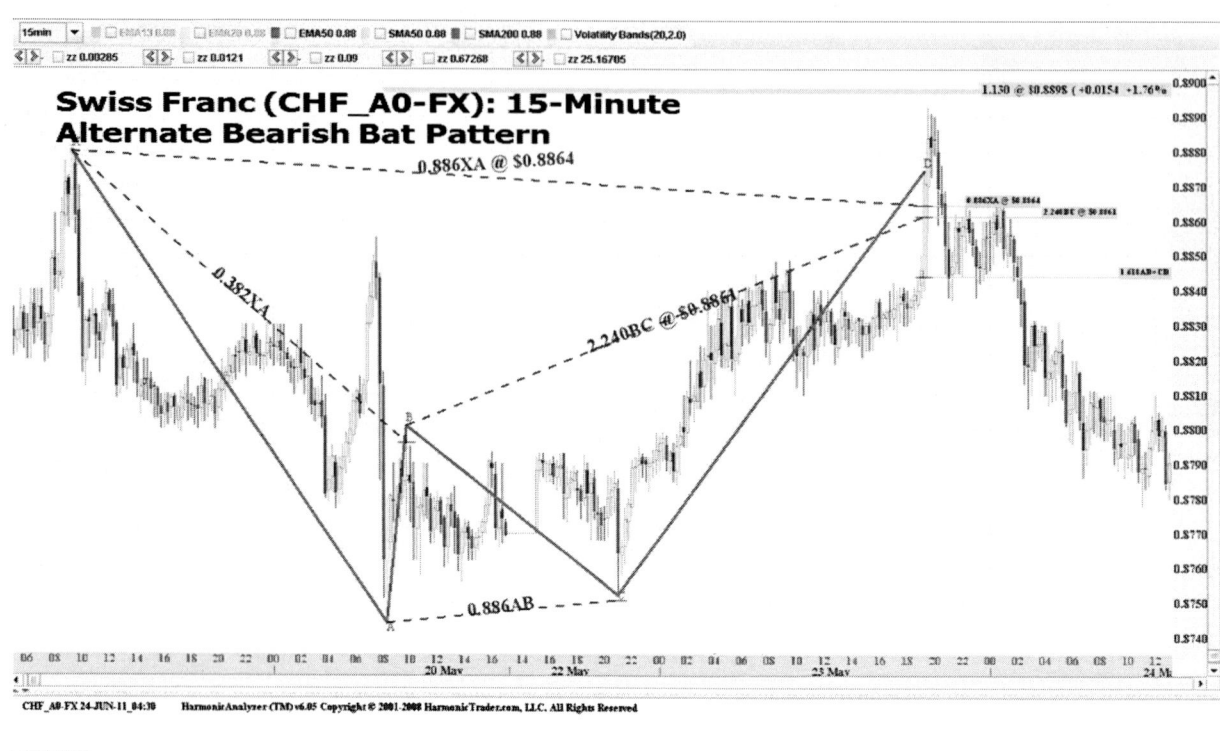

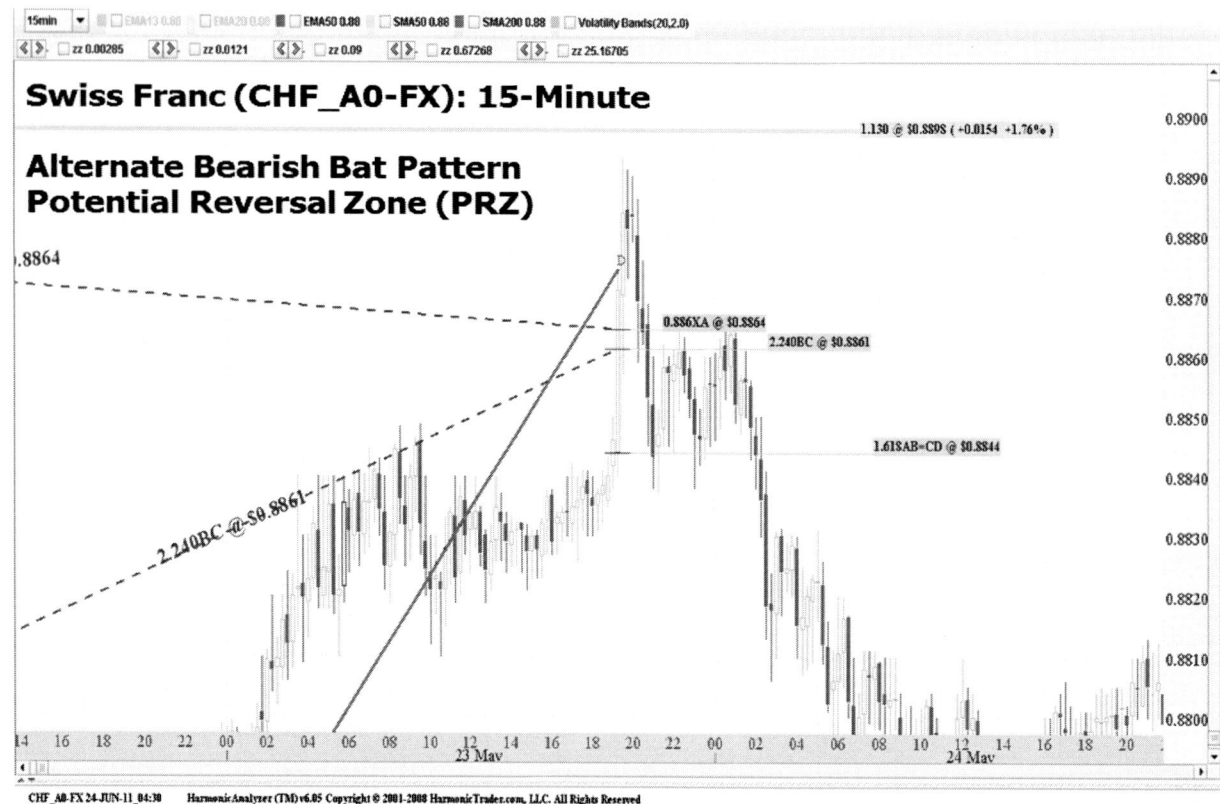

Harmonic Trading Volume 3: Reaction vs. Reversal

Crab Pattern

Elements:
B Point Ratio: 0.382-0.618
AB=CD Type: AB=CD-1.618AB=CD
BC: 2.618-3.618
XA: 1.618
Stop Loss > 2.0XA (Depends upon AB=CD)

Bullish Crab   Bearish Crab

Notes:
- Expect PRZ test to exceed 1.618XA with volatile price action.
- Utilize the area beyond the 2.0 XA as make-or-break stop loss limit measure especially when the reversal at completion point is extreme. In these cases, price action MUST REVERSE immediately after exceeding 1.618 XA general retracement area.
- B Point Alignment not less than 38.2% but can be up to 61.8% B point.

Harmonic Trading Volume 3: Reaction vs. Reversal

Bullish Crab Pattern

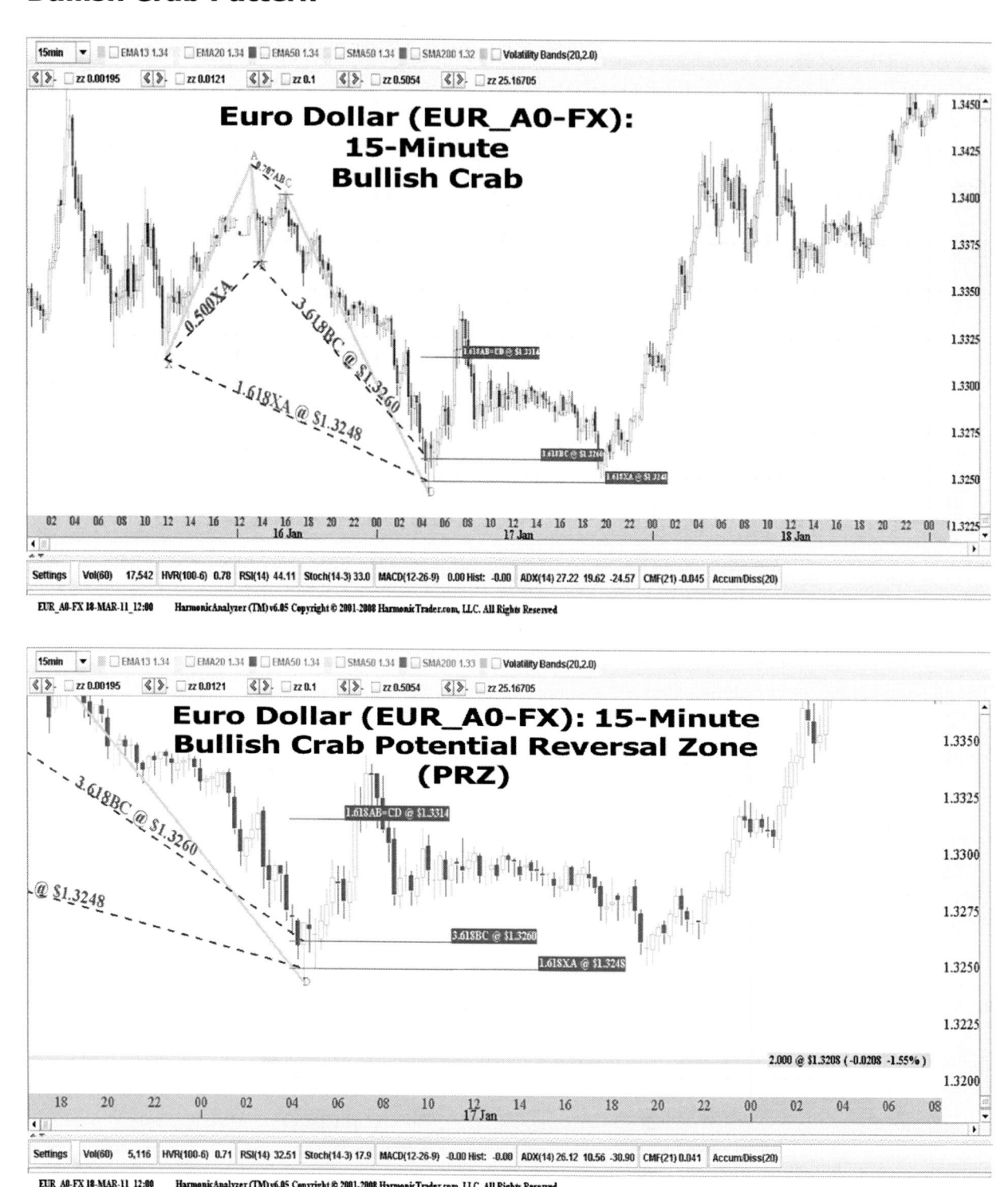

Harmonic Trading Volume 3: Reaction vs. Reversal

Bearish Crab Pattern

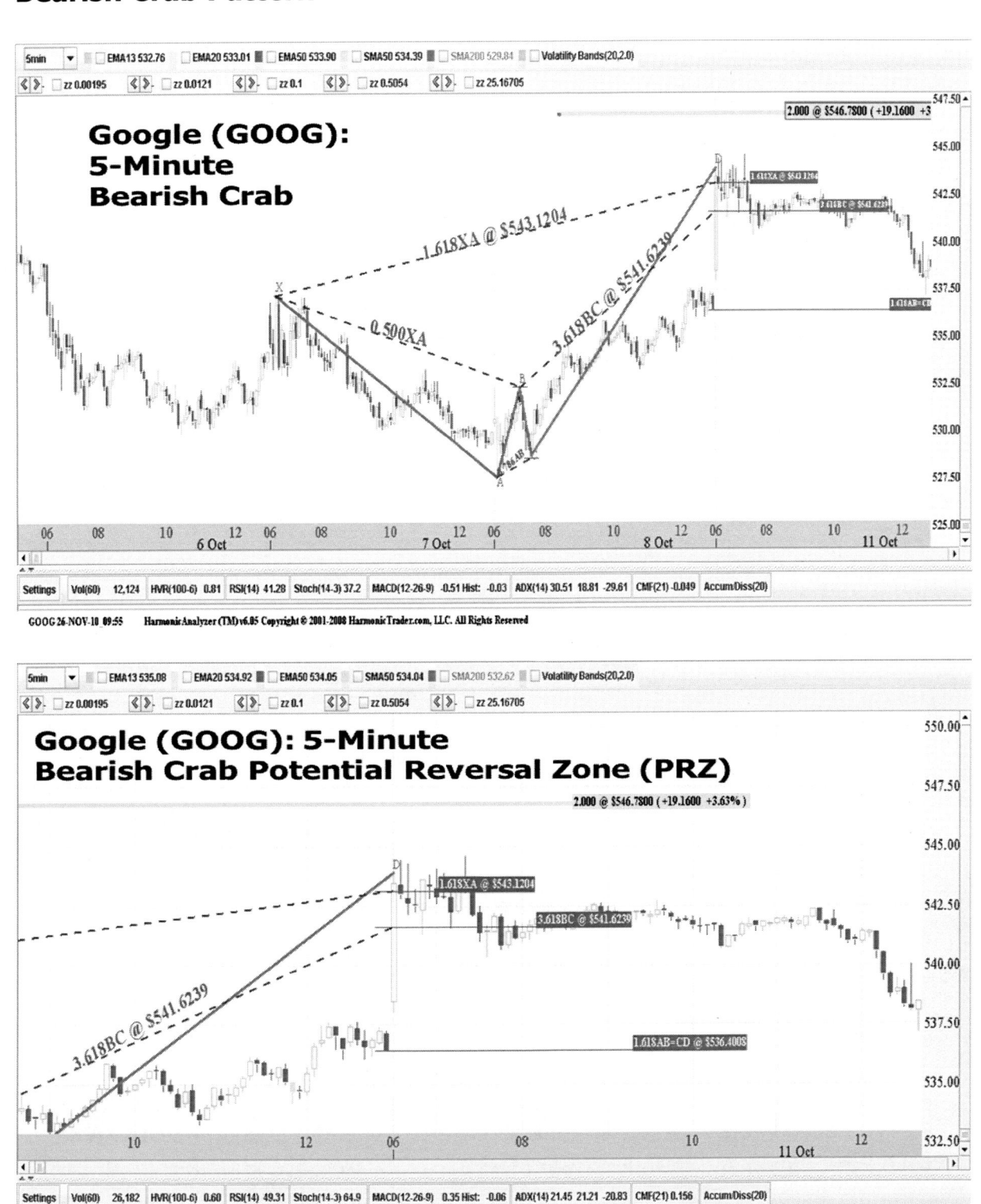

Harmonic Trading Volume 3: Reaction vs. Reversal

Deep Crab Pattern

Elements:
B Point Ratio: 0.886 (+5% Tolerance)
AB=CD Type: AB=CD-1.618AB=CD
BC: 2.0-3.618
XA: 1.618
Stop Loss > 2.0X (Depends upon AB=CD)

Bullish Deep Crab

Bearish Deep Crab

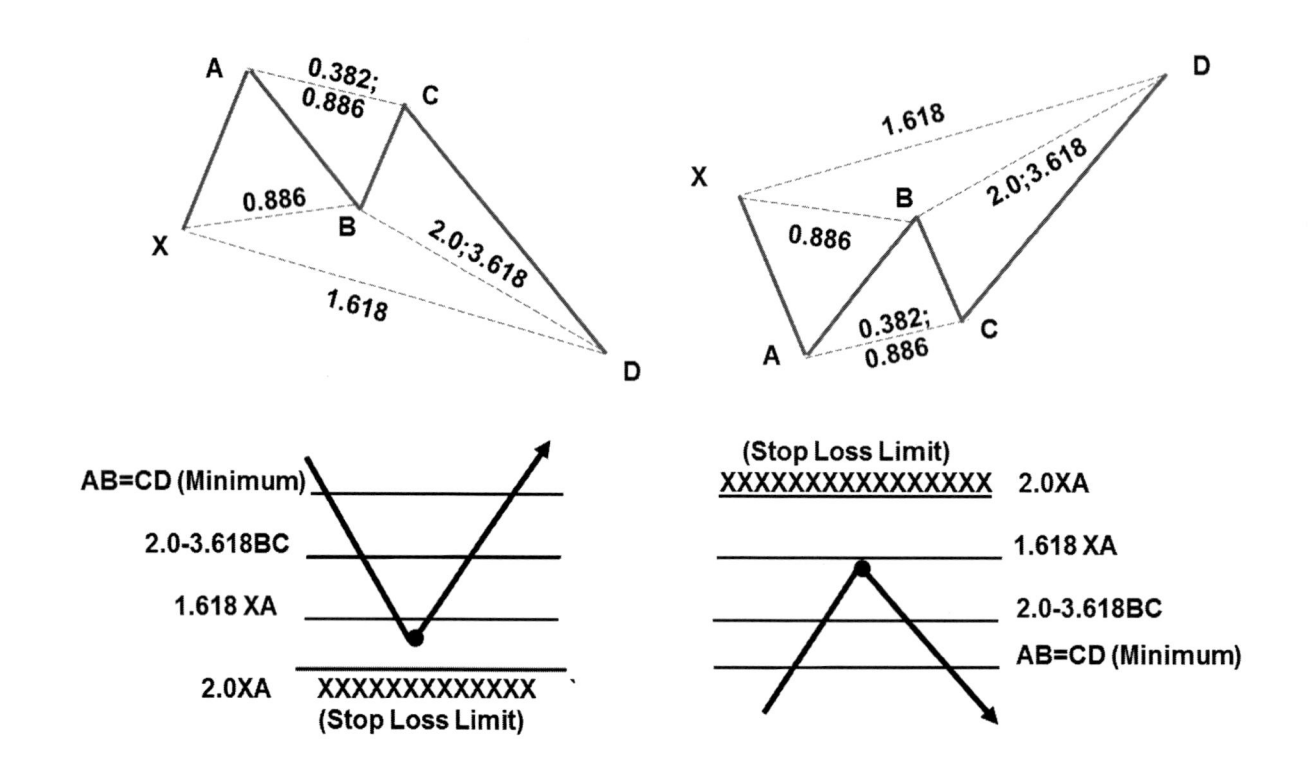

Notes:

- B point @ 0.886 XA Retracement is a minimum that must be t estedd to trigger the structure and possesses +5% tolerance.
- Utilize 2.0 XA as make-or-break stop loss limit measure.
- Price action MUST REVERSE immediately after exceeding general 1.618 XA area.
- B Point Alignment @ 38.2%XA or LESS up to 5% max above 61.8% level.

Harmonic Trading Volume 3: Reaction vs. Reversal

Bearish Deep Crab Pattern

Harmonic Trading Volume 3: Reaction vs. Reversal

SPECIAL SITUATION: Crab/Deep Crab@1.902XA

The 1.902 is an additional measurement that I first encountered in Bryce Gilmore's *Geometry of Markets* (Traders Press 1989). I found it worked extremely well in extension patterns like the Crab that experienced strong price action at completion point. It is a complementary tolerance measure effective in specific situations.

Elements:
AB=CD Type: AB=CD-1.618AB=CD
BC: 2.0-3.618
XA: 1.618-1.902
Stop Loss: > 2.0 (Depends upon 1.618-1.902XA)

Bullish Crab@1.902XA

Due to the extremity of this structure type, it is common to observe extreme price action as the pattern completes. The key is to observe the price behavior as all the numbers at the harmonic support are tested and include the 1.902 measure as an additional tolerance limit beyond the 1.618.

Bullish Crab Pattern
Potential Reversal Zone (PRZ)@1.902XA

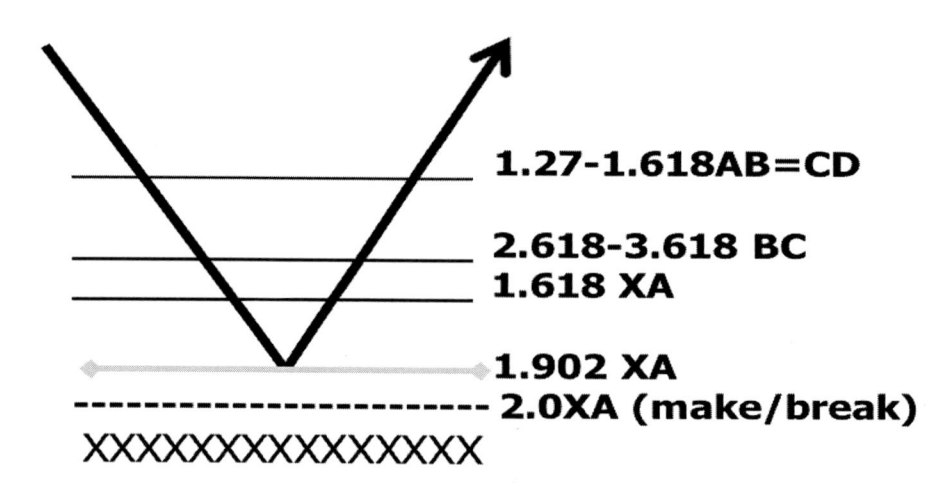

1.27-1.618AB=CD

2.618-3.618 BC
1.618 XA

1.902 XA
2.0XA (make/break)

Copyright HarmonicTrader L.L.C.

Harmonic Trading Volume 3: Reaction vs. Reversal

Harmonic Trading Volume 3: Reaction vs. Reversal

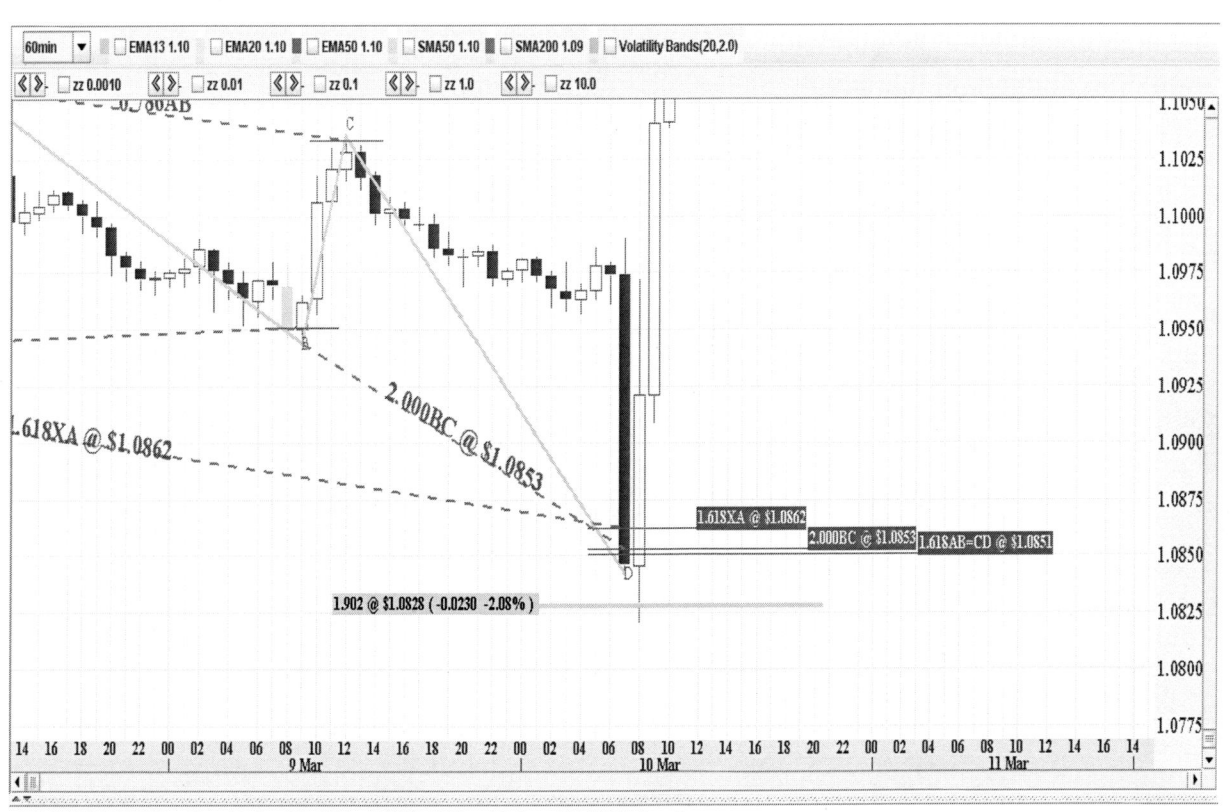

Bearish Crab@1.902XA

The 1.902 measure increases the acceptable tolerance of extreme price action, especially when reversals test the 2.0 stop loss limit. It is important to remember that stop losses are placed beyond these levels. Therefore, it is essential to assess price action as the pattern completes to gauge the validity of this additional tolerance beyond the ideal completion point.

Bearish Crab Pattern
Potential Reversal Zone (PRZ) @1.902

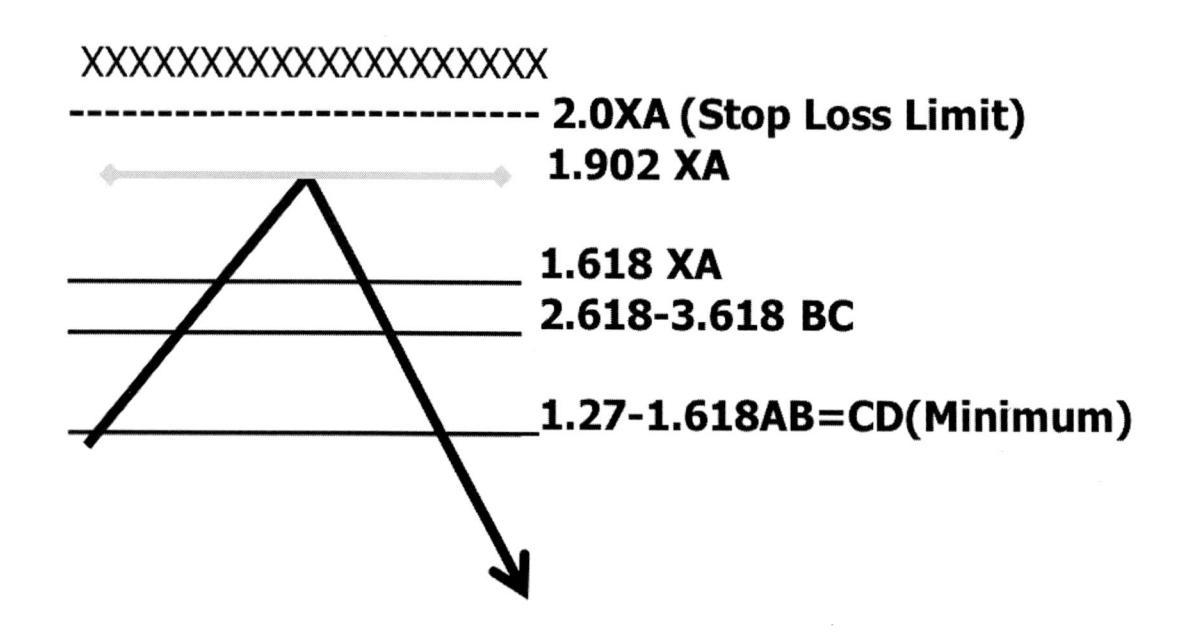

XXXXXXXXXXXXXXXXXXX

---------------------------- 2.0XA (Stop Loss Limit)

1.902 XA

1.618 XA

2.618-3.618 BC

1.27-1.618AB=CD(Minimum)

Harmonic Trading Volume 3: Reaction vs. Reversal

Bearish Crab@1.902XA

Harmonic Trading Volume 3: Reaction vs. Reversal

Butterfly Pattern

Elements:
B Point Ratio: 0.786 (+/-3% Tolerance)
AB=CD Type: AB=CD-1.27AB=CD
BC: 1.618-2.24
XA: 1.27
Stop Loss > 1.414XA (Depends upon AB=CD)

Bullish Butterfly

- A 0.382; 0.886 C
- 0.786
- X B 1.618; 2.24
- 1.27
- D

- AB=CD (Minimum)
- 1.618-2.24BC
- 1.27 XA
- 1.414XA   XXXXXXXXXXXXX (Stop Loss Limit)

Bearish Butterfly

- X 1.27 D
- 0.786 B 1.618; 2.24
- A 0.382; 0.886 C

- (Stop Loss Limit) XXXXXXXXXXXXXXX 1.414XA
- 1.27 XA
- 1.618-2.24BC
- AB=CD (Minimum)

Notes:

- B point must be a precise 0.786 XA Retracement and requires a 3% tolerance to distinguish these structures.
- Utilize 1.414 XA as make-or-break stop loss limit measure.
- Favor the 1.414 level especially when the AB=CD exceeds 1.27 XA level.
- Due to the nature of the pattern price action MUST REVERSE immediately after exceeding 1.27 XA general area.
- B Point Alignment must be within the 3% parameters of the 78.6% retracement otherwise these structures will typically form a Crab at the 1.618.

Harmonic Trading Volume 3: Reaction vs. Reversal

Bullish Butterfly Pattern

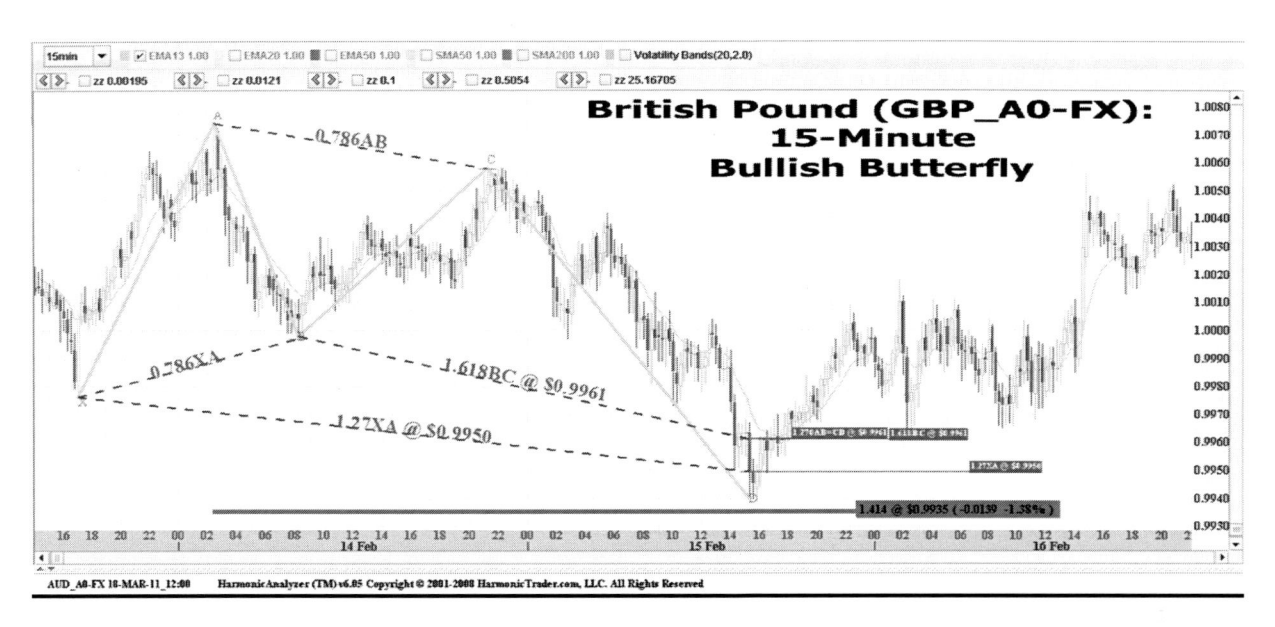

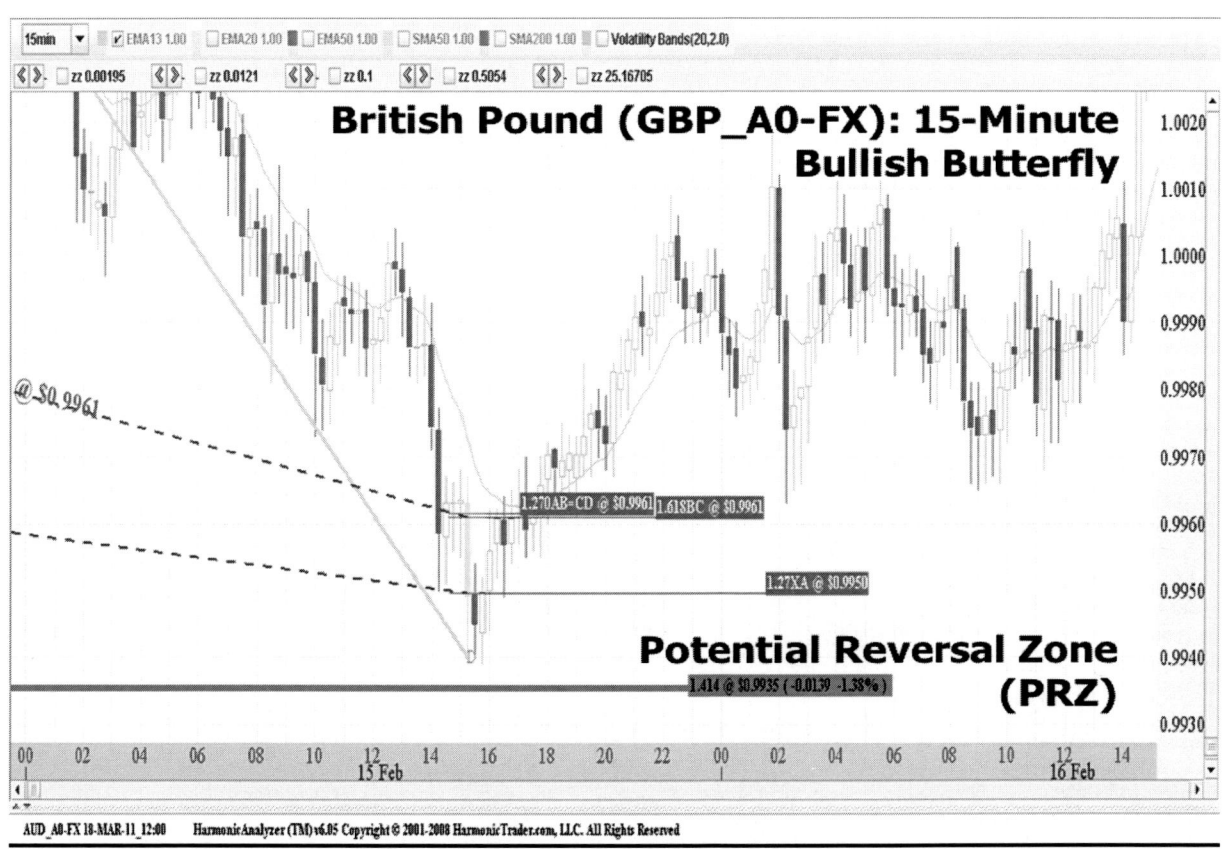

Harmonic Trading Volume 3: Reaction vs. Reversal

Bearish Butterfly Pattern

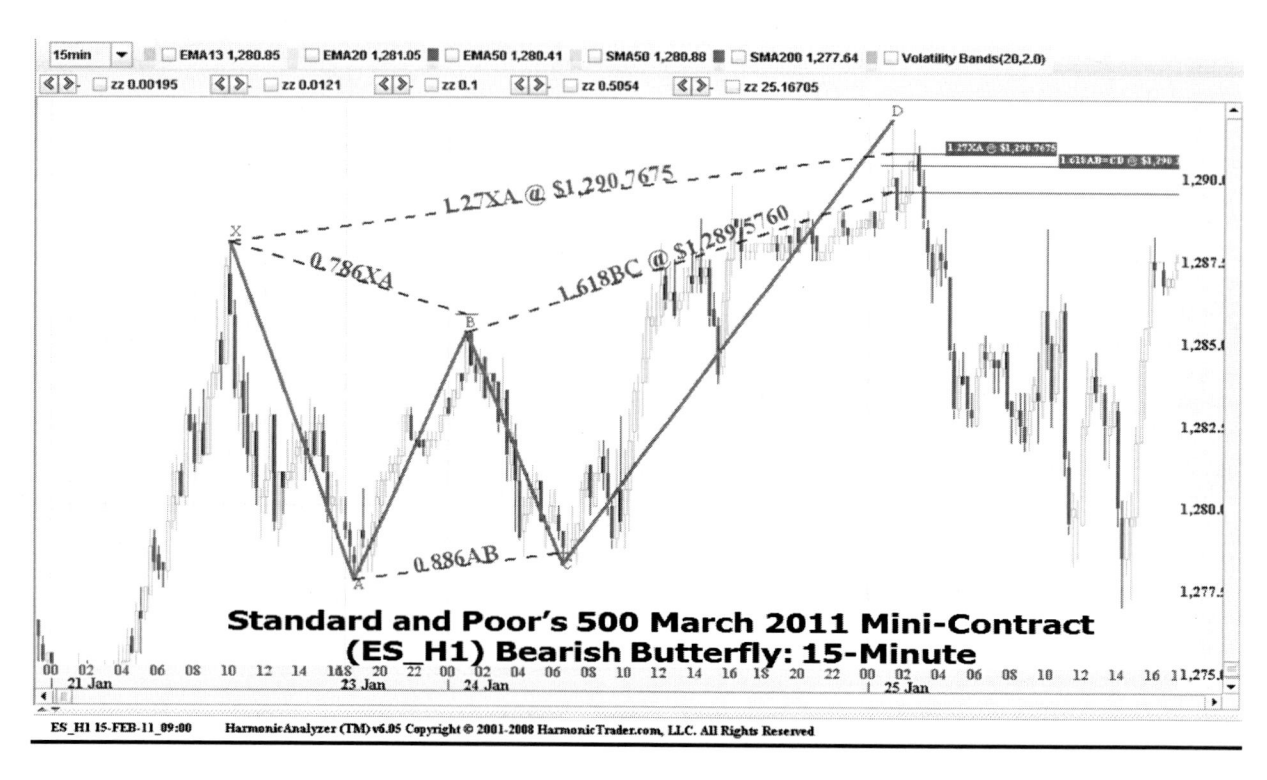

Standard and Poor's 500 March 2011 Mini-Contract (ES_H1) Bearish Butterfly: 15-Minute

Standard and Poor's 500 March 2011 Mini-Contract (ES_H1) Bearish Butterfly Potential Reversal Zone (PRZ) 15-Minute

Harmonic Trading Volume 3: Reaction vs. Reversal

Shark Pattern

The Shark Pattern is a new harmonic pattern that I initially released in 2011 in my *Patterns into Profits* course. Although I was aware of the price structure for quite some time, I needed to refine the identification parameters to discover the best opportunities. Essentially, the pattern is the primary structure that precedes a 5-0 formation. This structure is outside the typical M and W framework. It possesses a unique formation called an Extreme Harmonic Impulse Wave that retests defined support/resistance while converging in the area of the 0.886 retracement – 1.13 extension. In all cases, the completion point must include the powerful 88.6% support/retracement as a minimum requirement. In addition, the unique extreme Harmonic Impulse Wave employs a minimum 1.618 extension.

This combination with the 88.6% retracement defines a unique structure that possesses two profound harmonic measures to define the minimum level. In many cases, the price action will retest the initial starting point of the pattern and define excellent opportunities to take advantage of a market that has moved to far too fast within a limited period of time. These structures typically possess over-extended price action that utilizes the "natural" state of the Extreme Harmonic Impulse Wave which is typically categorized with reactionary trading behavior.

This pattern frequently defines excellent opportunities but these reversals are often sharp and require specific management strategies to capitalize on the phenomenon. In many situations, the price action will retest the prior support/resistance level and typically result in a limited counter trend move. This structure should be handled differently than the standard M and W patterns. In fact, the overall expectations in price action should be short-lived and seek to capture the clearest opportunities. The Shark pattern yields many accurate and aggressive reactions that can be successfully traded as long as a more active management is applied.

Trading The Shark Pattern

The Shark Pattern is represents a temporary extreme structure that seeks to capitalize on the extended nature of the Extreme Harmonic Impulse Wave. Since it precedes the 5-0, the eventual 50% level acts as the optimal profit target. Once executed, the position requires an active trade management strategy. Confirmation at the pattern's completion point demands a demonstrative change in price action character immediately following minimum test of 88.6% retracement and the 1.618 Extreme Harmonic Impulse Wave. After these have been tested, the price action typically will exhibit a change in direction that can be quite volatile. As long as the minimum measures have been tested, the reversal must be anticipated quickly thereafter. It is common for price action to exceed the minimum levels but the overall determination of the pattern's validity depends upon the price action at the completion point.

1.13 Extension – The Failed Wave

The 1.13 extension usually represents a failed breakout (shake-in) or breakdown (shake-out) of an established prior resistance or support point. The 1.13 harmonic ratio is the inverse of the 0.886 and it is as important in specific situations. The 1.13 ratio represents a critical structure outside the M and W types that is effective in pinpointing divergent reversals.

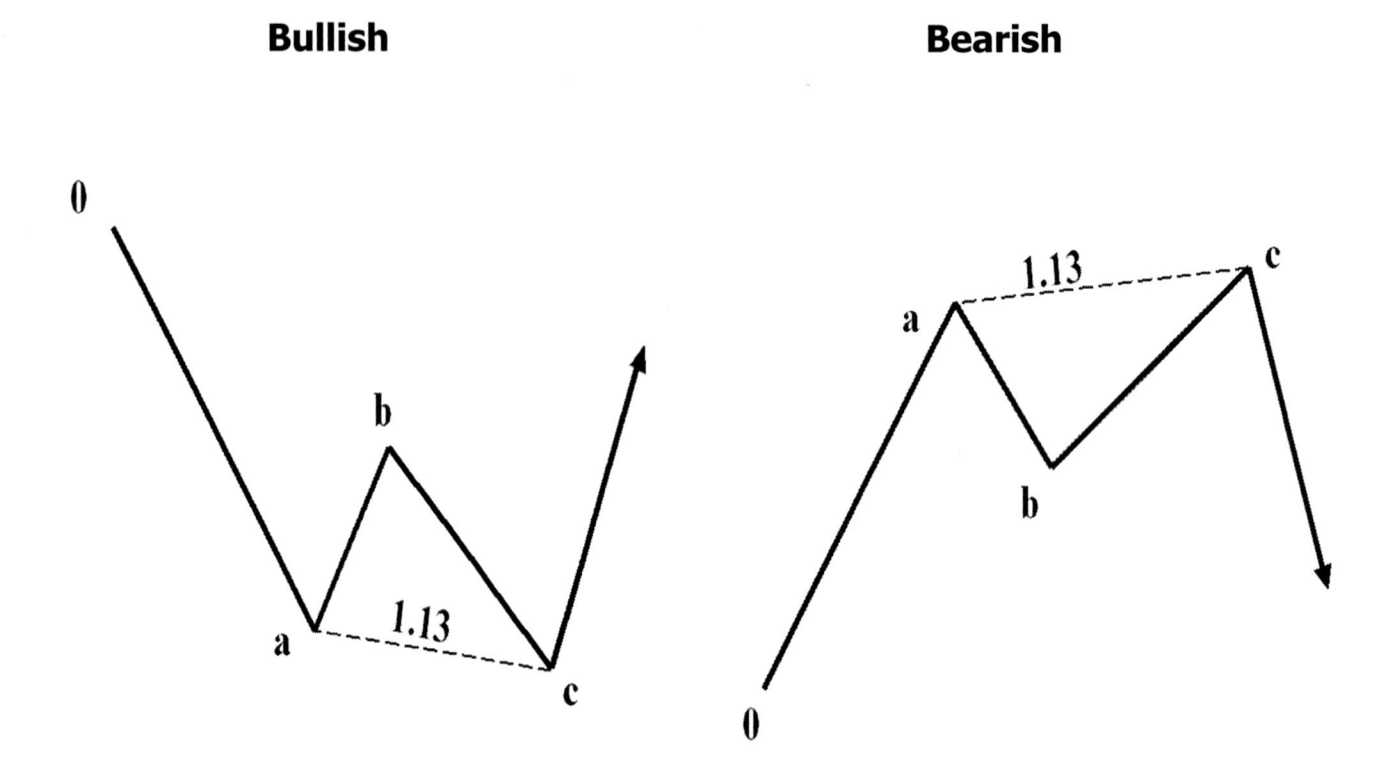

Bullish   **Bearish**

A divergent reversal unfolds when the secondary test does not have the strength to continue in the direction of the primary trend. The 1.13 extension represents a make-or-break level in many retests of clear support and resistance. In fact, price action that exceeds a critical 1.13 extension level frequently will continue farther to the 1.27 or 1.618 areas.

Harmonic Trading Volume 3: Reaction vs. Reversal

Harmonic Impulse Waves

Harmonic Impulse waves are sharp, short-lived price movements that adhere to specific ratios. These structures should be treated in the same manner as complex patterns, as they are unique structures outside the realm of M and W structures. These formations are most accurate in specific harmonic situations.

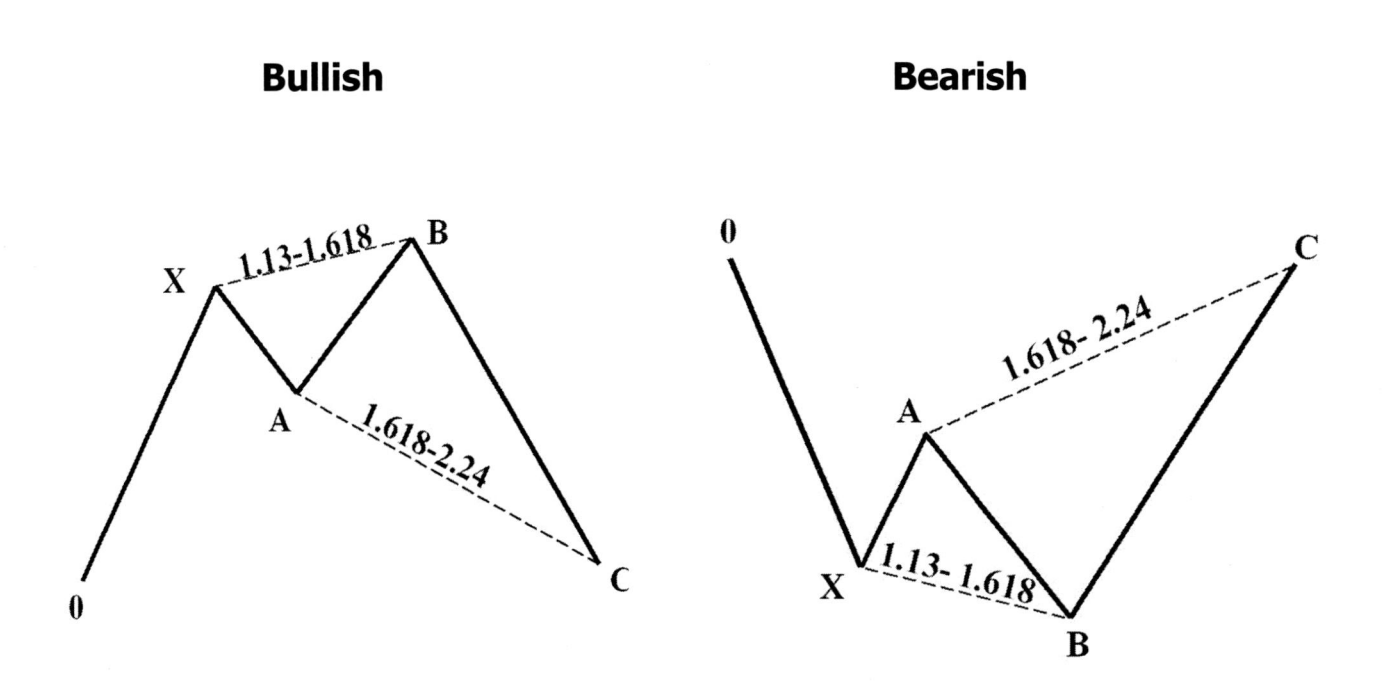

Bullish   **Bearish**

Starting with a preceding 0XAB segment, the Extreme Harmonic Impulse is an accelerated extension that reaches to a minimum of a 1.618 level to as far as a 2.24 limit. This structure is a critical component of Shark and 5-0 Patterns.

Shark Pattern Management

Because the Shark pattern is a reactive trading opportunity, it requires an active – if not automatic – management strategy. The optimal profit objectives must anticipate a reaction to the 50–61.8 % to test the 5-0 Pattern Potential Reversal Zone (PRZ). Specifically, the initial profit objective for the Shark Pattern should be the LESSER OF the 50% level or the Reciprocal AB=CD Pattern – whichever comes first. Typically, the initial profit objective will be the first price measurement in the 5-0 Potential Reversal Zone (PRZ). Although other discretionary strategies can be employed to determine if a larger

Harmonic Trading Volume 3: Reaction vs. Reversal

reversal as possible, the management of the Shark pattern seeks to capture the highest probabilty price segment automatically. Although it can be difficult to automatically secure profit targets, it is essential to maximize these opportunities in this pattern. Although I publicly released this pattern years ago, this is the first time I have detailed the important differences that optimize these decisions.

Bullish Shark Pattern

It is important to note that I have added an additional measure at the 0X retracement of a 38.2 – 61.8% at the A point. Since this is outside of the normal M and W measures, it does help to differentiate Shark structures as valid opportunities.

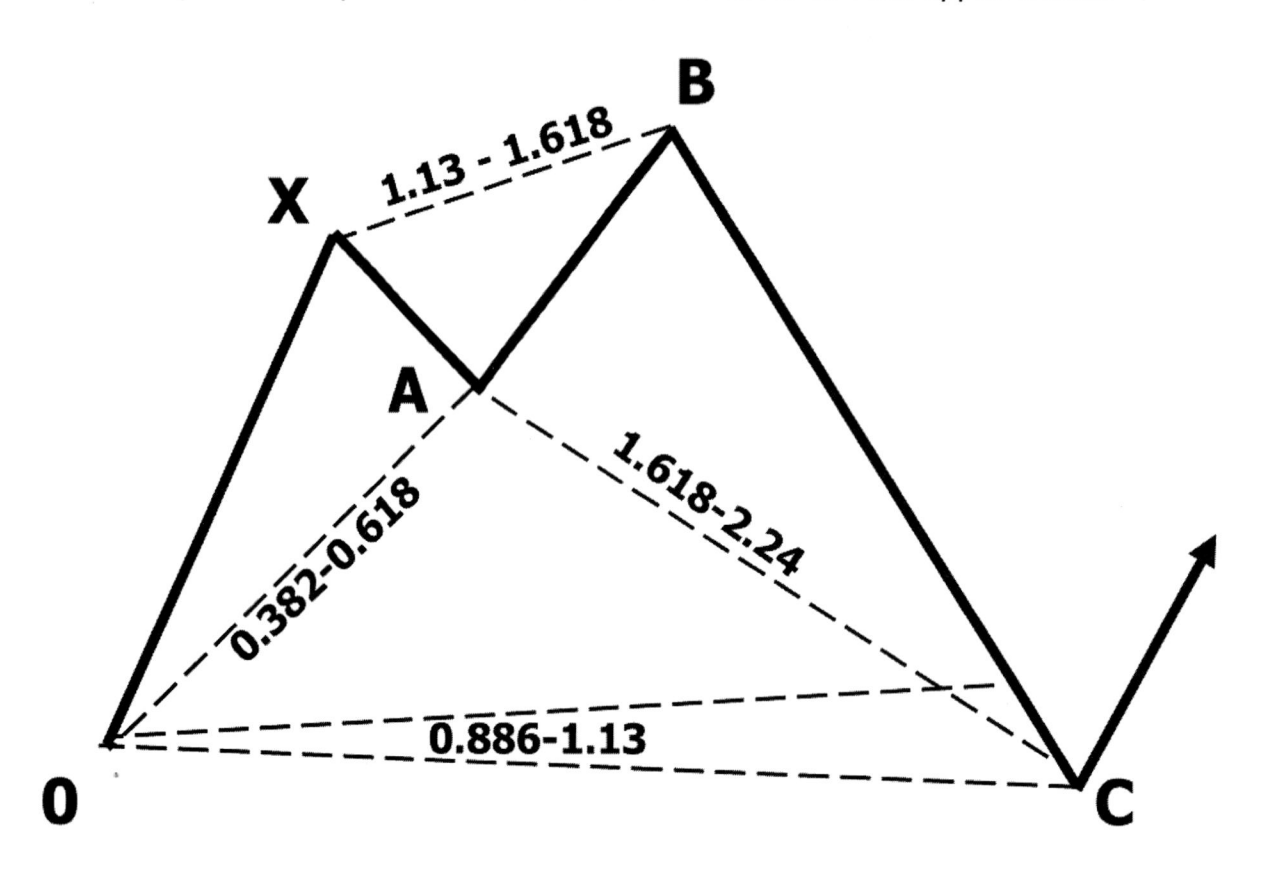

The Shark is an excellent structural formation but does require some specification to avoid invalid possibilities. The key technical event is the retest of the initial pattern point at 0. Depending upon the impulsive leg, the 0B measurement will occur after the 88.6% retracement has been tested. There can be some variation where price action exceeds the 1.0 level and reaches for the 1.13 but this depends upon the impulsive structure. We will look at some combinations throughout this material the primary price

Harmonic Trading Volume 3: Reaction vs. Reversal

event that is unfolding in the structure is a sharp retest of the initial point that possesses some powerful reactive harmonic phenomenon.

Bullish Shark Pattern Potential Reversal Zone (PRZ)

The Shark pattern defines a unique conglomeration of impulsive and reactionary harmonic structures that provide definitive entries. The bullish Potential Reversal Zone defines the harmonic support at same area as the retest of the initial point pattern. Essentially, this alignment of structures identifies an opportunity to buy at established support. Although the 88.6% retracement is an important minimal consideration, the larger focus should analyze price action in the area of the 1.0 XA level as well.

Bullish Shark Pattern
Potential Reversal Zone (PRZ)

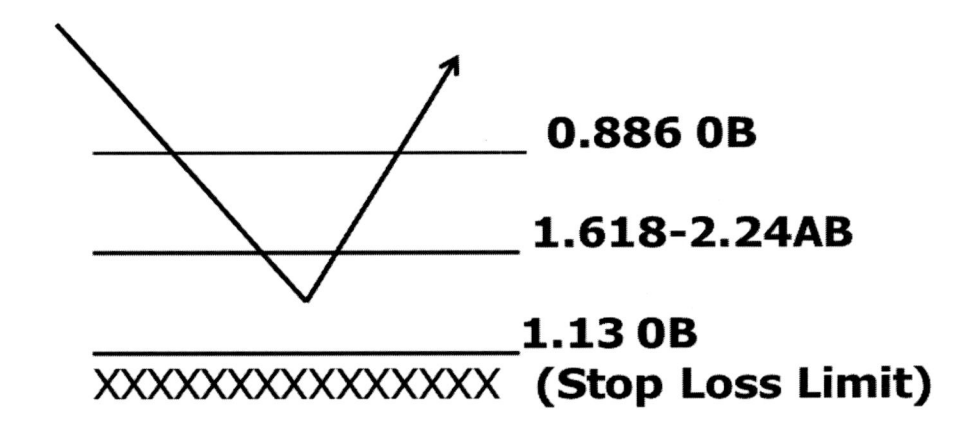

0.886 0B

1.618-2.24AB

1.13 0B

XXXXXXXXXXXXXXX (Stop Loss Limit)

Copyright HarmonicTrader L.L.C.

The key in determining whether to execute at the 88.6% retracement or the 113% extension is to analyze the impulsive minimum 1.618 extension. Depending upon where this completes, it will dictate whether the Shark pattern will complete at the prior initial low or there will be a situation of extended price action to the 1.13 level. If the minimum 1.618 impulsive wave completes before the 88.6% retracement, then 2.0 or 2.24 would be use to best compliment the harmonic support. Regardless of how far the price action trades beyond the minimum levels, the key in all reversals is to see demonstrative price action that continues in the countertrend direction following completion of the pattern.

Harmonic Trading Volume 3: Reaction vs. Reversal

Euro U.S. Dollar (EUR/USD): 15-Minute
Bullish Shark Pattern

The following example of the Euro/Dollar possesses all of the ideal elements of structure. The AB impulsive leg was a 2.24 extension that completed before the 0B 88.6% retracement. Since the minimum 1.618 impulsive leg was satisfied, the completion of pattern was focused on the 88.6% level.

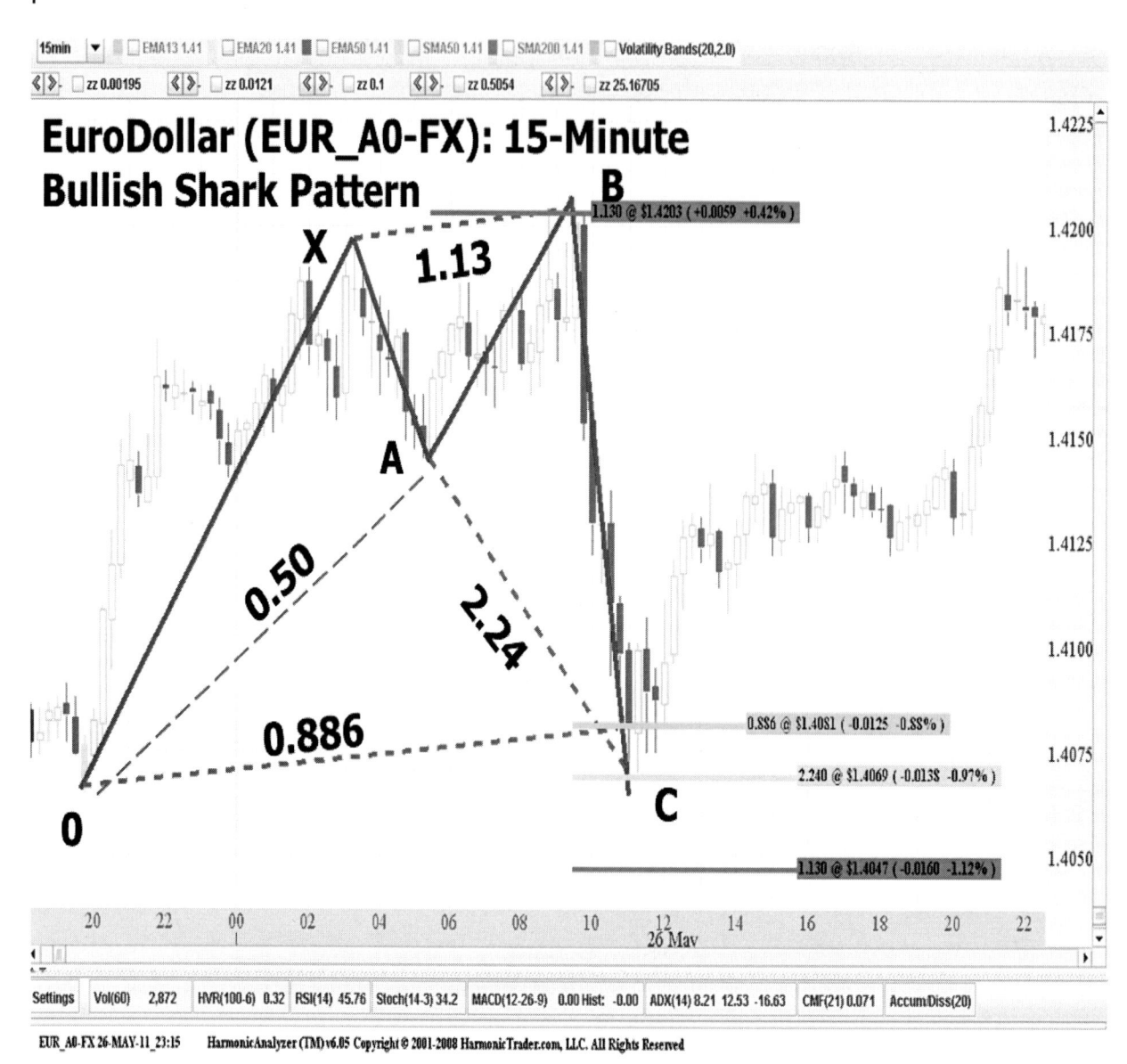

Harmonic Trading Volume 3: Reaction vs. Reversal

Euro U.S. Dollar (EUR/USD): 15-Minute
Bullish Shark Pattern Potential Reversal Zone (PRZ)

As I have mentioned previously, the Shark pattern is a structure that typically precedes a 5-0 formation. We will outline the 5-0 pattern later in this chapter but it is significant confirmation in the handling of Shark pattern opportunities. In fact, the 50% retracement is utilized as the initial target for the Shark. This underscores the importance of recognizing the Shark as a reactive structure first and foremost.

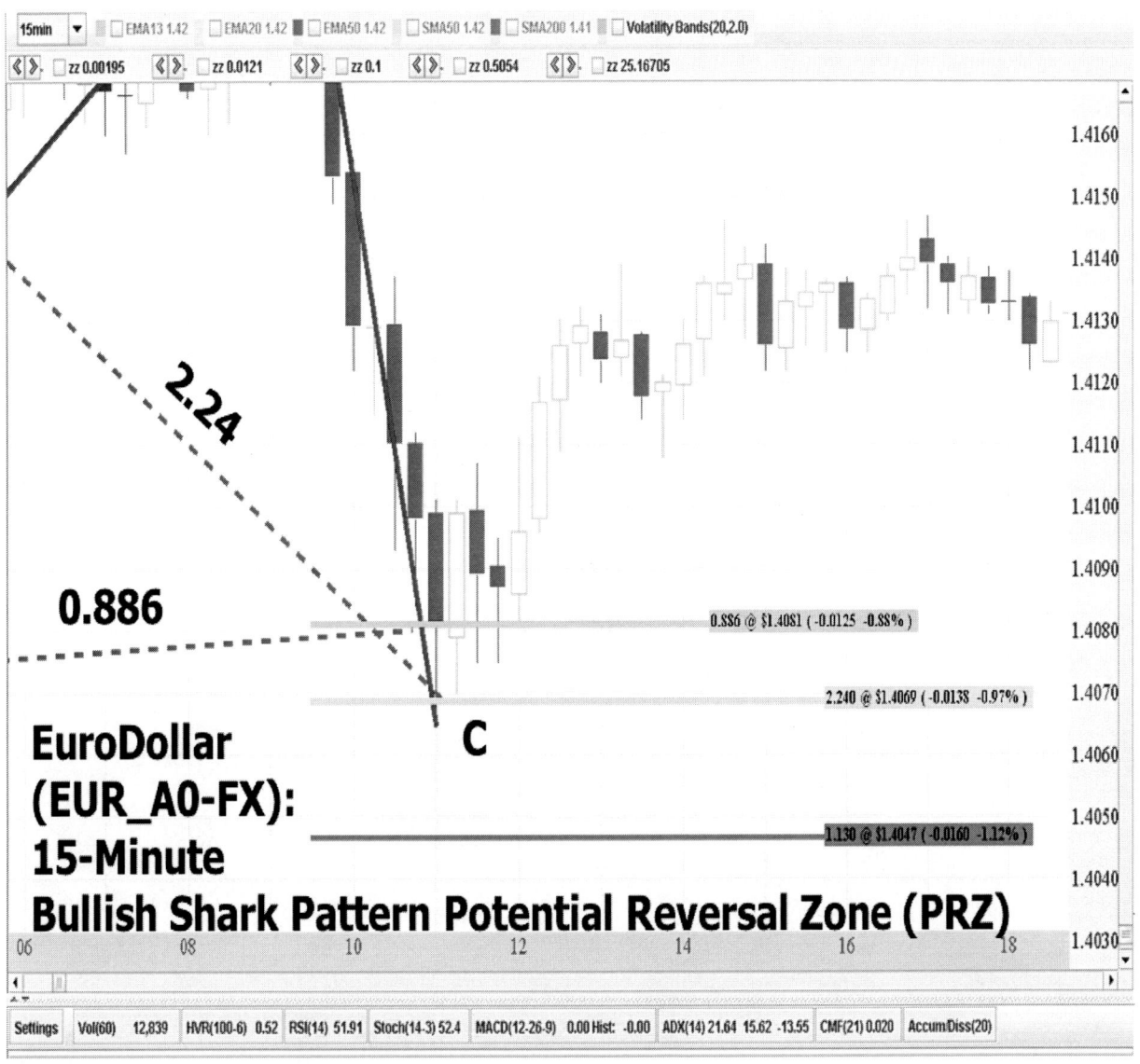

Harmonic Trading Volume 3: Reaction vs. Reversal

Euro U.S. Dollar (EUR/USD): 15-Minute
Bullish Shark-> Bearish 5-0

In this example of the Euro on a 15-minute chart, the initial reversal from the Shark pattern at 1.4070 served as sharp intraday support while the 50% ratio of the pattern defined an important minimum target. Although it is possible for 5-0 patterns to fail, they most commonly experience consolidation that requires immediate trade management at the predetermined profit target under most conditions. After gaining experience with these trades, it will become clear that the best decision is to capture partial profits at a minimum at these price objectives.

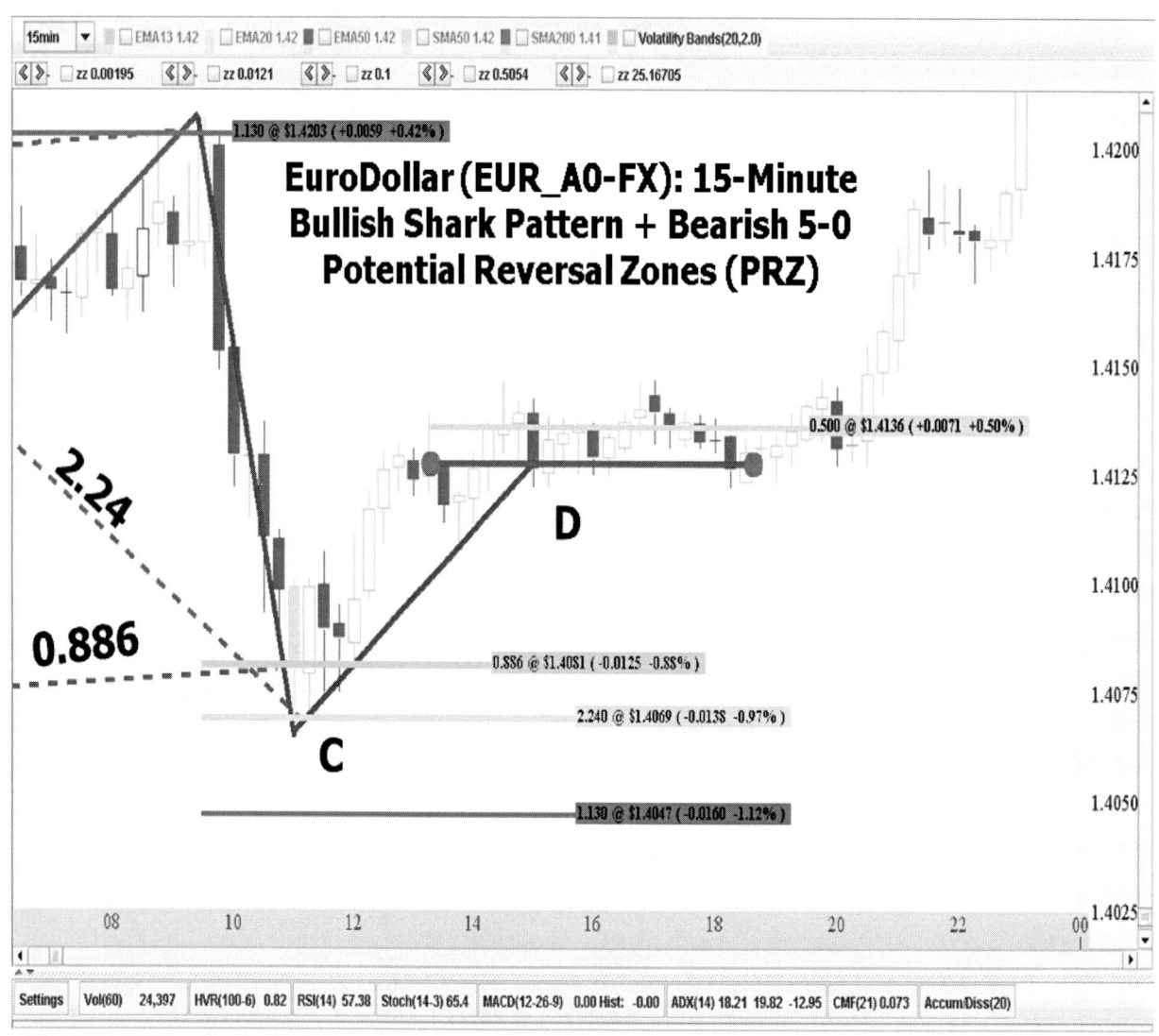

Harmonic Trading Volume 3: Reaction vs. Reversal

Bearish Shark Pattern

The key in defining the Bearish Shark is to distinguish the minimum impulsive leg relative to the 0B retest. Depending upon where the 1.618 minimum impulsive leg completes, the extent of the price action exceeding the initial point of the pattern can be clearly determined.

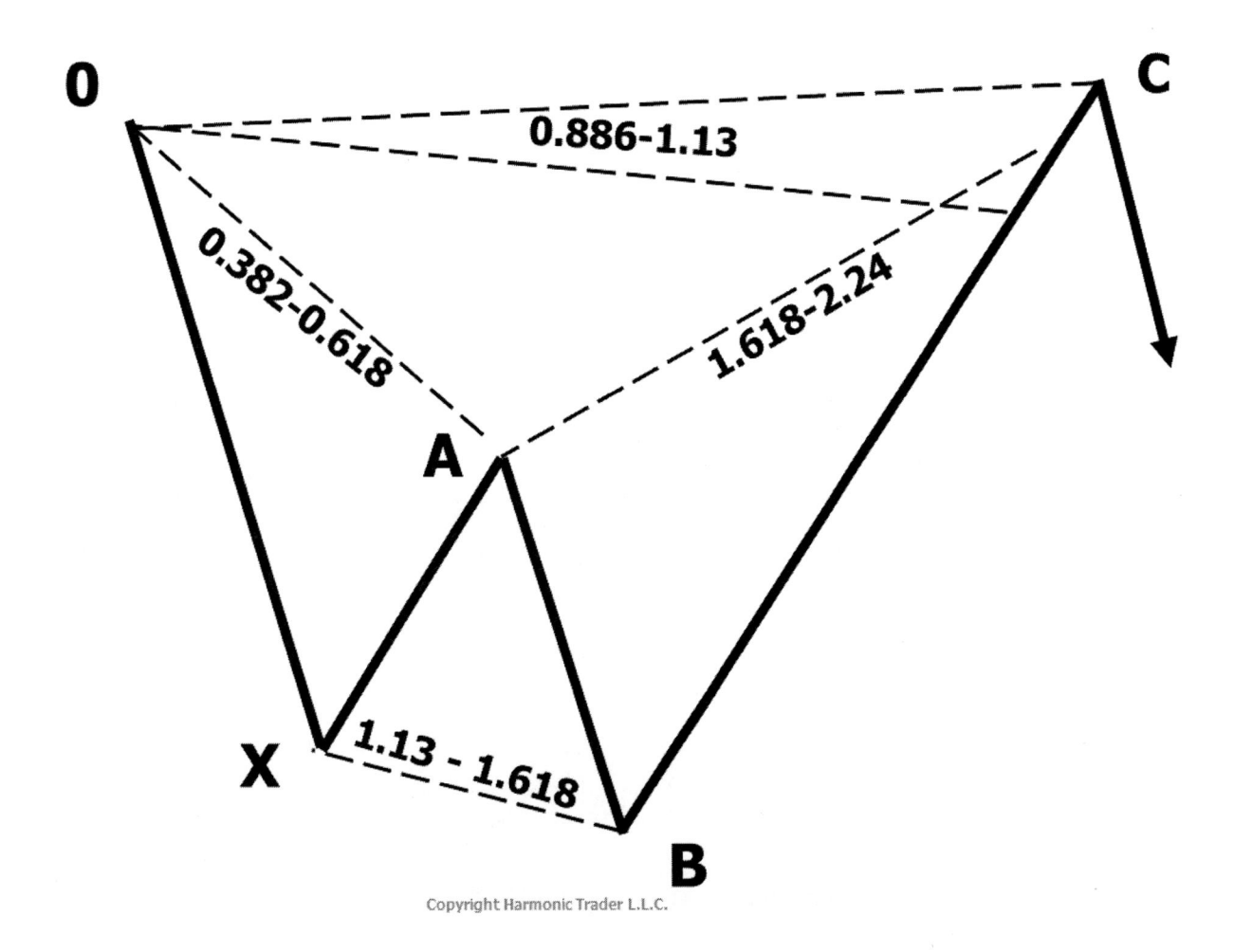

Harmonic Trading Volume 3: Reaction vs. Reversal

Bearish Shark Pattern Potential Reversal Zone (PRZ)

Generally, the price action in the Potential Reversal Zone will require confirmation at the pattern completion point but the overall determinationn of whether the reversal will be a retracement at the 88.6% level or an extension at the 1.13 XA measure will be dictated by the impulsive leg. In most cases, I expect the Shark to retest the initial point of the pattern (1.0 0B). Therefore, price action that exceeds the 88.6% level is common for these structures.

Bearish Shark Pattern Potential Reversal Zone (PRZ)

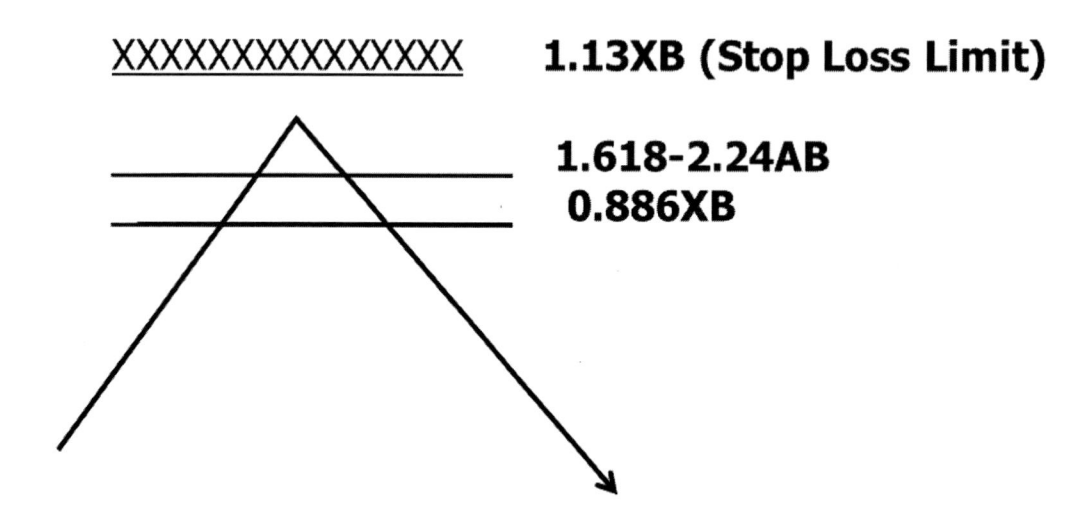

XXXXXXXXXXXXXX 1.13XB (Stop Loss Limit)

1.618-2.24AB
0.886XB

Copyright Harmonic Trader L.L.C.

Harmonic Trading Volume 3: Reaction vs. Reversal

Canadian Dollar (USD/CAD): Daily
Bearish Shark Pattern

The following example of the Canadian Dollar on the daily chart possesses perfect structure and exemplifies the reactive nature of the pattern.

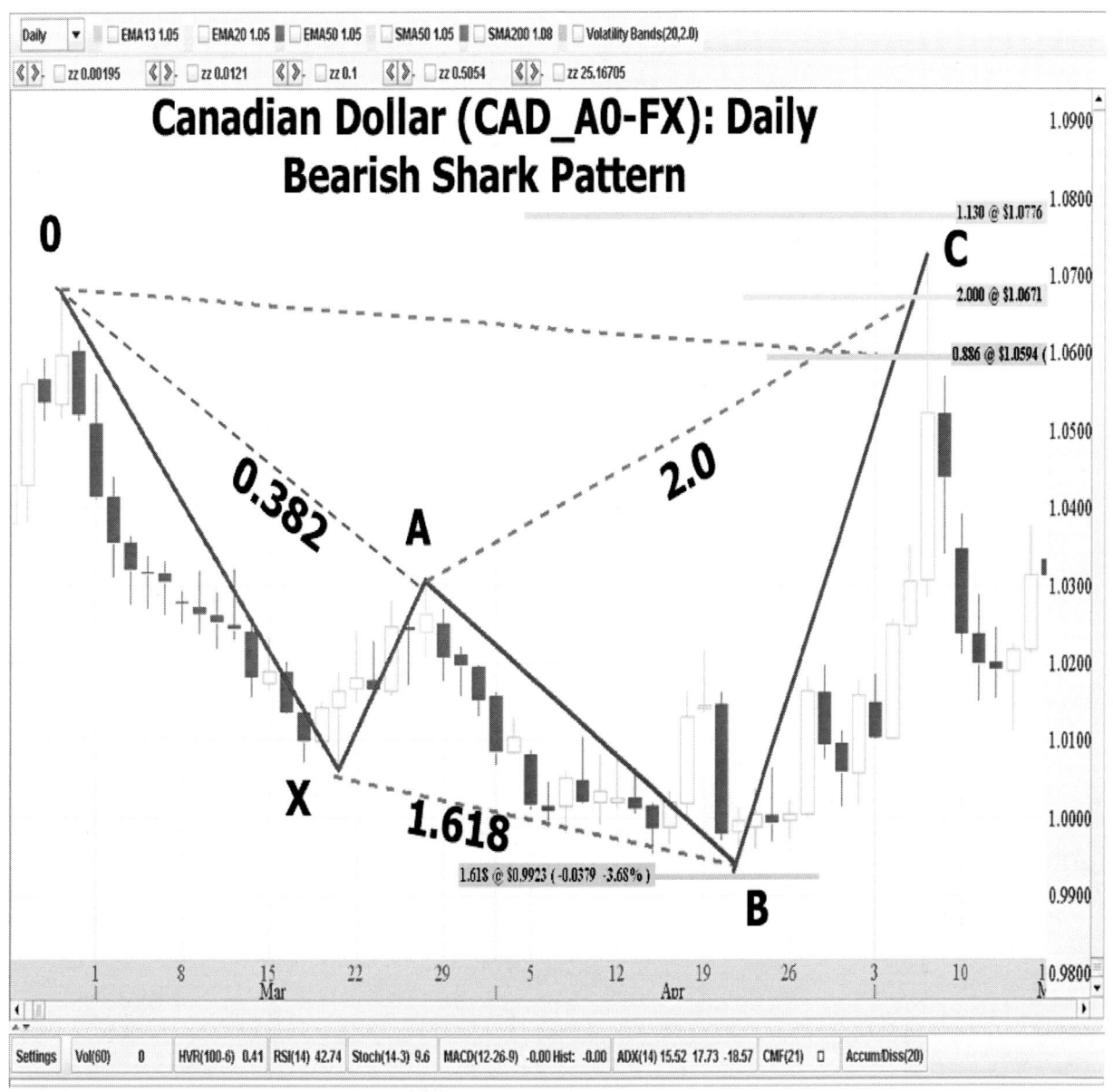

Harmonic Trading Volume 3: Reaction vs. Reversal

Canadian Dollar (USD/CAD): Daily
Bearish Shark Pattern Potential Reversal Zone (PRZ)

Although the 1.618 impulsive leg preceded the 88.6% retracement, the alignment of these measures defined the 1.06-1.07 area - close to the initial point (1.0 0C) of the pattern - as the preferred area for completion. It is important to note that the price action exceeded these minimum measures but reversed on the exact day it tested the entire zone.

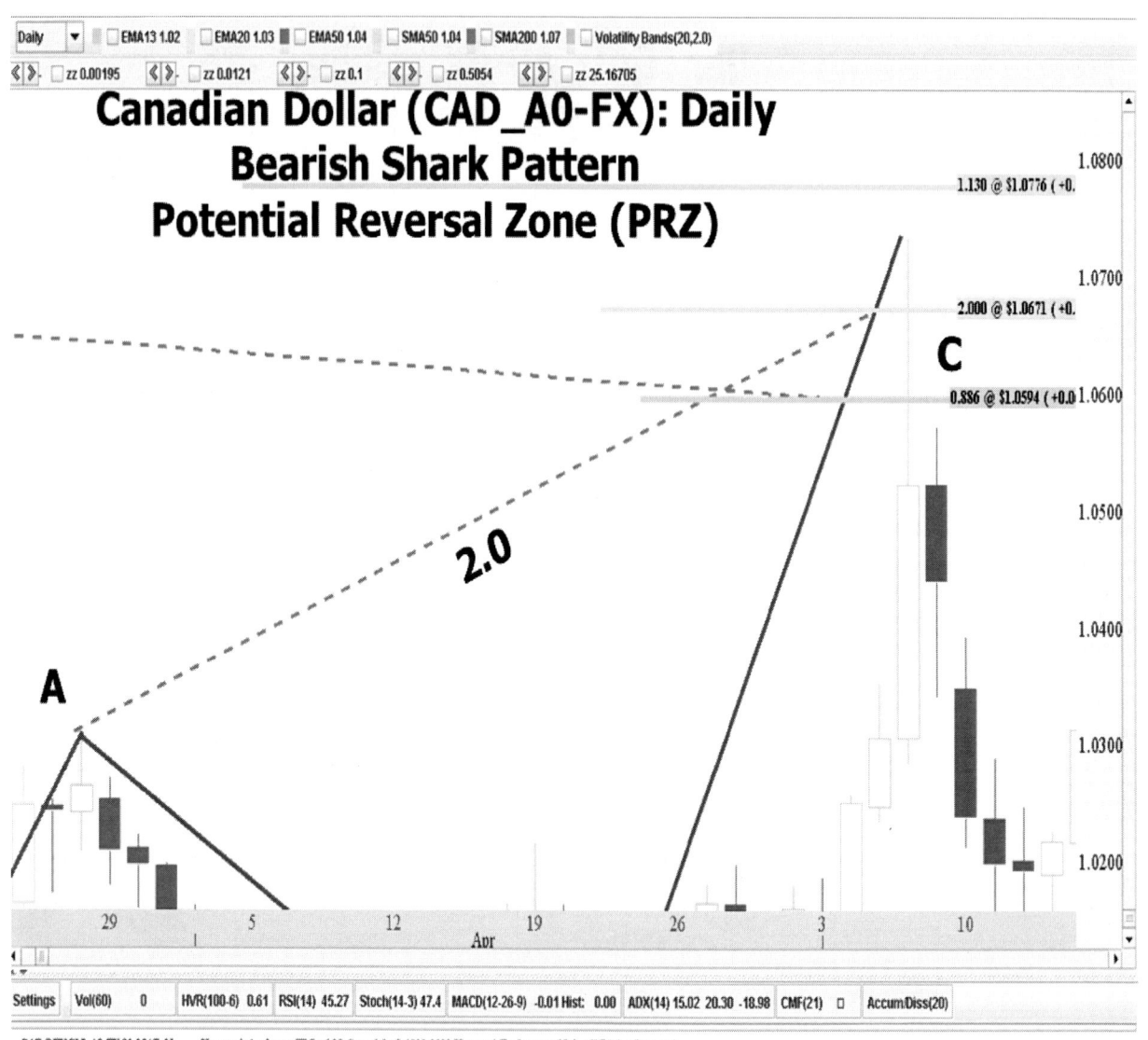

Harmonic Trading Volume 3: Reaction vs. Reversal

Canadian Dollar (USD/CAD): Daily
Bearish Shark > Bullish 5-0

Regardless of the timeframe, the Shark pattern always incorporates the minimum 50% level as its profit target. In this instance, the pattern will morph into a Bullish Shark into a Bearish 5-0 structure. Again, these situations are best captured with automatic profit targets on a portion of the position at a minimum. On this daily chart, the reversal was severe and exceeded the minimum 50% level. This is typical but automatic profit objectives secure these reactive moves most efficiently.

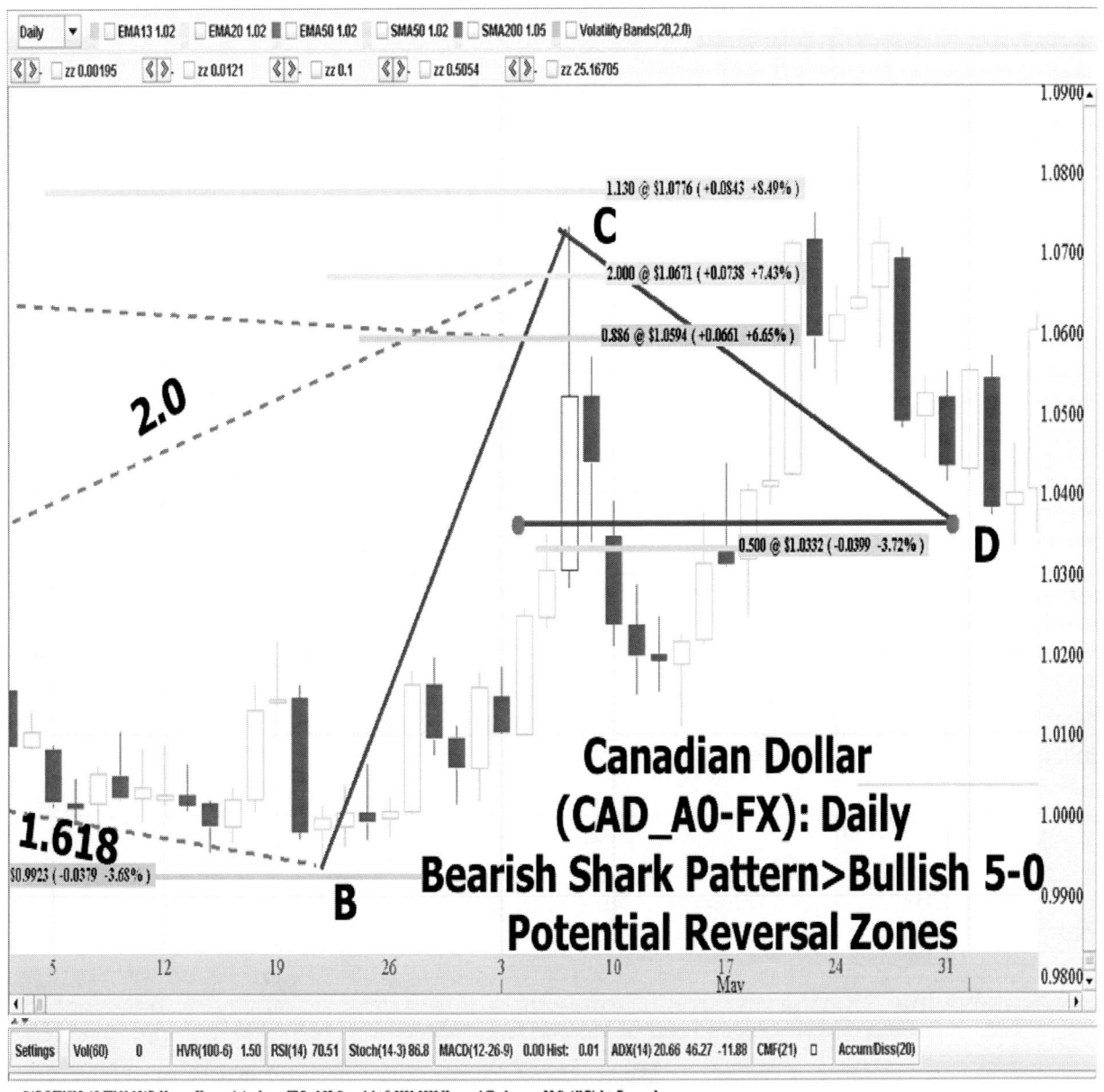

Harmonic Trading Volume 3: Reaction vs. Reversal

Shark Pattern Conclusion

The Shark is a distinct structure but different than the M&W harmonic pattern types. The completion of the structure serves as the precursor to the 5-0 Pattern. Thus, these two patterns are related to each other, especially since the 5-0 defines the optimal profit target for the Shark. The pattern works extremely well retesting prior support/resistance points (0.886/1.13) as a strong counter-trend reaction opportunity that provides clear yet short-lived moves. Remember, the extended AB Extreme Harmonic Impulse Wave must be at least a 1.618 (can be as much as 2.24) but these are typically extreme price action. The 1.618 serves as the definitive price segment in the structure as long as the minimum 88.6% 0B retracement is tested. The 1.13 0B extension serves as a maximum limit that must not be exceeded. Most importantly, the execution in the Shark PRZ will depend upon the price action as it tests the minimum levels. The reversal may unfold beyond the minimum measures but the area for the stop loss limit must be established just beyond the 1.13 extension. Due to its reactionary nature, it is essential to automatically capture the profit objective at the first measurement in 5-0 within the Potential Reversal Zone (PRZ). Finally, the Shark represents Harmonic Trading history, as this the first book where I have released the advanced specifications of the the pattern.

5-0 Pattern

The 5-0 pattern was originally presented on HarmonicTrader.com in 2003 and released to the public in an article on TradingMarkets.com in March 2005. (http://tradingmarkets.com/recent/are_you_a_fibonacci_fan_youll_like_this_pattern-655968.html) The 5-0 requires an exact alignment and ideal symmetry. *Harmonic Trading Volume Two* (2007) defined the exact alignment of ratios and all aspects of the structure. This nature of this pattern is a relatively new discovery in the field of Technical Analysis. Although other interpretations of extended structures have been presented in previously, the exact rules for the 5-0 pattern are unprecedented and exemplify why Harmonic Trading is different from the rest.

5-0 Pattern Basics

The 5-0 structure is different from the M-type and W-type alignments in the other patterns but the same Harmonic Trading principles apply. The measurements employed with the 5-0 place greater emphasis on different price segments than the other patterns. For example, the 0B point AND the BC projection determine the validity of the structure. The initial XA leg of the structure typically possesses a 1.13, 1.27, 1.41 or 1.618 extension. The Reciprocal AB=CD pattern - a variation of the regular structure – is utilized to define the Potential Reversal Zone (PRZ). The 50% XA retracement is the defining limit at the pattern's completion point but the 61.8% XA retracement is included in the determination of the setup, especially in the Stop Loss determination.

Reciprocal AB=CD Pattern

The Reciprocal AB=CD measured by first counter-trend move within an established trend. It typically resembles a lazy "Z" or "S." The Reciprocal AB=CD is more of an estimation that must be complemented by other harmonic measurements and it is applied to non-M &W-type structures. Also, it is effective in distinct price channels to gauge the predominant reactive counter moves that can define important continuation zones within a primary trend. Remember, these are approximation measures that are employed in specific situations. Other distinct measures must be included with this pattern type but it is effective in structures such as the Shark and the 5-0.

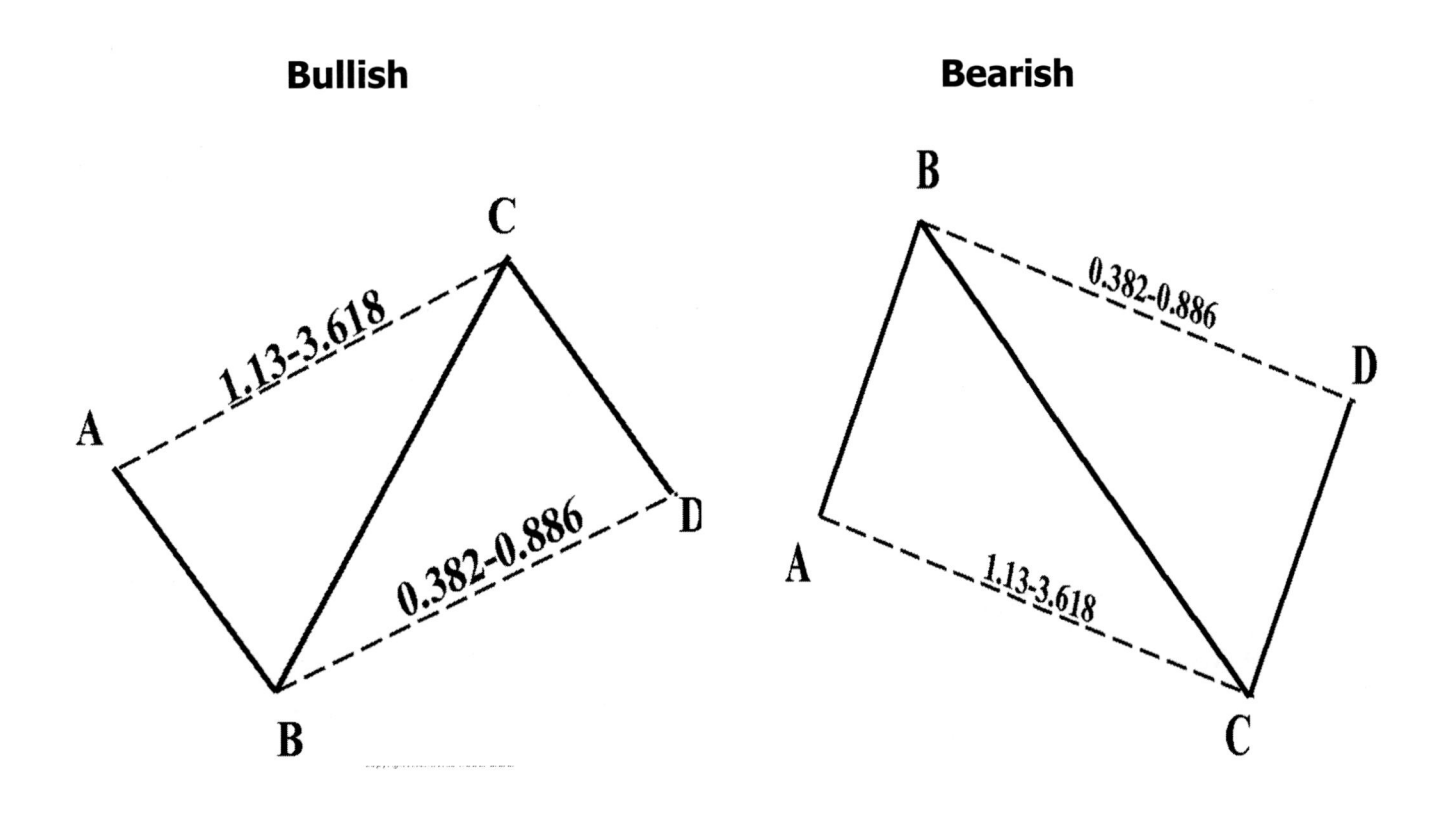

Bullish

Bearish

Harmonic Trading Volume 3: Reaction vs. Reversal

Bullish 5-0 Pattern

The Bullish 5-0 pattern is an extremely effective formation but it must be identified properly. There are a number of situations that can closely resemble this structure but if any individual point of the formation fails to satisfy the pattern ratio requirements, it must be dismissed. However, when clear formations develop with the correct measurements, these harmonic zones are extremely accurate. In particular, the incorporation of the 61.8% retracement provides a dynamic means of identifying important continuation levels.

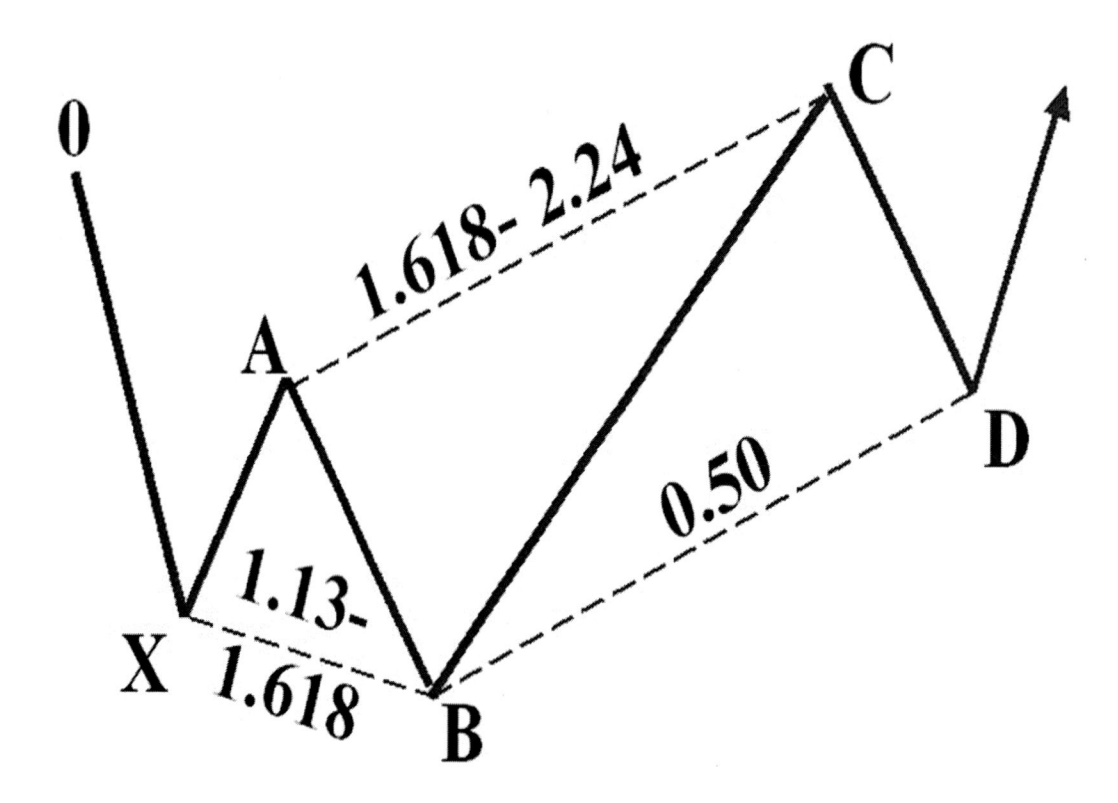

Harmonic Trading Volume 3: Reaction vs. Reversal

Bullish 5-0 Pattern Potential Reversal Zone (PRZ)

If the 61.8% retracement is the most powerful ratio of all Harmonic Trading measures, its importance within the 5-0 pattern is the most effective of all price structures as it truly serves as a critical make-or-break stop loss cosideration. Depending upon where the Reciprocal AB=CD completes, the exact termination point for the execution of the structure will vary. In the bullish pattern, if the Reciprocal AB=CD completes before the 50% retracement, the execution will be immediately at this level. However, a Reciprocal AB=CD that completes lower than the 50% level will always include the 61.8% retracement as the optimal entry price for the trade. Although the stop loss in both situations is beyond the 61.8% level, each total determination depends upon the Reciprocal AB=CD.

Bullish 5-0 Pattern Potential Reversal Zone (PRZ)

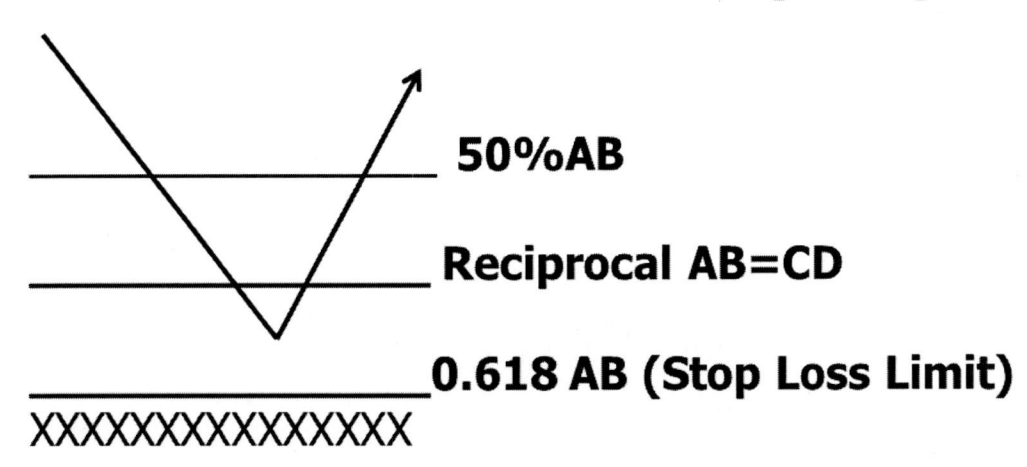

- 50%AB
- Reciprocal AB=CD
- 0.618 AB (Stop Loss Limit)

Copyright HarmonicTrader L.L.C.

Harmonic Trading Volume 3: Reaction vs. Reversal

Australian Dollar (AUD_A0-FX): 60-Minute
Bullish 5-0 Pattern

The following chart exemplifies the structure of a 5-0 Pattern and the concise reversal behavior that must ideally unfold in the harmonic support. AUD/USD possessed an ideal structure that reversed at the 50% level at the 0.9750 which was confirmed by the Reciprocal AB=CD at 0.9775.

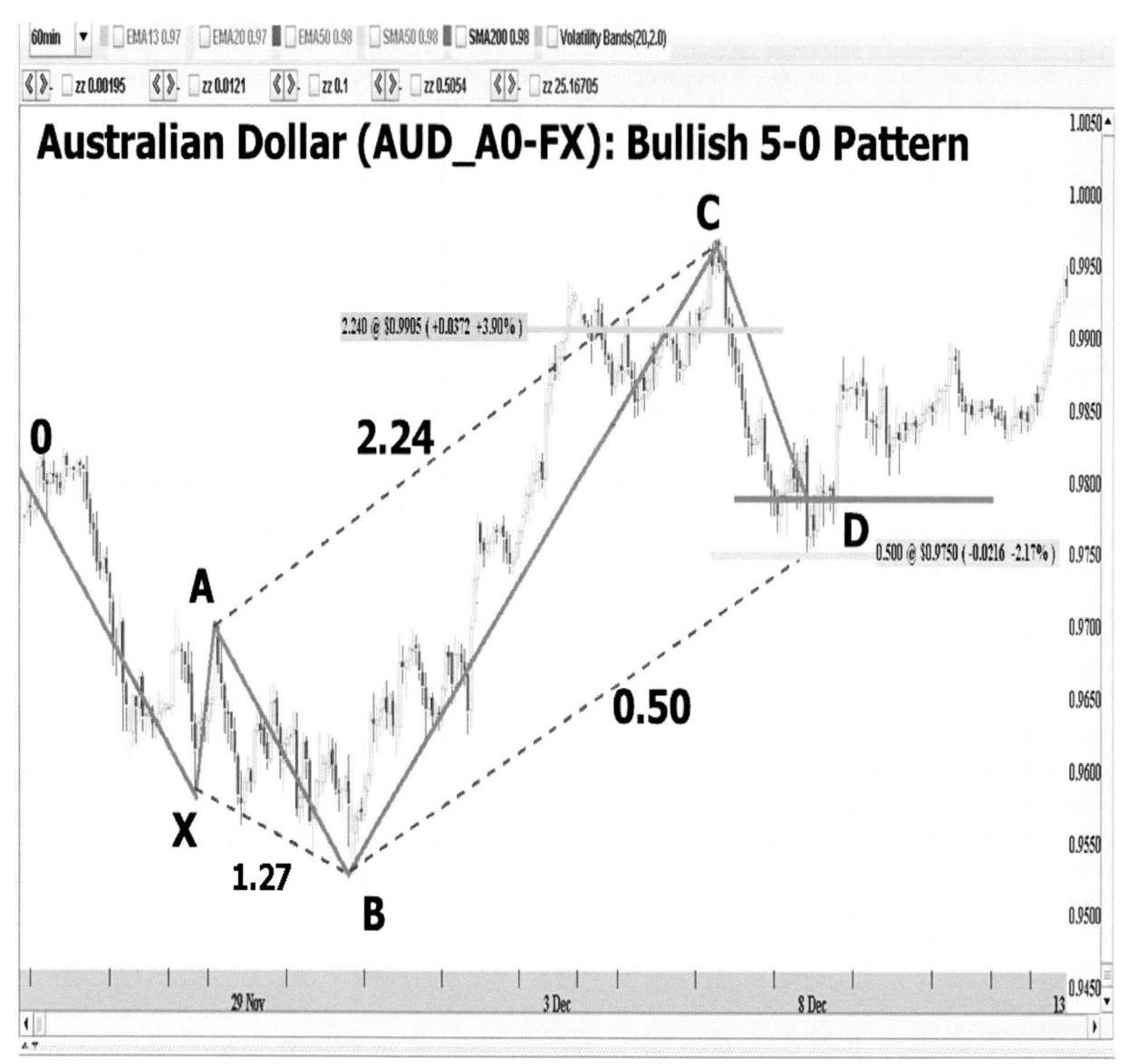

Harmonic Trading Volume 3: Reaction vs. Reversal

Australian Dollar (AUD_A0-FX): 60-Minute
Bullish 5-0 Pattern Potential Reversal Zone (PRZ)

This following chart shows the price action in the Potential Reversal Zone (PRZ) of the 5-0 Pattern. The price action stabilized as it tested the zone, reversing immediately after it tested the 50% retracement.

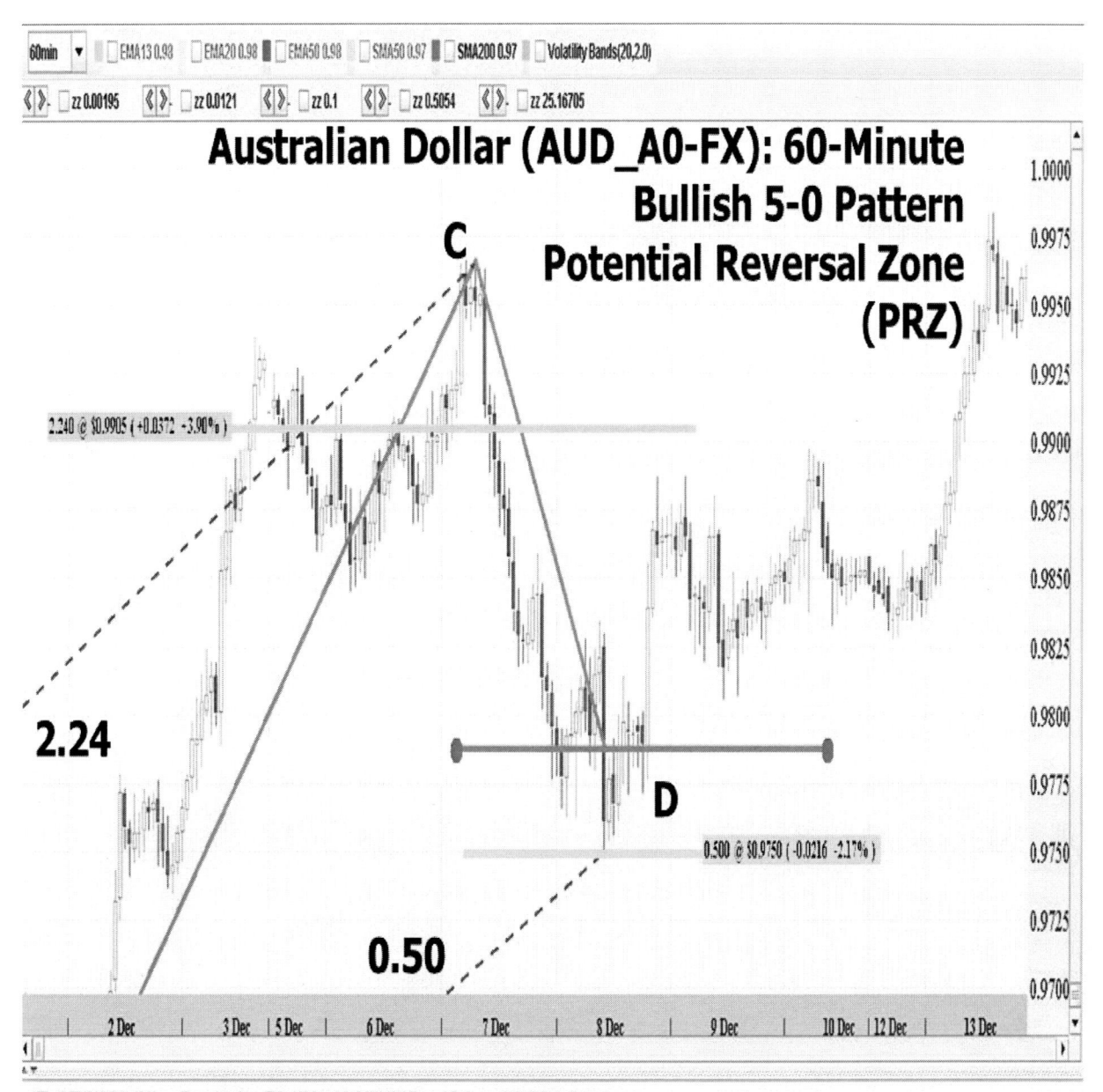

Harmonic Trading Volume 3: Reaction vs. Reversal

Bearish 5-0 Pattern

The Bearish 5-0 structure is an excellent continuation pattern within established trends. Although the execution of the opportunity is determined by the Reciprocal AB=CD, the 61.8% bearish retracement will always be the most important measure in the set up. At a minimum, it serves as the defining area for the stop loss level and is vital in the determination of the validity of the trade, especially on the initial test of the Potential Reversal Zone.

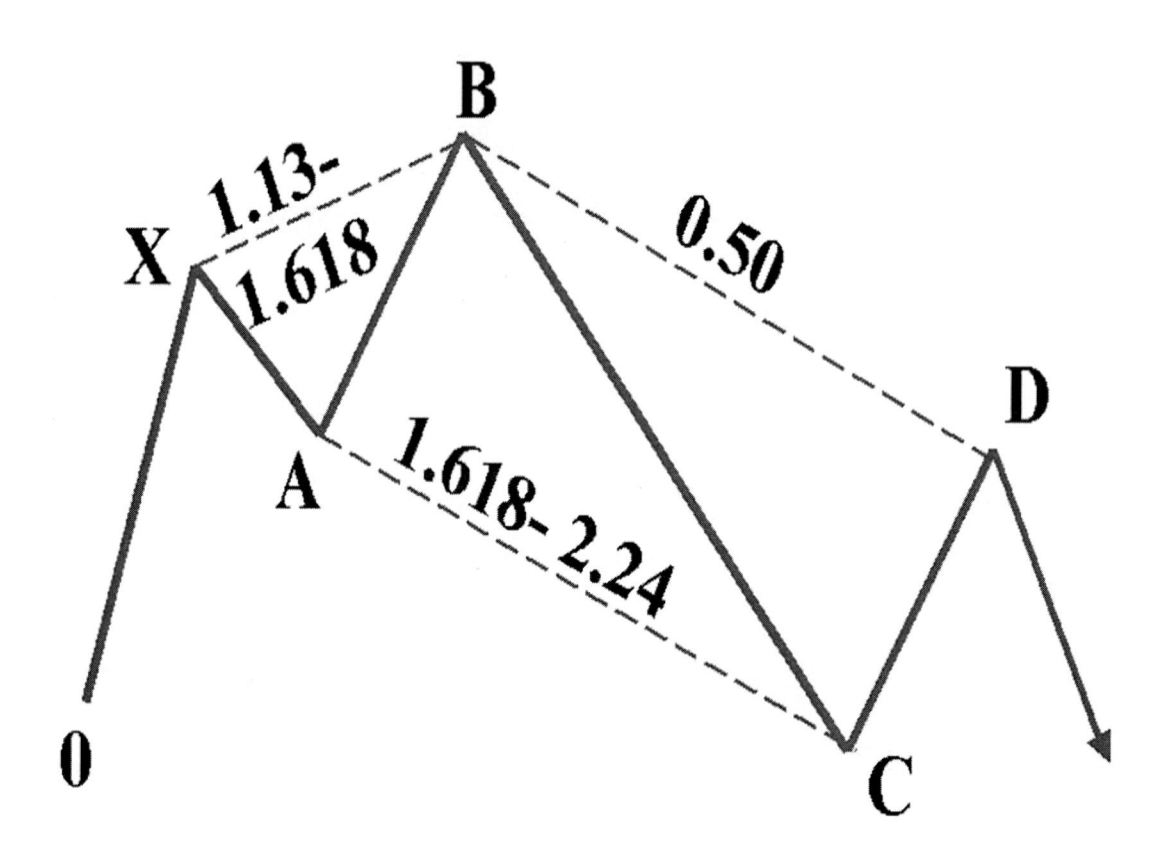

Harmonic Trading Volume 3: Reaction vs. Reversal

Bearish 5-0 Potential Reversal Zone (PRZ)

In the Bearish 5-0 Potential Reversal Zone, the 61.8% limit will be the top end of the resistance in every situation. The only difference will be whether or not the Reciprocal AB=CD defines the execution closer to the 50% or higher. In most cases, the Reciprocal AB=CD will converge closely to the 50% ratio but if it is above that the execution will default to the 61.8% price level.

Bearish 5-0 Pattern
Potential Reversal Zone (PRZ)

XXXXXXXXXXXXXXX **0.618XA (Stop Loss Limit)**

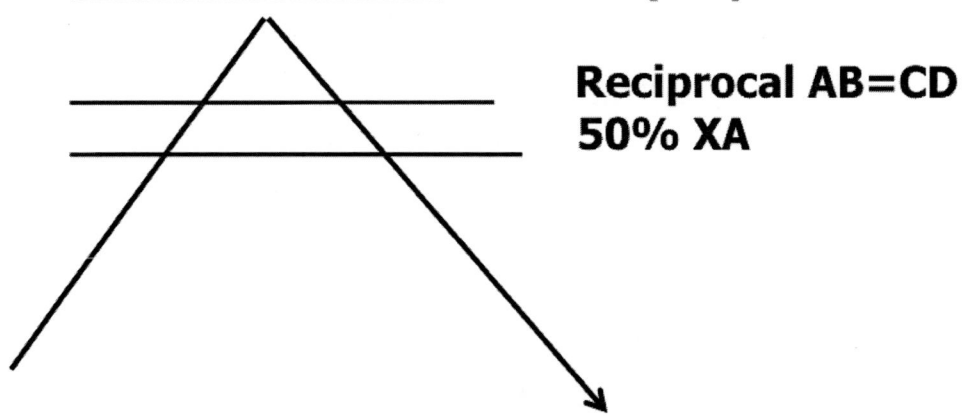

Reciprocal AB=CD
50% XA

Copyright Harmonic Trader L.L.C.

Harmonic Trading Volume 3: Reaction vs. Reversal

Gold ETF (GLD): 15-Minute
Bearish 5-0 Potential Reversal Zone (PRZ)

The following 15-minute chart of the GLD exemplifies the continuation nature of the structure. After an extended decline, the price action formed a distinct bearish 5-0 at the 134 level where the formation pinpointed the acceleration of the downtrend. The Reciprocal AB=CD was slightly below the 50% level which defined the Potential Reversal Zone for the harmonic resistance. The most important aspect of this example is to note the immediate effect that the resistance had on the price action. The inability of the GLD to trade above these levels was the first sign that the pattern was proving to weigh heavily on the short-term rally. After several hours of sideways consolidation in the zone, the price collapsed and accelerated lower.

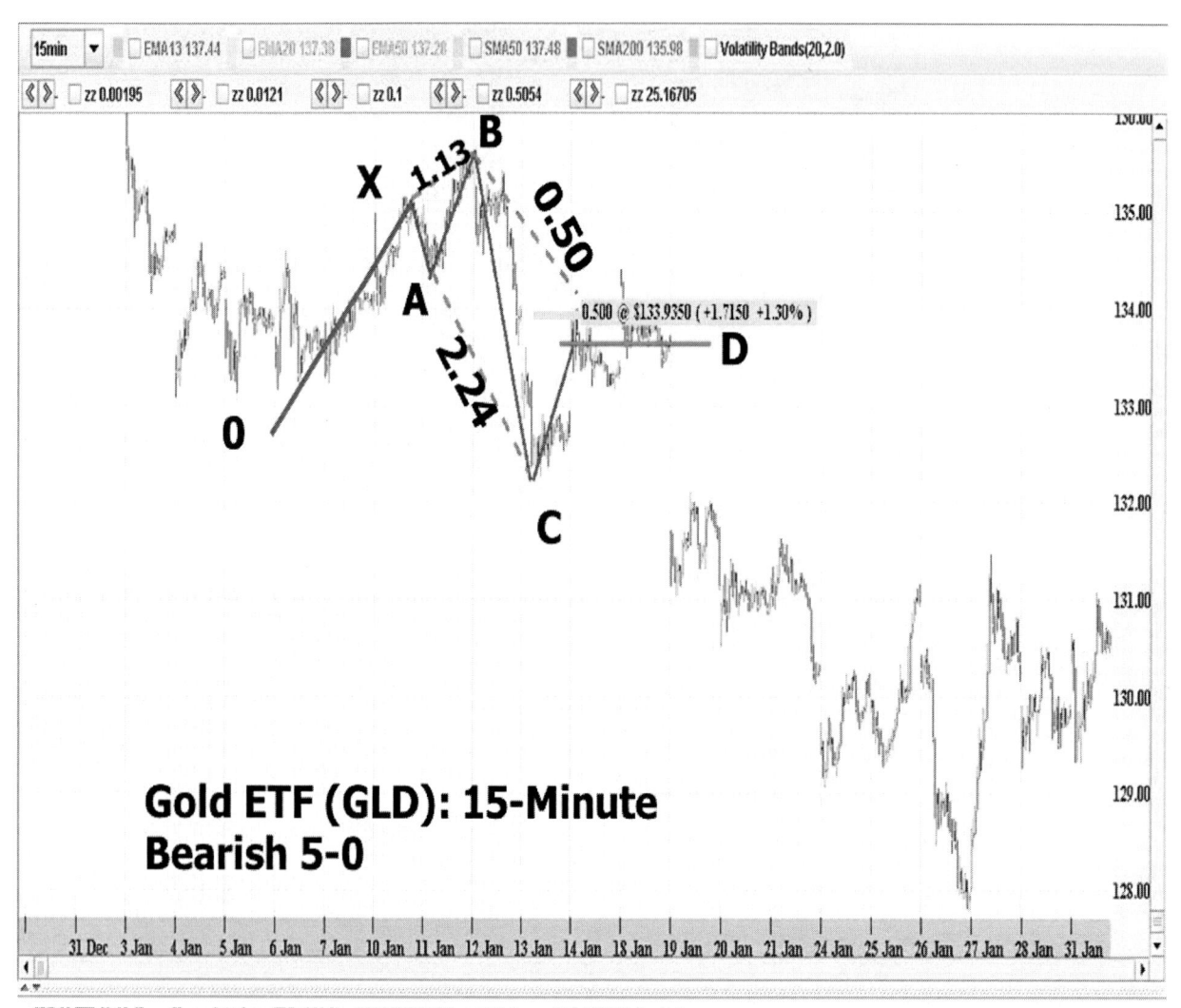

Harmonic Trading Volume 3: Reaction vs. Reversal

Gold ETF (GLD): 15-Minute
Bearish 5-0 Potential Reversal Zone (PRZ)

This type of price action is common in most harmonic patterns when the initial reaction seemingly stalls at the exact zone. Although these are early signals, the distinctive change in the character of the uptrend at the Potential Reversal Zone was quite clear. These situations are comprehended readily with experience but this type of price action should be closely monitored as an early sign of pattern validation.

Harmonic Trading Volume 3: Reaction vs. Reversal

Harmonic Head and Shoulders Pattern

The most famous complex price pattern is the Head and Shoulders formation. Technicians have studied this structure for decades. However, all presentations of this formation have presented various Zig-Zag definitions without any ratio measurements. I always found this application to be too vague for precise trading opportunities. Although I believe the pattern has merit, it is typically featured in well-chosen examples by those whom employ it in their chart analysis.

Over the years, I have experimented with various ratio applications in relation to its basic structural rules. The premise of categorizing Head and Shoulders formations based upon their proportional ratio alignment seemed sensible to me initially. Although I will not get into classic rules that were originally presented, my interpretation employs reciprocal harmonic ratio relationships of the formation to more precisely identify when these patterns are actionable trading opportunities. Much like the precepts M and W-type patterns, similar structures that possess varying measurements must not be treated uniformly. I found this to be true for variations of Head and Shoulders formations as much or even more so than harmonic patterns. Clearly, those Head and Shoulders Patterns that lack symmetry and structure are less reliable than the variations that possess clear harmonic relationships. In my opinion, the harmonic Head and Shoulders Patterns eliminate many invalid candidates and provide precise measures to analyze the completion of the opportunity. This will lead to less opportunities to consider but the harmonic ratio requirement will highlight these unique situations which are ultimately more actionable in terms of real executions.

Head and Shoulders Pattern analysis has marked an important step in the evolution of pattern recognition strategies within Technical Analysis. The vague interpretations and after-the-fact application have evolved to the point where other methods can complement the basic premise of the structure. Essentially, the pattern represents a trend failure where three unique pivot points market the sequential change in price action. Certainly, established Head and Shoulders Patterns can be effective in denoting important turning points within the larger trend. However, the application of harmonic ratios helps to pinpoint the exact completion – at the right shoulder of the pattern – where the final reversal will ensue. Furthermore, the ancillary stop loss and profit target consideration define the parameters of the situation more precisely, as the primary focus is to capitalize on distinct harmonic patterns and indicators that complement the area for the completion of the right shoulder.

I have held this belief for a long time that any technical strategy geared to providing an actionable signal must possess a definable limit as to when it is immediately validated. In terms of classic price formations, I have tinkered with various alignments over the years to create a definable means to validate structures as trading signals. In this book, I have gone to greater lengths to provide other classifications for states of price action during the trade execution and trade management phases. I strongly encourage Harmonic Traders to consider the importance of this degree of categorization as a means to handle any market environment. My emphasis with this detailed analysis is to ascertain the precise signals and termination points that outline all of the natural possibilities relative to harmonic levels that facilitate decisions throughout the trading process. Essentially, harmonic pattern requirements filter out many invalid opportunities that avoid random situations and follow only those that possess distinct formations. For the Harmonic Head and Shoulders Pattern, the application of proportional harmonic ratios eliminates random situations that may have previously been considered. The harmonic types are measurable and provide structural signals that complement the basic premise of what the Head and Shoulders Pattern encompasses.

Within Technical Analysis, pattern recognition strategies tend to be vague in their application. I believe any trading strategy must be able to measure levels uniformly and define requirement that pinpoint ideal opportunities. However, the real trading world frequently fails to follow ideal models. Whether we are analyzing wave structures, trendlines, wedges or simple support/resistance, there must be other considerations that signal when such structural analysis does not unfold as expected. Hence, structural trading techniques must be designed to anticipate situational realities that diverge from the ideal model. Harmonic Patterns provide the flexibility to anticipate pattern failures, especially when early price action fails to manifest individual confirmation at the completion of the structure. Although these filtering strategies may result in less opportunities, the definitive requirements that dictate valid complex harmonic situations reduce uncertainty. Furthermore, it is possible to pinpoint those conditions that adhere to only the requirements that validate a structure as truly harmonic.

In my opinion, the original rules for the Head and Shoulders structure lacked the precision to pinpoint exactly where pattern completed. In fact, the confirmation for the structure does not occur until the primary trendline has been violated. In addition, standard technical rules for the expected move project their respective targets well after the fact. The Harmonic Trading measurements can close the gap to precisely measure price pattern and/or critical harmonic ratio levels at the right shoulder to define an exact completion of the opportunity. In doing so, the Harmonic Head and Shoulders possesses clearer metrics and actionable levels based upon a projected completion for the structure.

Much like the specifications of the M&W formations, the Head and Shoulders structure must possess an exact alignment that validates these movements as a pattern. As I mentioned previously, the structure starts at the end of an extended trend. After forming an initial pivot point referred to as the *Left Shoulder*, the price action establishes the extreme low or high - known as the *Head*. Typically, the extreme price level will be a demonstrative if not volatile inflection point. The left shoulder and head typically are distinct in their formation and establish the foundation for the completion of the structure. The *Right Shoulder* must not exceed the Head within the formation and the expected retracement should reach the same price as the left shoulder pivot point. Although the interpretations of these rules can outline numerous possibilities, the structural principles provide a foundation to apply more precise strategies that validate these situations. Furthermore, the application of harmonic ratios at all point refine various structures into specific types in a precise manner. Most notably, the integration of such measures helps to make the Head and Shoulders formation a more actionable pattern closer to the reversal at the final pivot point.

Bullish Harmonic Head and Shoulders Pattern

The bullish pattern is commonly referred as an inverse Head and Shoulders. In the reciprocal application of Harmonic ratios, the two most important characteristics of the structure are that it should possess *Reciprocal Ratios* and ideal symmetry to distinguish these patterns. The extension that forms from the left shoulder to the head of the formation represents the primary ratio to calculate the ideal ratio for the right shoulder retracement. Earlier in this material, I reviewed the reciprocal nature of C points to the BC extension with AB=CD structures. The harmonic ratio at the C point establishes the ideal extension measure for the AB=CD completion point. In the Head and Shoulders formation, the Reciprocal Ration of the Left Shoulder extension defines the ideal Left Shoulder retracement.

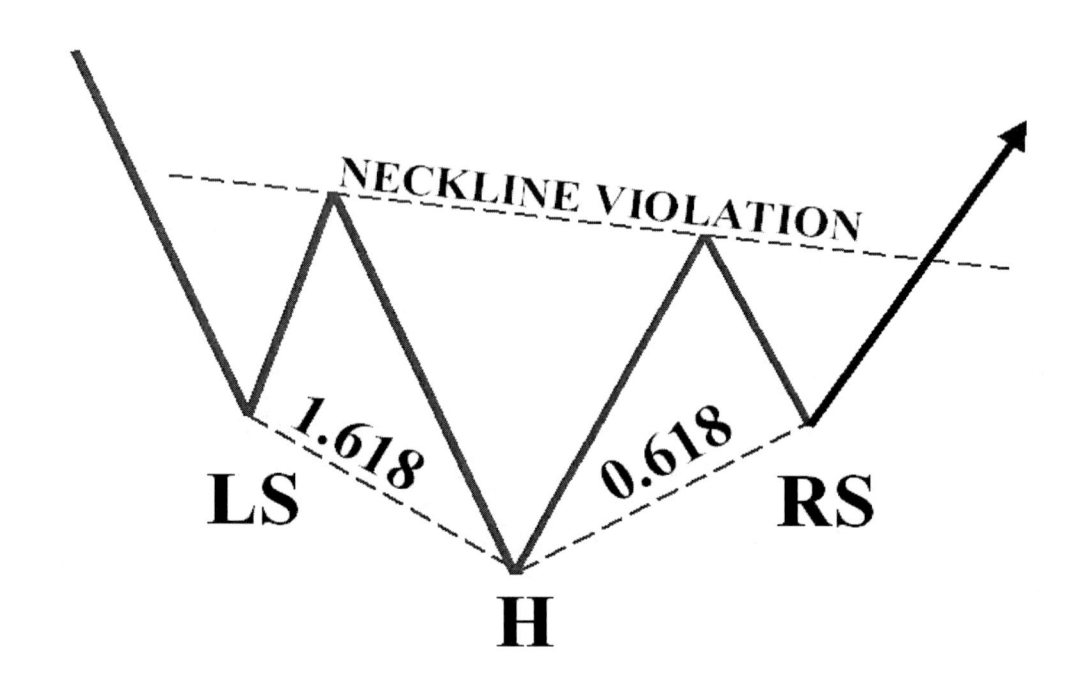

Also, it is quite common to see a bullish pattern form at the right shoulder retracement, which would signal a more complex harmonic scenario than a singular ratio. These are interesting situations that do unfold regularly but the most important aspect of the harmonic application to the Head and Shoulders pattern is to recognize only the clearest of structures with Reciprocal Ratios as valid trading opportunities.

Harmonic Trading Volume 3: Reaction vs. Reversal

Crude Oil (CL_#F): 5-Minute
Bullish Harmonic Head and Shoulders Pattern

The following chart in Crude Oil exemplifies the structure and proportion that a Harmonic Head and Shoulders Pattern must possess. In this case, the left shoulder defined a 1.41 extension at the head of the pattern and established the 70.7% retracement at the right shoulder to validate the proportion.

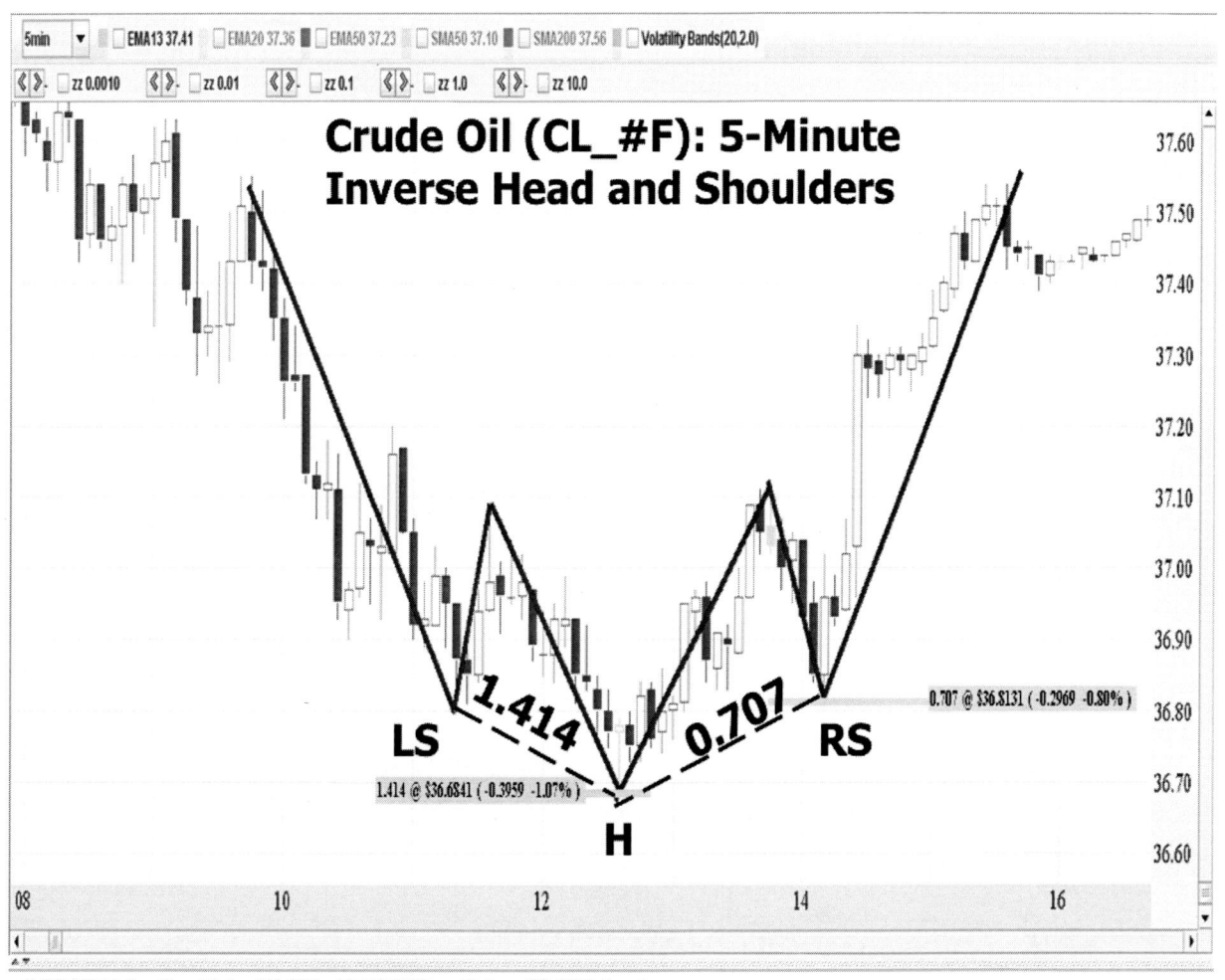

Harmonic Trading Volume 3: Reaction vs. Reversal

Bearish Harmonic Head and Shoulders Pattern

The historic dilemma with the Head and Shoulders pattern underscores a general frustration of ambiguity within Technical Analysis. For years, people have attempted to quantify exactly what the Head and Shoulders pattern really means. In my research, I encountered many individuals trying to outline Head and Shoulders patterns that simply did not possess the ideal elements as prescribed in the original interpretation. I believe that the pattern was presented in attempts to define a specific structural market environment. Although there is more to the pattern than the simple formation, I believe that its classification based upon precise ratio measurements is a leap forward in its application.

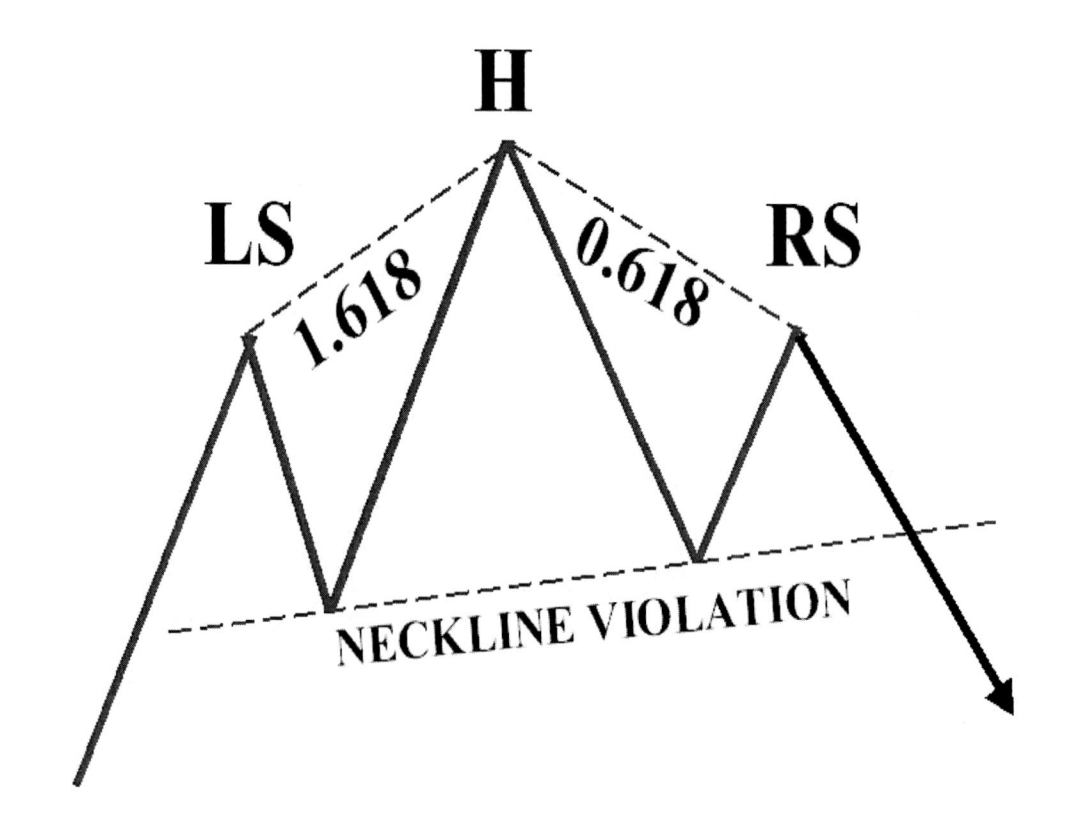

Harmonic Trading Volume 3: Reaction vs. Reversal

Australian Dollar/Swiss Franc (AUDCHF_A0-FX): 60-Minute Bearish Harmonic Head and Shoulders Pattern

It is important to note that the symmetry was quite ideal in this situation. Not to mention, the right shoulder of the structure possessed the reciprocal of the ratio exhibited by the left shoulder. The previous 60-minute chart of the Australian Dollar/Swiss Franc formed an ideal Head and Shoulders pattern but the execution of the opportunity was validated in particular due to the ratio relationship of each shoulder. Although these are simple advancements, I believe that any structural signal must be entirely quantifiable to be of actionable value, and these proportional ratio strategies can help traders employ this formation more effectively.

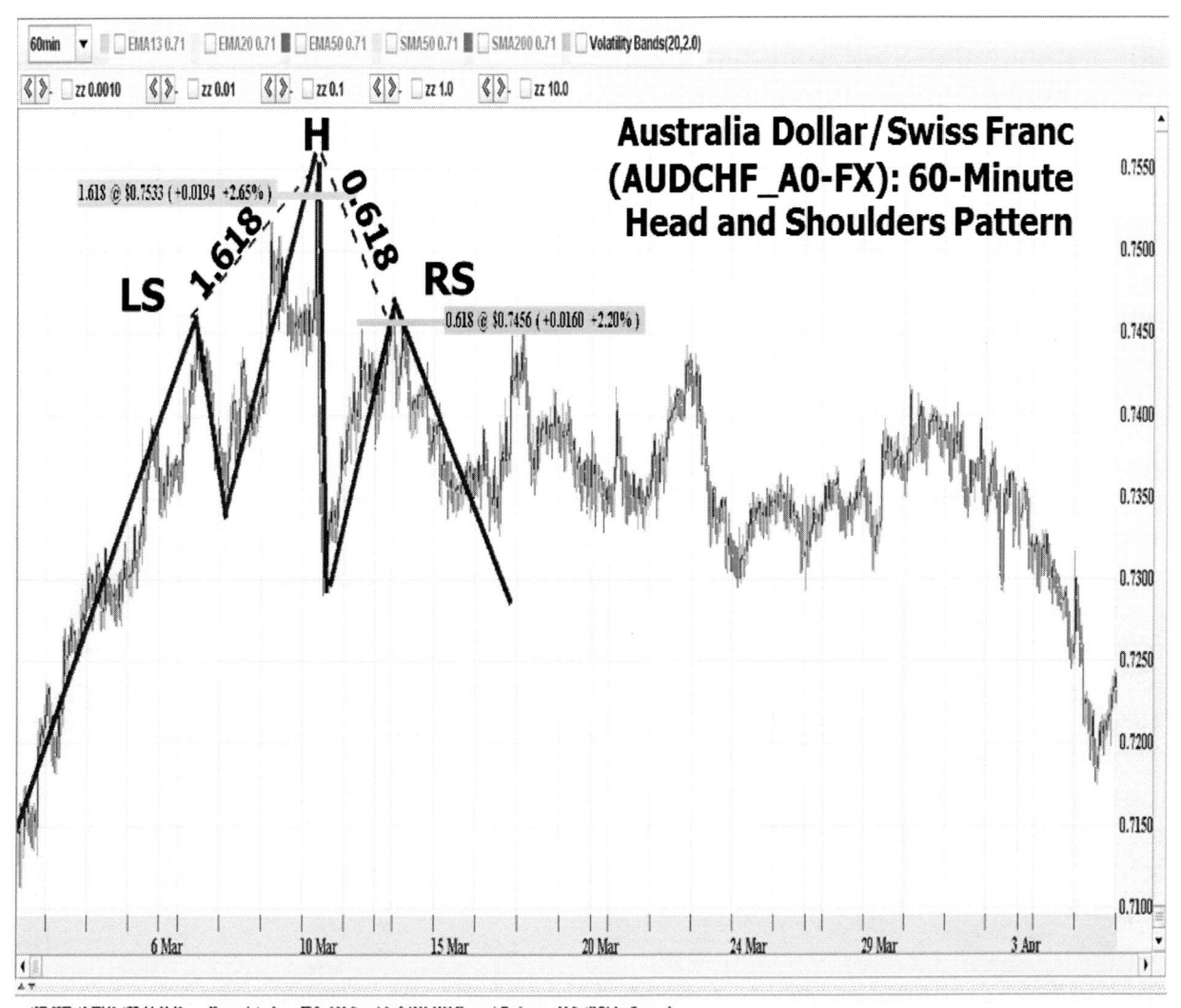

Harmonic Trading Volume 3: Reaction vs. Reversal

Standardized Harmonic Trading Identification Measurements Conclusion

Although I have discussed pattern identification rules in each of my books, I felt it necessary to present a quick review of all parameters that define these structures as Harmonic Trading opportunities. I purposely outlined the exact measures for each pattern to provide a thorough resource for traders to know what really constitutes a harmonic pattern OPPORTUNITY. Furthermore, I thought it was necessary to reinforce the realities of these patterns and emphasize the limitations of each structure. Of course, there will always be some allowance for real-world trading beyond measured objectives. However, these structures possess the requirements that denote what constitutes a harmonic opportunity. In addition, these structural conditions establish a standardized harmonic pattern framework.

A number of standardized identification measures have proven quite effective over the years in a number of types of structures. For example, the Shark and the 5-0 go a long way in analyzing those pattern possibilities outside of the M and W formations. Not to mention, the Harmonic Head and Shoulders pattern is another example of how simple measured relationships can provide greater technical information regarding the overall state of price action. For decades, many were aware of the phi (0.618/1.618) ratios as potential individual support/resistance. However, the application of this ratio never advanced beyond the simple measurement until they were incorporated into harmonic patterns. Their relationship as Reciprocal Ratios in Harmonic Head and Shoulders Patterns is another example of a more complex phenomenon at hand. Therefore, these advanced applications categorize price structures as unique technical entities are designed to convert recognizable phenomenon into actionable strategies.

The standardization of harmonic patterns is essential to defining what is truly a valid opportunity from a random structure. In fact, the current public perception seems to fail to understand the importance of following only those patterns that possess the proper measurements. It is critical to understand that these rules filter most invalid opportunities in advance. For me, these standardized measurements constitute my primary trading advantage and consistently provide a framework to facilitate decisions. Although I am continually analyzing structural measurements as precisely as possible, my fundamental assessment is based upon these harmonic identification standards first and foremost. In doing so, the basic foundation that harmonic patterns have provided is now the primary step within a larger analytical perspective that incorporates other critical measures of equal importance at the execution and management phases of each opportunity.

Chapter 3
Advanced Harmonic Trading Execution Strategies

Every trader must have a sound reason to enter a position. No matter what type of methodology is employed, all successful traders define those variables that signal opportunities consistently and reliably. Within the Harmonic Trading approach, we establish a variety of measured variables and readings that define states of potential price behavior. Harmonic patterns are one example that measures unique cyclical formations with prescribed ratios to consistently identify accurate price ranges for anticipated moves. This predictive ability is derived from a comprehensive measurement framework and an overall assessment of multiple conditions of the market. Applying proven strategies that can be statistically quantified, it is possible to identify market conditions when they manifest characteristics of complex models that have been historically substantiated.

In this book, I discuss a variety of standardized measures and general statistical expectations that help to establish the proper framework of expectations for any market environment. Most of the strategies presented herein are the result of refining multiple variables to uncover those situations that have yielded the most significant results consistently over time. In fact, it is one of the reasons why I have waited so long to present much of these concepts. In my own research, I tinkered with the initial foundation of many of these ideas for quite some time before optimizing all parameters of the opportunity. In this material, I will expand upon the existing foundation of strategies and present detailed research on exact situations within particular stages of the Harmonic Trading process. For this discussion, I am only outlining the most comprehensive relationships to outline complex environments clearly. Beyond pattern identification, the other stages of the trading process can be measured to complete the framework to define profit objectives and stop loss limits.

The Harmonic Trading execution strategies encompass a variety of considerations much the same manner that pattern identification rules define possible entry levels for trading opportunities. I consider the execution phase the most difficult skill set to master, as decisions are compressed within a relatively small time period. Although this challenge can be overcome through thorough preparation, the execution process typically experiences the greatest degree of human error. Therefore, successful navigation of the execution phase requires defined skill sets and confirmation signals that validate what the structural pattern measures are suggesting.

Harmonic Trading Volume 3: Reaction vs. Reversal

The execution phase starts with the confirmation of an anticipated price reaction from the completion of an established harmonic pattern. There are numerous confirmation strategies that can be employed but the best measures with harmonic patterns typically reflect a similar environmental reading to that of the price structure. One way to think about it is that an execution seeks to capitalize on the reaction to a particular technical stimulus – a catalyst that precedes the price move. The completion of a harmonic pattern can be considered as a type of technical catalyst. Harmonic patterns tend to define the natural limits of any price move, especially on the initial completion of the structure. Technical indicator readings such as Relative Strength or the Harmonic Strength Index that test their relative extremes at a pattern's completion point can effectively gauge intensity of a particular price move. As I will discuss later in this material, the primary objective of this integration is to isolate the parameters of both readings to define larger reversals versus minor reactions. The integration of harmonic confirmation strategies is the most essential consideration during the execution within a pattern's zone. In fact, all Harmonic Trading executions must include some combination of confirmed price action at the completion of the structure with a coordinated technical formation that confirms the pattern signal. It is essential to refine these situations further and categorize indicator readings to the same degree as harmonic patterns. Luckily, most of this work has been automated to isolate these complex situations, and it is possible to follow a number of generated signals that define those opportunities with the greatest potential in advance. The integration of price and environmental measures creates a clearer framework of expectations to guide trading decisions. Both harmonic patterns and indicator strategies are effective analytical approaches in their own right. In concert, they are vastly more precise and define a larger comprehension of market direction.

Expectations within the Harmonic Trading Process

I have always emphasized importance of measuring the market to define expectations. It is the only way to consistently guide trading decisions and have confidence in the actionable signals your analysis is generating. Furthermore, it is essential to consistently "get in the right ballpark" on most trades – that is, your analysis does not put you in situations where you get blown to pieces instantaneously. Although mistakes may be made, the overall facilitation of one's analysis must effectively identify opportunities with defined price parameters in advance. Although anything can happen in the market, a reliable trading skill set must include a clear understanding of various trading situational possibilities. Most harmonic patterns possess finite outcomes that in any situation fall into one of a few possibilities that guide trading decisions based upon probable future price action. When harmonic patterns are isolated, the parameters of the opportunity are well-defined – if not mechanical – where the decisions are based upon the interpretation of the price action at each respective level. In this manner, Harmonic Trading is a defined process with a specific procedure, and it must be treated as such.

The prescribed expectations that harmonic pattern instill is a critical element in the natural strategic advantage. The application of these expectations into actionable opportunities is more a matter of discipline as much as education. The trader must be prepared to take action according to the defined skill set of the harmonic pattern framework. Although a simple understanding of required actions at each step of the process will facilitate decisions effectively, there are essential considerations at each stage to successfully identify, execute and manage harmonic pattern opportunities. Each step possesses defined measures that distill infinite possibilities down to one or two clear causes of action. In fact, all harmonic measurements are designed to eliminate the impossible and focus on those finite possibilities within any situation. The simple understanding that all trading situations possess finite possibilities instills a degree of confidence by simply quantifying the unknown to a greater degree. Later in this chapter, we will examine the various strategies help explain these finite possibilities and clarify how this larger understanding of expectations can signal those flawed situations well in advance. Furthermore, this comprehension helps to limit losses by identifying those scenarios that are not exhibiting anticipated response.

Simply stated, if in doubt, get out! Those situations that do not provide clear structural levels and/or distinct confirmation immediately at the completion of a harmonic pattern opportunity typically signals a price structure that is unlikely to yield any measurable move. Although it is common for price action to nominally pause at these levels, the possibility to capture any degree of profit is muted. When those situations become obvious, the trader must exit the position at breakeven or with a small loss and be happy that they were smart enough to make the assessment of a flawed scenario rather than hoping it would work out. Again, we will address these strategies in detail but the general expectations of each step of the process are essential in optimizing trading decisions, especially when market conditions can easily create confusion.

The Harmonic Trading Process

The Harmonic Trading Process defines the step-by-step considerations that are faced during the identification, execution and management of a position. All methodologies must outline the specific conditions that validate an actionable trading opportunity. When it comes to harmonic patterns, the identification measurements that dictate the validity of the opportunity also are relevant in execution and management decisions. The most important aspect is that traders realize the entire scope of strategies at each stage of the harmonic pattern opportunity.

1. **Trade Identification Expectations:** The most important aspect of this initial step is to properly measure pattern structures with harmonic ratios to define the execution price range. For new traders, this may require a period of study to fully understand the individual measures of each pattern structure and how other confirmation methods can validate those with the greatest potential.

2. **Trade Execution Expectations:** As the shortest phase in the trading process, the execution of a harmonic opportunity must assess multiple factors simultaneously. The most important initial step is to identify exact pattern completion point – known as the Terminal Price Bar(T-Bar). Immediately following the completion of this price bar, the anticipated reversal must be demonstrative within a limited period of time. We will review this concept in detail momentarily but the Terminal Bar is an essential singular price point upon which secondary calculations can facilitate the analysis of price action and ultimately the execution of trade. Furthermore, confirmation factors must be coordinated with price action to gauge the actual real-world trading behavior against the model of harmonic measurements. We will discuss numerous scenarios that provide enormous insight to determine best opportunities later in this material.

3. **Trade Management Expectations:** After properly identifying a distinct harmonic pattern opportunity and coordinating execution confirmation strategies, the trade management parameters facilitate a defined understanding of what is possible. Throughout the management phase, it is imperative to employ the exact rules which instill the proper expectations maximize the handling of the position and minimize loss. It is important to note that there are clear strategic assessments that must be considered in advance before even executing the opportunity. Respective timeframes as well as specific price action must be analyzed to gauge the probable future price action. Although these strategies are not complex, they must be clearly understood to thoroughly understand the possibilities of the harmonic pattern opportunity.

Potential Reversal Zone (PRZ) Review

The Potential Reversal Zone (PRZ) is the founding principle of Harmonic Trading. The concept represents the ultimate technical premise by identifying opportunities based upon the market's own price action. Harmonic Patterns define clear price levels in such a manner, and can consistently pinpoint where to enter a position within a precise range.

Harmonic Trading is absolute in the nature of its classification of what constitutes a potential trade opportunity. In my opinion, 80% of all trading mistakes are made in the identification of a particular opportunity. I believe these are avoidable mistakes, as well. One of the most common errors is not identifying patterns correctly. Hence, the execution is flawed because the proper levels of support/resistance are not accurately measured. Although our harmonic pattern software has eliminated these mistakes, the recognition and understanding of the specific ratios and measurement strategies that constitutes a valid opportunity facilitates execution decisions. As I mentioned previously, the standardized rules eliminate flawed opportunities based upon a strict interpretation of harmonic structures to validate the execution. If the structure does not possess the required measurements and show signs of confirmation upon the immediate completion of the pattern, the opportunity is to be avoided. In most cases, the best opportunities do not unfold until well after a pattern has completed anyway.

This concept was one of the initial discoveries within the Harmonic Trading approach. Once identified, the potential opportunity is monitored until the price action tests all of the numbers in the Potential Reversal Zone (PRZ) to mark the official completion of the structure. These harmonic measurements create a price range to focus on and observe other affirming phenomenon in the same precise area as the completion of the pattern. However, one singular price bar does not define the entire trading opportunity, as the significance of Potential Reversal Zone highlights the critical area where to expect some degree of a reaction at a minimum. Within the PRZ, the critical focus occurs immediately after the pattern completion point - known as the Terminal Price Bar (T-Bar).

Terminal Price Bar (T-Bar)

The Terminal Price Bar represents a definitive interval of price action that marks the projected reversal area within the context of the relevant pattern that is completing. I outlined this concept in *Harmonic Trading Volume 1*. As most people already know, the Terminal Price Bar represents the exact completion of the pattern. Simply stated, the structure is only an actual trading opportunity at the completion of this data point.

If we consider all patterns as a collection of individual data points – which they are, we must be able to identify the precise set of trading history that is meaningful and material in the identification of a pattern's exact completion. In particular, the Terminal Bar represents an important advancement within the Harmonic Trading approach. The concept is more than a single price bar. Complementary strategies can be integrated at the completion of the Terminal Bar to confirm opportunities beyond the simple identification of patterns. The confirmation strategies effectively pinpoint the precise level for the execution. Other strategies such as indicator confirmation techniques, trendline analysis and time projections can facilitate harmonic pattern identification signals to an even more advanced degree. Regardless, the Terminal Bar concept is the most critical step tin the execution process with the realization that the identification of patterns is only a starting point.

The concept of ratio alignments and strict measurement classifications has advanced the general pattern concepts of the past, as Harmonic Trading has become known for yielding precise technical information as measured by the market's own movements. There are not many methodologies that even attempt to identify market moves in such an exact manner. As anyone who is really trading, the translation of ideas into profits involves some real-world challenges that require reliable information and clear predictive capabilities to define probable future direction for any position in the market. Every trader must know when to get in, have an idea how long to stay in the position, optimize the entry to minimize loss and maximize profit with proper management strategies.

> **"An ideal reversal usually tests all of the numbers in a Potential Reversal Zone (PRZ) on the initial test. The predominant trend usually reverses from this initial test of the entire PRZ and continues in the reversal direction shortly thereafter. In an ideal reversal, the price bar that tests all of the numbers in the PRZ is called the Terminal Price Bar(T-Bar)."**
>
> *Harmonic Trading Volume 1* pg. 185
> Scott M. Carney Copyright 2004
> Financial Times Press 2nd Ed. 2010

The concept of Potential Reversal Zone (PRZ) is the most important price range that is measured in Harmonic Trading and serves as the basis for most trading decisions. However, the Terminal Bar serves as the optimal price marker to determine the validity of the overall zone. Although this price range is relatively small within the total price history that comprises most patterns, the precision of focusing precisely after the Terminal Bar within this "window of opportunity" is another reason that Harmonic Trading is so effective. Such precise techniques outline the most important price levels within any trend.

For some, the Potential Reversal Zone (PRZ) takes time to integrate into existing trading strategies, as it certainly requires discipline to wait for a pattern's completion. However, most traders begin to comprehend the other important characteristics and distinct relationships that typically materialize within these ranges, providing substantial confirmation of the larger timeframe opportunities. For example, it is common for a Potential Reversal Zone (PRZ) to comprise only 3-5% of the total range of the pattern. Also, this finite range is frequently about the same amount with respect to time. It is in the commonality of price behavior in these situations that facilitates the analysis during the various trading phases, and defines consistent characteristics that provide early signals of validation.

Terminal Price Bar in the Potential Reversal Zone (PRZ)

I first discussed the concept of the Terminal Price Bar in my book, *Harmonic Trading Volume 1*. The principle of what the Terminal Price Bar represents has been a major step forward in the refinement of Harmonic Trading strategies to pinpoint exact price levels that represent significant change. Remember, the Terminal Price Bar is the price bar that tests the extreme range of Potential Reversal Zone (PRZ) – that is, the price bar that ultimately tests the final number been established price range.

It is very common for harmonic patterns to experience a degree of consolidation as the pattern completes. In these cases, it is common for the price action not to immediately test the entire Potential Reversal Zone (PRZ) and require some consolidation before reversing. In fact, the price action can linger for some time and then test the final number that defines the zone at the pattern completion point. In some cases, the price action will test all of the numbers in a single bar. These are the most ideal cases while more complex reversals benefit from such standardization by categorizing price action behavior at the completion of these opportunities.

Terminal Price Bar Tips

- The price bar that tests the last measured number of the entire Potential Reversal Zone (PRZ) is the official Terminal Price Bar.
- The T-Bar marks the price level where the pattern can be considered officially complete and look to execute immediately thereafter (T-Bar+1).
- The T-Bar can test the entire PRZ at one time or require some consolidation before testing all of the harmonic measurements.
- Acceleration in the anticipated reversal must be realized in the price action after the entire range is tested to validate a reversal.
- Assess the Potential Reversal Zone (PRZ) measurements closely in relation to the price action, particularly the relative AB=CD structure in comparison to the XA and BC calculation.
- Assess Confirmation Factors simultaneously with reversal progress in the PRZ.
- Price action must exhibit a change in "character" by expressing individual price action shortly after completing the Terminal Price Bar of the pattern that confirms the anticipated direction. For example, a bearish pattern must exhibit individual bearish price bars immediately following the completion of thr Terminal Price Bar as an early indication of some type of countertrend reaction.

Harmonic Trading Volume 3: Reaction vs. Reversal

Terminal Price Bar Psychology

The Terminal Price Bar concept fits into a framework where a valid opportunity must exhibit the required price action to confirm the structural price level. The signals that validate Potential Reversal Zones must exist to generate an execution and they serve as evidence for what the pattern is dictating. Although it can be a challenge at first to maintain the discipline to find situations and wait for them to complete, the ability to apply a predetermined plan is when a novice Harmonic Trader truly graduates to a professional skill set. Therefore, the associated psychology and expectations involved with the Terminal Price Bar create definitive limits, especially when a situation is not working out.

When the price action cannot confirm the anticipated reversal, traders must ask themselves whether or not they are correctly reading the signals the market is providing. Sometimes, traders fail to make the correct assessment and/or admit what is clearly happening immediately following the Terminal Price Bar as they lose sight of the individual importance of this price analysis in real world conditions. Of course, confusion can happen to everyone. However, the key is to continually improve your understanding of the significance of the Terminal Price Bar within the PRZ during the execution phase. As experience bolsters trading comprehension, the ability to capitalize on such information becomes easier and overall consistency is established.

The Terminal Bar psychology focuses on what is possible at all times. The mind must be in a constant state of possibility that seeks to optimize all decisions based upon the relevant signals that the market provides in general. The challenge can be if the trader ignores information that is presented in front of them. It is a common human error within the trading process but one that continually motivates the integration of acting upon the information presented by harmonic expectations to turn analysis into profits. When it comes to the Terminal Price Bar, we must think of this singular data point as the "Execution Light Switch" that turns the trade opportunity ON! Simply stated, the trade opportunity becomes valid immediately AFTER the completion of the T-Bar. In doing so, the expectations of the harmonic pattern and the relative confirmation strategies create a definable price range of predictable behavior.

Defined Trading Realm

Finally, it is important to note that it is only within this price range that these assumptions are valid. Beyond these price limits, the anticipated behavior must be considered incorrect and money management strategies must kick in to minimize losses. In this process, the trader is responsible for their actions and must handle situations accordingly. The trader's primary job involves this transition of measuring identifiable phenomenon and converting it into actionable and executable opportunities. Although this may be the single greatest challenge for all traders, the key is to analysis into action, and awareness is always the first step in any solution. If we are able to precisely measure all aspects throughout the Harmonic Trading process, it is possible to isolate those consistent factors that dictate success and limit failure. These measures can be compiled to create a Defined Trading Realm.

Any methodology that seeks to measure the market and find opportunities based upon specific measures is attempting to establish parameters that help quantify particular market movements as unique environments. Volume, Moving Averages, MACD and Elliott Waves are all examples of technical strategies that are attempting to measure unique situations in an attempt to define trade opportunities. Most of these measures are of no value on their own. However, they do possess some merit in combination with other considerations.

From a Harmonic Trading perspective, the most important focus is the price range of support or resistance as defined by the pattern. Beyond this, indicator analysis is the primary means of confirming the pattern at hand. The structural information provided by the measurements of the pattern define the entry for the trade and help ascertain the stop loss for the entire set up. All of these measurement strategies eliminate the impossible first and then define the remaining possibilities that can be considered. The Defined Trading Realm of harmonic measures provides this insight by establishing proper expectations and defining price objectives for each step within the process.

There must be a degree of clarity before any trade can be executed. That is, the position considered possesses overwhelming technical measures that clearly outline the critical price levels of the opportunity before its completion. Within the Harmonic Trading approach, we employ patterns to define price levels for identification, price action and indicator analysis for execution, and predetermined targets and trendline considerations to dictate management. Each step possesses specific price levels that are measured in advance that help to guide decision-making process. The Defined Trading Realm is the window of opportunity where all price parameters of entry, exit and stop loss targets are known in advance.

The Defined Trading Realm is important because it instills discipline regarding the measurement strategies to be as exact as possible, particularly in the categorization of price action. As soon as the Potential Reversal Zone (PRZ) has been established, the Terminal Price Bar marks where the pattern completes and the point where specific confirmation strategies must confirm what the structural signals are suggesting. Furthermore, the confirmation of multiple signals reduces the noise of the market to define only those situations with the greatest potential for profit – focusing more on reversals and less on reactions.

Defined Trading Realm Expectations

Throughout the evolution of my trading experience, I've come to realize that consistent success comes from a superior identification methodology that has been tested thoroughly and applied uniformly. Many people argue that certain individuals are naturally more gifted to be traders and others. I completely disagree with this and tend to argue that the application of one's methodology is what defines success. Although some people may be more adept at implementing a system of strategies, the general litmus test of success depends upon if the actions taken are inherently effective.

Most important, the Defined Trading Realm establishes a framework for expecting success. A well-defined trading plan that consistently proves itself instills a great deal of confidence and engenders an attitude of clarity. Many traders do struggle throughout their career as they try to find those strategies that can define opportunities for them. During this trial and tribulation, traders must focus only on those methods that can lead to the realization of consistent success. Quite simply, a trader who is not achieving success does not possess the proper measurement strategies to analyze the markets. It is imperative for those individuals to stop trading and take a hard look at what they're doing. If their methodology is not providing them the signals necessary to accurately decipher price action and define opportunities, the trading analysis is simply expressing a random and erratic state. And, random analytical strategies always yield random results.

Effective trading strategies must able to consistently define clear opportunities that can dictate the relevant expectations to predict probable future price action. Any measurement of price behavior can be rationalized to possess certain strategic value. However, all strategic trading measurements must possess an ability to be applied uniformly across all timeframes and markets in order to avoid making assessments based upon random price action. This is why the harmonic measures are so critical within the Defined Trading Realm. If a particular strategy is accurate, the anticipated trading opportunity should be clearly implemented and possess elements of a well-defined situation. The ability to recognize complex variables and understand these various types will clearly define what type of market environment must be considered relative to the pattern.

The proper expectation based upon accurate measurements creates a perspective of anticipation that is a required element of trading success. Although anything can happen in the financial markets, price action can adhere to cyclical and structural patterns that provide likely outcomes of projected circumstances. Moreover, complementary technical readings and other critical price measurements can enhance a specific scenario and confirm the prevailing expectations of what has happened.

Again, I must stress that these are valid points to consider but are only helpful to the trader if they are employed according to the prescribed expectation framework. For example, a trader may understand that a pattern will likely fail when the situation lacks confirmation or immediately triggers a stop loss but not react to take the action necessary to appropriately respond to the situation. This is a case when human error simply overrules the overwhelming evidence of the Defined Trading Realm. We'll talk about this later in the material but it is a primary conflict that all traders must overcome. The Defined Trading Realm provides the parameters to assess the opportunity but it is still up to that person to execute strategies and expectations the market is presenting to them.

Defined Trading Segments

When all parameters of the trade are defined in advance, the known outcome defines what I call a "Defined Trading Segment." These Defined Trading Segments are areas on a price chart where the anticipated outcome is quite clear. It could be the next obvious harmonic target or the Potential Reversal Zone (PRZ) of a pattern as the price action is completing the CD leg. All traders are trying to analyze charts to identify specific conditions that form over time and anticipate their fruition. Within the Harmonic Trading approach, measured situations frequently materialize where the targeted objectives are quite clear even when the possibility may seem remote. These defined segments help to clarify the predominant trend direction, especially when the parameters of particular harmonic pattern identify situations where only one possibility seems relevant based upon the structural and technical condition at hand.

The defined price segment is even clearer when the obvious price target possesses multiple technical readings converge in the same direction. These variables are effective, especially as the primary factor signaling reversals that determine which patterns are profitable and which are not. Essentially, these overwhelmingly clear situations are the result of a deeper comprehensive understanding that comes with experience. Most traders are able to understand various aspects of trading processes but when the advanced strategies are integrated to basic price measurements, these situations present an incredible opportunity to capitalize on clear technical signals.

I want to emphasize the importance of the correct expectations at each harmonic price level. In this book, I have outlined a variety of situations that detail likely scenarios based upon complex measurements. I want to take that a step further and stress the direct interpretation of each measure within the gamut of harmonic ratio measurements. The simple price measures unto themselves provide standardized assessments of what to expect. This was a new concept when I initially introduced it in *The Harmonic Trader*. However, I would like to further emphasize this concept and apply it across all harmonic measurement strategies.

Harmonic Trading is a great deal more than just simple measurements. These measurements constitute the elements of analysis that is derived from the structural signals the market forms. As I mentioned previously, these labels or categorizations may seem obvious but no other market approach has attempted to describe price measurement integration. In fact, each measurement serves as a building block of evidence to describe situation at hand. If multiple measures signal the same conclusion, these of the situations have greater probability of being realized than other less clear examples.

Bullish Terminal Price Bar

The price bar that tests the lowest measured number of the entire bullish Potential Reversal Zone (PRZ) marks the price level where the pattern can be considered officially complete. The price action can test the entire PRZ at one time or require some consolidation before testing all of the harmonic measurements. The most important aspect is the pattern is considered complete when the final number in the entire range has been tested.

Bullish Terminal Price Bar

- Bullish price action is realized immediately after the entire range is tested.
- Focus on the critical harmonic measurements in the Potential Reversal Zone (PRZ) - particularly the AB=CD and the XA calculations.
- Assess Confirmation Factors simultaneously with reversal progress in the PRZ.
- Price action should exhibit a change in "character" closing ABOVE the PRZ shortly after completing the Terminal Price Bar of the pattern.

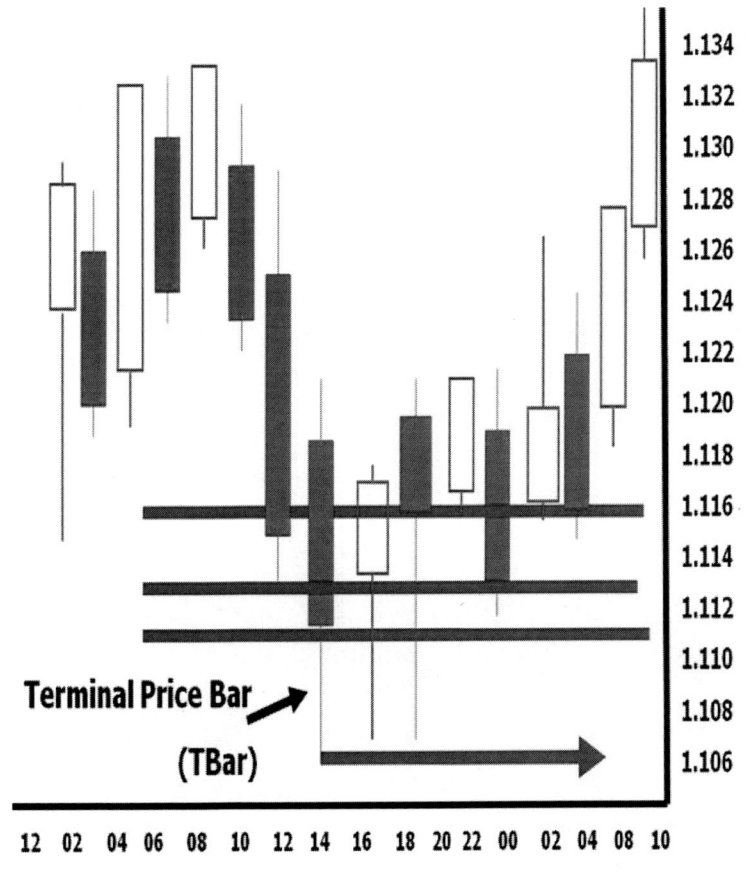

Copyright Harmonic Trader L.L.C.

Harmonic Trading Volume 3: Reaction vs. Reversal

Apple (AAPL): 5-Minute
Bullish Butterfly
Terminal Price Bar

The following 5-minute chart of Apple shows ideal reversal behavior at the completion of a short-term pattern. The price action formed a distinct pattern that defined the intraday completion point in the 306.50-307 range.

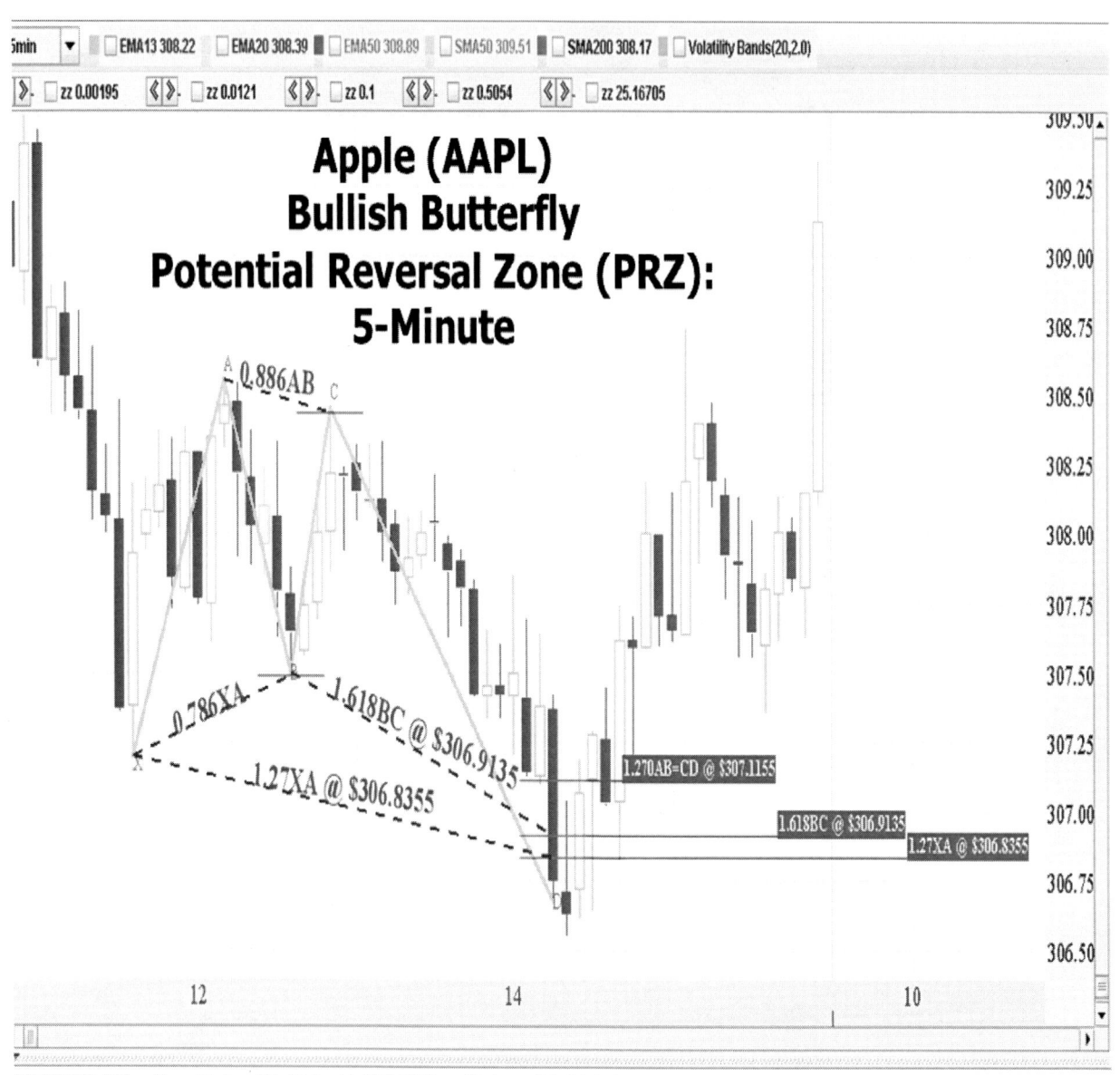

Harmonic Trading Volume 3: Reaction vs. Reversal

Apple (AAPL): 5-Minute
Bullish Butterfly Potential Reversal Zone (PRZ)
Terminal Price Bar

The following chart of the price action in the Potential Reversal Zone (PRZ) shows how the price action stabilized after a sharp drop as it entered the range of harmonic support. The Terminal Price Bar was established after testing the pattern completion point. The reversal rallied higher within three price bars after the pattern was complete.

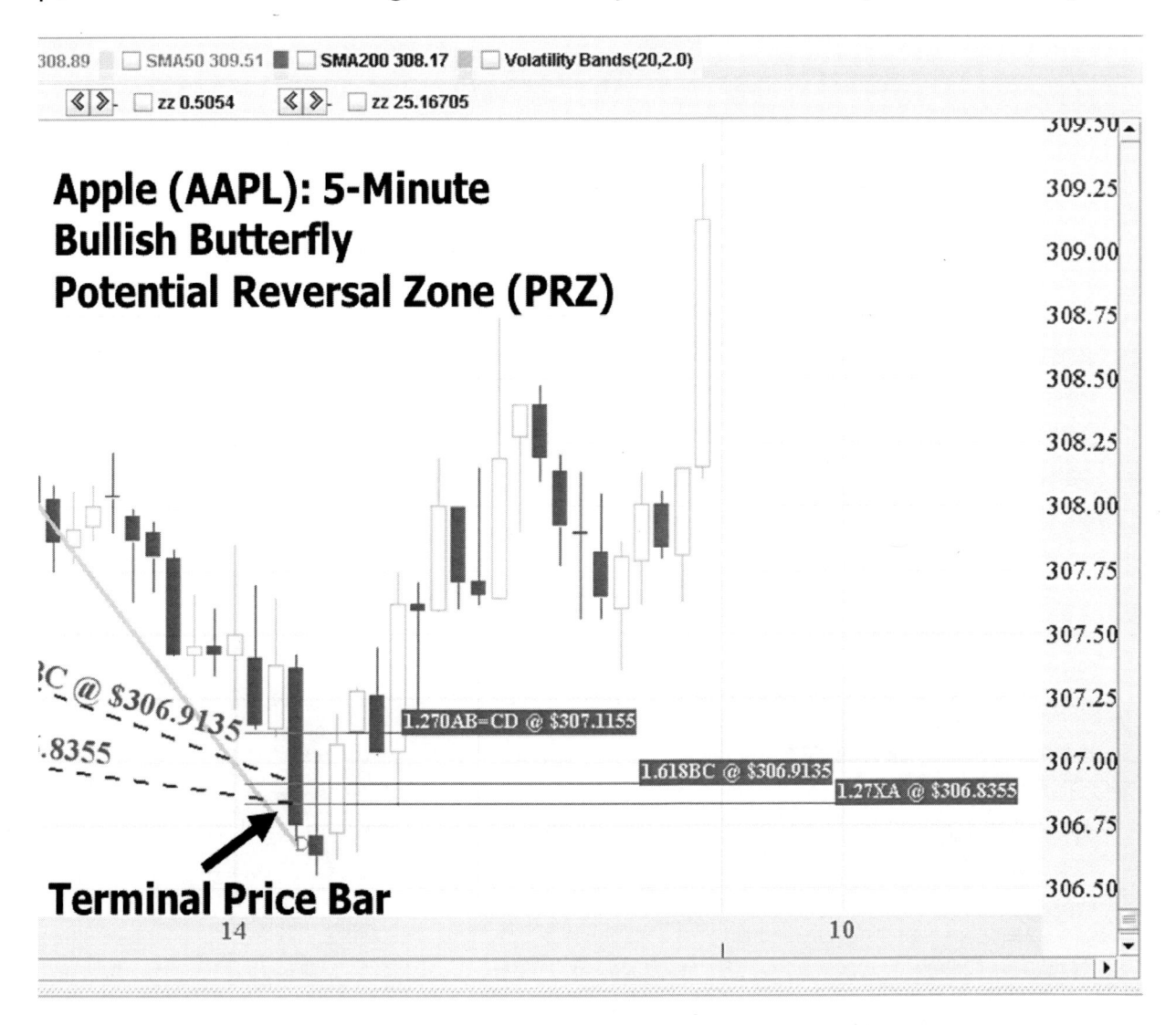

Harmonic Trading Volume 3: Reaction vs. Reversal

Bearish Terminal Price Bar

The Bearish Terminal Price Bar will signify the optimal resistance level to focus on within the overall zone. One important consideration as the pattern completes is the action immediately after completion of this individual bar. This requires close monitoring of the price action as it tests the Potential Reversal Zone. However, the reaction after this completes should be immediate. At a minimum, individual bearish price bars should begin to signal an early validation of the pattern at hand.

Bearish Terminal Price Bar

- **Bearish price action is realized after the entire range is tested.**
- **Assess the Potential Reversal Zone (PRZ) particularly the relative AB=CD structure in comparison to the XA calculation.**
- **Assess Confirmation Factors simultaneously with reversal progress in the PRZ.**
- **Price action must exhibit a change in "character" closing BELOW the PRZ shortly after completing the Terminal Price Bar of the pattern.**

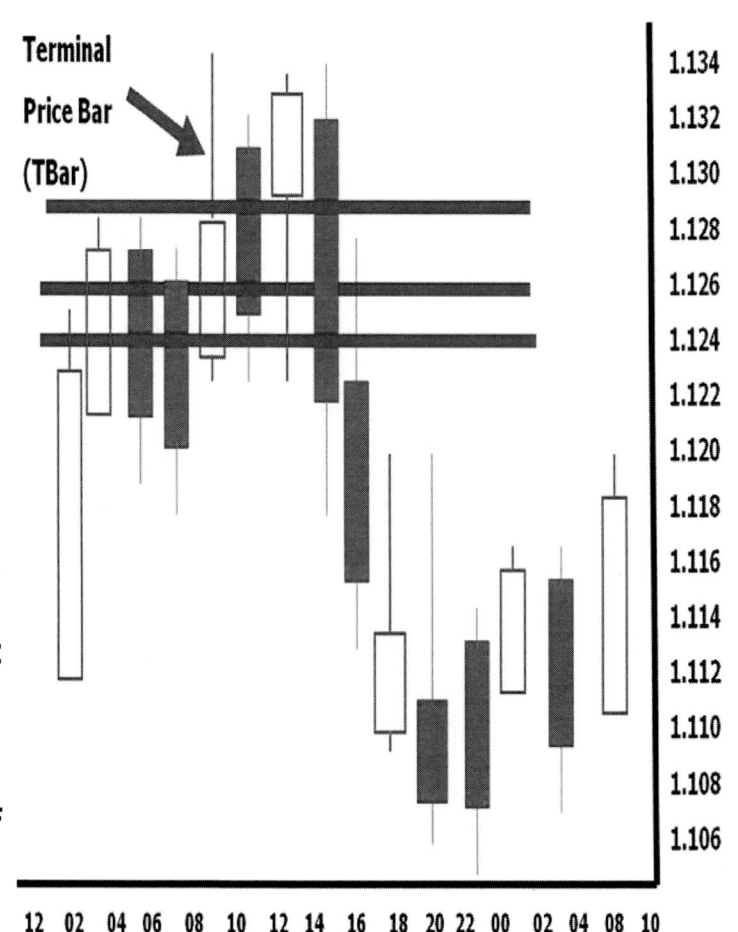

Harmonic Trading Volume 3: Reaction vs. Reversal

Swiss Franc vs. Japanese Yen (CHFJPY_A0-FX): 15-Minute
Bearish Butterfly
Terminal Price Bar

The following chart shows a distinct Bearish Butterfly pattern that completed on the 15-minute timeframe. This is an excellent example, as it shows a rather volatile reversal despite the distinct structure. The pattern completed in the 0.9285 area and stalled immediately after the Terminal Price Bar was well-established.

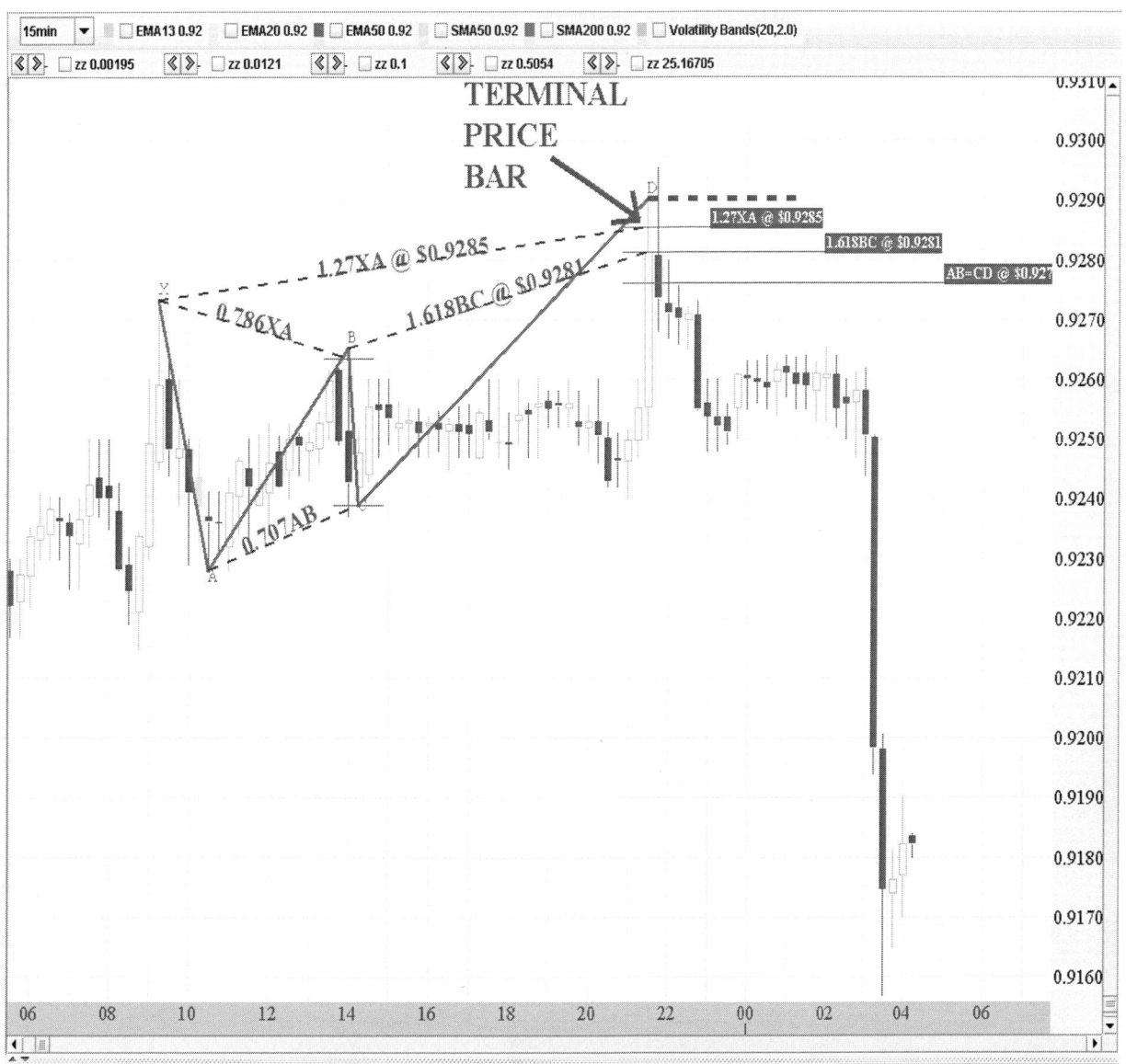

Harmonic Trading Volume 3: Reaction vs. Reversal

Swiss Franc vs. Japanese Yen (CHFJPY_A0-FX): 15-Minute Bearish Butterfly Potential Reversal Zone (PRZ)
Terminal Price Bar

The following chart demonstrates the importance of the Terminal Bar extreme to gauge how far price action can exceed a measured harmonic level to optimize executions and management. Despite the strong price action, the Terminal Bar pinpointed the exact level where to anticipate the reversal.

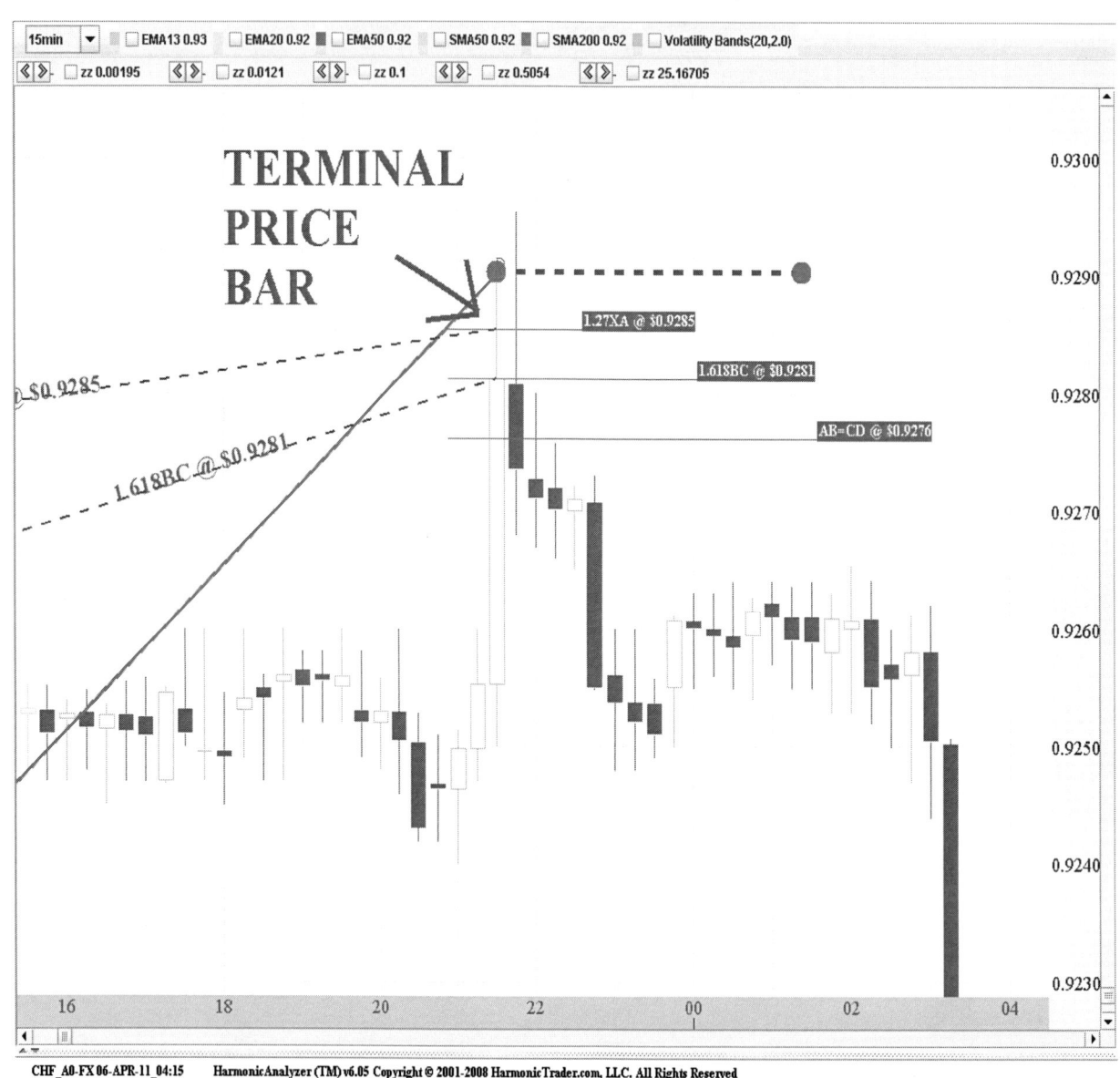

Harmonic Trading Volume 3: Reaction vs. Reversal

Terminal Price Bar (T-Bar) Overspill

I want to make a comment about the importance of assessing price action following Terminal Price Bar. It is quite common for the Terminal Price Bar to exceed the extreme of the Potential Reversal Zone (PRZ). Such price action can create some doubt regarding the ability of the pattern to mark an important reversal in the overall price trend of the market. The Terminal Price Bar is immensely significant in validating the entire price range where a reversal may unfold. The Terminal Price Bar typically sets the limit for any price action beyond the measured zone.

It is common for by section to exceed the Potential Reversal Zone (PRZ), especially on the initial test. Although there is some degree of what I refer to as technical "overspill" - the amount price has exceeded the ideal harmonic measured levels, this assessment is one of the most important considerations to consider at a pattern's completion point. Although harmonic patterns are quite precise, there will always be some degree of price action that exceeds the measured levels. The difference between the pattern's ideal entry point versus the extent of live trading that exceeded these levels requires skilled interpretation and confirmation strategies. It can be tricky to differentiate between price action that is clearly violating the projected completion point of a pattern versus a similar set up that requires a more consolidation beyond the Potential Reversal Zone (PRZ) before the entire scenario can unfold. However, the individual price action immediately following the Terminal Price Bar provides material information regarding how much room is permitted beyond the ideal calculations to determine the validity of any trade.

As I have discussed previously, I do believe the sum total of the all harmonic measurements offer comprehensive calculations of the natural trading cycles at hand. Harmonic Pattern measures converge at specific levels, outlining an "electrified atmosphere" where by price action uncannily reacts at the projected measurements and defined by harmonic zones of support/resistance. Once the Potential Reversal Zone has been established, the extent of the price action at the completion point validates the overall potential for the test of this structural level to yield a reaction or a reversal. The initial test of most patterns will yield a reaction at a minimum, as long as the individual price action immediately following the completion of the Terminal Bar and begins to shows reversal signs thereafter. The early action typically offers clues and frequently defines the validity of the trade. In fact, the Terminal Bar extreme creates an ideal integration of the PRZ measures to define a *permissible* price range to optimally execute the opportunity and optimize trade entries.

Permissible Execution Zone (PEZ)

After defining the official completion point of the initial test of a harmonic pattern, the realization of the trading opportunity begins. The assessment of the execution must occur quickly and in accordance with other clear confirmation signals. In fact, there are other important considerations beyond the price action of the pattern that must be assessed between the time the Terminal Price Bar has been established and a specific number of price bars thereafter. We must see price bars that confirm the pattern immediately following the completion of the Terminal Price Bar. For example, a bullish pattern that yields an initial reaction will typically consolidate after testing the pattern. Most reversals require a few individual bars to consolidate before any substantial move can be expected/. However, a few individual bullish bars after the Terminal Bar has been established would be considered as a vital sign of change within a critical harmonic zone. The changes within PRZs serve as the defining price behavior change to validate the structure well-before the resulting reaction is realized. As long as the price action changes course shortly after the Terminal Price Bar is established, the "reactive probability" of the pattern is increases with time. These small but significant signals happen repeatedly within the Potential Reversal Zone (PRZ) and help to define what I call the Permissible Execution Zone.

The area that comprises the Permissible Execution Zone is extremely small relative to the total size of the pattern. The PEZ represents an optimal range beyond the measured zone where a tolerance beyond the ideal levels attempts to pinpoint extremes with unique precision. The Permissible Execution Zone represents the optimal price range for a harmonic structure. Integrating confirmation strategies in these areas provides a few even more precise metrics within the larger price zone. These strategic measurements are designed to facilitate decisions during the execution stage of the trading process.

Permissible Execution Zone (PEZ) Tips

- PRZ+T-BAR Extreme = Permissible Execution Zone (PEZ)
- Potential Reversal Zone (PRZ) AND the extreme of the Terminal Price Bar identifies the ideal measurement area that accounts for the real-trading behavior within an acceptable tolerance beyond the ideal Potential Reversal Zone (PRZ).
- Improves Risk/Reward ratios by optimizing trading decision relative to current price action.
- Advances Harmonic Trading Execution Strategies from POTENTIAL REVERSAL ZONE (PRZ) to PERMISSILE EXECUTION ZONE (PEZ)
- Execute trades in this area STARTING AFTER THE TERMINAL BAR = T-Bar+1

The concept of the Permissible Execution Zone is the next level of optimization within the Harmonic Trading approach. Over the years, I have distilled a gamut of measurement strategies to pinpoint the most important measure cyclical areas that seek to minimize loss and maximize the. The Permissible Execution Zone reduces the entire trading process down to a precise window. The various readings at this exactly at this price level must dictate future possibilities that can be considered in any opportunity. The price history manifested here represents the definitive action for the larger trend.

Terminal Price Bar (T-Bar) +1

The most difficult aspect of any trade is the assessment and recognition of stop loss limit. Within the Permissible Execution Zone, stop loss limit could be comprised of two or three measures. Although most people know the standard stop loss limit as base upon the pattern measurement, there are other smaller factors that can be calculated that complement the Permissible Execution Zone relative to the stop loss limit. Again, the Terminal Price Bar serves as the initiating event in the Permissible Execution Zone. Sometimes, reversal can occur quickly while other situations may require greater consolidation. This is where the skills of the trader are required to be patient and wait for clear signs to confirm the scenario.

Permissible Execution Zone (PEZ) Psychology

The Permissible Execution Zone is the ultimate realization of the Defined Trading Realm. The ability to define and measure every stage of trading process provides price levels that guide trading decisions. All of these parameters must be determined before the trade is even executed. Realizing that the market can be measured in this regard instills a degree of confidence, as well.

There are many steps involved in the trading process. The identification principles within the Harmonic Trading approach are powerful enough to make any person feel as if they understand the market's movements. Problems can arise when variations of price action do not unfold consistently and a certain degree of doubt is instilled due to the inability to decipher price action. Or worse, Harmonic Traders fail to take action at the levels within the pattern framework. Regardless, the proper perspective realizes that opportunities are defined within this framework where prescribed strategies facilitate all trading decisions. Concepts such as the PEZ require that traders define price parameters in advance and validate trading executions based upon specific confirmation factors. Therefore, the criteria that dictate actions at specific PEZ levels guide executions to only those areas where the expected possibilities based upon the harmonic pattern at hand are outlined before the trade in entered.

Execution Triggers in the Permissible Execution Zone (PEZ)

The Permissible Execution Zone is determined by the Terminal Bar extreme and confirmed by RSI and/or HSI strategies that unfold in the same area. The various measurement techniques highlight valid execution zones when they complete within the defined harmonic area. The "execution trigger" is typically marked a distinct indicator extreme reversal that reacts in the same price level as the pattern at hand. The sequence of a pattern completion at the Terminal Bar is the final step in the identification process that establishes an immediate limit but the situation still requires a distinct indicator test within the zone to pinpoint the optimal entry. These technical readings typically unfold shortly after the Terminal Bar has completed and mark the precisely where the trade is to be executed. Once signaled, the management parameters instantly become the only considerations which include monitoring the price action relative to the stop loss and profit targets.

After establishing the Permissible Execution Zone, the penultimate signal before the actual trade will typically be some type of technical event that unfolds on the shorter timeframe. For example, a pattern that completes on a 60-minute chart will typically possess some type of concurrent signal on the 5-minute timeframe, providing early evidence of the larger reversal at hand. We will address these strategies later in this material, and such integration becomes easier with experience. The key is to measure all Harmonic Trading possibilities in advance. These parameters outline the tolerance limits permitted at harmonic levels of support and resistance to allow for real world trading action beyond the projected measures. However, the timely decisions required can be challenging in real-time situations, especially in short-term opportunities when the market is volatile.

Execution triggers in the PEZ do not materialize in every pattern formation. Although the lack of confirmation is a warning sign, it is important to remember that Harmonic Traders are responding to specific technical events and following the prescribed harmonic pattern framework that determines the ultimate execution entry within the Permissible Execution Zone. In other words, "No Trigger, No Trade!" In essence, the action of execution must be "triggered" by a "complementary indicator event" for the trade to be deemed a live opportunity. Harmonic Traders are responding to precise technical events within the optimized PEZ rather than simply guessing if a pattern will yield any substantial move. In this manner, the pattern's Permissible Execution Zone highlights the optimal structural support/resistance but the indicator confirmation in this area dictates the actual execution. Both assessments must express the same behavior at the measured area to define the strongest pattern candidates. This integration classifies the technical character among the phases of the Harmonic Trading process to assess price action relative to the expected outcome and stop loss, as long as the position remains in the trader's favor.

Harmonic Trading Volume 3: Reaction vs. Reversal

Bullish Permissible Execution Zone (PEZ)

The Bullish Permissible Execution Zone is extremely effective when harmonic support is exceeded beyond the ideal measures by the Terminal Price Bar, especially in extreme declines. The price action at the pattern completion point gauges how far to allow any further consolidation beyond the Potential Reversal Zone and the Terminal Bar extreme. This limit allows for those situations where the immediate test possesses strong price behavior but the harmonic pattern opportunity remains valid. Other confirmation signals can facilitate the analysis at this price level but the extra tolerance is extremely effective in optimizing executions and serves as the make-or-break harmonic support within the immediate trend.

Bullish Permissible Execution Zone (PEZ)

- **Assess Permissible Execution Zone (PEZ) established by the Terminal Price Bar extreme to define the beginning of the execution process.**

- **Anticipated reversal behavior must be exhibited immediately after the Tbar+1 unfolds.**

- **Analyze confirmation factors with respect to the defined trade parameters — Stop Loss, Profit Target and the measurements that define PEZ.**

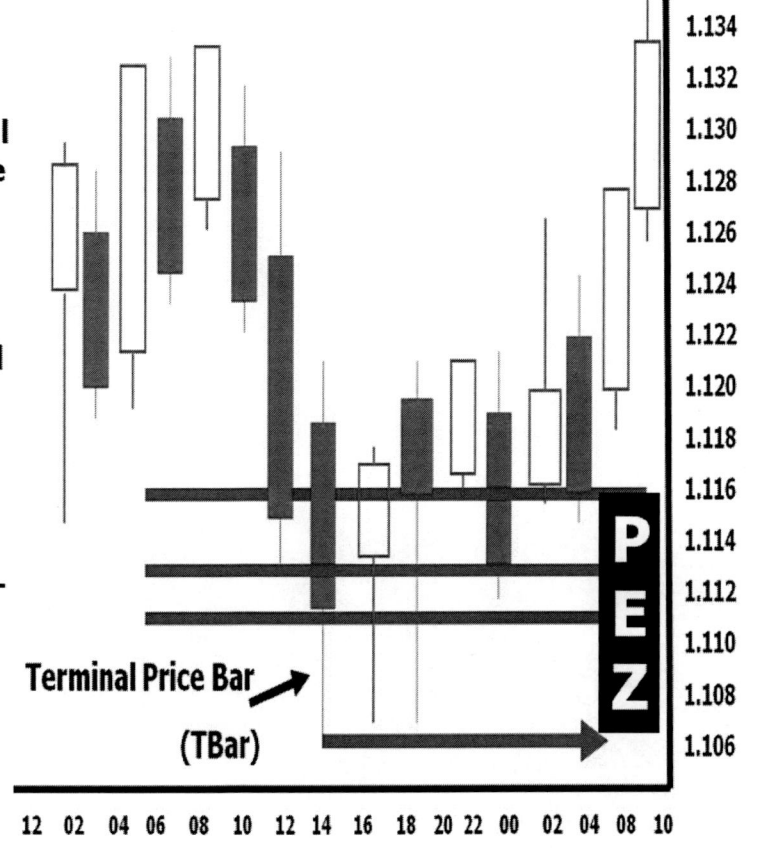

Harmonic Trading Volume 3: Reaction vs. Reversal

British Pound/Japanese Yen (GBPJPY_A0-FX): 60-Minute Bullish Deep Crab

The following chart examples of GBP/JPY possess a PRZ that defined support between the 155.70-155.15 level while the Terminal Price Bar exceeded this area on its initial test. This established an extreme low at the 155 level – 70 pips lower than the ideal support projected at the 1.618 projected. The nature of this price action beyond the ideal measure indicated a wider Permissible Execution Zone that optimized the entry below the PRZ. In fact, the price action was quite severe as it entered the zone of harmonic support. However, the price action stabilized immediately after testing the Terminal Bar was established.

Harmonic Trading Volume 3: Reaction vs. Reversal

British Pound/Japanese Yen (GBPJPY_A0-FX): 60-Minute
Bullish Deep Crab Permissible Execution Zone (PEZ)

The following chart of the price action in the Permissible Execution Zone reveals that the initial test nominally hit the stop loss limit but did not exceed this level. Remember, stop loss limits are assessed by standard measures but must be analyzed relative to the immediate action beyond the Terminal Price Bar. We will look at how to handle these situations a little later in the material but this exemplifies the optimization of real-world trading within the harmonic pattern framework.

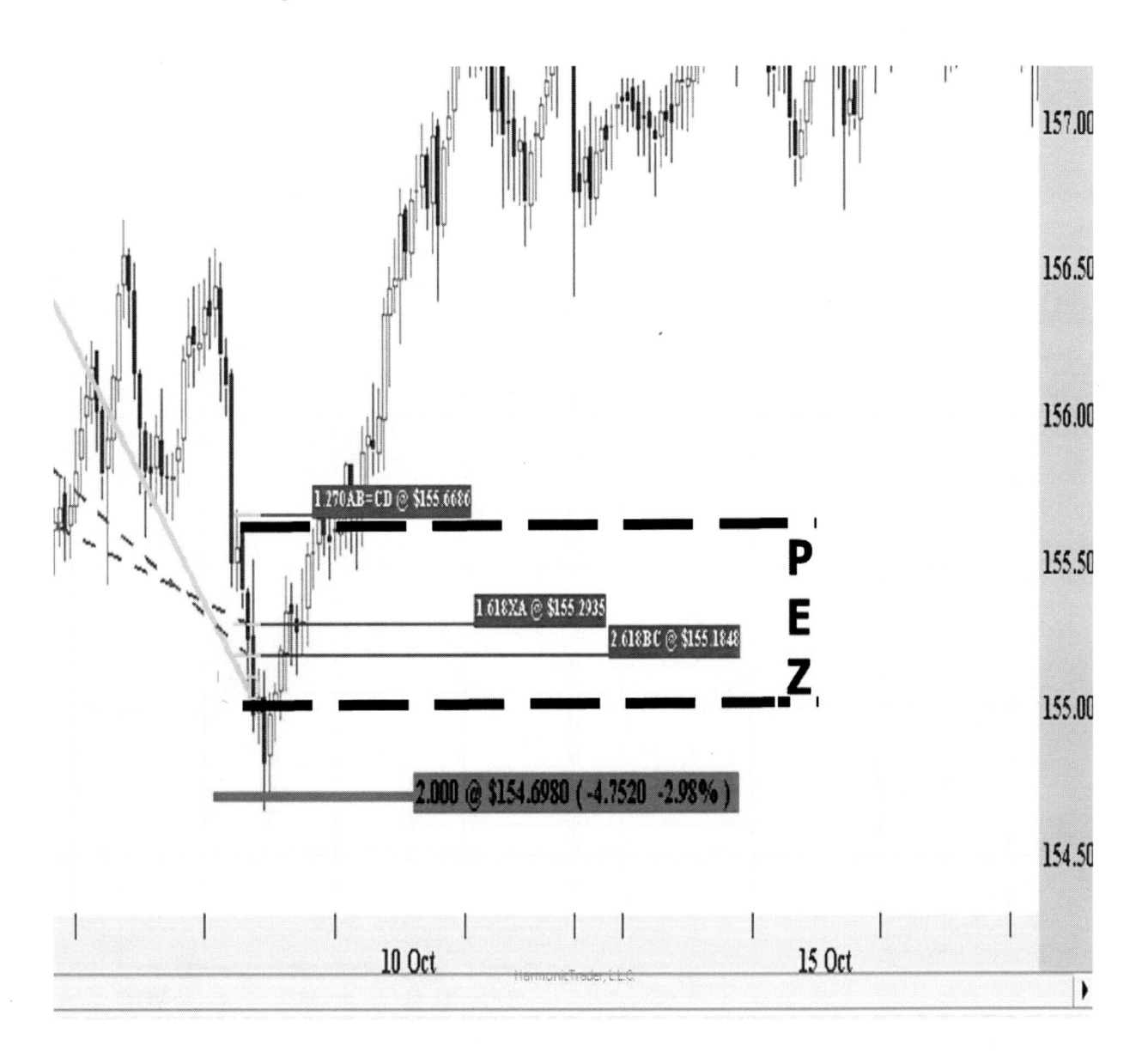

Harmonic Trading Volume 3: Reaction vs. Reversal

Bearish Permissible Execution Zone (PEZ)

Any assessment of the Bearish Permissible Execution Zone must focus on the individual price bars immediately after the pattern has completed. Harmonic resistance will be defined by the pattern's reaction as it enters the measured zone. A simple execution confirmation method is to wait for an individual bearish price bar as a means of confirmation within the consolidation in the harmonic resistance zone. These early price bar formations signal a larger move at hand. As experience develops, Harmonic Traders typically are able to execute based upon these confirmation strategies more readily, decisively navigating any market environment. As we review numerous examples throughout this material, it is important to note the immediate individual price behavior for confirmation to effectively signal valid trade entries.

Bearish Permissible Execution Zone (PEZ)

- **Assess Permissible Execution Zone (PEZ) established by the Terminal Price Bar extreme to define the beginning of the execution process.**

- **Anticipated reversal behavior must be exhibited immediately after the Tbar+1 unfolds.**

- **Analyze confirmation factors with respect to the defined trade parameters – Stop Loss, Profit Target and the measurements that define PEZ.**

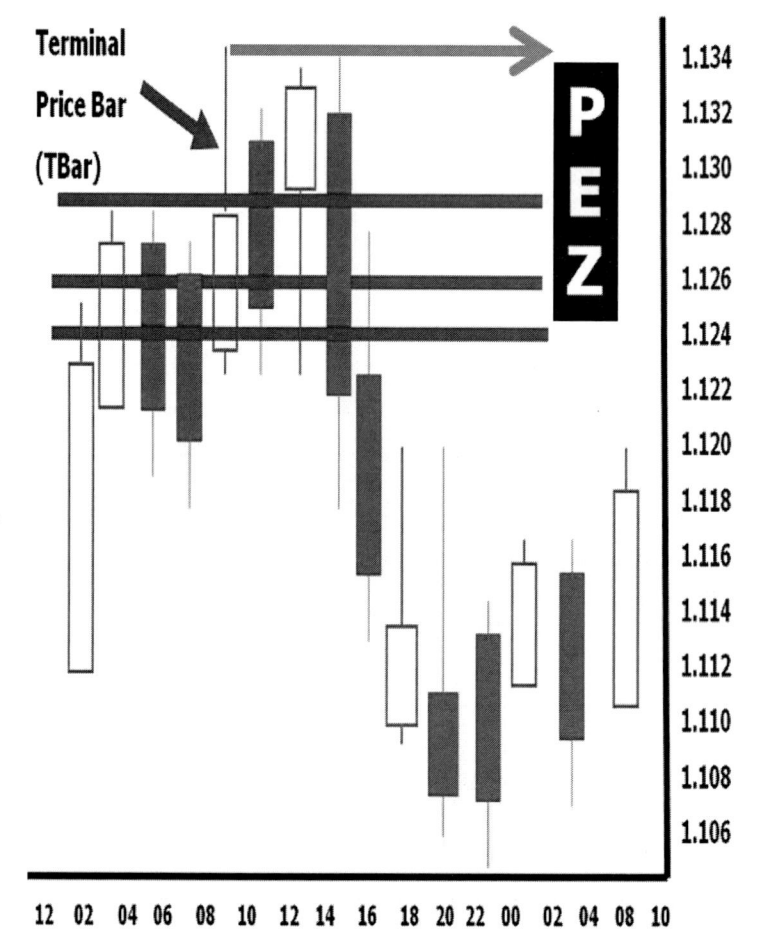

Harmonic Trading Volume 3: Reaction vs. Reversal

Australian Dollar/Swiss Franc (AUDCHF_A0-FX): 60-Minute Bearish Butterfly

The following chart of the Australian Dollar/Swiss Franc shows a distinct Bearish Butterfly pattern that manifested demonstrative reversal behavior at the harmonic resistance. Furthermore, the Terminal Price Bar slightly exceeded the Potential Reversal Zone on the initial test.

Harmonic Trading Volume 3: Reaction vs. Reversal

Australian Dollar/Swiss Franc (AUDCHF_A0-FX): 60-Minute Bearish Butterfly Permissible Execution Zone (PEZ)

The extreme of this price bar indicated that the immediate resistance should not experience much consolidation beyond the limits of the Permissible Execution Zone. The extreme of the Terminal Price Bar defined an extra 5-10 pips tolerance beyond the minimum limits of the Potential Reversal Zone. Therefore, the Permissible Execution Zone defined the acceptable tolerance of the real trading action to optimize the entry to favor an entry slightly above the measured levels. This trade defined the 0.9790 area as the ideal entry for the trade.

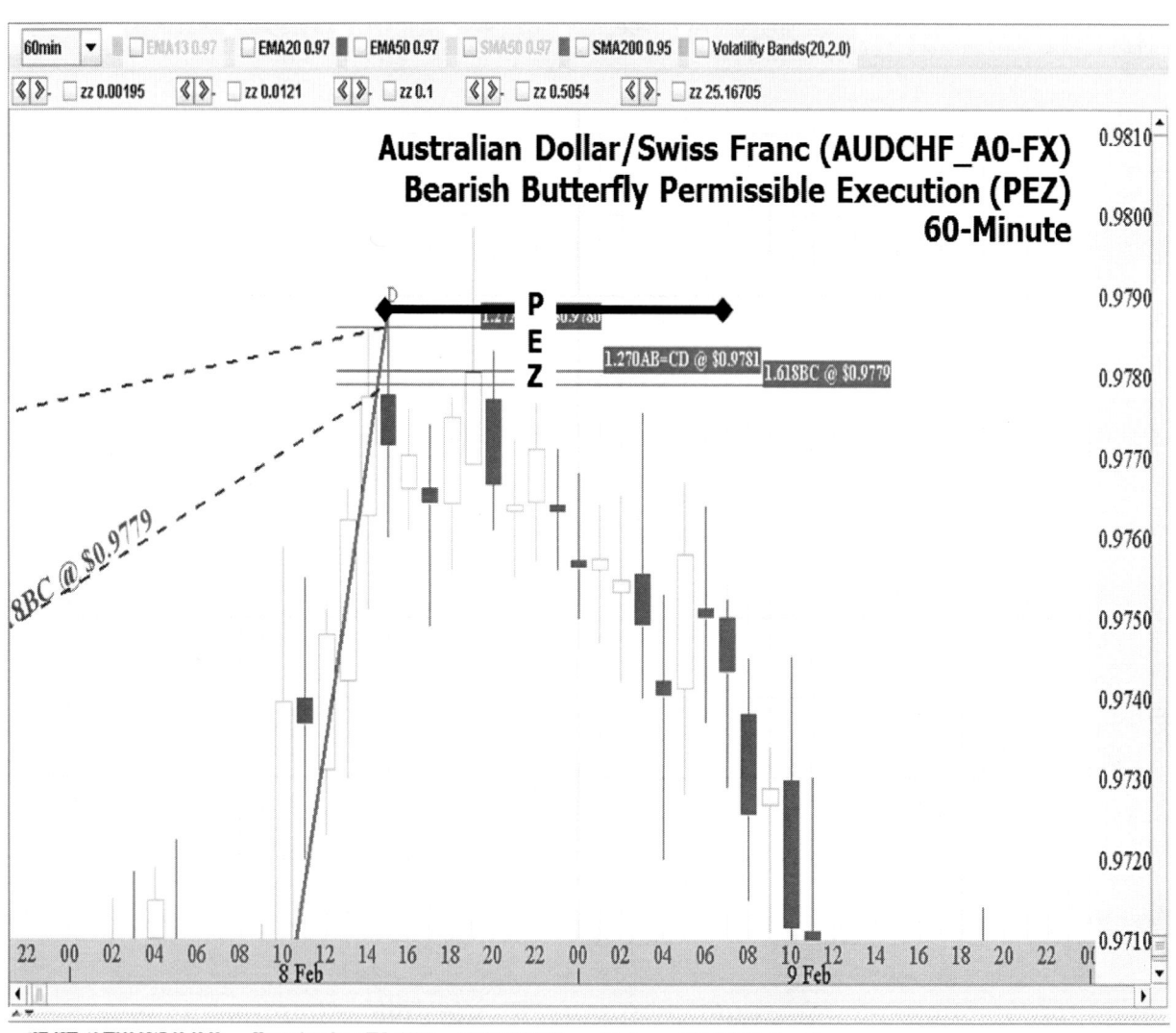

Harmonic Trading Volume 3: Reaction vs. Reversal

Advanced Stop Loss Considerations

All measurements within the harmonic pattern framework are directly related to each other and their proportional significance is often overlooked. The combination of ratios defines the natural limits of any price move, especially the relevant measures employed within stop loss assessments. The stop loss limits for each pattern are directly related to the ratios within the harmonic framework. For example, the Bullish Butterfly employs a 1.27XA as its primary projection to define the completion point of the pattern. If price action was to exceed this area beyond a 1.414, the ideal stop loss limit would be triggered and the pattern will be considered invalid. Stop loss limits are more of the general guidelines as they relate to patterns and may be integrated into trade management of the position differently depending upon the price action in the PRZ.

Standard Stop Loss Pattern Limits

Pattern	XA Ratio	Stop Loss Ratio
Butterfly	1.27	>1.414
Crab	1.618	>2.0
Deep Crab	1.618	>2.0
5-0	0.618	>0.618
Shark	1.13	>1.27
Gartley	0.786	>1.0
Bat	0.886	>1.13
Alternate Bat	1.13	>1.27

Harmonic Stop Loss Limits

The ideal stop loss ratio levels are dependent upon the Terminal Price Bar. The Potential Reversal Zone defines the price range for the completion of the pattern. Implicit within these measurements, the associated stop loss ratios that I have previously outlined serve as an essential management guideline in advance. However, the assessment of the real-world trading action beyond the ideal measures is an essential skill that must also incorporate the coordination of confirmation strategies to effectively optimize stop loss considerations. As with the identification rules for patterns, it is possible to define limits within Permissible Execution Zone that include the Terminal Price Bar to determine an appropriate stop loss limit. This is an important trading skill because there will be situations that require an active management approach to effectively handle volatile situations. There is no such thing as a perfect execution so that traders must be realistic

Harmonic Trading Volume 3: Reaction vs. Reversal

and understand that sometimes active market environments require dynamic adjustments to assess how price action is responding to the harmonic levels.

Terminal Price Bar Advanced Considerations

Over the years as I have refined the strategies, my focus has shifted from mostly an identification dominated trading approach where I spent most of my time looking for valid harmonic patterns to now mostly concentrating on the price action immediately following the establishment of Terminal Price Bar. The initial few price bars have enormous significance and the character of this action provides immediate insight into the nature of the pattern itself. The key is being able to know when to allow certain price action to consolidate in the general area of a completed pattern versus precise executions that require an immediate entry at the completion of the structure. In either situation, there will be a brief period shortly after executing the position where constant assessments of stop loss considerations and initial profit targets define the decision-making process.

Stop Loss Assessments

Many traders whom experience success early on and attempt to become more active trader and take on greater risk often begin to reach outside of their true level of ability typically will ignore stop loss limits as complacency sets in. The failure to employ stop loss limits in every trade is a quick road to disaster. At a minimum, this can lead to mistakes that impact trading psychology and overall confidence. The failure to maintain stop loss discipline is one of the biggest issues all losing traders face. Furthermore, those who are unable to integrate the Terminal Bar concept and stop loss assessments at the completion of harmonic patterns are typically those traders who do not possess the analytical skills required to selectively execute opportunities. Harmonic patterns that lack ideal structure or violate stop loss limits are to be avoided or exited quickly. It is always better to pass on any trades and only execute those that are overwhelmingly clear. When losses are encountered, the trader must go back and review the actions to assess the true effectiveness of their executions. In fact, it is only through such review that traders can realize the reasons for their mistakes and what needs to be changed so profit consistency can be achieved. Stop loss levels must be analyzed relative to the Terminal Bar to improve execution errors and correct the obvious mistakes while reinforcing effective trading habits.

This is particularly important within the Harmonic Trading management process. When price action does not unfold as expected, there will typically be clear evidence at hand of an impending failure. As we know, the most important consideration early in the reversal process is to assess how price action is unfolding beyond the Terminal Price Bar completion point. The management of the position depends upon the price action relative to the expected outcome based upon the harmonic pattern. All markets fluctuate from support to resistance and exhibit price behavior that changes in character based upon the relative position of the trend. The key issue for new Harmonic Traders is that they must distinguish the definitive conditions that dictate a reaction versus a reversal. When assessing a stop loss limit, it is common for price action to signal a failed harmonic level early into the reversal. Again, this depends upon the Terminal Price Bar as it tests the Potential Reversal Zone (PRZ) to establish the tolerance beyond the ideal measured level but price action that exhibits decisive continuation will signal a flawed opportunity. Sometimes, it is prudent to wait for these individual signals before even considering an execution. However, the most dramatic failures can be avoided easily. These situations unfold once the Terminal Price Bar exceeds the Potential Reversal Zone and fails to yield any considerable constructive individual price action in the anticipated direction of the new trend. We will look at some warning signals in the PRZ in this material but the obvious signs of price action must be respected.

Bullish Terminal Price Bar Failures

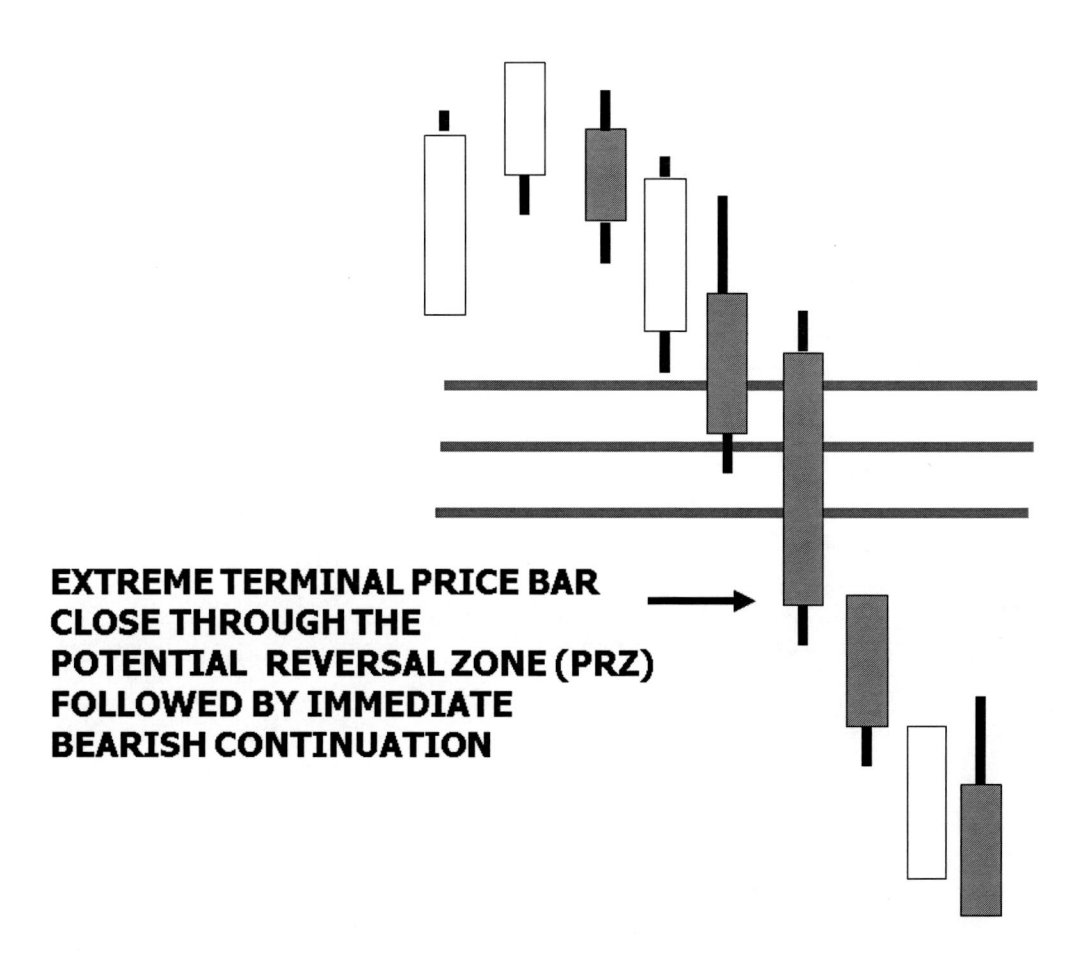

EXTREME TERMINAL PRICE BAR CLOSE THROUGH THE POTENTIAL REVERSAL ZONE (PRZ) FOLLOWED BY IMMEDIATE BEARISH CONTINUATION

Once price action establishes the Terminal Price Bar, the immediate continuation frequently signals an immediate failure. In the bullish case, any price action that continues in the direction of the downtrend should signal a potential failure at hand. The immediate bearish continuation should at least delay the execution until further confirmation can be established.

Australian/Canadian Dollar (AUDCAD_A0-FX): 5-Minute Bullish Butterfly Terminal Price Bar Failure

The following example of the Australian Dollar/Canadian Dollar shows a distinct Bullish Butterfly that declined through the Potential Reversal Zone and continued lower immediately after the Terminal Bar completed.

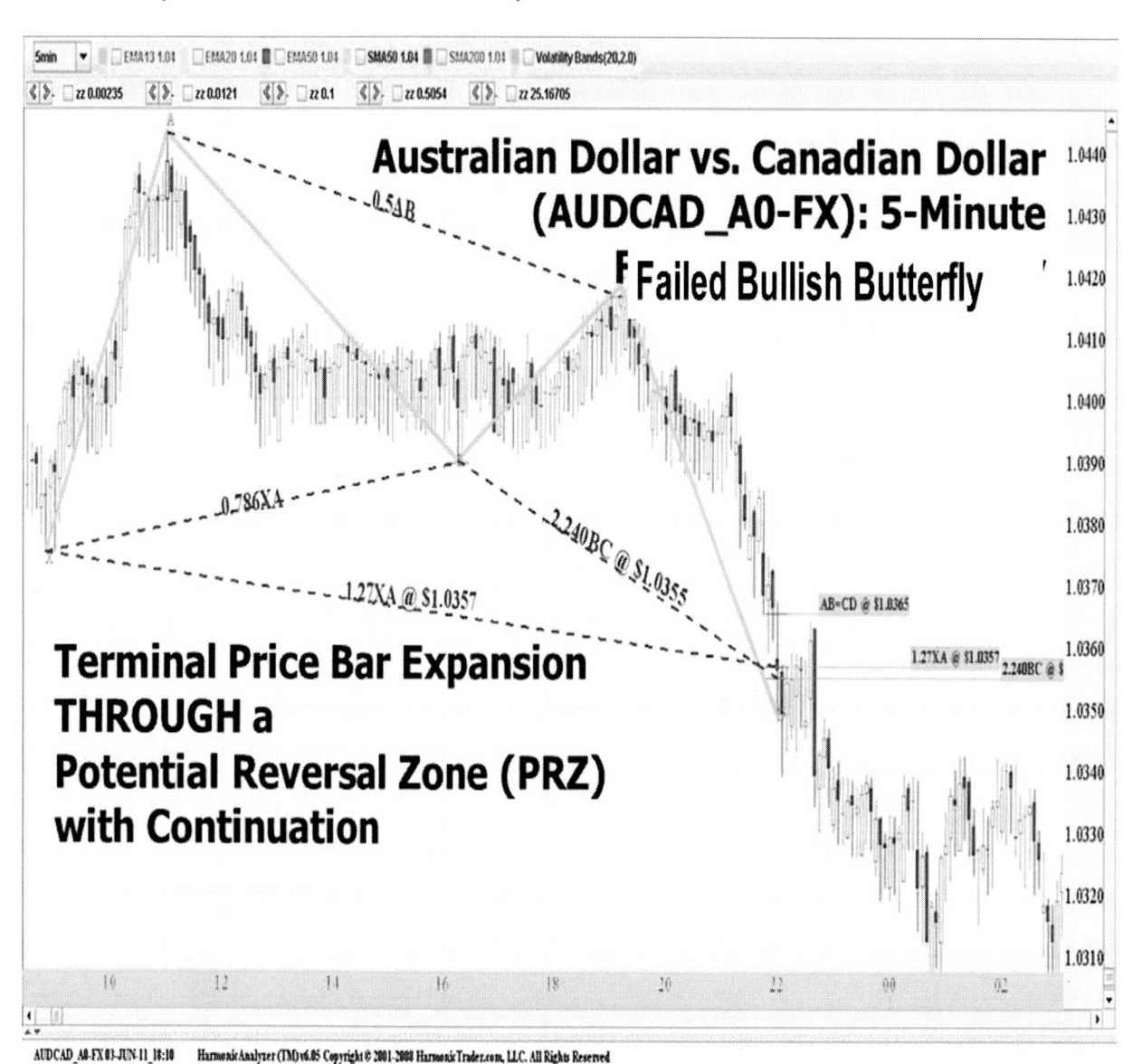

Harmonic Trading Volume 3: Reaction vs. Reversal

Australian/Canadian Dollar (AUDCAD_A0-FX): 5-Minute
Bullish Butterfly Potential Reversal Zone (PRZ)
Terminal Price Bar Failure

At a minimum, the stop loss should be adjusted to protect against dramatic drawdown or break even if possible. The goal at this point in the trade should be to limit risk, especially when the individual price action violates the Terminal Price Bar and continues in the direction of the predominant trend. The following chart of the price action in the Potential Reversal Zone that clearly shows how the harmonic support was violated, provided a brief consolidation and ultimately failed shortly thereafter.

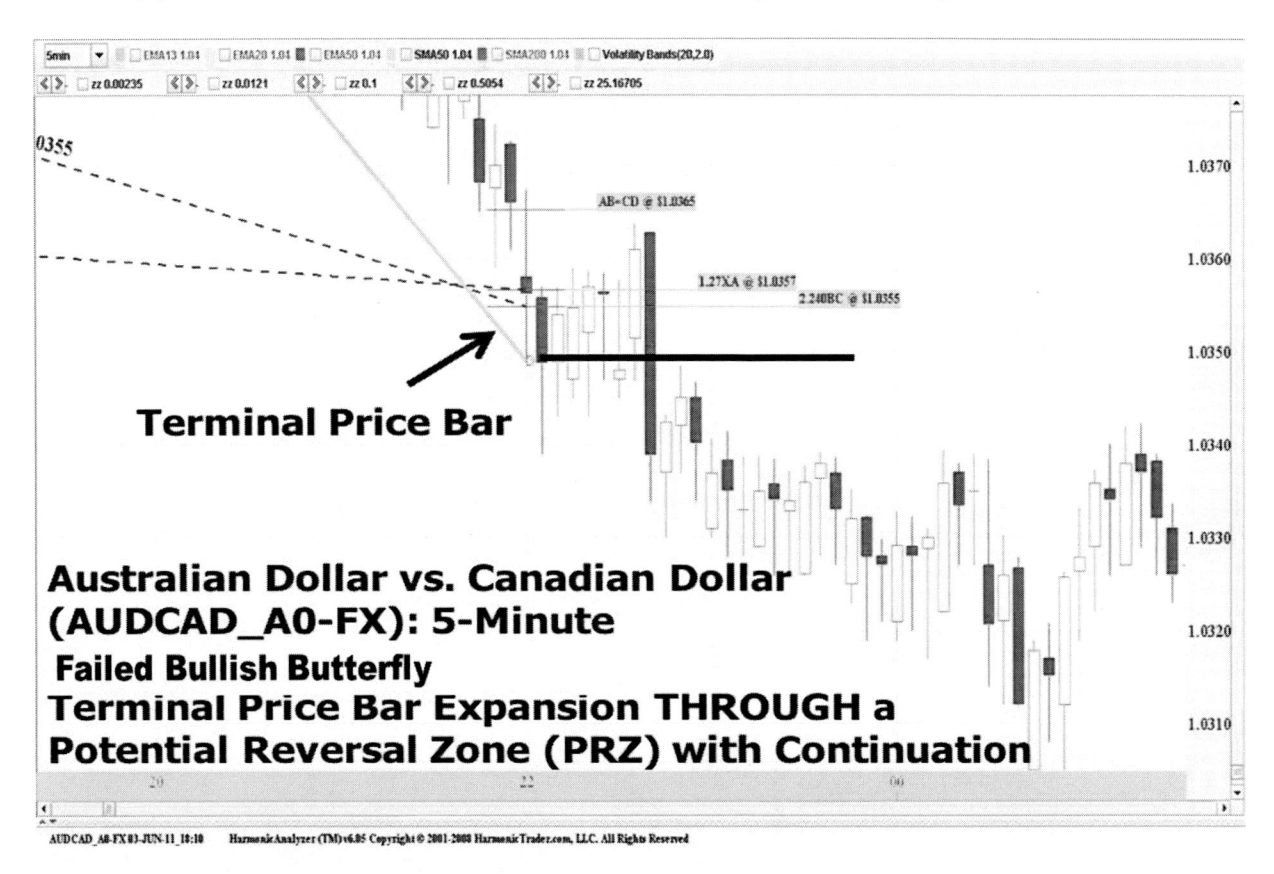

Australian Dollar vs. Canadian Dollar (AUDCAD_A0-FX): 5-Minute
Failed Bullish Butterfly
Terminal Price Bar Expansion THROUGH a Potential Reversal Zone (PRZ) with Continuation

We will look at how to handle these situations precisely with confirmation strategies to facilitate this analysis. However, the simple price action character exhibited overall weakness as the predominant trend continued lower following a nominal reaction beyond the Terminal Price Bar. The ideal support zone was measured between 1.0365 – 1.0355 on the following 5-minute chart. The Terminal Bar extreme defined the Permissible Execution Zone below this area at 1.0350. The execution of the opportunity favored the price range below the harmonic support. Even with this extra tolerance, it was clear that the price action was not responding and violated the Terminal Price Bar shortly after testing all the numbers in the PRZ to confirm the failure.

Harmonic Trading Volume 3: Reaction vs. Reversal

Bearish Terminal Price Bar Stop Loss Considerations

One of the primary challenges all Harmonic Traders face is to gauge the extent of the real-world price action beyond the ideal Potential Reversal Zone. The structural signal does possess a definitive completion point where the character of the price action must change. However, an immediate continuation beyond the Terminal Bar signals a flawed opportunity at hand.

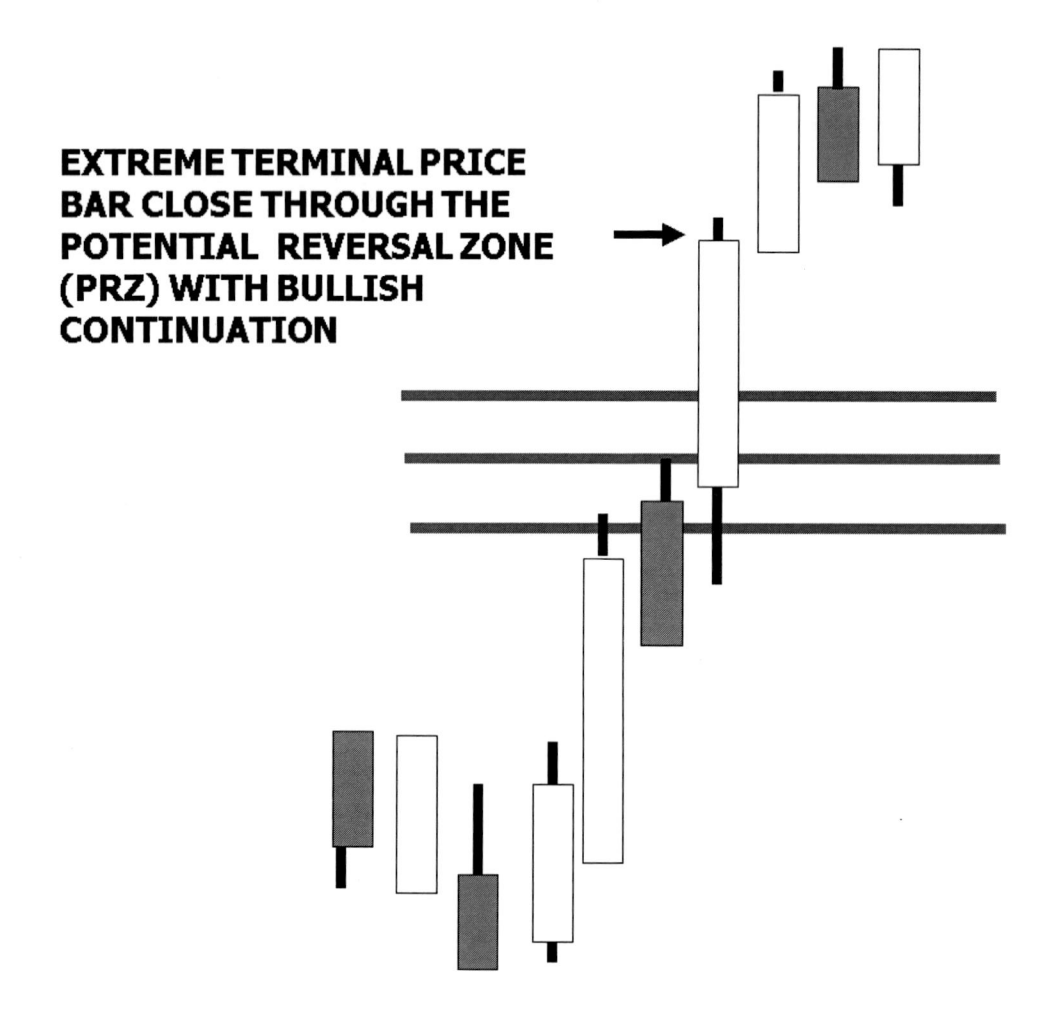

EXTREME TERMINAL PRICE BAR CLOSE THROUGH THE POTENTIAL REVERSAL ZONE (PRZ) WITH BULLISH CONTINUATION

Harmonic Trading Volume 3: Reaction vs. Reversal

U.S. Dollar/Japanese Yen (JPY_A0-FX): 5-Minute
Bearish Gartley Terminal Price Bar Failure

The following chart shows the strong price action at the completion point of the Gartley pattern. The Potential Reversal Zone (PRZ) defined the 80.25 area as critical short-term harmonic resistance. The price action traded through this zone as it completed the Terminal Bar, and continued higher, immediately negating the bearish pattern.

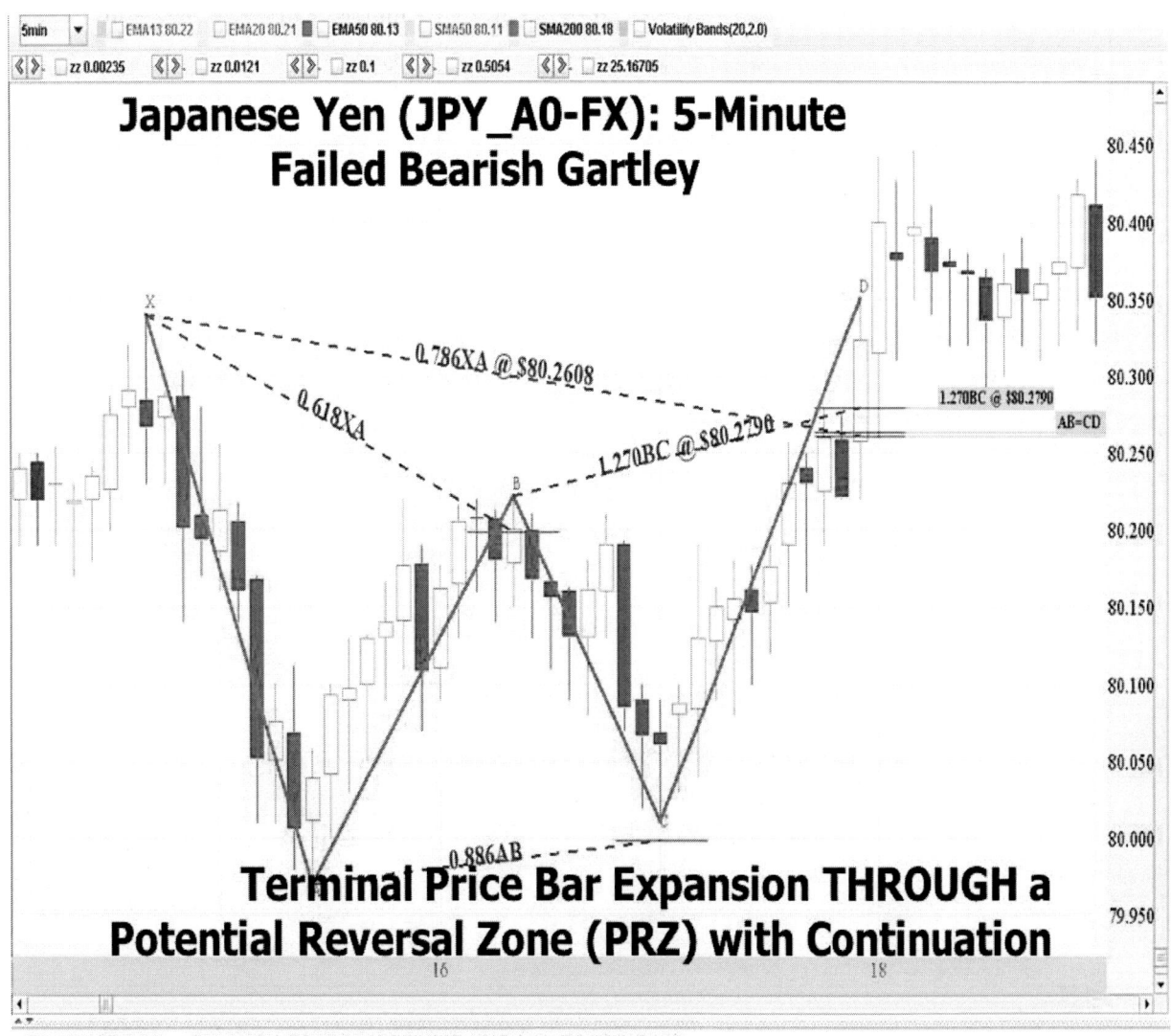

Harmonic Trading Volume 3: Reaction vs. Reversal

U.S. Dollar/Japanese Yen (JPY_A0-FX): 5-Minute
Bearish Gartley Potential Reversal Zone (PRZ)
Terminal Price Bar Failure

The failed Gartley in the US Dollar/Japanese Yen only required 10 minutes following completion of the Terminal Price Bar to demonstrate its strength. The peculiar aspect of the Terminal Price Bar in harmonic patterns is that it will exhibit extraordinary behavior beyond the norm to signal a flawed level of resistance.

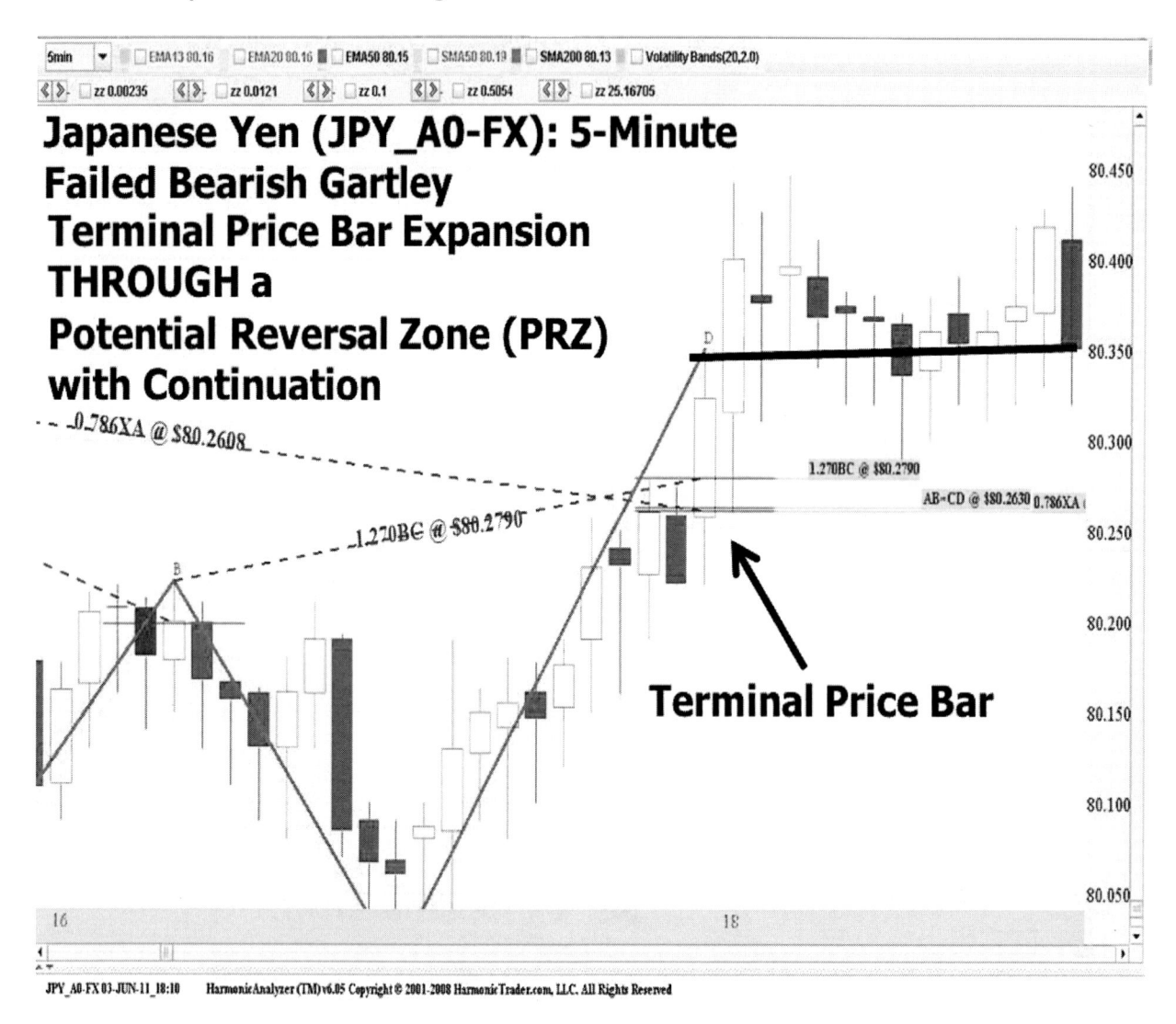

As we outlined in the chapter on trade execution, the price bar following the completion point of the pattern is where we begin consider the validity of the opportunity. However, any immediate continuation in the direction of the predominant trend will signal a delayed execution at a minimum. In this case, the price action rallied

Harmonic Trading Volume 3: Reaction vs. Reversal

sharply and never gave a chance to even confirm the reversal. It is also important to note that in most valid reversals there will be a brief consolidation phase to varying degrees before the reversal can ensue. Any immediate action beyond the Terminal Bar that fails to express countertrend behavior represents a warning of failed reversal at hand. The key is to monitor the position as the pattern completes and execute only if the individual price bars and specific confirmation signals validate the measured price level.

Advanced Harmonic Trading Execution Strategies Conclusion

Beyond the basic measurements of harmonic patterns, there is an important distinction that must be made at the completion point of the structure. One of the basic challenges for all Harmonic Traders is to distinguish how far beyond the ideal measurements can we allow for deviation from the harmonic model while still possessing a valid trade opportunity. Concepts such as the Terminal Price Bar, the Potential Reversal Zone and the Permissible Execution Zone address this issue clearly and provide parameters as the pattern completes to validate the price action. Furthermore, advanced calculations of the Terminal Price Bar exemplify the unique individual data points that provide relevant and accurate measures.

These proprietary concepts are founded in the principle that all parameters of the trade are established by the market's own price action. Most important, the measurable zone of harmonic price phenomenon consistently establishes the natural limits of price action on any time interval. The zones that these measures define provide a dynamic means of assessing how far the market can move in any one direction within a certain period of time before a counter reaction is required. These insights in combination with other standard measures clarify the overall probable future price direction and facilitate trading decisions throughout the process. Over the next several chapters, we will examine these advanced concepts and the proper situations to which they can be applied.

Chapter 4:
Harmonic Trading Reversal Types

Over the years, much of my research regarding harmonic pattern management strategies resulted in a similar categorization as patterns. A harmonic pattern completion must be distinguished as distinct types where the first test and completion of a pattern leads to a highly probable "reactive event" where some type of a reversal will occur. However, a reversal is not exactly accurate when describing this type of situation. A better term would be a reaction. In the philosophy of what harmonic measurements represent, the cyclical nature of price action mechanisms demands there be some type of response point from the structure.

As all traders understand, no price can move straight up or straight down. There must be buying to the selling and vice versa. These are the natural forces of the market. Therefore, every singular price move regardless of its direction must experience some type of inflection as part of its natural mechanism. The recognition of this natural phenomenon bolsters the argument for recognizing those measurements that reflect the natural cyclical movements – a.k.a. harmonic ratios – where only the relevant measurements are considered.

Definition of an Ideal Reversal

From a harmonic pattern perspective, the initial completion of the pattern represents a type of natural cycle. Even if that pattern is eventually violated, the formation of the structure can identify temporary profitable price segments consistently. However, one of the earliest challenges most Harmonic Traders face is what to expect completion of the pattern. Many whom have learned identification techniques are not aware essential strategies that facilitate execution and management decisions throughout the process. Ideally, price action should reverse after the entire range is tested, assessing the Potential Reversal Zone (PRZ) particularly at the XA retracement/projection (typically the largest leg of the pattern). It is essential to take particular note of the relative AB=CD structure in comparison to the XA calculation and coordinate effective confirmation signals such as indicators simultaneously with reversal progress in the PRZ.

Within the Harmonic Trading approach, the best opportunities for exact reversals of measured patterns occur on the initial reaction of the structure. We will outline these "Type-I" situations later in the material but it is important to understand there are differences basic reversal types between the first time a pattern completes as opposed to a secondary retest.

Harmonic Trading Volume 3: Reaction vs. Reversal

Following the establishment of the Terminal Price Bar, price action should reverse shortly after testing all numbers in the Potential Reversal Zone (PRZ), and test a minimum retracement range between 38.2% – 61.8% of the pattern to define - the *Initial Profit Objective*. Due to the nature of the initial reversal, the profit objective is aggressively and automatically managed. These reactive trades possess sharp and accelerated moves that can be executed time and time again to capitalize on powerful natural cyclical movements, that provide consistent characteristics of their beginning, middle and end.

Harmonic Pattern Reversal Types

Most of the finer strategies within the Harmonic Trading approach were developed over a process of many years – primarily out of trial and error. After the guidelines were established to measure exact patterns, other considerations for execution and management became more apparent. I noticed that there was a distinct difference between the first time a pattern completed supposed to a situation where there is a period of consolidation before the reversal. Similar patterns did not necessarily dictate that each would experience the same outcome. Rather, it was quite common for nearly identical pattern structures to experience varying results. Therefore, price structures unto themselves seemed to yield an unpredictable range of outcomes.

The gradual evolution from simple pattern identification to precise classifications of trading situations was facilitated by advances in software. In 2000, I started work on the first harmonic pattern software program, the Harmonic Analyzer. It is important to remember that there were very few software options and no programs that could automatically scan for harmonic patterns at this time. Most software platforms did not even possess basic Fibonacci measurement tools. I was able to program the algorithms and create a tool that automatically scanned and measured harmonic pattern structures. We were able to establish exact tolerance levels for structural variation to optimize results. After nearly 3 years of development, we were able to offer an unprecedented software program and unlock advanced execution and management relationships related to harmonic patterns with extreme accuracy.

In the beginning, my initial comprehension of the differences in patterns was limited. Although my suspicions were correct that price structures must be precisely measured to define unique technical situations, the extent of how much specification was required escaped me. Once the initial structural rules were designed, it was easy to classify every pattern type with its own explanation. There were definitive environmental variables that I found to consistently repeat and to signal profitable trades in advance to facilitate execution and management, as well. Thus, the patterns for defining the price levels became more of a starting point for execution considerations, while the confirmation triggers were acting as the final determinate of the trade.

A common experience for many traders is to measure a pattern properly, execute at the completion point, experience a sizable but brief reactive move only to give it all back as price action quickly retests the pattern. These are common early learning experiences that traders must overcome and learn from to be able to manage harmonic

Harmonic Trading Volume 3: Reaction vs. Reversal

price action effectively. For myself, I had to test various theories before I realized certain consistent reactions were unfolding following the completion of pattern. These repeated observations led to the basic Harmonic Trading process model that anticipates pattern completions in a particular sequence. Starting with the identification of a distinct pattern, the Potential Reversal Zone (PRZ) must be accurately measured. The key completion of the Terminal Price Bar acts as a trading alert – the light switch that turns the trade on – to represent the official starting point for the execution. Within that brief window of the consolidation range established by the Potential Reversal Zone (PRZ), the price action must be closely monitored along with other confirming indicators readings to determine the nature of the consolidation.

Serial Bullish Reversal

An ideal bullish reversal typically occurs in the clearest structural opportunities. When a bullish pattern defines harmonic support, the strongest reaction expressed in the price action will change course dramatically on the first test of the completion point. These reversals are associated with price action that reverses sharply and forms a successive pattern of higher highs and higher lows as the bullish price bars exhibit demonstrative continuation in the anticipated direction.

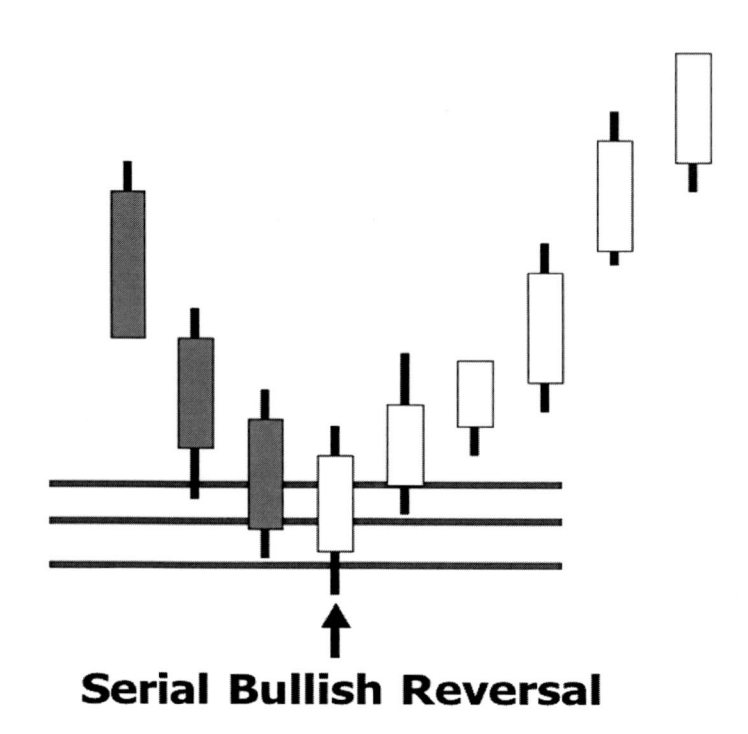

Serial Bullish Reversal

Harmonic Trading Volume 3: Reaction vs. Reversal

The key is to gauge the price action as the Terminal Price Bar is established. There are complementary strategies that help to define when these reversals will occur. However, the safest course of action is to monitor each price bar beyond the completion point. Until the initial reversal fails to continue in the countertrend direction, it is to be assumed that the pattern reversal will continue. We'll take a look at exact management strategies that help make these distinctions. But, it is essential to assume that all initial tests of significant harmonic pattern opportunities will yield a serial reversal until proven otherwise.

Gold ETF (GLD): 15-Minute
Bullish Gartley Serial Bullish Reversal

This following daily chart of the Gold ETF shows an ideal Bullish Serial Reversal. The GLD formed a Bullish Gartley that reversed exactly at the Potential Reversal Zone (PRZ). The price action tested all of the numbers and reversed at the low range of the harmonic support. The Terminal Price Bar stabilized shortly thereafter and the ensuing continuation of the new uptrend climbed steadily in the days that followed.

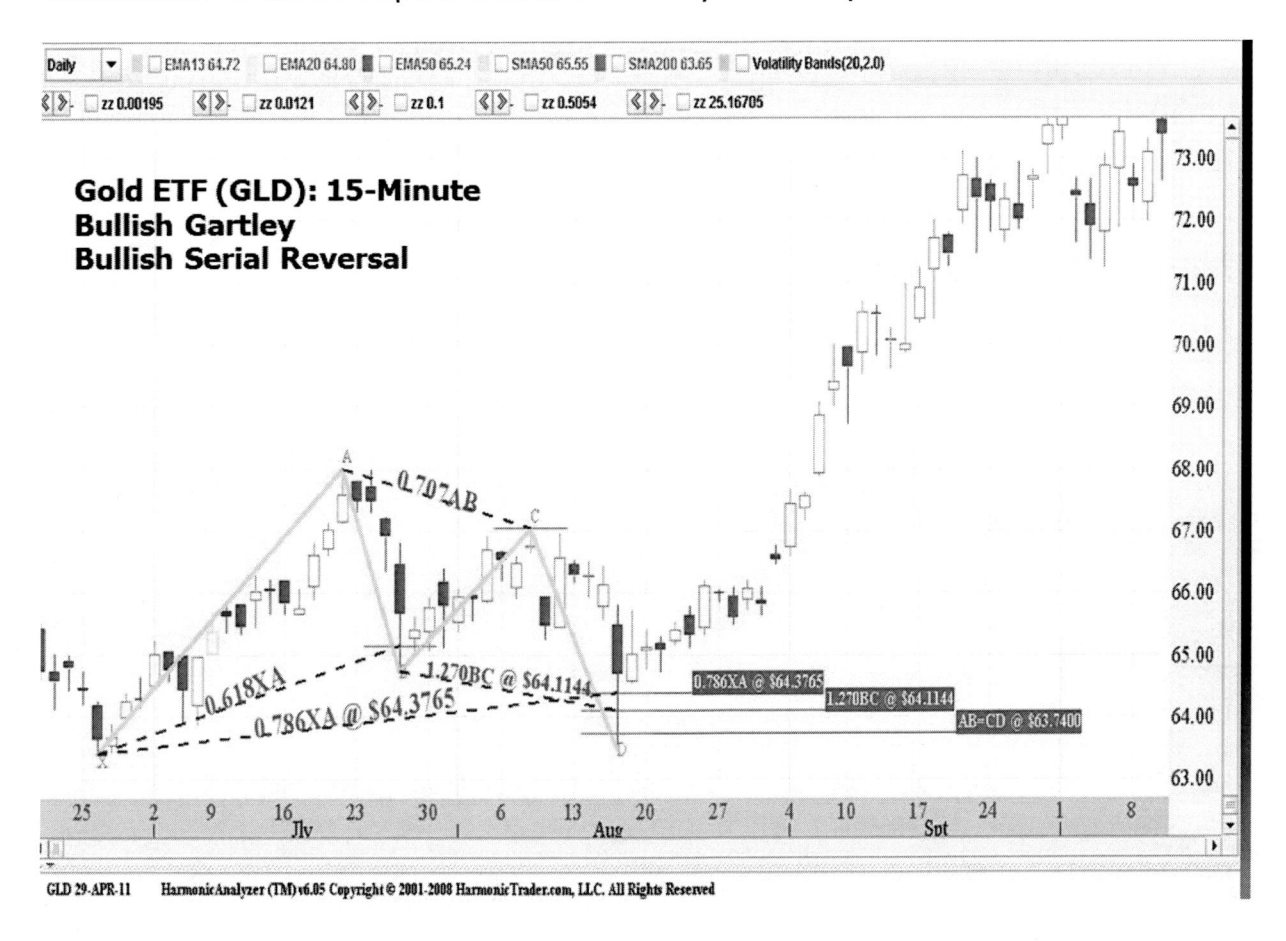

Harmonic Trading Volume 3: Reaction vs. Reversal

Gold ETF (GLD): 15-Minute
Bullish Gartley Potential Reversal Zone (PRZ)
Serial Bullish Reversal

This chart shows the price action in the Potential Reversal Zone (PRZ). Despite the extreme price action, the Terminal Price Bar was established on the day that it tested all of the numbers. Due to the volatility of the move, this may have been a tricky execution. Regardless, the execution for the bullish continuation was quite clear.

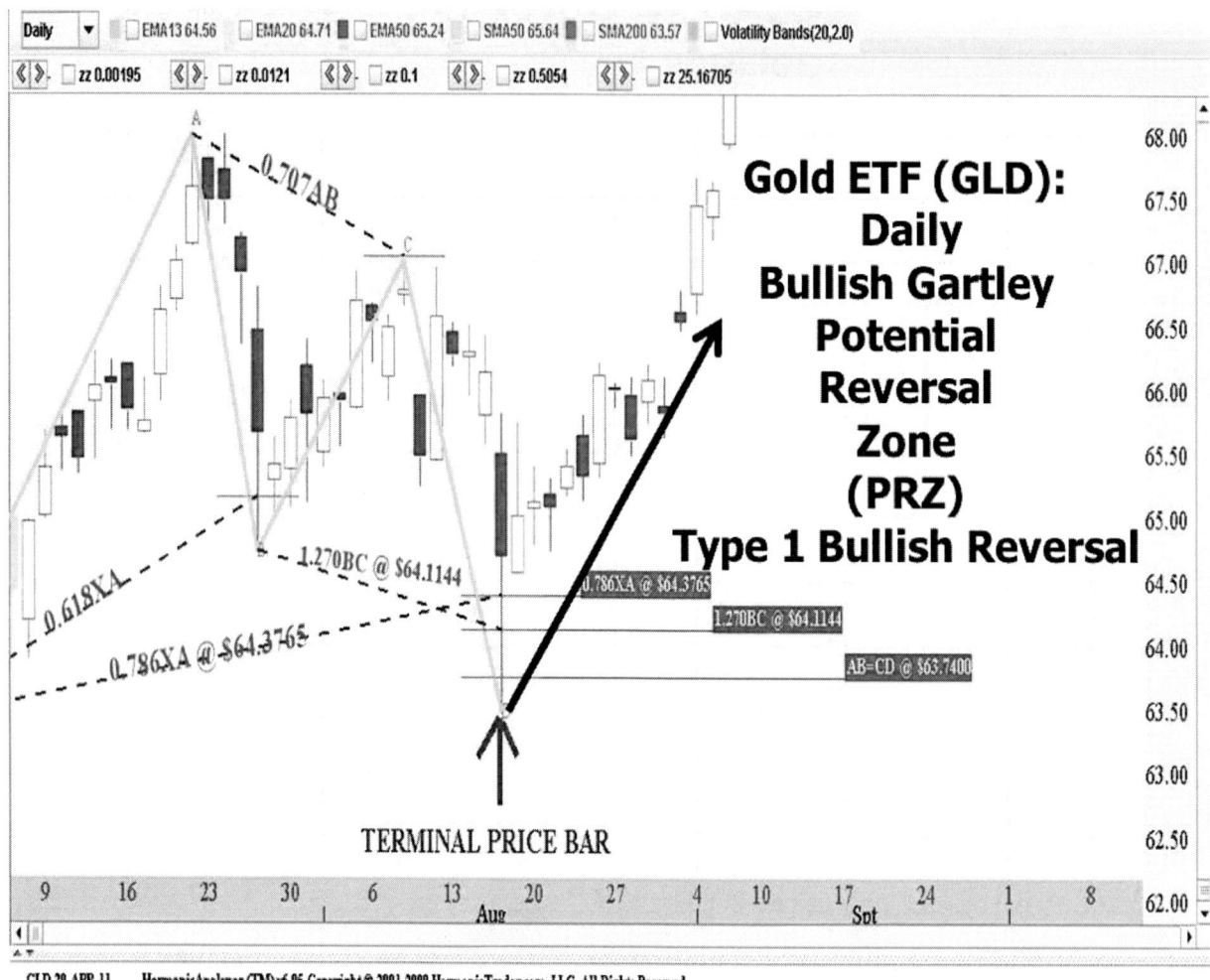

The reversal climbed steadily higher, as each successive price bar formed a pattern of higher highs and higher lows. When trading behavior moves in such a linear fashion, it frequently is signaling potential strength beyond the initial reaction. The clearest serial reversals will typically follow in this fashion with overwhelming bullish continuation.

Harmonic Trading Volume 3: Reaction vs. Reversal

Serial Bearish Reversal

The key technical event that must occur is some type of individual resistance at the numbers defined by the pattern where each price bar fails to move higher above the Terminal Price Bar and begins to slowly roll over. The serial bearish reversal will exhibit a pattern of lower lows and lower highs in the successive price bars following the completion of the pattern.

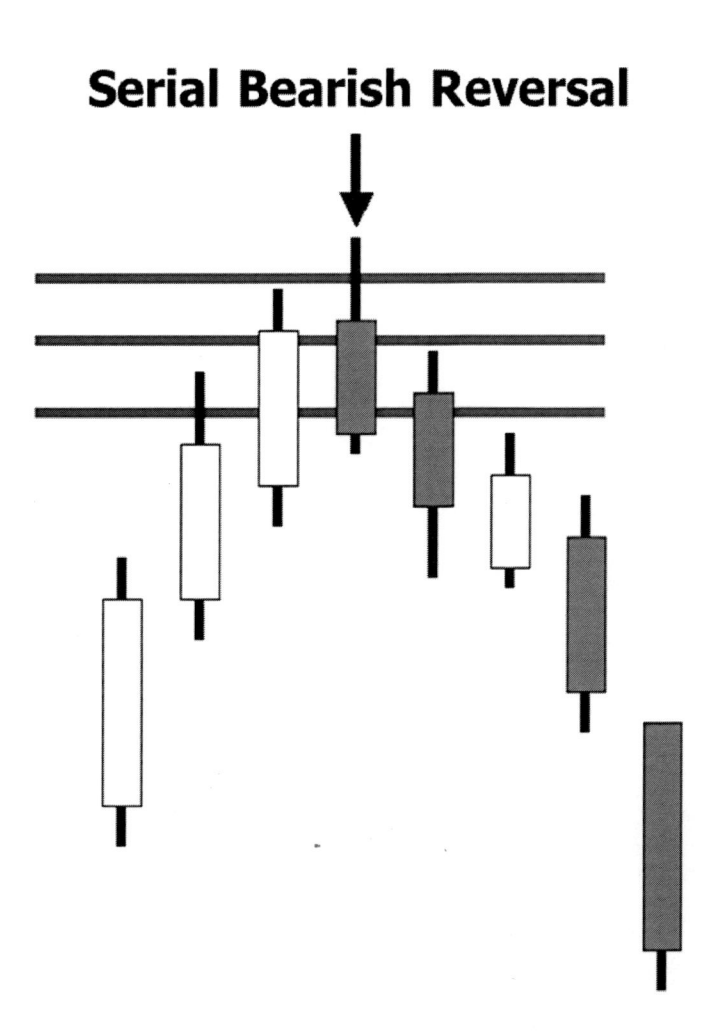

Serial Bearish Reversal

In most cases, the initial reaction of most harmonic patterns will exhibit some type of serial reversal after testing all of the numbers at the pattern's completion point. The key to capitalizing on the situations is to understand when these movements will yield minor reactions versus larger reversals. Again, we will look at detailed strategies later in this material that incorporate these ideas. For now, it is important to be aware of the type of price behavior following completion of a harmonic pattern opportunity.

Harmonic Trading Volume 3: Reaction vs. Reversal

Microsoft (MSFT): Daily
Bearish Butterfly
Serial Bearish Reversal

The following daily chart of Microsoft exhibits an ideal serial reversal. The pattern was quite distinct with three measurements defining the Potential Reversal Zone (PRZ) in the 26.50-27.30 area. Immediately after testing all the numbers at the pattern completion point, the price action rolled over and declined steadily thereafter.

Harmonic Trading Volume 3: Reaction vs. Reversal

Microsoft (MSFT): Daily
Bearish Butterfly Potential Reversal Zone (PRZ)
Serial Bearish Reversal

The next chart that shows the price action in the Potential Reversal Zone (PRZ). The Terminal Price Bar was established with a peak of 27.40. In combination with the other numbers in the zone, the harmonic resistance was established in this area. The most interesting aspect is the price action immediately following the Terminal Price Bar.

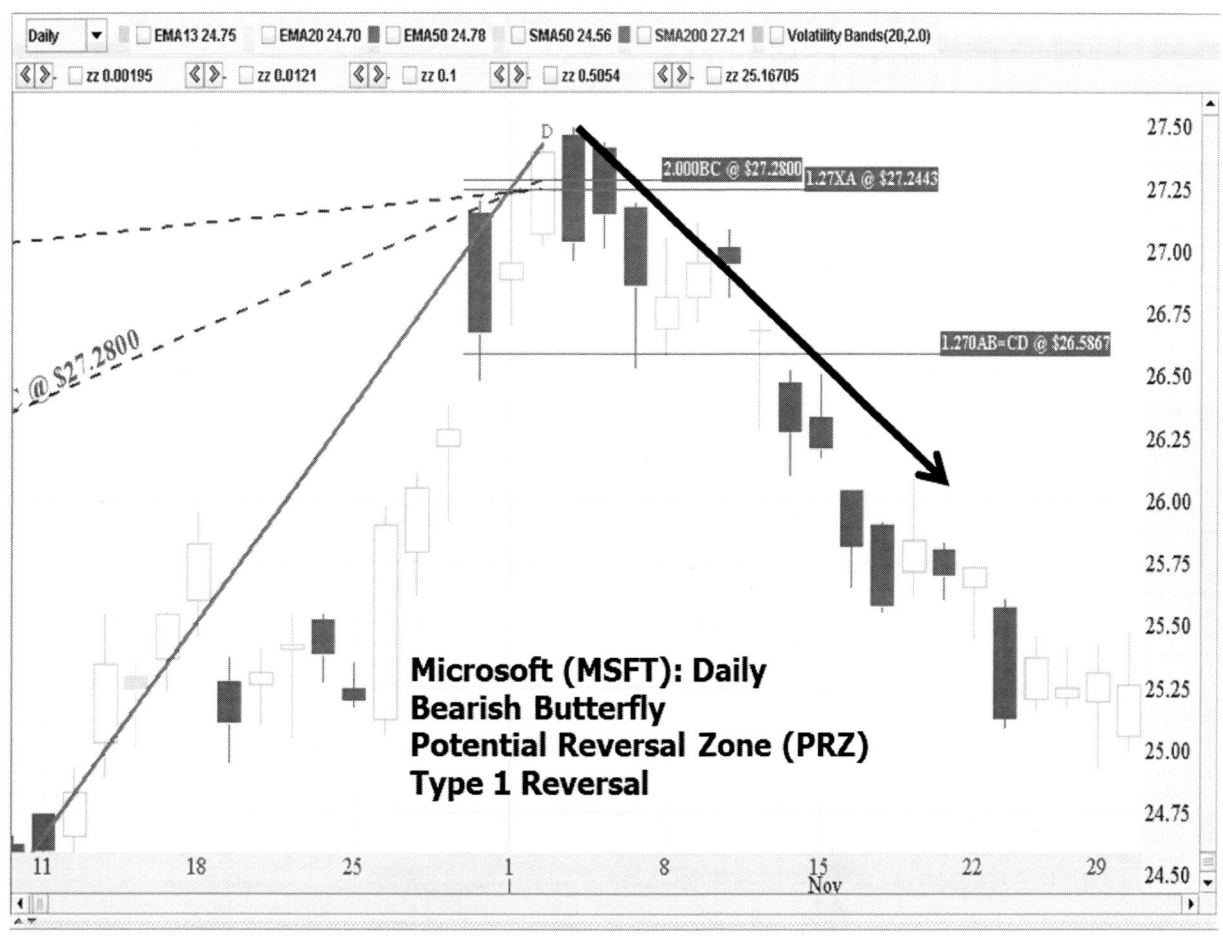

In this case, the single reversal bar was incredibly significant and pinpointed the first confirmation that the pattern's resistance was taking effect. In essence, the character of the new trend begins to change in situations like these, and can be completely confirmed after the second or third price bar. By the end of the second day, MSFT failed to make a new high for the move. Within a few days, the reversal continuation accelerated. Of course, there are more strategies to consider immediately following completion of this initial reaction but the Serial Reversal does help to define proper expectations regarding immediate reactions at distinct harmonic levels.

Harmonic Trading Volume 3: Reaction vs. Reversal

Divergent Reversal

One of the most powerful methods to analyze price action is the ability to ascertain those reversals that require extra consolidation at the pattern's completion point while still signaling a valid opportunity. It is common to witness a final price divergence in the PEZ where a retest of the Terminal Bar extreme marks an important confirmation of the harmonic level. The gamut of divergence analysis in price action, sector analysis and other relative measures is a broad but powerful approach to compare critical variables that can validate important turning points in the financial markets. When it comes to price action, there are many instances where a small series of individual trading points forms a "micro-mechanism" that consolidates within zones of harmonic resistance and support. The divergent reversal requires that price action establish an initial range that experiences a brief consolidation to retest the limits of these parameters but is a unique price mechanism that typically precedes more substantial moves.

Bullish Divergent Reversal

The Bullish Divergent Reversal involves a process of multiple price bars establishing, retesting and ultimately confirming a particular harmonic support level that stabilizes a downtrend. In most cases, the divergent reversal will provide more complex sequence of individual price bars that represents a more significant cyclical turning point.

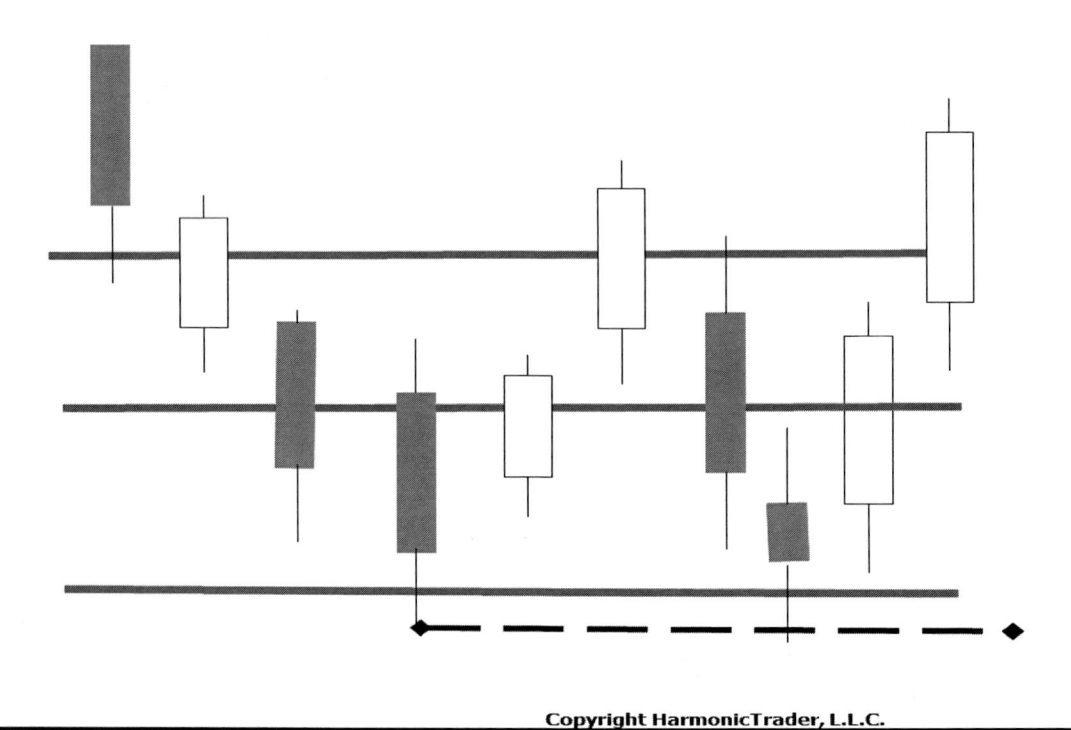

Harmonic Trading Volume 3: Reaction vs. Reversal

After establishing an important low that is usually preceded by a steady decline, price action will usually require a few individual intervals to stabilize the downtrend. Although the degree of this consolidation can vary, it typically unfolds within a 3-5 price bar window following the completion of pattern.

Euro vs. U.S. Dollar (EUR_A0-FX): 15-Minute
Bullish Crab
Divergent Bullish Reversal

The following chart of the Euro/Dollar on a 15–minute chart shows distinct Bullish Crab pattern that required a secondary test. After the initial reaction, the price action retested the entire harmonic support and initial point of the first reaction.

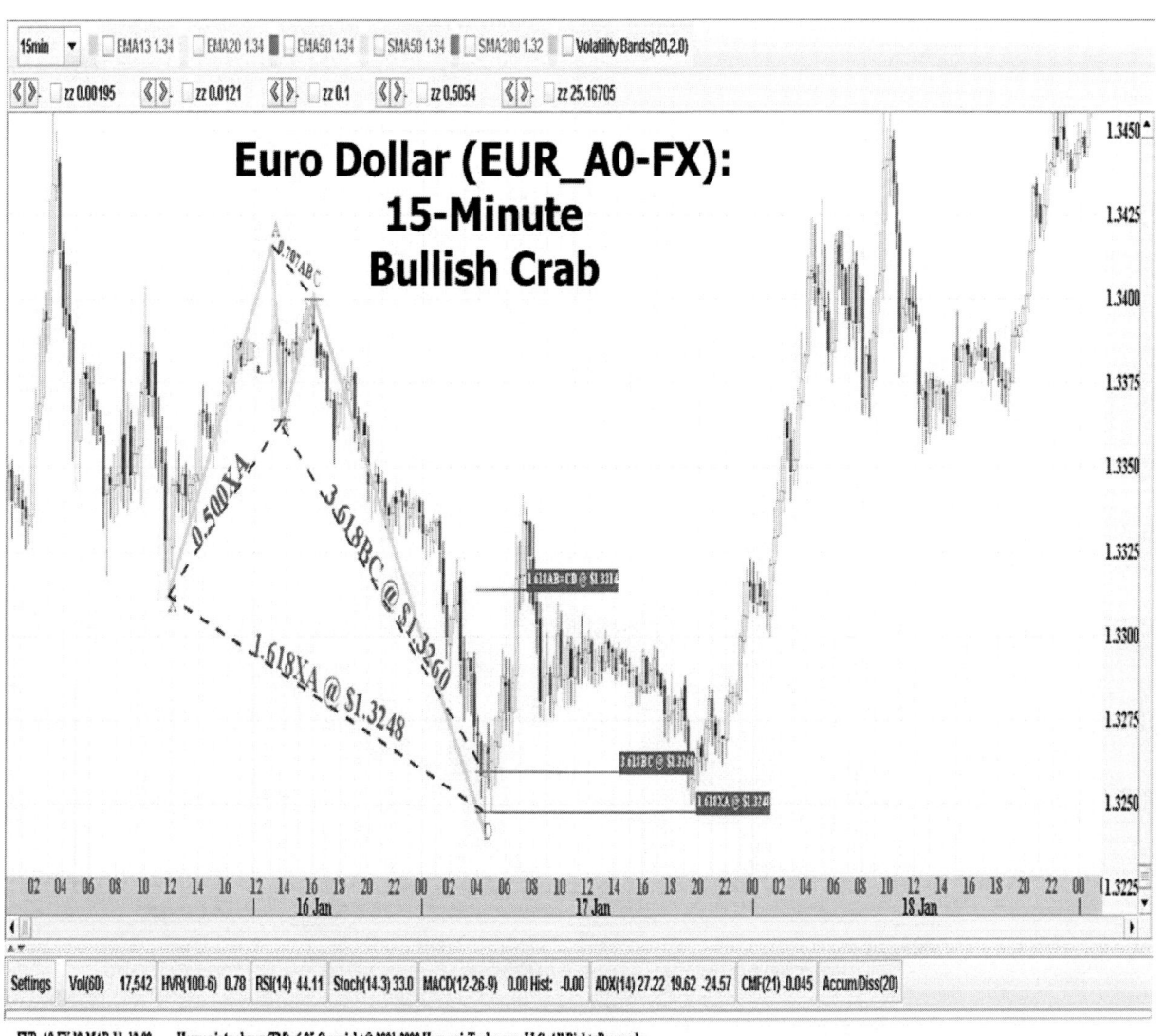

Harmonic Trading Volume 3: Reaction vs. Reversal

Euro vs. U.S. Dollar (EUR_A0-FX): 15-Minute
Bullish Crab Potential Reversal Zone (PRZ)
Divergent Bullish Reversal

The following chart shows the price action in the potential reversal zone. The Bullish Crab was a distinct pattern that experienced an initial reaction at the completion of the pattern but required a secondary test before a larger reversal could unfold. The support that was established by the initial test was confirmed with a retest of the lowest measured at the ideal harmonic support. In fact, this was an exact retest but it is common for divergent situations to nominally exceed the initial level. The key characteristic of this retest is to optimize executions based upon the Terminal Bar extreme and anticipate a slight violation before a larger reversal can ensue.

Harmonic Trading Volume 3: Reaction vs. Reversal

Bearish Divergent Reversal

The Bearish Divergent Reversal is quite common in those pattern completions that require several price bars to resolve the overall resistance zone. Typically, the Terminal Price Bar will be established on the initial test of the Potential Reversal Zone. Following a brief reaction, the follow-through beyond the Terminal Bar will typically experience a pausing behavior that trades within the limits of the Potential Reversal Zone. After this brief consolidation, the retest of initial peak will typically fail and exhibit accelerated bearish behavior thereafter. The real challenge in this type of reversal can be overcome by monitoring the tight consolidation within the limits of Potential Reversal Zone. Depending upon the results of the immediate secondary retest, the full effect and potential of the bearish divergent reversal can be realized shortly after the initial Terminal Price Bar has been established. In combination with larger pattern measurements and other confirmation strategies, this simple price mechanism acts as a confirming variable to substantiate price levels as an absolute technical event.

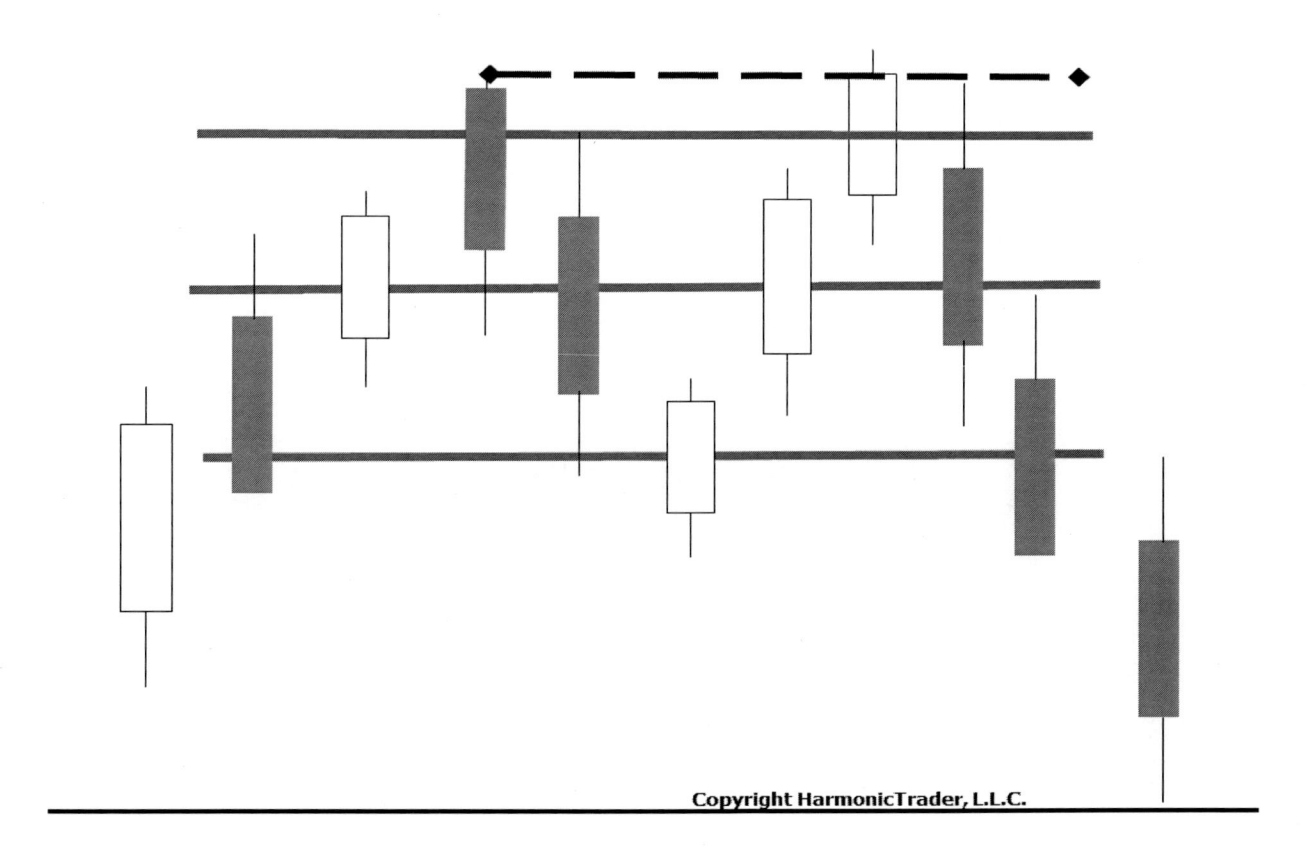

Harmonic Trading Volume 3: Reaction vs. Reversal

Euro vs. U.S. Dollar (EUR_A0-FX): 15-Minute
Bearish AB=CD
Divergent Bearish Reversal

It is interesting to note that the following chart of the Euro/Dollar exemplifies this type of divergent price move before the acceleration of the substantial reversal. This formation can be tricky to trade because the retest can make it seem that the pattern is about to fail. However, this is when a prepared trading plan identifies reversal types and exact price limits IN ADVANCE to optimize decisions to handle situations properly. In this case, the price action stalled immediately after completing the pattern. After a brief reaction, the price retested the Potential Reversal Zone and confirmed the harmonic resistance by immediately rolling over after hitting the T-Bar extreme

Harmonic Trading Volume 3: Reaction vs. Reversal

Euro vs. U.S. Dollar (EUR_A0-FX): 15-Minute
Bearish AB=CD Potential Reversal Zone (PRZ)
Divergent Bearish Reversal

The following chart of the price action in the Potential Reversal Zone exemplifies this situation. The harmonic resistance defined the 1.4930 level as the top range that immediately capped the intraday rally. Within five price bars after the completion of the pattern, the reversal accelerated sharply.

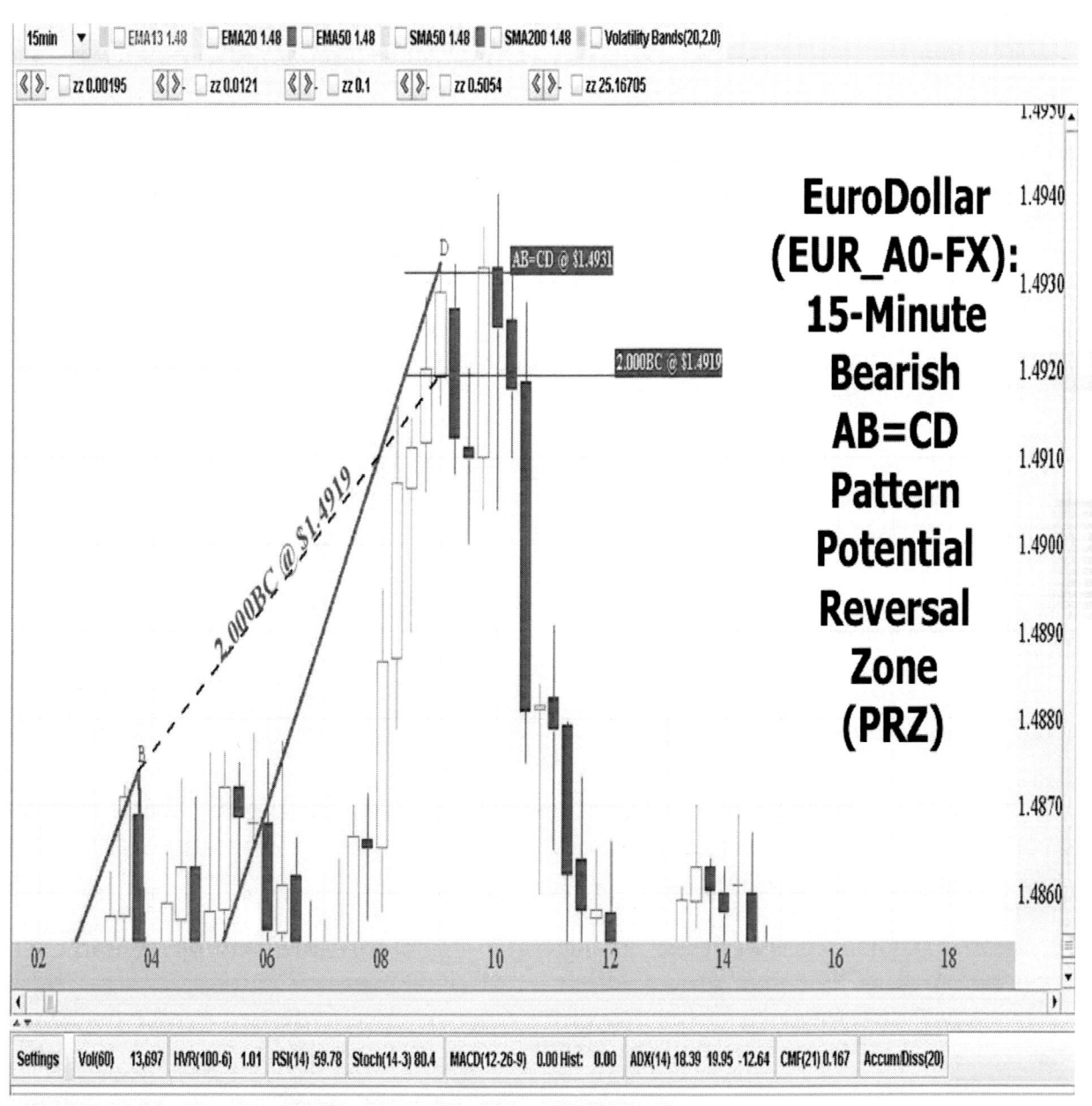

Harmonic Trading Volume 3: Reaction vs. Reversal

196

Type-I Reversal

One of the most profound advancements in my discoveries with harmonic patterns was not apparent to me until several years after the release of my first book, "The Harmonic Trader." I outlined a system of harmonic patterns with precise identification rules but the execution parameters and management classifications lacked comprehensive strategies to optimize decisions. At first, I spent quite a bit of time monitoring common traits and repeating characteristics that were observable with the most significant harmonic patterns. Eventually, I recognized that harmonic patterns exhibited common price reactions while larger reversals were associated with other readings and structural signals. Like patterns, reversals unfolded within a process after the point of completion. I realized there was an enormous difference in the potential for a profitable move if price action was completing the first time as opposed to a secondary retest.

Known as a Type-I harmonic pattern, initial completions frequently manifest a character in the price action that changes course aggressively from the Potential Reversal Zone (PRZ) with demonstrative and distinct countertrend behavior. Although Type-I reactions are excellent opportunities, they must be handled a bit more aggressively and automatically. In fact, a price reaction following the completion of the Terminal Price Bar typically will automatically test the initial profit target only to retest the entire pattern completion point before triggering a larger reversal.

A Type-I completion is a unique event within Harmonic Trading. The first time that price action tests a distinct harmonic pattern is the most important consideration of any structural opportunity. The Terminal Price Bar is the basis for any execution of a harmonic pattern. The price action immediately following the Terminal Price Bar provides immediate and accurate insight to what might occur beyond completion point. Although some may argue that the weighting of certain data might be biased, especially since all price history must be considered, the individual data immediately following the completion point of any pattern will determine its validity.

Type-I Reversal Trade Management Considerations

The effectiveness of harmonic patterns can be quite impressive. A Type-I reversal involves price action that is testing a Potential Reversal Zone the first time. After the reversal extreme is established, price action begins to initiate a counter-trend direction (T-Bar+2,3) without retesting Potential Reversal Zone (PRZ). Although there may be some consolidation after Terminal Bar has been established, the immediate and clear continuation must be demonstrated within 3 to 5 price bars no matter to provide those early signs of confirmation. This is one of the singular most important events that must occur to get any harmonic pattern reaction to manifest into a larger reversal.

Since the Type-I reaction is typically an immediate pattern reversal, there are predetermined strategies and preferences that are required for each situation to establish the limits of the opportunity. Type-I reversals tend to be quick and demonstrative after completing the pattern, as they usually experience the narrow time window to enter the trade at the optimal level. The focus must be on the Terminal Price Bar to execute immediately thereafter, as long as Stop Loss and Automatic Profit Targets are defined in advance.

I will be talking about specific strategies later in this chapter that dictate when to take profits aggressively versus when to allow more time for these situations to resolve themselves. In general, the Type-I reversal requires a short timeframe with an aggressive approach that includes automatic profit objectives established at the predetermined ratio measurements of 38.2%&61.8% as measured by the pattern.

Type-I Bullish Reversal

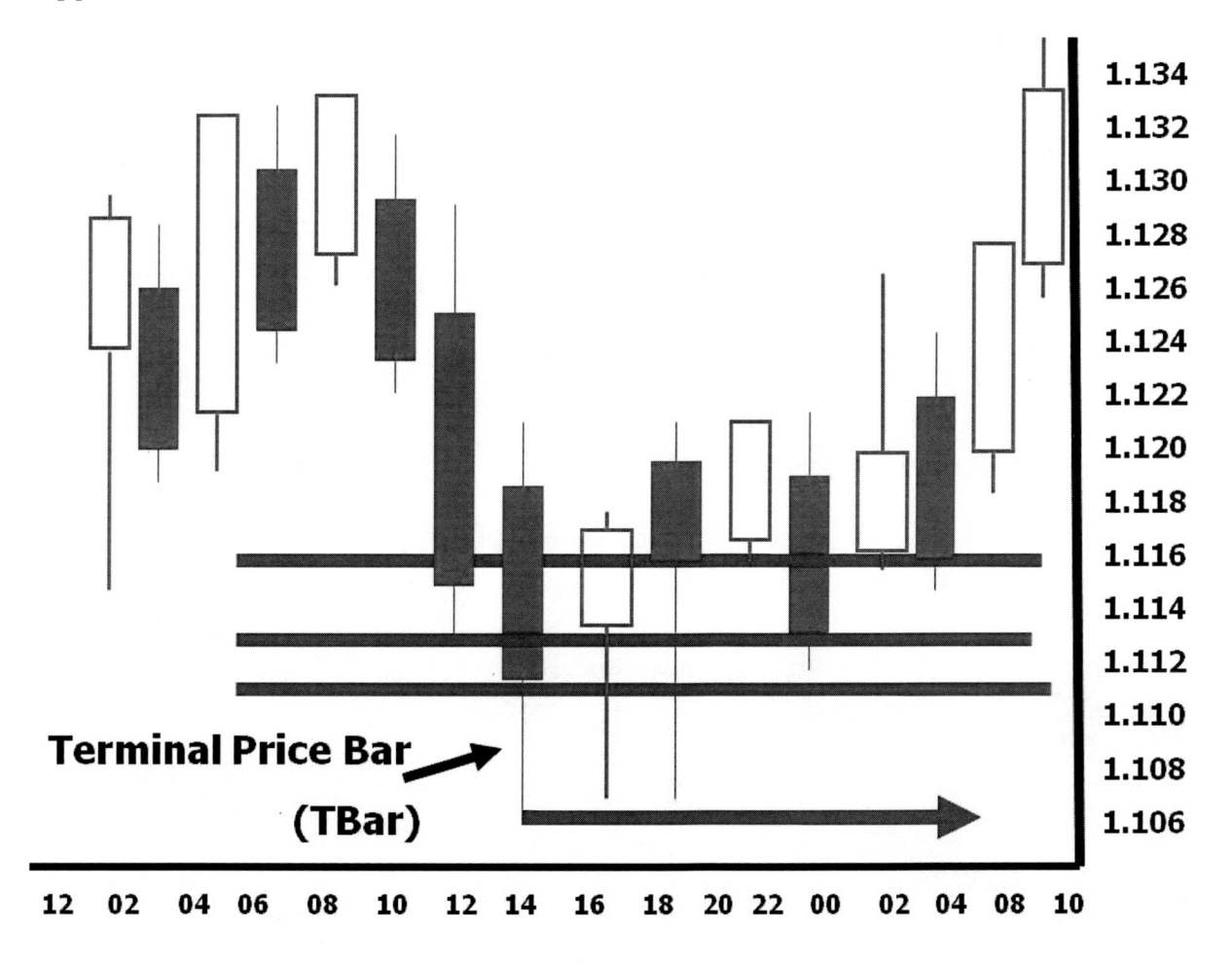

The Type -1 reversal requires a degree of preparation in order to capitalize on the situations. Sometimes, price action can quickly trade through the harmonic support area, reverse and not offer a great deal of time to get in on the position. I recommend setting

Harmonic Trading Volume 3: Reaction vs. Reversal

automatic price alerts as the Potential Reversal Zone (PRZ) is being tested in order to stay on top of these situations.

Australian Dollar (AUD_A0-FX): 60-Minute
Bullish 5-0 Pattern
Type-I Bullish Reversal

An interesting note about the analysis of Type-I reversals relates to the significance of the immediate price action following the Terminal Price Bar. There are not too many situations where the first few ticks following the completion of a pattern are so significant relative to a much larger data set. The following chart of the AUD/USD exemplifies the Type-I reversal behavior.

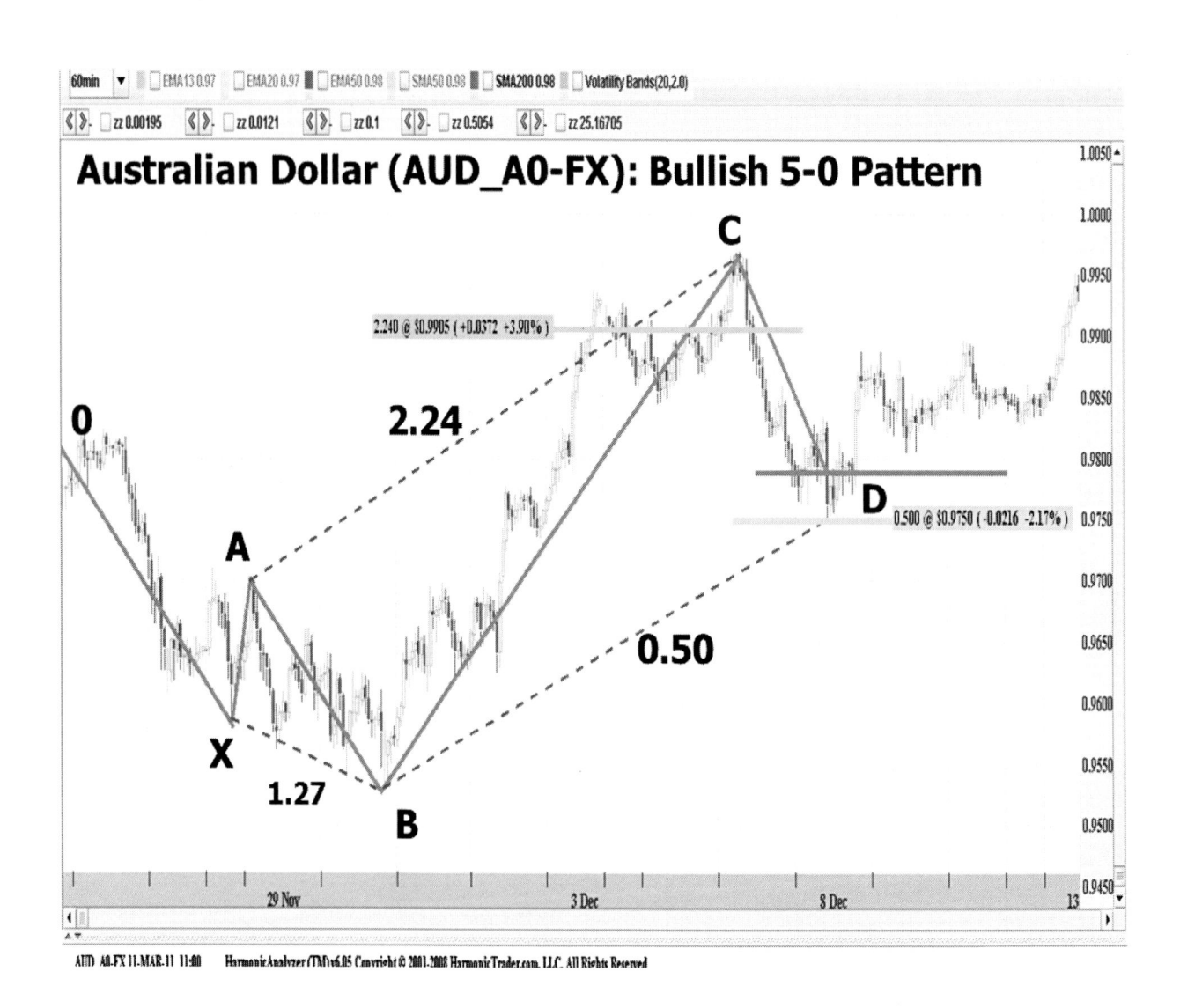

Harmonic Trading Volume 3: Reaction vs. Reversal

Australian Dollar (AUD_A0-FX): 60-Minute
Bullish 5-0 Pattern Potential Reversal Zone (PRZ)
Type-I Bullish Reversal

The following chart of the price action in the PRZ exemplifies the true nature of a Type-I bullish reversal. The price action reversed immediately after testing the low range of harmonic support. The 5-0 pattern reversed exactly at the 50% retracement at the 0.9750 level despite a final volatile sell-off. Regardless, the immediate stabilization marked the early price confirmation for the setup.

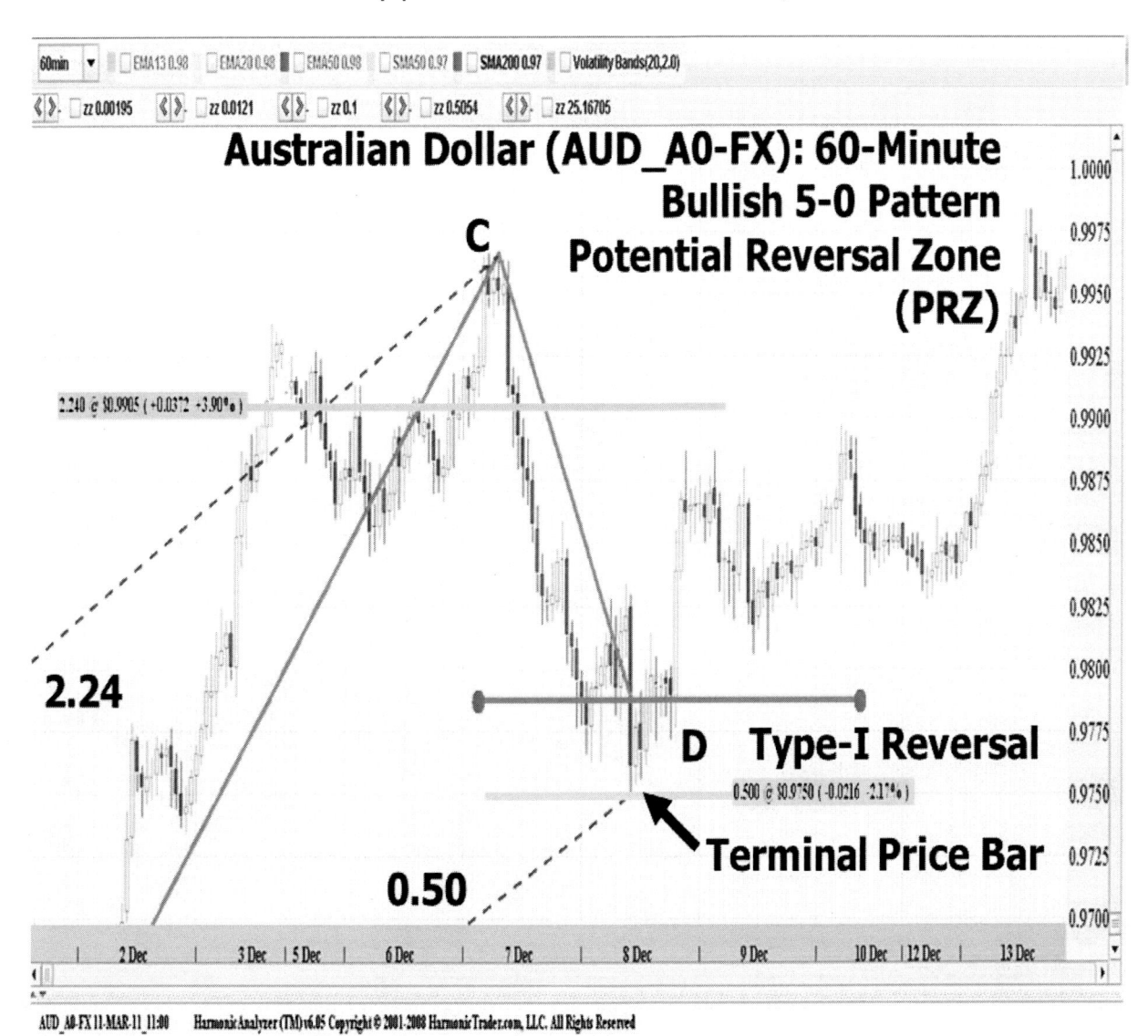

Harmonic Trading Volume 3: Reaction vs. Reversal

Type-I Bearish Reversal

The Type-I Bearish Reversal is defined by the price action in the harmonic resistance zone as soon as the Terminal Price Bars has been established. The key technical event that must occur is some type of individual price bar reversal at the completion point of the pattern where each price bar fails to move higher above the Terminal Price Bar and begins to slowly roll over.

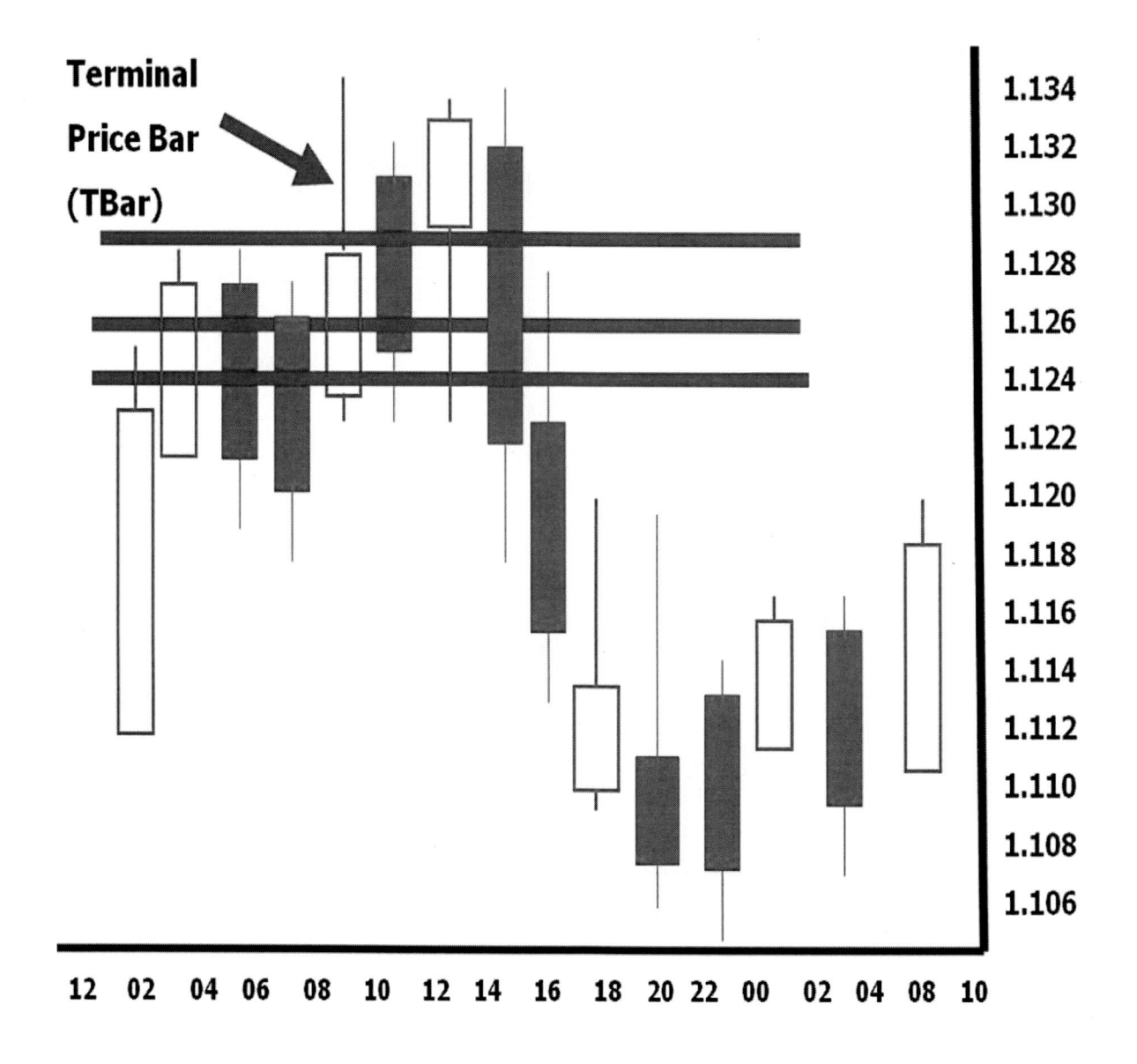

Harmonic Trading Volume 3: Reaction vs. Reversal

British Pound/Japanese Yen (GBPJPY_A0-FX): 5-Minute
Bearish Bat Pattern
Type-I Bearish Reversal

The following example of the British Pound/Japanese Yen on the 5-minute chart demonstrates the characteristics of a Type-I reversal. The price action stalled immediately after testing all of the numbers in the PRZ. This defined harmonic resistance in a tight area between 156.50 – 156.60 on the intraday chart.

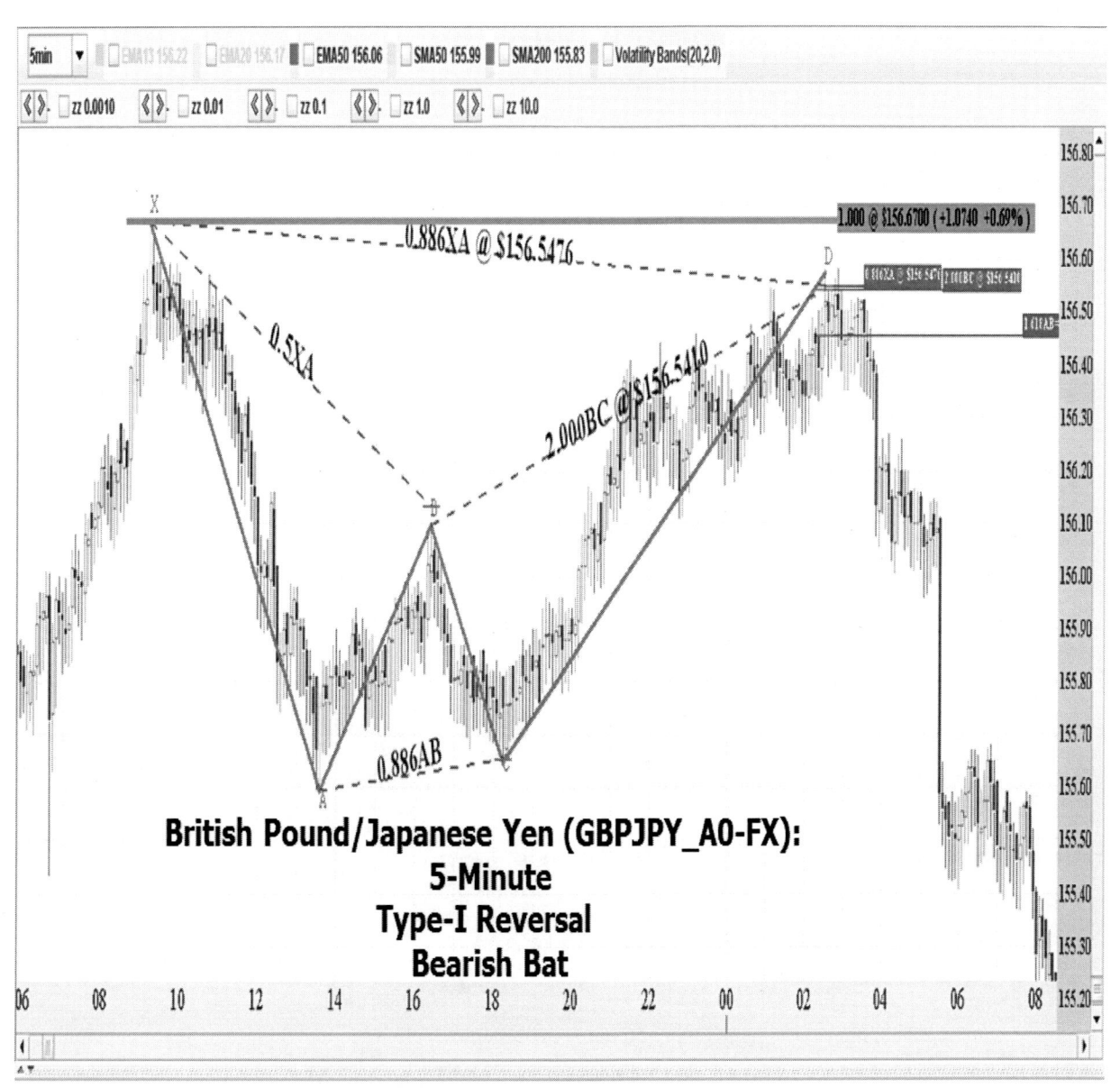

Harmonic Trading Volume 3: Reaction vs. Reversal

British Pound/Japanese Yen (GBPJPY_A0-FX): 5-Minute
Bearish Bat Pattern Potential Reversal Zone (PRZ)
Type-I Bearish Reversal

The price action in the Potential Reversal Zone possessed the ideal individual behavior to signal an early confirmation. These are the common characteristics of an immediate Type-I reversal. Sometimes, it can be advantageous to simply wait for an individual price bar confirmation following the completion of the pattern. Price action that materializes in the PRZ in the direction of the anticipated pattern typically serves as one of the first signals that the opportunity is valid.

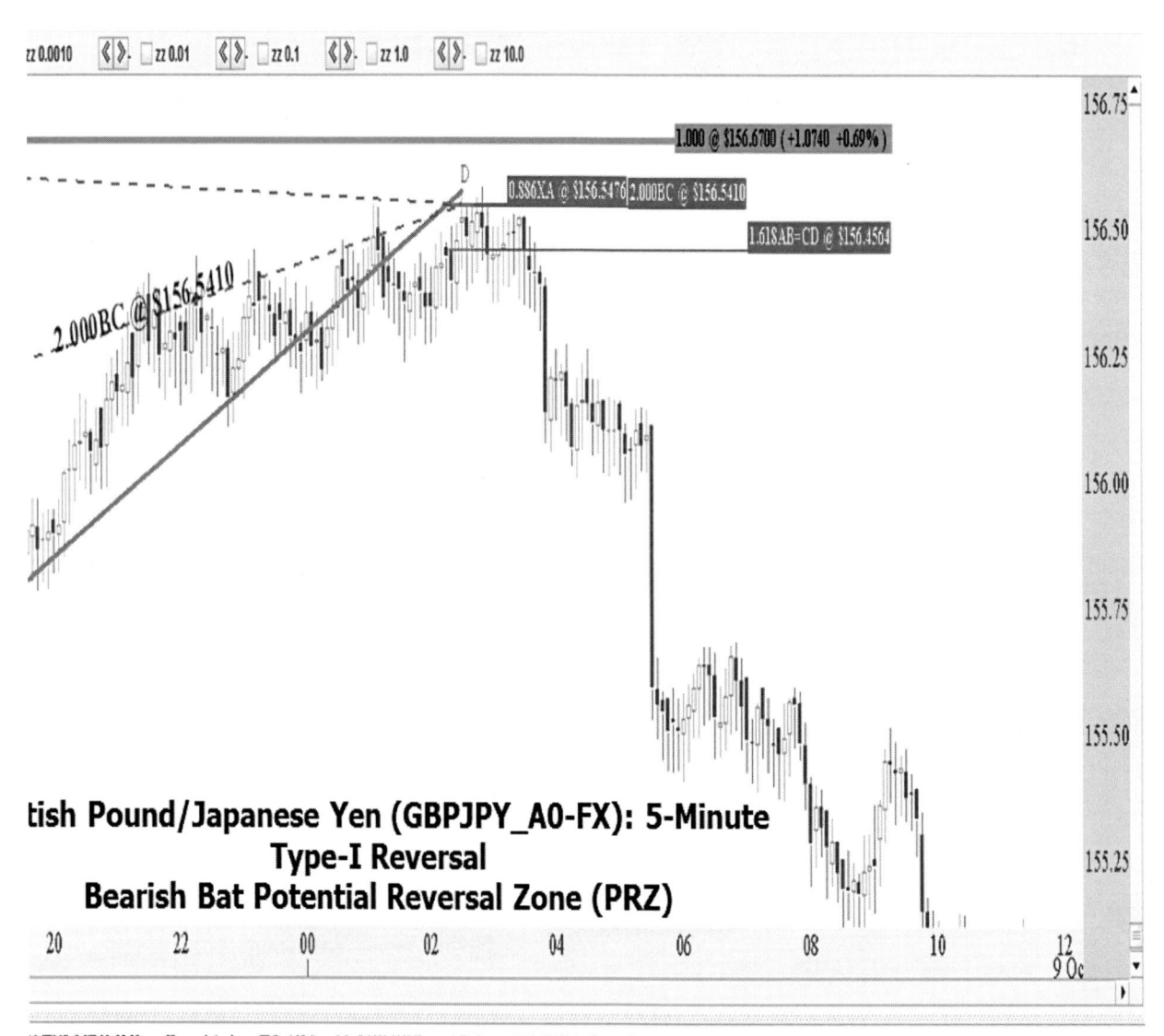

Harmonic Trading Volume 3: Reaction vs. Reversal

Type-II Reversal

The Type-II reversal is an entirely separate technical entity that retests the PRZ. In doing so, the Type-II reversal establishes its own Terminal Price Bar and requires specific confirmation strategies to unfold immediately as the pattern has completed. The combination of secondary smaller patterns that form between the Type-I and Type-II completion points can be expected and utilized to confirm the initial structural readings of the Type-I reversal.

Bullish Type-II Reversal

The Bullish Type-II reversal will typically unfold after the initial profit targets of the Type-I have been realized. Regardless of the Type-I reaction, the secondary test must focus on the exact point where the price action reenters the original reversal zone. Once price action retests this area, the execution is considered as a live trade opportunity but managed slightly differently.

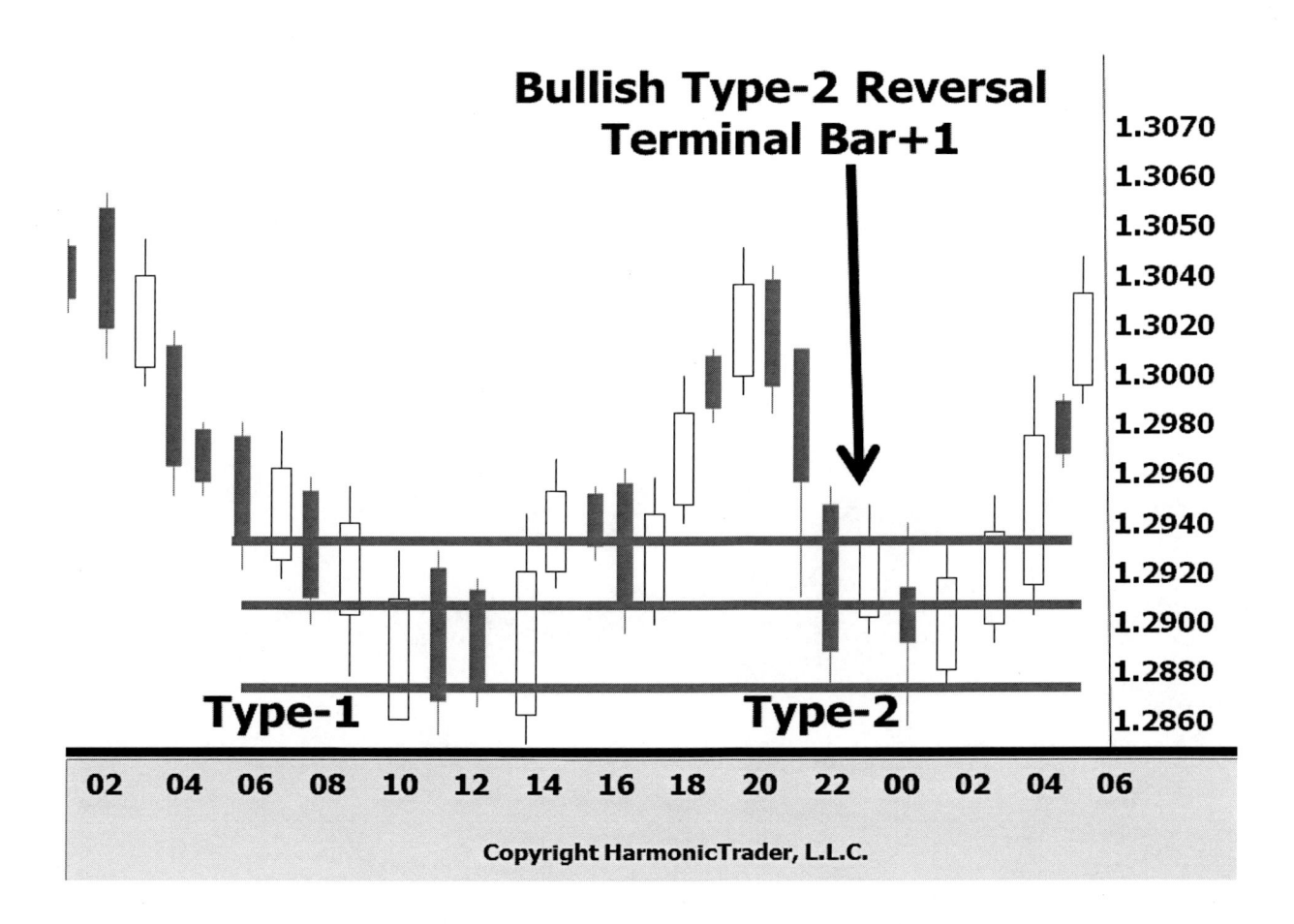

Harmonic Trading Volume 3: Reaction vs. Reversal

Canadian Dollar/Japanese Yen (CADJPY_A0-FX): 15-Minute
Bullish Deep Crab
Type-I & Type-II Reversal

The following example of the Canadian Dollar/Japanese Yen shows the ideal scenario of the Type-I and Type-II harmonic reactive phenomenon. The expectations of the Type-I reversal are reactive and short-lived in all cases, although CADJPY reversed sharply from the initial test of the harmonic support. The management required aggressive tactics, as the price action rolled over to retest the entire first reaction. Although the Type-II reaction requires more time to reverse, this scenario has the greatest potential for a larger move due to the confirmation of the initial test.

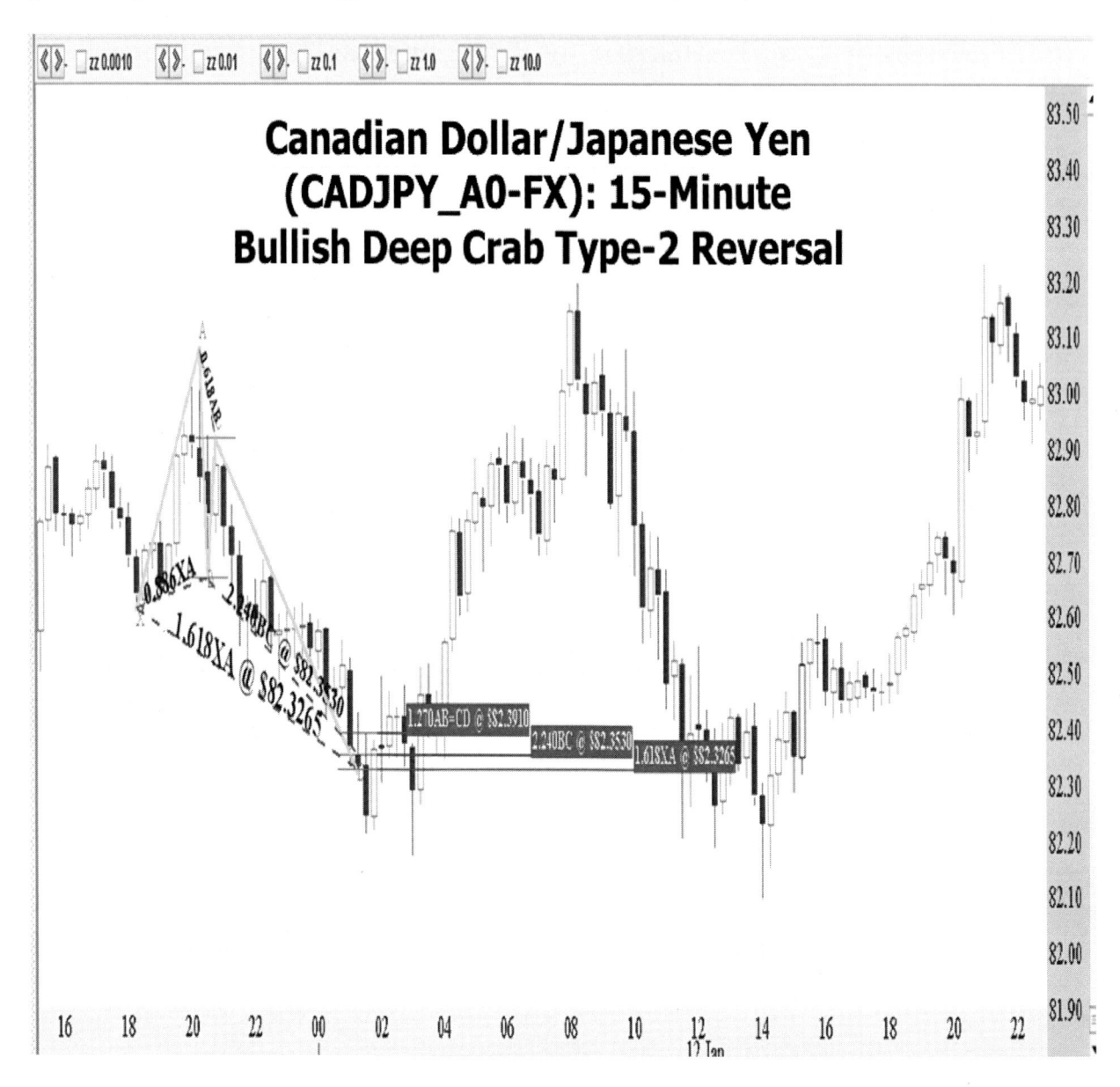

Harmonic Trading Volume 3: Reaction vs. Reversal

Canadian Dollar/Japanese Yen (CADJPY_A0-FX): 15-Minute Bullish Deep Crab Potential Reversal Zone (PRZ) Type-II Reversal

On the second retest of the original Potential Reversal Zone, the price action stabilized immediately the harmonic support just under the 1.618 at 82.30. After some consolidation, the reversal rallied sharply and continued well above the initial 38.2%/61.8% profit objectives. It is important to note the primary uptrend from the low of the retest served to mark the sustained move beyond the minimum price objectives.

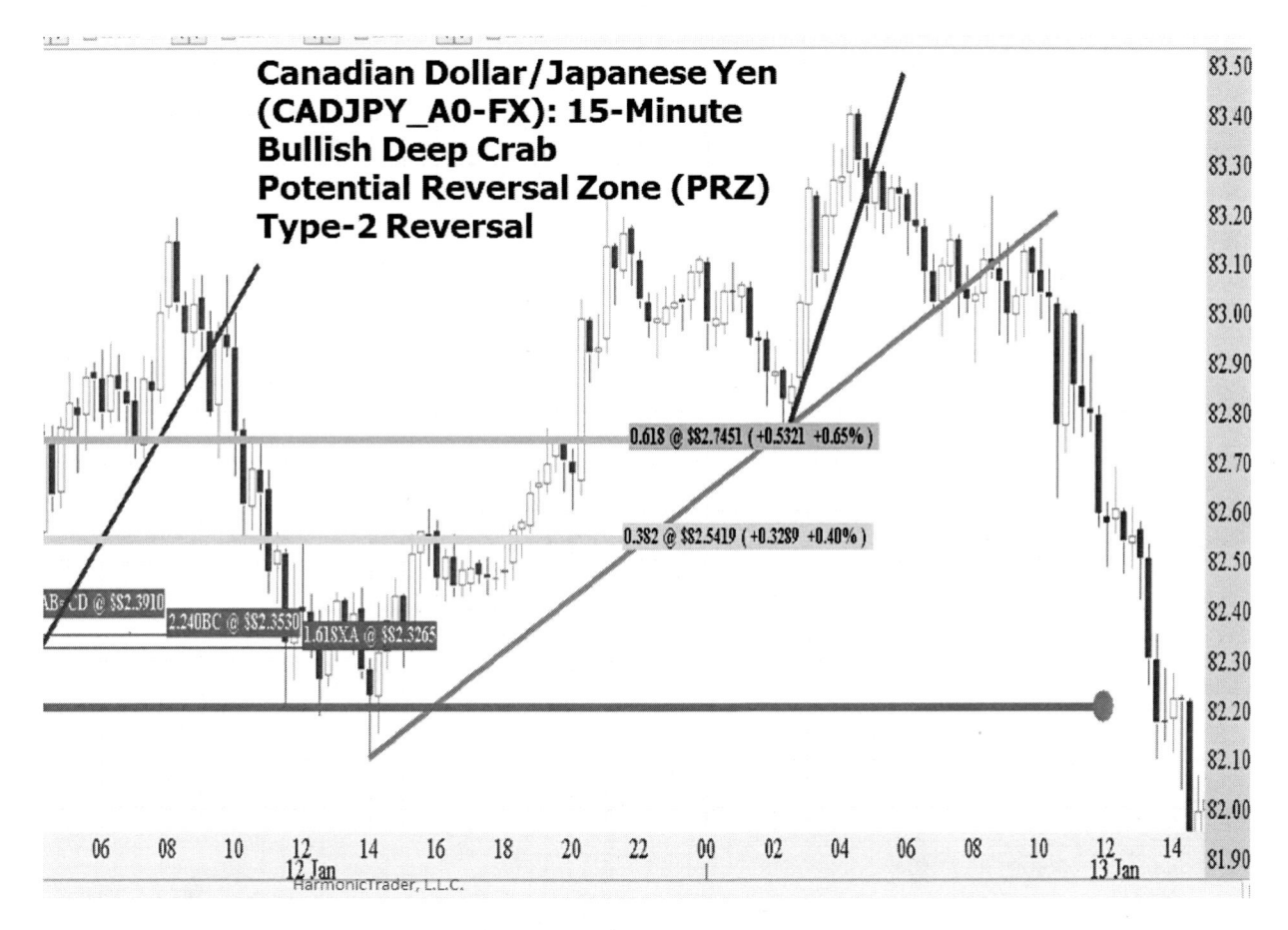

In Type-II situations, it is important to allow more consolidation as the reversal unfolds. Although the retest may not be as precise as the initial completion, the Type-II reversal demands that PRICE and INDICATOR CONFIRMATION validate the opportunity. These situations require more time but potentially offer more reward, as the second target is the typical Type-II profit objective. Defined as the 61.8% retracement of the pattern, the expectation for larger moves are due to the secondary confirmation that occurs at the retest. In fact, Type-II REVERSALS are the precise harmonic situations where the potential for a larger move after a harmonic pattern has been confirmed. Similar execution assessments will be employed on the retest of the original PRZ, but the

Harmonic Trading Volume 3: Reaction vs. Reversal

management associated with Type-II reversals will require more discretionary assessments – much more than in Type-I reactions. Most notably, the reversal trendline that develops following the retest will be a dynamic factor that projects the overall progress of the harmonic pattern reversal. Trendlines can be employed simply but are more effective with the profit targets to define the ideal framework to manage the trade. We will examine detailed strategies in the material regarding trade management. However, trendline strategies can be employed to manage any position and mark the optimal make-or-break levels in a variety on situations.

Bearish Type-II Reversal

Bearish Type-II reversals are associated with a secondary test that commonly exceed the initial peak. After the Type-I reaction has completed, the eventual retest will establish a "Type-II Terminal Price Bar" after testing all the numbers of the original Potential Reversal Zone. Once this occurs, the price action following the completion point of the retest should be demonstrative PRICE and INDICATOR reversal trend direction.

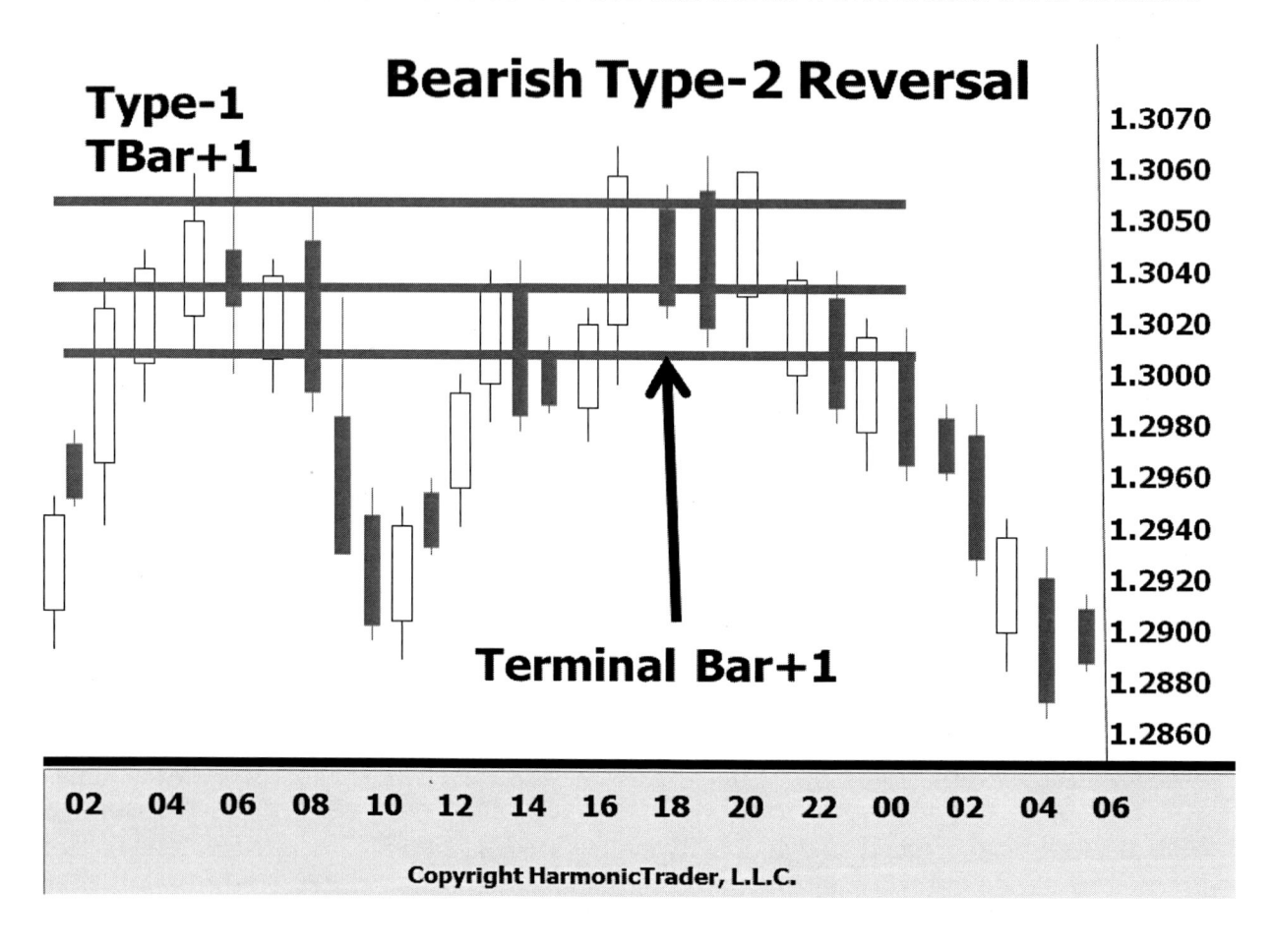

Harmonic Trading Volume 3: Reaction vs. Reversal

Swiss Franc/Japanese Yen (CHFJPY_A0-FX/): 60-Minute
Bearish Gartley
Bearish Type-II Reversal

The following chart Swiss Franc versus the Japanese Yen demonstrates the Type-I /Type-II phenomenon. Even in a volatile environment, the initial reaction from the pattern was a typical Type-I move that retested the PRZ inn dramatic fashion.

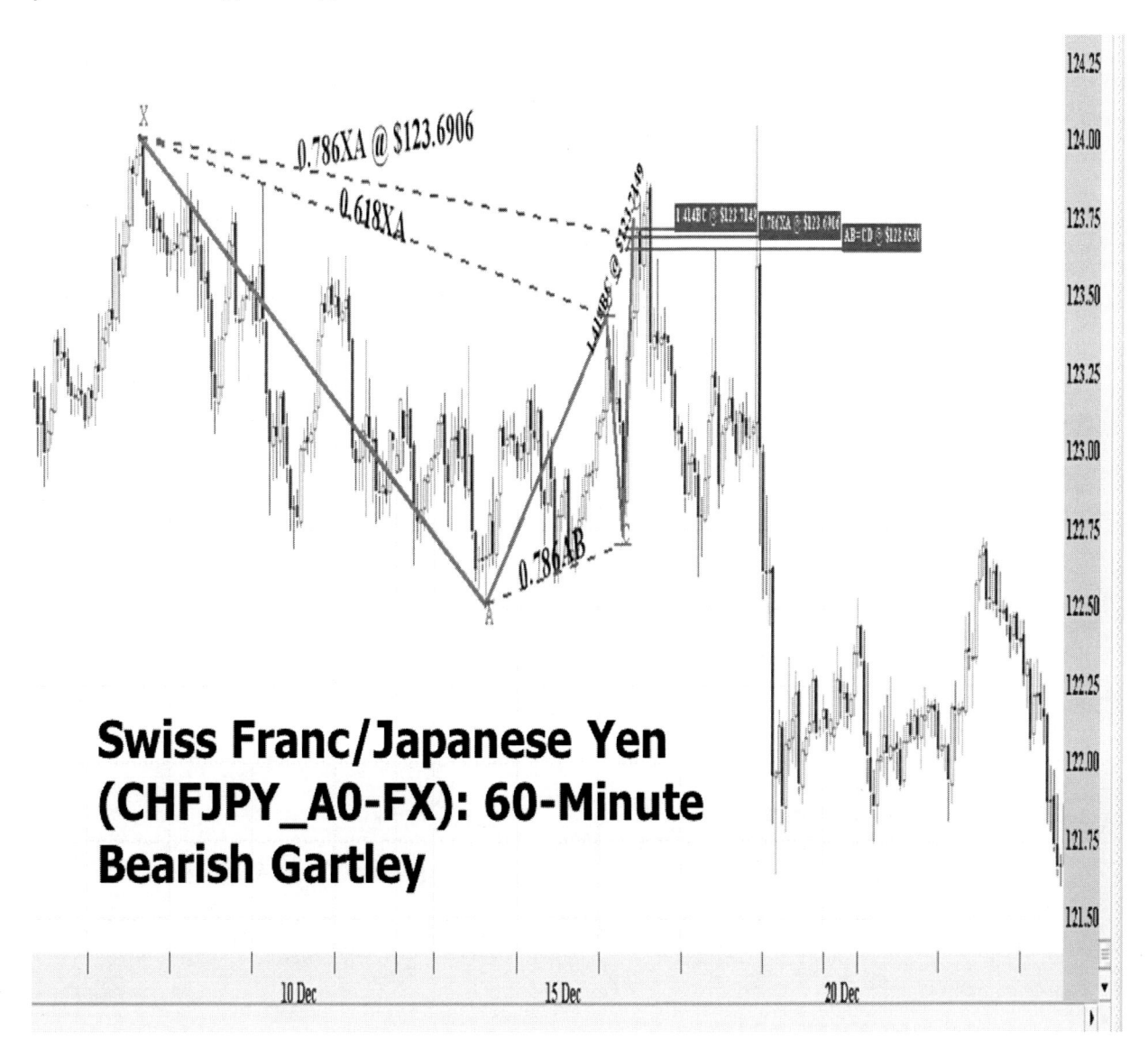

Harmonic Trading Volume 3: Reaction vs. Reversal

Swiss Franc/Japanese Yen (CHFJPY_A0-FX/): 60-Minute
Bearish Gartley Potential Reversal Zone (PRZ)
Bearish Type-II Reversal

The Bearish Gartley formed a distinct pattern on the 60-minute chart. The price action experienced a sharp reaction on the initial completion of pattern. After the initial reaction was complete, the secondary test reversed violently after testing the original Potential Reversal Zone. These situations can be difficult due to the volatility but the Harmonic Trading plan defines these price objectives in advance. Furthermore, the recognition of reversal types facilitates decisions effectively even in the most reactive of environments.

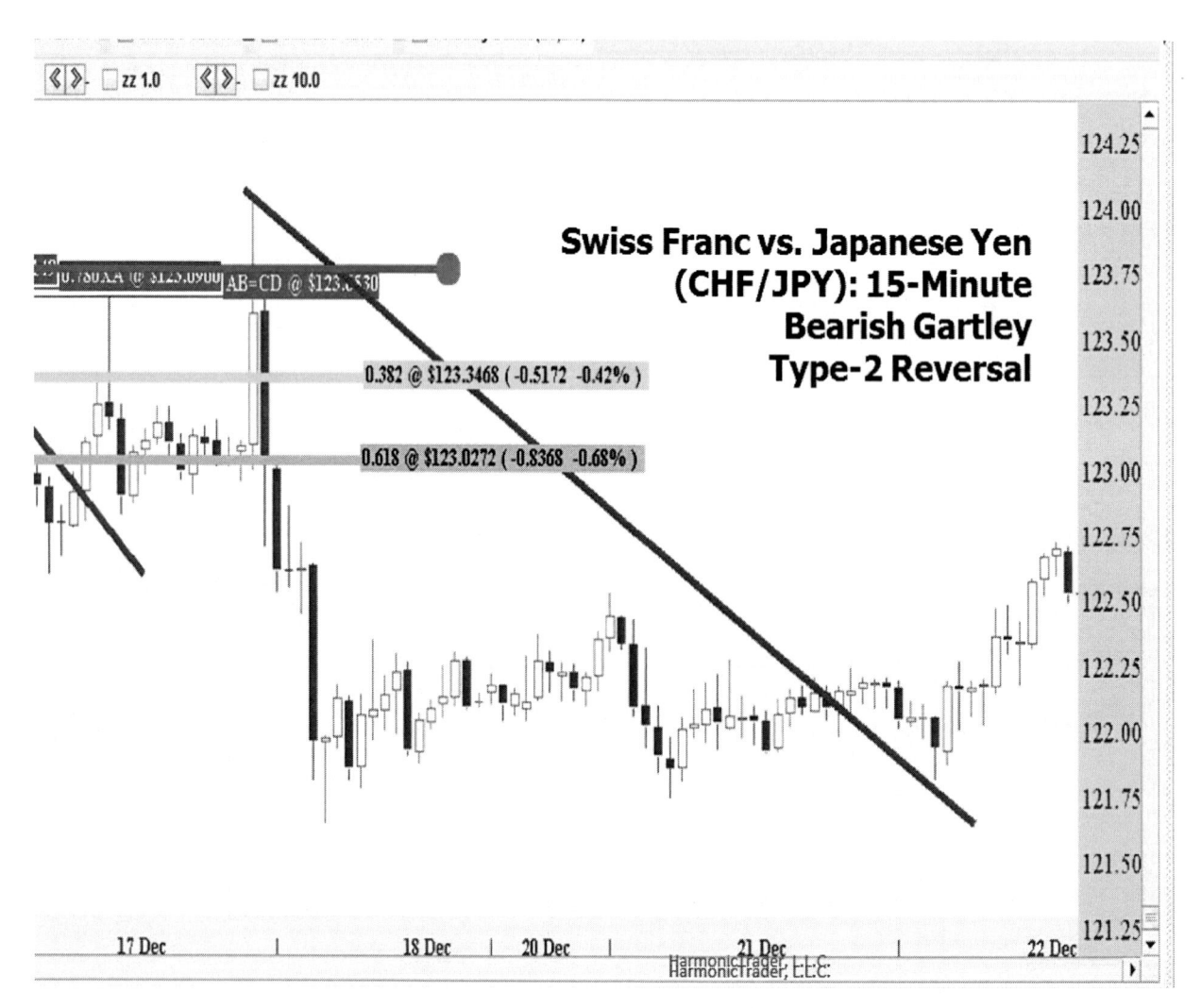

Harmonic Trading Volume 3: Reaction vs. Reversal

Harmonic Trading Reversal Types Conclusion

As I've outlined in this material, there are clear differences between immediate reversals and those that require consolidation. This distinction has created an effective means to quickly recognize those opportunities that will provide an immediate and clear reaction as opposed to those that will take longer to materialize. Furthermore, the basic understanding of the natural harmonic reaction most structures experience dictates the importance of categorizing whether the pattern is completing for the first time or undergoing a secondary retest of the established price level.

These are guidelines that took years of research and tinkering to truly define the consistent characteristics that facilitate the analysis of a reversal from these harmonic pattern distinctions. Not to mention, these strategies have become effective tools for traders to maximize multiple harmonic pattern opportunities and exemplify the type of measurements outside of the basic structural considerations that are essential part in navigating reactions and reversals.

Most importantly, the harmonic pattern execution framework facilitates decisions in a standard process that is as precise as identification strategies. Although there will be some differences depending upon market and time interval, these strategies are uniform and apply to all situations that may be encountered. The most important take away from this material is that harmonic pattern reversals must be differentiated and distinguished to optimize executions. Furthermore, demonstrative confirmation strategies at the completion of the harmonic pattern levels are among the most effective means to validate the opportunity in any execution. I recommend Harmonic Traders master the Type-I strategy and develop the skill to execute after the Terminal Bar is established. Although this window of execution can be truncated, the clear confirmation signals that unfold with the initial pattern completion provide further evidence that the structure will yield a minimum reaction. In the next few chapters, we will look at the strategies that pinpoint confirmation signals in the Potential Reversal Zone (PRZ) and the detailed trade management strategies that standardize actions in specific situations.

The Type-I Reaction vs. the Type-II Reversal concept is an essential aspect of the entire methodology. There are specific expectations that facilitate decisions in each situation. A reaction mentality will aggressively manage these positions and understand that there is a limited time to this scenario. The reversal mentality will employ a larger expectation about the potential profit objective but these situations require more time and distinct indicator confirmation in every case. Regardless, the harmonic pattern framework defines the entry, stop loss and profit targets in advance for both types. I frequently remind traders that harmonic patterns typically offer two opportunities – ONE REACTION, ONE REVERSAL. Within this perspective, these Harmonic Trading execution strategies provide the accurate insights required to make consistently effective decisions, especially in those trading environments that can be overwhelmingly confusing.

Chapter 5:
Advanced Indicator Analysis in Harmonic Trading

When I first released the pattern identification rules, I was exclusively committed to the study of price action. Other than looking at basic Volume readings, most of my research focused on the combination of price structures. This proved to be more than expected as the amount of detail required to break down the various pattern categorizations required a period of years to truly validate consistent harmonic behavior. In fact, I waited until 2004 before releasing Harmonic Trading Volume One due to the five-year testing period required to formulate the entire gamut of strategies that defined an entire framework. Once the price structure strategies were validated, I focused more on other technical approaches that I had studied long-before exploring patterns, and explored distinct relationships that consistently unfolded at the completion of harmonic patterns. Although I had been aware of indicator extremes as a means to assess market movements, the true value of this analysis was evidently clear in harmonic pattern situations.

In my opinion, this integration was the defining moment when Harmonic Pattern Theory became a larger field of study, now commonly referred to as *Harmonics*. The enhanced specification of strategies beyond simple structural identification has been essential in expanding comprehensive harmonic techniques applied in both execution and management. Harmonic Patterns are even more significant as point of reference for these stages in the process than the simple identification of a price structure. In fact, the search for deeper relationships in the areas of trading has led to unique discoveries beyond pattern recognition. The proprietary research of indicators such as Harmonic Strength Index (HSI) has advanced the overall effectiveness of the methodology. HSI readings complement the completion point of harmonic patterns and define the optimal level within a pattern's zone. When extreme indicator readings reverse from the corresponding extreme at or just after the Terminal Bar has completed, the execution can be considered valid and signals immediate confirmation of the pattern at hand. Harmonic Strength Index is just one type of strategy that distinguishes harmonic price action phenomenon relative to extreme readings. The integration of this analysis enhances the proper expectations to a precise degree and defines more complex but consistent harmonic pattern behavior.

When I initially researched indicator strategies, I explored relationships in Stochastics, MACD, ADX and others with the singular goal to expose those technical measures that provided the clearest signals at the completion of the pattern. Although most indicators have some value, I was able to quickly eliminate most, as they simply lacked the consistent qualities to measure price behavior as it related to harmonic movements. However, the Relative Strength Index (RSI) was one of the very few that possessed overwhelmingly clear relationships with harmonic levels. At the time, RSI was one of the primary indicators offered by most charting software. However, I was not completely aware of its origin or formula that explained why it worked so well with harmonic patterns.

Welles Wilder's book, *New Concepts in Technical Trading Systems (1978)* is a technical masterpiece if only for the indicator formula he shared in this material. Although this book contained mostly mathematical equations, it is one of the most important works that has established the foundation for modern technical indicators as they are known today. In fact, Mr. Wilder can be considered as the forefather of technical indicators due to the number of strategies he released in that book. ADX, RSI and many of the commonly known indicators came from this book. Not to mention, he has become known for other ideas such as Delta Cycle Theory which denotes important timing points within a trend.

These ideas represented a unique shift in market analysis in general, as formula such as RSI effectively revealed relationships based upon past history to analyze market movements. Not to mention, this was during a time when technical ideas were relatively unknown and charting software was just starting to emerge.

Mr. Wilder's focus on relative price analysis was an effective concept that still has potential analytical value in today's markets. When related to specific harmonic pattern situations, extreme RSI conditions define a unique opportunity where both structural and indicator signals confirm the same expectation for a reaction/reversal. For me, I was interested in any type of measure that could isolate distinct behavior within the zones of harmonic and support and resistance, as I was searching for only the most consistent variables. Of all indicators, Wilder's RSI signaled these situations. As I researched it further, I analyzed the individual components of the formula to understand how the indicator expresses its readings. In general, the RSI formula measures the relative performance of an immediate average versus that of a trailing average of greater length. Simply stated, the indicator compares what is happening now versus what is happening in the past to define <u>internal changes in price</u>.

RSI is an ingenious concept that identifies changing conditions that frequently precede major price moves. Although these signals require more than a single extreme reading to define a true change in the immediate trend, its value related to harmonic patterns is remarkable. Once I understood its importance in relation harmonic measurements, I aggressively tinkered with structural identification and numeric classifications that refined pattern situations to an exact degree. Much like pattern structures, the indicator analysis evolved into a framework of expectations that facilitated decisions throughout the trading process. Depending upon the condition of RSI, I was able to compare price movements relative to the degree of the indicator reading to more clearly ascertain the possibility that a pattern could yield a nominal reaction versus a significant reversal. Furthermore, I realized that indicator interpretations like these possessed similar harmonic structures, revealing insightful characteristics in the price action and the relative extremes in the market. In combination with harmonic pattern zones, the various type of RSI readings helped to define the "environment" in which harmonic patterns complete.

Such categorizations provided accurate and distinct expectations of probable future price action depending upon the indicator type. We will examine these strategies in detail later in this material. However, the importance of this analytical integration can not be understated. In fact, harmonic pattern opportunities – real trades – must possess some type of indicator confirmation – RSI, Harmonic Strength Index or other technical measure in every instance! These strategies constitute what is required to validate confirmation and highlight the larger potential for reversals from minor reactions.

Relative Strength Index (RSI)

In Wilder's book, he revealed the exact formula for the Relative Strength Index (RSI) and discussed some optimal strategies applied to the markets. The indicator was devised as a means of calculating the change in momentum of price movement as it relates to a predetermined time period. According to Wilder's definition, he employed a 14-period average. Although I will discuss different time periods later in this material, it is important to note that the indicator does not compare the Relative Strength of two securities. Rather, RSI measures the internal strength of the price action of an individual issue on a specific timeframe. RSI is a price-following oscillator that ranges between 0 and 100, typically topping out above 70 and reversing below 30 at extreme lows. The indicator reversal signal usually materializes in the indicator readings before the underlying price action reverses. This is even more valid when the indicator structural readings are differentiated.

Relative Strength Index (RSI) Formula

$$RSI = 100 - \{100/(1+RSI)\}$$

$$\text{Relative Strength} = \frac{\text{Average \# of Closes Up}}{\text{Average \# of Closes Down}}$$

(#: Typically based upon a 14 period)

RSI Extremes

The Relative Strength Index is an oscillates between 0 and 100. Welles Wilder defined these limits in his 1978 book, *New Concepts of Technical Trading Systems.* He outlined the nature these readings at the extreme levels and described conditions that tend to signal an impending change in trend. His Overbought and Oversold definitions are the standard for the indicator.

- **Overbought ≥ 70:**
  Price action that possesses an RSI reading at or above the 70 level.

- **Oversold ≤ 30:**
  Price action that possesses an RSI reading at or below the 50 level.

Expectations at Relative Strength Levels

In my own research, I employ these same parameters but I have classified indicator structural readings which possess specific implications in their own right. These refinements of RSI formations were effective in differentiating specific types of reversals as well as establishing proper expectations regarding probable future price action, especially when harmonic patterns completed at these extremes. In the same way that ratio measurements of price segments define certain expectations of what can happen, indicator readings possess similar interpretations that accurately define complex technical environments. In fact, these strategies offer a comprehensive framework of expectations which can be employed as a trading system in its own right. Together, indicator strategies complement harmonic price zones for the most effective application of these measures.

Oversold RSI Reading: 0-30 Range

The oversold range in the Relative Strength Index between 0-30 is an absolute level that was defined by Welles Wilder when he introduced the indicator. Due to the nature of the calculation, the indicator reading cannot exceed 0. The definition of an oversold reading of 30 or below is a mandatory requirement that must be realized to validate the extremity of the situation. I have encountered situations that fall just shy of the extreme and fail to signal a confirmation. The exact reading must register a value that is actually less than 31. In fact, a valid reading of 30.65 for example, can mark a valid confirmation. Although the clearest of extreme readings are to be favored, it is important to note that any reading of 30 or less qualifies as a valid oversold extreme. The most important event is triggered by the indicator reversal, since this is typically the early signal of a change in trend. More notably, indicator extreme tests that dramatically exceed the 30-minimum level on the initial test and typically signal a deeper move at hand. Therefore, the nature and degree of these extreme tests also dictates what can be expected among reversal possibilities.

Overbought Relative Strength Reading: 70-100 Range

The overbought range for the indicator is defined by a reading that tests at or above the 70 level and reverses from that extreme shortly thereafter. Depending upon the indicator's structural type, the extreme test may require varying levels of time before confirming the reversal. Again, these are the subtle differences that shape expectations and define confirmation variables. The most important consideration is the price action behavior after the reversal has completed. RSI readings can register extreme readings, reversing from the overbought zone at 70 as price continues to climb. This underscores the expectation that the trigger is an early signal and must be confirmed with a reaction in price. Furthermore, indicator assessments typically will require more time to gauge whether or not the reading will generate a price move of significance. However, this underscores the effectiveness of indicator integration to highlight complex harmonic pattern scenarios that define reliable trade opportunities.

Mid-point at the 50-Level

Price action at the 50-level can dictate a great deal regarding the state of the primary trend. One of the easiest ways to examine indicator readings in this area is to utilize the mid-level at the 50 level to gauge trend continuation. If price is clearly in a bullish trend, RSI should hold above the 50-level, as it fluctuates between the midpoint and the extreme 70-limit. This reflects a condition of a strong primary trend where pullbacks are normally brief pauses within the overall direction of the move. In distinct bearish trends, RSI should stay consistently below the mid-point 50-level. As price declines, it is common to observe Relative Strength readings that bounce between the 30-limit and the 50-limit.
Another important consideration that involves the midpoint 50-level is the determination of complex Divergence and Confirmation situations. Mr. Wilder discussed the importance of multiple indicator tests as more important than a single extreme. From the harmonic perspective, I have differentiated these multi-segmented indicator readings and analyzed those situations where two extreme readings are separated by a minimum test of the 50-level. Referred to as RSI BAMM, I will outline the details of this strategy later in this material but the significance of multiple indicator extremes must not be understated. Therefore, it is always essential to examine any indicator extreme test relative to the prior reading and the type of formation in the overbought/oversold zone.

Deep Extreme RSI Readings: 80/20

I have experimented a great deal with Relative Strength and deconstructed the formula in numerous ways. I have tested various components to adjust time preferences, price calculations and implement harmonic modifiers that quantify the natural limits of the indicator readings. For quite some time, I've been aware of small yet critical differences in severe RSI readings that expand in the extreme indicator zones beyond oversold readings below 20 and overbought readings above 80. These distinctions are determined by the behavior of the price action immediately after it tests the extreme limit. Similar to the differentiation of harmonic pattern types, overtly dramatic and "deep" extreme indicator tests must be handled differently. For example, an RSI reversal from 70 will possess different corresponding price behavior than a more extreme 80 reading. As I will outline later in this material, the structural formation of indicator readings will establish an even more detailed framework of precise expectations to facilitate decisions. These considerations serve as effective guidelines to define the total harmonic pattern framework.

I have outlined a number of situations with the RSI BAMM strategy that exemplify these types of situations. For example, an RSI reading that exceeds the 80/20 level and forms a complex structure will require much more time to confirm any possibility of a reversal. In fact, these situations typically require an eventual retest of the initial test of the harmonic price level before a larger reversal can ensue. These specific scenarios relative to harmonic patterns can be even more revealing. The proper minimum expectations of both indicator and pattern analysis provide a clearer picture of what can be expected. Although most initial reactions will be short-lived and require some degree of consolidation, this integrated comprehension promotes a realistic expectation for any harmonic pattern trading opportunity.

Twice the Distance in Half the Time...

One of the most helpful guidelines that I employ when monitoring price action, especially early reversal behavior following the execution of a trade is to gauge the progress of the indicator reading in relation to price. Since RSI can reliably be an early signal, the progress of price usually unfolds in a delayed manner until a thorough consolidation phase unfolds at the pattern's completion point. However, it is possible to assess to assess the validity of a harmonic pattern reversal from the indicator progress relative to price movements in the Potential Reversal Zone (PRZ). For example, a successful reversal from a bearish pattern with RSI confirmation will typically experience price action with a reading that reverses from the 70 level. Although the indicator may provide early confirmation, the acceleration of the reversal typically does not occur until the reading violates the mid-point at the 50-level. In essence, the magnitude of price movement from the pattern will not be the same as RSI declines from 70 to a 50 reading versus when the indicator drops from 50 to 30. Although these are effective management strategies, the categorization of "states of RSI" is another important distinction related to harmonic pattern reversals. In fact, I am sharing this proprietary insight for the first time and I will outline how to interpret these indicator readings later in this material. However, this unique phenomenon highlights definable RSI movements that are influential factors that can define the "character" of price action, especially in harmonic pattern reversal situations. The price behavior at the mid-point can identify an excitable state of trend acceleration. In general, RSI accelerations past the 50-level will result in a larger price move. In the situations, "price will go twice the distance in half the time" as the indicator accelerates into an extreme level. The basic assumption is as follows:

- **Bearish Trends:** When price declines with an indicator reading that declines from the midpoint line at 50 to the oversold extreme under 30, the bearish price trend will accelerate twice the price distance as it did from 70 to 50 in approximately half the time.

- **Bullish Trends:** When price increases with an indicator reading that goes from the midpoint line at 50 to the overbought extreme above 70, the bullish price trend will accelerate twice the distance as it did from 30 to 50 in approximately half the time.

Of course, these are general rules that will possess varying combinations. However, these expectations are reliable guidelines and help to monitor the price action especially after the execution of a harmonic pattern opportunity. Clearly, the magnitude of the price movement is not the same at each RSI reading. But, price does exhibit different behavior relevant to the trend when RSI readings correlate. This is one of the most reliable RSI assessments that helps monitor these strategies related to price behavior and gauges the extent of profit potential for any reversal. We will take a look at detailed trade management strategies later in the material but expectations such as these go a long way in defining what is possible within any market environment.

Most significantly, the strategies that explain distinct RSI phenomenon are reliable assessments even when patterns do not exist. This is where the selectivity to patiently wait for those overwhelming opportunities and the discipline to not attempt to trade those situations are less than ideal serves the trader's best interests in the long run. This may be difficult because there will be plenty of observational phenomenon that adheres to these concepts. Regardless, the goal is to identify those situations that possess overwhelming evidence of harmonic patterns and clear indicator confirmation to isolate the opportunities with the greatest probability based upon both metrics.

Coordinating Indicator Readings in the Potential Reversal Zone

Harmonic patterns define the price level for an anticipated reversal but valid trade executions require a clear indicator reaction at an extreme area for the most effective means of confirmation. Ever since I presented these integrated proprietary RSI strategies in my *Harmonic Trading Volume 2* book, the requirements that define pattern opportunities have become more specific - perhaps, a better word may be situational. Regardless, the advanced indicator conditions provide the most suitable environments for harmonic pattern reversals. Not only limited to RSI, other harmonic indicator readings build upon the foundation of this research and pinpoint price behavior in the Potential Reversal Zone to a more definable degree. Specific indicator confirmation strategies provide even more effective tools to assess harmonic pattern opportunities. The key is to understand in advance which variables and measures must be coordinated to mark valid confirmation. Although these events should occur simultaneously in the best confirmation situations, it is common to experience a delay in price action where the indicator signals early triggers of a potential change in trend. Regardless, there are a few standard comparisons that must be considered to completely integrate these confirmation strategies.

- **Coordinate Pattern Completion with an Extreme Indicator Reversal:** In these situations, we look for a reversal from the indicator extreme that matches up with the pattern's Potential Reversal Zone. If there is a bullish pattern, the extreme indicator reversal from the 30 level should be realized as the price action is testing the harmonic support. If there is a bearish pattern, the extreme indicator reversal must rollover from the 70 level and decline as the price action is testing a bearish pattern.

- **Confirm Price Action:** Although unique structures and complex readings can define comprehensive market opportunities, there are many situations where the trend of the indicator can confirm the overall direction of price. We will review some strategies as they relate to trade management later in this material. However, many important relationships are expressed in indicator readings that can signal the strength of the trend.

- **Differentiate Individual Indicator Readings at Extremes:** Outlined in my *Volume Two,* the type of indicator structure is critical in defining the extent of the extreme test. Much like harmonic patterns, indicator readings can form distinct structures at extreme levels that indicate the type of price action that can be expected as well as signal nominal reactions from potential pattern reversals. Furthermore, these strategies can be applied to manage positions optimally by instill the proper framework of expectations based upon the pattern AND indicator readings at hand.

Two Types of Indicator Formations at Extremes

I initially presented these strategies in my *Harmonic Trading Volume 2.* The categorization of extreme readings was an important advancement beyond simple indicator confirmation. The strategies in *Volume 2* – most notably, RSI BAMM – expanded the application of indicator readings in general, although RSI was the primary focus. The book distinguished structural indicator readings. There are two general classes of indicator structures that test the extreme levels – impulsive and complex. These formations possess unique characteristics and are excellent indicators of price character. Although both types require extreme Oversold (30 and below) or Overbought (70 and above) indicator tests, they are most effective at the completion of a pattern to serve as an early signal of an impending change in price direction. These measures must be analyzed simultaneously, as the extreme indicator test confirms the individual price action in the Potential Reversal Zone (PRZ) immediately after the Terminal Bar is complete.

Trigger Bar

The price point where the indicator reverses from the extreme is an important early sign of impending change, as this denotes the *Trigger Bar*. This is the price bar that marks the exact point where the indicator reversal from the extreme area can be considered as officially confirmed. Although anything can happen at that point, the harmonic pattern framework combines with such indicator behavior to define a unique phenomenon where some degree of reaction unfolds in both the indicator and price. When these elements are expressed by multiple readings, they distinguish unique technical environments.

The concept of the Trigger Bar is derived from the philosophy that all information required to define trade opportunities can be analyzed from the price action history. To that aim, I have analyzed many strategies and examined individual price bars at critical harmonic levels to confirm the larger signal that indicators can provide. Although most of this material has applied the concept to RSI, other obvious changes in various technical measures can be denoted. For example, a dramatic selloff that possesses an enormous Volume spike typically can signal a state of exhaustion where all of the sellers have exited the market. In this case, the only immediate reaction is an automatic rebound in price as the cyclical mechanism that unfolds following such a move. This reactive phenomenon is common at a variety of points but the price parameters must be quantifiable to denote the exact price level for these changes. In the Volume exhaustion example, the price bar that triggered the extreme surge would represent a significant price level that must be considered a relevant technical level. For harmonic patterns, the Terminal Bar extreme represents the trigger point for the opportunity. These are a few examples but exemplify how to pinpoint individual price bars that cause a demonstrative change in behavior related to a particular technical strategy.

Impulsive Indicator Structures

An impulsive indicator structure reflects price action that is experiencing a brief test of the extreme area that typically reverses quickly without any consolidating price action. The nature of the impulsive indicator structure forms a /\ or \/ in the extreme area. The clear confirmation occurs when the RSI reading reverses from the extreme zone. Although the impulsive structure can confirm a harmonic pattern opportunity with one test of the extreme, the optimal situations occur when there are multiple formations in price and indicator readings unfold simultaneously. Indicator confirmation with harmonic measurements will typically yield an early signal but provide a reliable indication of a change in price action. Impulsive indicator readings usually reverse from the extreme area within 1-3 price bars of the initial test. The nature of the indicator reversal is the critical factor that serves as the defining trait to validate the execution of a potential trade opportunity.

Bullish Impulsive Indicator Structures

An impulsive bullish indicator reading will typically test the extreme area under 30 and reverse immediately thereafter. It is quite common for these type of extreme tests to nominally exceed the minimum level at 30, register an oversold signal and reverse sharply. Although deeper RSI readings may still possess an impulsive structure, most of these readings will not exceed the 30 minimum level much.

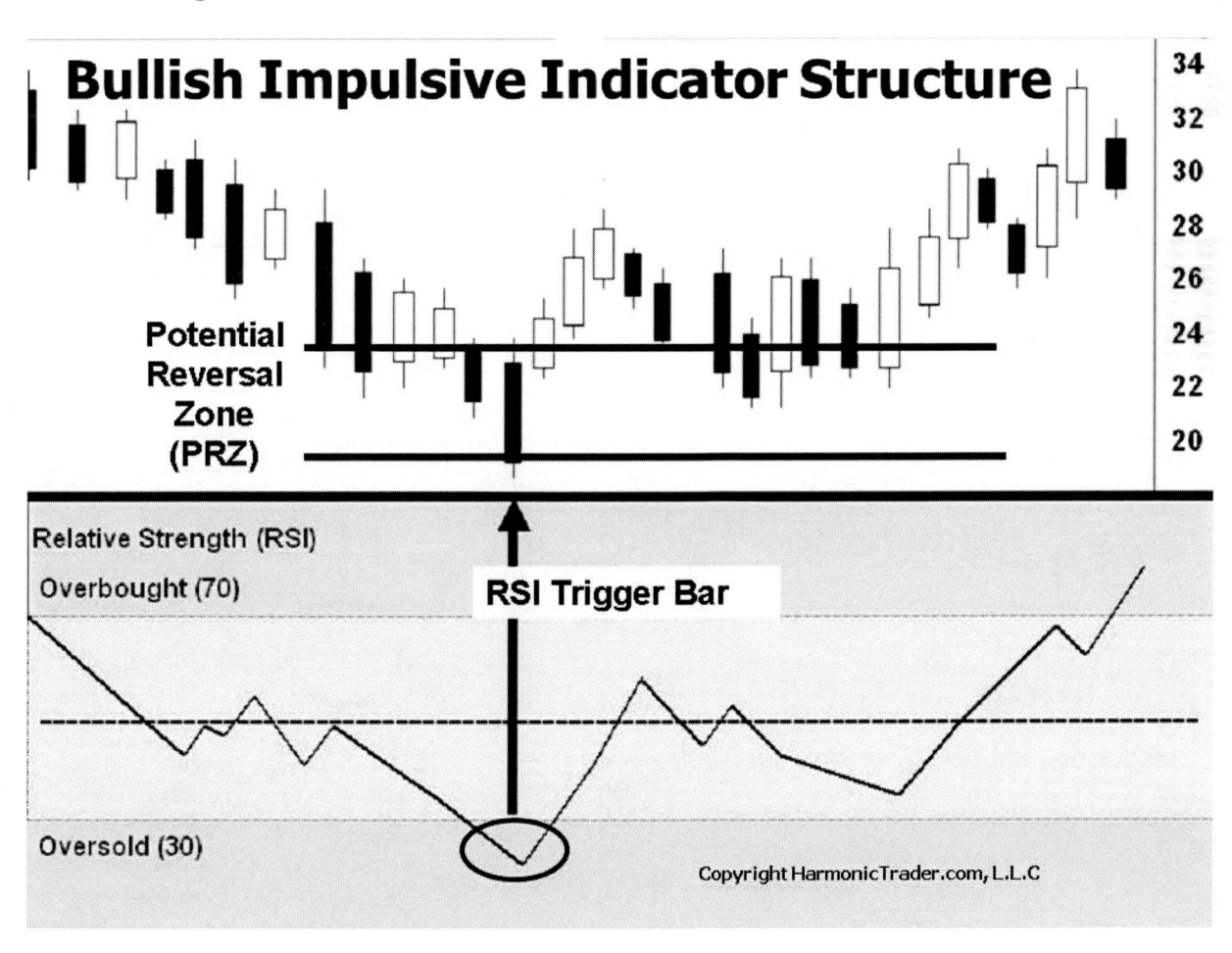

Harmonic Trading Volume 3: Reaction vs. Reversal

J.P. Morgan (JPM): 15-Minute
Bullish Deep Crab
Bullish Impulsive Indicator Structures

The following 15-minute chart of J.P. Morgan shows a distinct Bullish Deep Crab pattern with an impulsive RSI extreme test of the oversold limit that reversed immediately after completing the pattern. The indicator started to rally on the next bar and showed early progress before the price accelerated. These are the exact type of situations that must be coordinated to identify significant reversals in advance.

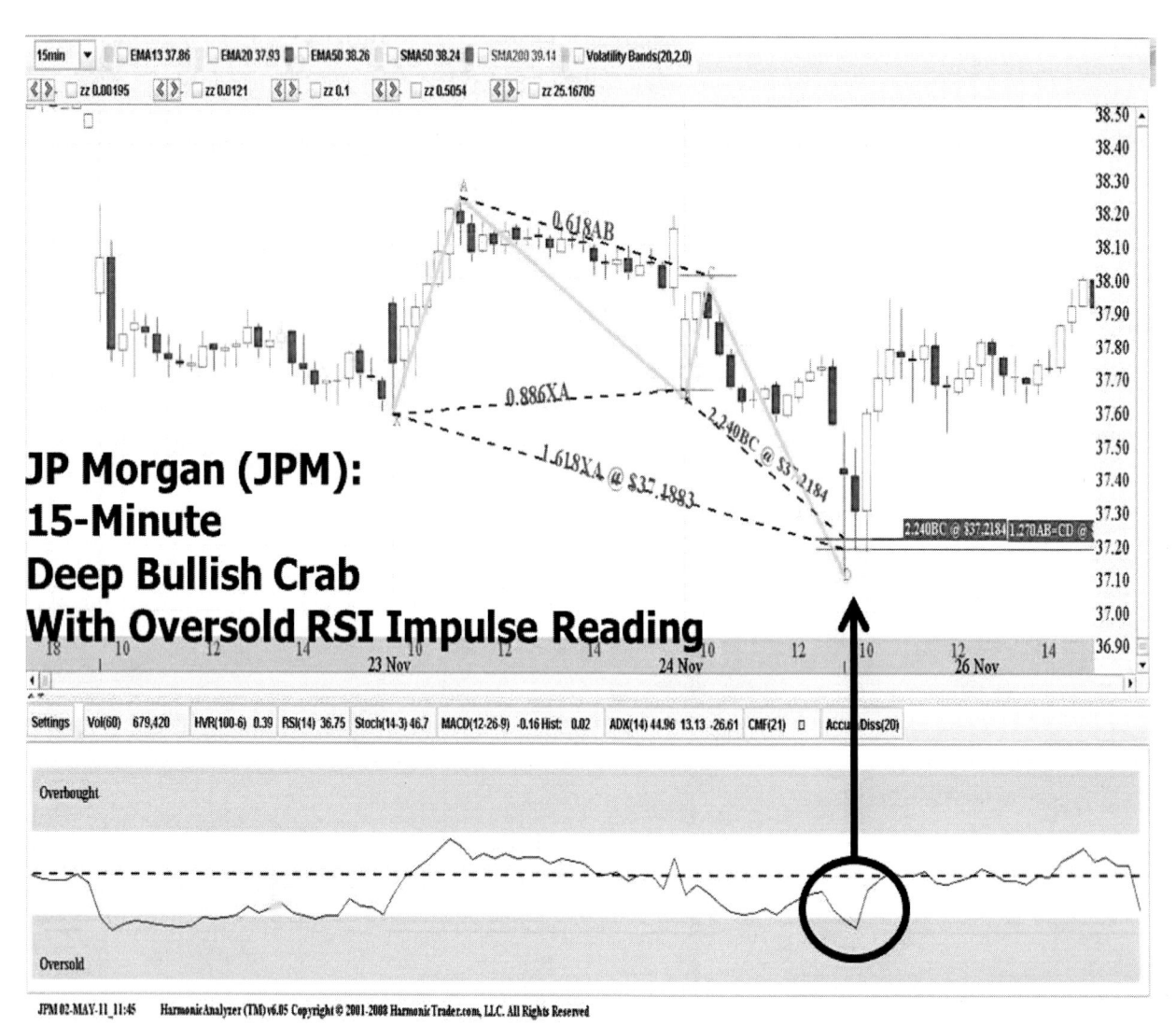

Harmonic Trading Volume 3: Reaction vs. Reversal

J.P. Morgan (JPM): 15-Minute
Bullish Deep Crab Potential Reversal Zone (PRZ)
Bullish Impulsive Indicator Structures

This chart shows the price action in the Potential Reversal Zone (PRZ) where the distinct Bullish Deep Crab marked an important harmonic support level. The price action stabilized immediately at the completion point of the pattern with an impulsive RSI extreme test of the oversold limit. The indicator reading immediately bounced after testing the 30-level with an impulsive structure, providing the early signs of a valid reversal at hand.

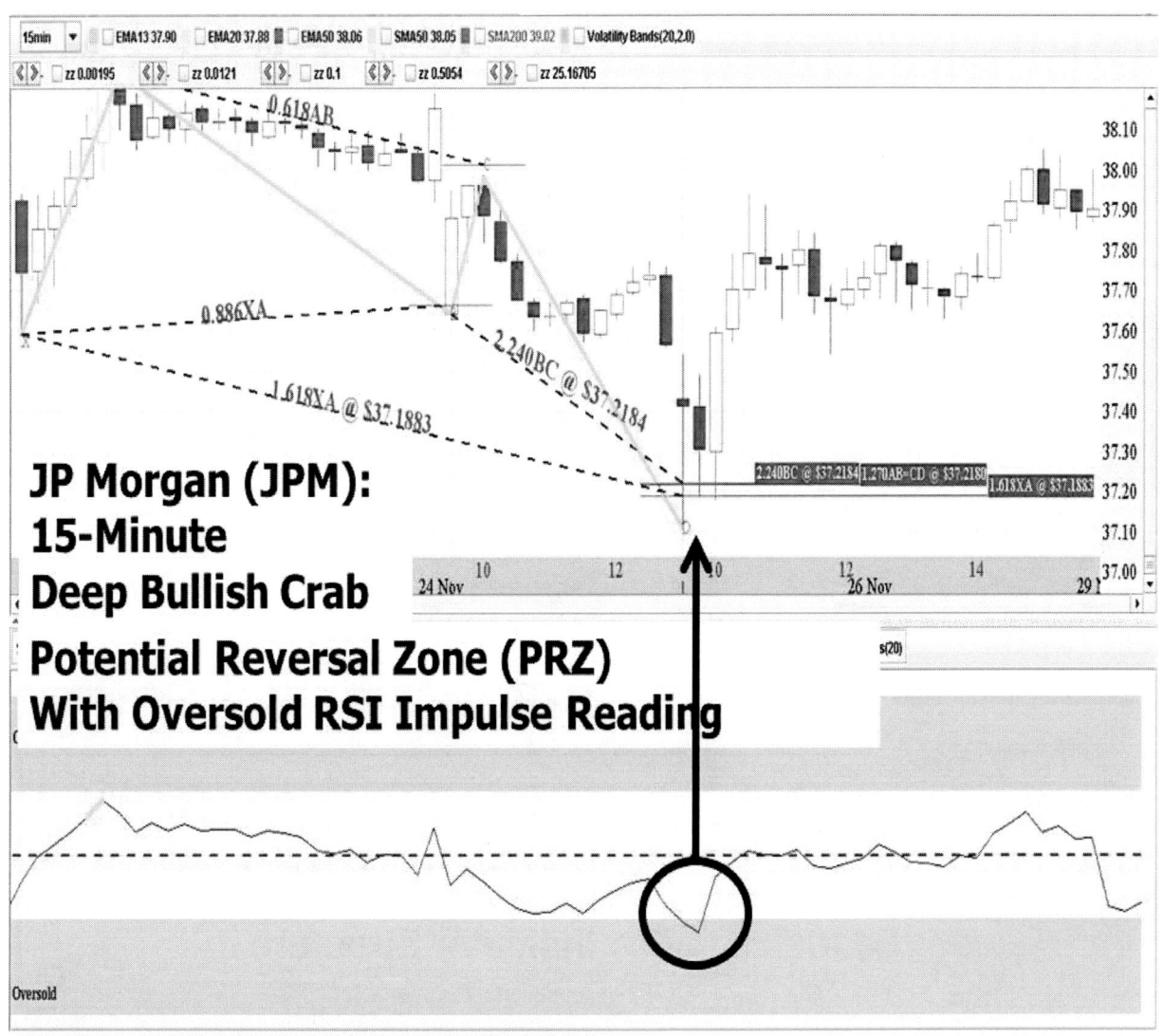

Harmonic Trading Volume 3: Reaction vs. Reversal

Bearish Impulsive Indicator Structure

The bearish impulsive indicator structure typically will be a quick test of the overbought limit above 70. This will be frequently associated with sharp price action where the indicator demonstratively reverses after testing the extreme limit. Impulsive readings can be early but do provide effective technical signs required to gauge the potential of a particular rally. Although a single indicator structure unto itself does not represent an actionable opportunity, in association with other price phenomenon and/or indicator readings, a more dynamic harmonic condition can be identified.

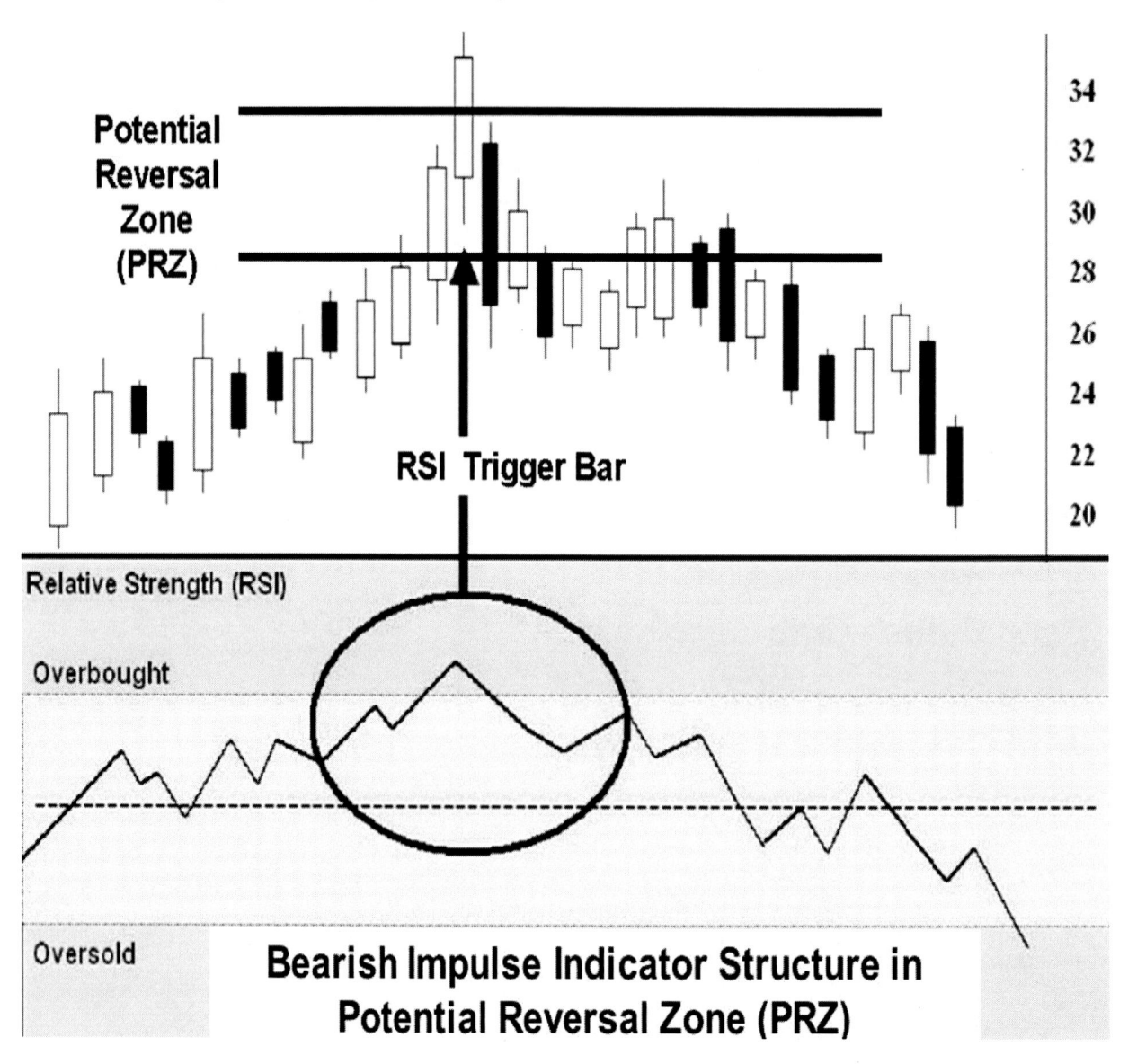

Bearish Impulse Indicator Structure in Potential Reversal Zone (PRZ)

Harmonic Trading Volume 3: Reaction vs. Reversal

Gold ETF (GLD): 5-Minute
Bearish Crab
Bearish Impulsive Indicator Structure

The following 5-minute chart in the continuous Gold contract shows a distinct Bearish Crab pattern with an impulsive RSI reading. As the price action was testing the harmonic resistance, the indicator reading reversed just above the 70-limit. The pattern was projected to complete in the 1388 area. The price action exceeded this area slightly as the 70-level was reached. Shortly thereafter, both the indicator and the price rolled over.

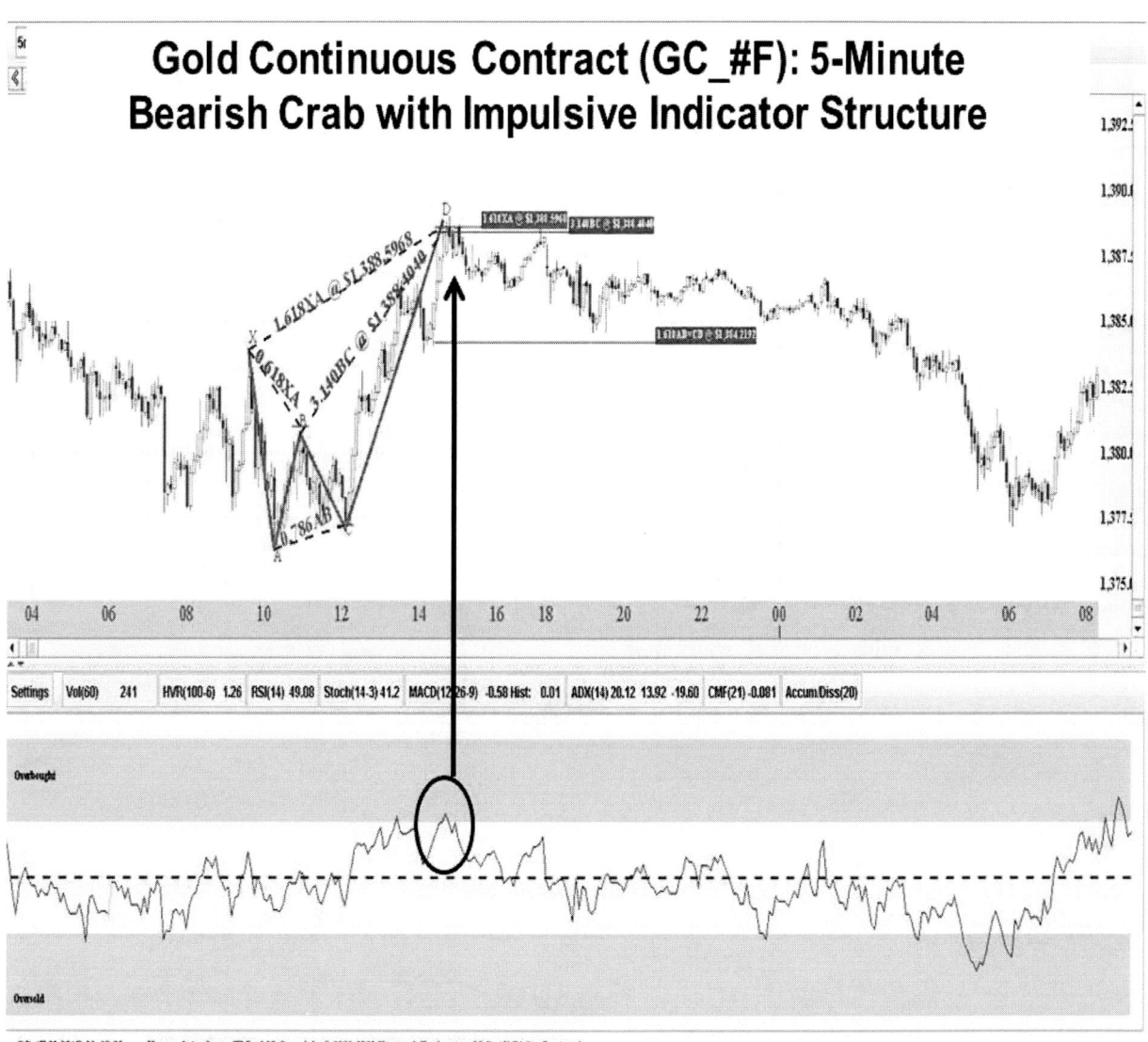

Harmonic Trading Volume 3: Reaction vs. Reversal

Gold ETF (GLD): 5-Minute
Bearish Crab Potential Reversal Zone (PRZ)
Bearish Impulsive Indicator Structure

The chart of the price action in the Potential Reversal Zone clearly shows how the indicator signaled the impending reversal as the price stalled after completing the Terminal Price Bar. These are critical and vital early signals of a valid pattern at hand. With experience, this coordination becomes easier and provides the insights necessary to know when a larger reversal will develop from an immediate Harmonic reaction. Coordinating the 70-test with the PRZ was the final move before the reversal ensued. After reversing from the 1389.60 level, the price action and corresponding indicator confirmed the dramatic move.

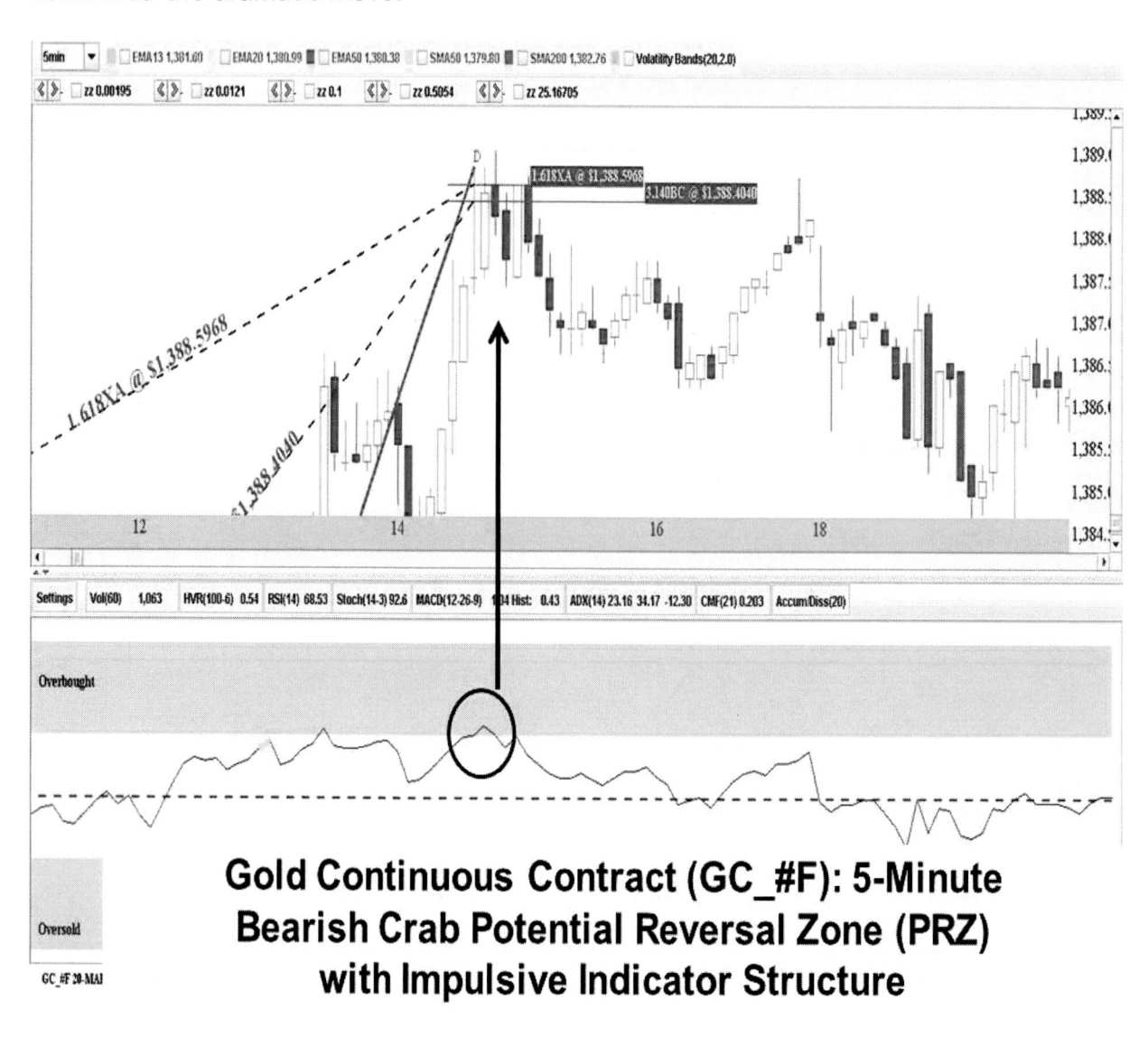

Gold Continuous Contract (GC_#F): 5-Minute
Bearish Crab Potential Reversal Zone (PRZ)
with Impulsive Indicator Structure

Harmonic Trading Volume 3: Reaction vs. Reversal

Complex Structures

Complex structures are those readings that exhibit an M-formation in the overbought extreme and a W-formation in the oversold zone. It is important to note that the entire M/W structure must take shape in the extreme zone. Otherwise, all other indicator structures can be considered as impulsive readings. Complex structures possess different expectations than impulsive formations in several ways. First, the complex formation usually requires more time to complete their reversal, as they are typically associated with deeper initial readings. Before the established price action can reverse, there will be a period of consolidation as the indicator tests the extreme limit. An indicator is not considered confirmed until it reverses completely from the extreme. In this situation, the exact price level where the indicator is "triggered" serves as another critical individual price bar within the Potential Reversal Zone (PRZ). Most important, complex structures define an initial area where the indicator reverses but the price reaction will only occur until the complex structure exits the extreme area.

Expectations of Complex Structures

Complex structures possess a defined expectation that typically requires a retest of the initial formation. As I will outline when we talk about RSI BAMM, the complex structure is a valid confirmation signal with harmonic patterns but requires a different perspective. In most cases, the reading will reverse according the RSI BAMM model from the extreme zone, react to the mid-point line at the 50-level before experiencing an eventual retest of the initial indicator trigger. Although this does not happen in every case, this general expectation does establish the proper bias and possibilities within the context of these environmental situations. If we understand that complex structures are likely to be retested, any corresponding price movement from this confirmation signal should possess a finite potential. This is particularly significant on the initial completion of a harmonic pattern that is confirmed by a complex indicator formation. The Type-I pattern corresponds with a complex structure in that both strategies anticipate secondary retest.

Bullish Complex Structures

The bullish complex RSI structure is a W formation that possesses all points under the 30-limit. In these situations, the price action will take more time to stabilize. The indicator will likely reverse early before the price confirms the new direction. This can be a challenge with complex structures however, the exact price level where the indicator reverses from the extreme serves to reinforce the measured harmonic pattern zones. Since complex structures are typically retested, it can be assumed that an initial reaction that experiences a reversal out of the extreme oversold 30-level will signal an impending change in price direction. Although this reaction experiences resistance once it exceeds the midpoint line at the 50-level, the most ideal cases will eventually retest the original bullish reaction. We will look at some combinations of the structures but the simple awareness of these expectations helps to facilitate decisions throughout the trading process.

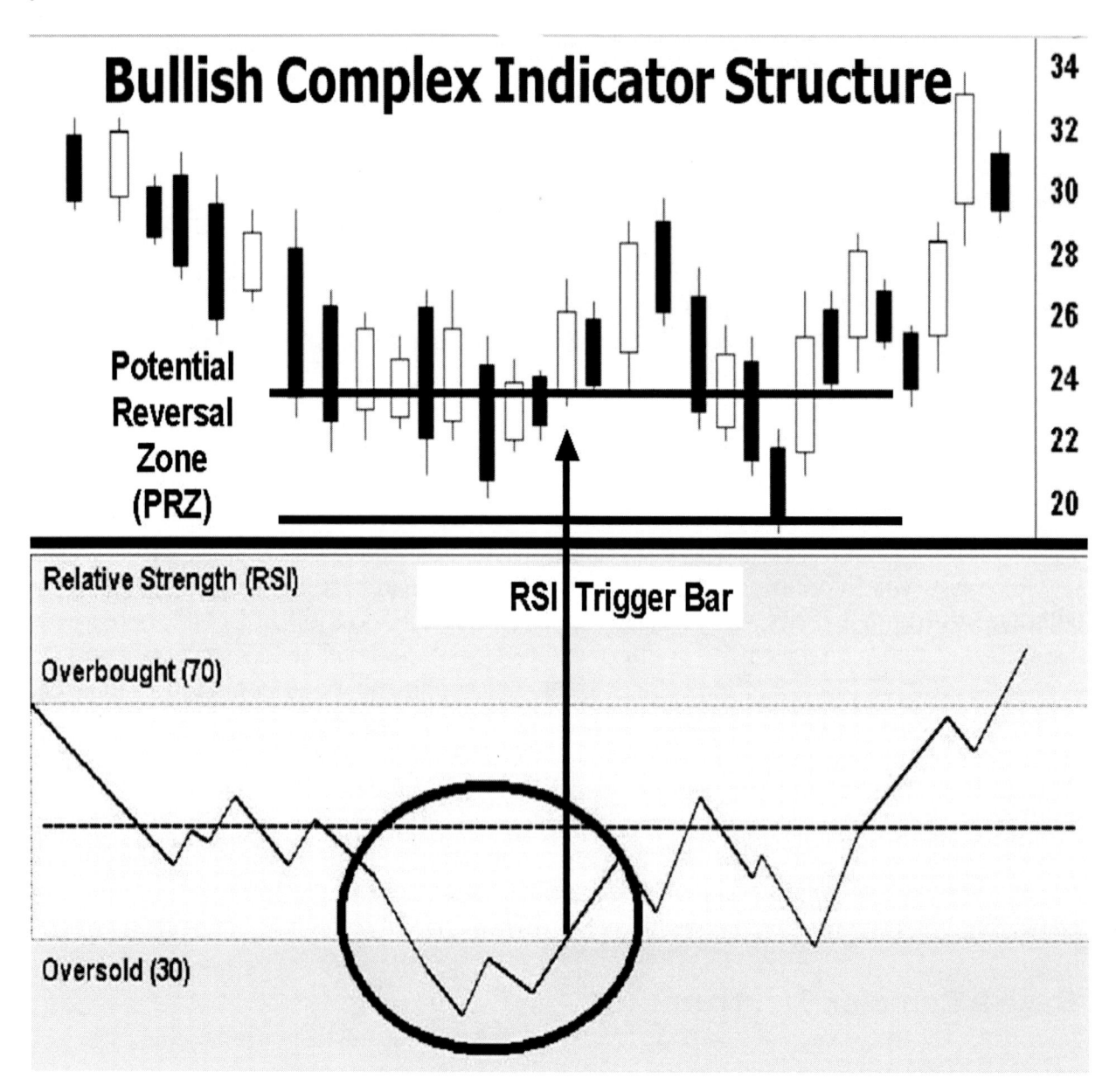

Bullish Complex Indicator Structure

Potential Reversal Zone (PRZ)

Relative Strength (RSI)

RSI Trigger Bar

Overbought (70)

Oversold (30)

Canadian Dollar (CAD_A0-FX): 15-Minute
Bullish Butterfly
Bullish Complex Structures

The following chart of the Canadian Dollar shows a distinct Bullish Butterfly pattern with a complex structure at the RSI oversold extreme. It is important to note how the final decline into the harmonic support zone exceeded the area slightly while the indicator stabilized. In the trade management material, we will look at how to handle these situations precisely but the coordination of the price action and the indicator in the Potential Reversal Zone defined the exact area for the opportunity.

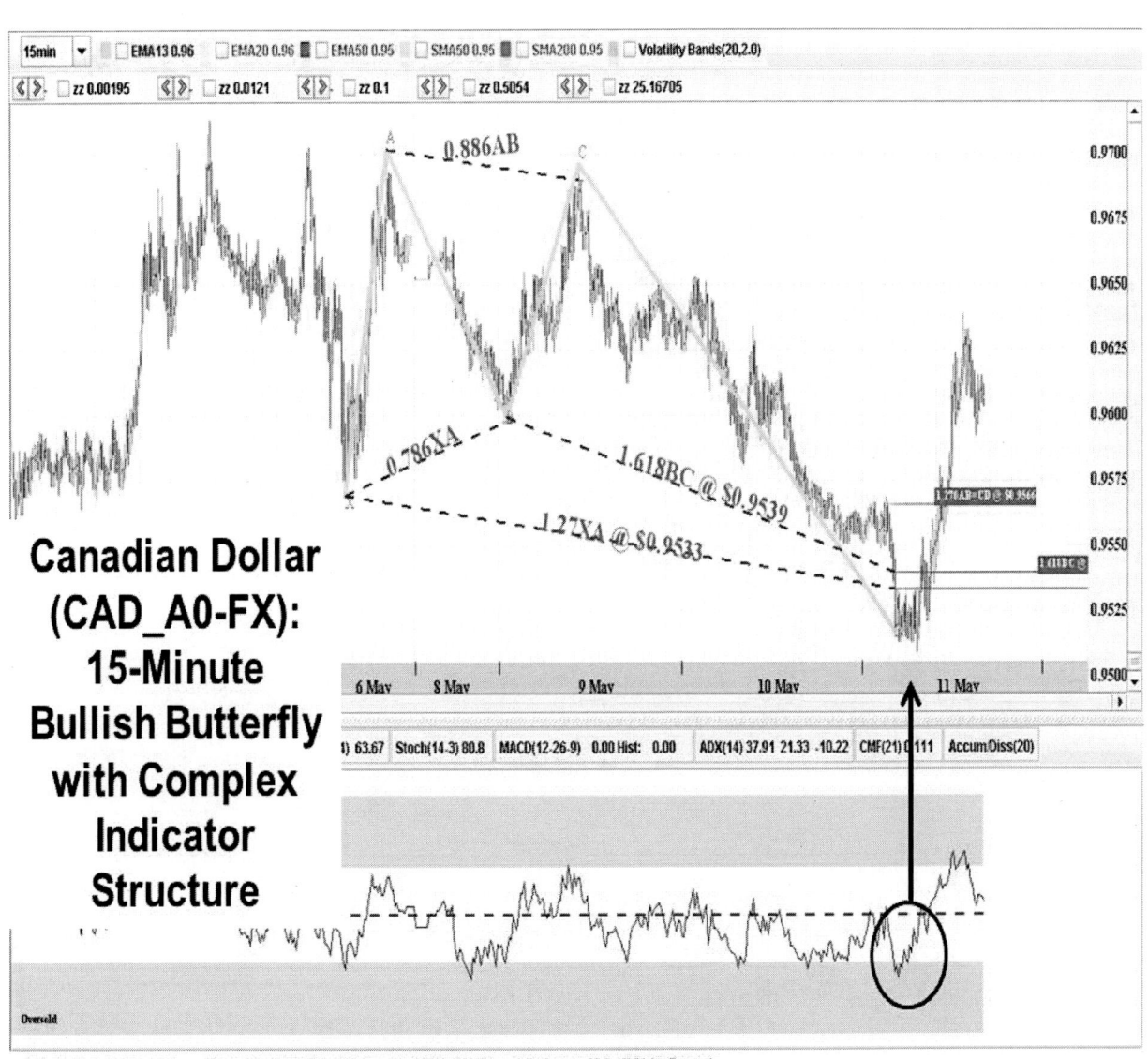

Harmonic Trading Volume 3: Reaction vs. Reversal

Canadian Dollar (CAD_A0-FX): 15-Minute
Bullish Butterfly Potential Reversal Zone (PRZ)
Bullish Complex Structures

The interesting aspect of this example was how the complex structure identified the RSI Trigger Bar which was slightly below the Potential Reversal Zone. Although the price exceeded the ideal harmonic support, the formation of the complex indicator reading signaled that this reversal would require more time at a minimum. The assessment of price as the indicator stabilizes is the key consideration in confirming the execution. Not to mention, the management of the trade is facilitated effectively by monitoring the progress of the indicator as it moves out of the extreme.

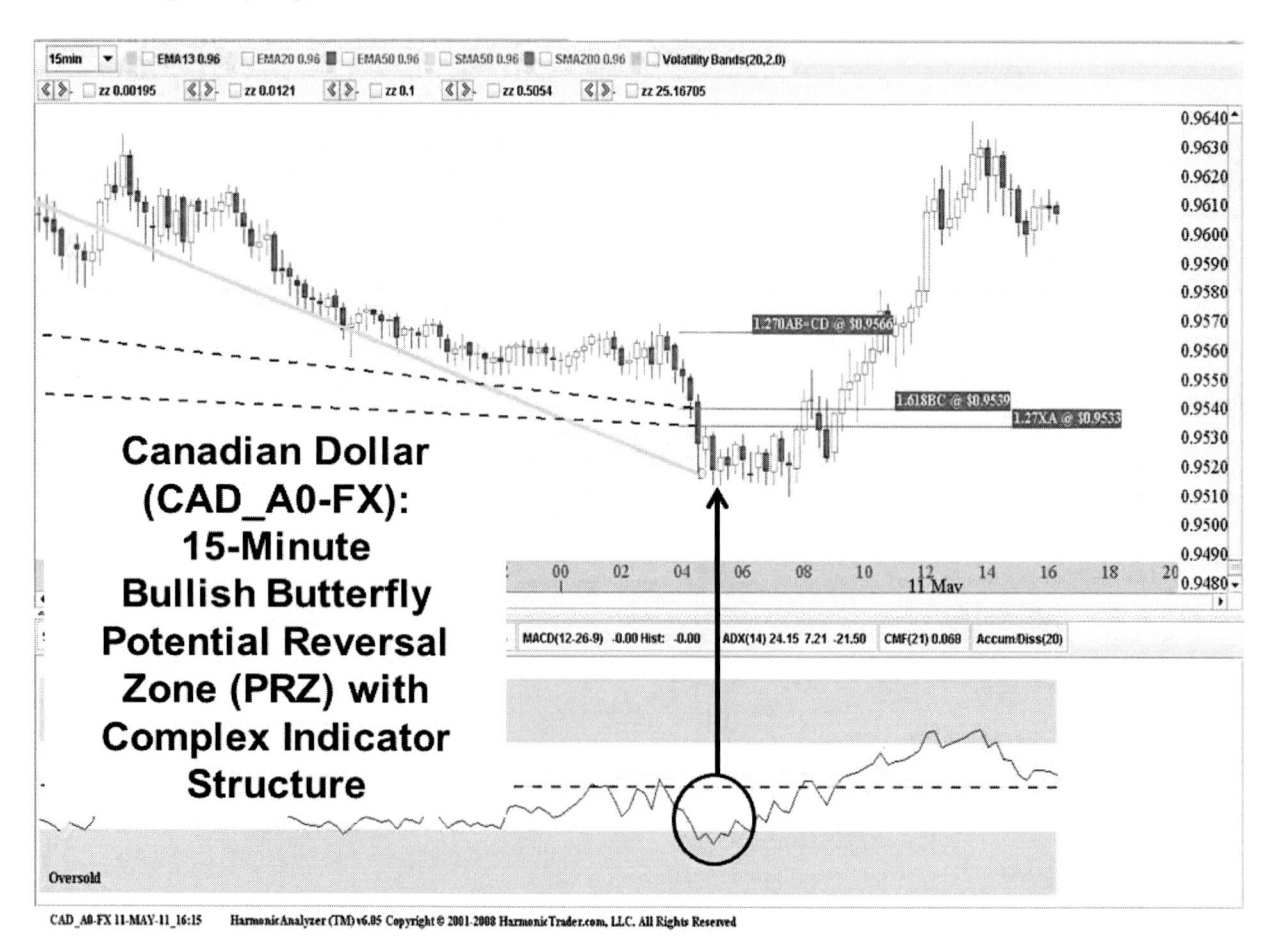

Canadian Dollar (CAD_A0-FX): 15-Minute Bullish Butterfly Potential Reversal Zone (PRZ) with Complex Indicator Structure

This chart shows the price action in the Potential Reversal Zone in the 0.9530 area with the distinct W structure that reversed three bars after the exact pattern completion point. As the indicator started to turn up, the price stabilized at 0.9520 just below the bottom range of the harmonic support. The RSI trigger bar provided the additional confirmation just below the ideal price measures for the optimal entry in the trade. Not

Harmonic Trading Volume 3: Reaction vs. Reversal

to mention, this example demonstrated the acceleration in the reversal as the RSI indicator rallied above the 50-midpoint line. This is an excellent way to monitor the progress of the consolidation after it reverses from the entire PRZ.

Bearish Complex Structures

Bearish complex structures are excellent early signs of a change in trend. Although the indicator reading forms an M-type structure in the extreme overbought zone, the strength of the price action to penetrate the higher extremes and form a complex reading signals a strong move at hand. In fact, the formation of a complex structure typically signals that the predominant trend will continue until the indicator can clearly reverse from the extreme. The RSI Trigger Bar is the price bar that marks the exact reversal from the zone, and it serves as a potential trigger point for the acceleration of a reversal. The exact peak of the RSI Trigger Bar serves as the price level resistance established by the reversal in the indicator. This is a concept that I first outlined in *Harmonic Trading Volume 2*, and I have incorporated it with patterns to optimize executions and manage reversals more effectively.

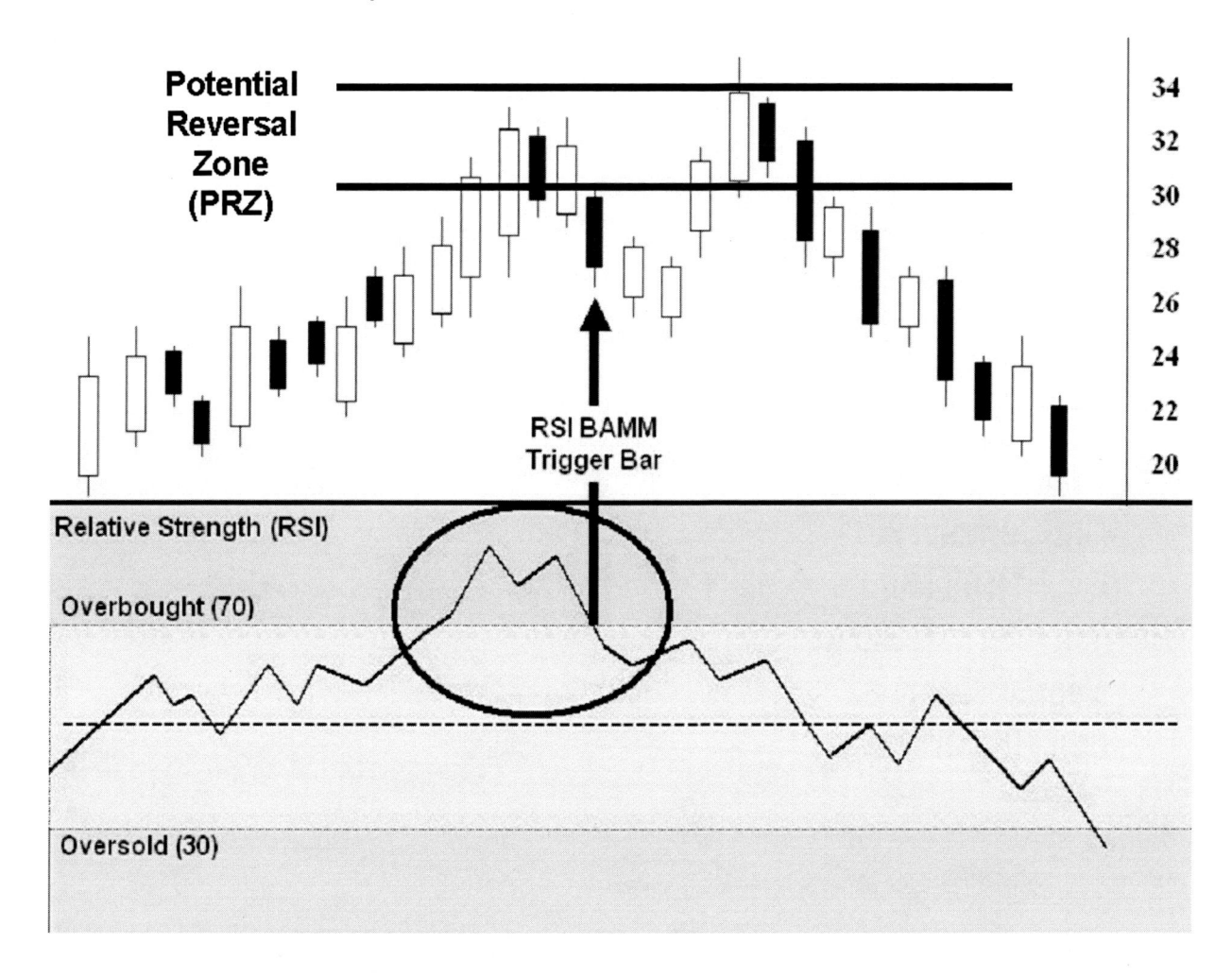

Harmonic Trading Volume 3: Reaction vs. Reversal

Standard and Poor's 500 Index Emini Futures (ESH1): 60-Minute Bearish Alternate Bat
Bearish Complex Structure Confirmation

The following chart of the S&P 500 shows an excellent example of a complex structure defining an early confirmation before the completion of the Alternate Bearish Bat pattern.

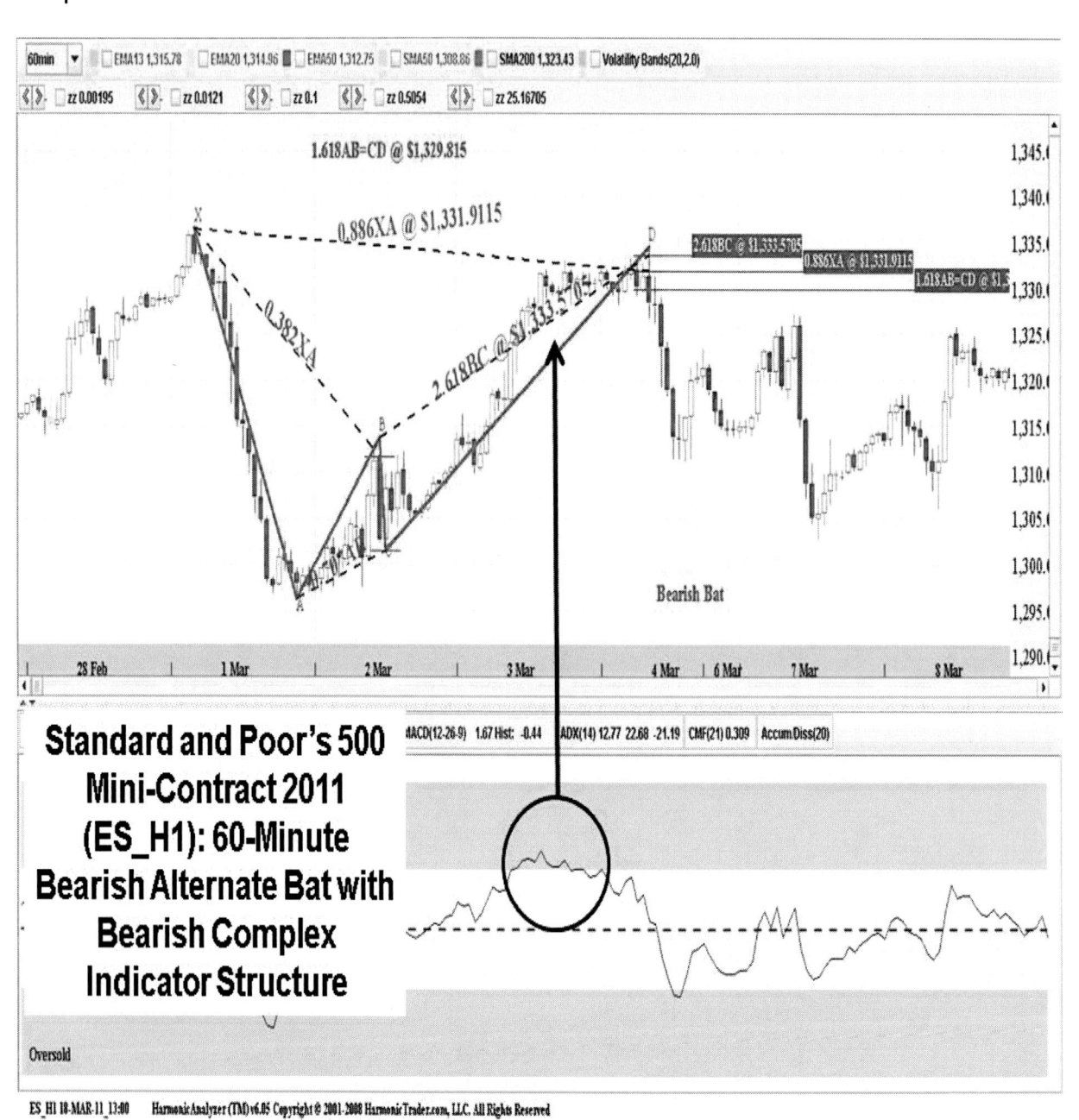

Harmonic Trading Volume 3: Reaction vs. Reversal

Standard and Poor's 500 Index Emini Futures (ESH1): 60-Minute Bearish Alternate Bat Potential Reversal Zone (PRZ)
Bearish Complex Structure Confirmation

This chart of the price action in the Potential Reversal Zone shows the indicator reversal before the exact completion of the pattern. The harmonic resistance defined the 1333.57 area as the zone for the short of the position. Interestingly enough, the complex structure provided an early confirmation with the trigger bar clearly signaling that the area just above 1330 was an excellent resistance zone.

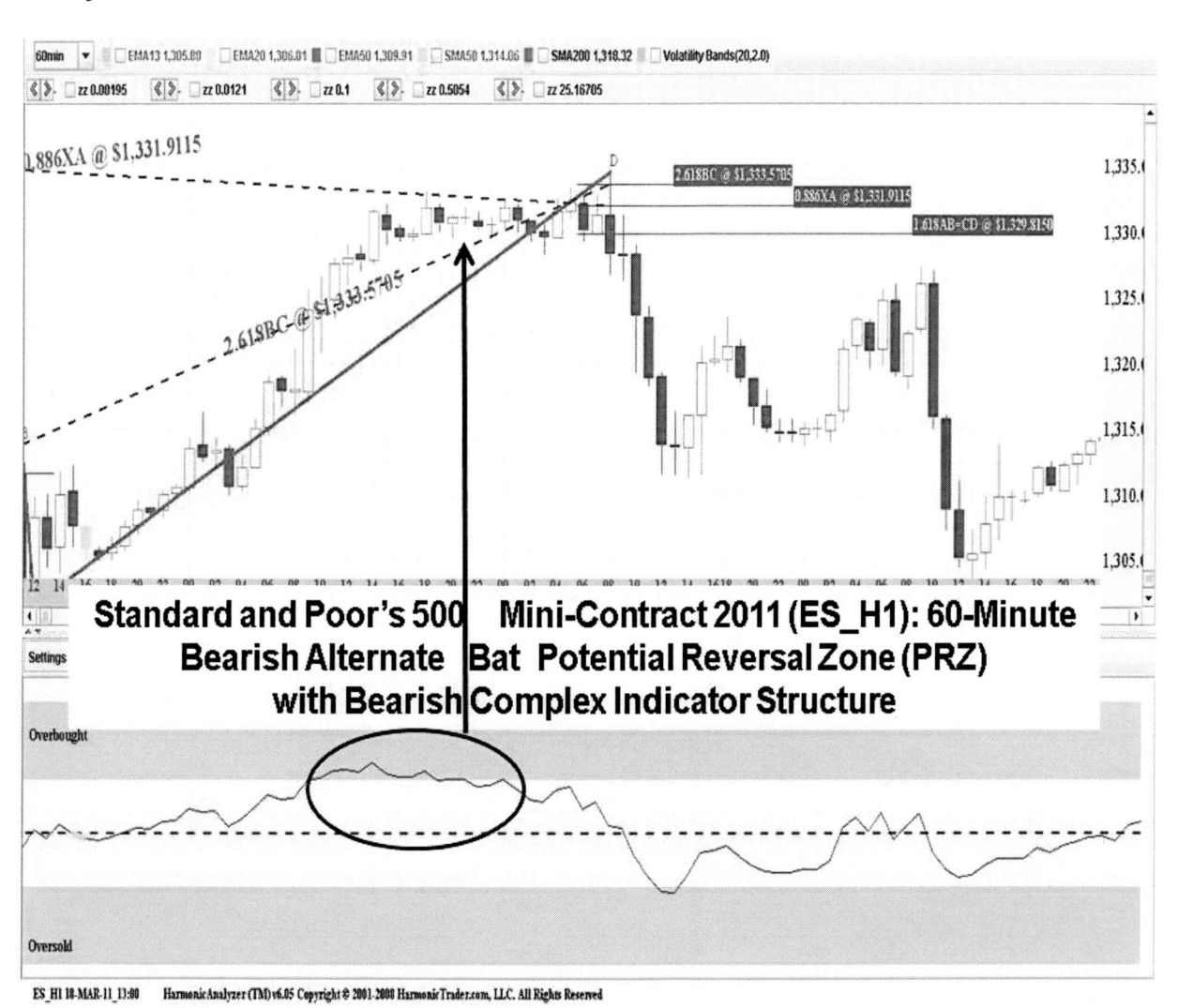

Again, it is critical to observe the progress of the indicator as it moves out of the extreme zone. In this case, the RSI reversal was demonstrative well before the pattern even completed and the downtrend progress accelerated dramatically once the indicator violated the midpoint 50 – level.

Harmonic Trading Volume 3: Reaction vs. Reversal

As with all harmonic strategies, it is important to note that this phenomenon occurs in all markets and on any timeframe. Throughout this book I feature a variety of charts that look at harmonic situations in currencies, stocks, indices but all markets possess this phenomenon. The strategies can be applied to all but I advise only the most liquid markets be considered for valid opportunities to minimize risk. As the prior example demonstrated, harmonic price action phenomena occur repeatedly. Clear opportunities like these represent the type of relationships that highlight the opportunities with the greatest potential. The most important consideration is that proper pattern AND indicator strategies work together to formulate proper expectations in any situation with the objective of isolating those with the greatest potential to yield a large reversal than a mere reaction.

RSI Breakout

As I have discussed various interpretations of Relative Strength in relation to price, one basic concept that all traders should master is a simple coordination of the indicator trend and the price trend. As RSI tests the overbought extreme, it signals an early reversal typical before it is expressed in the price.

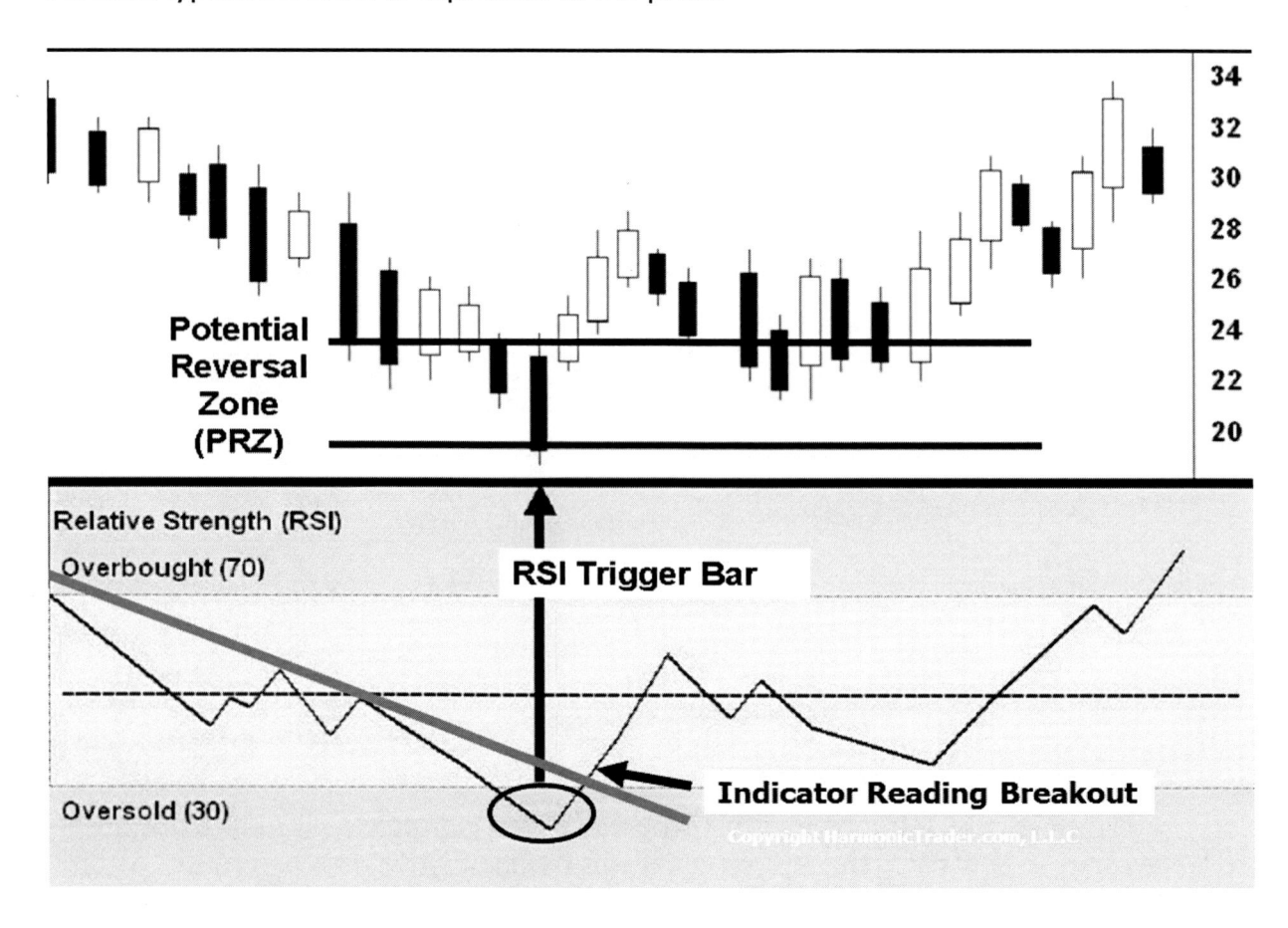

Harmonic Trading Volume 3: Reaction vs. Reversal

Standard and Poor's 500 Index Emini Futures (ES#F): 15-Minute RSI Breakout Confirmation

In the following example of the S&P 500, the continuous contract on the 15-minute chart exemplified the correlation of price and RSI. Clearly, the indicator stabilized and broke out of its downtrend before it was realized in price. These types of early indications are effective in confirming distinct trend reversals such as this. Although the larger confirmation is not official until the downtrend is violated, these strategies effectively coordinate multiple measures to define clear opportunities.

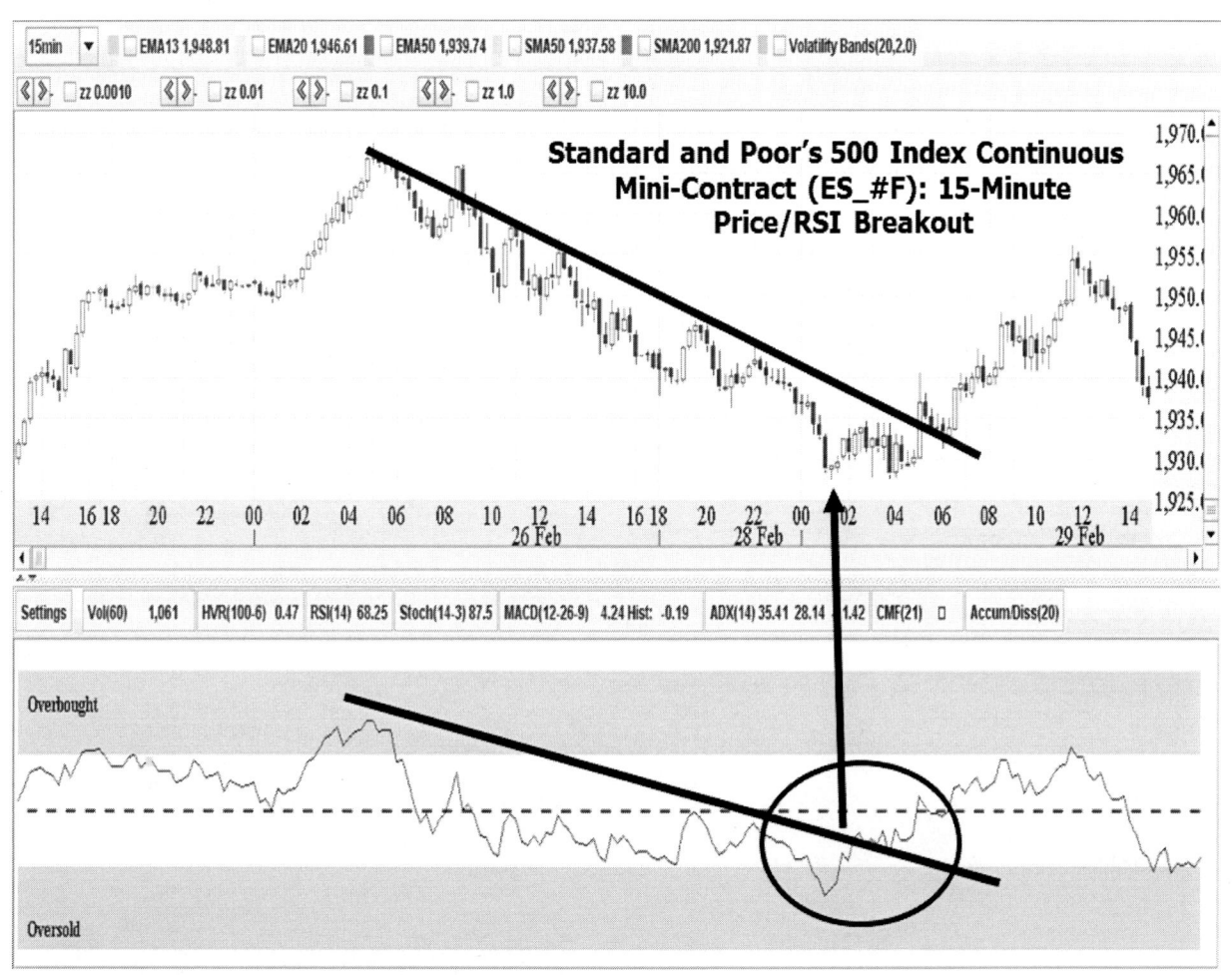

It is possible to monitor extreme price and indicator reversals simultaneously. Such integration is advantageous because it clarifies where these changes occur and delineates the area where price confirmation can be anticipated. In combination with harmonic patterns, these trendline assessments are effective in defining limits relative to any Potential Reversal Zone. Furthermore, these observations help to define the early stages of reversals before they are completely realized.

Harmonic Trading Volume 3: Reaction vs. Reversal

RSI Breakdown

There are multiple ways to monitor indicator progress but the identification of the primary trend is most meaningful when compared to the dominant direction price. These observations help to define various price segments as well as establish categories of different technical situations. When we monitor the uptrend in the indicator reading Relative Strength, the most ideal situations manifest an extreme reading above 70 level at the completion of a harmonic pattern opportunity. The breakdown in the indicator is typically an early signal but it is frequently confirming a more substantial reversal in the price action shortly thereafter.

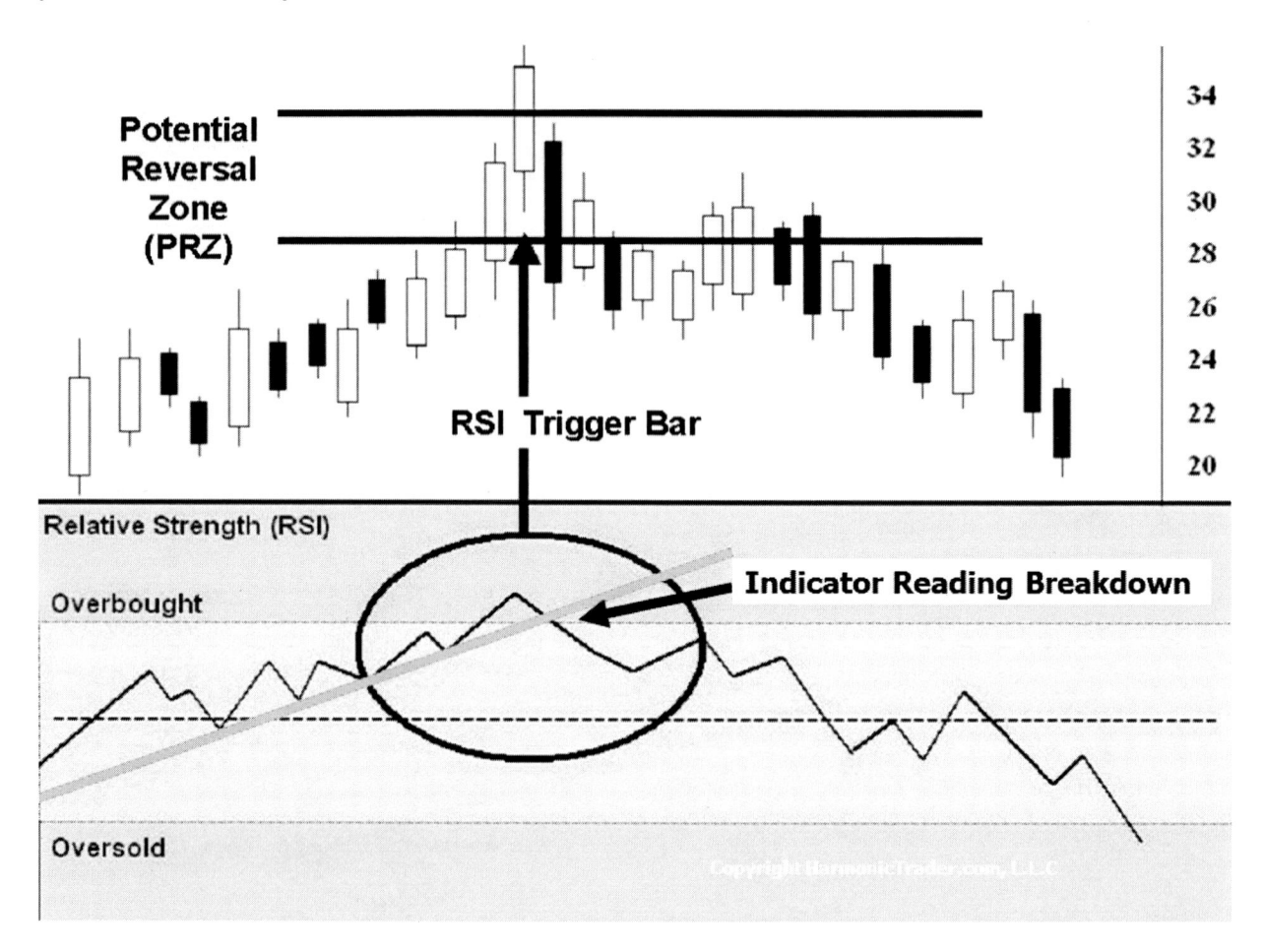

The assessments regarding the breakdown in the indicator are generally the same for both impulsive and complex types. Although impulsive situations can provide sharp reactions when both price and indicator trends are violated simultaneously, the most important identifier will be the trigger bar that denotes when the indicator reading declines below 70 level to confirm the extreme reversal. Again, these interpretations become easier with experience but the early violation in the indicator is a reliable trigger signal of impending change in the predominant trend.

Harmonic Trading Volume 3: Reaction vs. Reversal

NASDAQ 100 Index (^NDX): Daily
Bearish RSI Breakdown

The following daily chart of the NASDAQ 100 index exemplifies the relationship between price and RSI. When RSI breaks down following an extreme test, it is typical for price to follow. This is the most effective coordination to confirm trend violations in the Relative Strength Index.

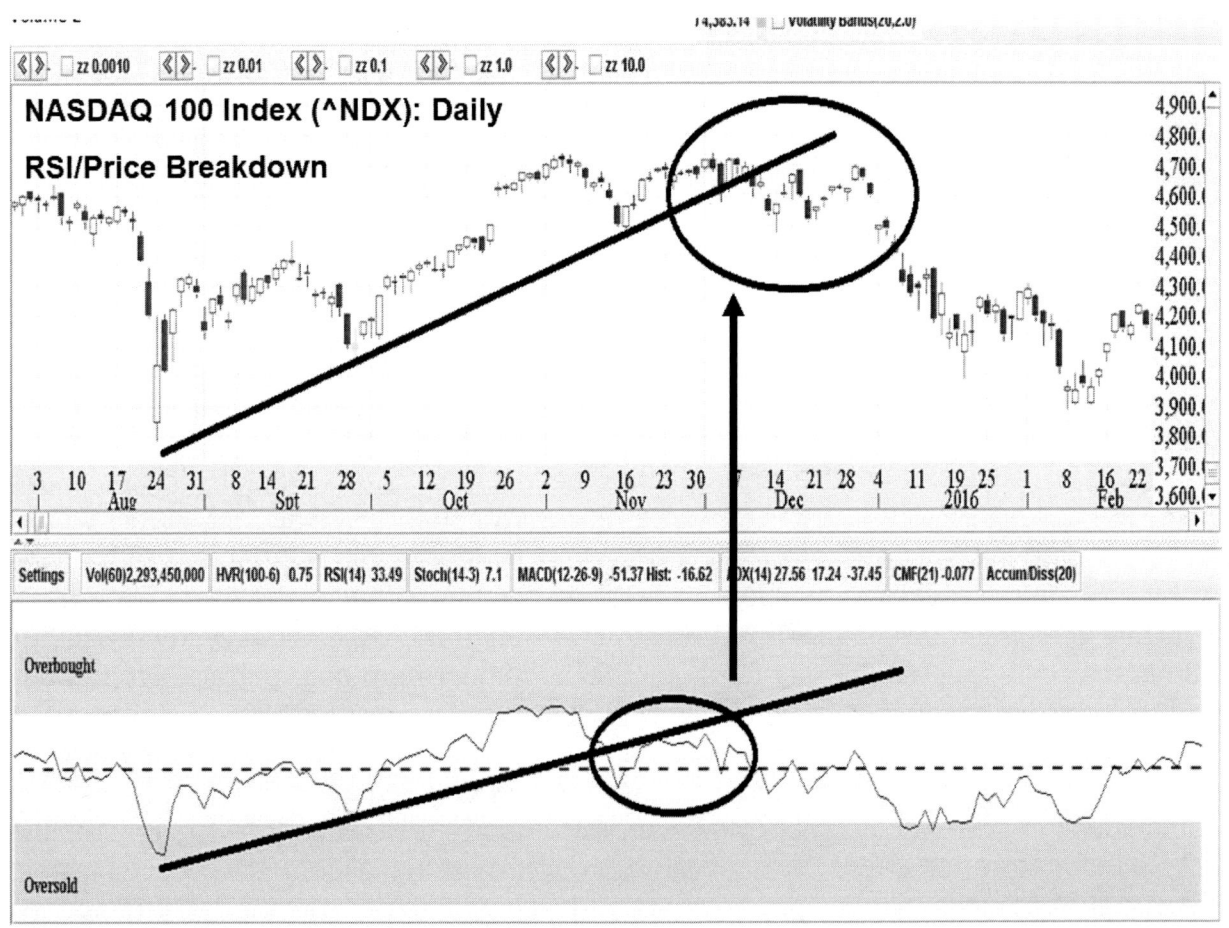

RSI BAMM Review

One of the biggest breakthroughs for me personally has been the RSI BAMM strategy. The RSI BAMM approach has its own set of rules but has been designed to be coordinated with harmonic patterns. These ideas evolved over a number of years to define unique situations of Divergence or Confirmation with harmonic proportions. Whether a pattern or single ratio is employed, the series of extreme indicator tests that reverse in tandem indicate a confirmed reaction at hand. The combination of price

Harmonic Trading Volume 3: Reaction vs. Reversal

measurements and indicator assessments provide an integrated framework to identify a larger market condition. Although this phenomenon requires multiple elements, it clearly defines how these trading cycles can be quantified and categorized to discover unique situations for harmonic pattern reversals.

Originally introduced in my *Volume 2 (2007)*, RSI BAMM principles have evolved immensely, where the importance of indicator confirmation is essential to confirm reliable technical information at a pattern's completion point. Although I have covered this material previously, I believe it is important to briefly review the basics of the RSI BAMM strategy as these principles will be applied to other technical measures and serve as the primary framework to assess other indicator confirmation strategies.

RSI BAMM is an acronym that is defined as Relative Strength Index Bat Action Magnet Move. The concept outlines specific situations of technical Divergence and Confirmation, where multiple structural indicator reading formations correspond with prescribed price action that pinpoints critical reversal zones much like harmonic patterns. In this case, the combination of defined indicator formations with harmonic price action isolates a unique situation that can highlight important consolidation zones well-before the trend reverses. Some aspects of the RSI BAMM process unfold in nearly an automatic fashion, exhibiting a particular character in these complex yet definable harmonic environments. Although the RSI BAMM technique employs other measures than patterns, the integration of these tools is remarkably effective within the basic harmonic framework.

At a minimum, Relative Strength has been an important filter to isolate those patterns that are reversing from their respective Potential Reversal Zone (PRZ) with a corresponding extreme indicator test. However, multiple indicator reading formations within RSI BAMM situations manifest unique and complex situations that are even more effective when harmonic patterns materialize. Although the indicator strategy possesses numerous technical insights on its own, the additional harmonic pattern proportions define an even more specific strategy with the dynamic relationships that this price behavior can possess.

I have discussed this unique indicator phenomenon at harmonic pattern completions in previous material. However, it is important to emphasize the unique and automatic nature of these prescribed harmonic pattern alignments. Once certain structural formations take shape, price action frequently experiences a "magnet effect" when 4 of the 5 essential measured pattern points are established. These situations will materialize in the final leg of most harmonic patterns where the acceleration to the completion point is realized as the structure completes. There are numerous examples of "automatic" harmonic movements that unfold within the pattern framework. In combination with RSI BAMM strategies, these techniques underscore the effectiveness of harmonic pattern optimization.

Although the entire RSI BAMM methodology is complex, the essence of the strategy is simple. Relevant price and technical measures define clear Divergence or Confirmation situations where harmonic pattern reversals have greater potential. When these multiple conditions occur together, a minimum harmonic pattern reaction can be more readily anticipated. The mandatory requirements that validate RSI BAMM situations define the price parameters that separate random movements from significant price structures. In the same manner as harmonic patterns, RSI BAMM must unfold in a precise sequential fashion.

RSI BAMM Requirements

The most important element of the RSI BAMM strategy employs harmonic measurements to define TWO unique extreme indicator reversals separated by at least one test of the mid-point line at the 50-level. Each test is classified as complex or impulsive, as these formations distinguish specific Divergence/Confirmation conditions that follow a prescribed set of rules in the same manner as harmonic patterns. The initial extreme reading typically will mark the most severe important inflection point of the situation, although price action may continue in the predominant trend. A secondary indicator test is anticipated that must not exceed the initial extreme reading. Between these two reversals, the double extreme test must be separated by a minimum reaction to the mid-point at the 50-level.

RSI BAMM 50-Midpoint Retest Requirement

The RSI BAMM mid-point at the 50-level is extremely important in the categorization of the oscillator readings within the RSI index. RSI oscillates between 0-100, and marks the 70-limit to define overbought situation and the 30-level as an oversold condition. RSI is an extremely effective indicator but does produce excessive readings that can distort the picture. One of the most important discoveries within the categorization of RSI indicator readings presented in *Volume Two* was the importance of the 50-level as a qualifying condition that distinguishes each extreme reading.

Early in my RSI BAMM research, I noticed that the most significant combination of extreme readings was separated with a minimum test of the 50-midpoint level. As I began to experiment with different RSI structural reading formations, I realized the structural significance to distinguish situations. In this scenario, the extreme indicator reading forms a double RSI pattern. I strongly encourage Harmonic Traders to investigate these differences and respect the importance of the midpoint. There are other applications for the midpoint that help to facilitate trade management decisions. In these instances, the assessment of extreme RSI tests must include the midpoint 50-line retest as a structural requirement before the secondary test to validate the scenario.

Although we will discuss the mid-point requirement in detail later in this chapter, the importance of the 50-level retest is one of the most important conditions applied to RSI BAMM analysis. Multiple indicator tests of an extreme area that are not separated by a test to the 50-midpoint line represent a less substantial technical situation than those formations that adhere to the RSI BAMM rules. The 50-limit retest also represents a structural requirement that isolates the most significant "environmental" opportunities.

Harmonic Trading Volume 3: Reaction vs. Reversal

These observations are particularly effective when assessing executions and analyzing management parameters relative to harmonic patterns. Defined price segments – expressed as harmonic patterns or simple ratio measurements- at various points within the RSI BAMM process frequently exhibit indicator readings that offer clear signals of the impending reversal direction. At times, RSI BAMM measures can indicate volatile reactive behavior while other formations dictate an environment where consolidation can be expected. For example, a bullish pattern that possesses a Potential Reversal Zone with a Relative Strength reading that is well-below the 30-level will require much more time to complete the reversal and stabilize in the PRZ before progressing to the minimum profit objective. In these cases, the indicator reading must reflect signs of a reversal before the price can be anticipated to change trend. Although executions may be delayed as the reversal consolidates within the price limits of the Potential Reversal Zone, the progress of the indicator reading is the defining confirmation that determines the likelihood of an initial reaction to turn into a larger reversal.

The RSI BAMM methodology was developed in the same vein as harmonic patterns. The repetition of multi-segmented structures provided definable circumstances that could be measured and ascertained consistently. Although concepts of technical Divergence and Confirmation have been discussed for decades, these interpretations are more appropriately applied within the harmonic pattern framework. These strategies represent advanced harmonic techniques to clarify vague harmonic pattern situation as more precise trading opportunities.

RSI BAMM Sequence

The RSI BAMM sequence of each extreme indicator test must be distinguished, as the type and alignment of these formations dictate the type of confirmation to be expected. Both Divergence and Confirmation are significant technical conditions but the management of these situations will differ depending upon the indicator type and the harmonic pattern at hand. Finally, the completion of RSI BAMM that corresponds with an immediate pattern Potential Reversal Zone (PRZ) represents a unique technical price level where a larger potential price reaction can be expected. The combination of these strategies precisely pinpoints critical changes in the larger trend, as well.

RSI confirmation is usually marked by specific multiple tests of an indicator extreme BEFORE the larger price reaction unfolds. RSI BAMM must adhere to the prescribed series of movements before the signal can be validated.

1. **1st Test of RSI Extreme**
2. **Reverse to Mid-Point at the 50-Level**
3. **2nd Test of RSI Extreme (not exceeding initial indicator inflection point)**

At various points of the RSI BAMM sequence, price action can take on a particular character – consolidating/accelerating within the predominant trend depending upon the type of formation the indicator exhibits. As we discussed previously, complex and impulsive indicator structures define varying expectations in the same manner as different harmonic patterns. Within the RSI BAMM approach, the type of formation at the initial test will dictate the type of Divergence/Confirmation unfolding.

Although the two indicator tests may possess different structural types, the RSI BAMM sequence may not vary from these requirements. Otherwise, the scenario will be invalidated. Most significant, the indicator retest to the mid-point line at the 50-level has been an effective primary differentiation variable as it applies to indicators in its own right. In the RSI BAMM, it is the absolute structural requirement that distinguishes these situations. Furthermore, these complex scenarios define effective expectations and pertinent interpretations about the potential for dramatic change in price behavior much like harmonic patterns. The differentiation of the specific indicator formations can signal changes in potential price behavior, especially when these relationships are exhibited at specific extremes.

RSI BAMM Types

RSI BAMM Divergence/Confirmation is mostly defined by the initial extreme indicator reading. Simple and Complex RSI BAMM formations will possess the same alignment but employ different combinations of indicator structures. The initial test of the first indicator will dictate the type, as the reading will register a deep impulsive reading or complex structure that trades well into the extreme. If simple, both readings will be impulsive formations. Complex RSI conditions are marked by an initial complex formation that possesses different expectations than impulsive readings. Regardless of RSI BAMM type, all formations must possess two distinct extreme tests that are separated by a minimum reaction to the mid-point line at the 50-level. Although other considerations are vital to assess valid RSI BAMM situations, the minimum retest to this level separates random indicator fluctuations from significant confirmation structures.

- **Simple Confirmation**
- **Complex Confirmation**
- **Simple Divergence**
- **Complex Divergence**

RSI BAMM Simple Confirmation

The RSI BAMM Simple Confirmation formation possesses <u>two impulsive indicator readings that are separated by a minimum test to the midpoint line at the 50-level</u>. The requirement that each test is separated by a minimum reaction to the midpoint line at 50 is essential in differentiating nominal impulsive readings from valid RSI BAMM confirmations.

RSI BAMM Bullish Simple Confirmation

RSI BAMM Simple Confirmation is comprised by two IMPULSIVE oversold extreme reversals where both the indicator and price retest at a higher level above the initial low. As price initially declines and the RSI indicator enters the oversold zone, the impulsive indicator reading will typically establish a short-term low. After the initial indicator reaction rolls over after testing the minimum 50-midpoint line, the secondary retest is initiated. The secondary test will reverse from a price retracement as the indicator retests initial extreme level.

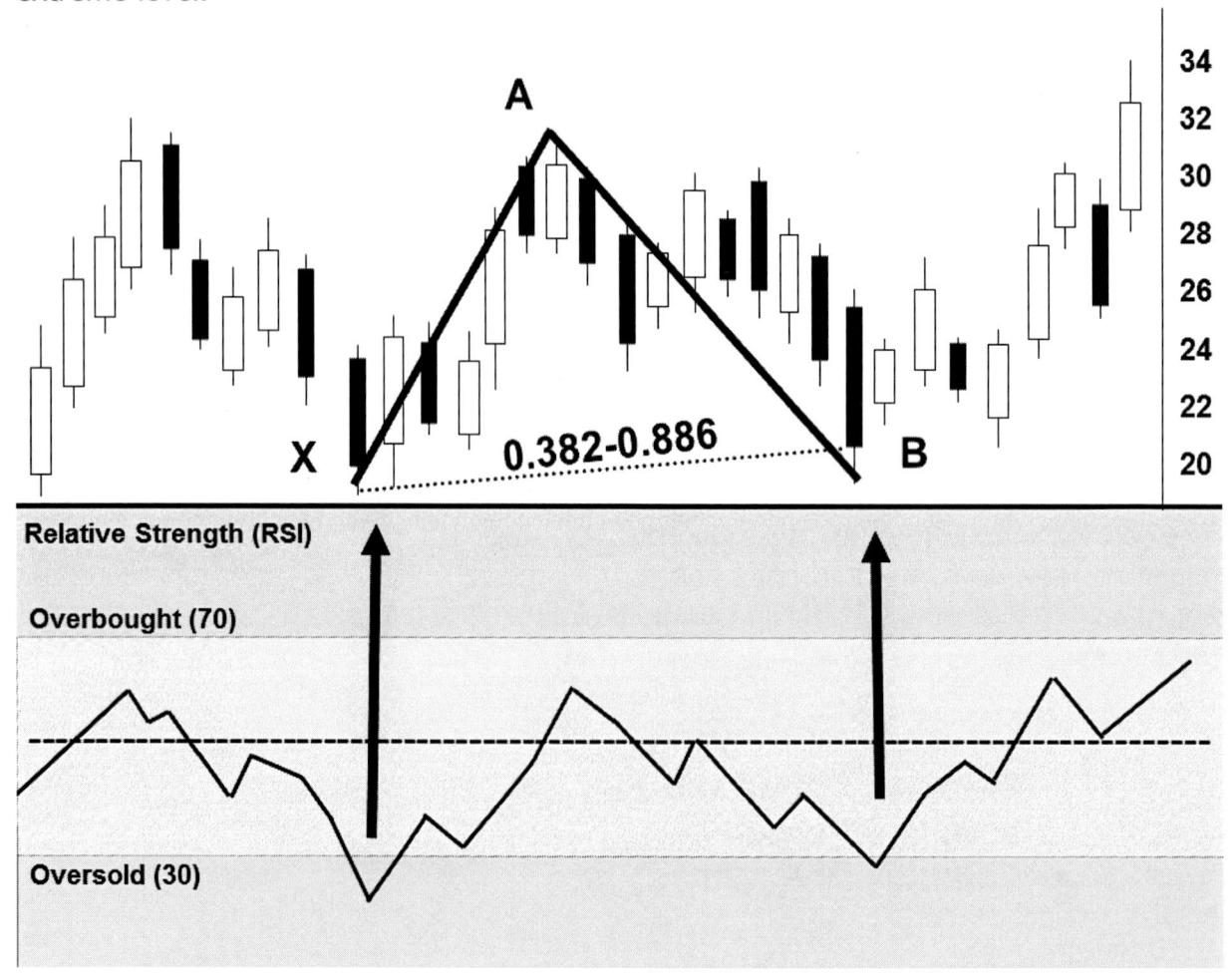

After the initial extreme indicator reversal, the corresponding retest will include a bullish retracement. The two successively higher readings in price AND RSI CONFIRM the harmonic support. In this case, the price retracement and the rising indicator readings define the environmental condition where the harmonic support has been confirmed and the reversal is strengthening.

Harmonic Trading Volume 3: Reaction vs. Reversal

New Zealand Dollar (NZD_A0-FX): RSI BAMM Bullish Simple Confirmation

The following chart shows an ideal RSI BAMM Simple Bullish Confirmation in the New Zealand Dollar that reversed at a 61.8% retracement. The most important aspect of these two formations is the minimum retest back to the mid-point line at the 50-level. The initial impulsive reading defined support at the 0.6760 level. After a period of consolidation, the indicator retested the oversold extreme with another impulsive reading that reversed slightly above the initial reversal.

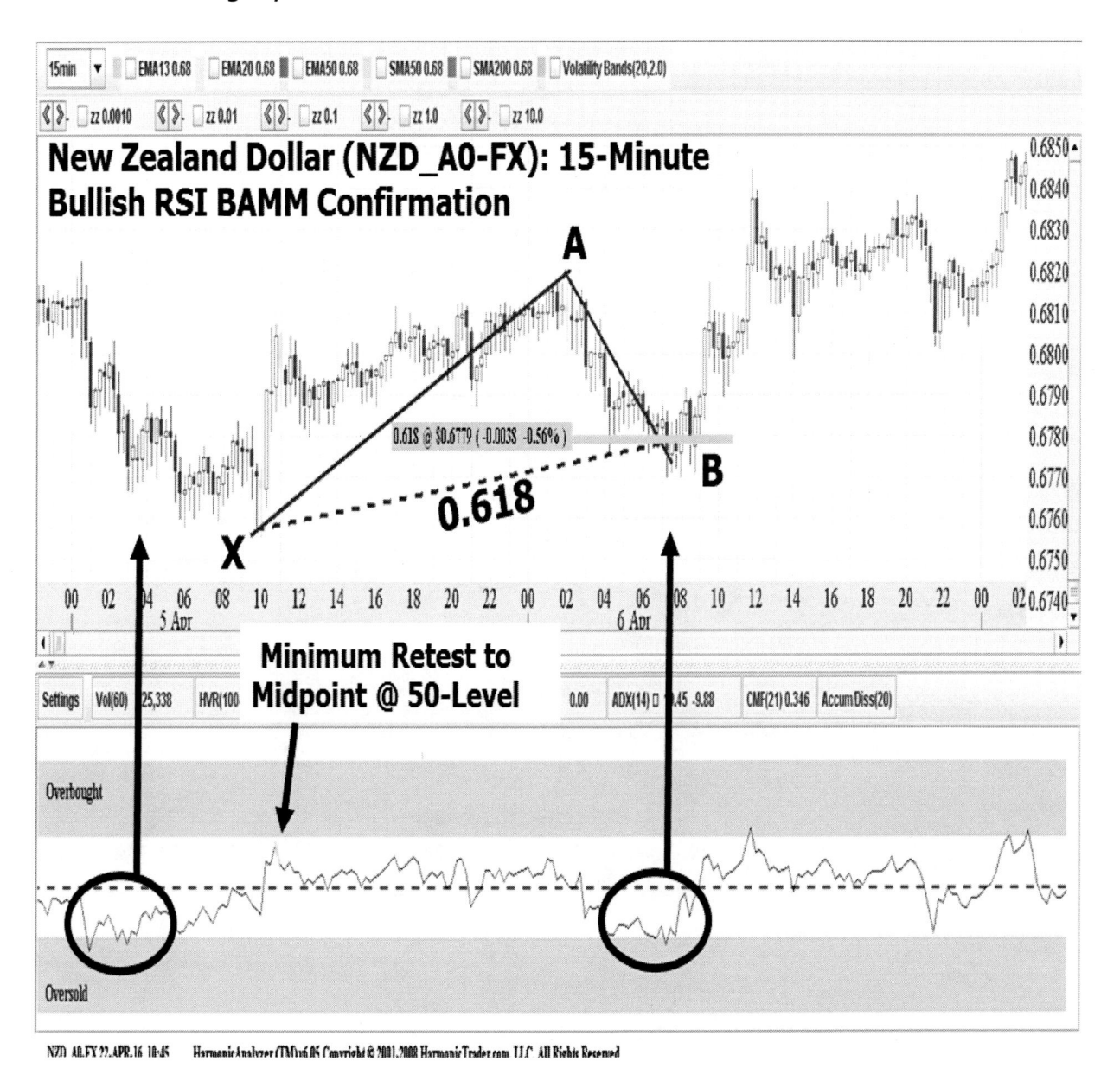

Harmonic Trading Volume 3: Reaction vs. Reversal

RSI BAMM Bearish Simple Confirmation

The Bearish RSI BAMM Simple Confirmation is comprised of two extreme indicator tests that are successively lower as overall trend declines from an important retracement. Although these situations frequently possess distinct patterns that help to confirm the continuation price level, the key technical event is triggered by the secondary reversal from the overbought indicator extreme.

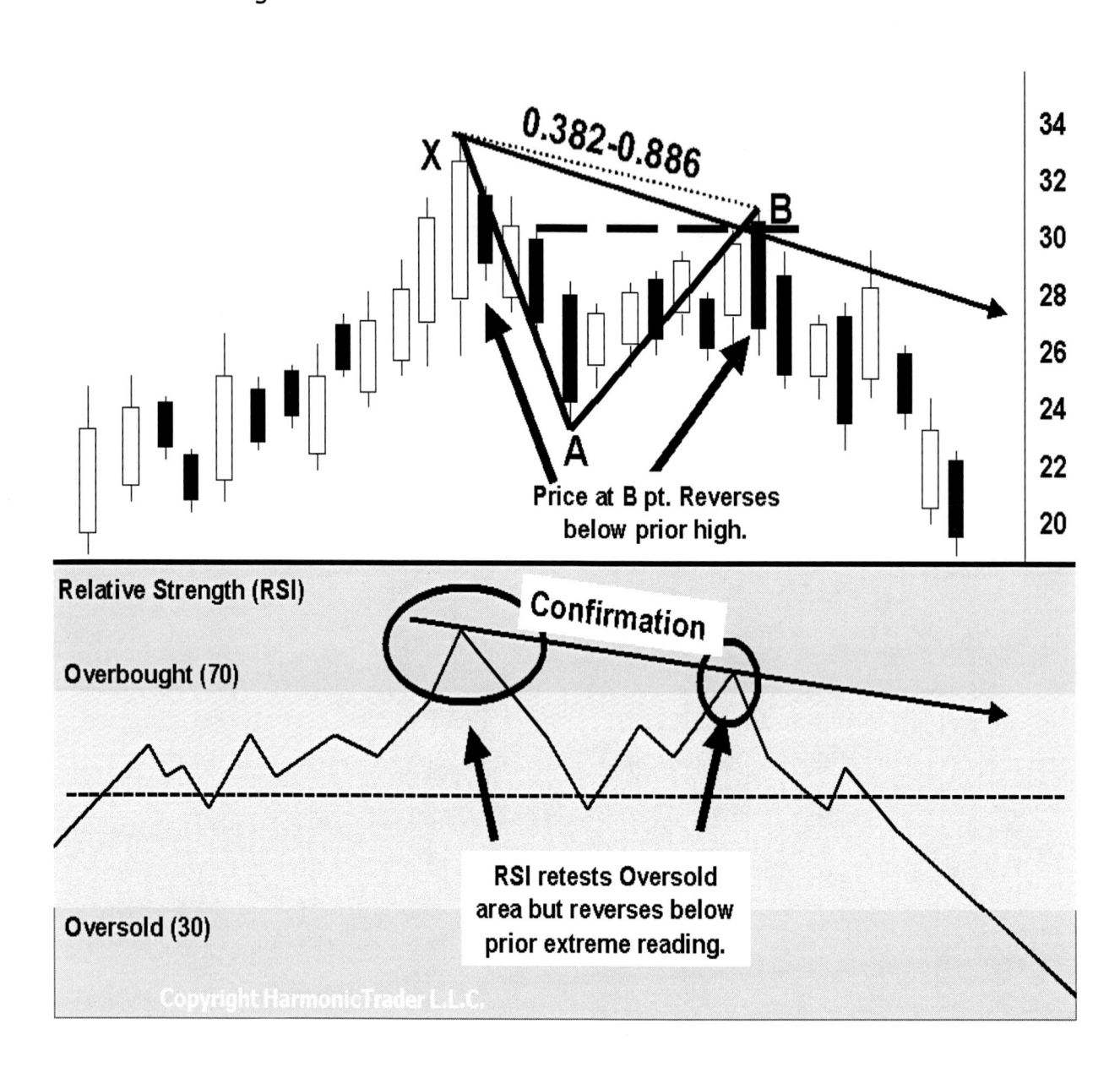

Harmonic Trading Volume 3: Reaction vs. Reversal

Boeing (BA): Daily
RSI BAMM Bearish Simple Confirmation

The following chart of Boeing possesses a clear harmonic pattern that was confirmed by the Bearish Simple RSI BAMM Confirmation. The overwhelmingly distinct successive impulsive readings identified an important environmental characteristic of the harmonic resistance established by the Bearish Bat pattern. These relationships developed over the course of several months but the daily reversal accelerated quickly following the completion of the pattern as the secondary test of the indicator confirmed the failure at hand.

Harmonic Trading Volume 3: Reaction vs. Reversal

RSI BAMM Complex Confirmation

The RSI BAMM Complex Confirmation is initiated with a complex RSI indicator structure as the initial reading. This begins the process where an immediate reaction to the mid-point line at the 50-level must be realized before a final impulsive retest of the RSI extreme is realized. This situation is unique because the secondary retest of the impulsive indicator reading confirms the more substantial complex formation.

RSI BAMM Bullish Complex Confirmation

The RSI BAMM Bullish Complex Confirmation situations possess successively higher RSI readings where the secondary impulsive indicator retest reverses at an important price retracement. There are many times where a simple AB=CD structure or complex pattern can confirm this area.

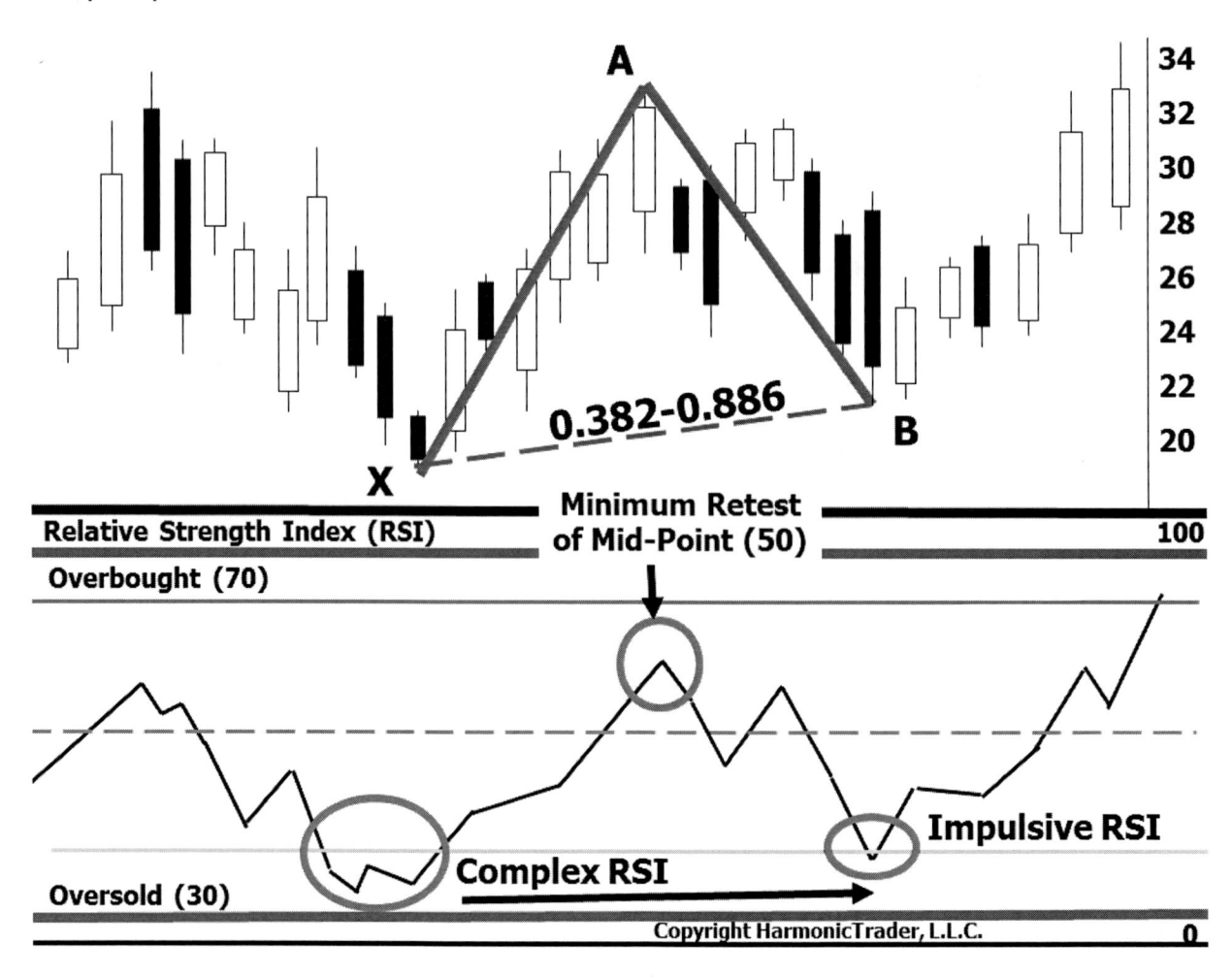

Harmonic Trading Volume 3: Reaction vs. Reversal

British Pound/U.S. Dollar (GBP_A0-FX): 15-Minute
RSI BAMM Bullish Complex Confirmation

In this example, the British Pound formed an ideal RSI BAMM Complex Confirmation at an important 61.8% retracement. In this case, the initial complex reading stabilized close to the 1.4100 level. After an extended consolidation phase where the indicator reading satisfied the retest of the midpoint at the 50-level, the price action retraced the initial rally. The secondary test of the indicator reading formed an impulsive structure that quickly reversed from the oversold extreme. In fact, it is important to note how the indicator reading itself established a clear uptrend following this confirmation and provided an early signal of the trend strength well before the price was realized. This type of awareness can help clarify those situations where harmonic measures are more important and yield a larger reversal than a nominal reaction with RSI BAMM confirmation.

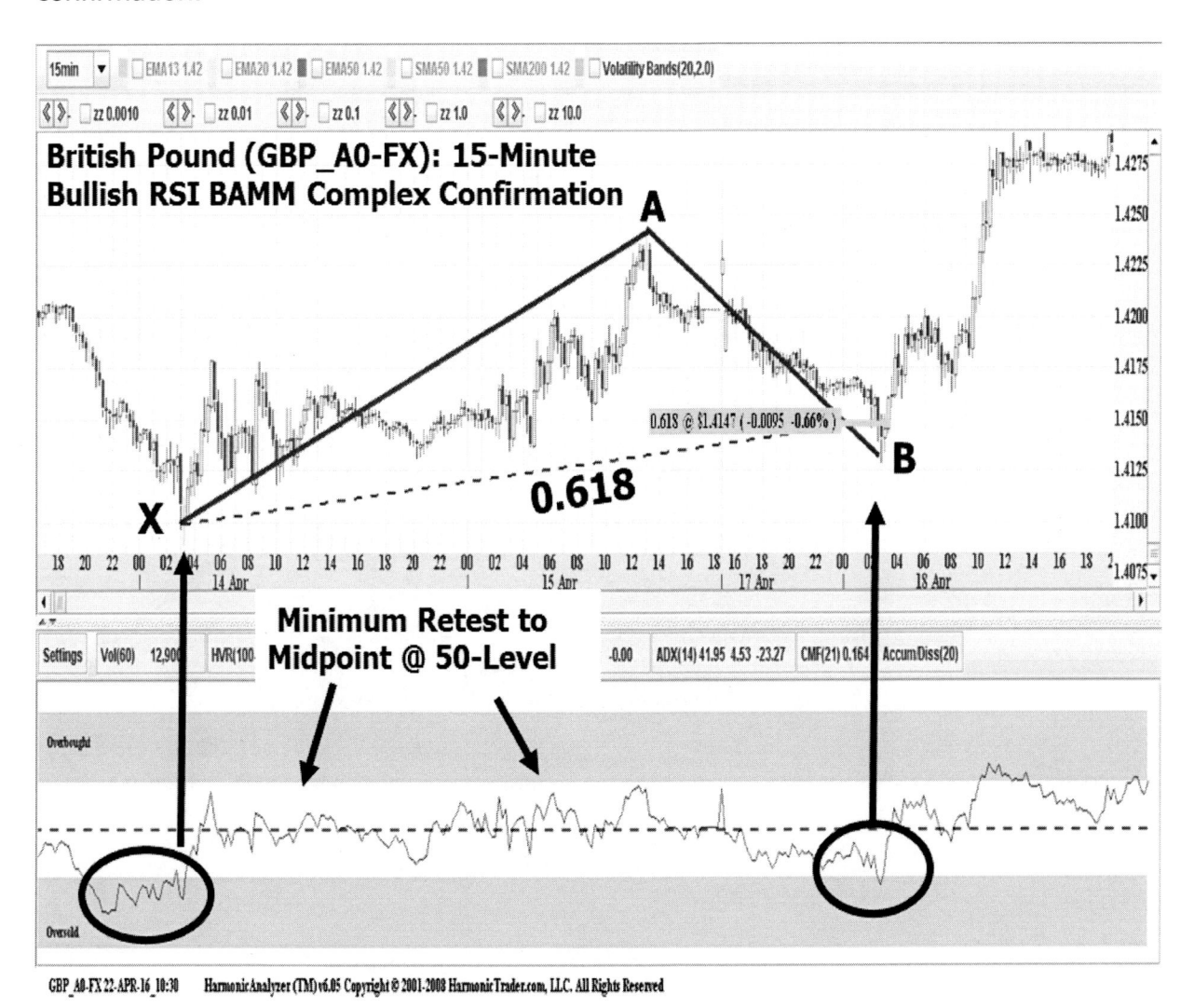

Harmonic Trading Volume 3: Reaction vs. Reversal

RSI BAMM Bearish Complex Confirmation

RSI BAMM Bearish Complex Confirmation situations possess two successive declining RSI extreme reversals where a key price retracement defines the resistance for the secondary test. Retracement patterns that materialize on the secondary test of this RSI formation provide some of the best confirmation situations.

Harmonic Trading Volume 3: Reaction vs. Reversal

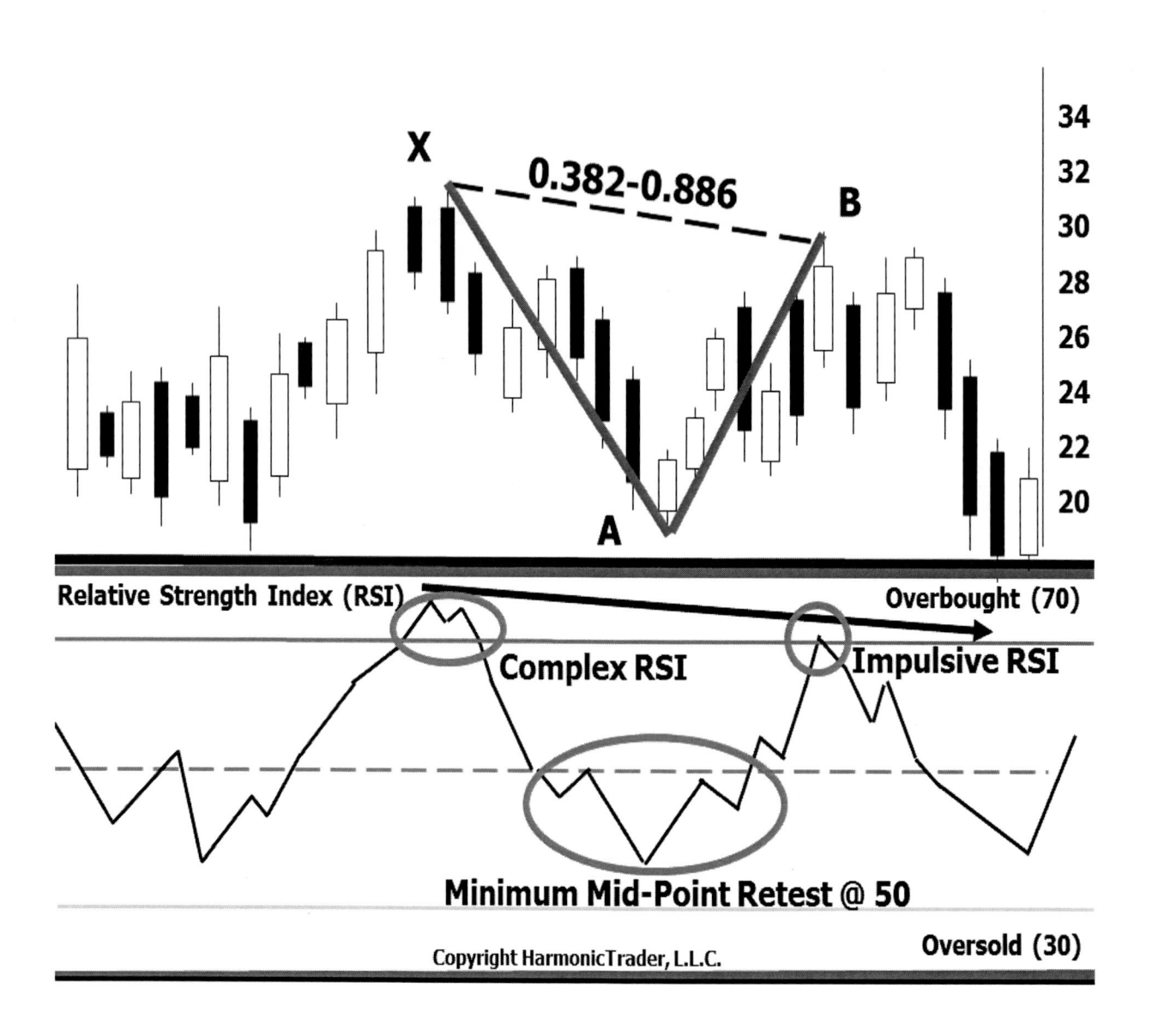

Standard and Poor's 500 Emini (ES#F): 15-Minute
Bearish 5-0 Pattern
RSI BAMM Bearish Complex Confirmation

The following 15-minute chart of the continuous contract in the Standard & Poor's 500 E-mini exemplifies a clear Bearish Complex RSI BAMM Confirmation. The Bearish 5-0 pattern was confirmed in an ideal fashion as the second indicator reading reversed from the extreme overbought area below the prior complex structure. In fact, the complex structure that marked the peak registered a reading at 75 while the secondary retest briefly hit the 70 level then sharply reversed thereafter. Again, it is important to notice the immediate price response following the completion of the pattern and focus on the indicator behavior, as the sharp RSI reversal indicated the weakness ahead.

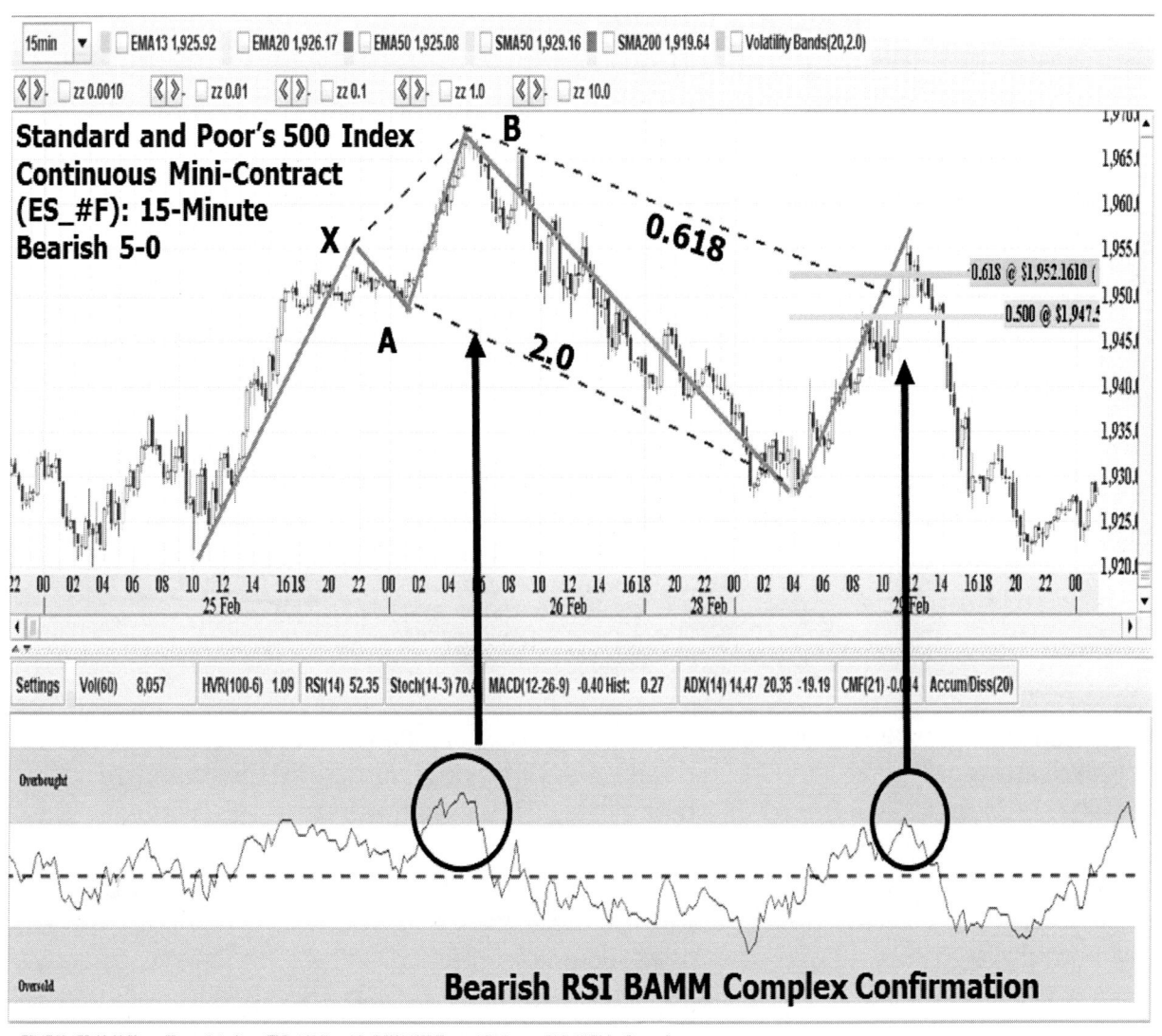

Harmonic Trading Volume 3: Reaction vs. Reversal

248

RSI BAMM Bullish Simple Divergence

One of the most powerful price action mechanisms the market exhibits is the phenomenon of Divergence. This occurs when an indicator reading reverses from an extreme level while the price continues in a final phase of the predominant trend. The indicator divergence marks an early but critical insight into the strength of the predominant trend. In combination with harmonic patterns, these represent some of the most precise opportunities.

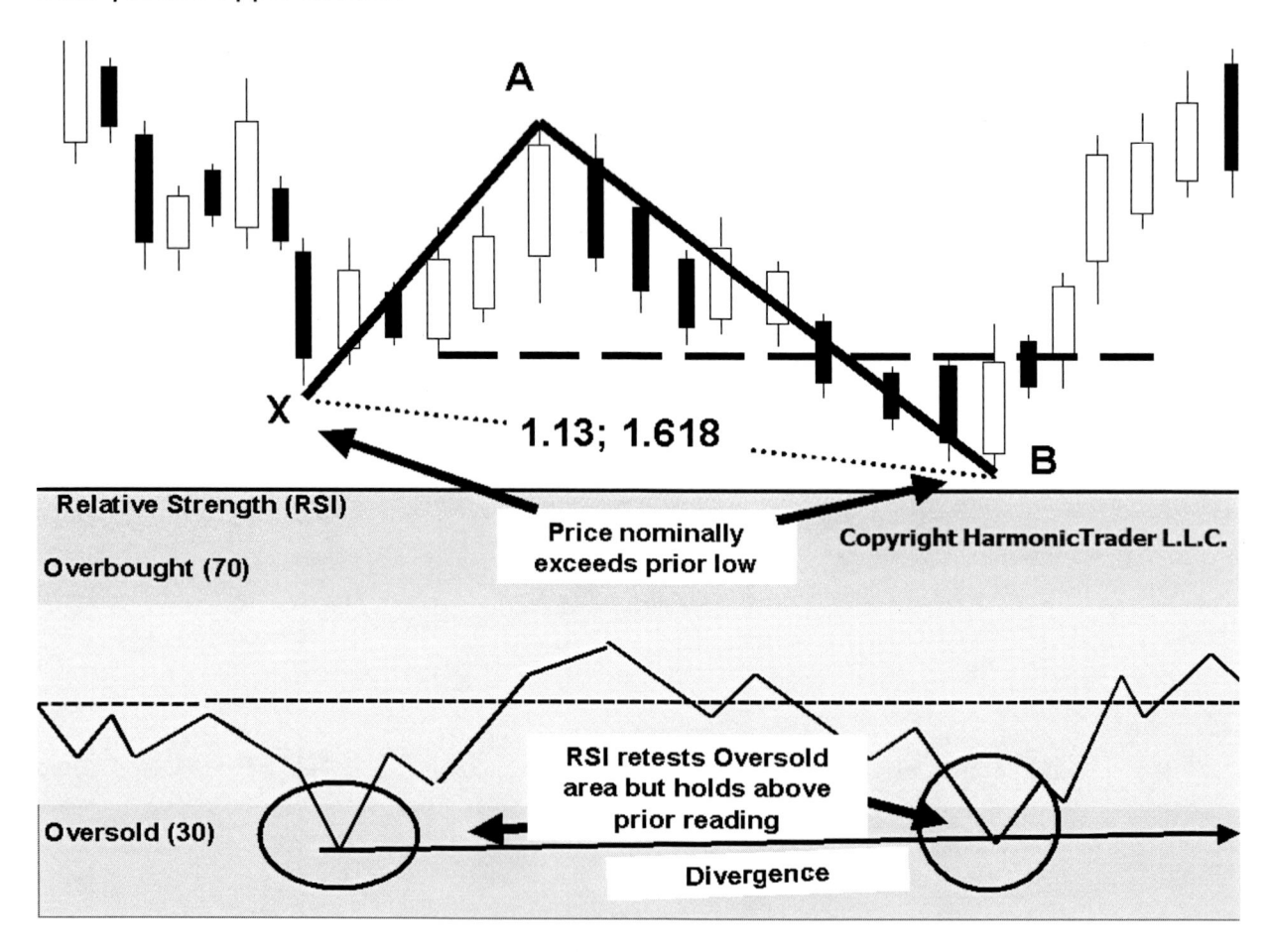

I initially outlined this concept in *Harmonic Trading Volume 2* and presented detailed strategies that help refine this phenomenon. Although the basic structural requirements are the same as all other types, the key difference in this variation is the projection of the price reversal. Typically, the price will reverse within a pattern that possesses a 1.13-1.618% expansion range as an RSI impulse structure rallies sharply after testing the Oversold level (<30). Although the price trades to a nominal new low, the impulsive retest above the prior complex reading is an important structural development that indicates strength not weakness. Bullish Divergence will possess successively higher indicator readings as the final price decline completes an extension pattern.

Harmonic Trading Volume 3: Reaction vs. Reversal

Standard and Poor's 500 Emini (ES#F): Daily
RSI BAMM Bullish Simple Divergence

The following daily chart of the Standard & Poor's 500 index shows a fantastic RSI BAMM Bullish Divergence. The index formed two successive impulsive indicator readings over the course of several months. The price action exceeded the initial low to the 1.13 extension while the indicator reading reversed from the oversold extreme at a slightly higher level. The minimum retest in the indicator reading to the mid-point at the 50-level was the deciding factor that distinguish these two tests as a potentially powerful harmonic support zone.

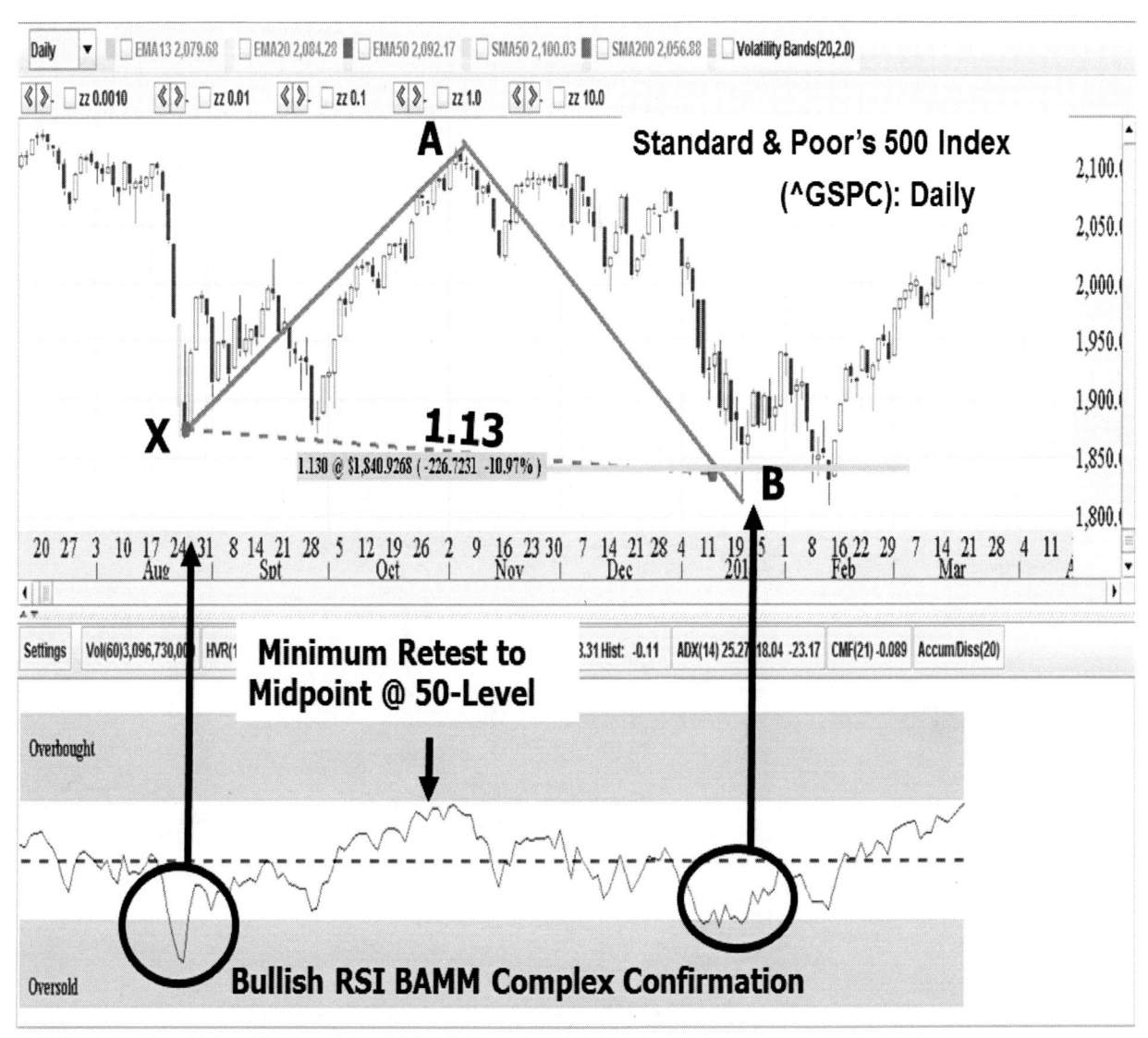

Harmonic Trading Volume 3: Reaction vs. Reversal

RSI BAMM Bearish Simple Divergence

Bearish Simple Divergence commonly materializes after an extended trend. Each extreme impulsive indicator test must be separated by a minimum retest of the mid-point at the 50-line to isolate random moves from distinct diverging readings. These formations are critical formations that define a change in trend well before it is expressed in price. Therefore, these double impulsive tests are significant, especially at the completion of a harmonic pattern, and must be considered more substantial than any singular reading.

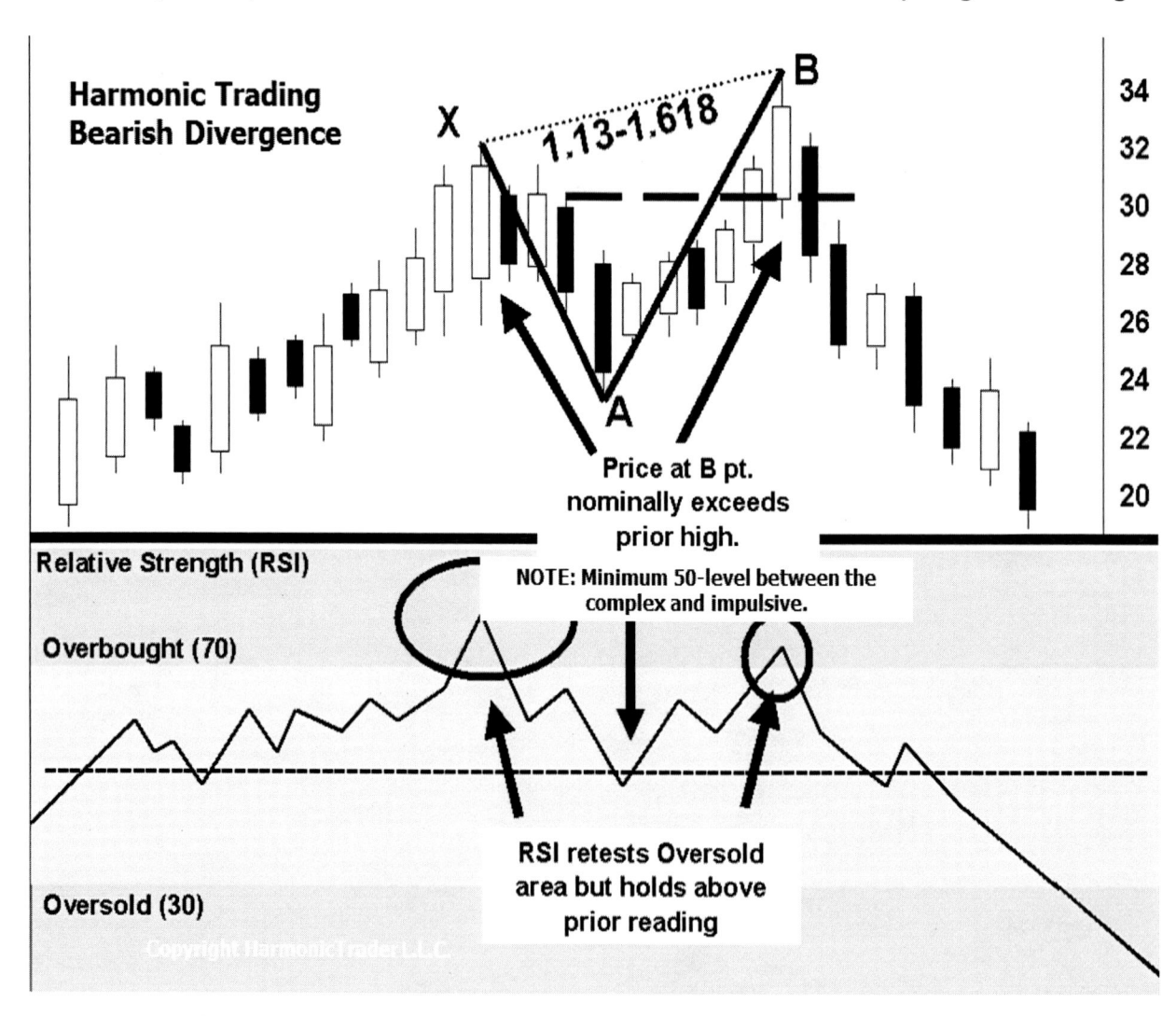

Harmonic Trading Volume 3: Reaction vs. Reversal

Crude Oil (CL #F): 15-Minute
RSI BAMM Bearish Simple Divergence

The following chart of the continuous contract in Crude Oil exemplifies what an ideal RSI BAMM Simple Divergence should look like. The indicator registered two successively lower impulsive RSI tests at the oversold extreme while the price action rallied to a 1.618 extension. As the indicator reading became weaker, the price to a nominal new high that was inherently flawed. These situations present some of the best reversal opportunities as the price extends into an area where the indicator weakness defines a larger reversal at hand.

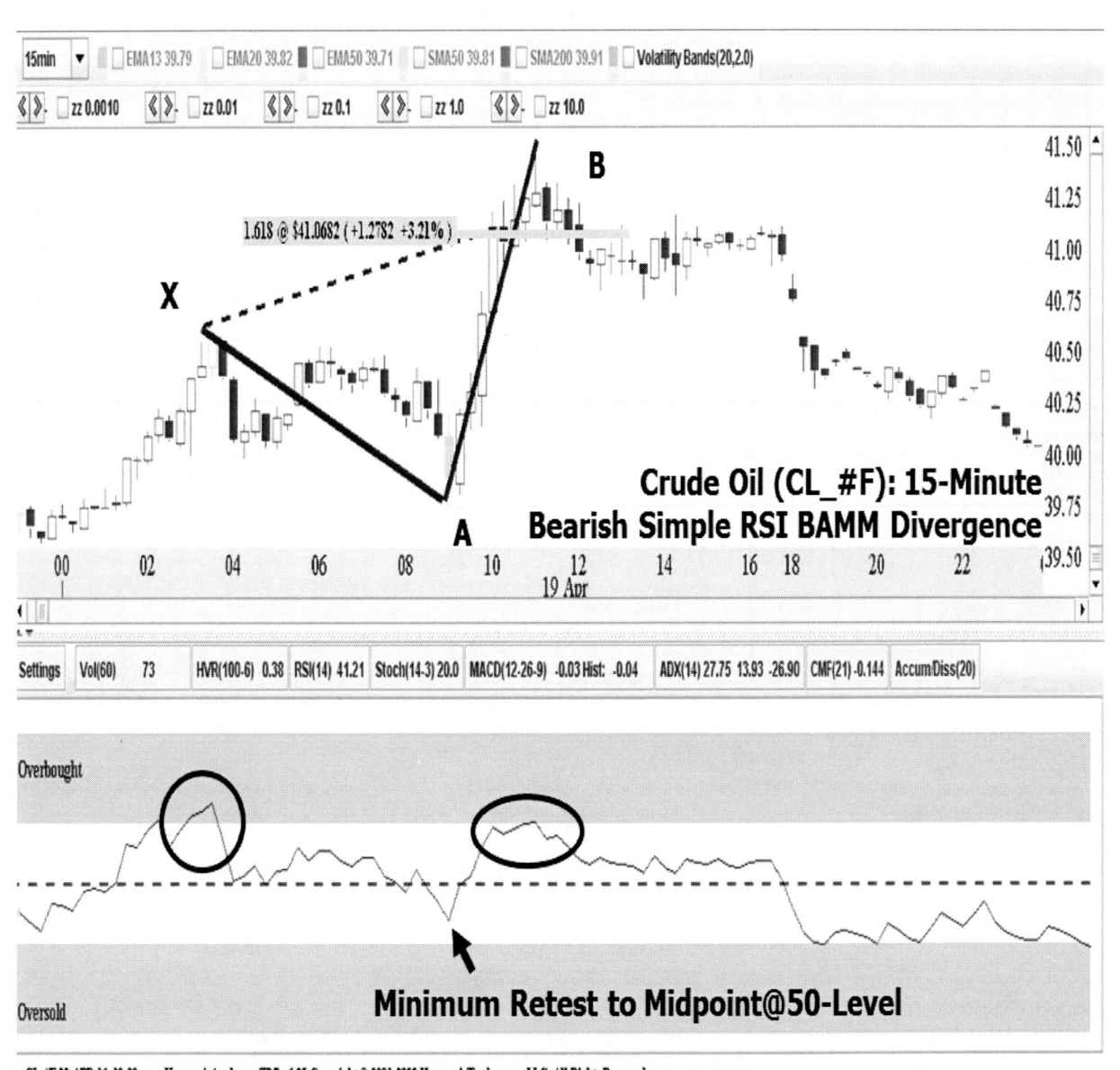

Harmonic Trading Volume 3: Reaction vs. Reversal

RSI BAMM Bullish Complex Divergence

The RSI BAMM Complex Divergence is the most advanced model to describe any indicator condition within the Harmonic Trading approach. Diverging indicator and price relationships define unique conditions for harmonic pattern reversals. I outlined these advanced relationships in my *Volume 2* book, and it still represents one of the most powerful harmonic pattern confirmation strategies. The RSI BAMM Divergence framework has enabled me to define harmonic pattern opportunities in an unprecedented fashion. In fact, these concepts have been the impetus for an entire body of advanced work that defines Harmonics in the financial markets unlike ever before.

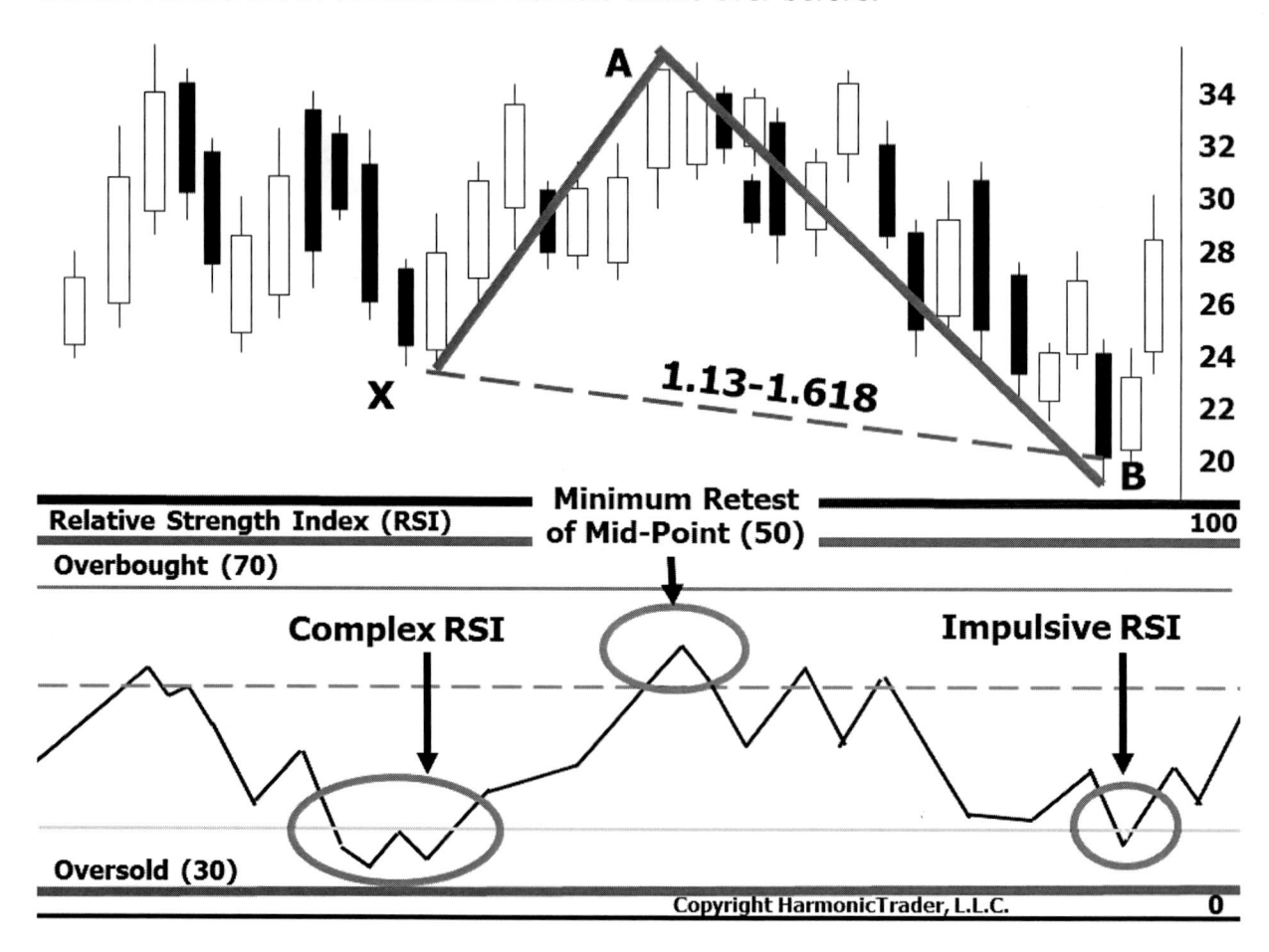

After a bullish complex indicator reading has materialized and the minimum retest of the 50-level has been satisfied, the eventual retest of the oversold extreme must possess an impulsive formation. As the RSI impulsive reading reverses at a slightly higher level than the initial complex structure, price action will decline to a nominal new low. Again, this is one of the most powerful technical situations the markets can provide. The last decline is weak where the sellers are exiting positions at prices that are near the termination point of the trend. These conditions possess some of the strongest market elements that create phenomenal price moves. The RSI BAMM approach accurately

Harmonic Trading Volume 3: Reaction vs. Reversal

defines where the price will terminate by assessing either the 1.13 or 1.618 projections. Although the completion of the entire RSI formation may be an early signal at times, it's coordination with a clear harmonic pattern is the best application of these conditions.

Dow Jones Industrial Average (YM#F): 15-Minute
Bullish Shark
RSI BAMM Bullish Complex Divergence

The following intraday chart of the Dow Jones Industrial Emini futures continuous contract shows an excellent example of a Bullish Complex RSI BAMM Divergence situation. The Bullish Shark identified excellent harmonic support and the impulsive indicator reading reversed above extreme low of the initial complex structure. The secondary test required some consolidation but the harmonic pattern pinpointed the price level for the reversal.

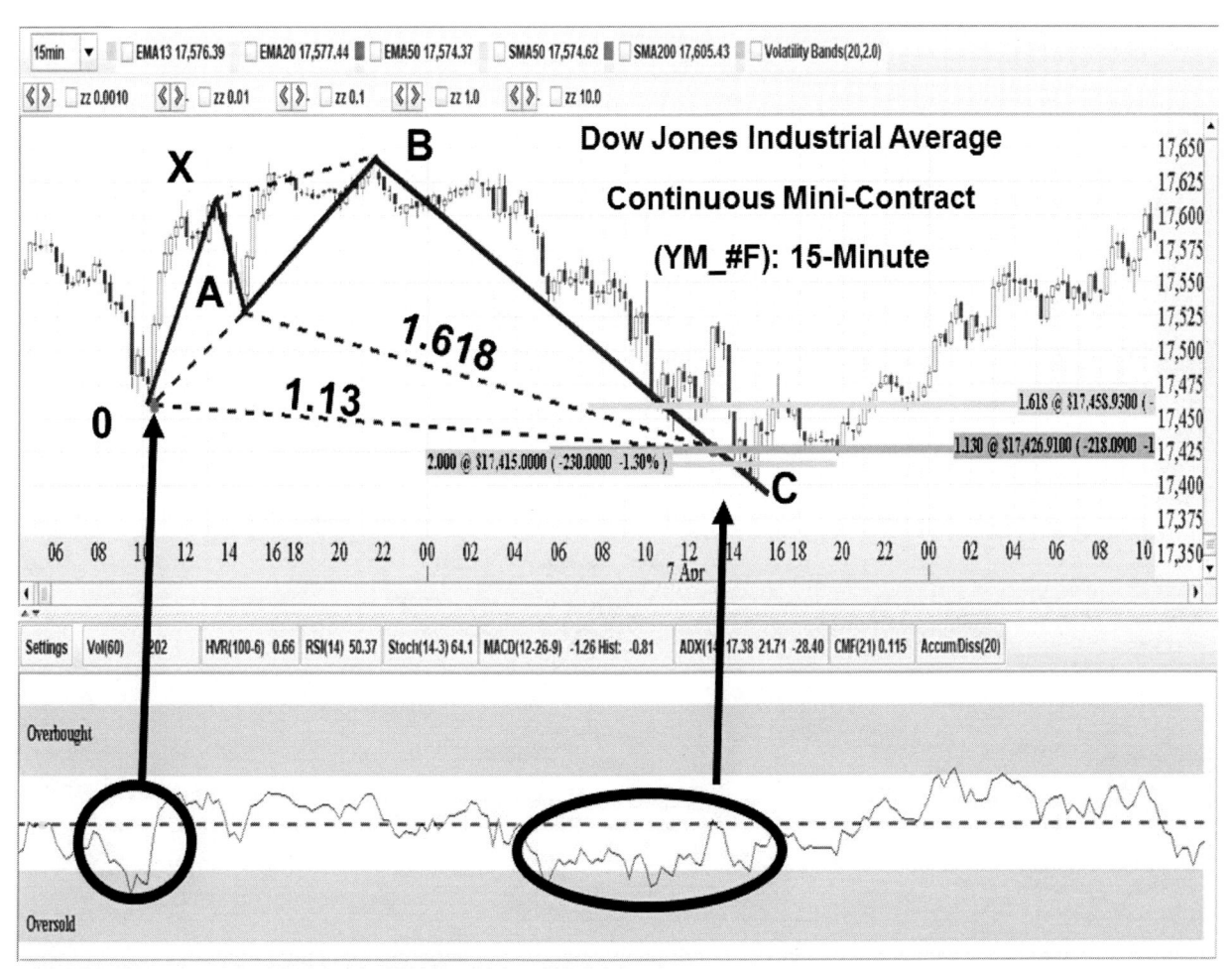

Harmonic Trading Volume 3: Reaction vs. Reversal

RSI BAMM Bearish Complex Divergence

The RSI BAMM Complex Divergence is a powerful combination of a complex formation followed by a distinct impulsive retest that is separated by reaction to the mid-point line at the 50-level. As the successive RSI extreme reversals are decreasing, price rallies to nominal new high but it is inevitably doomed due to the weakening internal strength as manifested by the indicator. These are fantastic trading opportunities and I recommend that all Harmonic Traders study this illustration to single out these opportunities as particularly significant.

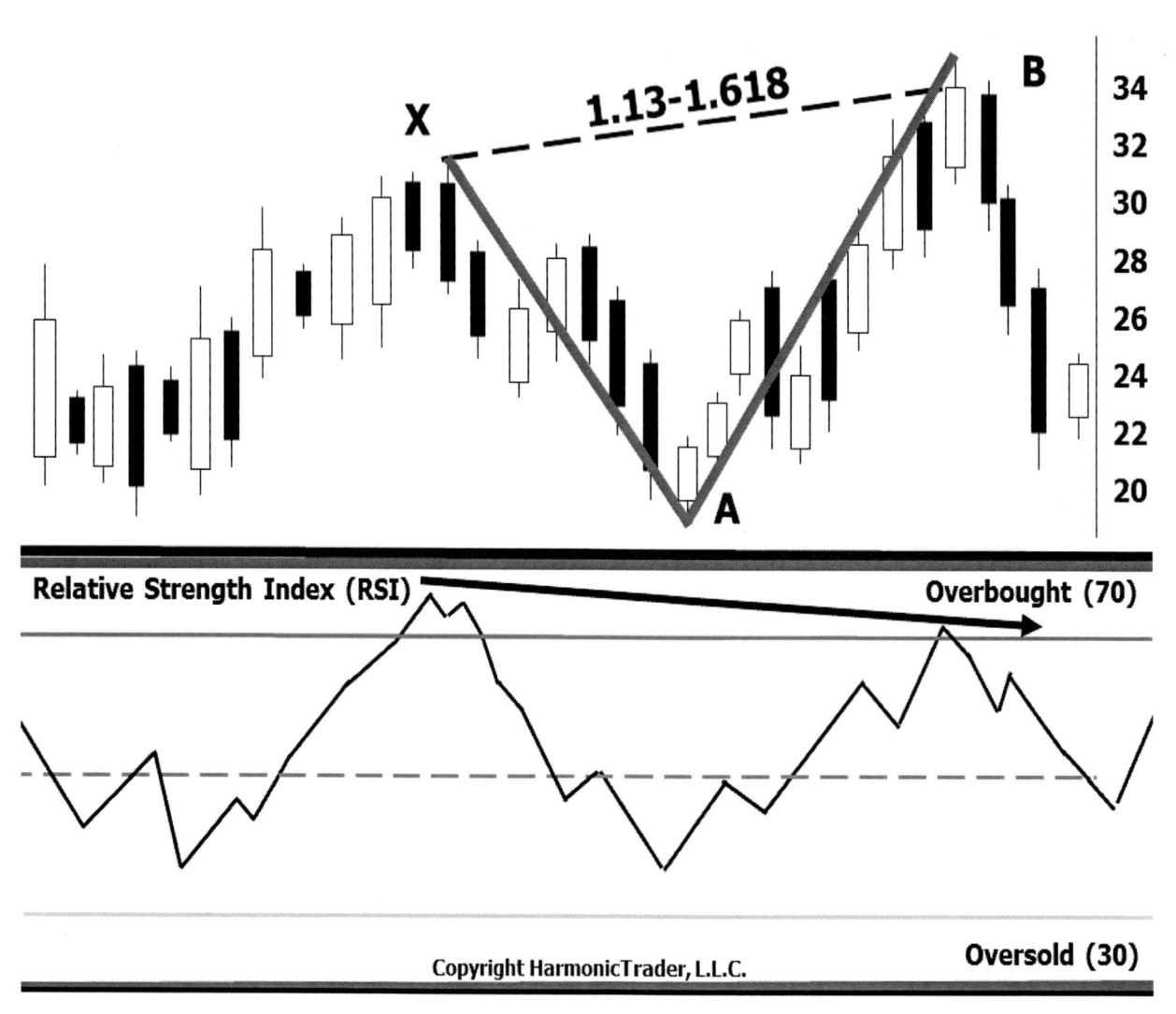

Harmonic Trading Volume 3: Reaction vs. Reversal

Standard and Poor's 500 E-mini (ES#F): 60-Minute RSI BAMM Bearish Complex Divergence

The following example of a Bearish Complex RSI BAMM Divergence in the Standard & Poor's 500 Index E-mini contract exemplifies all the conditions of this situation. The initial complex reading reversed from the overbought extreme. The minimum retest to the mid-point line at the 50-level preceded the final impulsive overbought extreme reading. The price action rallied to nominal new high while the indicator reversed from a reading that was lower than the prior extreme. The indicator reversed demonstratively following the secondary retest and indicated weakness at hand. These situations are excellent defining those rallies that are inherently doomed and become failed breakouts providing a greater potential for a large reversal.

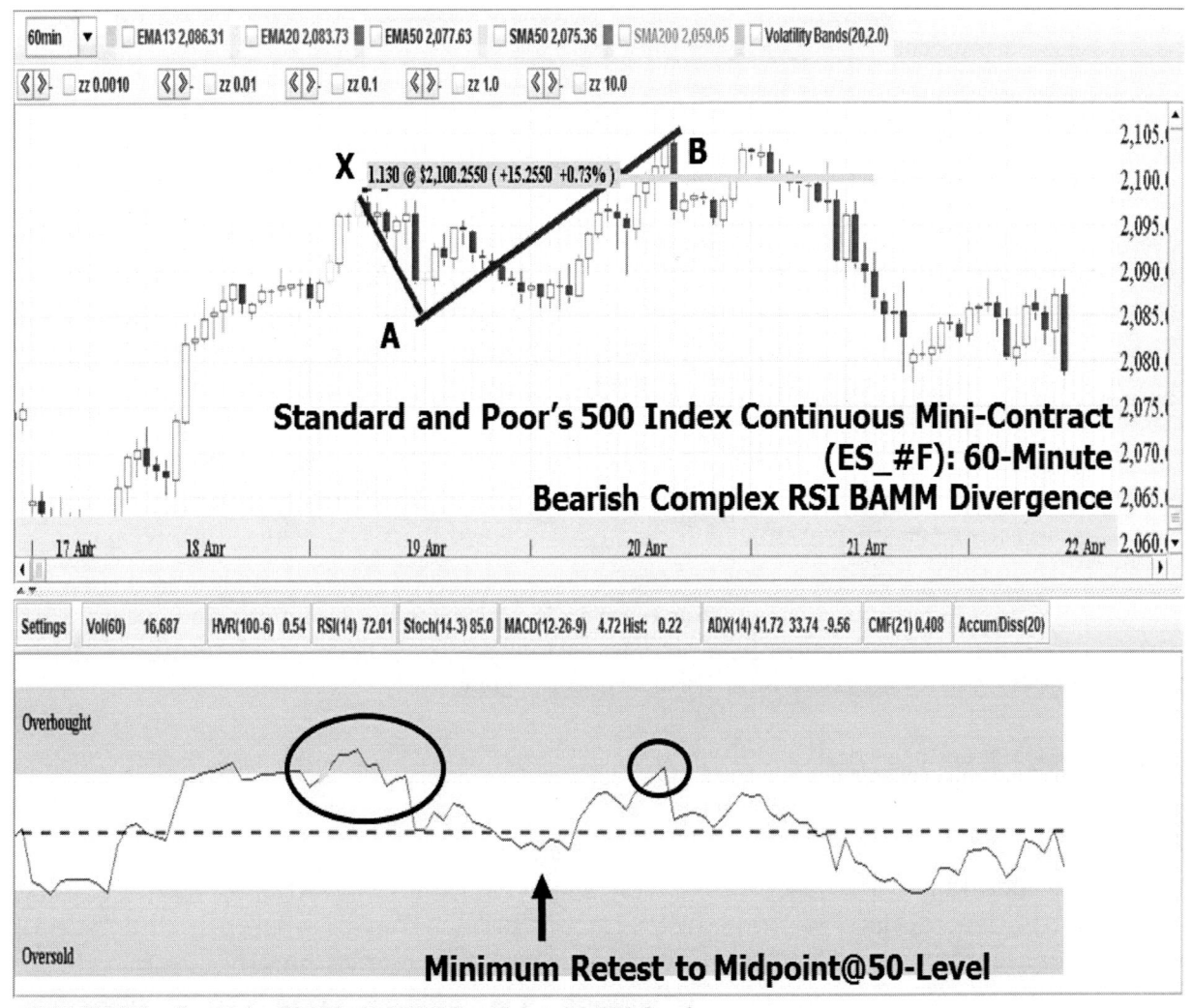

Harmonic Trading Volume 3: Reaction vs. Reversal

Harmonic Anticipations

The harmonic pattern framework and sequence of steps within RSI BAMM establish specific guidelines for each scenario to dictate when certain situations may yield a reaction while other condition lead to a more substantial reversal. This is the constant "Reaction versus Reversal" assessment that all traders must determine in the execution and management of any position. Certainly, more harmonic pattern situations will yield short-lived, counter-trend opportunities that must be managed aggressively. These Type-I situations highlight the reality of what to expect from harmonic patterns as most situations will require multiple tests of a price level before establishing a larger reversal. Therefore, the fundamental reactive anticipation regarding most harmonic pattern moves will facilitate a more responsive handling of any position and ultimately optimize decisions, as a conservative management will protect against losses and seek to capture profitable moves without hesitation.

The "temporary" nature of harmonic price behavior in situations like these establishes the proper individual expectations regarding what is possible from any harmonic pattern. As it relates to RSI BAMM, the various stages of the Divergence/Confirmation can be delineated to identify trade opportunities on smaller timeframes and capitalize on this phenomenon as it unfolds. The combination of pattern types and indicator readings distinguish reactive structural signals to an even more precise degree. Although we will review these advanced strategies further in this chapter, a larger harmonic comprehension can be attained to properly anticipate those conditions that typically yield reactions within the harmonic pattern framework as opposed to larger reversals. In most cases, the natural harmonic reaction phenomenon realized at the completion of critical pattern and indicator readings will define short-term "pausing" opportunities. Regardless of the longer-term trend, these harmonic reactions can yield a great deal of information about any potential opportunity. Furthermore, the larger relationships and categorizations of indicator readings with harmonic pattern types to establish the proper *Reaction versus Reversal* mentality. By no means do I feel that the RSI BAMM methodology is as comprehensive as the pattern identification rules. However, the fundamental expectations of how structures materialize in price and indicator readings facilitate decisions at each stage of the trading process.

Advanced RSI BAMM

As most know, the RSI BAMM strategy employs complex and impulsive indicator readings to define varying degrees of Divergence/Confirmation. Although most technical assessments can be derived from the harmonic price behavior related to the type of indicator readings at hand, all situations will provide clear price parameters to validate the opportunity. These strategies are more situationally–specific opportunities that require other conditions to be present to generate a valid trade signal. More than simple pattern identification, the defined expectations for each measurement within the RSI

BAMM approach represents an advanced framework within which to analyze harmonic structures. Once identified, it is possible to capitalize on the expected RSI BAMM sequence as it develops. Shorter-term opportunities frequently materialize within longer-term Complex RSI BAMM situations, as these structures define finite market movements in the same manner as harmonic patterns.

Advanced Bullish RSI BAMM Breakout

Since Complex RSI structures possess limited expectations following the completion of the reversal from the extreme area, an eventual retest is expected in all instances. Of course, a secondary retest will not unfold in this manner every time. However, this primary expectation instills an active management perspective at the initial completion of harmonic pattern to optimize the handling of these reactions. As was outlined earlier in this chapter, complex formations typically experience a short-lived reaction that eventually experiences a retest of the initial price level. Although the minimum expectation of all complex reversals is an eventual retest of the mid-point line at the 50-level, many interesting pattern relationships frequently pinpoint the retest and outline the final phase of the RSI BAMM. In many instances, a simple Bullish AB=CD Pattern will mark the price where this retest phenomenon initiates.

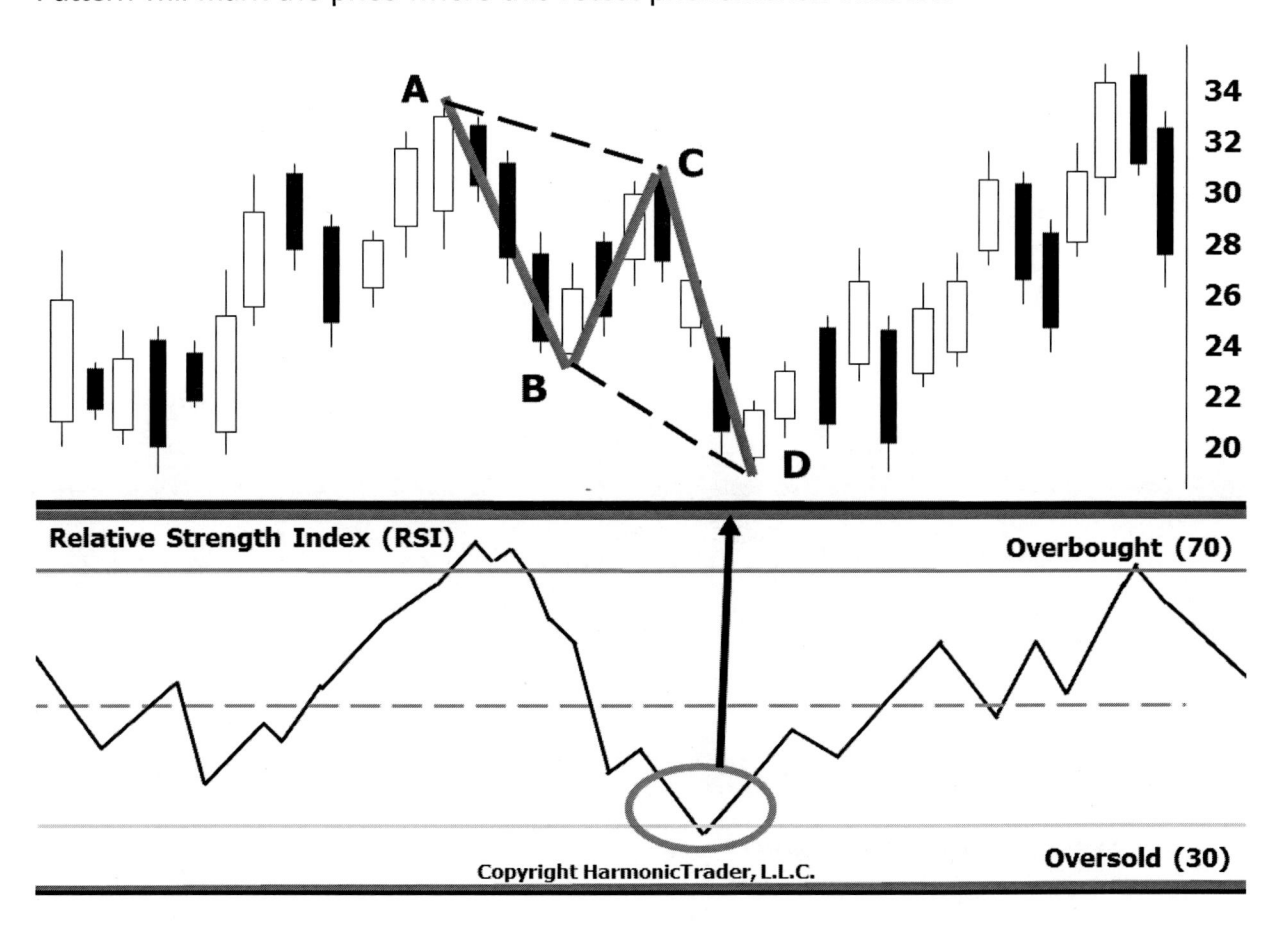

Harmonic Trading Volume 3: Reaction vs. Reversal

Microsoft (MSFT): Daily
Bullish Gartley
Advanced Bullish RSI BAMM AB=CD Breakout

The following daily chart in Microsoft exemplifies this phenomenon. In fact, the situation possessed more than just a Bullish AB=CD. The Bullish Gartley pattern that developed within the RSI BAMM complex set up was quite distinct and realized a sharp reversal. The AB=CD just under the $43 level After the complex structure was established, the indicator reading reversed all the way back to the oversold level as the price action formed a distinct AB=CD. When patterns such as these materialize between important extreme readings, the probability for a significant reversal is certainly greater with well-defined objectives in both the price and indicator readings.

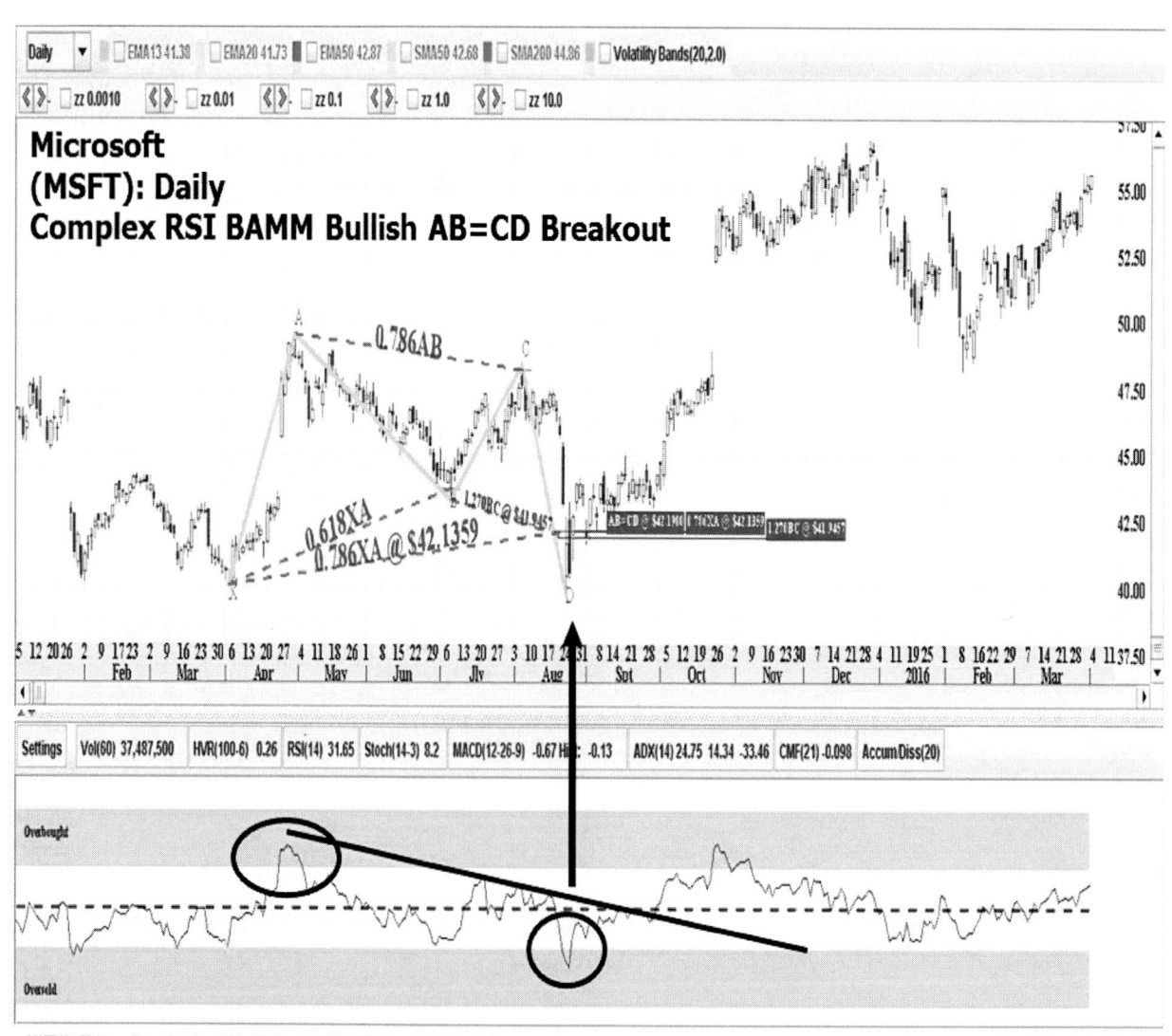

Harmonic Trading Volume 3: Reaction vs. Reversal

Advanced Bearish RSI BAMM Breakdown

After the complex RSI reading stabilizes under the 30 level, the corresponding breakout and price reaction will typically form a distinct AB=CD structure after establishing the initial low. These can be difficult situations to foresee an opportunity especially when the previous decline has been quite severe but a steep reaction from the initial complex indicator extreme can signal an unsustainable move, as well.

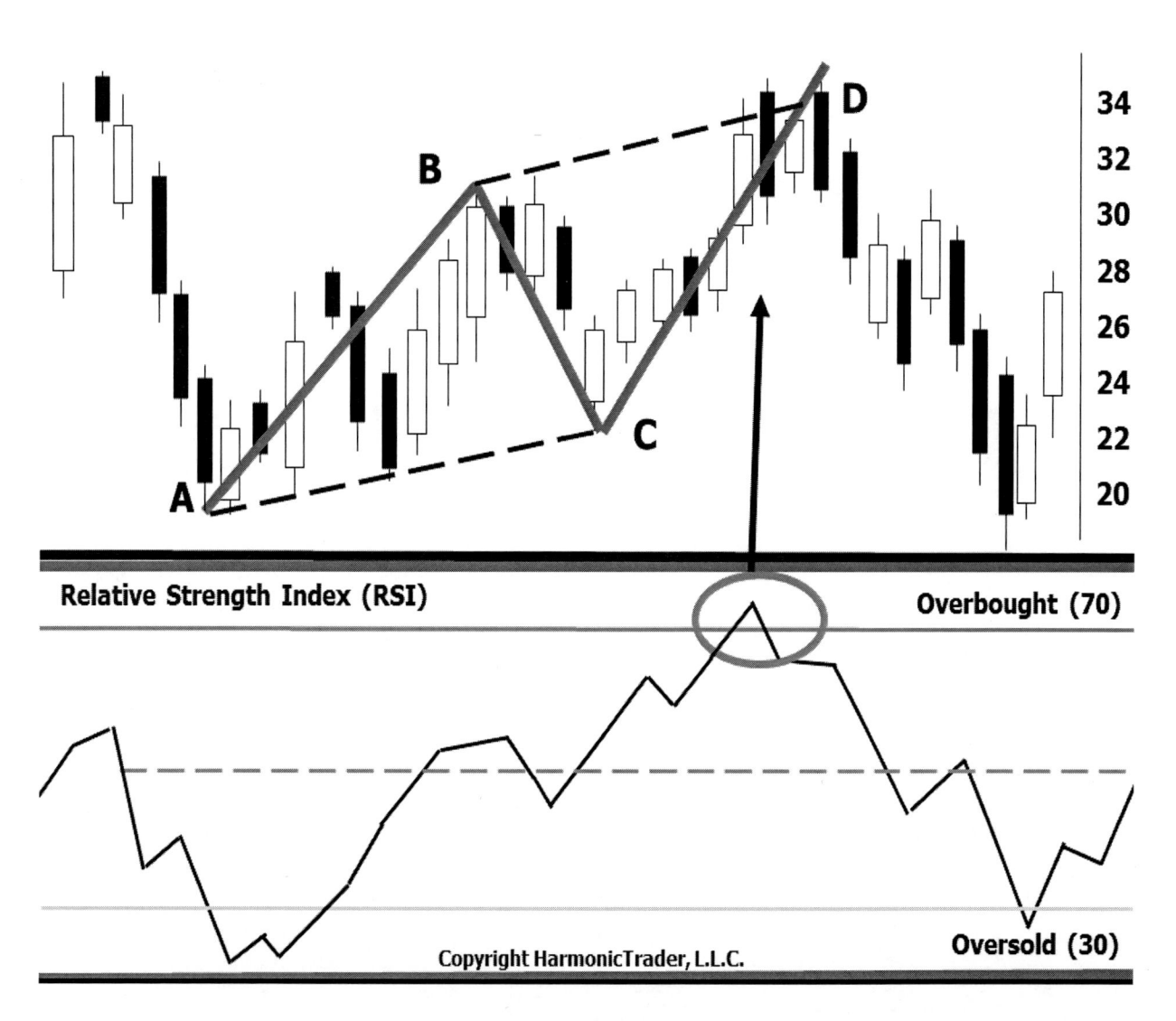

The eventual retest of the complex RSI indicator in combination with a minimum Bearish AB=CD pattern defines an important limit for the reaction. Again, it is important to understand that the minimum retest limits are often exceeded. In fact, it is quite common for the corresponding reaction of the indicator to test the other extreme. The key factor is where the pattern structure completes. This will pinpoint the minimum price target for the reaction and help confirm when the indicator begins to roll over.

Harmonic Trading Volume 3: Reaction vs. Reversal

Euro/British Pound (EURGBP_A0-FX): 15-Minute
Bearish AB=CD
Advanced Bearish RSI BAMM Breakdown

The following chart of the Euro/British Pound formed an exact AB=CD structure that marked the resistance of the initial reaction. In comparison, the complex formation reversed from the oversold extreme, tested the mid-point line at the 50-level before beginning the eventual retest. Although the price action gradually declined lower, the steady downtrend of the RSI reading clearly highlighted the bearish nature of this retest.

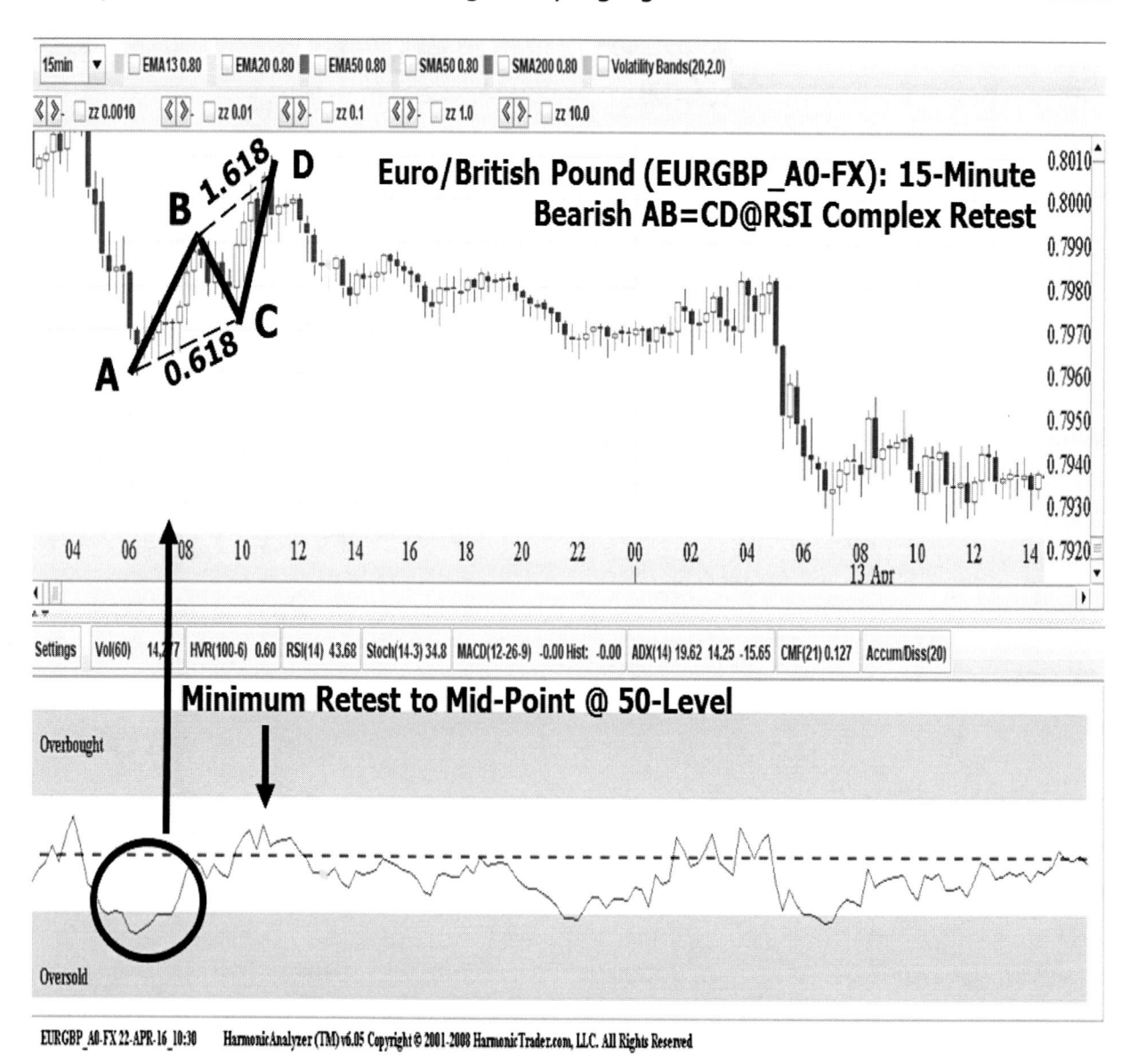

Harmonic Trading Volume 3: Reaction vs. Reversal

Advanced Indicator Analysis in Harmonic Trading Conclusion

My integration of Welles Wilder's Relative Strength measure with harmonic patterns was an enormous step forward in the analytical process of determining what truly defines a profitable harmonic opportunity. As I have outlined throughout this book, the key distinctions that are required to determine reactions from reversals, which must include considerations other than price measures. I believe that RSI is an ideal oscillator to gauge how far a market has moved in a specific period of time. However, the indicator's formula is somewhat static in its manifestation of readings and does not materialize in every instance. Sometimes, multiple tests of an extreme area can trigger false signals. Although I believe that these can be filtered to avoid mistakes, the true strength of any indicator analysis corresponds with structural measurements. Together, these assessments can define the predominant market direction and separate random market movements from significant price behavior. Furthermore, these integrations have created a more detailed analytical framework and led to advanced discoveries that further the understanding of harmonic patterns to an even greater degree.

Chapter 6
Harmonic Strength Index (HSI)

Harmonic Indicator Analysis

There are many shortcomings of technical indicator analysis as a stand-alone methodology. Most notably, the indicator unto itself is not a reliable signal on its own. In my *Volume 2* book, I outlined the unique RSI BAMM strategy of Divergence and Confirmation. However, I became frustrated by some of the limitations of this analysis since the phenomenon did not unfold ideally in as many situations as I wanted. Therefore, I set about to establish a new technical measure that would express natural extremes of price movements.

Although the proprietary ideas were derived from the Relative Strength Index formula, the unique refinements changed the elements of the overall calculation to reflect critical reactive changes of harmonic behavior. Effective on in their right, I have continued to maintain the application of these measures to harmonic pattern zones. with technical measures, especially those that employ harmonic ratios. I have found that indicators that possess a harmonic modifier to their respective formula provide a more appropriate insight as to the environmental bias of market conditions, especially when patterns confirm these measures.

The process of this discovery and refinement started in my research with harmonic patterns and Relative Strength. When I was putting together the material for *Volume 2*, I spent a great deal of time refining indicator readings and uncovering similar structural relationships as I had done for harmonic patterns. The strategies required several years of refinement before I was comfortable with the established parameters to confirm harmonic pattern opportunities in this manner. Although I was satisfied initially with the results of Relative Strength readings, the concept of confirmation became increasingly critical as the primary means to validate which harmonic patterns possessed the greatest potential. As I experimented with harmonic relationships in indicators, I unlocked many interesting discoveries. In fact, the formula for the harmonic indicator measures relative trading history similar to RSI but expresses readings in an unprecedented manner. The indicator is called the Harmonic Strength Index (HSI).

Harmonic Strength Index (HSI)

The Harmonic Strength Index (HSI) indicator is a proprietary formula that is designed to act as an early validation measure WHEN harmonic patterns exist. This is the best application for the indicator, especially as extreme reversals confirm pattern completion points. Quite simply, HSI is the next phase of Harmonic Trading. HSI is a broader expression of harmonic price behavior in the financial markets. The Harmonic Strength Index formula was refined over the course of a few years. Although the formula evolved from its original incarnation, the essential strategic concept has remained as the foundation for the goal of what is being measured. That is, the indicator is expressing the natural limits of any price segment with respect to its relative harmonic complex formula to express areas where minimum reactions can be expected. The additional ratio measures and reconfiguration of the RSI formula led to a smoother expression of readings that moved from one extreme to the next. The Harmonic Strength Index (HSI) is dramatically different in its measure and expression than RSI. However, I cannot over emphasize the importance of Welles Wilder's Relative Strength Index formula and, more importantly the principles of the indicator.

Adapted from the Relative Strength formula, the basic concepts that measure HARMONIC overbought and oversold levels became an interesting focus for my research. For years, I exclusively focused on Relative Strength as my primary indicator for confirmation and I was able to develop proprietary strategies based upon the principles garnered from this indicator. Therefore, I certainly acknowledge that none of this would be possible without the immense contribution of Mr. Wilder's RSI formula.

Most of my advanced RSI interpretations were developed years after the release my first two books. Advanced confirmation strategies such as RSI BAMM presented in *Volume 2* (2007) mark the expansion of strategies outside of the harmonic structural framework but, they accurately describe the ideal natural technical limits of any situation and define environments where harmonic patterns have the greatest potential for a sizable reversal. I have expanded upon the initial breakthrough of the Harmonic Strength Index to develop other ideas, and establish an official introduction to the trading world of what is now known as the subject of *Harmonic Indicators*. In the years to come, I look forward to sharing more of these proprietary advancements, especially with our harmonic pattern software tools.

Harmonic Strength Index Basics

The Harmonic Strength Index is a significant relative measure that is best applied within the window of opportunity established by the pattern. This is the objective of the Harmonic Strength Index, as well but the readings are designed to act as an early signal that corresponds with the completion of patterns to distinguish reactions from larger reversals.

The Harmonic Strength Index is an indicator that generally ranges between 0-100. These extremes are defined by unique harmonic levels that measure temporary overbought and oversold market conditions at the 88.6 and 11.3 indicator levels, respectively. The key challenge is to coordinate the price response following a pattern completion relative to the extreme HSI indicator reading. Patterns work well when this indicator confirmation unfolds immediately after the Terminal Bar has completed because the structural signal is defining a unique reaction to the measured harmonic level.

Reading the Harmonic Strength Index (HSI)

The HSI analysis focuses on a few distinct levels as it generally ranges from 0 to 100. Although the indicator can exceed these extreme levels, <u>the most important aspect of the reading is when it reverses from an extreme range.</u> To complement the 0-100 limit, I have created new price levels of the 11.3 and 88.6 to define extreme HARMONIC indicator conditions. These measures are designed to reflect the harmonic limits of the indicator in the same manner as RSI. The indicator is similar to Relative Strength in that it trades from one extreme to the other. However, Harmonic Strength Index was designed to incorporate ratio measures that filter out some of the excessive variation and noise typically found in Relative Strength. In essence, I was looking for a formula that would express the directional potential that patterns possess. Although I still feel that Relative Strength possesses important technical aspects of any market, the Harmonic Strength Index improved upon the environmental expression that substantiates proper expectations and clearly defines directional bias based upon the indicator reading at hand. In particular, the indicator is typically a leading signal that precedes the price reversal. Most important, the indicator reading possesses its greatest predictive capabilities at the completion point of patterns. This is an important distinction because the reversal of the indicator typically precedes price. Furthermore, the entire indicator reversal out of extreme zone must be registered before even considering a reaction price. This is the primary technical that is most effective when it coincides with completion of a harmonic pattern. Let's take a look at parameters that define Harmonic Strength Index.

Harmonic Strength Index (HSI) Oversold: Bullish Confirmation

The oversold zone in the Harmonic Strength Index is delineated by the 11.3 reading. Although the indicator can exceed the area below 0 and go negative, the defining event is the actual reversal above the minimum 11.3 level once the extreme test has completed. Even in these situations, the indicator reversal is an early signal of impending price action.

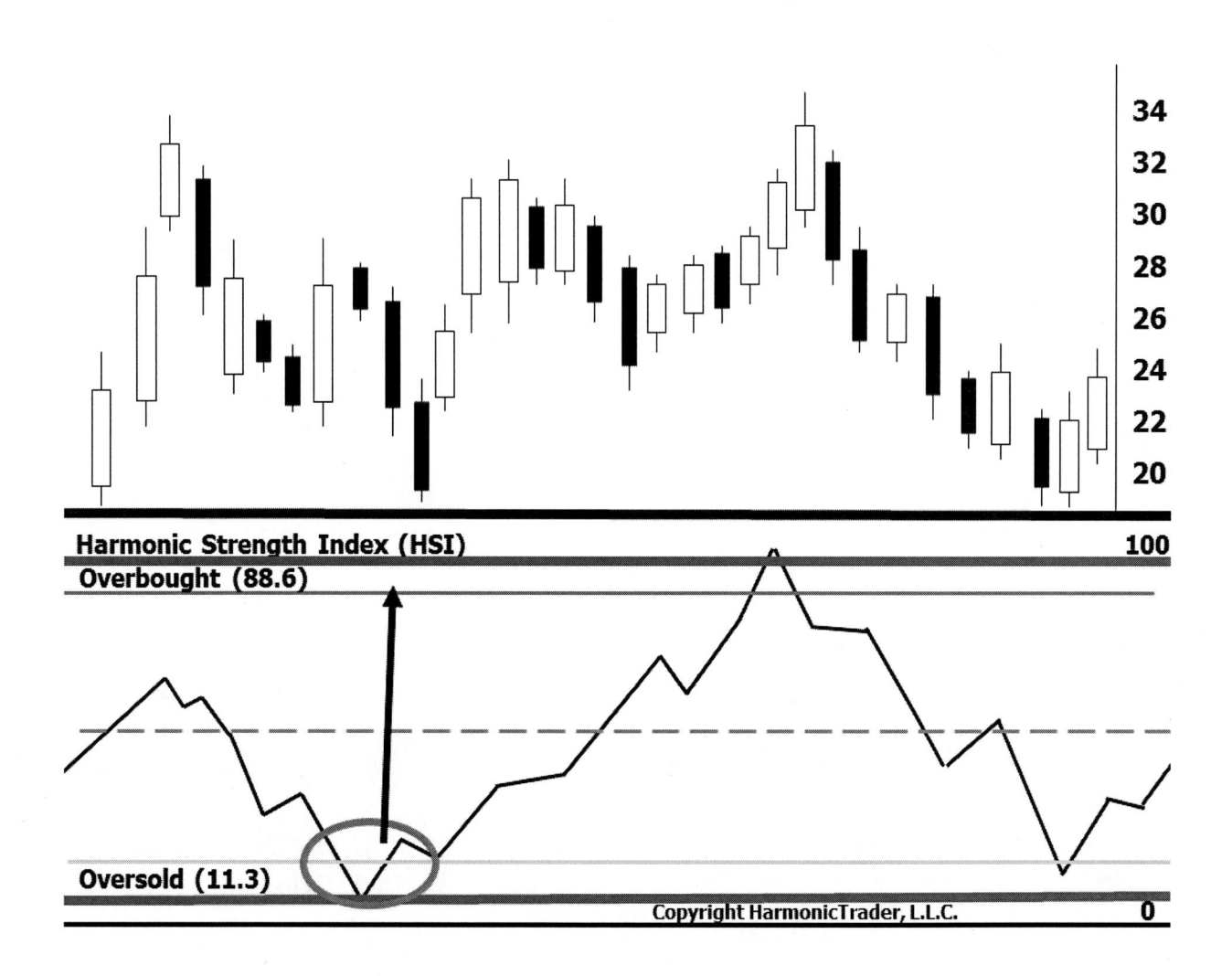

Harmonic Trading Volume 3: Reaction vs. Reversal

Google (GOOG): 5-Minute
Bullish Gartley
Harmonic Strength Index (HSI) Oversold: Bullish Confirmation

It is important to note that extreme tests that reverse below 0 from a negative reading typically signal a more exhaustive test of support. Also, these situations will require more time. The key is to focus on the individual HSI readings as the trading forms each price bar. As was the case for Google on the 5-minute chart, the HSI trigger was confirmed when the indicator reading reversed from the extreme in the direction of the pattern.

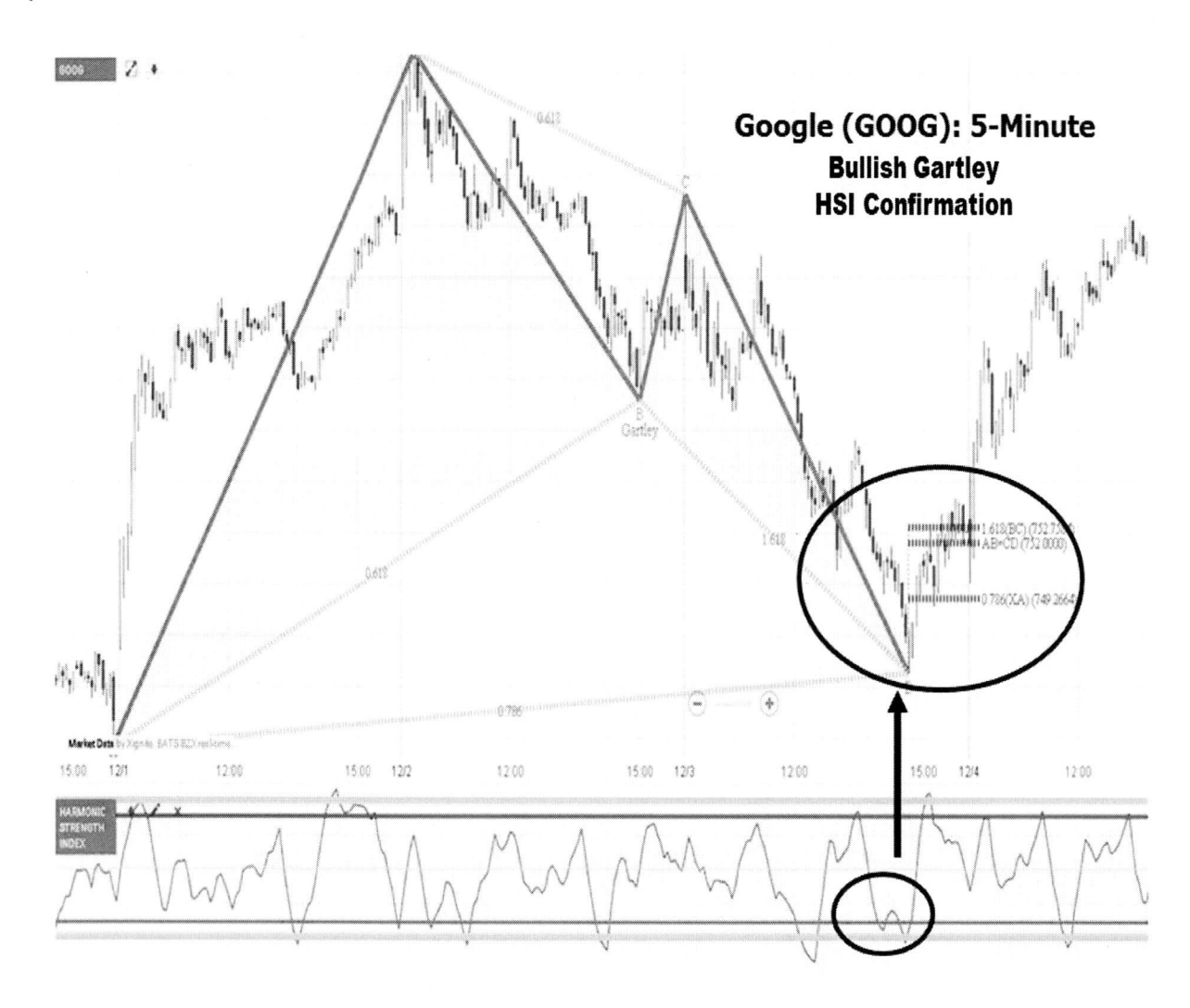

Harmonic Trading Volume 3: Reaction vs. Reversal

Google (GOOG): 5-Minute
Bullish Gartley Potential Reversal Zone (PRZ)
Harmonic Strength Index (HSI) Oversold: Bullish Confirmation

The price action in the Potential Reversal Zone (PRZ) was confirmed by the Harmonic Stength Index extreme reversal. The harmonic support and indicator oversold extreme reading pinpointed the ideal price level for the execution.

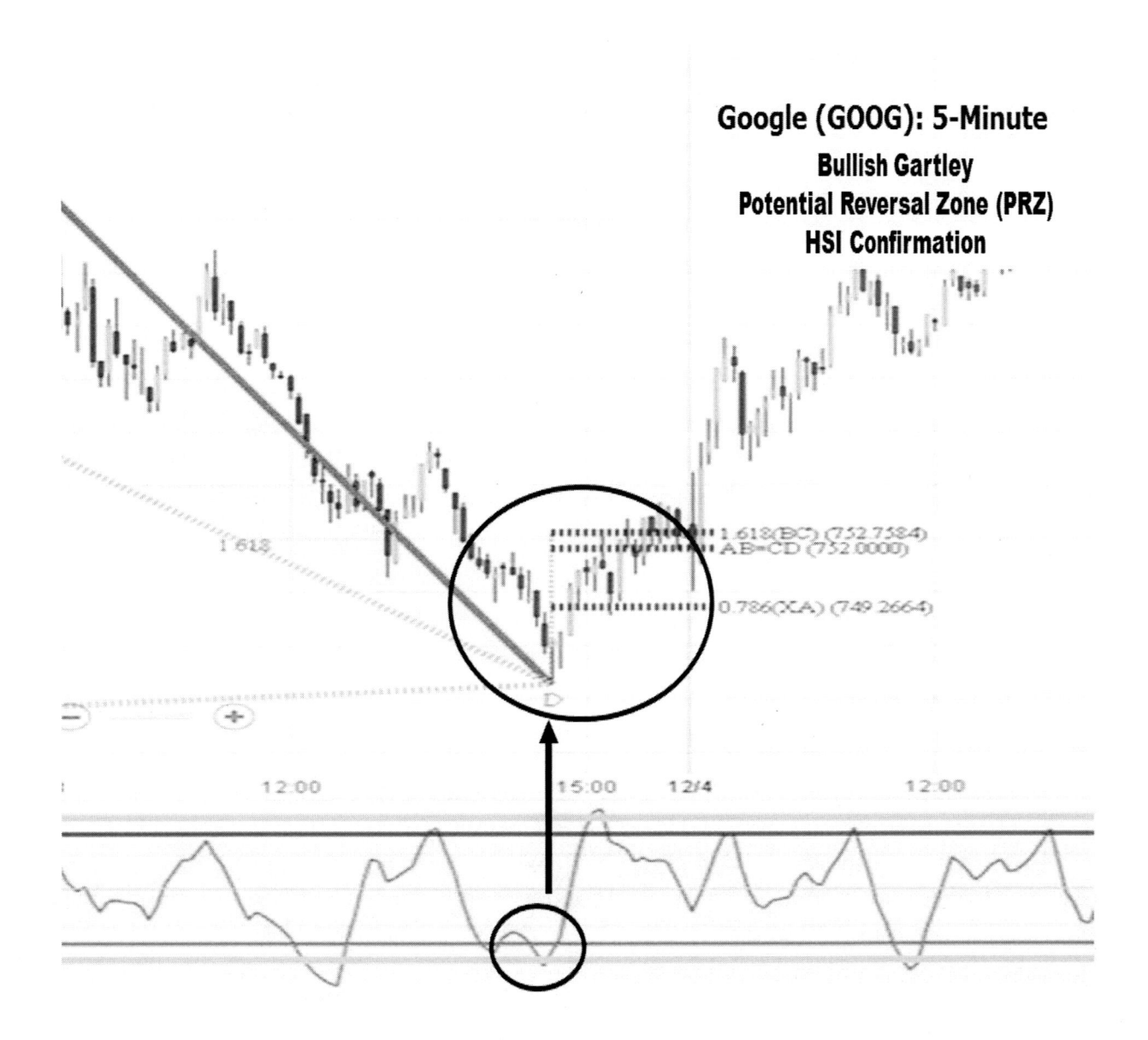

Harmonic Trading Volume 3: Reaction vs. Reversal

Harmonic Strength Index Overbought: Bearish Confirmation

An HSI reading is considered overbought AFTER the indicator reverses OUT of the entire zone. The overbought range starts at the 88.6 but it can exceed the 100 level. These structural indicator readings at the extreme tests typically reverse in a sequential manner as once the indicator reading peaks, the successive indicator readings will steadily decline.

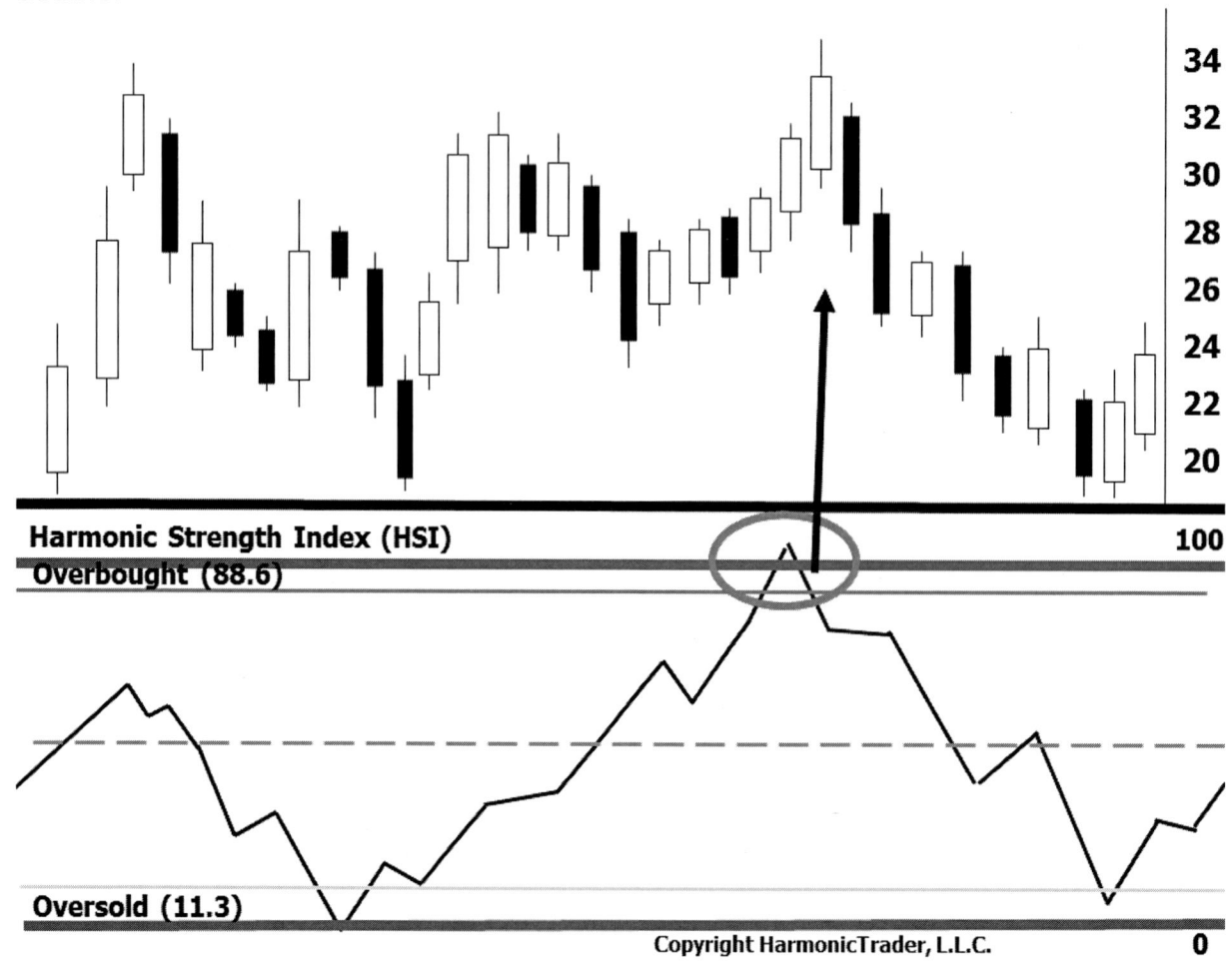

To generate an official overbought HSI reading, price action must exhibit a distinct reversal from the indicator after testing the 88.6 level at a minimum. Although the reading can trade as high as above 100 – or even 120, the key technical event that must occur to confirm the reversal is a reading that is trending out of this area. The indicator reading must enter the overbought zone and reverse shortly thereafter under the 88.6 minimum level. In its simplest application, these are the important singular events in each price bar that unfolds in the extreme zone of the Harmonic Strength Index that must be monitored and have particular significance when found with harmonic patterns.

Harmonic Trading Volume 3: Reaction vs. Reversal

Euro/U.S. Dollar (EUR_A0-FX): 5-Minute
Bearish AB=CD
Harmonic Strength Index Overbought: Bearish Confirmation

The following chart shows a Bearish AB=CD that possess ideal Harmonic Strength Index confirmation. The Harmonic Strength Index reading rolled over exactly in the Potential Reversal Zone. As the intraday AB=CD the pattern, the indicator clearly defined the short-term extreme.

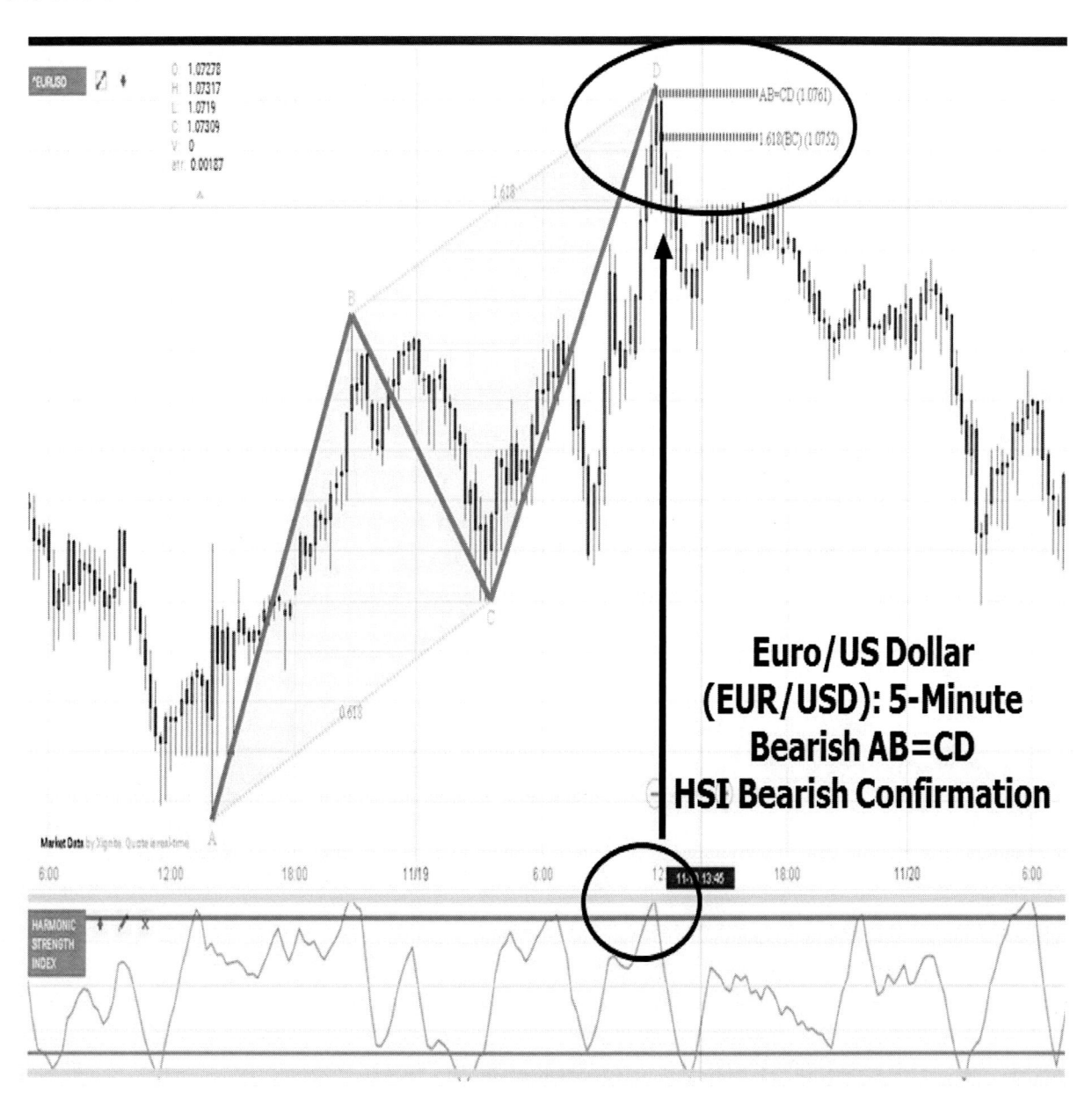

Harmonic Trading Volume 3: Reaction vs. Reversal

Euro/U.S. Dollar (EUR_A0-FX): 5-Minute
Bearish AB=CD Potential Reversal Zone (PRZ)
Harmonic Strength Index Overbought: Bearish Confirmation

The following chart the price action Potential Reversal Zone shows the individual price bars that completed in this harmonic resistance. Immediately after testing the entire area, the price action reversed sharply after the HSI reading declined under the 88.6 level. The exact AB=CD completion point pinpointed the reversal precisely at the Terminal Price Bar as the immediate reactive character in the harmonic resistance zone was a demonstrative change in character that the pattern was predicting. This is the exact type coordination required to validate reversals and define profitable opportunities.

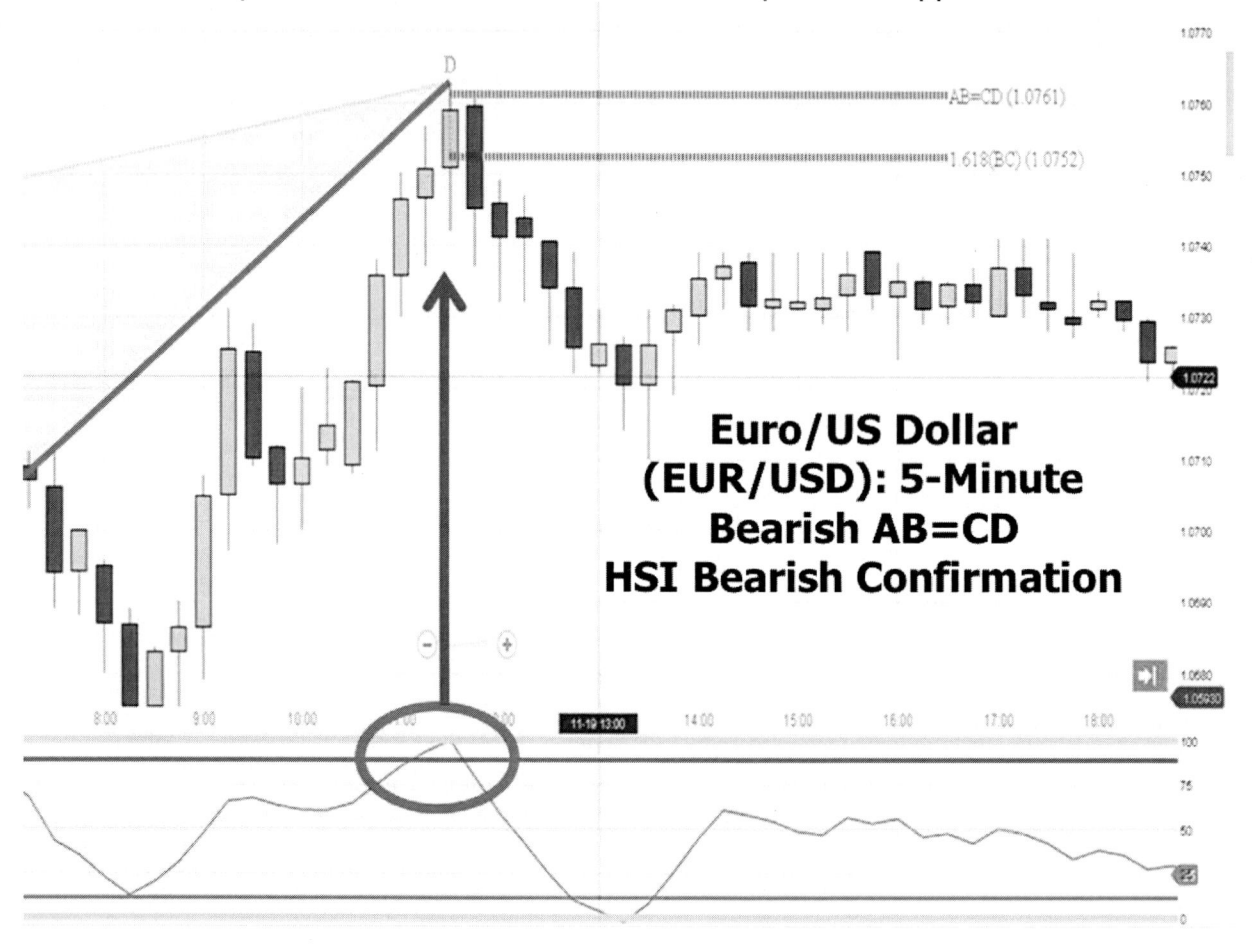

Euro/US Dollar (EUR/USD): 5-Minute Bearish AB=CD HSI Bearish Confirmation

It is important to note that the Harmonic Strength Index reading must reverse from the extreme zone before considering the trigger valid. Due to the nature of the indicator, the trend will typically not reverse before the indicator declines below 88.6 HSI level. In the case of EUR/USD, the indicator provided the early trigger of a valid opportunity at hand.

Harmonic Trading Volume 3: Reaction vs. Reversal

Harmonic Strength Index Mid-Line @ the 50-Level

Much like the interpretations of the midpoint line in Relative Strength, many of the same relationships do apply to the Harmonic Strength Index readings. Also, there are specific expectations and interpretations that are derived from a sequence of HSI indicator readings that distinguish specific environmental conditions. As is the case with the RSI BAMM for example, a double extreme indicator reading that is separated by a midpoint of 50 will represent the most significant BAMM-type formations. In addition, there are interesting relationships when the indicator reading maintains specific levels. For example, it is quite common to see bullish trending markets steadily rise and maintain a reading of all the 50-midpoint line. Conversely, bearish trends will exhibit price action that registers under the 50-midpoint line and fails to even reach the 88.6 line. These are a few traits of these readings, and other strategies will be presented to get the most out of this indicator.

Harmonic Strength Index Expectations

The primary situation where the HSI indicator works best is with a distinct harmonic pattern as defined by the Terminal Bar in the Potential Reversal Zone. In these cases, an extreme HSI reading triggers the reaction shortly after the indicator reverses. That is, many if not most cases will exhibit the indicator reversal occurring before price. This is important because the early signal provides advanced notice of the potential harmonic support/resistance. Furthermore, the indicator complements pattern reversal zones, as the environmental conditions within these extreme readings define important implications for the internal strength of the price action.

A lack of an HSI signal will identify any potentially failed situations in advance. When the indicator reading does not materialize at the completion pattern, the failure HSI to exhibit confirmation is an excellent example where the indicator is signaling a flawed structure. Although a reaction may unfold, more definable confirmation signals immediately after a Terminal Bar is established marks the optimal situations. The lack of an HSI trigger should reduce expectations at a minimum, as the pattern on its own holds less potential for even a reaction.

Another important consideration with the HSI indicator is that it frequently marks important continuation points within predominant trends – even when no structural signals provide reliable price levels these areas. All of these relationships become clear over time but the most important constraint involved with indicator reading itself is the actual trigger bar that marks the confirmation of reversal. Similar to Relative Strength, the price bar that results in the indicator reading reverse beyond the extreme level is a unique individual price point that must be considered. In fact, this assessment can confirm price parameters of the opportunity including the optimization stop loss limit at relative HSI readings. Of course, every HSI confirmation is not going to yield a sizable move but the extreme indicator reversal improves the probability of a successful reaction much in the same manner as RSI.

Serial Indicator Reversals

Due to the nature of the Harmonic Strength Index formula, the expression of these readings has been designed to exhibit a predominant bias and reflect states of price action that have moved too far in one direction within a specific period of time. Sometimes, the indicator will move dramatically with the price. In other instances, the indicator will move from one extreme to the next with very little price movement. These situations must be distinguished.

HSI is different from Relative Strength in that its formula has been designed to express these extremes as they relate to harmonic measures no matter how far price action has moved. In this regard, the indicator provides tremendous insight into the vitality of any price segment. Furthermore, the expression of this indicator in both extreme reversals and movement from extreme to extreme must be considered - *Serial.*

The general assumption of a serial indicator reading is that the individual readings will move in a successive numeric manner from one extreme to the next. As the indicator reading moves into an extreme area, the ultimate reversal at the 88.6-100 line and/or the 0-11.3 level cannot be determined until after the structure has reversed from the range. Typically, the individual readings will reverse from an extreme with successive readings.

One of the interesting aspects that was noticed in the development of this indicator was a unique ability of these extreme reversals to establish early countertrend signals in the individual readings well-before the price accelerates. As we have discussed, the indicator itself has been proven to be a leading signal that provides the definitive countertrend price level at the completion of a pattern. Once the HSI indicator has reversed, the Trigger Bar denotes the price level for this change and serves as the penultimate limit for the impending reversal.

I must emphasize the importance of waiting for the reversal out of the extreme. In the Harmonic Strength Index, as the indicator continues to register readings in the predominant trend the price will follow. In fact, a reading that enters the extreme zone will typically experience a price acceleration as each price bar registers a deeper level. For example, a market that has rallied quickly beyond the HSI extreme at the 88.6 level possesses inherent strength. Expansions beyond the minimum extreme limits of the 11.3 and 88.6 level result in price action that accelerates in a serial manner until the indicator reading can reverse.

In the HSI extremes, it is also important to make the distinction regarding the extent of the extreme reading that is registered. Depending upon whether the indicator reverses from 88.6 or from 100, the overall conclusion will be different. A reading that reverses from the 100 level may be considered more significant than just the 88.6 test. Regardless, the indicator will typically continue to trend higher in the extreme range until it has peaked. In the bearish example, a reading that hits the 88.6 level will continue higher with each price bar until the reading triggers a lower level. In our bearish example, price can rally above the minimum 88.6 level, continuing well-above the 100 level. As price accelerates in a dramatic fashion, each individual reading will continue successively in the predominant trend until expressing a decreasing value.

In these situations, the trend must be respected until the indicator demonstratively reverses from the overbought extreme. Again, this is a clear example of the early nature of the indicator to signal changes in price behavior but helps to avoid mistakes such as premature entries or attempting trades that lack confirmation. Assuming we were looking at a 15-minute chart, the indicator readings would continue to increase sequentially. Regardless if it is at 88.6 or 100, the key technical event unfolds when the individual indicator reading begins to roll over. The sequential indicator readings throughout the extreme reversal may look something like this:

Time	Price	HSI Reading
9:45 AM	103.22	77.08
10:00 AM	103.55	82.14
10:15 AM	103.79	89.10
10:30 AM	103.97	91.51
10:45 AM	104.11	100.77
11:00 AM	104.70	104.24 #
11:15 AM	104.73	93.21
11:30 AM	104.87	91.64
11:45 AM	104.48	84.95 $
12:00 PM	103.98	72.66

Although this is a hypothetical schedule of numbers, it demonstrates the serial characteristics of the indicator. HSI readings that exhibit this sequence of readings can be monitored to define the inflection point, especially when analyzed within a pattern's zone. Of course, this is an ideal scenario, HSI reversals unfold in such a serial manner. change when it happens, especially in the extreme zones. When we look at the illustration, notice the time and sales price readings that represent the high of each individual bar. The HSI readings that accompany the sequence of prices typically reflect this environmental assessment. It is important to note that as the price peaked, the

Harmonic Trading Volume 3: Reaction vs. Reversal

indicator reading will usually reverse as an early signal (#). It is quite common to see consecutive HSI readings diverge from the price extreme. This is an early but important trigger in the analysis of the indicator reversal. The key event is when the price falls out of the zone as denoted by the "$" mark at that readout time. These relationships will become clear with more experience but it is essential to closely monitor the individual readings as indicator reverses in the extreme zone.

Harmonic Strength Index (HSI) and Relative Strength (RSI)

The foundation for all my work has been to experiment with integrative techniques that compare various measurements to discover common characteristics to define unique market environments. These integrative conclusions are the basis for all Harmonic Trading decisions and represent advanced confirmation strategies for harmonic patterns. As I've mentioned previously, no indicator – RSI or HSI - can ever be considered as a standalone trade signal. However, there are distinct indicator formations that can confirm harmonic patterns to a specific degree. Obviously, HSI and RSI possess similar characteristics and possess a variety of interesting comparative relationships. Although it is not my desire to try to connect every signal, the clearest relationships are usually the most significant and have the greatest potential to unlock market signals.

There are a few ways to compare both measures. The strongest correlation is when both indicators confirm each other at extremes. However, there are many times when Harmonic Strength Index will register an extreme reading yet RSI will not. There are number of combinations that can form in these situations but the general take away is to focus on the price action as soon as the HSI trigger has been initiated. These are situations where HSI is indicating an "internally" exhaustive price segment that is usually a countertrend reaction. This is one of the most reliable advantages of HSI because it reveals hidden areas of support/resistance unlike any other indicator. Similar to the way that harmonic patterns can define "invisible" levels of support and resistance unlike any other methodology, HSI does the same for indicator readings.

When both trigger an extreme reading, there is a greater probability of confirmation. More importantly, the price level that marks the trigger which represents a technically more significant area that must be monitored. This is a situation where multiple technical readings that confirm the same assessment will be much more reliable than any singular measurement on its own.

Complex RSI with HSI Confirmation

One of the most common situations that can effectively confirm both methods is when price action forms a complex RSI structure with an impulsive HSI formation. The complex formation in the Relative Strength reading can take much longer and experience accelerated price behavior as it is in the final process of reversing. However, a Harmonic Strength Index reading that materializes in these situations can pinpoint the end of the consolidation typically associated with a complex RSI formation, and confirm the reversal in both indicator and price.

Bullish Complex RSI with HSI Confirmation

When a complex RSI formation exceeds the oversold level at 30, it can be difficult to know whether the price will merely consolidate or provide a decisive reversal. When HSI reverses from an extreme that corresponds with complex RSI structure, the Trigger Bar will mark the price action where a larger reversal can be realized, as these situations provide an even greater degree of bullish confirmation.

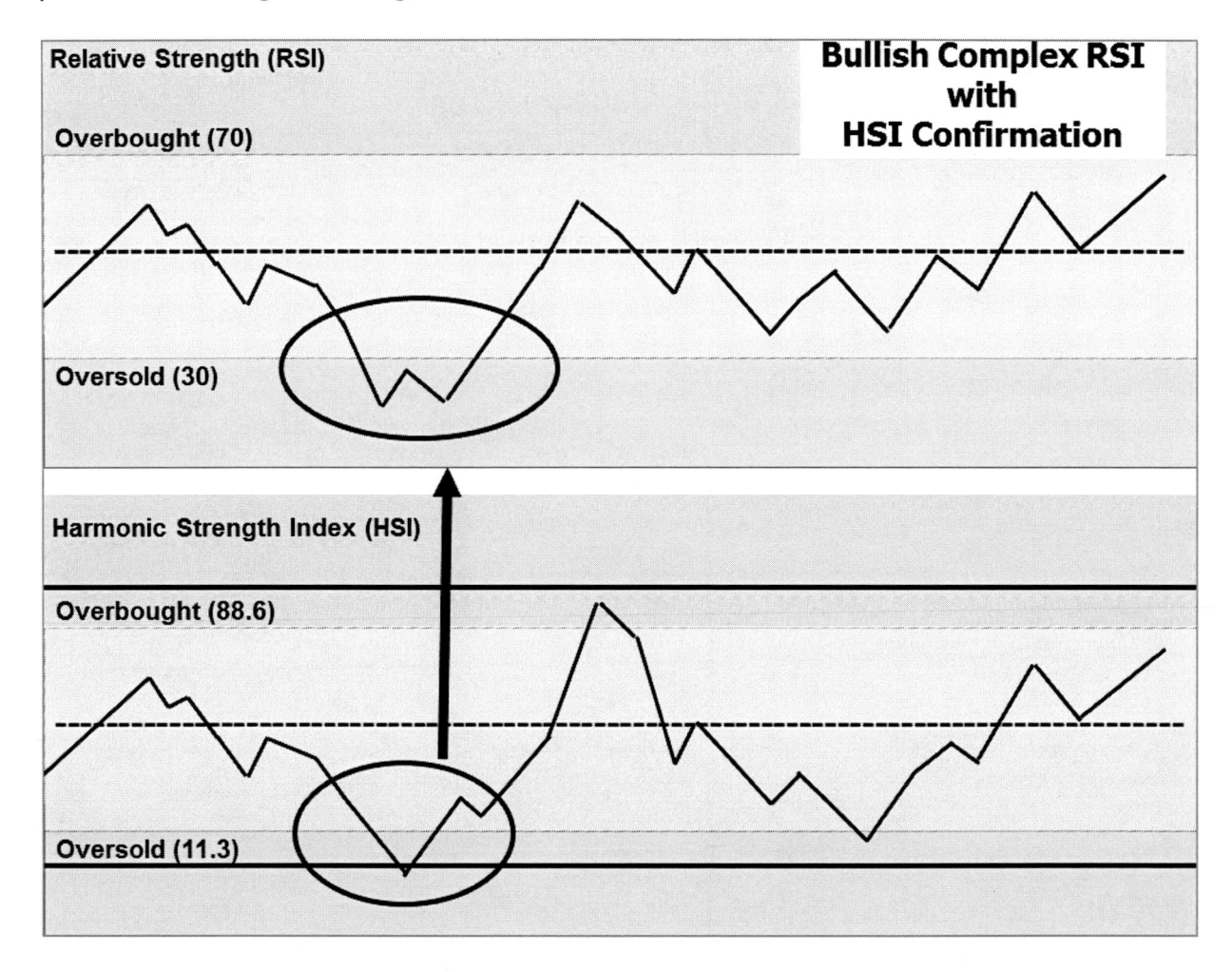

Harmonic Trading Volume 3: Reaction vs. Reversal

U.S. Dollar/Japanese Yen (JPY_A0-FX): 5-Minute
Bullish Complex RSI with HSI Confirmation

The following chart of the US Dollar/Japanese Yen shows a complex bullish RSI indicator reading that was confirmed by an extreme Harmonic Strength Index reversal. In this instance, the HSI reading was early but the Trigger Bar marked the initial stabilization level of the downtrend. The price action clearly responded after the RSI reading reversed from the oversold zone. When these multiple readings materialize in the same area, the price level must be monitored closely as potential harmonic support of significance.

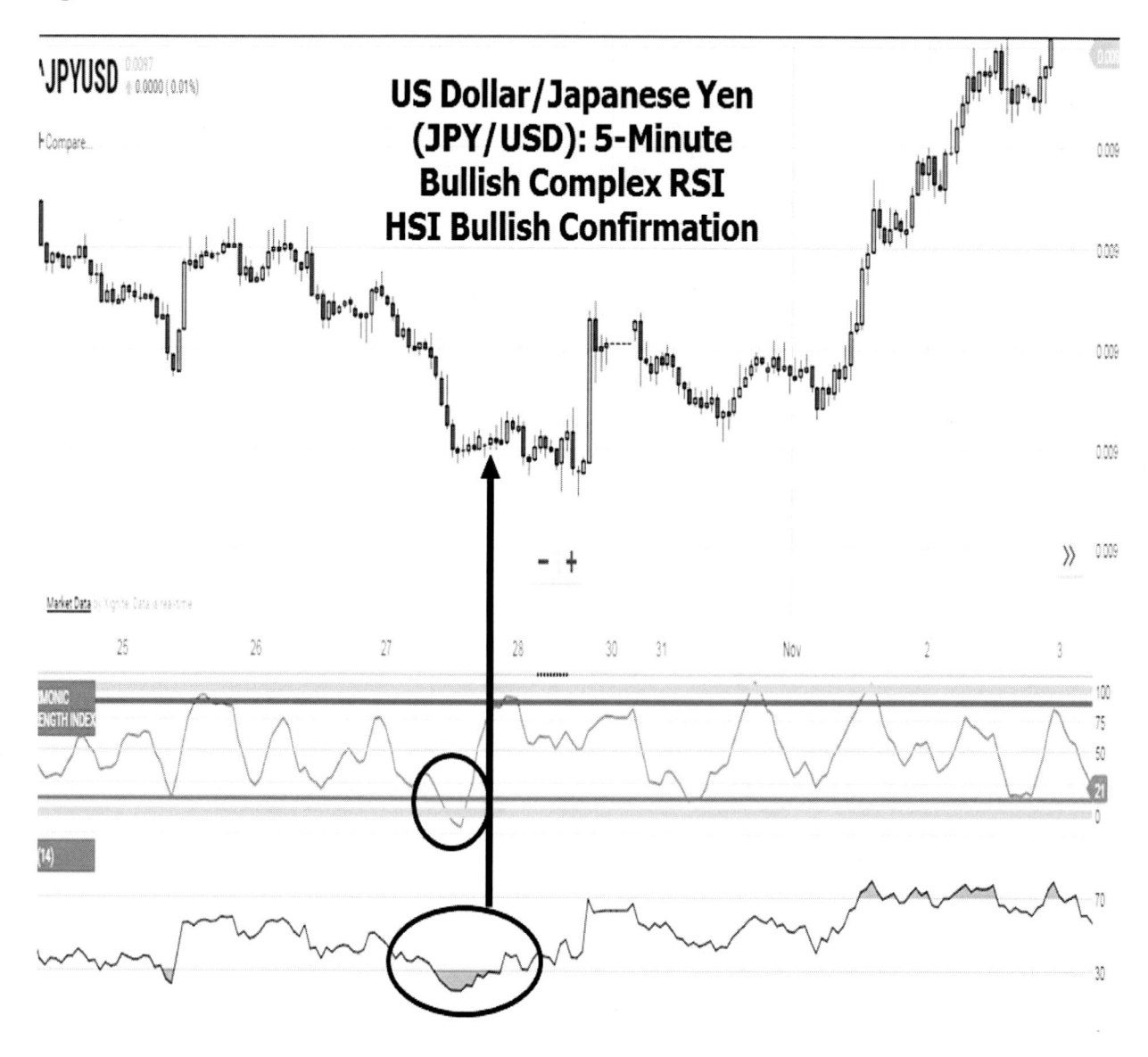

Harmonic Trading Volume 3: Reaction vs. Reversal

Bearish Complex RSI with HSI Confirmation

As a complex reading reverses from the overbought limit with a complex RSI structure above 70, an extreme HSI reading can pinpoint the indicator resistance. Although it is common for the HSI readings to be early, the combination of both formations is an extraordinary confirmation signal.

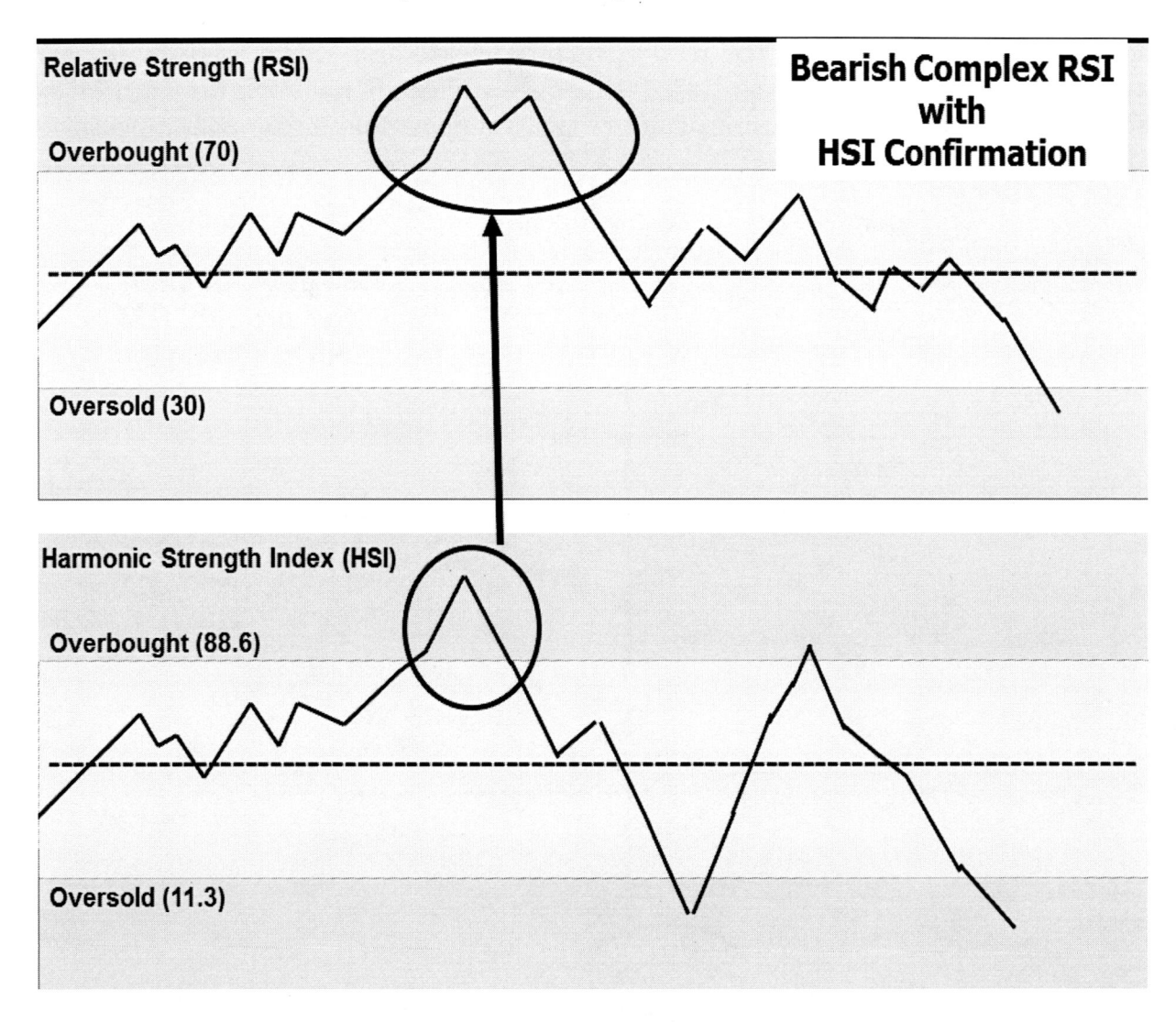

Harmonic Trading Volume 3: Reaction vs. Reversal

Tesla (TSLA): Daily
Bearish Complex RSI with HSI Confirmation

The following daily chart of Tesla demonstrates the long-term ability of the Harmonic Strength Index to confirm complex RSI readings. This was an interesting situation where the 88.6 level was tested briefly in the same area as the complex RSI formation. Once the complex RSI reading reversed from the extreme zone, the trigger was confirmed. The price action stalled immediately after the Harmonic Strength Index reversed while the complex RSI indicator readings required more time before declining below the 70-limit.

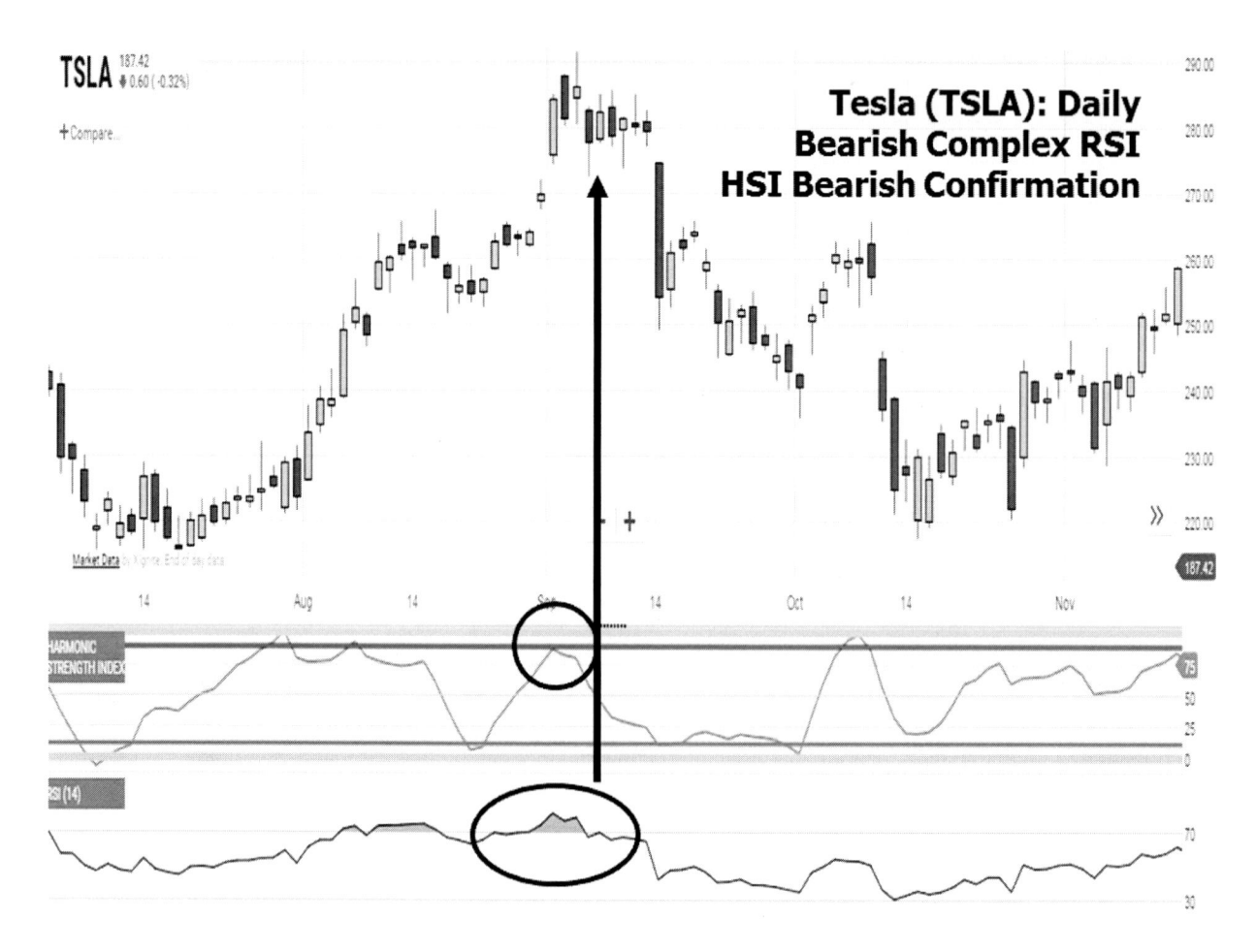

On a final note, is important to stress that these measures are the result of experimenting with dozens of different combinations to unlock consistent analytical tools that consistently identified the most critical points within any trend. The relationship of HSI versus RSI is a fantastic example of what is possible when you bring a comparative harmonic framework to a traditional technical indicator. These ideas alone could probably fill another book but that's not happening anytime soon!

Harmonic Trading Volume 3: Reaction vs. Reversal

Harmonic Strength Index Conclusion

The most important breakthrough that the Harmonic Strength Index encompasses is the significance these indicator readings possess relative to pattern measurements. There are a number of discoveries associated with HSI that express complementary strategies within the harmonic pattern framework. Over the years, I have introduced a several software applications that have gradually integrated new measures outside the basic pattern rules. Although pattern structures will always be the basis for any trading opportunity, indicator readings and their related assessments have expanded the analytical framework to highlight necessary confirmation strategies to identify those patterns that possess additional measures to identify those opportunities with the greatest potential.

The Harmonic Strength Index is a substantial breakthrough in assessing harmonic limits of how far the market can move in one direction within a certain period of time. I have outlined examples where the indicator can signal extreme moves well-before the price reacts from the completed pattern. Specifically, the Harmonic Strength Index extreme indicator reversal signals the most effective confirmation if it unfolds immediately in the area of the Terminal Bar.

As I previously mentioned, the presentation of the strategies and overall promotion of the indicator is intended to advance the knowledge - not sell a product. I make the indicator available on most software programs included with basic packages and offered reasonably as an individual add-on tool. Usually, I will provide free trials so that all traders can review the merits of the indicator for themselves. This is all I will say about the subject but there is an industry problem with individuals selling a variety of programs that have little trading value. I stand by my research and I know that this indicator can provide information unlike any other measure.

On a final note, the Harmonic Strength Index marks a new phase within the Harmonic Trading approach. As technology advances and programming becomes simpler, complex strategies can now be distilled to unprecedented levels. In fact, one of the hottest areas of research on Wall Street today is the programming of Artificial Intelligence with computers that actually learn. Many people have attempted to program neural–type networks for decades but the new framework in which many programs are offered have the capability to compile complex variables into simple algorithms. As this technology advances, trading automation and statistical verification will become commonplace.

Chapter 7:
Advanced Harmonic Trading Management Strategies

In *Harmonic Trading Volume 1*, I outlined a comprehensive trade management model. This was the result of several years of research after I released the harmonic pattern identification strategies in *The Harmonic Trader*. Many other measurements that define trade management parameters that have not been presented in any of my previous books. I have introduced a variety of concepts online, this is the first time I have compiled all strategies that define the ideal Harmonic Trading management framework in a book. These additional insights provide an even greater degree clarity for the overall Defined Trading Realm, especially as these price parameters relate to the management of harmonic patterns.

Although the management phase of the trading process can be the longest as price action can take time to establish a larger reversal, there are situations where these strategies are dictated by the volatility of the pattern completion and require an active management of the position. Other conditions may require more time to assess the larger reversal possibility. In either situation, the general categorization of management expectations depends upon how the actual price behavior reacts to the initial completion of the harmonic pattern.

After assessing all ideal harmonic parameters relevant to the Potential Reversal Zone, the behavior of the price action as it trades beyond the "execution window" must be monitored closely within the prescribed Harmonic Trading management parameters. Pattern-specific strategies must be employed in the same manner as identification and execution to optimized distinct scenarios. For example, a multiple unit exit strategy is a simple but effective means to capture sharp reactions by securing a portion of the position at an automatic profit objective while allowing more time for a large reversal to unfold. Employing discretionary management strategies, the trade remains open until the market signals that the reversal trend is no longer continuing. Although these general guidelines, these techniques constitue pattern-specific trade management strategies that are all measured in advance to define the potential limits of any opportunity.

Harmonic Trading Volume 3: Reaction vs. Reversal

Reversal Trendlines

Trendlines are extremely important for a number of reasons. They help define the predominant direction of any market on any timeframe. Trend channels provide a moving range of support and resistance, which is extremely effective in monitoring trending markets. Although there is some degree of interpretation required when assessing harmonic patterns, trendlines represent another structural measurement tool that can clearly detect changes outline important inflection points within the management process. Following the completion of a harmonic pattern, the new trend will typically exhibit a primary and accelerated trendline from the Potential Reversal Zone (PRZ) extreme.

- **Primary Trendline (≥45 Degree Slope):** This management trendline must possess a distinct and steady 45-degree slope projected from the reversal extreme at the Terminal Price Bar. Although price action will typically require more time to resolve the progress of the Primary Trendline, it does represent a dynamic price limit to assess stop loss adjustments as the trade unfolds. Most reversals will form a primary trendline initially as the price action changes trend.

- **Accelerated Trendline (≥60 Degree Slope):** After price action has initiated a reversal from the completion point of the pattern, the trendline that materializes after this consolidation marks an important basic determinant in the type of reaction that will unfold following completion of the pattern. In many cases, the price reaction will be quite sharp and follow a trendline that is greater than 60°. Although the slope of these trendlines may vary, the accelerated nature of this price move possesses a distinct and obvious character. In management situations, the violation of this trendline can trigger optimal profit objectives especially when integrated with other measurement strategies to effectively manage the position.

Manipulating the Slope of the Trendline

One common response I frequently hear from students in regard to the slope assessment of the trendline is that the magnification of the chart can be changed to adjust the degree of the trendline. First, let me say that if you are trying to adjust the charts magnification, you are probably already in trouble and need to get out of the trade! Seriously though, these basic concepts are more general assessments where the primary and accelerated trendlines will be obvious. Although the general 45° primary slope is an approximation, it should be less severe than the accelerated trendline. The different nature of these slopes will be obvious. In fact, the accelerated trendline is a steep, short-lived move that is unsustainable. Although this volatility may be due to any one of a number of factors, the clear character of the sharpness of the accelerated trendline cannot be disputed. Simply stated, most trend reactions that are volatile and steep in nature will experience some degree of consolidation before continuing in the same direction. When these accelerated trendlines are violated, a price retracement is inevitable.

Bullish Reversal Trendline Types

After the Terminal Price Bar has been established, the consolidation that commences beyond the pattern completion point begins to take on a degree of uptrend progress. Sometimes, the initial reversal can be sharp exhibiting a dramatic move. In most instances, these reversals are short-lived and must be managed accordingly. However, those reversals that can maintain a progress that upholds a minimum 45° primary uptrend will likely continue in that direction.

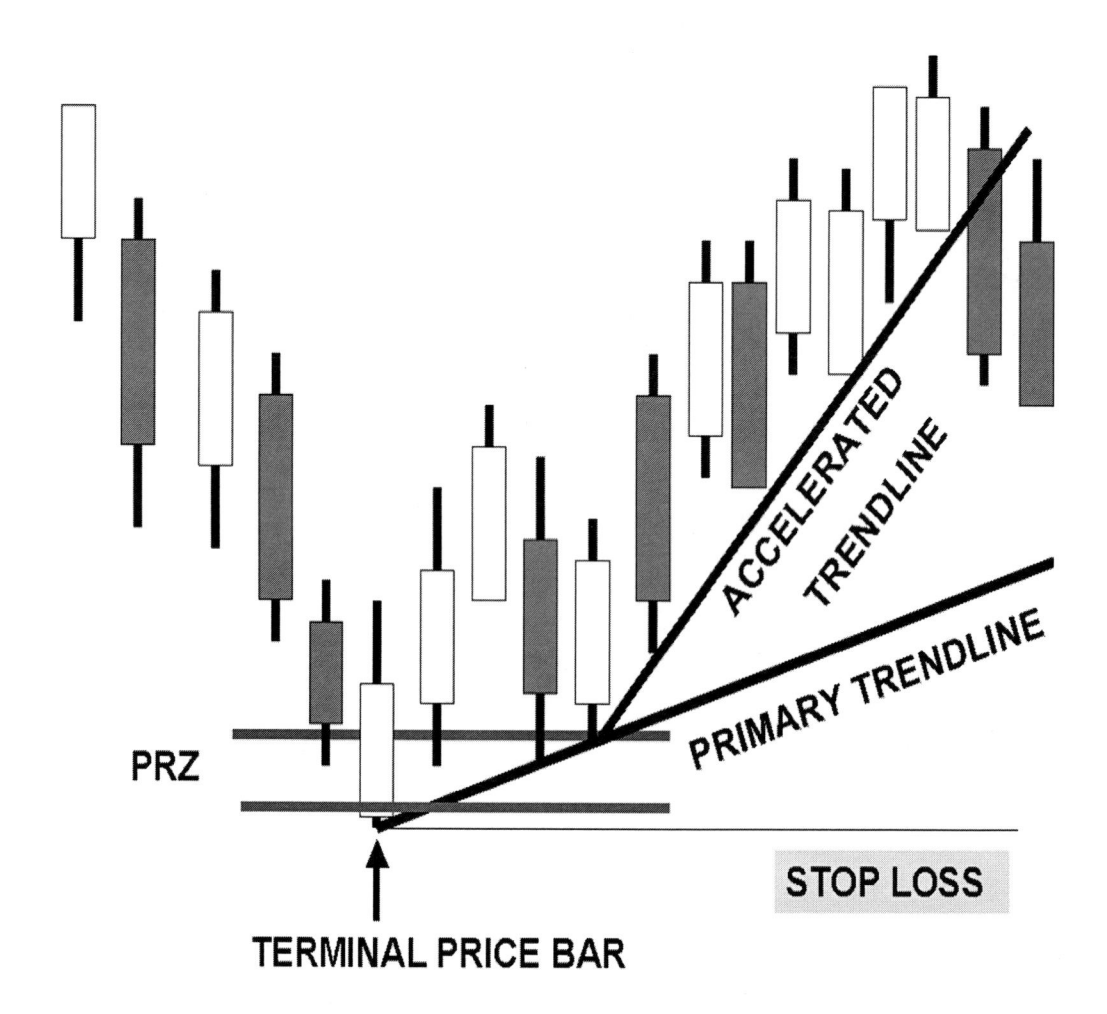

Harmonic Trading Volume 3: Reaction vs. Reversal

Gold (GC#F): 5-Minute
Bullish Alternate Bat Pattern
Reversal Trendline Types

The following chart shows an ideal Alternate Bullish Bat Pattern that experienced a sharp reversal soon after all the numbers were tested in the Potential Reversal Zone (PRZ). In the following example of the continuous contract in Gold, the reversal following the Alternate Bullish Bat possess a sharp trendline acceleration. The most important aspect in differentiating these trendlines is most pertinent in the optimization of profit management strategies, especially in Type-I situations.

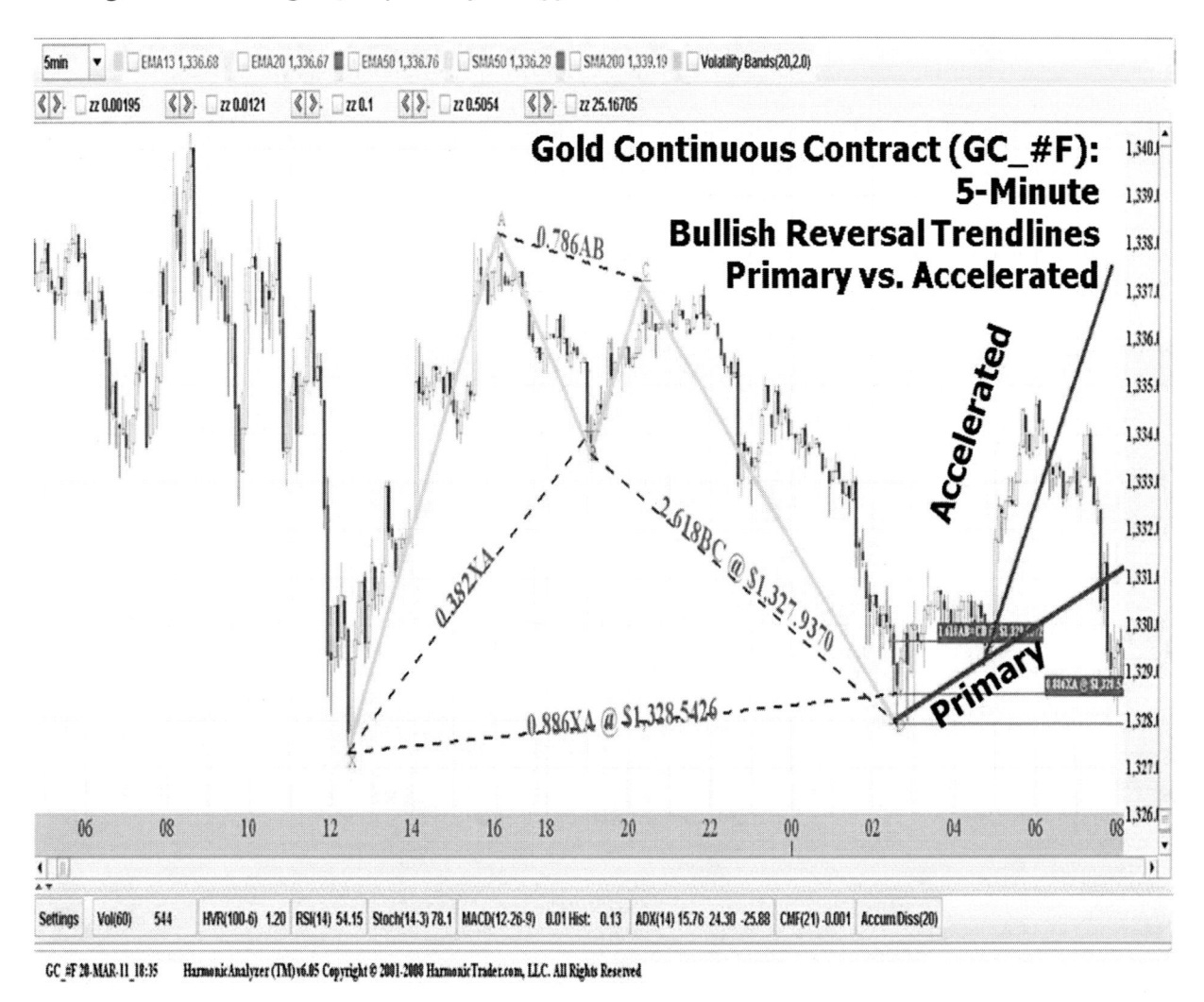

Harmonic Trading Volume 3: Reaction vs. Reversal

Gold (GC#F): 5-Minute
Bullish Alternate Bat Pattern Potential Reversal Zone (PRZ)
Reversal Trendline Types

The price action in the Potential Reversal Zone (PRZ) in this example demonstrates the effectiveness of the primary and accelerated trendline to gauge the extent of any reversal. In this case, the price action provided clear confirmation after the Terminal Price Bar was established. The price action stabilized on the initial test of the pattern and formed a steady 45° primary uptrend. After this brief consolidation phase, the reversal exhibited an accelerated move. However, the inability of the reversal to continue higher, especially after the accelerated trendline was violated, signaled the end of the reaction.

Harmonic Trading Volume 3: Reaction vs. Reversal

Bearish Reversal Trendline Types

After the Terminal Price Bar has been established, a simple primary trendline should be projected at a general 45° angle from the peak to gauge the progress as the reversal unfolds. It is quite common for price action to take on an accelerated nature and yield a sharp countertrend move, as it develops a steeper reversal trend. Again, these are extremely effective in those situations when the pattern is completing for the first time. The natural reaction at the completion point of a distinct pattern will typically provide a reaction that takes the form of a short-term trend.

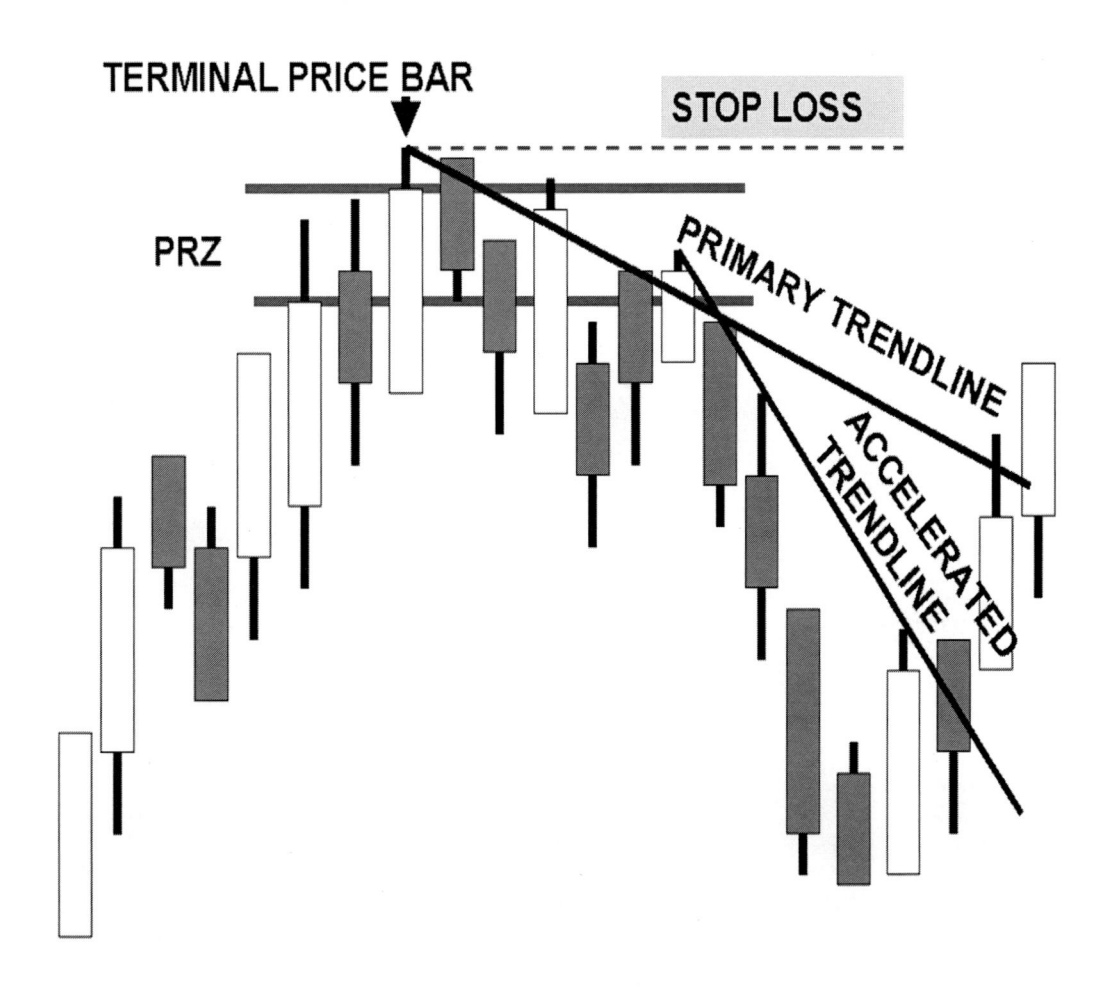

Australian Dollar/Canadian Dollar (AUDCAD_A0-FX): 15-Minute
Bearish Gartley
Reversal Trendline Types

This chart shows a Bearish Gartley on a 15-minute basis that formed a distinct pattern that exhibited ideal reversal trendlines following the completion of the structure. As soon as the Terminal Price Bar was established, the price action stalled in the Potential Reversal Zone (PRZ). After some consolidation, the reversal accelerated forming a steeper downtrend.

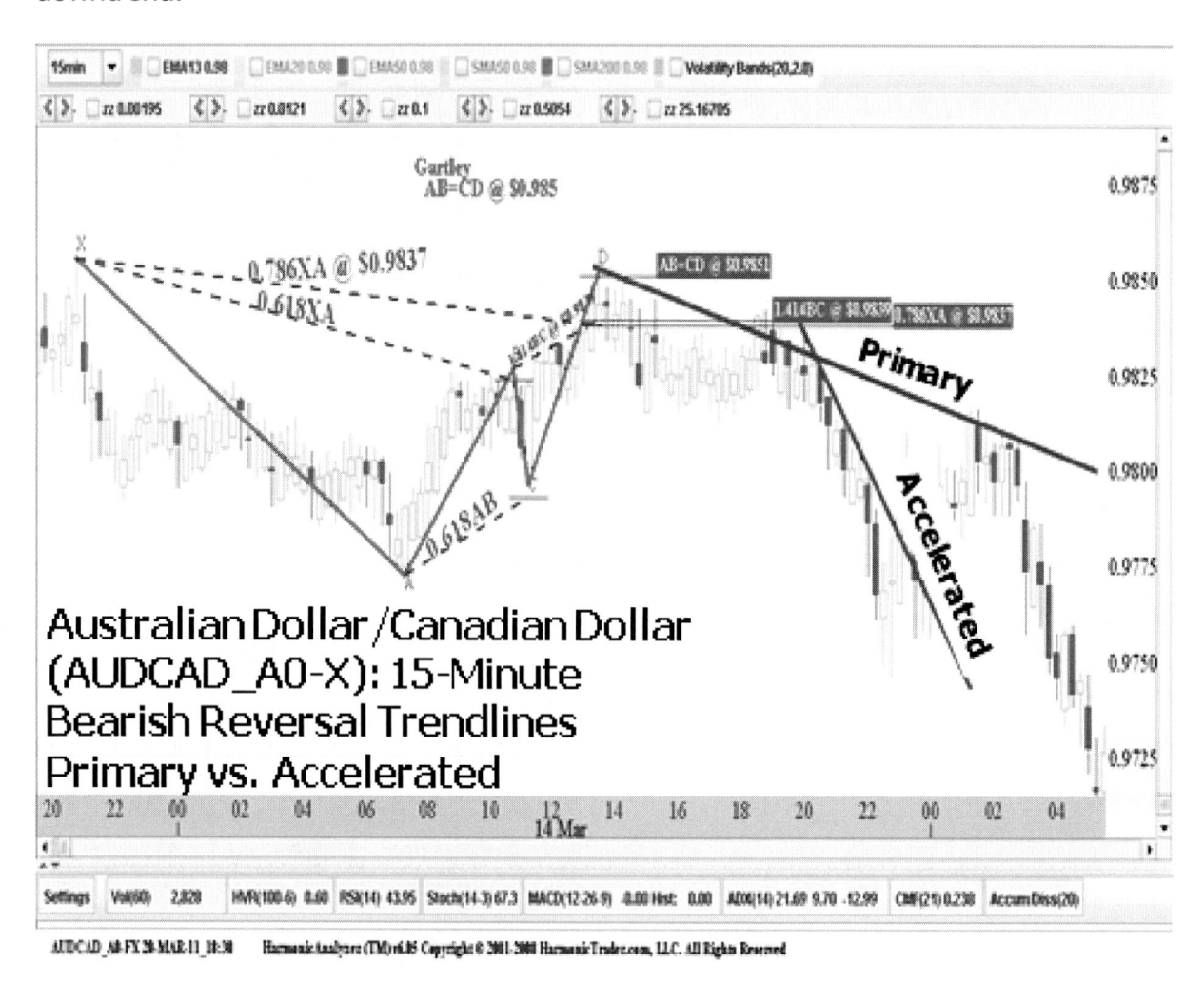

After a brief period of consolidation following the completion of the Terminal Price Bar in the AUD/CAD pattern, the primary reversal downtrend established a definitive make-or-break trailing stop area to assess the probability for a substantial decline. The reversal declined sharply lower and continued to trade below the primary reversal trendline.

Harmonic Trading Volume 3: Reaction vs. Reversal

Australian Dollar/Canadian Dollar (AUDCAD_A0-FX): 15-Minute Bearish Gartley Potential Reversal Zone (PRZ)
Reversal Trendline Types

The interesting aspect of this price action is how the trendline clearly guided the trade management in this situation. The progress of the reversal was able to maintain a primary downtrend and begin to accelerate, confirming the pattern as an important bearish continuation structure.

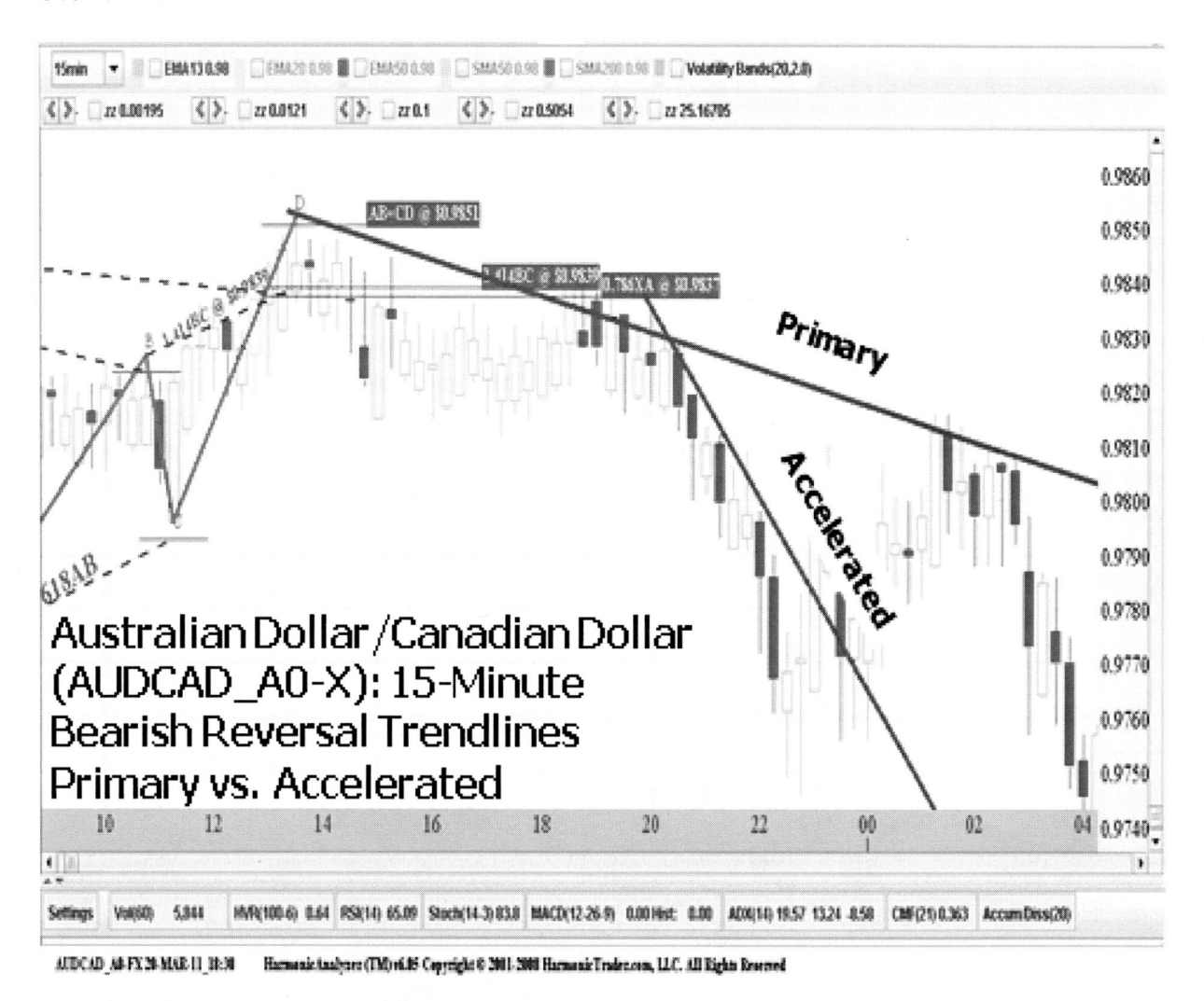

Although in most situations, a violation of the accelerated trendline would trigger some profit taking action, the primary downtrend line provided a clear trailing stop limitation to maximize the profit objective and manage the trade. We will look at some other advanced trade management strategies later this material that complement these trendlines.

Harmonic Trading Volume 3: Reaction vs. Reversal

Trade Management of Harmonic Trading Reversal Types

As we outlined in the Harmonic Trading Execution chapter, Type-I & Type-II reversal types instill the proper expectations to optimize the handling of any harmonic pattern. Although these are not terribly complicated, it is essential to follow these situational–specific strategies of the Type-I and Type-II guidelines. Furthermore, each reversal type possesses its own unique set of expectations and employs particular techniques unique to each reversal which facilitate trading decisions effectively. Ultimately, the predefined expectations and harmonic framework of measurements must determine those conditions where an active management strategy should be employed as opposed to a more passive approach that seeks to capitalize on longer-term situations by allowing more time for a reversal to unfold. Although each situation includes predetermined price parameters for every aspect of trade, each type is managed differently.

Harmonic Trading Trendlines: Type-I vs. Type-II Reversal

- **Type-I**: Since we manage these positions aggressively with automatic profit objectives and trailing stop management close to the primary trend, the importance of trendline assessments will be critical in capturing those temporary reactions and assessing potential for longer-term reversals. In most cases, an accelerated trendline violation will result in the close of the position. This incorporates the understanding that these scenarios are usually short-lived and provide a dramatic but temporary reaction. Furthermore, primary trendlines can be employed as a means gauge the true make-or-break for the position. In general, the Type-I philosophy is aggressive and prone for more intense management activity that secures profits when accelerated trendlines are violated.

- **Type-II:** The Type-II reversal represents a secondary retest that completely retests the original Potential Reversal Zone (PRZ). This confirmation of the established harmonic level will possess greater technical significance. However, these situations will experience accelerated trendline violations as we utilize the primary slope of the reversal to allow more time for these scenarios to resolve themselves. Also, smaller but complex formations such as other harmonic patterns forming on the retest of the Potential Reversal Zone (PRZ) can form on the retest of the primary trendline to confirm the reversal progress. The key in these situations is to utilize the accelerated trendline to secure a partial profit no matter what and allow another portion of the position to remain active until the primary trendline is violated.

Multiple Unit Management

Trade management of any harmonic pattern situation should employ closing positions with a multiple unit strategy of the original entry as a means to optimize profitability. Since Type-I reversals possess a more aggressive perspective, the profit management must be anticipatory. Understanding that these reversals are reactionary in nature, profitable moves that materialize quickly should be automatically closed at predetermined targets. Quite frankly, it does not matter what happens following the close of the trade. Sometimes, Type-I trades can be closed with the small profit or loss only to have the position work out in your favor. The only thing that matters is your result of whether the management of the position netted a profit or loss. Positions can always be reentered, especially in those situations that have overwhelming technical evidence to define the harmonic zone. In fact, most harmonic patterns offer two trade opportunities for each setup. For Type-II reversals, the price action must possess a full retest of the original zone AND an indicator confirmation signal. Patterns with HSI and/or RSI optimize the precise level within the Potential Reversal Zone (PRZ) retest. Some situations might seem to be failing if there is a lack of immediate reaction. These situations demand an indicator confirmation trigger to pinpoint the retest. Certainly, the best executions possess some type of extreme indicator reversal that highlights those conditions for the price to react from the completion pattern. These critical factors can facilitate whether to aggressively manage positions or dictate that more time is required for the reversal to be realized.

Within real trading situations, constant assessments must be considered of the optimal profit objective for the harmonic pattern. Depending upon the pattern type, specific trade management parameters define the framework of the pattern beyond its completion. In most cases, a partial management strategy that closes portions of the original position can secure an immediate reaction while allowing more time for the reversal to unfold. Although these decisions depend upon Type-I initial pattern completions as opposed to Type-II retest situations, a partial management of positions instill discipline and adheres to the trading plan defined in advance.

Type-I and Type-II harmonic pattern signals provide clear expectations and represent an most important aspect of this differentiation. However, it can be frustrating to know when to actively manage a position versus holding on to another for a longer period of time. While managing a trade based upon a harmonic pattern, it can be difficult to know in advance which situations will yield the monster "Home-Run" reversal and which ones should be actively handled to maximize the profit. Most harmonic patterns attempt to pinpoint clear reversal levels on the initial test that define clear reactive situations but these short-lived moves must be handled properly. In fact, this is the phenomenon that most new Harmonic Traders experience when they initially apply the measurements and are able to predict these reactions. Even if the price response is minimal, the sheer ability to predict where the market will react can be quite empowering. Now that the pattern rules are well known, most traders are able to discover these measures and identify trades at price levels with an unprecedented degree of certainty.

Harmonic Trading Volume 3: Reaction vs. Reversal

For most traders new to harmonic patterns, it only takes one trade to realize that these predictive capabilities comprise the structural foundation of any professional trader's skill set. More detailed analysis is required to know when to take a profit for short-term gain or to try to ride out any consolidation for a larger possible profit. Many of these decisions are determined by pattern and reversal types. Regardless, Harmonic Trading employs defined parameters in every situation to optimize the management of positions relative to pattern at hand.

Harmonic Trading Management Strategy Types

I. **Automatic Profit Targets:** Secure a profit automatically (with a limit order) at a predetermined ratio – 38.2% or 61.8% of the pattern – to ensure a winning trade on part of the initial position. Creates a "comfort zone" for the discretionary portion of the position.

II. **Discretionary Profit Targets:** The discretionary strategies employ secondary confirmation readings and trendlines to allow more time to assess price action signals that attempt to stay in the market as long as possible to realize the full potential of the reversal.

Harmonic Trading Management: Automatic Strategies

Most people who suggest that profit objectives should be randomly set at prior price levels without regard to the extent of the pattern ignore the fundamental basis of why these measurements work. In my *Harmonic Trading Volume 1* book, I quoted J.M. Hurst's *Principle of Harmonicity* where he put forth the proposition that price segments can be related to each other by small whole numbers. I have expanded upon this notion of replacing "small whole numbers" with harmonic ratio measurements. The key point here is that price segments can be measured and provide relevant technical information regarding probable future price action. Due to this relevance, profit targets can be accurately projected as long as they are based off the pattern itself not some random point.

Another consideration with automatic profit targets that is critical to success is the determination of the appropriate minimum level. Since the inception of my work, I have argued that the 38.2% retracement is an objective that represents the standard definition of any minimum harmonic measured moved. Although there are other types of measures that can use smaller Fibonacci – related ratios such as 23.6% or even the 11.3%, the general move of any material PRICE significance is defined as a 38.2% retracement measure.

The automatic Harmonic Trading Management strategies seek to capture the "Natural Harmonic Reaction" of any pattern. As I discussed earlier in the book, the automatic and natural reaction that price action experiences at the completion of most harmonic pattern opportunities provides a situation where there is enough time to assess the larger possibilities. This requires that opportunities are measured properly and executions are triggered at the measured price objectives. Although both reversal types employ automatic strategies to varying degrees, the strategy is most effective in securing profits within an optimized time period.

Automatic Harmonic Trading Management Tips:

Type-I vs. Type-II management considerations include the amount of time permitted for price action to completely express the full reversal following the completion of a pattern. The automatic strategy creates a management mechanism that is quite effective over the course of a population of trades, especially since it can reduce human error and facilitate more consistent profits. The obvious dilemma traders face is to determine if an automated profit strategy yields better results over the history of one's trading as opposed to trying to find the "home-run" situations.

- Automatic Objectives associated with Type-I patterns opportunities.
- Aggressive Harmonic Trading Management Strategy
- Seeks to capture the "Natural Harmonic Reaction" of the pattern.
- A more predictable process that is optimized by proper pattern identification and disciplined execution.
- Profit targets defined IN ADVANCE.
- Best for initial pattern completion (T-Bar+1).
- The profit objective should be measured as a ratio from the pattern off the reversal extreme (AD leg).

In Type-I situations, automatic profit targets will usually constitute the majority of the trade management. We will look at the overall Harmonic Trading management model later in this material but it is important to be aware of this phenomenon. Simply stated, the Type-I reversal yields reactive responses to the initial completion of any pattern while the Type-II retest possesses larger possibilities but still considers automatic profit targets to optimize these decisions.

Profit Anticipation

The key in the translation of harmonic measurements to identify structural signals as profitable opportunities requires a realization that a portion of the position must employ an automatic profit objective. Regardless of the reversal type, harmonic patterns require an automated management strategy simply due to their nature. Although some situations do identify remarkable opportunities, the realistic approach to all harmonic patterns is to treat them as temporary vehicles that yield clear execution parameters and profit objectives.

When I initially considered harmonic pattern management techniques, I would take a more passive approach and wait to see if something larger may develop in every situation. I found myself sitting on my hands although I was executing well-defined opportunities. My delay in capturing profits substantially hindered my overall performance. I believe traders will realize more consistent success if they incorporate the proper Type-I Reaction/Type-II reversal set of expectations where the measured management strategy that anticipates profit objectives in advance and closes out trades automatically with predetermined orders placed at the same time as the execution.

From a general trading perspective, the automatic management strategy anticipates the natural harmonic reaction and attempts to secure realistic profit amounts that most commonly fall within the range of a pattern's price limits. Furthermore, the prescribed ratio targets and other automatic strategies instill a greater degree of discipline in the management of the trade. Although people often disagree on the exact initial profit objective as measured by the pattern, it is clear that there are a few basic measurements that should be the basis for the automatic strategy. Most notably, the 38.2% and the 61.8% countertrend ratio measurements represent the minimum natural reactive harmonic targets to anticipate. Although this ideal framework is most appropriate in Type-I situations, it defines the standard expectation to define all minimum harmonic reactions.

We will address specific situations and how to optimize these measures in different scenarios. However, the ability to execute automatic profit objectives effectively demonstrates a larger comprehension regarding the entire trading process and exemplifies the realistic perspective required to maximize opportunities. In the same regard that I have stressed the framework of identification, execution and management, specific actionable trading strategies must be the elements that define any successful trading plan. Within this three-step Harmonic Trading process, all parameters are defined even before the entry of the position. The key is to execute according to the plan and focus on the price action as the price action approaches these levels. In all situations, automatically securing part of the position will facilitate the proper Reaction/Reversal assessments.

As a primary principle within the Harmonic Trading plan, I believe that the skills to master Type-I automatic management strategies on at least a part of every position fosters a proactive mentality. The Type-I fundamental expectation about most harmonic patterns is that there will be a profitable reaction that can only be captured through an aggressive management strategy. Considerations throughout the management process of reaction/reversal must adhere to the parameters of the harmonic pattern framework. Regardless of methodology, most successful traders whom I have encountered have a comprehensive understanding of how to define entry, exit and stop loss parameters that develop an overall assessment of the market's condition.

Harmonic Trading Volume 3: Reaction vs. Reversal

Bullish Automatic Profit Targets

This illustration exemplifies the simple measurements employed to define initial profit targets. This model was a result of years of research that measured the clearest reversals and most common limits of any pattern's reaction. These relationships will comprise the Type-I and Type-II targets where the minimum objectives for each reversal are the 38.2% and 61.8%, respectively.

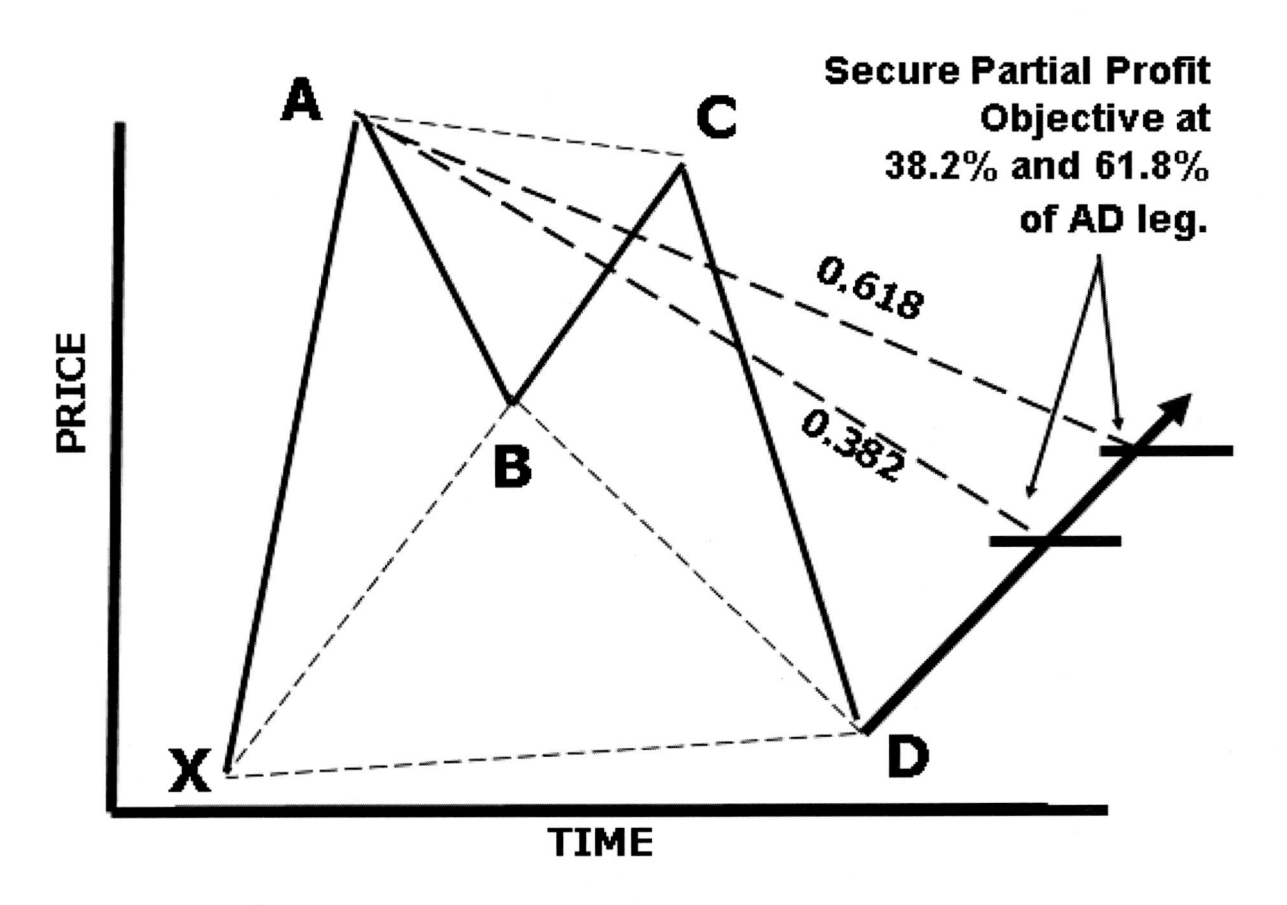

Secure Partial Profit Objective at 38.2% and 61.8% of AD leg.

Although the Type-I expected reversal should test the 38.2% pattern retracement level, this is serves as a minimum objective and the second target at the 61.8% level should be included to define the optimal profit zone for the reversal. At a minimum, some portion of the position should be covered at the first target. In the Type-II reversals, the automatic targets are still assessed but the execution of the position typically employs other confirmation assessments. Another advantage of these profit targets is that they provide a minimum objective to compare the associated stop loss limit and determine precise risk/reward percentages. Typically, harmonic patterns should possess a minimum 2:1 but preferably 3:1 risk-to-reward ratio. In fact, these are often overlooked considerations but clarify risk parameters and essential to select the best opportunities among the course of many trades.

Harmonic Trading Volume 3: Reaction vs. Reversal

Euro/U.S. Dollar (EUR_A0-FX): 60-Minute
Bullish Gartley Targets

The following Bullish Gartley in the Euro/U.S. Dollar exemplifies most common harmonic scenario in Type-I situations. The clear structure defined an ideal execution zone for the trade. Immediately following the completion of the pattern, the reversal rose sharply. The automatic targets - as measured from the peak of the pattern at the A point down to the reversal low - defined the 38.2% retracement at 1.3858 and the 61.8% retracement at 1.3927 as the minimum target objectives for the trade.

Even if part of the position was closed out early at the 38.2% level, the total profit trade realized an even sizable gain at the second target of 61.8% level. One interesting note about Type-I trades is that they typically experience some consolidation even if they eventually continue in the reversal direction. In this case, the price action reversed sharply and reached both targets shortly after completing pattern. Although the price action extended beyond these levels, the automatic profit strategies did optimize the amount of time required in the trade. Even if position was held, clearly there was extensive consolidation required before a larger reversal ensued. This is a perfect example of trying to optimize the amount of time in a particular position. This is a common dilemma that all Harmonic Traders face. It can be easy to assume that the automatic profit objective strategy will leave money on the table. However, my research shows that over the course of many trades, automatic profit objectives tend to be more efficient, as this management style capitalizes upon the natural harmonic reaction that is inherently volatile in character anyway. Therefore, the failure to establish profit targets in advance with limit orders does leave positions vulnerable to not capture profits, especially in Type-I volatile reactions are realized.

Bearish Automatic Profit Targets

The bearish model seeks to capture the reaction to the minimum 38.2% and 61.8% targets. It is important to note that these are minimum objectives, employed as an anticipatory strategy to optimize the trade management of harmonic patterns at predetermined targets.

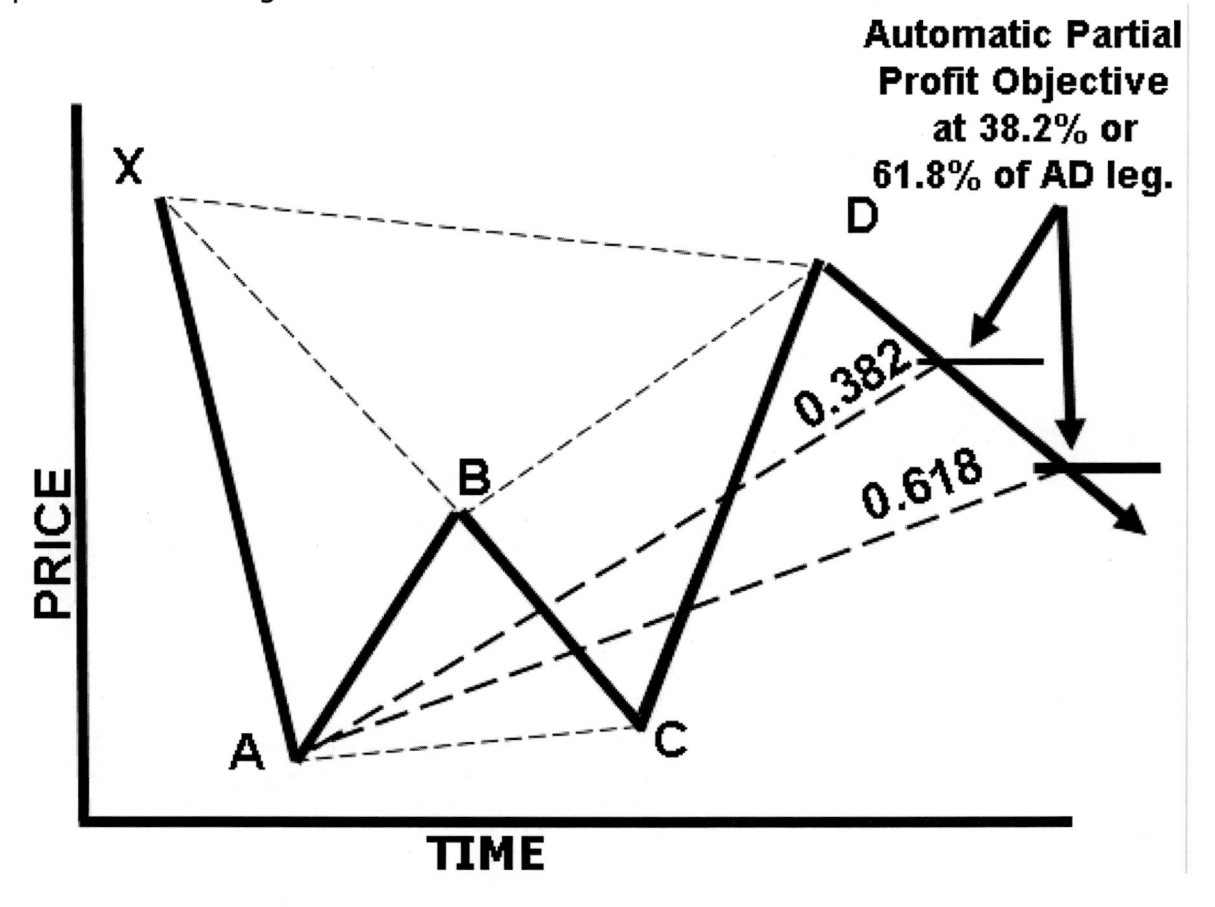

Harmonic Trading Volume 3: Reaction vs. Reversal

U.S. Dollar/Swiss Franc (CHF_A0-FX): 15-Minute
Bearish Butterfly Targets

The next example of the Swiss Franc shows a rather dramatic reversal at the completion of the pattern. Interestingly enough, the initial reactive thrust immediately tested both profit targets shortly after completing pattern. After a brief consolidation, the larger reversal was realized. One interesting aspects of this reversal is that it did not violate the distinct downtrend established from the Terminal Price Bar. In many management instances, the only consideration is monitoring a reversal trendline, especially after all price targets have been established.

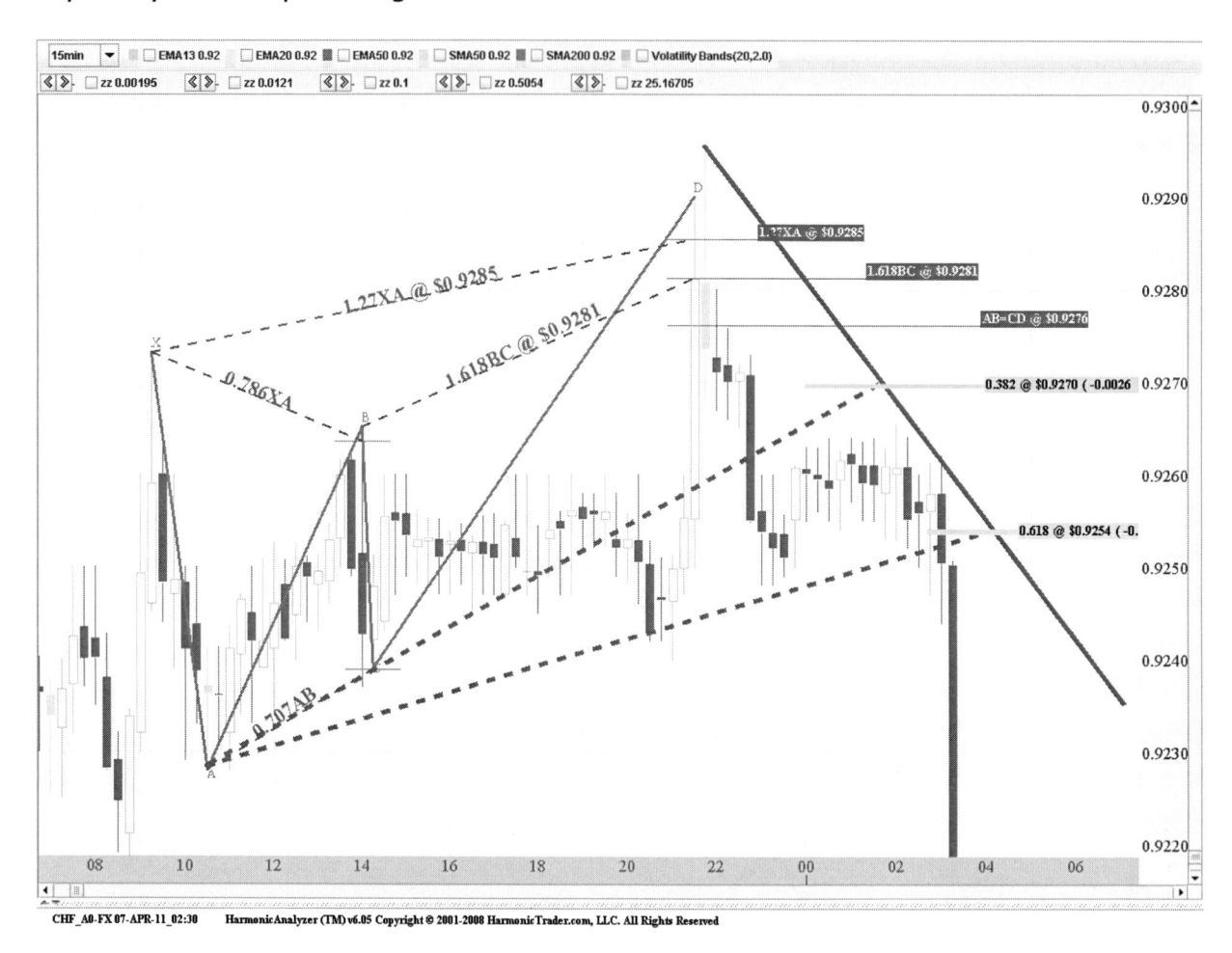

Harmonic Trading Management: Discretionary Strategies

Harmonic Trading discretionary management strategies employ secondary confirmation readings and trendlines to allow more time to assess price action signals that attempts to stay in the market as long as possible to realize the full potential of the reversal. There are variety of measurements and concepts that comprise these

Harmonic Trading Volume 3: Reaction vs. Reversal

discretionary strategies. Unlike the automatic profit targets established by the limits of the pattern, discretionary strategies involve a personal assessment of multiple variables. All traders must assess the internal debate of attempting to stay in a position longer to allow a larger reversal to develop. For example, certain price measurement comparisons must be assessed relative to trendlines that gauge the potential for a reversal to reach beyond a nominal reaction. In fact, the conglomeration of all of the strategies within the Harmonic Trading framework defines the larger assessment of the probable future price direction. There may be certain dominant factors that may serve as a primary basis such as demonstrative price action or strong execution confirmation that helps develop a clear bias to guide management decisions.

The discretionary strategies are designed to capture profit beyond the minimum targets. In this attempt to maximize profits, the risk required beyond the automatic pattern targets must be considered aggressively managed. Although some amount of profit will always be left on the table, the optimization of management decisions should always be guided by those strategies that consistently capture the majority of the possible move at hand.

Discretionary Harmonic Trading Management Tips:

- Discretionary Profit Targets can include other harmonic measures and strategies.
- Employs trendline analysis to manage the profit portion to stay in the market as long as possible to realize the full potential of a reversal.
- Exchanges immediate objective of automatic profit target for larger discretionary target.
- Assess "Giving Back Profit" vs. "Leaving it on the Table" allows more time for consolidation to realize larger reversal.
- More common in Type-II reversal management decisions.

Most important, the expectations of each reversal type are critical in guiding decisions throughout the trading process. Although automatic and discretionary strategies determine whether we actively manage a position or allow more time for the larger scenario to develop, the combination of assessments is the most effective means to maintain a balanced perspective that mostly expects reactive price moves that evolve into self-evident reversals. We will review strategies later in this material that detail the signs to trigger larger harmonic moves but the price action at each level will define the extent of the move.

Harmonic Trading Management of Type-I Reversals

As we have seen with the execution strategies, the management of Type-I reversals focuses primarily on the initial pattern completion - that is, the first time the price action tests the Potential Reversal Zone (PRZ) and establishes the Terminal Price

Bar to validate a harmonic pattern completion as a LIVE TRADE OPPORTUNITY! In most situations, we look to execute starting immediately after the Terminal Price Bar has been established (T-Bar+1) and anticipate that price action continues in counter-trend direction (T-Bar+5) without retesting Potential Reversal Zone (PRZ).

Bullish Type-I Harmonic Trading Management Model

Although I presented this model in *Harmonic Trading Volume 1* and outlined each of the management strategies, I have refined the overall application of these concepts to create a framework that distinguishes reactions as opposed to reversals. The goal of most Type-I trades is to secure profits at limited objectives. Before the position is even executed, the predetermined 38.2% & 61.8% profit target levels are established to automatically cover the position. Although this may seem counterintuitive to most traders, the recognition reversal types promotes an overall understanding that not all patterns are the same. Therefore, it is essential to identify those common parameters that help distinguish the early signals of probable future price direction.

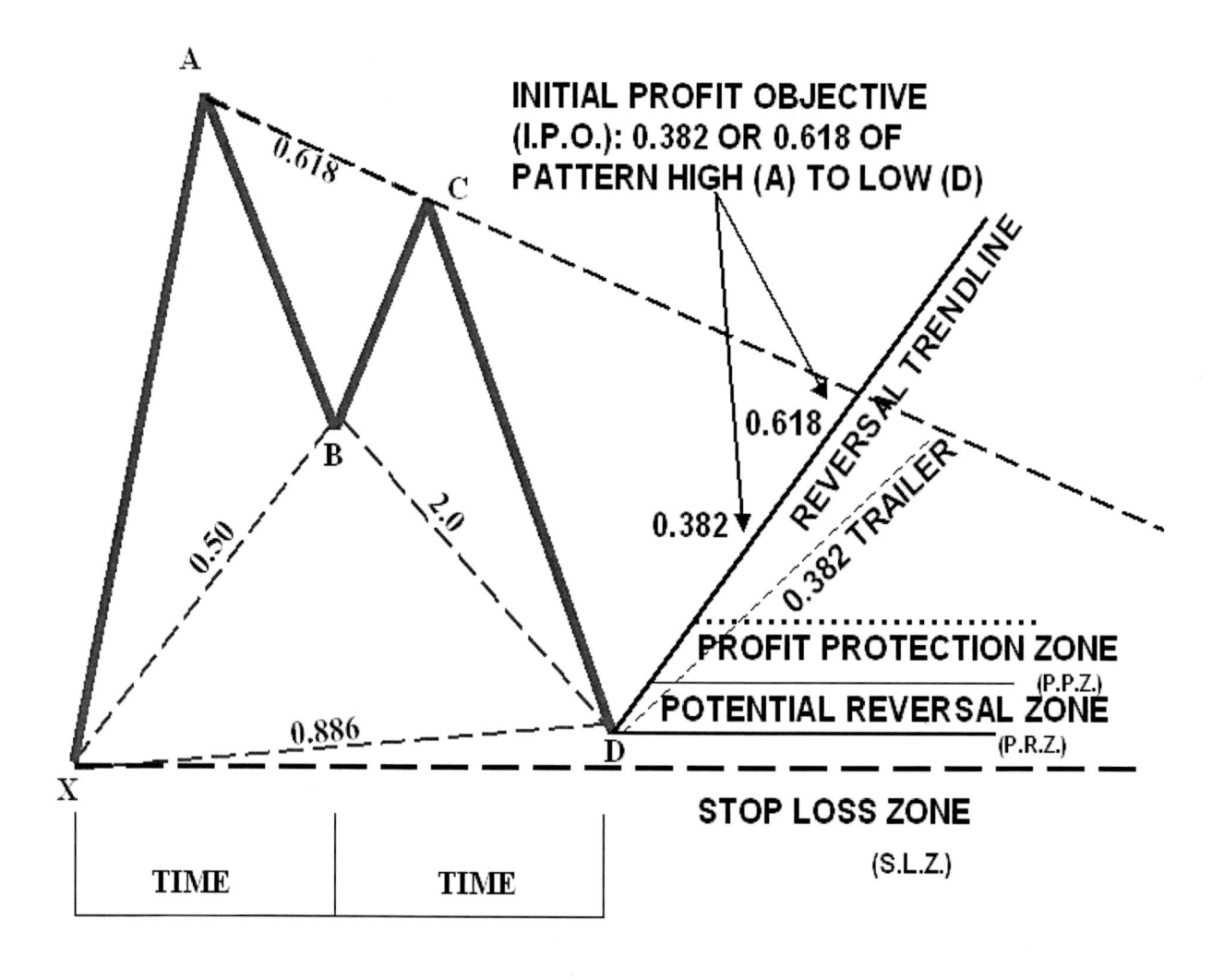

Harmonic Trading Volume 3: Reaction vs. Reversal

Canadian Dollar/Japanese Yen (CADJPY_A0-FX): 15-Minute Bullish Gartley
Type-I Harmonic Trading Management Model

The following example of the Canadian Dollar/Japanese Yen on the 15-minute chart exemplifies a Type-I reversal and affiliated management strategies. The pattern was quite distinct with a well-defined Potential Reversal Zone. These numbers defined the area at 83.65 as the ideal completion point pattern. The 38.2% and 61.8% targets were calculated for approximately 20 and 35 pips, respectively.

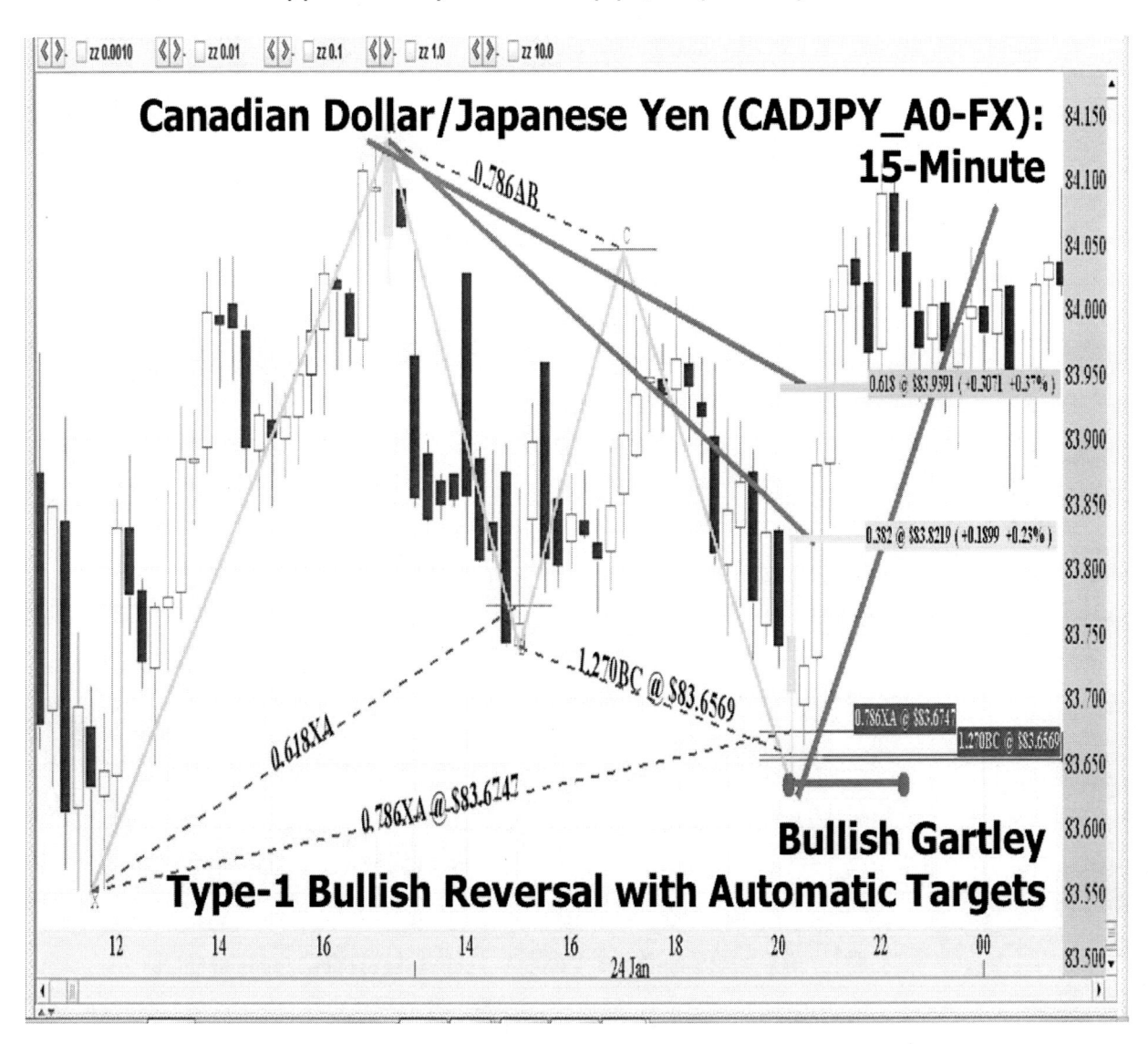

Harmonic Trading Volume 3: Reaction vs. Reversal

Canadian Dollar/Japanese Yen (CADJPY_A0-FX): 15-Minute
Bullish Gartley Potential Reversal Zone (PRZ)
Bullish Type-I Harmonic Trading Management Model

Although the price action rallied well above the 61.8% second target, price action stalled shortly thereafter and retraced most of those excess gains. Again, this is the challenge most Harmonic Traders face with these reversals. The automatic targets guarantee that certain profits are locked in yet remorse commonly sets in as the possibility for greater gain becomes apparent. In these situations, the Harmonic Trader must be realistic about what is attainable, utilize established profit targets to ensure gains are realized and then integrate lessons learned to capture more of these reactive moves while still maintaining a tight management policy throughout the process.

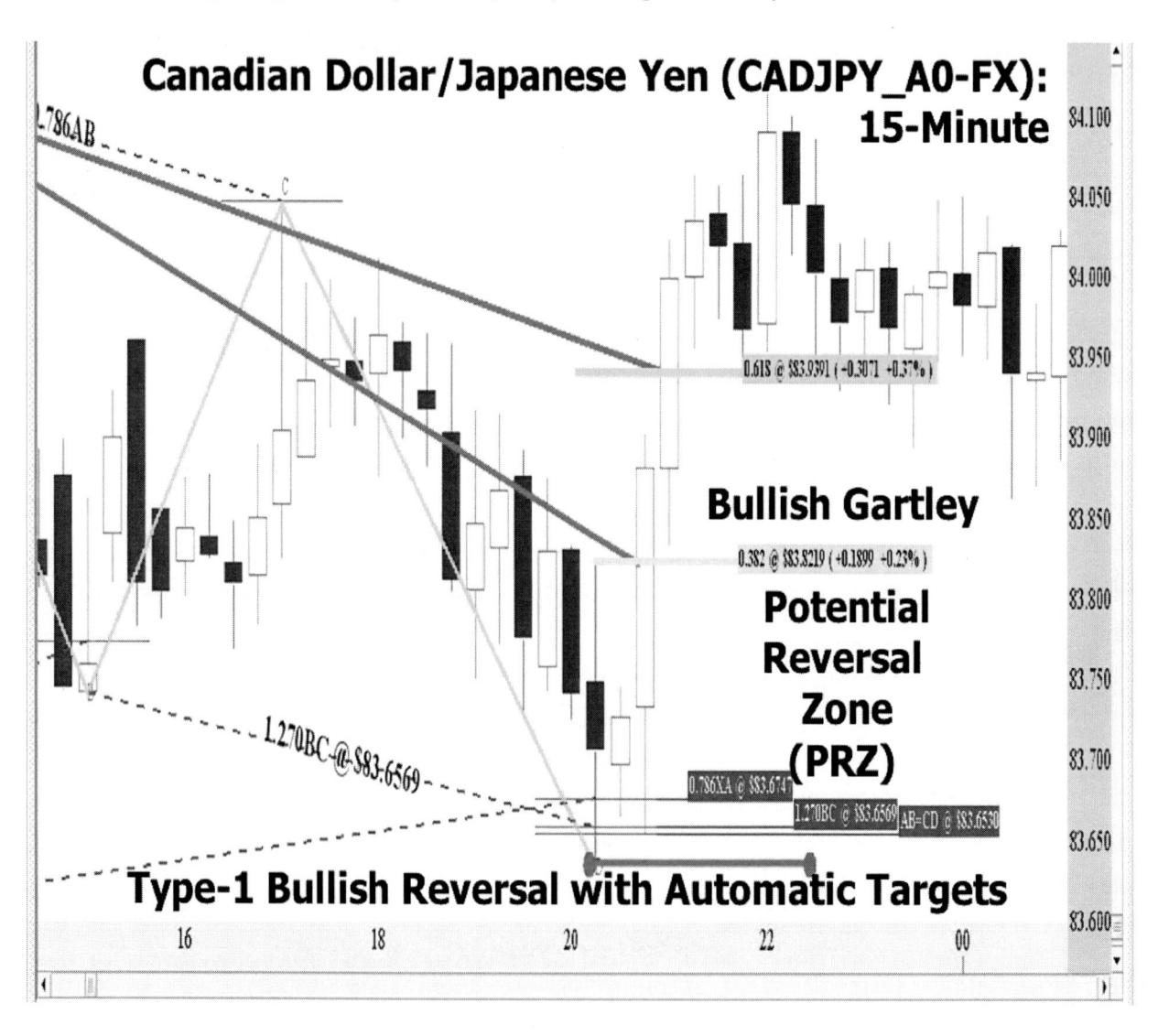

Harmonic Trading Volume 3: Reaction vs. Reversal

Bearish Type-I Reversal Management

The bearish management model outlines measurements and areas that include expectations of how to handle price action following the execution of a trade. The combination of trendlines and harmonic levels highlights the expected possibilities relative to the pattern at hand.

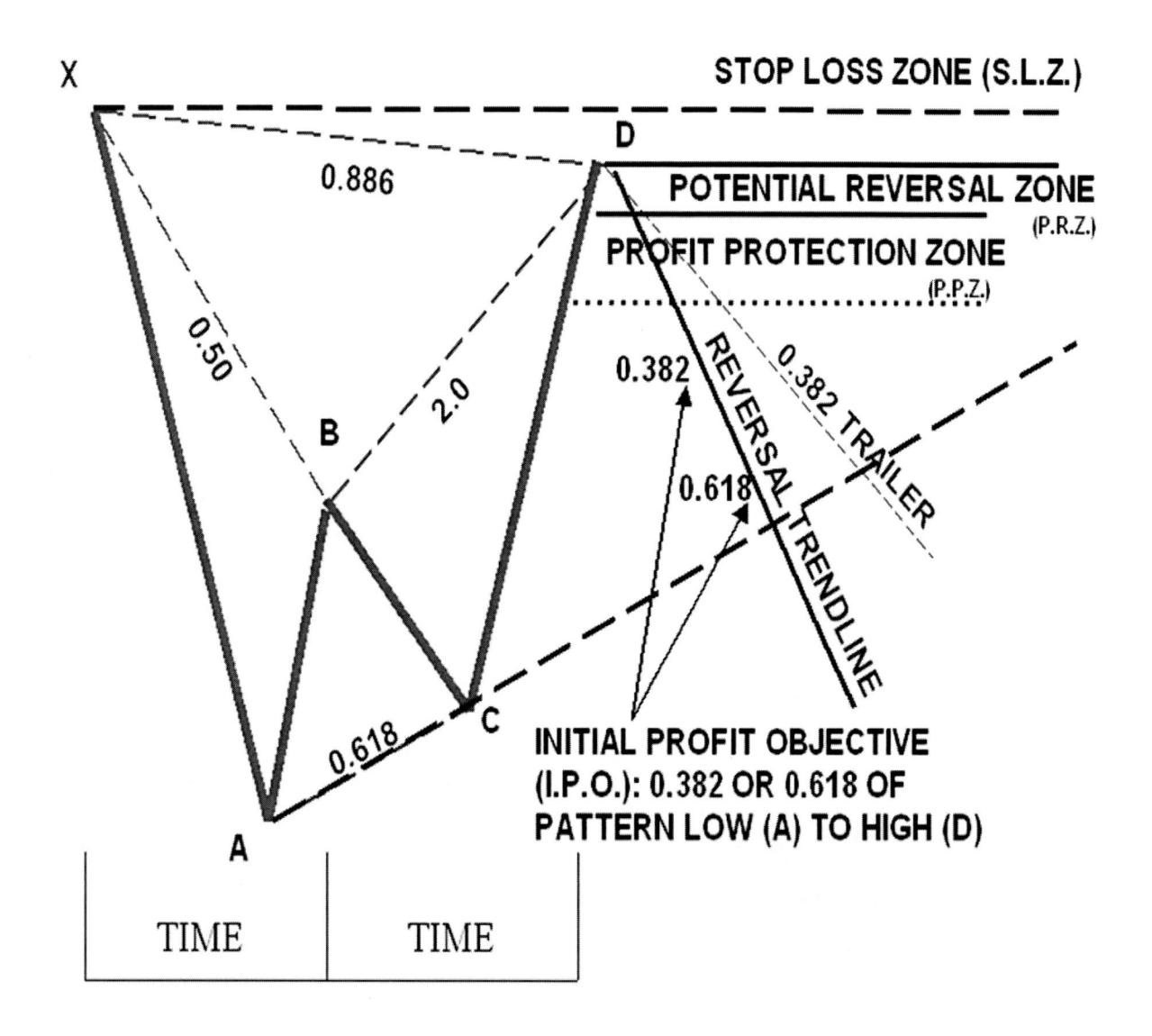

Clearly, the Type-I objectives define the 38.2% and 61.8% targets as the goal of the trade while not triggering the stop loss. Although concepts such as the Stop Loss zone, Profit Protection Zone and 38.2% trailing stop represent discretionary strategies, most of the automatic targets and trendline assessments will define actions in the Type-I management framework.

Harmonic Trading Volume 3: Reaction vs. Reversal

New Zealand Dollar (NZD_A0-FX): 15-Minute
Bearish Butterfly
Type-I Reversal Management

The following example of the New Zealand Dollar shows a common situation that most Type-I trades experience. The reversal was quite ideal at the completion of the pattern and the 38.2% initial profit target was realized after a brief consolidation. The initial reaction continued lower to test the 61.8% level. In these instances, the automatic targets would trigger that the profit is captured and trade is closed even though the larger reversal ensued later.

Harmonic Trading Volume 3: Reaction vs. Reversal

New Zealand Dollar (NZD_A0-FX): 15-Minute
Bearish Butterfly Potential Reversal Zone (PRZ)
Type-I Reversal Management

    The interesting aspect of this situation which is quite common in most Type-I management considerations is the fact that the price action consolidated after reaching the second target at the 61.8% level. This is a common phenomenon at either the 38.2% level or the 61.8% second target. The Type-I reversal expectation is that the initial reaction will likely experience some degree of a retest if it hits second target. At this point, the Type-II retest begins, requiring more time in any situation. Understanding this, our trade management parameters can be tightened to reduce risk required and capture profits more efficiently. In the case of NZD, the management beyond the 61.8% second target would be aggressive to secure the gain.

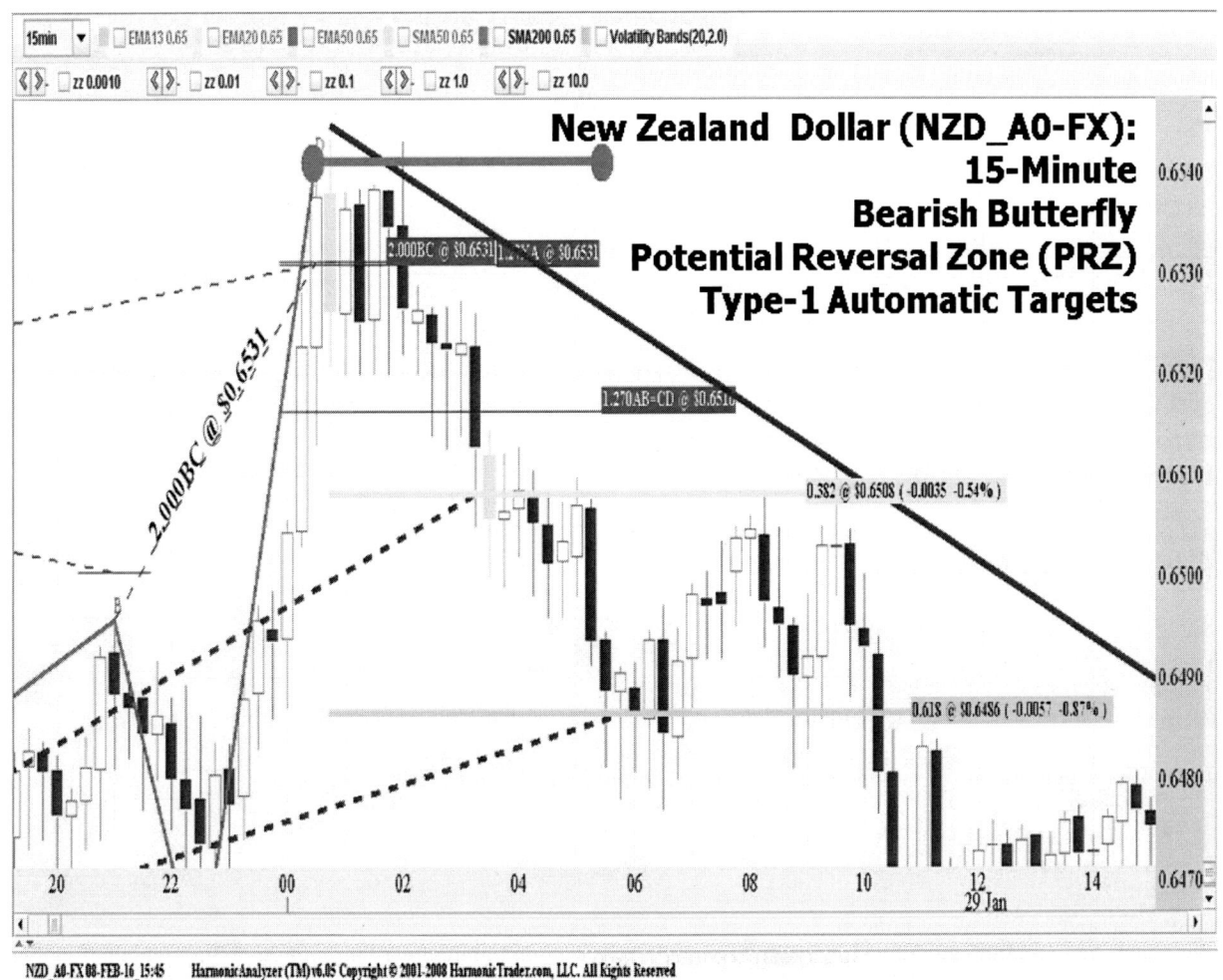

Harmonic Trading Volume 3: Reaction vs. Reversal

Type–II Reversals Management

The Type-II reversal is the most important event within a Potential Reversal Zone (PRZ). Since most pattern situations will experience some degree of the retest, the greatest impact realized from any pattern will not materialize until after this secondary test is completed. The management of these Type-II situations frequently requires confirming readings of the price levels established by the primary pattern. It is quite common for the price action to retest the Potential Reversal Zone to provide obvious confirmation in the most valid situations. It is important to note that the Type-II scenario will possess other measurements that help determine the overall validity of the setup. The secondary test of any Potential Reversal Zone (PRZ) will include other confirmation signals that help determine the overall situation. In addition, the Relative Strength readings and price action triggers that unfolded during the Type-I test will help to pinpoint the clear make or break level for the secondary test.

The price action following the Type-I reversal can actually help to define what the potential profit objectives might be for the Type-II scenario. Generally, if a pattern is going to yield a valid reversal it will be confirmed on the secondary test of that structure. The Type-II strategies are a bit more flexible, as the assessment of the price action must be considered relevant to the ideal harmonic levels. These situations require more time before a larger reversal can ensue. The primary technical event unfolds after the secondary test reenters the Potential Reversal Zone and establishes a Type-II Terminal Price Bar. In the same manner as the initial test, the price action during this retest establishes the permissible possibilities for the entire scenario as long as the price action continues in counter-trend direction beyond the Potential Reversal Zone (PRZ). The ability to apply this general model serves as an effective means to thoroughly analyze particular trade opportunities and define all relevant parameters required to facilitate trading decisions within the Type-II retest.

Type-II Reversal Management Tips

- The SECONDARY RETEST in price action that tests the Potential Reversal Zone (PRZ) after TYPE-1 REACTION.
- Expect larger possibilities for profit potential as the retest confirms the initial pattern as important structural signal to define support/resistance.
- Look for smaller pattern structures and important measurements that confirm the completion point of the primary pattern.
- IDENTIFY Primary Pattern Potential Reversal Zone (PRZ) and look for full retest of ALL #s.
- EXECUTE @ Type-II Terminal Price Bar+ 1 strategy and assess secondary confirmation factors to confirm retest of Primary PRZ.
- MANAGE with Discretionary Strategies to allow more time for larger reversal to unfold.

Harmonic Trading Volume 3: Reaction vs. Reversal

Bullish Type-II Reversal

The Type-II bullish reversal can be found in those clearest instances where an initial reaction to harmonic support experiences a pullback to retest the Potential Reversal Zone (PRZ). Although the most ideal situations will retest all of the numbers in the support range, the most common result is a nominal retracement that will typically form additional confirmation signals to help validate the opportunity. It takes some time to be able to ascertain when a Type-I reversal ends and a Type-II reversal begins but the clearest initial signal is when the first rally rolls over and violates a simple primary trend line. The price action on the secondary test possesses enormous implications for the potential support. It is quite common in failed situations where the secondary test rolls over sharply and declines below the Terminal Price Bar. As I will outline later in this book, there are clear signals to these opportunities.

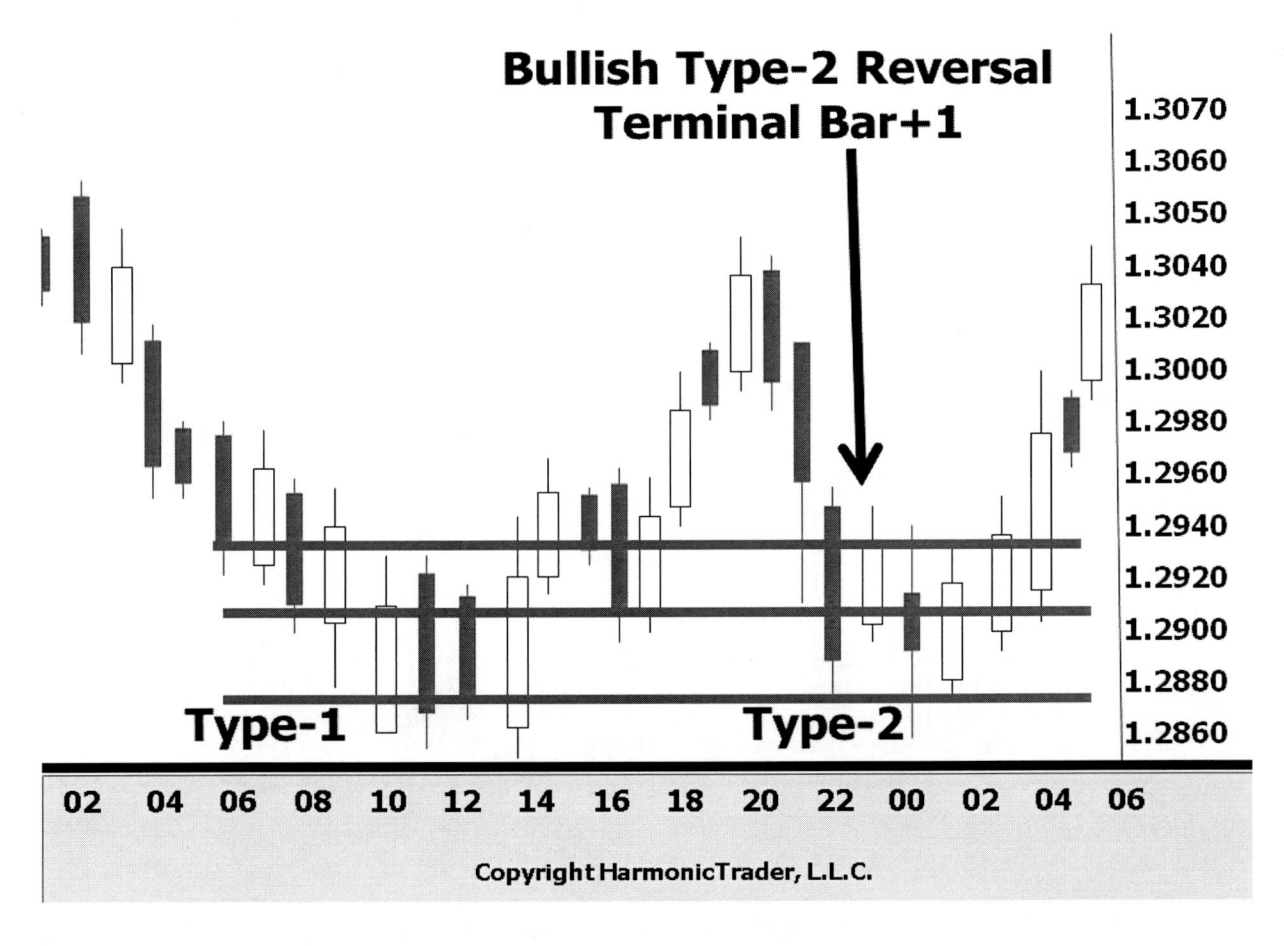

As the secondary retest is unfolding, the key event to denote the completion of the reversal is an entire test of the initial Potential Reversal Zone. At that point, the Type-II reversal has completed and we employ the Terminal Bar + 1 methodology to examine immediate entry points for the position. Sometimes, smaller patterns or other

Harmonic Trading Volume 3: Reaction vs. Reversal

identification measurements will confirm the support that is being retested. These are relevant and do help to confirm the retest of the Type-I support.

Canadian Dollar/Japanese Yen (CADJPY_A0-FX): 15-Minute Bullish Crab
Bullish Type-II Harmonic Trading Management Model

The Canadian Dollar/Japanese Yen on the following 15-minute chart formed a Bullish Crab pattern that experienced a sizable reversal on the initial completion. Despite the strength of the move, it quickly rolled over and retested the pattern's original Potential Reversal Zone. The price action stabilized at this harmonic support but required more consolidation before the larger reversal ensued. This example possesses all of the standard expectations for any harmonic pattern opportunity.

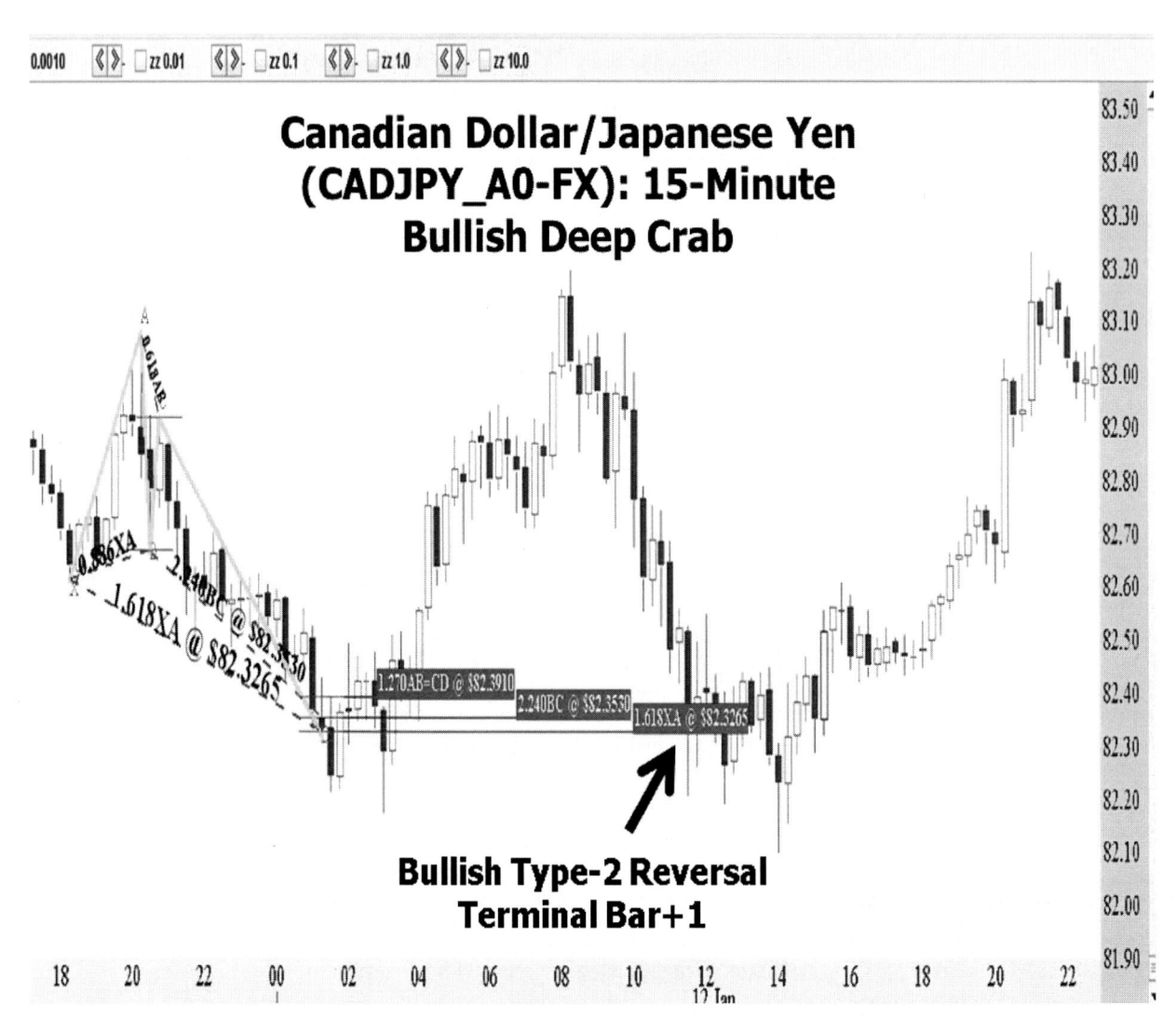

Harmonic Trading Volume 3: Reaction vs. Reversal

Canadian Dollar/Japanese Yen (CADJPY_A0-FX): 15-Minute
Bullish Crab Potential Reversal Zone (PRZ)
Bullish Type-I Harmonic Trading Management Model

The initial pattern yielded a sizable but short-lived reaction. The secondary test required more time but marked an important confirmation point for the harmonic support. As this framework becomes more ingrained into your trading plan, these situations become easier to execute and manage more efficiently. In this instance, the secondary test reversed sharply after completing the Type-II reversal. The execution price levels were essentially the same as the initial test, however the profit targets were managed differently.

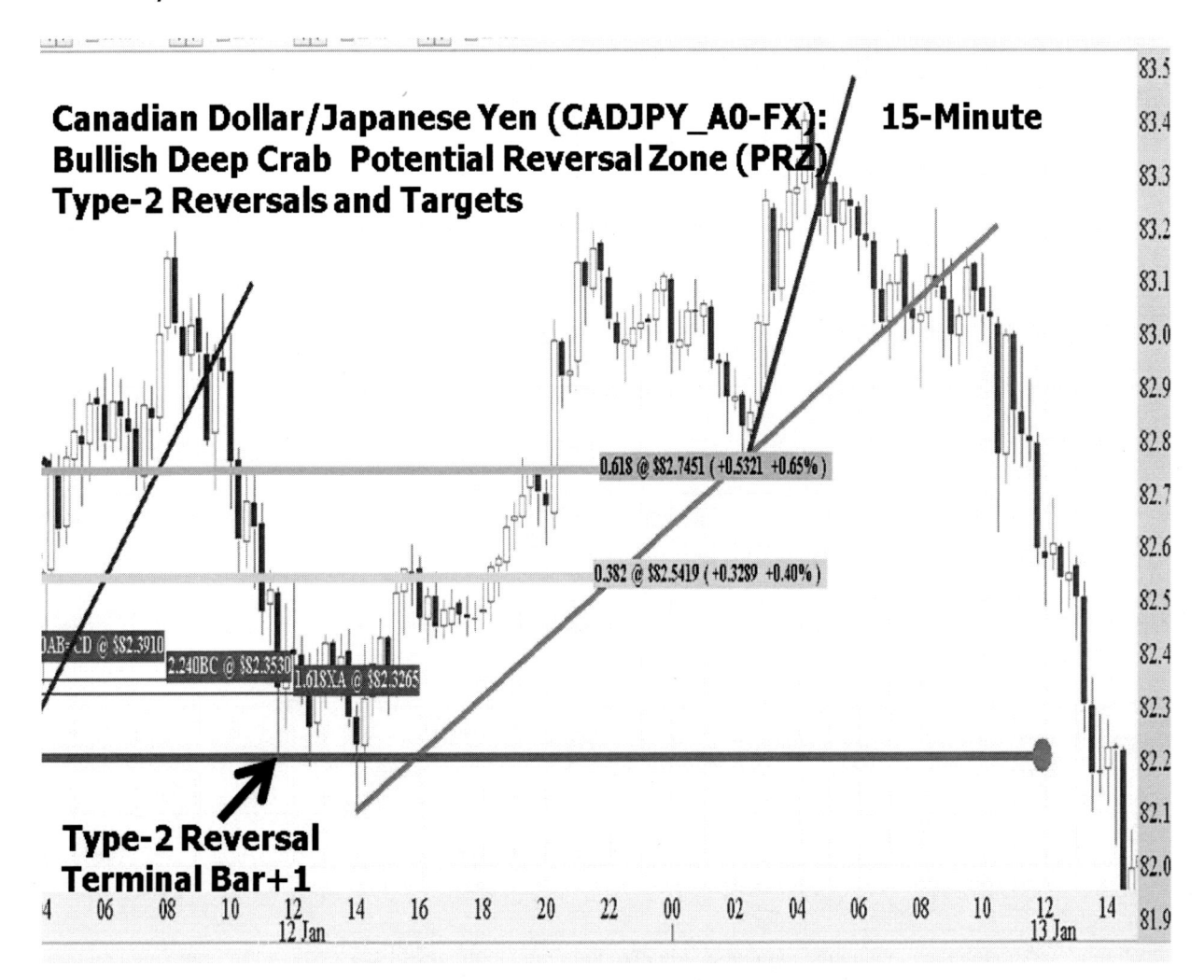

Although the typical 38.2% and 61.8% harmonic levels as measured by the extreme of the pattern served as important minimum objectives, the trendline analysis clearly maintained stop loss levels to stay in the trade as the reversal unfolded. The initial reversal rallied impressively where each individual price bar formed a successive pattern

Harmonic Trading Volume 3: Reaction vs. Reversal

of higher highs and higher lows in the anticipated trend direction. In Type-II situations like this, the initial portion of the position will likely be secured at the 61.8% minimum profit target. The second target is the expected and the automatic aspect of the Type-II trade management, although I still believe it is advantageous to automatically secure some portion of every trade at a predefined target while allowing discretionary strategies to facilitate decisions when to stay in the trade.

Bearish Type-II Reversal

After experiencing a reaction from the initial completion of the pattern, most Type-II reversals will require more time for the price action to unfold but the expectations of a larger reversal increase as the harmonic resistance is confirmed on the secondary test.

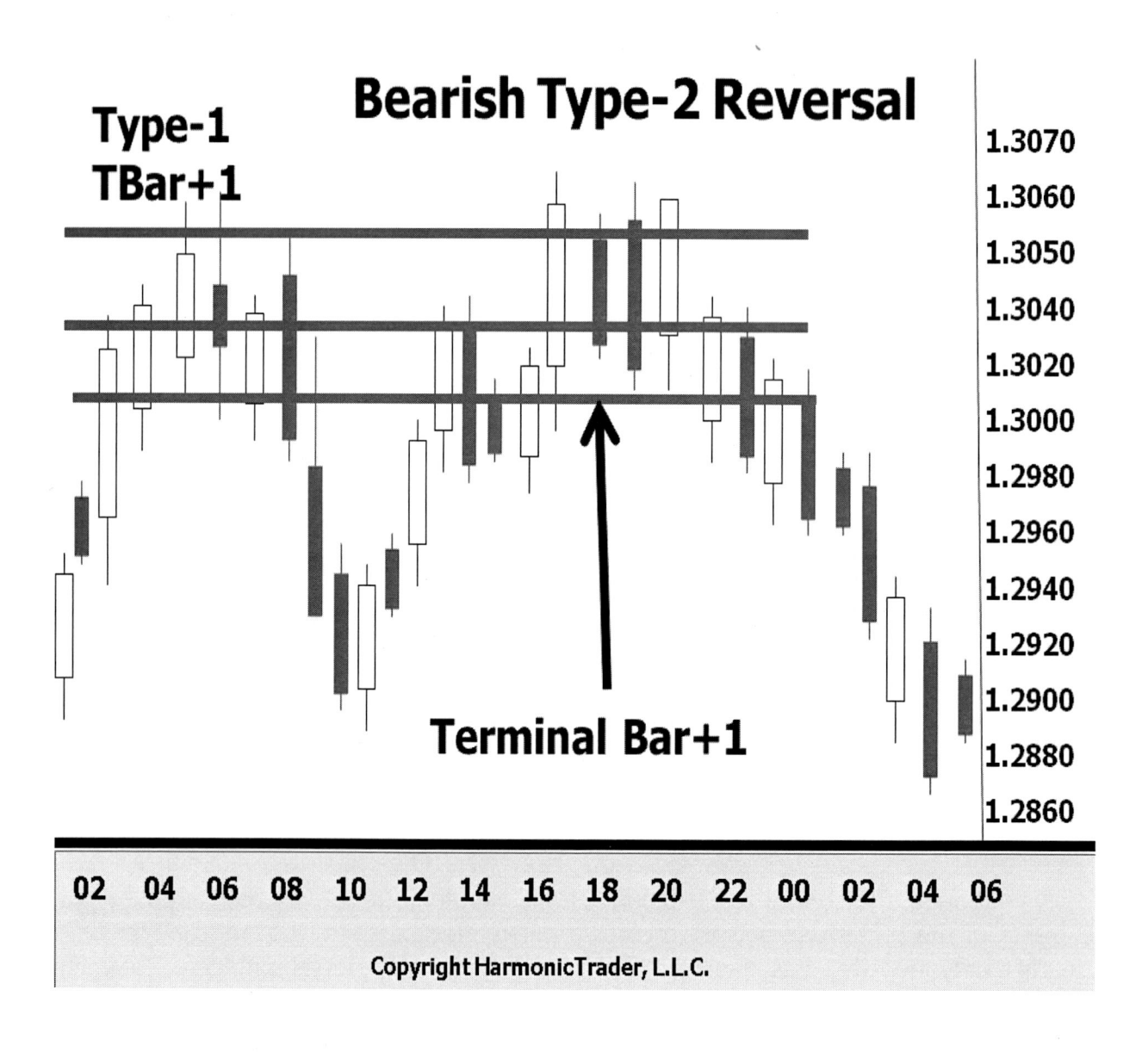

Harmonic Trading Volume 3: Reaction vs. Reversal

Swiss Franc/Japanese Yen (CHFJPY_A0-FX): 60-Minute
Bearish Gartley
Bearish Type-II Reversal

This following 60-minute chart of the Swiss Franc/Japanese Yen exemplifies the Type-I and Type-II phenomenon. For this case, let's focus on the Type-II phenomenon and the characteristics that triggered the reversal. Clearly, the pattern established initial resistance as the price action sharply reacted from the completion of the initial test of the Potential Reversal Zone.

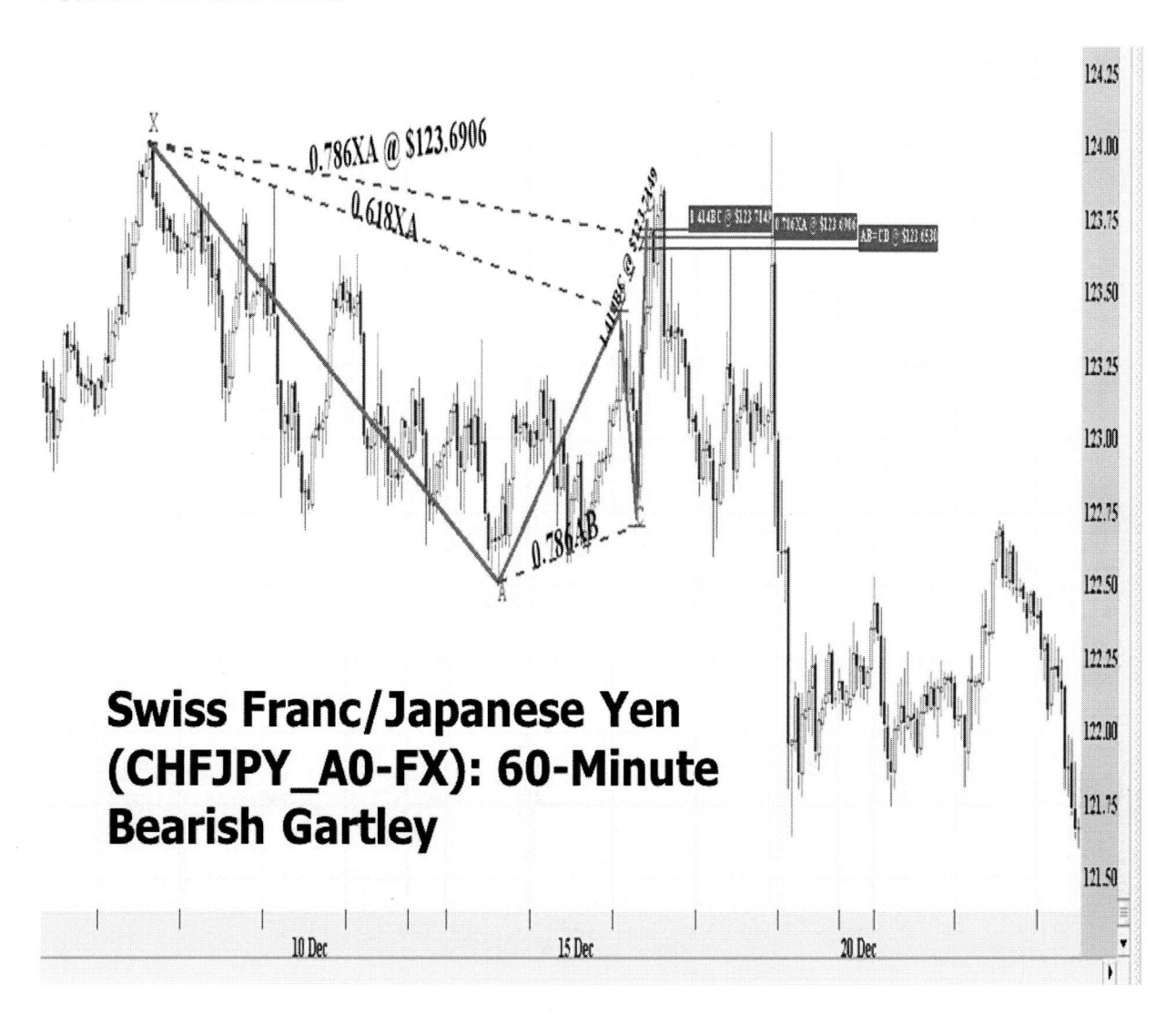

Harmonic Trading Volume 3: Reaction vs. Reversal

Swiss Franc/Japanese Yen (CHFJPY_A0-FX): 60-Minute
Bearish Gartley Potential Reversal Zone (PRZ)
Bearish Type-II Reversal

This chart of the price action in the PRZ demonstrates the power of an established harmonic level to affect price action. In the case of CHF/JPY, the Type-II reversal point clearly shows how the initial pattern marked substantial harmonic resistance. Although this reversal was sharp, the scenario was quite clear that the secondary test was to be respected and it yielded a much larger profit opportunity.

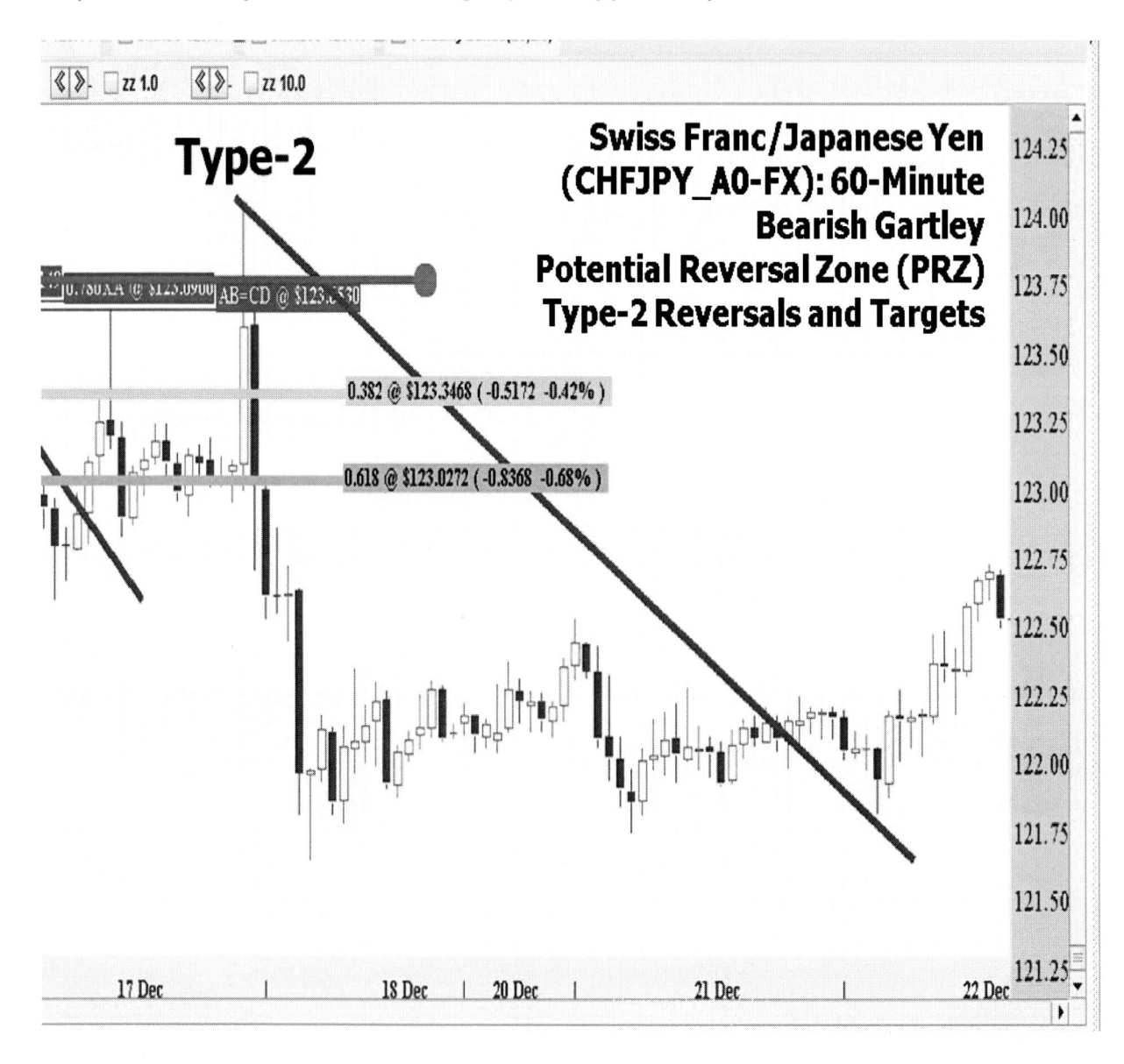

Harmonic Trading Volume 3: Reaction vs. Reversal

Type-III Reversals?

If there are Type-I and Type-II reversals, what happens when price action retests a Potential Reversal Zone (PRZ) for a third time? In most cases, a failed reversal of the Type-II retest will usually result in a complete failure of the pattern at hand. In essence, there are no Type-III reversals UNLESS THERE IS OVERWHELMNG INDICATOR CONFIRMATION. Typically, the Type-II Terminal Price Bar represents the stop loss limit for a "Type-III" reversal situation but the price level established by the initial completion of the pattern serves as the defining minimum limit in any situation. While the secondary retest is still a valid trading opportunity even if it does not possess any pattern structure to complement that Type-II area, the focus should still primarily be on the initial range of harmonic measures that established support/resistance from the initial test of the set up. It is important to note that a third test of any significant harmonic level should trigger suspicion regarding its integrity. Although some levels of support and resistance can experience what some technicians calling a "triple bottom," I believe that such consolidation typically fails the measured area. Clearly, the more consolidation required following the realization of the secondary retest, the less likely the reversal will unfold and is less likely to immediately reverse in the same way a Type-I scenario. In either case, the price action must exhibit the anticipated behavior shortly after reentering entering the Potential Reversal Zone (PRZ) on the secondary test. In addition, the Type-II Terminal Price Bar serves as an additional price level to consider and the ultimate make or break for the entire trade. The greatest advantage of the situations is that they require a smaller stop loss limit than Type-I situations.

Advanced Harmonic Trading Management Conclusion

I believe the Harmonic Trading management strategies represent some of the finest advancements of this book. The expectations established in the reversal types and the distinction in handling these situations are important proprietary distinctions that go a long way in determining *Reactions versus Reversals*. Many of these concepts include harmonic measurement strategies that are outside of the normal pattern considerations. Some of these concepts were a part of the initial discoveries presented in my first book, *The Harmonic Trader*. However, most of these ideas were developed after I released *Harmonic Trading Volume 1*. I feel that the material has completely clarified the subject of Harmonic Trading management. In the same way that the identification rules that become the standard for harmonic patterns, these are the prescribed rules and optimized framework to handle harmonic patterns.

Harmonic Trading Volume 3: Reaction vs. Reversal

Chapter 8
Harmonic Trading Timeframes

Now that we have thoroughly reviewed the basic concepts of trade identification and execution, we can focus on the advanced ideas that define the validity of any Harmonic Trading situation. First, the price action at the completion of the pattern is the most important determinant of a valid trading opportunity. As defined by the Terminal Price Bar, the price action in the Potential Reversal Zone (PRZ) serves as the early indication of what can be expected from any pattern. Second, the condition of the Relative Strength/Harmonic Strength Index readings at the completion of the pattern defines other expectations that must be assessed simultaneously. We can employ basic trendline analysis to determine the condition of the reversal and compare this to the predominant trend. Concepts such as the primary and accelerated trendline tools create make-or-break limits that guide trading decisions.

We must expect a price reaction within the Potential Reversal Zone (PRZ) as the first sign that this structure truly possesses harmonic qualities. Although most markets do exhibit harmonic patterns to some degree, it is essential to find only those situations that possess the clearest relationships. Again, this is where preparation helps to avoid mistakes and define the best opportunities in advance.

The key to remember is that we do not use every measurement strategy in every situation. Rather, we are trying to assess all opportunities from those three elements: Harmonic ratio relationships, *Market Sine-ature* and environmental technical confirmation. Many of the execution and management strategies integrate more complementary measures depending upon how the price action resolves the pattern completion point. Although it is not necessary to understand every aspect of each situation, a larger comprehension is derived from integrating multiple elements and being able to understand how the combinations relate to each other. Obviously, the degree of knowledge and understanding takes time but I feel that I have presented a framework that can be easily understood.

As we discussed previously, it is best to look at the most liquid and largest markets for these types of opportunities but the simple understanding of this framework enables Harmonic Traders to navigate complex environments and distill them into clear conclusions. A final perspective on further clarity necessary to understand the relative forces of any trade opportunity is to examine multiple timeframes to gain a relative perspective on the forces of price action from a larger timeframe and a shorter timeframe. Again, these are situational assessments where we employ particular timeframes at specific stages in the trading process.

This perspective is enormously helpful before and after a trade has been executed and the initial progress of a reversal can be monitored. Furthermore, other decisions such as profit targets and stop loss limits can be confirmed through this relative timeframe analysis. Finally, I want to point out that the subject of comparative timeframe has been discussed for decades. Although it is not necessary to incorporate every measure on each timeframe, the key is to define clear harmonic phenomenon that confirms the basic structural assessment. Analysis of comparative timeframe yields interesting insights and uncovers important technical price levels that may otherwise be overlooked.

Harmonic Trading Timeframe Types

1. **Primary = Timeframe that possess the clearest pattern structure.**
2. **Proximate** = The (lower) shorter timeframe after primary pattern has been identified.
3. **Distal** = The (higher) longer or larger comparative timeframe after primary pattern has been identified.

Harmonic Trading Primary Timeframe

One of the most common debates within the Harmonic Trading community is to ascertain exactly what is the ideal pattern size. Although I do believe that smaller patterns possess different expectations then larger structures, the most appropriate guideline is to establish a minimum. As I have discussed previously, I believe that the expectations that are associated with a sample size of at least 30 price bars due to Central Limit Theorem which provides a statistical requirement for a measurable sample size that can possess a higher degree of probability for normal distribution. Therefore, Harmonic Traders always want to use a pattern size that possesses rational behavior where normal expectations do not skew dramatically from analysis. As a basis for all pattern size assessments, the primary harmonic pattern to be assessed is the structure that develops on a timeframe that is 30 bars or more. As I discussed previously about the dilemma of two different timeframes having the same pattern, I always recommend to favor the interval which has the clearest confirmation strategies as well. Of course, the larger time interval will be more significant than the smaller, and we will look at how to compare multiple timeframes in this chapter. The key considerations with the Primary timeframe are to properly measure the pattern, identify the exact completion point with the Terminal Price Bar and understand the technical environment of the confirmation strategies to monitor the reversal.

An important trading tactic that must be assessed during the completion of the pattern is the analysis of the Terminal Price Bar. It is essential to identify the opportunity beforehand, monitor its progress as it enters the Potential Reversal Zone and literally link up the exact time completion with the price bar to monitor the patterns precise completion point. For example, an intraday pattern that materializes on a 15-minute chart will likely require two or three price bars to test an intraday pattern at a minimum. Specifically, the pattern itself can take an hour or two to complete depending on its size.

However, the recognition of the exact completion point where the first bar to test all of the numbers – the Terminal Price Bar completes, the possibility of the trade execution becomes *permissible* instantaneously. This is important because the price action that immediately follows this completion point provides immediate signals as to the validity of the potential price move. The coordination of multiple variables converges at the pattern's completion point - tick by tick as that individual price bar completes. It is at that point that the Primary timeframe becomes a live opportunity. Of course, there are a few other small triggers to observe as a final confirmation including RSI techniques that we have previously discussed. The key concept is to recognize that the identification phase ends at the immediate close of the primary timeframe price bar and the execution phase begins at the T-Bar+1.

Once the primary timeframe has been established, the price parameters for the trade must be assessed and the precise technical confirmation readings confirmed. As the price action tests the Potential Reversal Zone, the Terminal Bar will enter the Potential Reversal Zone and provide an insight as to how far beyond the harmonic level the real action will go before reversing. The Permissible Execution Zone as defined by that Terminal Bar extreme defines how much area beyond the ideal measurement of the pattern structure the price action can exceed before invalidating the trade opportunity. This is the importance of waiting for the Terminal Bar + 1 on the Primary timeframe as most valid reversals will provide an immediate trigger that validates the predicted reversal direction.

Harmonic Trading Proximate Timeframe

The Proximate timeframe is the (next) shorter timeframe – typically intraday – after Primary has been determined. The assessments on the shorter timeframe seek to optimize executions by identifying similar technical signals that the Primary is predicting. In fact, multiple harmonic phenomenon on varying time intervals is an excellent overall confirmation method that the opportunity at hand has greater potential for a larger reversal. The Proximate timeframe is typically at least one quarter the size the primary timeframe. For example, a harmonic pattern opportunity that develops on 60-minute timeframe will employ a 15-minute timeframe as the Proximate basis.

As I mentioned previously, these classifications are important because they define exactly what timeframes to examine. Although the comparisons may slightly vary, the important concept is to compare what is happening on a smaller timeframe relative to the clear pattern opportunity developing on the established primary timeframe. Sometimes, traders will focus on multiple lower timeframes and begin to confuse the analysis. In our example of the 60-minute chart, I would rather focus on what happens on the 15-minute basis and include the 5-minute basis as well. When we start looking at more than a few timeframes, the entire basis of the trade gets skewed.

Terminal Price Bar+1 on Proximate Timeframe

The most important event that unfolds at the pattern's completion point is the assessment of individual price bars on the Proximate timeframe that make up the "+1 bar" after the Terminal Bar has been established. Once the Terminal Bar has been established, the immediate timeframe must be regarded more seriously. For example, if a primary pattern developed on a 60-minute chart, we would examine the completion of the pattern at the top of the hour after it hits all of the numbers in the Potential Reversal Zone. If the 60-minute pattern tested all of the numbers in the Potential Reversal Zone at 10:49 AM, we must wait until the top of the hour at 11 AM before we can actually consider taking the trade. This is essential because we are able to establish the Terminal Price Bar and ensure that the early harmonic reaction signs will unfold to provide insight to the validity of the opportunity as it completes. After the Terminal Bar is established, it is possible to monitor the trade on the Primary timeframe and the Proximate timeframe as it nears completion. In this manner, we are able to assess the individual components of the exact completion point by breaking down the Terminal Price Bar and the +1 bar to decipher the immediate signals of confirmation. Remember, <u>Harmonic Trading executions are based upon the price action in the Potential Reversal Zone (PRZ) on the PROXIMATE timeframe</u>. This is an important strategic concept as it helps Harmonic Traders focus on the short-term price progress and the primary indicator of the larger reversal at hand. Also, the Proximate timeframe provides early indications of larger timeframe conclusions.

Harmonic Trading Distal Timeframe

The Distal timeframe is the (Next) furthest/longest timeframe – typically weekly, daily, 240-minute, 60-minute. It is most critical in long-term relative levels of support/resistance after the primary pattern has been determined. The larger price assessments on the DISTAL timeframe seek to reaffirm the primary structural pattern signal and establish the trade parameters of stop loss and profit target levels. Although profit targets are typically measured by the primary pattern, larger Distal timeframe price objectives do provide targets beyond the immediate initial harmonic Type-I and Type-II objectives.

The general process of coordinating the Distal timeframe does not get considered until after the Terminal Price Bar has been established. The action immediately following the Terminal Price Bar determines the validity of the execution while the complementary factors – especially RSI & HSI – must exhibit confirmation simultaneously as the price action reverses. Although the execution is monitored on the Proximate timeframe, the progress of the larger reversal can be monitored on the Distal timeframe especially when certain situations require more consolidation. There are number of ways to compare strategies and expectations but the confirmation strategies provide multiple elements that should also be expressed across all timeframes. Of course, these are the most ideal expressions of valid reversal behavior but the comparison of elements helps to uncover the significant technical events that are unfolding within the Potential Reversal Zone.

Three Harmonic Trading Timeframe Scenarios

The best way to demonstrate how to assess these three timeframes is to present the various trade types that possess a model approach of how to handle short-term versus long-term opportunities. These are general examples but do represent an ideal comparative approach to timeframe analysis.

1. **Intraday Trade** = Reference intraday timeframes typically 15-minute intervals that seek to capture price move over course of a few minutes to several hours. All positions are open and closed within the same 24-hour period.

2. **Swing Trade** = Reference Daily, 60-minute timeframes that seek to capture price move over course of several sessions to many days.

3. **Swing Position** = Reference Weekly, Daily, 60-minute timeframes that seek to capture price move over course of several weeks to many months.

Harmonic Trading Execution Timeframe Example: Intraday Trade

Let's examine typical timeframes that involve an intraday trade opportunity example. This is a common situation that active traders face every day. First, the most appropriate timeframe for short-term opportunities is a minimum 15-minute primary pattern.

- **Primary Timeframe = 15-minute interval**
- **Proximate (next shortest) Timeframe = 5-minute**
- **Distal (next longest) Timeframe = 60-minute**

Harmonic Trading Volume 3: Reaction vs. Reversal

Australian Dollar/Japanese Yen (AUDJPY_A0-FX): 15-minute Bearish Alternate Bat
Primary Timeframe

Although opportunities may develop on 5-minute or 1-minute timeframes, I feel that the risk reward ratios and obtainable profit targets are most reliably exhibited on a 15-minute timeframe no matter what the market. The following example of the Australian Dollar/Japanese Yen on the 15-minute Primary time frame shows an ideal Type-I scenario.

Harmonic Trading Volume 3: Reaction vs. Reversal

Australian Dollar/Japanese Yen (AUDJPY_A0-FX): 15-minute
Bearish Alternate Bat Potential Reversal Zone (PRZ)
Intraday Trade: Primary Timeframe

The following chart of the price action in the Potential Reversal Zone shows the immediate change in character as the pattern completed just shy of the 82 level. The initial 38.2% and 61.8% profit targets defined the 81.18 and 80.65 levels, respectively as the immediate management objectives for this scenario. As the reversal accelerated lower, it maintained a steady downtrend. You could say that this is the primary downtrend on the primary timeframe that helped maintain the management of the position. Clearly, the primary trendline indicated a larger reversal beyond a nominal reaction.

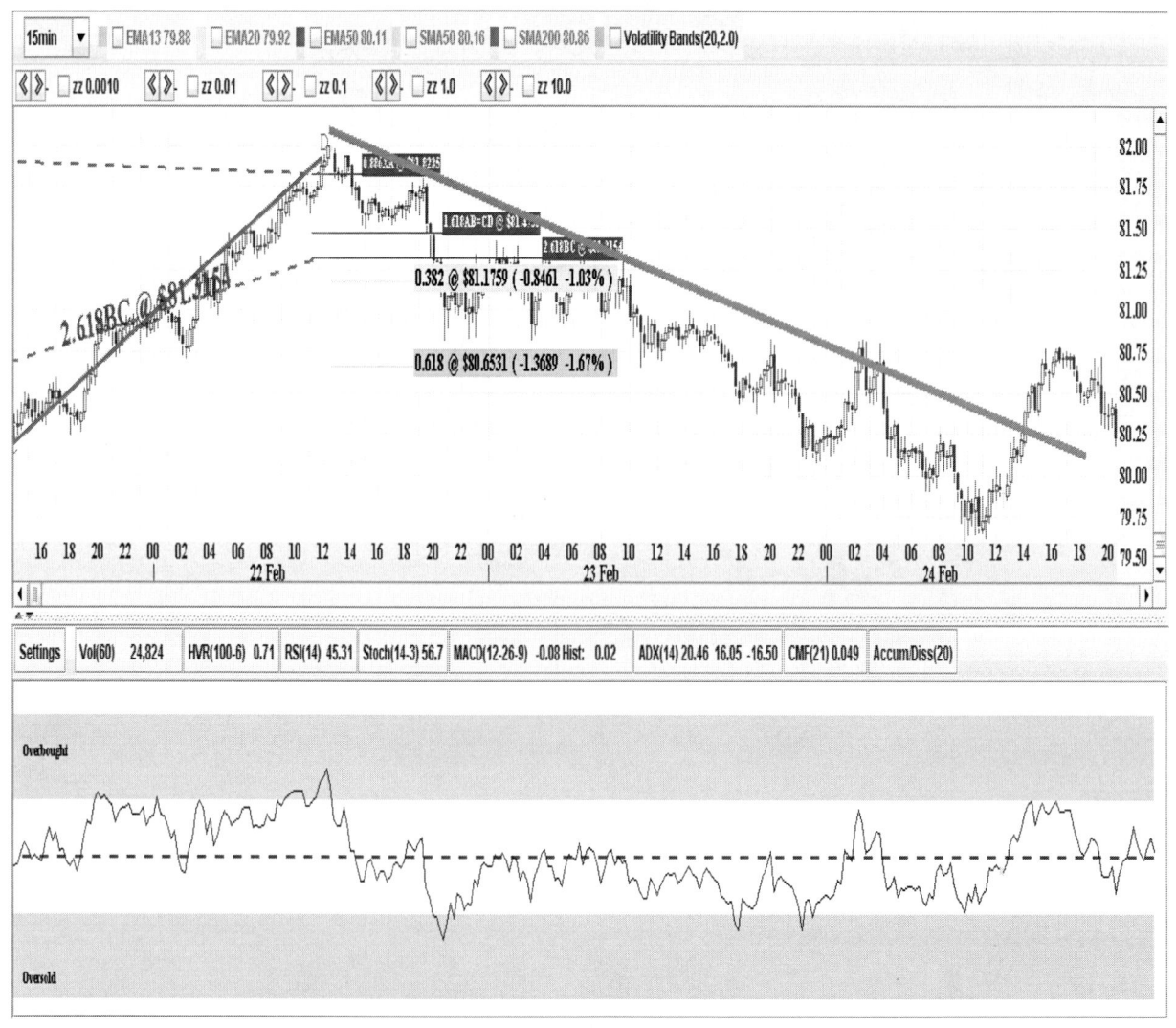

Harmonic Trading Volume 3: Reaction vs. Reversal

Australian Dollar/Japanese Yen (AUDJPY_A0-FX): 5-minute
RSI Confirmation
Intraday Trade: Proximate Timeframe

On the five-minute Proximate timeframe, the harmonic resistance established by the primary pattern find the area just under the 82 level was confirmed by a short-term extreme Relative Strength reading. Clearly, the indicator reading reversed sharply in this area and served as the early signal of a larger reversal at hand. These situations are common and must be recognized on the Proximate timeframe for early validation of the primary pattern.

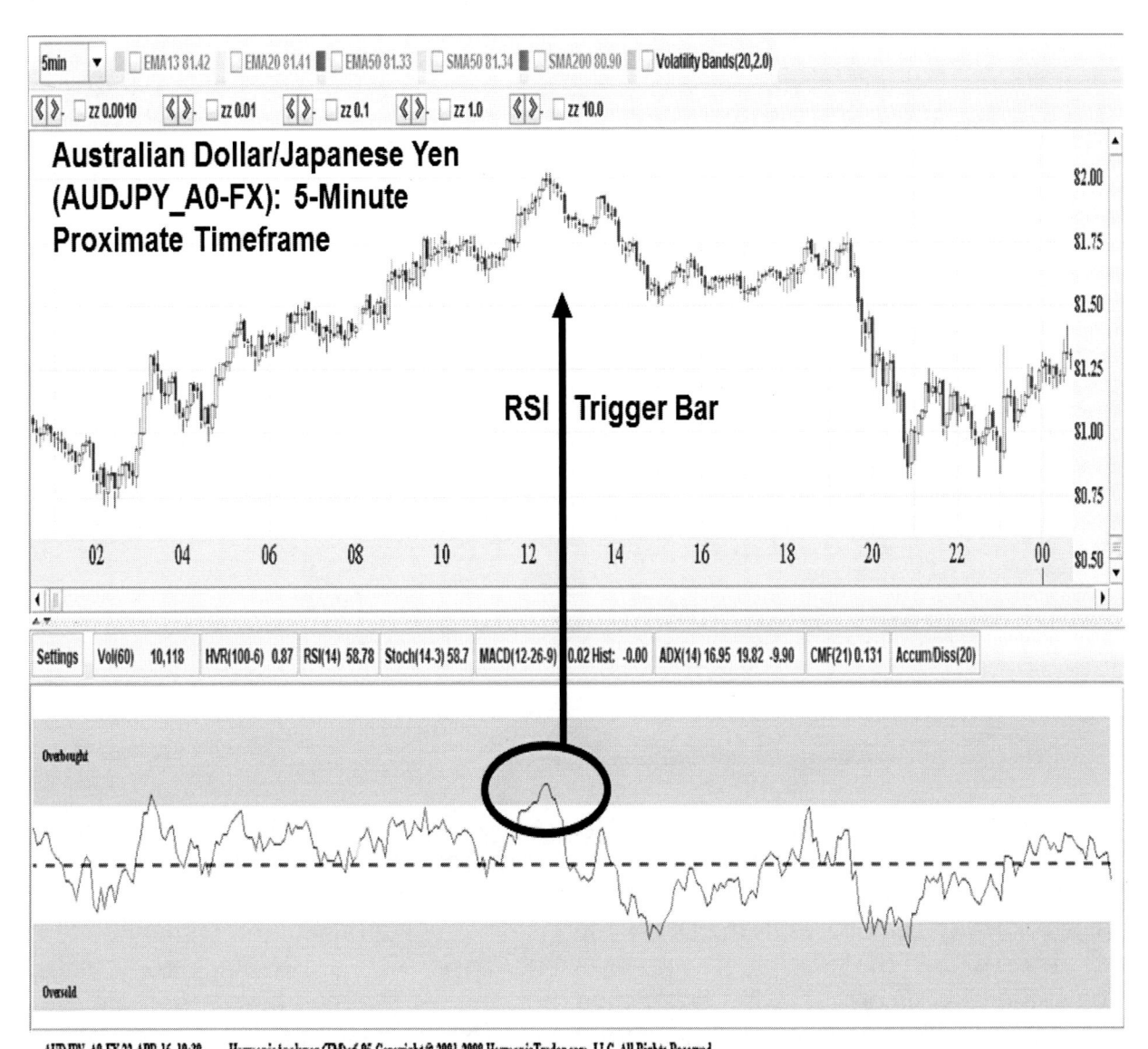

Harmonic Trading Volume 3: Reaction vs. Reversal

Australian Dollar/Japanese Yen (AUDJPY_A0-FX): 60-minute Bearish AB=CD
Intraday Trade: Distal Timeframe

In comparison to the longer timeframe, the situation possessed a distinct Bearish AB=CD pattern that marked the larger downtrend. Although it is difficult to see the primary Bearish Alternate Bat structure on this chart, the distinct downtrend was reinforcing the possibility of a continuation pattern. Furthermore, the distinct downtrend in the indicator was confirming the larger downtrend at hand.

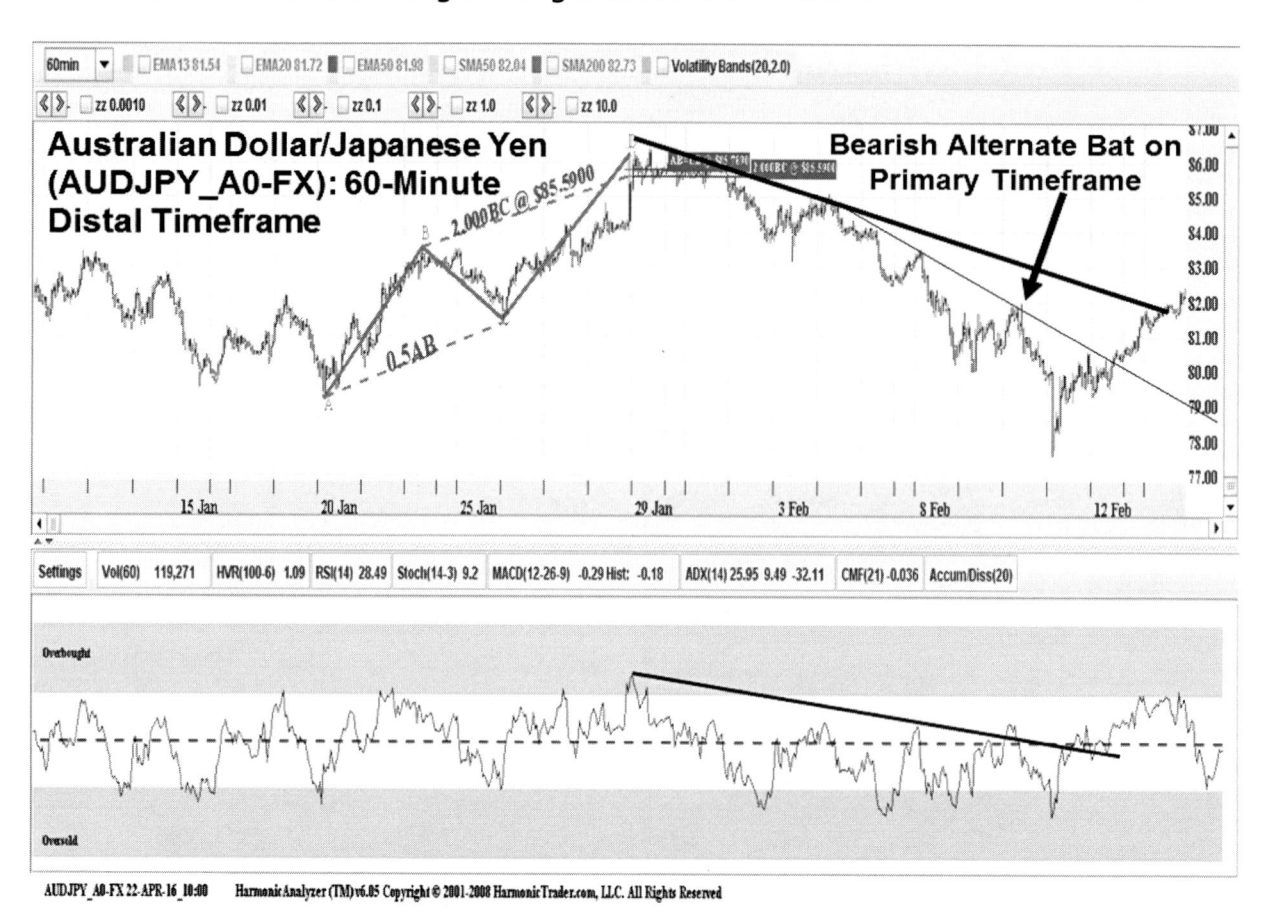

It is important to note that not every harmonic pattern opportunity requires the ideal scenario on each timeframe. This example demonstrates how shorter-term patterns within established trends can define excellent continuation opportunities. Although it is still essential to combine both the Distal and Proximate timeframes, the primary pattern will always be the minimum measurement basis for all trading possibilities. Comprehension improves with experience but the most important aspect of this coordination is to identify a harmonic pattern with an environmental element on at least to time frames for the most reactive conditions. In this example, the Proximate timeframe on the 5-minute chart possessed an ideal short-term Relative Strength reversal trigger.

Harmonic Trading Volume 3: Reaction vs. Reversal

After breaking down these possibilities, the most important technical event is a short-term extreme reading that reverses in the anticipated direction of the primary pattern.

Harmonic Trading Execution Timeframe Example: Swing Trade

A swing trade is a bit longer in nature and includes both intraday and daily charts. Typically, these positions will last anywhere from a few hours to several days. The best pattern situations will unfold on a 60-minute time frame and employ a Proximate timeframe that monitors the execution on a 15-minute basis.

- **Primary Timeframe = 60-minute interval**
- **Check Proximate (next shortest) Timeframe = 15-minute**
- **Check Distal (next longest) Timeframe = Daily**

Crude Oil (CL_#F): 60-Minute
Bullish Gartley
Swing Trade: Primary Timeframe

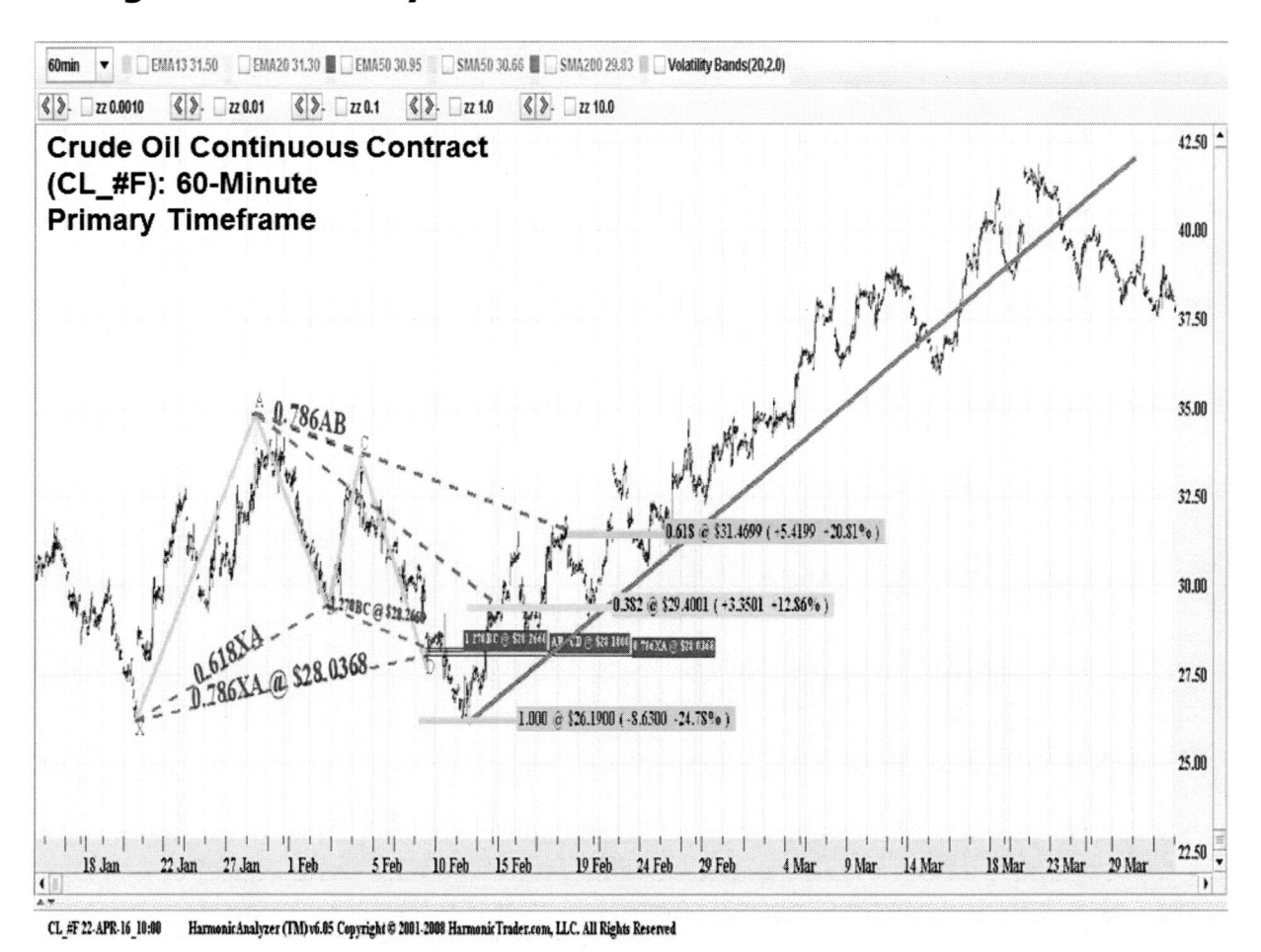

Harmonic Trading Volume 3: Reaction vs. Reversal

322

Crude Oil (CL_#F): 60-Minute
Bullish Gartley Potential Reversal Zone (PRZ)
Swing Trade: Primary Timeframe

This chart of the price action in the Potential Reversal Zone shows a consolidation that nearly exceeded the stop loss limit under the 1.0XA level. I believe this is an excellent example because it reflects a common situation where price action can exceed the ideal measures. One way to optimize these situations is to coordinate execution strategies at the completion point of the pattern. Despite the extra time required to establish the reversal, the price action continued higher after stabilizing just below the Potential Reversal Zone under the $28 level.

The Type-I reversal tested both profit objectives in short order while maintaining the primary uptrend throughout the next several days. Typically, some part of the position should be secured while simultaneously monitoring the reversal progress by staying in the trade as long as the primary trend is maintained.

Harmonic Trading Volume 3: Reaction vs. Reversal

Crude Oil (CL_#F): 15-Minute
RSI BAMM Divergence
Swing Trade: Proximate Timeframe

Analyzing the Proximate timeframe on the 15-minute chart, we see a clear RSI BAMM Complex Divergence that confirmed the primary harmonic support just under the $27 level. This is an excellent example of utilizing the Proximate timeframe as an immediate trigger in the price range of the Potential Reversal Zone. A short-term signal such as this within a longer-term harmonic price range is significant and represents an ideal trigger to confirm the execution.

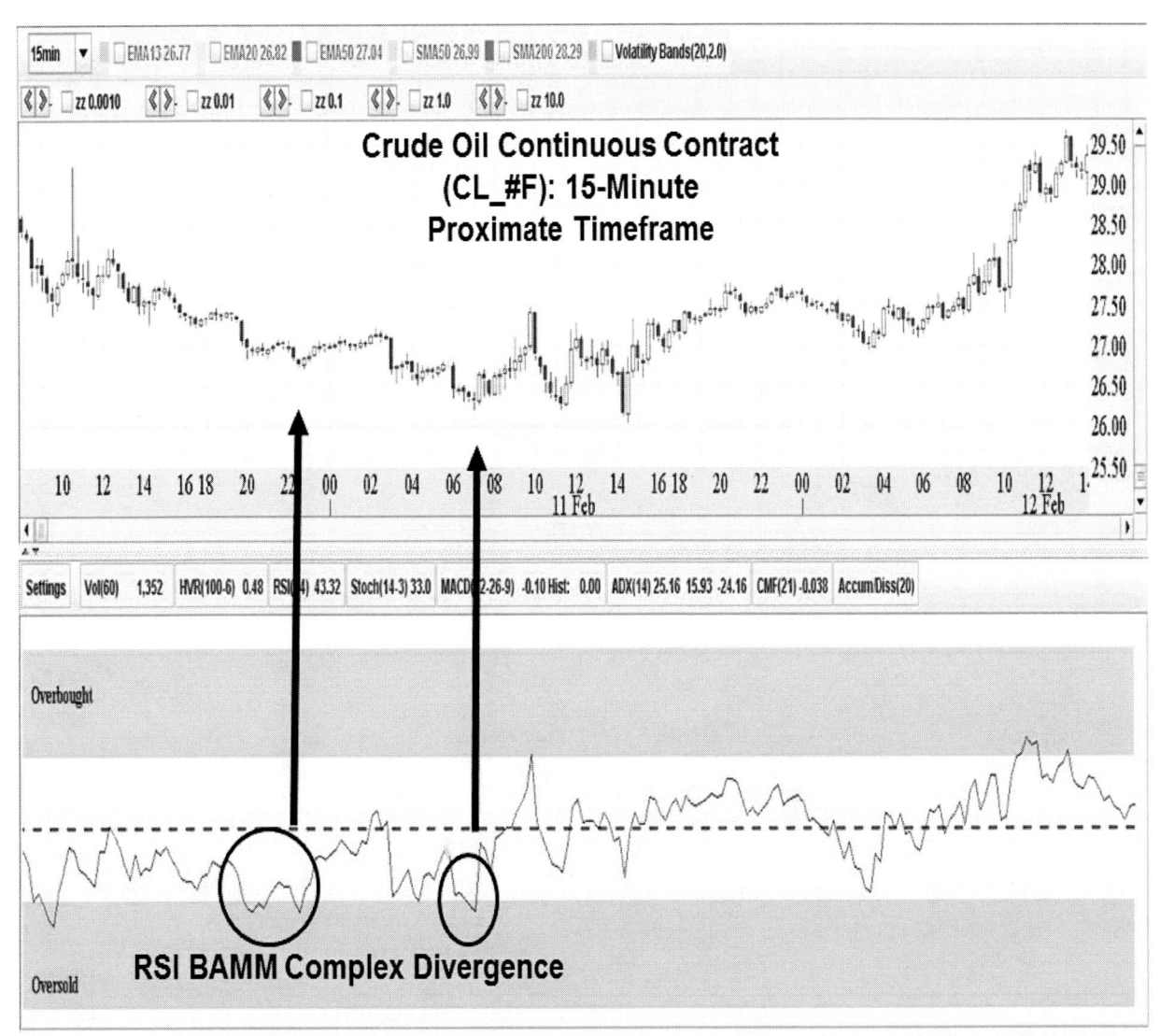

Harmonic Trading Volume 3: Reaction vs. Reversal

Crude Oil (CL_#F): Daily
Bullish Bat
Swing Trade: Distal Timeframe

When we look at the Distal timeframe, the same pattern structure materializes that appeared on the 60-minute chart. Clearly, a distinct Bullish Bat pattern materialized on the daily timeframe however the size of the pattern did not satisfy the minimum 30 bar required. As we have discussed previously, it is best to revert to the timeframe that possesses at least 30 bars. This pattern was only 16 bars but we can clearly see that the secondary test established the $26 level and led to a demonstrative reversal. Furthermore, the price action on the daily chart manifested overwhelming continuation immediately after completing the pattern. As the reversal progress continued, each daily bar formed a successive pattern of higher highs and higher lows that indicate the strength of the support.

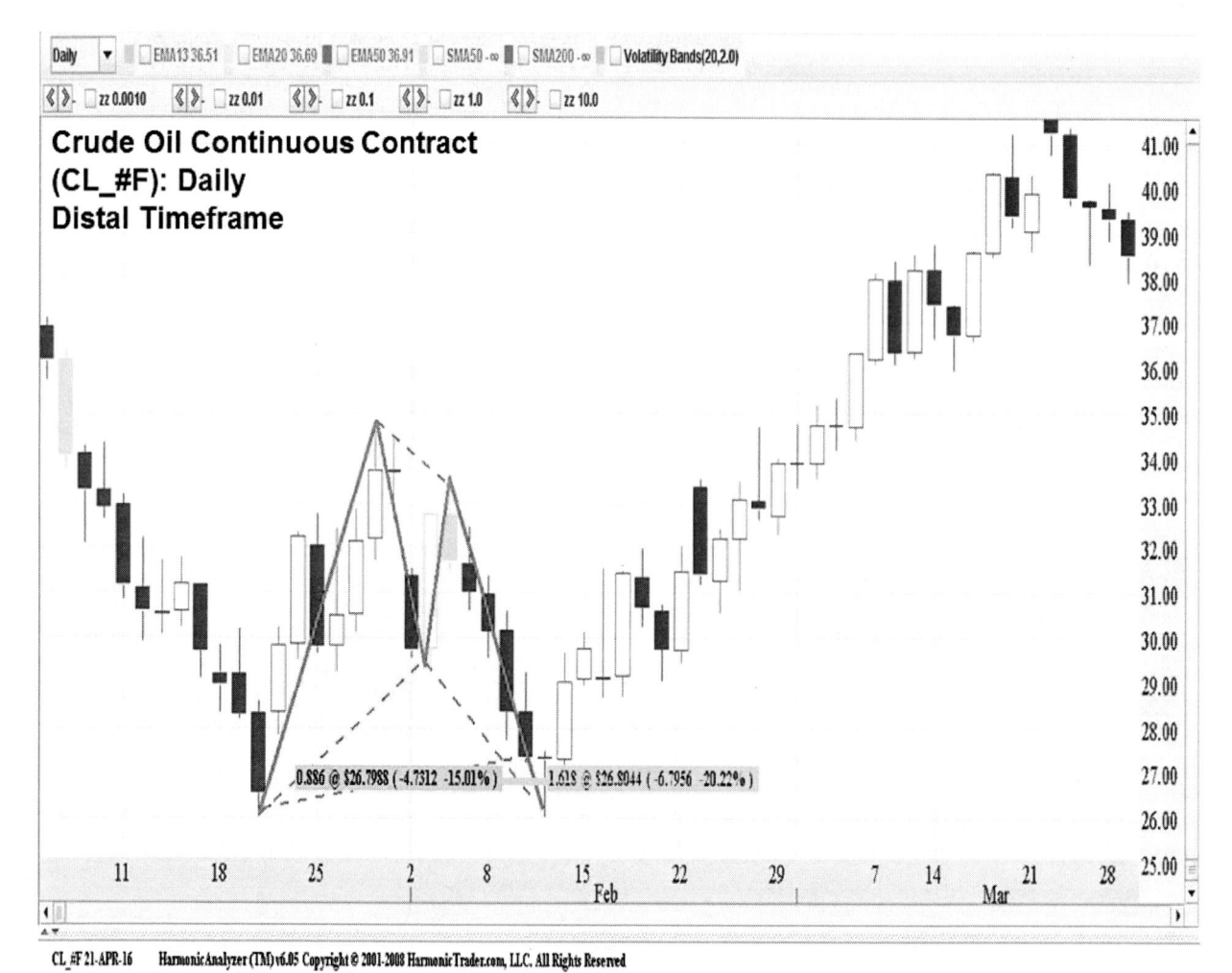

Harmonic Trading Volume 3: Reaction vs. Reversal

Position Trade: Primary Timeframe

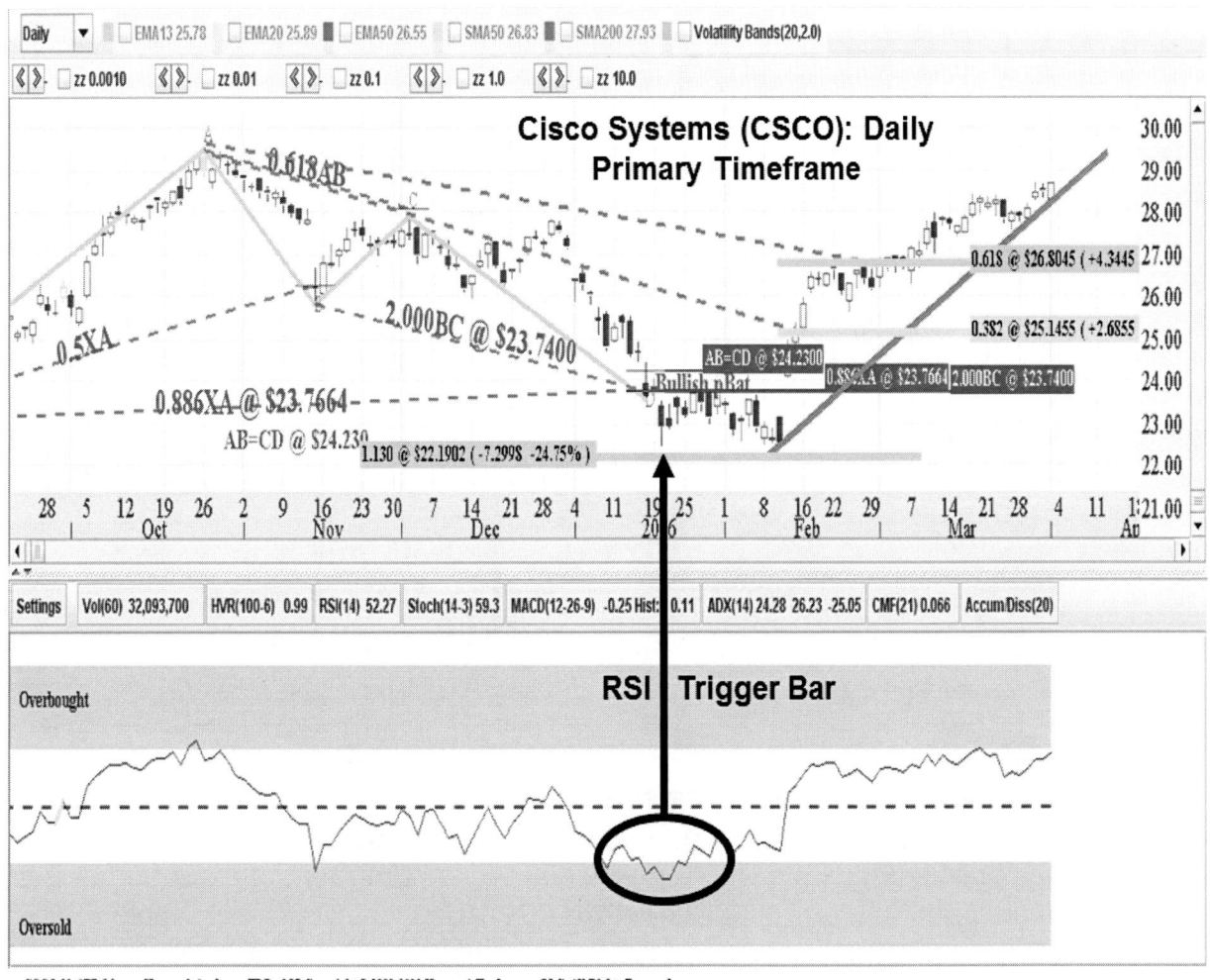

Longer-term opportunities unfold in the same manner as intraday opportunities. These situations are best applied to daily and weekly harmonic patterns. The identication, execution and management are applied uniformly regardless of timeframe. However, the longer-term patterns define the most substantial of harmonic opportunities that simply require much more time to unfold.

- **Primary Timeframe = Daily**
- **Proximate (next shortest) Timeframe = 60-minute**
- **Distal (next longest) Timeframe = Weekly**

Cisco (CSCO): Daily
Bullish Bat
Position Trade: Primary Timeframe

Harmonic Trading Volume 3: Reaction vs. Reversal

The daily Bullish Bat pattern in Cisco Systems represents an ideal situation, especially for opportunities in the stock market. I believe that stocks can be great trading opportunities because they exhibit the same properties as short-term patterns but they allow more time to handle the situation and manage the position,

Cisco (CSCO): 60-Minute
Bullish Gartley
Position Trade: Proximate Timeframe

On the Proximate timeframe, Cisco Systems formed a distinct Bullish Gartley with Harmonic Strength Index confirmation that confirmed the primary pattern.

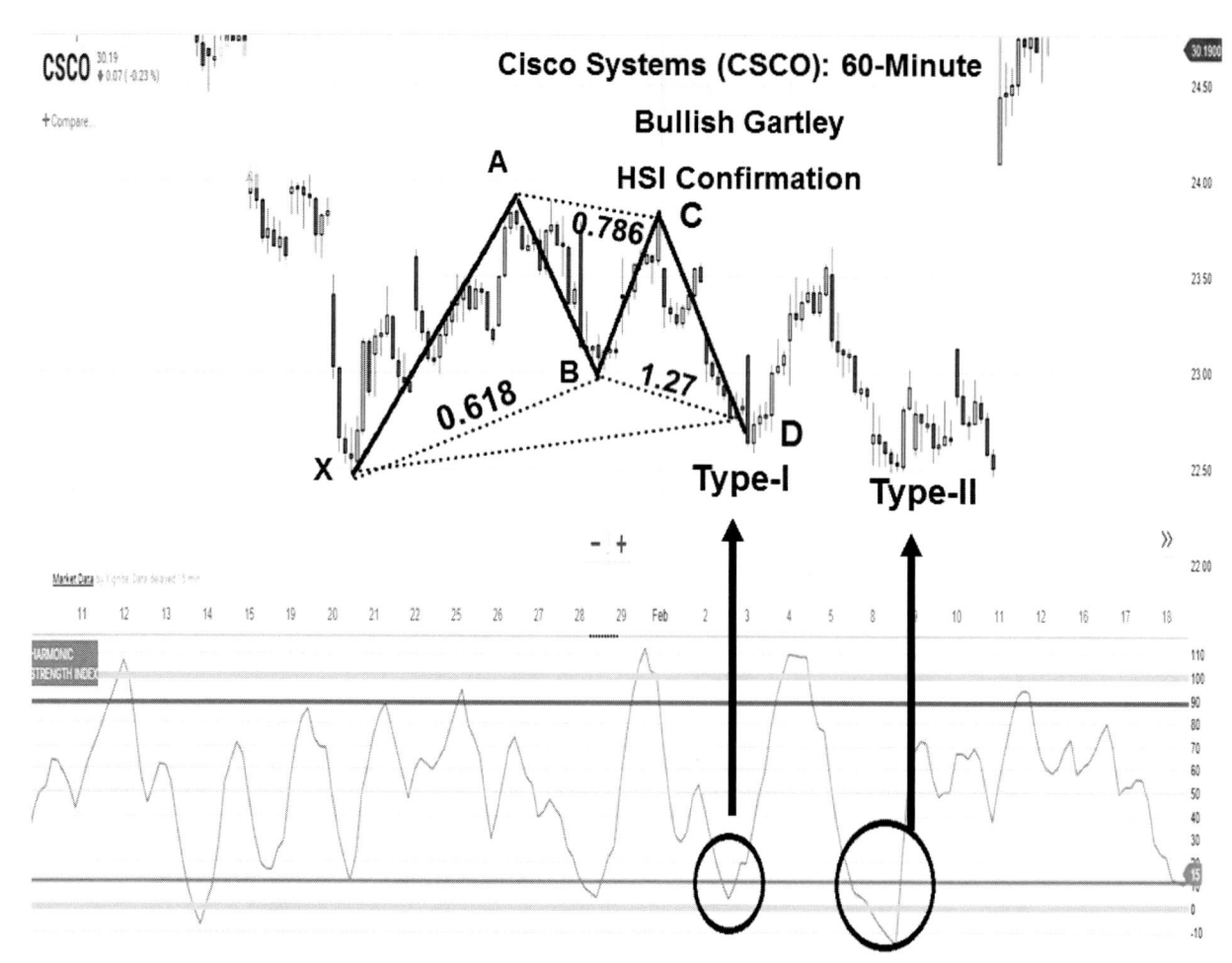

This 60- minute structure possessed a Type-I and Type-II retest before the larger reversal ensued. It is interesting to note how the intraday pattern still followed the basic trade management model but it was critical in optimizing the execution of the position. Although the intraday opportunity was distinct on its own, this example

Harmonic Trading Volume 3: Reaction vs. Reversal

demonstrates how the comparison of multiple time frames is extremely effective in the overall assessment of any opportunity.

Cisco (CSCO): 60-Minute
38.2% Retracement
Position Trade: Distal Timeframe

The daily pattern completed at an important 38.2% retracement on the weekly chart. This is another situation where the Distal timeframe provided a simple but significant measure that confirmed the smaller structure.

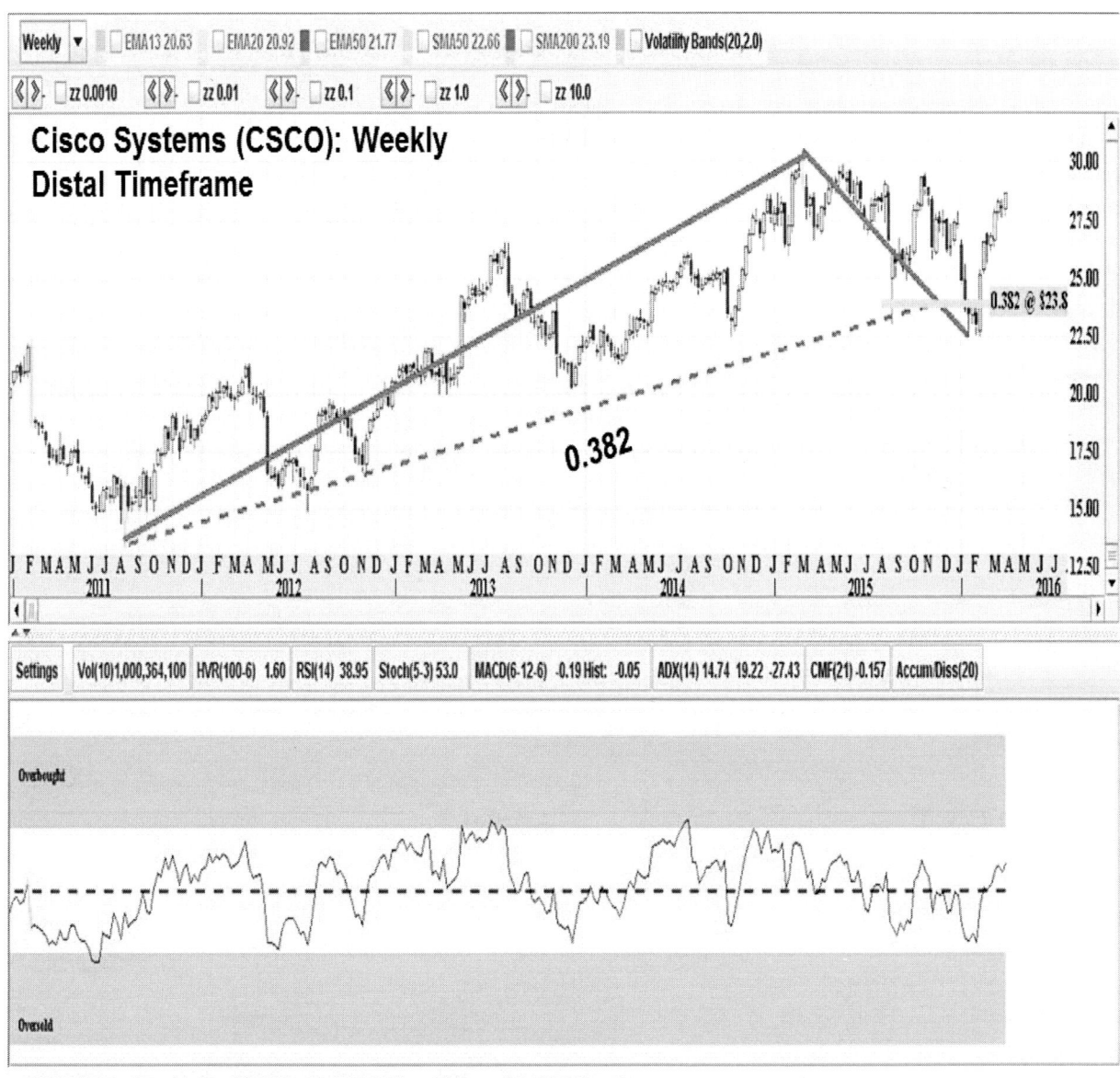

Harmonic Trading Volume 3: Reaction vs. Reversal

Such long-term reversal phenomenon is vital in identifying exactly where primary patterns have the most potential. The weekly trend was overwhelmingly bullish. Therefore, shorter-term structures provide excellent continuation patterns that have the potential of accelerating beyond nominal reactions to become larger reversals. Again, it is not essential to have patterns and indicator readings on every timeframe. The key is to coordinate the Proximate and Distal timeframe with an overwhelming harmonic opportunity on the primary basis. Of course, situations that have multiple harmonic measurements converging in the same area on multiple time frames will be more ideal. However, the primary focus should be to discover those conditions that confirm the primary pattern. Clear confirmation structures and indicator readings that develop on these time frames clarify expectations and optimize price parameters.

Harmonic Trading Timeframes Conclusion

For the purposes of Harmonic Trading, I have classified each timeframe with unique descriptions and expectations. My attempt to label these categorizations more specifically speaks to a larger effort to create a discipline around this understanding. I have replaced general terms for specific references that better describe the situation on that specific time interval. The key in this comparative timeframe analysis is to identify the harmonic measurements and environmental indicator phenomena that are unfolding simultaneously. Simple comparisons such as a harmonic pattern completing on a shorter timeframe in the same area as a larger harmonic pattern would represent a meaningful additional signal to confirm the trade. There are many combinations like this but the key is to identify what is happening on the longer-term perspective as well as the shorter-term timeframe.

Conclusion

I want to emphasize that my starting point in all of this was unlocking the harmonic price relationships that are exhibited in the market's structural price movements. Although pattern rules are standardized effective structures, the most profound ratio relationships in combination with the environmental indicator analysis optimize the market conditions with greatest probability. The most element of this measured framework is that it defines high probability expectations a finite market universe. That is, the comprehensive harmonic situations have limited possibilities. This narrows decisions variables to one of a few options designed for consistent conclusions. In my opinion, any methodology must be able to consistently "get in the right ballpark" where risk is defined and profit objectives are understood before any trade is executed. Since we are employing ratios that are manifested throughout the universe, the natural harmonic model of cyclical behavior creates a framework possesses accurate automatic price parameters that reduce errors. I believe that 80% of all mistakes in trading are eliminated through proper identification of market conditions first and foremost. The other 20% is reduced through the proper coordination of execution confirmation and a clear understanding of profit possibility.

We have covered many new techniques and advancements that build on the basic pattern foundation. The entire methodology creates an understandable framework and trading skill set that provides the following:

- **WE NOW HAVE A DEFINED PROCESS** to identify, execute and manage trade opportunities.
- **WE NOW UNDERSTAND** how to interpret price action and confirmation signals to optimize trade decisions.
- **WE ACCEPT FULL RESPONSIBILITY** to follow the Harmonic Trading Plan to capitalize on the opportunities the market's signals provide.
- **WE WILL NOW FOLLOW THROUGH** to improve trading skills through further study and regular review of trades.
- **WE HAVE A GLOBAL COMMUNITY OF HARMONIC TRADERS** who understand the natural harmonic advantages and are the type of individuals who understand the natural advantage of these principles.

Throughout this book, I have presented those strategies that can separate harmonic reactions from larger reversals. No matter what the end result, it is important to understand that there are absolute and finite strategies that must be implemented properly to capture the phenomenon. Regardless of a brief reaction or home-run reversal, the essence of Harmonic Trading is the fact that we can and do measure all parameters of the opportunity. Instead of trying to be a trader who relies on "artistic" abilities, success depends upon refining an effective strategic plan. Why would you risk money in any business venture without a plan? Yet, I see this happening time and time again by new traders.

Harmonic Trading Volume 3: Reaction vs. Reversal

The Future of Harmonic Trading

The goal of this book was to present the strategies that offered consistent variables that defined clear situational opportunities. Over the past 20 years, this harmonic framework – that started with simple price differentiation of M and W structures - has evolved into an entire optimized process. The long-standing challenge of knowing which patterns possess greater potential has been the motivating factor throughout my research. My continued focus on specific trading situations has been the key component that has unlocked these relationships.

I feel that this material has advanced the foundation of Harmonic Trading to facilitate a larger comprehension of this phenomenon as it relates to new measures. Clearly, we are not just focusing on harmonic patterns anymore. The advanced strategies can be referred to as Harmonics, especially related to indicators. The deeper evolution of these strategies presented in *Harmonic Trading Volume 2* (2007) marked the inception of techniques beyond simple pattern analysis. Although price patterns unto themselves are extremely effective, the larger comprehension garnered from harmonic indicator readings has defined unique situations where these advanced insights provide a clearer perspective. In the same manner that harmonic patterns are not a singular decision variable, the multiple integration of these strategies is the process that Harmonic Traders is the key to mastering the entire measured framework. This material facilitates this advancement and enables early initiates of harmonic patterns to grasp the deeper comprehension more readily.

Although I have been developed these strategies from years of study, the most profound future direction for this material will encompass a greater statistical research that assesses definitive market classifications. Much of my work has been market dependent, where time intervals, pattern specifications and other filters have provided exact parameters to assess statistical results. The challenge within my own research has caused me to define all parameters of the Harmonic Trading process exactly. Each situation must be defined according to market, pattern type and other situational variables that distinguish it is a unique technical entity. Otherwise, the results will be comparing those situations that possess different variables. As I have mentioned previously, this is a concern for most of the results that are being presented currently and general statistics about harmonic patterns. To further enhance the general understanding of Harmonic Trading probabilities, results must be derived from those parameters that can classify both price and environmental variables consistently. This is the number one challenge for harmonic patterns and for most trading strategies currently promoted today. Therefore, the future for this approach and all trading strategies that analyze the market will be validated by a more precise statistical framework to assess their overall effectiveness.

Many of the strategies that were presented in this book were derived from those relationships that yielded remarkably consistent results. Concepts such as RSI BAMM, reversal types and other complementary measures must be measured relative to pattern structures uniformly to optimize trading decisions within the harmonic pattern framework. Clearly, the empirical evidence of the importance of harmonic ratios to yield reliable and consistent information of future probable price action is overwhelming even in the hands of the novice trader. I believe this is the immediate appeal of these measures, as Harmonic Traders are able to experience some predictive capabilities with the application of simple pattern measurements. Although there are many other strategies that must be incorporated to experience success, the inherent advantages of these harmonic measurements can be easily incorporated. However, the more precise situational opportunities represent the future of Harmonic Trading and the continued optimization of those variables that most reliably guide decisions throughout the process.

Market Mechanisms Review

Throughout this material, I previously talked about the market mechanisms that price action can exhibit to define a complex technical condition. Specifically, the collection of technical events comprised by population of price data that exhibit and manifest these important signals to dictate the overall trend direction. Market mechanisms such as pattern structure direction, RSI BAMM combinations and other distinct categorizations provide the analytical tools to interpret price history for accurate assessment of future prices.

Ever since my earliest interest in Technical Analysis, I have always suspected that the market expresses various types of trading conditions that encompass more than a single move or individual price bar. In fact, I associate various moves in the financial markets in the same way that the weather can change. A rainstorm that is on the horizon does not happen at once. A decline in the market usually requires a formation phase that possesses consistent variables to signal potential of a change in trend. As clouds develop and storms take shape, the pace and duration of bad weather goes through various stages in its completion.

My awareness of these stages of trading was shaped by my initial impressions as a CRT operator in the options pits of the Philadelphia Stock Exchange. In the late 1980s, I spent a summer internship in the options pit as a quote operator. (The market maker would bark out the changes in price but it was not automated.) Although rather mundane especially when the market was quiet, I was one of the people responsible for punching in the changes in price into the computer. When a flurry of activity was about to begin, I noticed a series of market fluctuations that preceded the larger price acceleration. Interestingly enough, various local traders would initially circle the market maker pit and probe the scene to assess the opportunity. The most interesting aspect of watching this process unfold was the unique capitulation phases that were frequently compressed in time as price accelerated. We were dealing with option prices that fluctuated frequently, especially when premium collapsed to the point where the contract was worthless. This is a unique issue to options in general. However, the sheer magnitude of losing an entire contract value over the course of a few hours was remarkable. As I began to comprehend the larger monetary implications, I realized that there was enormous opportunity fluctuating in a short period of time. I learned that any price value in the market has a short-lived equilibrium and the changes that occur exhibit consistent characteristics. The entire process is quite fluid but it requires a dynamic degree of flexibility that takes experience and discipline to capitalize on opportunities.

These early experiences were instrumental in developing my perspective and understanding of how markets function. My ability to develop clear expectations were derived from those early experiences on the floor of a real exchange, and has been a primary inspiration to comprehend these dynamics on charts to the real-world trading process that unfolds. In doing so, I believe that I have been able to maintain a realistic set of expectations to refine only those relationships that provide reliable measures in any market environment.

The Promise of the Harmonic Trading Process

The promise of the Harmonic Trading process provides a framework to measure and analyze any market condition. Outlining most of the critical trend environments and technical triggers that facilitate the trading opportunity, the strategies in this book advance harmonic analysis of price zones to a more precise focus on the execution triggers and management skills that isolate advanced harmonic conditions.

One of the reasons Harmonic Trading has been widely accepted is due to its ability to be consistently effective and provide step-by-step model that considers only the most relevant technical information. I believe it's essential to memorize the harmonic patterns and understand the subtle differences that distinguish each situation. Many of the basic concepts that are derived from the measurement strategies are common knowledge within the Harmonic Trading community. However, my goal in this material was to provide precise tools that optimize executions and management decisions beyond simple identification.

Beyond Pattern Identification

As the awareness of harmonic patterns has grown, the identification measurements have provided people with an ability to understand price action in a unique and new manner. The common experience is that most individuals who take the time to investigate harmonic patterns and ratio measurements should not ignore the confirmation strategies that explain the optimal context for the entire methodology. I believe the advancement of software technology has enabled traders to learn more quickly and focus on selectivity to define the best opportunities. After I created the first harmonic pattern program, the Harmonic Analyzer, I was able to focus on the strategies that helped define valid reversals. The technology alone was an enormous advantage, as I no longer had to spend time searching for situations that satisfied identification rules. For new Harmonic Traders, they have an advantage in that they are able to learn the identification guidelines more readily while incorporating advanced execution and management skills to effectively handle each opportunity. With today's technology, it is possible to integrate Harmonics in a way that was not possible 20 years ago.

Trading is an Imperfect Process

Regardless of the effectiveness of this methodology, I readily admit that "Harmonic Trading is an imperfect process." The understanding of this one concept will serve to justify all emotional responses and clarify mental confusion regarding any missed opportunity. It is important to note that the means by which success is measured in the market is relative. As Harmonic Traders, it is important to understand that the world in which we are operating is not perfect. When we relate this basic acknowledgment to our actions, it is possible to understand that our performance will never satisfy the best-case scenario. Simply stated, we cannot expect to be 100% correct 100% of the time. There will be missed opportunities. There will be money left on the table. There will be trading decisions that could have been maintained more effectively. However, we are human. Our advantage and clear comprehension are derived from the basic understanding that we need to be right not perfect to succeed as profitable traders. Any extreme emotional influence that distorts trading abilities must be understood that nothing is perfect or even fair in the financial markets. I always believe that the mantra that "*Trading is an Imperfect Process*" fosters a realistic attitude that does not permit excuses. Sometimes, personal mistakes or misunderstanding can lead to substantial issues in applying even the basic strategies to define opportunities. However, this is most effectively handled by reviewing past decisions and future opportunities within the measured harmonic pattern framework to improve trading abilities.

Focus on the Process

Despite the fact that it is an imperfect process, all considerations regarding trading can be resolved through definition, responsiveness and clarity of one's trading plan to guide decisions before they are encountered. Although I understand why emotions can be troublesome to certain individuals more than others, I would always argue that one's ability to be successful in the markets depends upon the effectiveness of their trading plan. If that is a Harmonic Trading plan, an automated robot or a long-term 401(k) investor who is riding the ups and downs for the long haul, I believe the satisfaction of one's endeavors in the markets comes down to process employed. Is the market frustrating? Are you able to identify those price levels that consistently define important inflection points or trend continuation areas? Do you have confidence in the analysis that you put forth – in advance – to execute with real money? If the answer is not a straightforward yes, your entire trading process must be mastered and improved until more consistent results are obtained.

Standardization of Measurements

The initial ideas of pattern differentiation presented in *The Harmonic Trader* led to a wider focus of providing measurement guidelines for each step of the process. As I mentioned previously, I feel this is more a framework with respect to harmonic patterns but I have seen a number of other additional technical methods that have provided excellent confirmation signals. I'm always curious to see how people integrate harmonic patterns but I do believe that most respect the alignments and rules that validate opportunities. However, more than any other principle that should be emphasized, there must be a standardization to each pattern that has a prescribed set of measurement requirements to validate the trading opportunity. The standardization comes from my decades of work that has categorized these structures as specific technical measures. Much of the clarification that was presented in the earlier material regarding the Potential Reversal Zone (PRZ) for each pattern for example, is designed to clarify the framework of these measurements. Other concepts further the understanding of these limits to add natural parameters to the perspective of the environment in which patterns complete.

Define Your Own Success

Throughout my career, I have met people in every aspect of this industry. I have had the pleasure to get to know retail and institutional traders from around the world. Also, my work has enabled me to confer with some of the top professionals in the industry. I'm grateful for all of these experiences. Some of these individuals are worth hundreds of millions of dollars while most of the people I encounter are regular folks. To me, it does not matter how much money any person has. My involvement with the financial markets has been rewarding on many levels with like-minded traders who share the same passion to learn and profit from these endeavors. The common trait that I have seen in most successful traders is that they define their own success. This is important because the most confident traders who truly know what they are doing understand all parameters of the situation they are operating in. They know what they want. They know how to get what they want. And they do it without excuses. The most successful traders are self-determined individuals who accept no excuses in the face of the pursuit of their goals. It's not an easy task but those who persevere eventually win.

The problem has been the promotion of unrealistic ideals about trading and the perceived Wall Street culture in general. In the past few years, movies such as "The Wolf of Wall Street" idolize less than reputable individuals who care nothing for knowledge of the market and focus on manipulation of others to earn their money. Incredibly, the main character in that movie is now revered as a great salesman, despite a few years in jail. I won't even mention his name because I have no respect for him nor the taint he has left on an industry that I hold in high regard. Yes, I hold the trading industry in high regard but I have very low expectations. Why do I say this? Simply stated, money makes people do crazy things. Over the course of a few decades in this industry I have learned that those who persevere and stick to their guns are the ones who make it. Other manipulators and bad actors who seem intent on hurting those that truly want to learn never last.

As a former Registered Investment Advisor, I have always upheld a fiduciary responsibility to be of serious mind and intent when conferring about potential opportunities in the market. I believe any individual whom intends to represent themselves as a market professional must do so in the highest of ethics with the sincerest of intentions. Unfortunately, the norm today is for internet marketers and less credentialed individuals to focus their time on promotion of incorrect ideas. My focus has always been about the work. I care about the ideas that are presented in public and I have decades of experience with the strategies that I present. I stand by my life's work with a fiduciary commitment to put forth only the most effective harmonic strategies.

Countless traders have studied the basic harmonic pattern measurements. However, the entire harmonic pattern framework of execution and management rules are as essential to facilitate success. I believe that the methods in this material expands beyond the initial foundation of measurements to confirm opportunities to an unprecedented degree. In this regard, *Harmonic Trading Volume Three* represents the most comprehensive presentation of harmonic pattern situations, distinguishing not only exact structures but unique characteristics of the environments within which they complete. Through such precision, we can understand and expose the natural limits of the financial markets to an unprecedented level. In this pursuit, the harmonic pattern framework becomes the guiding decision-making basis for all trade opportunities.

Bibliography

Carney, Scott M. *Harmonic Trading Volume 1*. Second Edition Princeton, New Jersey: Financial Times Press, 2010. (Original 2004)

Carney, Scott M. *Harmonic Trading Volume 2*. Second Edition Princeton, New Jersey: Financial Times Press, 2010. (Original 2007)

Carney, Scott M. *The Harmonic Trader*. United States of America: Harmonic Trader Press, 1998.

Cootner, Paul H. *The Random Character of Stock Market Prices*. Cambridge, MA: MIT press, 1964.

Douglas, Mark *Trading in the Zone: Master the Market with Confidence, Discipline and a Winning Attitude.* New Jersey: Prentice-Hall publishing, 2000.

Edwards, Robert D. & McGee, John Technical Analysis *of Stock Trends*. Fifth Edition, Boston, MA: John McGee, 1966.

Gann W.D., *How to Make Profits in Commodities*, New York, New York: New York Institute of Finance, 1942.

Gann W.D., *Tunnel Thru the Air*, Pomeroy, WA: Lambert-Gann Publishing, 1927.

Gartley, H.M., *Profits in the Stock Market*, Pomeroy, WA: Lambert-Gann Publishing, 1935.

Hurst, J.M., *J.M. Hurst Cycles Course*, Greenville, S.C.: Traders Press, 1970.

Hurst, J.M., *The Profit Magic of Stock Transaction Timing*, Greenville, S.C.: Traders Press, 1970.

Kane, Jim, *Advanced Fibonacci Trading Concepts*, Tucson, AZ: KaneTrading.com, 2003.

Merrill, Arthur, *Merrill Filtered Waves*. New York, NY: Analysis Press, 1977.

Morris, Greg *Candlestick Charting Explained*. New York, NY: Wiley Publishing, 1989.

Murphy, John J. Technical Analysis *of the Futures Markets*. New York, NY: New York Institute of finance, 1986.

Kaufman, Perry J. *Commodity Trading Systems and Methods*. New York, NY: Wiley publishing, 1980.

Lynch, Peter *One Up on Wall Street*. New York, NY: Simon and Schuster Publishing, 1986.

Patel, Manesh *Trading with Ichimoku Clouds: The Essential Guide to Ichimoku Kinko Hyo Technical Analysis* 1st Edition New York: Wiley Publishing, 2014.

Prechter, Robert, *Elliott Wave Principle*, Gainesville, Georgia: New Classics Library, 1978.

Pring, Martin Technical Analysis *Explained*, Second Edition. New York: McGraw – Hill, 1985.

Raschke, Linda Bradford & Connors, Larry *Street Smarts: High Probability Short-Term Trading Strategies* 1st Edition. M Publishing Group, 1996.

Schwager, Jack D. *A Complete Guide to the Futures Markets: Fundamental Analysis,* Technical Analysis, *Trading, Spreads and Options*. New York: Wiley Publishing, 1985.

Wilder, J. Wells New Concepts in Technical Trading Systems. Greensboro, NC : Trend Research, 1978.